LAUNCHING
NEW VENTURES

7e

LAUNCHING NEW VENTURES

An Entrepreneurial Approach

Kathleen R. Allen
University of Southern California

CENGAGE
Learning·

Australia • Brazil • Mexico • Singapore • United Kingdom • United States

CENGAGE
Learning®

Launching New Ventures: An Entrepreneurial Approach, Seventh Edition
Kathleen R. Allen

Vice President, General Manager, Social Science & Qualitative Business: Erin Joyner

Product Director: Michael Schenk

Senior Product Manager: Jason Fremder

Content Developer: Christopher Santos

Product Assistant: Jamie Mack

Marketing Director: Kristen Hurd

Marketing Manager: Emily Horowitz

Marketing Coordinator: Christopher Walz

Art and Cover Direction, Production Management, and Composition: Lumina Datamatics

Intellectual Property

   Analyst: Diane Garrity

   Project Manager: Sarah Shainwald

Manufacturing Planner: Ron Montgomery

Cover Image: ©Ensuper /Shutterstock

For product information and technology assistance, contact us at **Cengage Learning Customer & Sales Support, 1-800-354-9706**

For permission to use material from this text or product, submit all requests online at **www.cengage.com/permissions**
Further permissions questions can be emailed to **permissionrequest@cengage.com**

Library of Congress Control Number: 2014955990

ISBN-13: 978-1-305-10250-7

Cengage Learning
20 Channel Center Street
Boston, MA 02210
USA

Cengage Learning is a leading provider of customized learning solutions with office locations around the globe, including Singapore, the United Kingdom, Australia, Mexico, Brazil, and Japan. Locate your local office at: **www.cengage.com/global**

Cengage Learning products are represented in Canada by Nelson Education, Ltd.

To learn more about Cengage Learning Solutions, **visit www.cengage.com**

Purchase any of our products at your local college store or at our preferred online store **www.cengagebrain.com**

Printed in the United States of America
Print Number: 02   Print Year: 2016

BRIEF CONTENTS

Part IV Planning for Growth and Change   381

CONTENTS

Part II Feasibility Analysis   63

Part IV Planning for Growth and Change   381

Chapter 16 FUNDING STARTUP AND GROWTH   383

Chapter 17 PLANNING FOR GROWTH AND CHANGE   418

Case Studies   453

Appendix   523

PREFACE

The sixth edition of this book came out in 2011 (copyright 2012), three years after the financial crash and well into a global economic downturn. A strong turnaround has yet to materialize and so entrepreneurs, who tend to thrive in negative circumstances, are still the hope for the economic future of most nations around the globe. As I noted in the previous edition, the developing world has wholeheartedly embraced entrepreneurship as a way to pull itself out of this enduring economic malaise. The world we live in today is vastly different from the one that existed when I wrote the first edition of *Launching New Ventures* in 1995 as we headed toward the dot com boom and continuing economic prosperity. Nevertheless, I would argue that the future of the United States and certainly the world lies with entrepreneurs who start the innovative businesses that create jobs and produce products and services to fuel the economy. For the foreseeable future, we will live in a world characterized by high degrees of uncertainty rather than the more predictable risk with which we had grown comfortable for several decades. Entrepreneurs are comfortable with risk because they can calculate probabilities and outcomes for the risks they face. Uncertainty, on the other hand, has no probabilities associated with it; it can't be calculated or predicted. To survive in a world of uncertainty, entrepreneurs must develop businesses that are fast, lean, adaptable, and flexible. Whether a new venture operates in the Internet world, the life sciences, manufacturing, or services, entrepreneurs need to compress the product development timeline, get to an early prototype quickly and cheaply with the minimum number of features needed to meet the customer's requirements, continually refine their business models, and find ways to get traction as fast as possible. An uncertain business environment means more than ever that the winners will be those who launch businesses as entrepreneurs in the true Schumpeterian sense of the word: disrupting what has gone before, looking for the unexpected, and creating new value.

The evidence for the benefits of entrepreneurship is clear when we study its impact on society and on the economy. However, the evidence is not so clear when we look at entrepreneurship in the academy. As educators and practitioners, we assume more benefits than we can actually quantify. In the preface of the previous edition, I referred to an important article written by one of the early leaders in the field. It bears repeating here because the problem persists. Researcher and Professor Dale Meyer wrote about the field of entrepreneurship as a discipline in a provocative article for the *Journal of Small Business*

Management called "The Reinvention of Academic Entrepreneurship." He lamented the lack of rigorous metrics for measuring the impact of entrepreneurship education on students and society, the heavy reliance on neoclassical economic paradigms, and the blurring of the boundaries between entrepreneurship and small business management. He called for more emphasis on creative, self-organizing processes that entrepreneurs employ to craft complex, adaptive business systems. I wholeheartedly agree with Meyer's assessment. Today, the term *entrepreneurship* has been diluted by overuse in contexts that have nothing to do with new venture creation. *Entrepreneur* is being co-opted by everyone, including the media, to describe what is more traditionally referred to as a small business owner, a successful musician, or an effective product manager. The rationale for this dilution is that if you think like an entrepreneur, you're an entrepreneur. I believe that this rationale confuses entrepreneurship with creativity and innovation. In every edition of *Launching New Ventures,* I have attempted to remain true to the Schumpeterian view of the entrepreneurial process as "creative destruction." Now, more than ever before, the world needs entrepreneurs, in the strictest sense of the word—those who challenge the way we think about business, who create innovative business models that solve new problems, and who excel at sense-and-respond processes in the face of great uncertainty.

With all the knowledge we now have about how to operate effectively in a global market, how to build successful companies with extraordinary valuations, and how to innovate, we still have so much more to learn. And that is perhaps why so many of us enjoy the field of entrepreneurship because it is messy, chaotic, and in a constant state of change. We are continually challenged to revise our ideas—what we knew to be true—in the face of almost daily changes in the countless variables that affect the complex launch and growth of a new business.

Launching New Ventures, Seventh Edition, represents the most current thought, ideas, and practices in the field of entrepreneurship. In fact, ever since its first edition, *Launching New Ventures* has endeavored to extend the boundaries of what we know about entrepreneurship and to celebrate the uniqueness and creativity of entrepreneurs.

CONTENT, ORGANIZATION, AND UNIQUE COVERAGE

Launching New Ventures is organized around the process of creating a startup, from the recognition of an opportunity to the launch of the business. It is designed to help readers organize and plan for venture creation by mentally (and sometimes physically) engaging in the various activities that entrepreneurs typically undertake. This book has never sought to be all things to all people. It has a very specific emphasis on pre-launch activities—those things that entrepreneurs do to prepare to start a business and secure their first customer. The reason for this emphasis is that the decisions made to prepare the business for launch will have a significant impact on how successful that launch is. So this book explores activities such as opportunity creation and feasibility analysis in more depth than the average book on entrepreneurship. The book also takes a distinctly entrepreneurial view of new businesses as opposed to a small business perspective. In a complex, global world, new business owners, whether their business might be the next Google or simply a small restaurant, need to think like an entrepreneur. They need to be opportunity-focused, innovative, growth-oriented, and constantly looking for new ways to create and capture value for customers. Today the entrepreneurial mindset is essential for survival and growth.

Part One introduces the foundations of entrepreneurship and entrepreneurial opportunity, which are important to understanding the decisions that entrepreneurs make, the environment in which they make those decisions, and the tasks they must undertake before starting a new company. In Chapter 1, readers will learn the nature of entrepreneurial ventures and how they are distinct from other types of businesses as well as the role of entrepreneurship in the economy. Chapter 2 dispels many myths about entrepreneurs and helps readers understand the characteristics and behaviors that work for and against entrepreneurs. Readers also learn about the entrepreneurial mindset, which is so critical for a successful startup. Chapter 3 introduces the subject of opportunity and how entrepreneurs create and shape opportunities for themselves.

Part Two addresses the heart of entrepreneurial activity, the testing of a business model through feasibility analysis. It opens with Chapter 4, "Analyzing the Industry and Market" where readers will learn how to study an industry, the environment in which the new business will operate, and follows that with a discussion of how to effectively conduct market research to understand customer needs and levels of demand. Chapter 5 focuses on the design, development, and testing of a business model as well as how innovation happens in all the components of the business model. Chapter 6 explores the way entrepreneurs develop products and services; it considers product development using lean methodologies, prototyping, and the minimum viable product. Chapter 7 considers ways to protect a startup's assets through intellectual property rights. Chapter 8 looks at how to build an effective founding team and also discusses how to determine what gaps in experience and expertise may exist in the management team and how to compensate for them with such solutions as strategic alliances and independent contractors. Chapter 9 closes this part by addressing the startup resources entrepreneurs must gather and how to calculate the required capital and other resources needed to launch the venture and operate it until it achieves a positive cash flow from the revenues it generates.

Part Three deals with business design, those activities that take place once you know you have a feasible venture. It begins with Chapter 10, which describes how to move from a feasibility analysis to preparing a business or execution plan. Chapter 11 deals with the design of an entrepreneurial company, considering how entrepreneurial businesses are organized, how entrepreneurs determine the best business location, and how they develop their initial human resource capability. Chapter 12 focuses on how products and services are produced and addresses issues related to planning the startup operations of a new business, such as production, quality control, customer service, outsourcing, and managing the supply chain. Chapter 13 looks at the legal form of the business and discusses the advantages and disadvantages of sole proprietorships, partnerships, and corporate forms. Chapter 14 deals with the role and implementation of the startup marketing plan and how to promote new products and services effectively with limited resources. It pays particular attention to the role of new media, including social networks and search engine marketing. The chapter also addresses personal selling and customer relationship management. Chapter 15 explores the increasingly important topics of vision, ethics, and social responsibility. The value system of a new business shapes the culture of the business and the image it will have to live up to as it builds its reputation. Readers will be challenged to define a vision for a new venture based on the values they believe to be important. They will also gain a greater understanding of the need for ethics and social responsibility in any business. Part Four explores planning for growth and change in the new organization. It begins with Chapter 16, which looks at how to fund a startup as well as a rapidly growing venture, including the cost and process of raising capital, venture capital, and the IPO market. Chapter 17 deals with exploration and exploitation growth strategies for entrepreneurial ventures. It also pays particular attention to growing by going global and concludes with a discussion of harvest and exit strategies.

SPECIAL FEATURES IN THE SEVENTH EDITION

The seventh edition contains a variety of features of value to instructors and readers.

1. *Chapter Objectives* highlight the key topics for each of the chapters.

2. Entrepreneur *Profiles* that begin each chapter provide real-life examples to illustrate the application of chapter concepts and to inspire readers. Smaller-scale examples are also scattered throughout the chapters to maintain the real-life tone of the book.

3. *"Global Insights"* and *"Social Entrepreneurship: Making Meaning"* boxed inserts highlight additional examples, companies, and organizations that have taken a global or a socially responsible approach to entrepreneurship.

4. The *New Venture Action Plan* serves as a reminder of the tasks that need to be completed at particular stages of the entrepreneurial process.

5. *Questions on Key Issues* at the end of each chapter provoke interesting discussions.

6. *Experiencing Entrepreneurship* is a series of activities at the end of each chapter that give readers a chance to learn about entrepreneurship by getting involved in entrepreneurial activities and interacting with entrepreneurs and others in an industry of special interest to the reader.

7. Four new *Case Studies* have been added to the seventh edition to reflect a wider variety of businesses and types of entrepreneurs. The cases are followed by discussion questions.

NEW TO THIS EDITION

The following are the major changes to the seventh edition.

Overall Changes

- The seventh edition has some changes in chapter order for better flow.
- Chapter 6 from the fifth edition has been split into two chapters to make way for a more in-depth treatment of prototyping and the minimum viable product (now Chapter 6) and a more in-depth treatment of intellectual property (now Chapter 7). Chapters 15 and 16 from the fifth edition have been combined to present a complete discussion of funding for both startup and growth (Chapter 16), and Chapters 17 and 18 from the fifth edition have been combined to reflect the natural relationship of growth and change (Chapter 17). The seventh edition now has 17 chapters.
- The seventh edition has eight cases, four of which are new to this edition and reflect companies started and built since 2006. Command Audio, Google Inc., Homerun.com and B2P were retained from the previous edition.
- More international and environmental/sustainability examples have been included.
- Examples and data have been updated; most of the beginning Profiles, as well as a most of the boxed inserts, are new or have been revised to reflect current company data.

Chapter by Chapter Changes

- Chapter 1: All statistics have been updated, as well as the inclusion of the most recent market trends: digital anonymity, the return to domestic manufacturing, big data, and the Lean Startup movement. The opening Profile on WhatsApp and the Social Entrepreneurship box on Angaza are new for this edition.
- Chapter 2: A new Global Insights box features Nordic entrepreneurs who started born global companies as well as new examples in all the chapter sections and updated statistics. Chapter 3: Profile 3.1 presents a new story of young British entrepreneur Nick D'Aloisio. The new chapter title, Creating an Opportunity, underscores the proactive nature of opportunity for entrepreneurs. They don't wait for opportunity; they create it. The chapter has been reorganized to include a new section on opportunity/ideation and a more substantial treatment of the problem-solving process.
- Chapter 4: This chapter now focuses on industry and market analysis, which was Chapter 5 from the sixth edition, to better prepare readers for the business model discussion in Chapter 5. The profile on Gemvara has been enhanced and updated and a new Social Entrepreneurship Box on Medic Mobile has been added. All resources have been updated, new examples included, and a new figure describing an ethnographical approach to customer discovery and solution validation has been included. Chapter 5: This chapter focuses exclusively on business model development. A new opening Profile

showcases Amazon.com as a business model innovator and a new Global Insights Box looks at business models in the developing world. The chapter features an in-depth treatment of hypothesis testing and adds a new section on innovating with business models. There are a number of new figures including a revised business model canvas that incorporates the work of both Alex Osterwalder and Ash Maurya.

- Chapter 6: This chapter was renamed "Prototyping and Validating a Solution" to reflect an emphasis on product design and development issues. Intellectual property now has its own chapter. New box features include Profile 6.1 about an online social learning company Grockit and a Global Insights box on APOPO. In addition to updating examples, the chapter features a new chapter section and associated figure on product development tradeoffs as well as an in-depth discussion of the minimum viable product.

- Chapter 7: This chapter is devoted to intellectual property and ways to protect the startup's assets. It opens with a new profile on the trademark infringement case between Pinterest and Pintrips and includes a new Global Insights Box on intellectual property in China. All statistics and laws have been updated with more current examples.

- Chapter 8: This chapter is now about the founding team. It opens with a new profile on Fandeavor and includes a new Social Entrepreneurship Box on Vera Solutions. The chapter incorporates important research on founding teams conducted by Noam Wasserman and addresses the issue of entrepreneur scalability. Chapter 9: Now titled "Calculating Startup Capital Requirements," has been completely reorganized to move more effectively through the process of determining the amount of funding required to launch the business. A new profile on Barefoot Winery and a new Global Insights Box on migration as a source of entrepreneurship have been added. A new section on risk mitigation is also included.

- Chapter 10: This chapter opens Part III on business design by discussing the preparation of a business plan. A new profile about the failure of a South African startup and an in-depth discussion of proof of concept demonstrations are included. The chapter also includes a new approach to the elevator pitch as well as a discussion of TAM, SAM, and SOM, the various markets being addressed. Chapter 11: Profile 11.1 focuses on culture and has been enhanced and updated for this edition. A new Global Insights Box about Chinese entrepreneurship has also been added.

- Chapter 12: Opening Profile 12.1 on an entrepreneur who turned the wine industry upside down is new, as is the Social Entrepreneurship box featuring five socially responsible startups. A more in-depth treatment of supply chain management has been added and the chapter has been complete refreshed.

- Chapter 13: Profile 13.1 opens with a new story about an entrepreneur whose success came when she fought back after a major lawsuit. A Global Insights box on the legal forms of organization in the UK is also new. All laws have been updated

- Chapter 14: Profile 14.1 is new with an interesting startup experiment in marketing. A new section on journey mapping the customer experience has been added as well as social media marketing through video. The social media metrics section has been enhanced to reflect the latest tactics. The chapter has been completely refreshed with new examples. Chapter 15: This chapter closes the part on Business Design and is now the chapter on ethics and social responsibility. A new profile on a socially responsible for-profit business, Hearsay Social, opens the chapter and an updated Global Insights box on Turkish company AirTies is included. The entire chapter has been refreshed with new examples.

- Chapter 16: Opening Profile is new about a software company that makes big data analytics easily accessible to smaller businesses, and the Social Entrepreneurship box on Room to Read has been updated. The chapter has been reorganized to begin with the topic of financial planning. All statistics on investment have been updated and an expanded section on crowd funding has been added. The valuation section has been completed reworked and a new section on the concepts of divergence and dilution has been added. Chapter 17: The final chapter opens with a new profile story on Annie's Homegrown and its bumpy growth path. The Global Insights box is also new and looks at the growth of startups in Africa. This chapter now combines the topics of growth and change because they normally occur together, and the chapter has been tightened up to discuss only the most important topics from the original two chapters.

SUPPLEMENTAL MATERIALS

Key instructor ancillaries (Instructor's Manual, Test Bank, and PowerPoint slides) are available on the support website located at www.cengagebrain.com, giving instructors the ultimate tool for customizing lectures and presentations.

The Instructor's Manual is a comprehensive and valuable teaching aid, featuring chapter summaries and author notes, chapter objectives, brief chapter outlines, answers to end-of-chapter questions, suggestions to end-of-chapter activities, supplementary lecture materials, and Case Study teaching notes.

The Test Bank, revised and updated, includes a variety of true/false, multiple choice, and short answer questions in varying levels of difficulty, which emphasize the important concepts presented in each chapter.

The PowerPoint® Presentation provides instructors with comprehensive visual aids for each chapter in the book. These slides include outlines of each chapter, highlighting important figures, concepts, and discussion points.

Visit the text Web site at www.cengagebrain.com to find instructor's support materials and study resources to help students practice and apply the concepts they learned in class. The password-protected site contains resources for both students and instructors. For students it provides online interactive quizzes and flashcards. For instructors it includes downloadable Instructor's Manual and Test Bank files, as well as downloadable PowerPoint® Presentations.

ACKNOWLEDGMENTS

Many people helped make this seventh edition of *Launching New Ventures* happen—entrepreneurs, university students, professors, and, of course, the publishing staff at Cengage. In particular, I would like to thank Development Editor Chris Santos, who kept me on track through a very fast production schedule. In addition, I want to express my appreciation to Jason Fremder, Product Manager, and our Project Manager at Lumina Datamatics, Joseph Malcolm.

I want to thank the instructors who used the sixth edition and provided feedback, as well as my students at the Lloyd Greif Center for Entrepreneurial Studies at the University of Southern California, who willingly share their ideas and comments with me. I also want to thank those instructors who provided formal manuscript reviews at various stages of the revision process for this and previous editions:

Donna Albano
Atlantic Cape Community College

Jackie Anderson
Davenport University

Joseph S. Anderson
Northern Arizona University

Rachel Bates
Wichita Area Technical College

Richard Benedetto
Merrimack College

Edward Bewayo
Montclair State University

Bruce Dickinson
Southeast Technical Institute

Janice Feldbauer
Austin Community College

Todd Finkle
University of Akron

Isaura Flores
UNT Dallas

Susan Fox-Wolfgramm
San Francisco State University

Frederick D. Greene
Manhattan College

Jeffry Haber
Iona College

Jo Hamilton
Franklin University

Steven C. Harper
University of North Carolina at Wilmington

Timothy Hill
Central Oregon Community College

Sandra Honig-Haftel

Joseph Hruby
Baldwin Wallace

Lilly Lancaster
University of South Carolina–Spartanburg

Victor L. Lipe
Trident Technical College

Tom Lumpkin
University of Illinois at Chicago

Clare Lyons
Hagerstown Community College

Steven Maranville
University of Houston–Downtown

Ivan J. Miestchovich, Jr.

University of New Orleans

Stephen Mueller

Texas Christian University

Eugene Muscat

University of San Francisco

Terry Noel

Wichita State University

Robert Novota

Lincoln University

Fred B. Pugh

Kirksville College of Osteopathic Medicine

Juan A. Seda

Florida Metropolitan University

Michael Sperling

Stanly Community College

Randy Swangard

University of Oregon

Charles N. Toftoy

The George Washington University

Lynn Trzynka

Western Washington University

Barry L. Van Hook

Arizona State University

John Volker

Austin Peay State University

Bill Waxman

Edison Community College

Mark Weaver

University of Alabama

David Wilemon

Syracuse University

Dennis Williams

Pennsylvania College of Technology

Doug Wilson

University of Oregon

Gene Yelle

UMUC

And finally, I would like to thank my husband, John; and our children, Rob, Jaime (a writer herself), Betty, and Greg for their love and support.

K.R.A.

ABOUT THE AUTHOR

Kathleen Allen, PhD is a professor of entrepreneurship at the USC Marshall School of Business and founding director of the Marshall Center for Technology Commercialization. Allen works with scientists and engineers to identify markets and applications for their technologies, develop commercialization teams, and prepare them to launch ventures and seek funding. Her expertise in technology commercialization is now being applied in projects with the U.S. Navy and the U.S. Department of Homeland Security. She is the author of more than 15 books in the field of entrepreneurship and technology commercialization. Her personal entrepreneurial endeavors include co-founding two successful companies in commercial real estate brokerage, development, and investment, and two technology-based businesses that commercialized patented technologies. Dr. Allen served as entrepreneur-in-residence to a major aerospace firm, currently serves as advisor to several private companies, and is director of a NYSE company. In 2014, she was selected as Entrepreneurship Educator of the Year by the U.S. Association for Small Business and Entrepreneurship. Allen holds a PhD with a specialty in entrepreneurship, an MBA, an MA in Romance Languages, and a BA in music.

PART I

ENTREPRENEURSHIP AND OPPORTUNITY

The Road to Startup

Simplified

Find a Problem

Make sure it's significant and compelling

Engage with Potential Customers

Observe
Listen
Focus on problems

Develop

The solution in a physical form—a prototype
Test it with customers

Build the Product and Get It Ready to Sell

Include feedback from customers in the design and development

Develop and Test

How will you make money?
If necessary, whom do you know who can contribute capital to your business?

Look for Partners

Who can share resources and help you get to market faster?

Develop a Marketing Plan

What is the best way to reach customers?

Decide on the Legal Form for the Company?

How to split equity?
Roles and responsibilities

Hit the Market and Learn If Your Business Model Works

Get market feedback and revise if needed
Retest the model

CHAPTER 1

Understanding Entrepreneurship

"I think a good entrepreneur has a very clear grasp of what the goal is, an unwavering sense of the goal, an utterly agile approach of getting there."

JOHN KATZMAN, CEO NOODLE EDUCATION

CHAPTER OBJECTIVES

- Define entrepreneurship.
- Explain the role of entrepreneurship in economic growth.
- Distinguish entrepreneurial ventures from small businesses in terms of their purpose and goals.
- Describe the evolution of entrepreneurship.
- Identify today's broad trends in entrepreneurship.

WHATSAPP: FROM DAVID TO GOLIATH

On February 19, 2014, social networking giant Facebook acquired WhatsApp, a texting service, for $19 billion in the largest acquisition of a venture-backed company in history. At $19 billion, WhatsApp now exceeded the value of American Airlines, Marriott International, and a host of other iconic companies. Needless to say, the startup world was energized even if they didn't completely understand why Facebook needed to pay such a premium.

Jan Koum, a 38-year-old Ukrainian immigrant who began his life in the United States on food stamps, was not your typical New Millennial app developer in an accelerator waiting to be acquired. Born in Kiev, Ukraine, he grew up in a small village where his father was a construction manager. Their home had no hot water and they used the phone only when they had to because it was monitored by the government. At the age of 16, during a difficult time politically, Koum and his mother fled to the United States where she became a babysitter and Koum swept floors at a grocery store. By the age of 18, Koum had taught himself how to program and he joined a hacker group. Eventually he enrolled at San Jose State University, and in 1997, he met what would be his co-founder, Brian Acton, who worked at Yahoo!. Through nine years at Yahoo!, the two discovered that they did not enjoy advertising platforms—"dealing with ads is depressing." As a result, in 2007 they left the company.

The idea for WhatsApp was inspired by Apple's App Store and the potential for a whole new industry. Drawing on his experiences in the Ukraine where close friends stayed in regular contact but were charged exorbitant fees for texting and then they were monitored, Koum wanted to find a way to provide free and open access to people to communicate via text messages. In 2009, WhatsApp was born. By the end of 2009, the duo had updated the app to enable sending photos and their user growth increased, even when they decided to charge $1 for the app. By early 2011, WhatsApp found itself in the Top 20 of all apps in the Apple Store as their app went viral. It was at that point that Koum agreed to take $8 million from Sequoia Capital with the promise that he wouldn't be forced to use an advertising model. By 2013 with 200 million active users, they did a second round of funding in which Sequoia invested another $50 million, bringing WhatsApp's valuation to $1.5 billion. Interestingly enough, because Koum had stuck to a subscription model, their accumulated revenues now exceeded their Series A funding.

Koum did not set out to be acquired by Facebook; however, once you take venture capital, those decisions are not yours alone. It's easy to see why Facebook wanted WhatsApp. Slow to embrace the mobile platform, Facebook's users were demanding a more mobile friendly version of Facebook. What's more, both Facebook and WhatsApp are big drivers of smartphone use in India, Latin America, and Southeast Asia, so it was a natural alliance. However, there is one issue that users worry about going forward. Will Facebook respect WhatsApp's privacy policy, which is much different than Facebook's? Because its voracious appetite for customer information is well known in the industry, Facebook has been accused of slippage when it comes to user privacy. Koum is adamant that the values that inspired WhatsApp in the first place will not change. The company will not store customer information—not even phone numbers—or any messages. They only store undelivered messages and only for 30 days.

Facebook now owns WhatsApp, but Koum sits on the board of directors of Facebook while running WhatsApp somewhat independently. His commitment to privacy remains strong, but with the disclosure that some encryption flaws that exposed chat histories on the Android phone and a finding that messages sent over Wi-Fi or other public channels can be decrypted using known methods, that commitment is being severely tested.

Sources: Olson, P. (February 19, 2014). "The Rags-to-Riches Tale of How Jan Koum Built WhatsApp into Facebook's New $19B Baby," *Forbes,* http://www.forbes.com/sites/parmyolson/2014/02/19/exclusive-inside-story-how-jan-koum-built-whatsapp-into-facebooks-new-19-billion-baby/; Bajarin, B. (March 17, 2014). "The Value of Facebook and WhatsApp: Connecting the Unconnected," *Time,* http://time.com/27337/the-value-of-facebook-and-whatsapp-connecting-the-unconnected/; Johnston, C. (March 18, 2014). "WhatsApp's Idealism and Facebook Realism: A Study in Contrast," *ARS Technica,* http://arstechnica.com/business/2014/03/whatsapp-says-privacy-is-a-promise-it-can-keep/.

The WhatsApp story in Profile 1.1, although a rare event by any measure, clearly illuminates the excitement of entrepreneurship today and goes a long way toward explaining why so many people want to become entrepreneurs. The lure of success and wealth is enticing, but the reality is that most entrepreneurial businesses do not end up like WhatsApp. In fact, WhatsApp is only one example of what success looks like in the world of entrepreneurship.

What is entrepreneurship? Today the term is being applied to all types of businesses, from the one-person, home-based business to the Fortune 500 company. Because the term *entrepreneur* carries with it a positive connotation, there is a tendency to attach it to any activity that involves starting or innovating. Frequently, people say "I'm being entrepreneurial" when what they mean to say is that they're being creative. From one of the earliest definitions of entrepreneurship, proposed by Austrian economist Joseph Schumpeter, we learn that entrepreneurship is a form of "creative destruction." Breaking down old ways of doing things to create new value.[1] In the early years of the field of entrepreneurship as a discipline, the focus was on the startup of new ventures and the associated activities that defined those ventures.[2] Some research tackled the psychological and sociological traits of the entrepreneur in an attempt to define *who* the entrepreneur is, whereas other research asserted that what the entrepreneur *does* is more important.[3] Later, many definitions focused on the pursuit of opportunity and its exploitation.[4] One definition by Harvard professor Howard Stevenson that still embodies the essence of entrepreneurship is: The process by which individuals—either on their own or inside organizations—pursue opportunities without regard to the resources they currently control.[5]

This definition suggests that entrepreneurship is more than simply starting a business; it also encompasses a mindset or way of thinking and a set of behaviors. That way of thinking is usually opportunity-focused, risk taking, innovative, and growth-oriented. Although entrepreneurship is still most commonly thought of in the context of starting a business, the entrepreneurial mindset can be found within large corporations, in socially responsible nonprofit organizations, and anywhere that individuals and teams desire to differentiate themselves and apply their passion and drive to executing a business opportunity. The behaviors that entrepreneurs undertake include creating opportunity, gathering the resources required to act on that opportunity, and driving the opportunity to completion. At its core, entrepreneurship is about a novel entry into new or established markets and about exploiting new or existing products and services.[6]

Entrepreneurship is not unique to any country, gender, race, age, or socioeconomic sector. Entrepreneurs can be found in some form in every country, in every age group, and (increasingly) in women as often as in men. The entrepreneurial fever does not distinguish between the rich and the poor; in fact, it touches anyone who has the passion to be self-employed or anyone who is determined to be independent and to take charge of his or her life. The entrepreneurial way of thinking can be understood and practiced, and the skills and behaviors of the entrepreneur can be learned and applied. The only characteristic of entrepreneurs that is arguably intrinsic is passion, the drive to achieve something. Passion cannot be taught or practiced; it simply exists when the right elements come together—for example, when an entrepreneur creates a business opportunity and devotes his or her full attention and resources to bringing it to life. Passion is found in successful people in all disciplines—great musicians, artists, writers, scientists, and teachers. It is what drives a person to go beyond expectations and to be the best that person can be.

This chapter explores entrepreneurship as a phenomenon and lays the groundwork for the skills and behaviors that are fundamental to the remainder of the text.

1.1   THE ROLE OF ENTREPRENEURSHIP IN THE ECONOMY

To understand the role that entrepreneurship plays in the economy, it is important to describe the process that entrepreneurs undertake as they create and exploit opportunity. Figure 1.1 depicts a view of this entrepreneurial process. As displayed, it is not a linear process but rather something more like a dynamic system with complex moving parts. Entrepreneurs initially work in Phase 1 to find a problem in a market or an industry. Once a significant problem or need is discovered, they do initial research to understand the industry, the potential market, and any issues they might face in the areas of intellectual property, regulation, or in developing a technology in the case of a technology solution. However, these preliminary activities do not occur in a vacuum. Instead, they are often intertwined with the activities in Phase 2, which focus on validating the hypotheses the entrepreneur has made about the customer, the solution, and the proposed business model. The results of these efforts to research and validate hypotheses will ultimately provide important information about sources of revenue and major drivers of cost. When the activities in Phases 1 and 2 give the entrepreneur sufficient confidence that this business is feasible, it's time to consider the design of the business and to create a plan for execution of the concept. This means having the right team and partners in place as well as choosing the best time to launch the business.

FIGURE 1.1   The Entrepreneurial Process

Phases	PHASE 1: Environment, Discovery & Opportunity	PHASE 2: Business Model Development and Testing	PHASE 3: Business Design, Planning, and Execution
RESEARCH	**Critical Industry Forces** Suppliers, Buyers, Competitive Rivalry, Barriers to Entry, Threat of Substitutes Trends: Technological, Political, and Social	**Value Proposition: The Solution** Applications, Product/Service Offerings Benefits to Customer	**Business Process Flow** Customer Acquisition to Delivery Business Activities
	Market: Pains/Problems Market Size and Growth Competition Trends	**Customer Segment Identification and Validation** Addressable Market Segments Benefits to Each Customer First Customer Customer Channels	**Key Resources Required and Timing** Physical—Plant and Equipment Capital—Working and Investment Human—Headcount
	Intellectual Property, Regulatory, and Technology Validation Patent Decisions, Regulatory Impact Technology PlatForm Development Field Tests and Pre-Clinical tests Technology validation	**Technology Application Validation** Field Tests with Customers Animal Trials Clinical Trials	**Operations** Manufacturing/Operations Plan Marketing Plan Management Plan Contingency Plan Execution Plan
OUTCOMES	**Revenue Sources and Drivers** Number of Sources Type Size Speed to achieve		**Strategic Partners** Independent Contractors Strategic Alliances Investors
	Cost and Profitability Drivers Type Size Importance		**Launch Strategy** License Start a Business Sell Joint Venture
	Startup Capital Requirements		
EXECUTION	**Management Team** **Board of Directors/Advisors** Expertise, Experience, Network		**Market Timing** When to launch

The successful execution of the entrepreneurial process results in a new venture; however, the process of testing and validation continues as the new business responds to a dynamic environment that includes all the variables external to the business that can impact its growth. Some of those external variables include the economic environment, competition, new laws and regulations, labor supply, and sources of capital, to name a few. As the leader, an entrepreneur essentially plays two roles—that of the catalyst, initiating and driving the process, and that of a ringmaster in a three-ring (or more) circus, managing the process through all its changes as the business grows.

This complex entrepreneurial process provides many benefits to society. Chief among these benefits are economic growth, new industry formation, and job creation. The following sections offer some insight into these contributions.

1.1a   Economic Growth

Early economists recognized that technology is the primary force behind rising standards of living[7] and that technological innovation would determine the success of nations in the future. For many years, economic growth was explained solely in terms of inputs of labor and capital. However, in the 1980s—referred to by many as the Decade of Entrepreneurship—the work of Paul Romer and others identified technological change as a critical element of a growth model that responds to market incentives.[8] Romer asserted that technological change happens when an entrepreneur identifies new customer segments that appear to be emerging, new customer needs, existing customer needs that have not been satisfied, or new ways of manufacturing and distributing products and services. (See Figure 1.2.) Identifying these needs offers the opportunity to invent new technology solutions that change the way we do things. Clearly the Internet was one of those technologies, as were fiber optics and the artificial heart. However, it is not just the invention of new-to-the-world technologies that spurs economic growth. Innovators who find ways to improve on existing products, services, and business models or help customers become more efficient also contribute to a vibrant economy.

FIGURE 1.2 Entrepreneurship and Technological Change

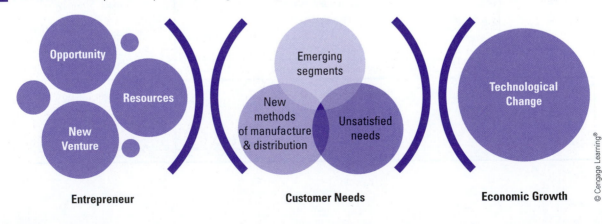

Another way that new technologies have produced huge economic benefits is by lowering the cost of information and transportation, enabling a broader range of goods and services to be traded anywhere in the world. In fact, today very few markets enjoy freedom from competition in the global arena. For example, where local markets in Florida and California once dominated the market for fresh fruits, today consumers are frequently unaware that much of their fresh produce comes from Chile, New Zealand, and other parts of the world. Even service companies cannot escape the impact of the global economy. Russia, China, and India, for example, are dominant players in the software programming industry by transmitting their services electronically and economically to anywhere in the world.

1.1b   New Industry Formation

New industries are another important outcome of entrepreneurship and technological change. An industry is simply the people and companies that engage in a category of business activity such as semiconductors, medical devices, or food services. New industries are born when technological change produces a novel opportunity that enterprising entrepreneurs seize. For example, Apple's iPhone, introduced on January 9, 2007, spurred the development of the mobile app industry, which is now one of the fastest growing sectors in the broader software industry. In 2013 alone, the industry grew 115 percent.[9] The iPhone itself was an innovation built on the know-how of many earlier inventions. Nevertheless, Apple saw the opportunity to change the way we use phones by essentially putting a very powerful computer into everyone's hands and then encouraging developers to create unique programs exclusively for the device.

Industries don't last forever. Much like humans, they have life cycles—they're born, they grow, they decline, and they die. Figure 1.3 depicts the generic life cycle of an industry. The earliest stage of an industry is a time of rapid innovation and change as young firms struggle to become the industry standard bearers with their technology. As these entrepreneurial firms achieve noticeable levels of success, more and more firms desiring to capitalize on the potential for success enter the industry. As the industry grows, it generally becomes more fragmented as a result of so many firms competing for position. Then, at some point consolidation begins to occur as the stronger firms begin to acquire the smaller firms and the weaker firms die out. Eventually, the number of firms in the industry stabilizes and the firms mature. If innovation in the industry ceases to occur, the industry output may actually begin to decline. However, if new, disruptive technology is introduced, the industry may now have a new platform on which to innovate and grow again.

Why are so many more firms created than an industry can support? The answer lies in not knowing which new firms will be successful in securing adoption of their new technologies, products, or services. In the case of incremental innovations, or improvements on existing products, research has shown that incumbent firms are generally more successful than new firms, but, with disruptive, new-to-the-world technologies, it is anyone's guess who the survivors will be.[10] When a disruptive technology wins the standards war in an industry, it can

FIGURE 1.3
The Industry Life Cycle

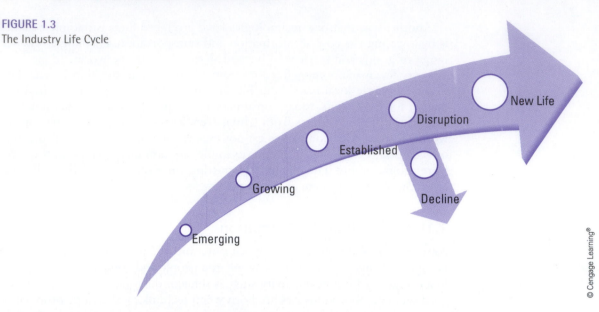

New Life

Disruption

Established

Growing

Decline

Emerging

© Cengage Learning®

make obsolete previous technology almost overnight. For example, the battle between HD DVD and Blu-ray ultimately left HD DVD in the dust. More recently, when the wireless industry transitioned to 4G technology, there was a battle between Qualcomm's Ultra Mobile Broadband (UMB) and a European rival, which had developed Long Term Evolution or LTE, which was compatible with the GSM communications standard used by about 80 percent of the world's wireless subscribers. Within a year, Qualcomm decided to cede its space to LTE. LTE became the standard in 2008.

1.1c   Job Creation

Entrepreneurial ventures are responsible for job creation that is disproportionate to the net total new jobs created in the United States over the past 25 years. The U.S. Small Business Administration (SBA) defines a small business as one with fewer than 500 employees, which by many standards is not very small and includes both high-growth technology ventures and small "mom and pops"—quite a range indeed. The European Union uses a lower cutoff point of 250 people. Nonetheless, businesses classified as small by the U.S. SBA definition represent 99.7 percent of all employers and pay more than 45 percent of the total U.S. private payroll. They have generated 65 percent of net new jobs over the past 15 years.[11] It is important to note, however, that the vast majority of net new jobs created by the small business sector are created by a few rapidly growing young firms called "gazelles" or high-impact businesses. These young businesses generally have sales that double over a four-year period with employment growth of two or more times over the same period.[12] High-impact businesses account for 5 to 6 percent of all businesses, but they account for nearly all net new job creation.[13]

Economic data from 2010 indicate that there were 5,717,302 (99.7%) employer firms with fewer than 500 employees and 17,236 (3%) large employer firms in existence. Businesses with fewer than 20 employees account for approximately 18 percent of all jobs, while businesses with 20–499 employees (considered small businesses) account for about 30.7 percent of all jobs. The largest firms with more than 500 employees provide 50.9 percent of all jobs. Overall, entrepreneurial firms with fewer than 500 employees account for 49.1 percent of all jobs.

Table 1.1 depicts the number of employer firm startups (in business for less than a year) in the United States from 2005 to 2010. It is interesting to note that while the number of employer firms remained fairly consistent over the entire period, the number of employer firm startups declined overall—remaining relatively constant from 2005 to 2007, then declining in 2008 and again in 2009, and rising only a bit in 2010. During the period, startups accounted for between 9.0 percent and 11.1 percent of all employer firms.[14] However, if you consider net job creation, that is, factoring in firm contractions and death, startups created about 19.5 million jobs, whereas existing companies destroyed about 23.1 million jobs, which resulted in an overall net loss of 3.4 million jobs.[15] One explanation for this loss is the fact that approximately one-third of startups close by the second year and fewer than half still exist after five years.[16]

Data from the U.S. Census Bureau from 1998 to 2011 demonstrates that the age of the business is more important in understanding job creation and employment than the size of the business. Essentially, firms less than two years old are fairly volatile in both job creation and destruction, much more so than larger established firms, especially in the first five years.[17] Therefore, it is not necessarily small businesses as a whole that create jobs but young businesses that are growing. Startups are generally job destroyers in the first five years, but the firms that survive tend to grow and add net new jobs over time.

TABLE 1.1
Number of Employer Firms by Startups and Non-Startups 2005–2010

YEAR	#EMPLOYER FIRM STARTUPS	#EMPLOYER FIRM NON-STARTUPS	TOTAL # EMPLOYER FIRMS	SHARE OF EMPLOYER FIRMS THAT ARE STARTUPS
2005	644,122	5,339,424	5,983,546	10.8%
2006	670,058	5,352,069	6,022,127	11.1%
2007	668,395	5,381,260	6,049,655	11.0%
2008	597,074	5,333,058	5,930,132	10.1%
2009	518,500	5,248,806	5,767,306	9.0%
2010	533,945	5,200,593	5,734,538	9.3%

Sources: U.S. Small Business Administration, "Statistics of U.S. Businesses, U.S. Dynamic Data, U.S. Data: Employer Firm Births and Deaths by Employment Size of Firm, 1989–2010," at http://www.sba.gov/advocacy/849/12162; U.S. Bureau of the Census, "Statistics of U.S. Businesses: Latest SUSB Annual Data, 2009, U.S. & States Totals," November 2011, at http://www.census.gov/econ/susb/historical_data.html; and U.S. Bureau of the Census, "Statistics of U.S. Businesses: Latest SUSB Annual Data, 2010, U.S. & States Totals," October 2012, at http://www.census.gov/econ/susb/.

Given that we do business in a global marketplace, it's important to know something about international entrepreneurship. The annual *Global Entrepreneurship Monitor* employs samples that represent about 75 percent of the world's population and 90 percent of the world's GDP. The study divides countries into three groups based on where the country stands in terms of growth and they look at early-stage entrepreneurial activity.[18] In the 2013 report, they identified three categories of countries: factor-driven, efficiency-driven, and innovation-driven.

■ **Factor-driven economies** rely on unskilled labor and the extraction of natural resources for growth. Here businesses are normally created out of necessity and so these countries tend to have very high entrepreneurial activity rates relative to other types of economies. Examples are Zambia and Nigeria, which have entrepreneurial activity rates at a high 39 percent of the adult population.

■ **Efficiency-driven economies** are those growing and in need of improving their production processes and quality of goods produced. Examples are Argentina, Russia, and South Africa, although the highest entrepreneurial activity rates were found in Latin America and the Caribbean.

■ **Innovation-driven economies**, which are the most advanced, are where businesses compete based on innovation and entrepreneurship. Examples are the United Kingdom, Singapore, Israel, and the United States. The highest levels of entrepreneurial activity are found in Trinidad, Tobago, and the United States.

Entrepreneurship occurs in all three categories, but it is clearly driven by different factors in each, and those factors determine the types and size of businesses found in those countries. One consistent finding is that across all type of economies, there are more people in the 25- to 34-year-old age group with intentions to start a business.

1.2   THE NATURE OF ENTREPRENEURIAL STARTUPS

Entrepreneurial ventures and small businesses are related, but they are not the same in most respects. Both are important economically but each provides different benefits and outcomes. Schumpeter described entrepreneurs as equilibrium disrupters who introduce new products and processes that change the way we do things, while small-business owners typically operate a business to make a living.[19] Examples of small businesses are small shops, restaurants, and professional service businesses. They form what has been called the "economic core."[20] In some cases, they're known as lifestyle businesses or "mom and pops," not only because they tend to stay small and geographically bound, but more because their owners make a conscious decision to remain small. As a result, they tend to be slow growing and often replicate similar businesses already in the market.

It should not be forgotten, however, that even high-impact ventures start small. The difference is that the high-impact entrepreneur's goal is not small.

In general, high-impact entrepreneurial ventures have three primary characteristics. They are:

- Innovative
- Value-creating
- Growth-oriented

An entrepreneurial venture brings something new to the marketplace, whether it be a new product or service. It creates new value in a number of important ways. Entrepreneurs create new jobs that don't merely draw from existing businesses, and by finding niches in the market, entrepreneurs serve customer needs that are currently unserved. Moreover, entrepreneurs typically have a vision of where they want their businesses to go, and generally that vision is regional, national, or (more often) global.

Choosing what kind of business to start is very important, because that choice influences all subsequent decisions and determines what kinds of goals you are able to achieve. For example, if you intend to grow a business to a national level, you will make different decisions along the way than if the intent is to own and operate a thriving restaurant that competes only in the local community. Generally, running a small business requires good management skills on the part of the owner, who must perform many of the tasks associated with the business as it grows. By contrast, entrepreneurs often do not have the skills to handle the management aspects of the business and prefer to hire experts to carry out that function, leaving the entrepreneur and the founding team free to innovate, raise capital, and promote the business. Chapter 2 will address the behavioral characteristics of entrepreneurs.

1.2a   Risk and the Entrepreneurial Venture

It's impossible to talk about entrepreneurial ventures without considering the effects of risk as risk is an inherent part of the entire entrepreneurial process. What changes over time with more information and validation from the market is the impact of that risk. Figure 1.4 depicts the relationship between the amount of risk in a new venture and the impact of that risk.

Much of new venture risk occurs early in the creation process. Borrowing a term from product development, we can call the period of time prior to launch and startup the *fuzzy front end*, which simply means that the activities undertaken at this point are often unclear and subject to change as more information is obtained. The fuzzy front end has been modeled in economic terms. Simply put, the amount of investment an individual is willing to make in a new product—or, in this case, in a new venture—is a function of the probability of its success, the value of that success, and the cost of failure $[\text{Inv} = f(\text{PS} + \text{VS} + \text{CF})]$. A change in any one of these values will alter the economics of the bet.[21] The nascent entrepreneur uses the time spent in the fuzzy front end to calculate the probability of success as an entrepreneur; what that success will mean in terms of return on his or her investment of time, money, and effort; and what the risk or cost of failure might be. Those probability estimates are highly subjective;

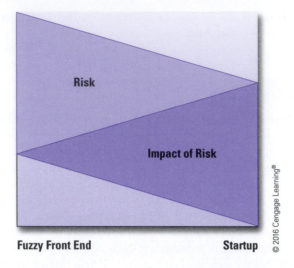

Risk

Impact of Risk

Fuzzy Front End   Startup

© 2016 Cengage Learning®

however, if the nascent entrepreneur uses the time in the fuzzy front end to gather information about the industry and market, test the business model through feasibility analysis, and determine the conditions under which he or she is willing to move forward and start the business, much of the subjectivity will be eliminated. Moreover, the risk of startup will be reduced, and the probability associated with the three outcomes will be more accurate.

Nevertheless, the impact of the risk taken is relatively small at the fuzzy front end but grows exponentially as the new venture gets closer to startup. More is known at startup, which reduces risk, but what risk remains has a larger impact because to achieve startup, more resources must be invested; consequently, the loss is greater should the venture fail after launch.

It is not entirely clear what actually prompts an individual to become a nascent or budding entrepreneur. Even with the risk assessment and risk mitigation that are part of preparing to launch a new venture, there appears to be no uniform mechanism that consistently results in an individual deciding to put forth the effort to launch a business. One individual may choose to enter the nascent stage despite a high level of risk. Another may choose to reject the nascent phase even under conditions where the perceived risk involved is low. Nascents appear to emerge from the population through both push and pull factors. *Push* is the mechanism that drives an individual to become a nascent entrepreneur because all other opportunities for income appear to be absent or unsatisfactory. In other words, it's a necessity. *Pull* is the mechanism that attracts an individual to an opportunity and creates a "burning desire" to launch a business and capture a market. Recent research has found that ability expectancies play a more significant role than outcome expectancies in whether a nascent entrepreneur launches a business.[22] In other words, entrepreneurs come to the new venture process with perceptions about their ability to undertake the tasks required to start the business independent of the probability of failure, and those perceptions drive whether or not the business actually launches.

The intent to start a business is not in itself enough to make it happen. Due to the challenging nature of the endeavor, many potential entrepreneurs drop out of the process as they move from intention to preparation and then to execution. In addition, a high number of entrepreneurs give up before the new business makes the transition to an established firm.[32] Again Figure 1.4 enables us to see from an investor's perspective that if an investor funds a venture at the fuzzy front end or pre-startup, the risk is high. That risk declines as the new venture answers many of the questions that surround its viability as a business. Ironically, the investor is inclined to invest at startup or beyond when the risk is smaller, but impact of a failure at that point is actually greater.

1.2b   New Business Failure

The SBA reports that about half of all new businesses will survive five years or more, and approximately one-third will survive 10 years or more. So it is clear that survivability increases with age.[23] Furthermore, while the rate of startups has increased, the rate for small business failures has declined. Nevertheless, other studies have found that only about 45 percent of startups were still alive after five years.[24] Bloomberg reports that 8 out of 10 entrepreneurs fail within 18 months, an 80 percent failure rate.[25] This disparate range of failure rates is likely due to differing definitions of failure and from lumping all types of businesses into the sample.

One of the biggest reasons for new business failure is that entrepreneurs come up with a solution looking for a problem. They haven't identified a real need in the market that they can address with their business concept. Another reason is that the solution they are offering is not unique or compelling. In other words, it is often a "me-too" solution that does not offer anything different from what is already in the market. Yet another reason is that they haven't identified and tested a business model that actually works. All of these factors lead to failure. But beyond these factors, entrepreneurial ventures face the liability of newness. The fact is that the firms that are most likely to survive over the long term are those that display superior levels of reliability and accountability in performance, processes, and structure. Because these factors tend to increase with age, failure rates tend to decline with age.[26] Young firms have a higher chance of failure because they have to divert their scarce resources away from the critical operations of the company in order to train employees, develop systems and controls, and establish strategic partnerships. Another body of research sees failure as a liability of adolescence, claiming that startups survive in the early years by relying on their original resources, but that as those resources are depleted and the need to find new and different resources increases the company's chances of failing also increase.

Failure is a fact of life that must be dealt with. The vital issue for entrepreneurs is not avoiding failure but minimizing the cost of a possible failure and recovering quickly. That comes from starting with a robust business model and testing it in the marketplace prior to starting the business.

SOCIAL ENTREPRENEURSHIP: *MAKING MEANING*

Solving a Tough Problem in Africa

Mobile phones have penetrated Africa in a big way, growing at a rate of about 30 percent per year. But keeping those mobile phones charged is a costly proposition. In East Africa, for example, the typical family may spend 30 percent or more of their annual income on lighting and cell phone charging, according to Lesley Marincola, CEO of Angaza, a company founded in Nairobi, Kenya, in 2012 that is working to solve that problem. With its PAYG (pay-as-you-go) platform, it overcomes the price barrier to solar and other sources of energy by accepting energy prepayments, which avoid the service costs associated with traditional loans. Using their own cell phone, customers can send payment information to their PAYG-enabled solar devices. One of Angaza's customers is a farmer named Stephano who uses his cell phone for business. Because traditional kerosene is dangerous to his family's health, he was able to switch to Angaza's product SoLite to provide clean light and to charge his phone. Now he can pay for energy based on his needs, and it's actually costing less than kerosene.

Source: Angaza Design, www.angazadesign.com.

It is important to understand how entrepreneurship has evolved over time as a discipline even while its economic benefits have remained relatively constant. The next section presents a summary of key changes in the entrepreneurial landscape.

1.3   A BRIEF HISTORY OF THE ENTREPRENEURIAL REVOLUTION

The United States was founded on the principle of free enterprise, which encouraged entrepreneurs to assume the risk of developing businesses that would make the economy strong. However, it was not until the 1980s that the word *entrepreneur* came into popular use in the United States, and an almost folkloric aura began to grow around men and women who started rapidly growing businesses. These formerly quiet, low-profile people suddenly became legends in their own time, with the appeal and publicity typically associated with movie stars or rock musicians.

Today's entrepreneurs are no different. Elon Musk has changed the game for the space industry by creating a lower-cost solution for sending cargo and satellites into space. Under the leadership of Jeff Bezos, Amazon.com completely disrupted the brick-and-mortar retail industry. Entrepreneurs such as these shake up the economy and change the game for everyone. They look for unsatisfied needs and satisfy them. Figure 1.5 summarizes the entrepreneurial evolution that has taken place since the 1960s, paving the way for the innovation economy that has been the envy of the world.

FIGURE 1.5 The Decades of Entrepreneurship

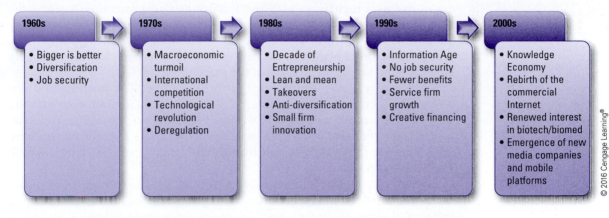

FIGURE 1.5 The Decades of Entrepreneurship

1960s
- Bigger is better
- Diversification
- Job security

1970s
- Macroeconomic turmoil
- International competition
- Technological revolution
- Deregulation

1980s
- Decade of Entrepreneurship
- Lean and mean
- Takeovers
- Anti-diversification
- Small firm innovation

1990s
- Information Age
- No job security
- Fewer benefits
- Service firm growth
- Creative financing

2000s
- Knowledge Economy
- Rebirth of the commercial Internet
- Renewed interest in biotech/biomed
- Emergence of new media companies and mobile platforms

© 2016 Cengage Learning®

1.3a The Decades of Entrepreneurship

In the *mid-1960s*, gigantic companies were the norm. General Motors in the 1960s was so large that it earned as much as the 10 biggest companies in Great Britain, France, and West Germany combined.[27] The reason why U.S. companies enjoyed such unrestricted growth at that time was that they lacked competition from Europe and Japan. Therefore, job security for employees was high, and companies tended to diversify and grow very large by acquiring other businesses.

The *1970s* saw the beginning of three significant trends that would forever change the face of business: macroeconomic turmoil, international competition, and the technological revolution. A volatile economic climate, the likes of which had not been seen since World War II, dominated the 1970s. The Vietnam War economy brought inflation, the dollar was devalued, food prices skyrocketed as a consequence of several agricultural disasters, and the formation of OPEC sent gas prices up 50 percent. Furthermore, by the late 1970s the Federal Reserve had let interest rates rise to a prime of 20 percent with the result that there was no borrowing, no spending, and a recession that spilled into the 1980s, bringing with it an unemployment rate of 10 percent.[28] To compound the effects of the economy on business, by 1980 one-fifth of all U.S. companies faced foreign competitors that had far more favorable cost structures with much lower labor costs. Imports, particularly in the automobile and machine tools industries, were suddenly taking a significant share of the market from U.S. businesses.

The third event affecting business at that time was the technological revolution brought about by the introduction in 1971 of the Intel microprocessor, the Mits Altair personal computer in 1975, and the Apple II computer in 1977. Microprocessors succeeded in rendering whole categories of products obsolete—such things as mechanical cash registers and adding machines, for example—and effectively antiquated the skills of the people who made them.

Increasing the pressure on business, the government ushered in a new era of business regulation with the Environmental Protection Agency, the Occupational Safety and Health Agency, and the Consumer Product Safety Commission, all of which increased costs to businesses. On the opposite front, deregulation forced planes, trucks, and railroads to compete, and in general big companies no longer had control of the marketplace.

By the *early 1980s*, business was in terrible shape. The Fortune 500 saw a record 27 percent drop in profits.[29] Large mills and factories were shutting down; manufacturing employment was declining; and yet, ironically, productivity remained the same or actually increased. New, smaller manufacturers were still generating jobs—and not only manufacturing jobs, but service jobs as well. How was this possible?

To become competitive, the smaller, more flexible, entrepreneurial manufacturers had hired subcontractors who could perform tasks such as bookkeeping and payroll more efficiently. These service firms developed to support the needs of the product sector, but they also inspired the creation of other service firms: People who work often need day-care or maid services, so even more jobs were being created.

With the creation of all these jobs, it is no wonder that the 1980s was called the true Decade of Entrepreneurship by many, including the father of modern management science, Peter Drucker, who was not alone in asserting that the United States was rapidly and by necessity becoming an entrepreneurial economy.[30] On the heels of the emergence of Silicon Valley and its legendary entrepreneurs, the mainstream press began to focus on business activities, creating many popular magazines such as *Inc.* and *Entrepreneur*.

Responding to this entrepreneurial drive, big business in the 1980s found it necessary to downsize and reverse the trend of diversification it had promulgated for so long. If big companies were going to compete with the dynamic, innovative smaller firms and fend off the takeover bids so prevalent in the 1980s, they would have to restructure and reorganize for a new way of doing business. This restructuring and reorganizing actually resulted in improved performance, increased profits, and higher stock prices. It also meant, however, that many jobs would no longer exist, employees would receive fewer benefits, and the only "secure" jobs left would be found in civil service.

Toward the end of the 1980s, researchers observed that young entrepreneurial ventures were internationalizing much earlier than expected and at a much smaller size.[31] A significant number of these ventures were in high-tech industries.[32] Large-sample empirical research revealed that directors and managers with significant international experience played a strong role in the internationalization of entrepreneurial ventures at startup.[33] All these events moved this country toward a period in the 1990s that required the vision, the resources, and the motivation of the entrepreneur to seek new opportunities and create new jobs in a vastly different global environment electronically linked via the Internet.

More than perhaps anything else, the *1990s* were characterized as the Information Age. The commercial Internet emerged midway through the decade, and suddenly global competition and resources were more readily available than ever before. The Internet made entrepreneurship and the ability to compete alongside large established companies in the same markets a reality. Furthermore, with more and more jobs being shipped overseas, employees learned that job security was no longer a fact of life. U.S. companies quickly discovered that their competitiveness lay in the control of information and new ideas, and clearly the Internet was to play an important role in this new view of the world. The late 1990s brought the "dot com" bubble and the rush of the venture capital community to position itself for what appeared to be a new way of doing business. At the same time, the interest in non-Internet-related technology was waning as investors saw a much quicker return on their investment in the world of e-commerce.

The ***new millennium*** ushered in what many referred to as the *knowledge economy*, brought about by increased globalization and the competitive shift to more "knowledge-based economic activity."[34] In the new economy, the primary resource was knowledge rather than raw materials and physical labor. Differences in economic performance in regions of the world could largely be explained by the presence or absence of entrepreneurship capital, which was essential to the development of new business models that monetized knowledge. Entrepreneurship capital was characterized by social networks that linked entrepreneurs to educational institutions, industries, network brokers, and to resources. California's Silicon Valley and the North Carolina Research Triangle are two examples of environments that have long prospered from knowledge-based economic activity and a high level of entrepreneurial enterprise.

The knowledge economy of the early 2000s was also described by low-cost competition from Asia and Central and Eastern Europe that came about when transfer costs were driven down in the telecommunications and computer sectors, making it easier and less expensive to move capital and information. Consequently, most routine tasks in production and manufacturing were now more efficiently accomplished in low-cost locations.

Without a doubt, the early 2000s were also influenced by the commercial Internet. In 1998, the media declared that dot com was the business of the future—that it would change the way business was conducted forever. By the spring of 2000, the dot-com bubble had burst and funding for dot-com ventures virtually disappeared overnight. However, what remained was a distribution channel that had huge potential and merely required good business models to sustain it.

Renewed interest in non-Internet-related technologies was one of the results of the dot-com crash of 2000 as investors turned to solid technologies that could be protected through patents and developed a growing interest in green tech, biotech, and biomedical devices that spread into the second decade of the new millennium. Marketer Joe Pine characterized this second decade of the new millennium as the "experience economy." Companies are looking for ways to give their customers an authentic experience. As it turns out, mobile is a platform that is well suited to experiences because mobile devices like smartphones are with users wherever they go. With mobile devices dominating the market, more entrepreneurs are looking for ways to solve problems associated with search, e-commerce, social networks, and communication on mobile devices.

1.4   CURRENT ENTREPRENEURIAL TRENDS

In the previous edition of this book (2012), major trends were global economic turmoil, green power, the women's market, and the Gen Y consumer movement called *mass mingling*. Clearly those trends are still relevant, but four new trends, among many trends, have emerged that will also affect the decisions entrepreneurs make about opportunity, business models, and strategies to sustain their businesses: (1) digital anonymity, (2) domestic manufacturing, (3) big data, and (4) the lean startup movement.

1.4a   Digital Anonymity

Today indiscriminate sharing of personal information on social networks is at the top of the hype cycle. The typical mobile user checks his or her email on a smartphone 150 times a day and global mobile traffic as a percentage of total Internet traffic has now reached more than 15 percent with the trend line curving steeply upward. Facebook can claim more than a billion global active users, 60 percent who log in daily and have an average of 200 or more friends. About 350 million photos are uploaded daily, but that pales in comparison to the 100 hours per minute of video that is uploaded to YouTube.[35]

With so many people sharing the most intimate details of their lives with the world, something was bound to disrupt the trajectory of online sharing. The year 2013 saw NSA leaks, hackers targeting consumer credit cards, and blanket inquiries into individual's personal lives through their online connections, to name a few. These invasions of privacy and more have inspired whole new platforms based on giving the user a digital experience that can be anonymous, deleted, and secure. For example, Snapchat, a photo messaging app, enables users to send a photo or video with text to a specific group of people and control the time limit for how long they can view the Snaps, from one to ten seconds. When the time limit ends, the Snap is no long available and is deleted from Snapchat's servers. In this way users can control their digital footprints.

On the business side, ArmorText provides an encrypted platform for companies who want to communicate through text messages in a secure environment that meets the requirements of government regulations such as HIPAA in the healthcare field and FINRA in financial services. New search engines such as DuckDuckGo offer the opportunity to search the Internet without being tracked, which is particularly important in countries that watch what citizens do on the Internet. Going forward, entrepreneurs should expect to see more offerings related to privacy and security.

1.4b   Return to Domestic Manufacturing and Craft

In the United States, "Made in America" is making a comeback. In a 2014 report on U.S.industrial manufacturers, PricewaterhouseCoopers found a reason to be optimistic that the United States may experience a renaissance in manufacturing.[36] Some of the contributing factors include affordable labor, higher shipping costs, and innovation introduced by manufacturing startups like Tesla Motors, which employs robots to keep costs down. Many entrepreneurs are finding that bringing their manufacturing home, called in-shoring, reaps benefits in speed and more control over the process. For example, a San Francisco–based apparel company, Everlane, which sells to customers online, is now manufacturing half of its product line in the United States. If Everlane gets a plug from TV show or even praise from an online blog, it can respond quickly to the surge in demand that typically follows. That would not be possible if Everlane had to rely on its overseas manufacturer.

A study by the Boston Consulting group finds that more than half of large manufacturing firms are planning to return some of their production to the United States to take advantage of skilled labor and reduced costs of transportation.[37] What this means for entrepreneurs is that they may be able to keep their manufacturing domestic and they may be able to find manufacturing partners with excess capacity that they can tap into until their business is making money.

One of the key technologies in the manufacturing space that is surging in interest is 3D printing using advanced materials. These printers, which have been around a while, lay down particles of wood, plastic, or metal in very thin layers that build up into whatever object is being created. One of the leaders in this effort is Nike, which is changing the way we look at mass production. The company is able to produce prototypes at speeds never before seen, bringing down the typical development time from six weeks to two days.[38] Entrepreneurs are even finding that 3D printing can be a cost-effective way to make products in small quantities. Summer Powell designs jewelry on a 3D computer screen and then uses a New York printing service to produce the jewelry out of nylon on a 3D printer. Then Powell adds some finishing touches and sells the jewelry online through Etsy.com or in local boutiques in San Francisco.[39]

As manufacturing regains prominence in the United States, it will not look like the manufacturing of 20 years ago and entrepreneurs will have an important role to play, whether it's with 3D printing applications (also called *additive manufacturing*), advanced robotics that are reducing the need to outsource overseas, software solutions, service integration, or making sense out of big data. Technology is bringing down the cost of manufacturing and the opportunities to innovate are enormous.

1.4c   Big Data

Big data is the term now being used to describe the rapidly growing mass of information that companies and individuals are stockpiling and storing. With an increasing number of devices gathering information, we are now experiencing what is called *data exhaust*, which is simply the data that goes into the Internet every time we send a text, search a website, or tweet. IBM reports that our devices give birth to 2.5 quintillion bytes of data every day. That is equivalent to 531 million DVDs. In fact, it is estimated that by 2020, the rate at which we produce data will mushroom to 35 zettabytes, or 7.35 trillion DVDs.[40]

Of course, all of that data, whether it's structured data such as reports or unstructured coming from multiple sources, needs to be catalogued, stored, and analyzed. So rich with possibility is this trend that specialized funds such as Data Collective have been launched to provide investments in big data start-ups that can find ways to monetize data. Entrepreneurs who can gain access to unique data and insights that no one else has can create a strong competitive advantage. Furthermore, new database systems are needed because legacy systems from major vendors were not developed to effectively handle the speed, volume, or variety of data being produced online. There are now opportunities to disrupt the current systems with systems that are faster and more flexible.

Data is now considered an asset class for most businesses, so this trend will converge with the trend toward privacy and security. One of the biggest challenges going forward is figuring out how to extract revenue from that data.

1.4d   The Lean Startup Movement

Although the lean startup movement seems to be a hot trend in the startup world, it actually had its origins in a famous management approach used by Toyota called *lean thinking*. The three key principles of lean are 1) minimizing waste in time and resources, 2) continuous improvement through experimentation and pivoting in new directions, and 3) systems thinking or looking at the big picture. Throughout the 1980s and 1990s, lean found its way into all kinds of businesses until Eric Ries, a software entrepreneur, introduced lean to the startup world with his book aptly named *Lean Startup*. In it he focused on how to get to the customer quickly with minimum viable product (MVP) to get feedback (validation) and iterate (pivot) to a more successful outcome. According to Ries, the key question to be answered is "Should we build this product?" Moreover, "Can we build a sustainable business around this set of products and services?" He asserts that the key activities of a startup are "build-measure-learn."[41] The methodology favors "experimentation over planning, customer feedback over intuition, and iterative design over traditional 'big design up front' development."[42]

The lean startup movement generally attempts to take a scientific approach to startup and to create a brand around the approach. It was quickly adopted by Silicon Valley technology companies and Ries became a frequent speaker and advisor on the topic. Even the U.S. government began looking for ways to take a lean approach to government programs. The biggest criticisms of the movement are that the approach itself has not been validated due to the difficulty of controlling for all the variables that might impact the process. Reid Hoffman, LinkedIn founder, was reported as saying that the movement is good for entrepreneurs, who are not Steve Jobs or Elon Musk, the role models for many technology founders today.[43] In some cases, lean has been misinterpreted by entrepreneurs as an excuse to bring incomplete products to market that have no real value.

As the lean startup movement begins to move out of the startup space and into Fortune 500 companies, worldwide organizations, and government agencies, it will probably be required to adhere to metrics that have been missing from its experience in the startup world. Some of the tenets and tools of lean are incorporated in some fashion in this book, most notably in Chapter 5; however, this book does not adopt any trend wholesale. Instead you are encouraged to pick and choose the ideas and tools that best suit your situation and needs.

1.5   LOOKING AHEAD: THE ORGANIZATION OF THE BOOK

Starting a new venture is a process that begins long before the business ever opens its doors. That process is rarely linear but rather a more iterative—even chaotic—process; however, the entrepreneurial process does have direction and goals. This book is divided into four sections that reflect the key elements of the entrepreneurial process.

Part One Chapters 1 through 3 focuses on entrepreneurship and opportunity. Chapter 1 serves as an introduction to the field of entrepreneurship and the environment in which entrepreneurs start new ventures today from a macro perspective. Chapter 2, another foundational chapter, explores the entrepreneurial journey from the entrepreneur's perspective, a micro perspective, and helps you prepare for this journey by dealing with the human side of entrepreneurship as a mindset and a way of life. In Chapter 3, the process of entrepreneurship begins and we look at how opportunities are generated through the development of creativity and problem-solving skills.

Part Two (Chapters 4 through 9) explores feasibility analysis for new ventures in detail by examining the various types of hypotheses and tests that entrepreneurs use to determine the conditions under which they can launch their businesses. It includes all the areas of the business that must be researched and understood in order to increase the chances of a successful launch.

Part Three (Chapters 10 through 15) focuses on the elements of business design and operations, and it addresses how to develop a business plan or execution strategy for the startup. Chapter 15 also introduces ways to incorporate ethics and social responsibility into the business.

Any successful business undergoes growth and change, so Part Four (Chapters 16, 17) focuses on these related issues. Chapter 16 looks at how to fund startup and growth and architect a harvest strategy for the entrepreneur and any investors. Chapter 17 explores how to plan for growth and change.

Entrepreneur skills are key not only to economic independence and success but to business survival. The marketplace puts a premium on creativity, initiative, independence, and flexibility. Entrepreneurs who develop those behaviors and display those characteristics will be more likely to succeed.

New Venture Action Plan

- Read broadly about entrepreneurs and new ventures to get ideas for what makes a successful venture.

- Interview an entrepreneur to better understand the entrepreneurial mindset.

- Research new trends, particularly in an industry in which you're interested.

Questions on Key Issues

1. Define the term *entrepreneurship*.
2. How do entrepreneurial ventures differ from small businesses?
3. As the mayor of your community, what incentives would you put into place to encourage entrepreneurship?
4. Describe the current environment for entrepreneurship in your country. Compare that environment to another country in a different part of the world.
5. Which of the entrepreneurial trends discussed in the chapter will have the biggest impact and why?

Experiencing Entrepreneurship

1. Interview an entrepreneur in an industry or business that interests you. Focus on how and why this entrepreneur started his or her business. Be sure to include the following:

   a. Contact information

   b. The entrepreneur's name, address, title, company name, and phone number

   c. Background

   d. How did you find this person and why did you choose her or him?

   e. Why is this person an entrepreneur?

   f. What influenced the entrepreneur to identify and pursue this opportunity?

   g. How did the entrepreneur's background (family history, prior education, and work experience) affect the opportunity discovered?

   h. Describe the opportunity that the entrepreneur decided to pursue and the process the entrepreneur used to evaluate the opportunity.

   i. How did the entrepreneur evaluate the opportunity?

   j. What criteria did the entrepreneur use to decide whether to pursue the opportunity?

   k. What were the perceived risks of this opportunity and how did the entrepreneur expect to manage them?

   l. What did the entrepreneur do to turn the opportunity into a business?

   m. Identify specific activities the entrepreneur undertook to develop the opportunity into a business.

   n. Identify when the entrepreneur did these activities (provide dates: month and year).

   o. Identify important contacts and individuals who were helpful during the startup process.

   p. What major problems did the entrepreneur encounter along the way?

   q. How were these problems solved?

   r. What advice would the entrepreneur give to someone thinking about pursuing an opportunity?

   s. Why was this entrepreneur successful?

2. Analyze how the factors in question 1 affect the entrepreneur's success.

Relevant Case Studies

Case 6 Groupon

Case 7 HomeRun.com

CHAPTER 2

Preparing for the Entrepreneurial Journey

"Success isn't permanent, and failure isn't fatal."

MIKE DITKA, PROFESSIONAL FOOTBALL COACH

CHAPTER OBJECTIVES

- Dispel myths about entrepreneurs.
- Understand the many pathways to entrepreneurship.
- Make entrepreneurship a way of life.
- Prepare to become an entrepreneur.

PROFILE
2.1

ONE JOURNEY THAT INSPIRED AN INDUSTRY

Sometimes you start out wanting to launch a simple business and end up creating an entire industry. At least that's what happened to lifelong friends Adam Lowry and Eric Ryan who combined contemporary design and eco-friendly ingredients to produce a line of liquid soaps and cleaners called Method Home that is now worth over $100 million. Lowry is a chemical engineer with a focus on the environment, while Ryan is a marketing guru with experience at Gap and Saturn, among other companies.

It was the late 1990s in San Francisco when the two Michigan-born-and-bred friends began brainstorming potential products to reinvent. They used a technique that entrepreneurs often use when they want to see something from a different point of view: They took the most mundane household cleaners and said, "What if we…." That process led to the idea that, unlike the dominant products from Procter & Gamble and Clorox that contained harsh, toxic chemicals, their cleaners would be eco-friendly and have beautiful, contemporary designs—in other words, both style and substance. In Lowry and Ryan's view, going green did not mean that the consumer had to suffer. Green could be stylish and practical.

Their first product came out in the midst of the recession of 2001, funded with seed capital of $90,000 that they had raised from friends and family. In true entrepreneurial fashion, they had mixed the products up in a bathtub and delivered them in an old pickup truck. However, in the process, they had used up all their capital. They even remember a dinner with their first investors where they couldn't find a credit card that wasn't maxed out—they had to use their persuasive skills to convince the restaurant owner that they were good for it.

Within a year, they had battled their way into distribution in 800 stores with products that used natural ingredients—palm oil, coconut oil, and corn oil—bottled in attractive, recyclable containers. Lowry and Ryan knew that their core strategy had to be around brand building and that they were going head-to-head with the dominant players in the market. To succeed, they needed to attract one of their favorite designers, Karim Rashid, who turned out to be intrigued by their bold mission and agreed to come on board as the chief creative officer.

Design was one component of their brand-building strategy; speed and innovation were the other critical elements. To achieve all three, they developed a system of 50 subcontractors so they could introduce new products quickly and pull failed products off the shelves just as quickly. Today, they sell more than 130 products in over 8,000 stores. In 2012, Method merged with Ecover to create the world's largest green cleaning company. Taking green to the max, in 2014 the company broke ground on its first Leed-certified U.S. manufacturing plant on Chicago's south side.

Sources: "Method Breaks Ground and Unveils Designs for Its First U.S. Manufacturing Plant," *Method Press Release*, March 4, 2014, www.methodhome.com; "How Two Friends Built a $100 Million Company: The Rise of Method Home," *Inc.com*, June 29, 2010, www2.inc.com/ss/how-two-friends-built-100-million-company; Heffernan, M. "Messy Guys Make Millions Selling Green Cleaning Products," *Reader's Digest* www.rd.com/money/messy-guys-make-millions-selling-green-cleaning-products; and; Van Schagen, S. "An Interview with the Founders of Method Green Homecare Products," March 13, 2008, www.grist.org/article/fighting-dirty/PALL/print.

Entrepreneurship is a personal journey that begins in the mind of an individual. It is a personal journey because business is fundamentally about people— their hopes and dreams, how they interact, make decisions, plan for the future, deal with conflict, and so on. In fact, all of entrepreneurship can be reduced to people. From the entrepreneur's motivation to start a business to the decisions made about growth, customers, facilities, employees, and the exit from the business, everything comes down to people and their needs and motivations. Entrepreneurs' needs and motivations must be satisfied by their startups or they will not have the motivation to persist in their efforts. The new venture must also satisfy the needs of customers or they won't be motivated to buy. Would it surprise you to learn that Amazon.com is ranked number one of the top 100 global brands across seven major industries for best customer experience? This rating did not happen by accident. In fact, there are at least five reasons why this company succeeds where others do not. (1) The customer comes first and every employee understands this, (2) they make the customer experience as easy as possible, (3) they personalize the experience by recommending items based on customers' previous purchases, (4) they reach out to try to save the customer money by letting them know when the price of something they're interested in has gone down, and (5) the company engenders a high degree of trust. That kind of relationship with customers comes from the recognition that business is fundamentally about people.

Entrepreneurs quickly learn the importance of people when they try to put together a founding team. Assembling the right team can, more often than not, make the difference between success and failure. It is very difficult today to start a new company as a solo entrepreneur; mostly because any single person rarely has all the knowledge and skills required to move quickly and make the decisions that will lead to success, so assembling a great team is more critical than many entrepreneurs believe. As part of an enormously successful team, Eric Schmidt stays in the background when it comes to the press about the company he co-founded with his much younger partners Sergey Brin and Larry Page—Google. Brin and Page brought youthful exuberance and new ideas while Schmidt brought business experience and capital. This is a team that believes in creating a family in their workplace environment—"it's easier to get a family united behind a cause than a bunch of employees," says Schmidt.[1] In the fast-moving Internet marketplace, having a team with compatible values and a laser focus on the company vision is a sure route to success.

How large and how fast to grow the business is very much a personal decision. Entrepreneurs who want to balance work with a personal life may choose to start a business that generates significant revenues but does not require a great deal of people and physical assets to manage. That was the position that Julie Fredrickson took. Fredrickson is the co-founder and CEO of playAPI, a New York–based enterprise software company launched in March 2012. She serves clients such as Gap, American Express, and Kate Spade. Unlike many entrepreneurs today, she is not a workaholic; Fredrickson limits her work day to 10 hours or less and keeps her weekends free.[2] Her company builds digital marketing and brand building campaigns that drive customer engagement using game mechanics. PlayAPI may not grow as fast or become as big a company as many entrepreneurs aspire to achieve, but her goal is to have a successful business *and* a successful life.

The decision about when and how to exit the business is also a very personal one because it is based on the entrepreneur's goals and values. Some entrepreneurs start many ventures in their lifetimes, so they experience the exit multiple times. Others, like Bill Gates of Microsoft (co-founder/CEO from 1976 to 2000) or Michael Dell of Dell Computers, (founder/CEO from 1984 to 2004 and again from 2007 to the present), stay with their businesses for years, choosing not to exit. And still other entrepreneurs see their exit strategy change in response to unforeseen circumstances. In July 1999, John Lusk co-founded Platinum Concepts, Inc with some of his classmates from the Wharton School of Business at the University of Pennsylvania. Their core product was the MouseDriver, a computer mouse shaped like a golf-club head. Lusk's goal was to build the company up as fast as he could, exit in two years, and sell the company to another business. His plan forecasted the company's revenues skyrocketing to $10 million in 6 months. Unfortunately, this did not happen within his predetermined timeframe. It took approximately 18 months to build any sales for the MouseDriver. As a result, Lusk altered his exit strategy, deciding not to sell the company but instead to spend more time diversifying the product line and getting his products into the mass market. Ultimately, Lusk sold the company in 2003 to a large East Coast gift distributor.[3]

As you can see, there really is no place in the entrepreneurial process that is not affected by people. This chapter explores the personal journey to entrepreneurship, what it takes to become a successful entrepreneur, and the many ways to approach entrepreneurship throughout a career.

2.1   SAYING GOODBYE TO STEREOTYPES

Given the frequency with which entrepreneurs are discussed in the media, it is not surprising that stereotypes have developed around them. Not all of these stereotypes are flattering, and most are simply false. In fact, research has failed to identify that stereotypical entrepreneur. There are no psychological or sociological characteristics that can predict with any certainty who will become an entrepreneur or who will succeed as an entrepreneur.[4] This section attempts to dispel some of the myths surrounding entrepreneurs so that the entrepreneurial journey can begin on a solid, factual foundation.

2.1a   Myth 1: It Takes a Lot of Money to Start a Business

One false assumption about entrepreneurship is that it takes a lot of money to start a business. Nothing could be further from the truth. For example, Lori Bonn Gallagher parlayed her love of travel and finding unique jewelry into a multimillion dollar business. Starting with $1,000 worth of samples of hand-blown glass jewelry that she discovered in France and a successful selling strategy, Gallagher secured a deal with Nordstrom to begin selling her imported jewelry in the United States. Today her jewelry is designed at her headquarters in Oakland, California, manufactured in Bali, and sold in retail outlets such as Nordstrom, Discovery Store, and Boston's Museum of Fine Arts museum shop (www.loribonn.com).

Other factors such as the management team and the market being addressed are far more important than your initial resources. In fact, some research has determined that it is not specifically the amount of capital an entrepreneur possesses at startup that is important but rather how many resources of all types (founding team, network of contacts, connections in the value chain, etc.) the entrepreneur can access and/or control.[5]

2.1b   Myth 2: It Takes a Great Idea

Jim Collins's research, which was documented in the bestseller *Built to Last*, dispelled the myth that it takes a great idea to start a business. In fact, most of the great businesses that have been successful for at least 50 years—companies such as Walt Disney, Sony, and Merck—didn't start with a great idea. They started with a great team who simply wanted to create an enduring company. Venture capitalists will often say that they will take a great team and a large market opportunity in a fast-growing area over a great idea any day, because it takes a superior team to execute a successful business concept and it takes customers in a fast-growing market to create a great return to the investors.[6] Usually it's not the idea but the execution plan that makes the business a success. Marc Benioff did not invent software as service, but his company Salesforce.com found the pain in hosted solutions and removed it. Instead of having to buy applications to handle each function in the business, companies can access hosted services that can be customized to meet their specific needs. Benioff's success was not a great idea but rather solving a big problem with great execution.

2.1c   Myth 3: The Bigger the Risk, the Bigger the Reward

Students of entrepreneurship often hear that risk is correlated with reward—the greater the risk taken, the greater the reward expected. Certainly, it appears that investors hold that point of view. But *risk* is a relative term, and the goal of most entrepreneurs and investors alike is to reduce the level of risk in any venture. In fact, investors *expect* entrepreneurs to do what it takes to reduce the risk for them such as testing the market, acquiring the first customer, and investing some of their own capital in the business, and no one expects the business to be worth less because risk was reduced. It is actually to entrepreneurs' advantage to reduce risk for investors so that they, the entrepreneurs, can retain more of the equity when it comes time to negotiate for an infusion of capital.

2.1d   Myth 4: A Business Plan Is Required for Success

There is no question that lenders, investors, and others want to know that an entrepreneur has done his or her homework before they're willing to risk their capital. It is also true that an operating business that wants to secure a loan from a bank will likely have to produce a business plan. But many entrepreneurs have started highly successful businesses without having a formal business plan in place—including recognizable companies such as Pizza Hut and Crate and Barrel that have survived for decades. Others have launched websites and been "in business" within a day, making money within a couple of weeks. The prevalence of business plan competitions and courses requiring a formal business plan obscures a potentially troubling fact: Researchers do not agree on the relationship between a completed business plan and new venture success. Some believe that a plan takes time away from more valuable activities like validating the customer and business model. Others argue that a plan helps facilitate resource acquisition. The middle ground seems to be that a formal business plan is not always required to launch a successful business, but as an execution document, it may be very helpful in planning for growth. The issues of the business plan will be presented in more depth in Chapter 10.

2.1e   Myth 5: Entrepreneurship Is for the Young and Reckless

Many people believe that if they haven't started their first business by the time they are 30, it is too late. They think that the energy, drive, resources, and risk involved are suitable only for the young. And with stories like Yahoo Inc.'s acquisition of 17-year-old Nick D'Aloisio's mobile-app company, the impression is that Silicon Valley, at least, is a haven for the very young. But interestingly enough, The Founders Institute, a startup incubator based in Mountain View, California, reports that the average age of its participants is 35; it was 29 when they started in 2009. When Y Combinator, an accelerator, looked at a recent batch of entrepreneurs, it found that the ages ranged from 18 to 43.[7] In fact, the Kauffman Foundation studied 652 American-born heads of technology companies launched between 1995 and 2005 and discovered that the average age of the founder was 39 at startup.[8] Going beyond technology to include non-technology ventures, the *Kauffman Index of Entrepreneurial Activity* from 1996 to 2011 found that the share of entrepreneurs in the 55- to 64-year-old age group grew from 14.3 percent to 20.9 percent, while the number of entrepreneurs in the 20- to 34-year-old age group was at its lowest in the same period.[9] What this suggests is that entrepreneurship can be a lifetime endeavor for anyone who wants to enjoy the excitement of building something from scratch—watching it grow and become successful.

2.1f   Myth 6: Entrepreneurship Cannot Be Taught

This myth is a corollary to "Entrepreneurs are born, not made." Both are wrong. There is a lot about entrepreneurship that can be taught, including specific skills and behaviors. People who don't naturally have the skills of a successful entrepreneur can certainly learn and apply them. Management guru Peter Drucker asserted, "The entrepreneurial mystique, it's not magic, it's not mysterious, and it has nothing to do with the genes. It is a discipline. And, like any discipline, it can be learned."[10] Scholarly research over a number of years has supported that claim. In fact, a 2008 twin study by Nicolaou and Shane using 870 pairs of identical twins and 857 pairs of same-sex fraternal twins to study entrepreneurial activity, found that entrepreneurs are about 40 percent born and 60 percent made.[11] The born part was not deterministic but rather explanatory; that is, their results pointed to strong evidence for the effect of environmental factors, including genetics, on entrepreneurial propensity. Practically speaking, the born part is what cannot be taught, the passion to persist and achieve as well as the willingness to take risk. Some have called it the "fire in the belly." And indeed, what motivates someone to leave Harvard University to start a business (like Bill Gates of Microsoft) or to revolutionize social networking (like Facebook founder Mark Zuckerberg) cannot be learned. It is simply part of a person's makeup as it is in any successful person in any field of endeavor.

2.2   PATHS TO ENTREPRENEURSHIP

Entrepreneurs are as varied as the kinds of businesses they start and the precipitating events that led them to become entrepreneurs in the first place. In general, people start businesses either out of necessity or driven by opportunity. In the United States, opportunity-driven entrepreneurship is far more prevalent than in efficiency-driven or factor-driven economies such as Brazil and Uganda, where entrepreneurship frequently happens out of necessity.[12] When capital markets make it difficult to find funding, entrepreneurs are less likely to start new ventures from scratch. By contrast, they are more likely to start new ventures on their own when the incentives inside large organizations are weak or nonexistent, when the opportunity requires significant individual effort as in the invention of a new technology, and when normal scale advantages and learning curves do not provide advantages to the large organization.[13] Entrepreneurs also choose the startup process when industry entry barriers are low, when the environment is uncertain, and when the opportunity they seek to exploit involves a breakthrough or disruptive technology that will make previous technology obsolete.

There are many paths to entrepreneurship, and in the following sections we briefly look at four broad categories that differ from the traditional path: the home-based entrepreneur, the serial entrepreneur, the nonprofit entrepreneur, and the corporate entrepreneur.

2.2a   The Home-Based Entrepreneur

It might sound strange to refer to a home-based business as entrepreneurship. And in most cases, you would be right because many of these are hobby businesses, consulting, and freelance-type businesses; but many others are entrepreneurial ventures that compete in the same arena as brand-name businesses with large facilities. Technology has made it possible to do business from virtually anywhere, so entrepreneurs don't have to work in traditional office spaces to start or run businesses. Moreover, home-based business owners can tap into more resources than ever before from their desktops or mobile devices to locate help for any problem they may be facing, from finding business forms to seeking legal advice to learning how to start and run a business. In addition, U.S. tax laws have become more accommodating to home-based business owners who can take a deduction for their home office space and appropriate business expenses.

According to the Small Business Administration, 52 percent of small businesses are home-based. Given that there are 28 million small businesses (fewer than 500 employees), that's 14,560,000 businesses.[14] Many entrepreneurs with aspirations to grow their businesses start from home to save on overhead and reduce the risk of startup. Once the concept has proved itself, they often move out to acquire facilities and other resources that will support the growth of the company and the addition of employees. Some of the more famous businesses that started out home-based are Apple, Hershey's, Mary Kay Cosmetics, and the Ford Motor Company. However, some home-based entrepreneurs choose never to have traditional office space but rather prefer to stay mobile and do business from their home, boat, car, or vacation home.

2.2b   The Serial or Portfolio Entrepreneur

Many entrepreneurs enjoy the pre-launch and startup phases so much that when those activities are over and running the business takes center stage, they become impatient to move on to the next startup. It's the thrill of starting a business that keeps them going; they prefer to leave the management issues to someone else. An entrepreneur who starts one business and then moves on to start another is called a *serial entrepreneur*. Often these entrepreneurs start another business that builds on the experience from the first venture or builds on a specific expertise that the entrepreneur possesses or has acquired through a previous venture. Venture capitalist Vinod Khosla is one example. He co-founded Sun Microsystems; then he left to become a general partner at Kleiner Perkins Caufield & Byers, a Silicon Valley VC firm, until 2000. Then in 2004, he formed his own firm Khosla Ventures, which invests in technology. Another example is the founders of Airbnb, an online marketplace that enables you to rent your house or apartment for any length of time. They became entrepreneurs with their first venture, selling election-themed cereal boxes in 2008, before moving to the Airbnb concept. One could argue that they were true "cereal entrepreneurs."[15]

An entrepreneur who owns a minority or majority stake in several ventures is called a *portfolio entrepreneur*.[16] Portfolio entrepreneurs often create a lot of churn in their portfolios as they seek out new business opportunities that link to their existing businesses. They tend to be constantly on the hunt for new opportunities.[17] Certainly U.S. entrepreneur Elon Musk is in this category, having co-founded PayPal, then going on to found Tesla Motors, Solar City, and SpaceX. Also in this group is Naveen Jain, who founded Intelius, a Web security firm; Infospace, which provides metasearch and private-label Internet search services; and Moon Express, which is planning to mine the moon for rare elements.

2.2c   The Nonprofit Entrepreneur

Today many enterprising people are turning to nonprofit types of ventures to realize their entrepreneurial dreams. Nonprofit, socially responsible businesses typically focus on educational, religious, or charitable goals. They generally seek tax-exempt status so that they can attract donations from companies and individuals who believe in their mission. Contrary to popular belief, nonprofit businesses can and should make a profit, but that profit must stay within the company rather than be distributed to the owners. Jennifer Staple-Clark founded Unite for Sight in 2000 while she was a sophomore at Yale University. The nonprofit is now a leader in "providing cost-effective care to the world's poorest people including more than 65,000 sight-restoring surgeries."[18] Chapter 12 explores nonprofit ventures in more depth from a legal perspective.

2.2d   The Corporate Entrepreneur

Entrepreneurship is no longer viewed solely as the startup of a new, independent firm; it can also occur inside an existing organization. Known as corporate entrepreneurship, this phenomenon is now regularly studied by the research community, and increasingly, large organizations are finding it necessary to provide for entrepreneurial activity to remain competitive.[19] Corporate ventures are distinct from other types of projects that large firms take on. For one thing, they generally involve innovation and activities that are typically new to the company so the risk of failure is high. There is also a high degree of uncertainty around such projects, so they are often managed separately from core business activities. Recognizing that it is nearly impossible to re-engineer and redesign an entire organization to be more entrepreneurial, many companies have chosen from several models to simulate the entrepreneurial environment required for innovation to occur[20]:

- **Opportunistic Model**: This is the common place where most companies start their efforts to be more entrepreneurial. They wait for project champions to emerge and suggest new business opportunities. Then they decide if they want to move forward and provide some support.

- **Enabler Model**: Google is an example of a company that sprinkles resources throughout the organization to encourage innovation and entrepreneurship at all levels while establishing clear criteria for the selection of opportunities to pursue.

- **Advocate Model**: Here the company acts like an evangelist, assigning ownership of a project or new business creation and providing modest seed funding to test it. DuPont, a global conglomerate, uses this approach to generate new sources of growth for the company.

- **Producer Model**: Some companies like IBM and Cargill establish formal organizations with dedicated funds and significant autonomy. This approach used to be called a "skunkworks," dubbed so by Lockheed Martin when it originated the idea years ago to develop its stealth fighter jet.

GLOBAL INSIGHTS

Nordic Entrepreneurship: Born Global Companies

More than ever before, we're seeing startups that serve a global niche market from inception. But nowhere has this been more apparent than in the Nordic countries of Norway, Denmark, and Sweden. They are home to some powerhouse companies such as Novo Nordisk, a Danish company that produces half the world's medical insulin; Oticon, the leader in hearing aids; and Swedish retail giants IKEA and H&M. These are just a few examples of Nordic entrepreneurial success. Some of the reasons for their success include a commitment to continuous innovation, taking the long view of success with many of the most successful businesses being family-owned for generations, a consensus-based management style, and a willingness to replace labor with machines. But even these successful entrepreneurs are concerned about their ability to keep up with the rest of the world. Most of these countries' successful ventures like Legos, the toy manufacturer, were founded decades ago. To keep up they need a new generation of entrepreneurial ventures in the works. Whereas in most of the world born-global companies are technology-based, in the Nordic countries they cross many non-technology industries. But like most born-global companies, the Nordic companies go global from inception because their home country does not provide a large enough market by itself to sustain them. In many ways, that is fortunate because research has pointed to the fact that born-global firms are more successful than firms that were not born global.

Sources: "Nordic Companies Have Coped Well with Globalisation, But Need New Blood," (February 2, 2013). *The Economist*. http://www.economist.com/news/special-report /21570837-nordic-companies-have-coped-well-globalisation-need-new-blood-global-niche; Tanev, S. (March 2012). "Global from the Start: The Characteristics of Born-Global Firms in the Technology Sector," *Technology Innovation Management Review.* http://timreview.ca/article/532

Those who choose the corporate entrepreneurship path will need to align with key decision makers in the organization; work with only the best, most motivated people; and do any job needed to make the project work.

This book is not intended to address the specific needs of corporate entrepreneurs, but recognizing opportunities, conducting feasibility analyses, and developing execution plans are as relevant in the corporate environment as they are in a startup.

2.3   THE CHALLENGES AND OPPORTUNITIES OF ENTREPRENEURSHIP

In Chapter 1 we referred to a good definition of entrepreneurship as offered by Harvard Business School professor Howard Stevenson more than three decades ago. It's worth repeating here for reasons that will soon be apparent.

"Entrepreneurship is the pursuit of opportunity without regard to resources currently controlled." Notice that nowhere in that definition is it talking about entrepreneurship as a personality trait or something you are necessarily born with. What the definition does suggest, and what is supported by research, is that entrepreneurs are more likely to come from poor or middle-class families than from wealth, because entrepreneurs historically have been used to doing without—bootstrapping or begging, borrowing, and bartering to get what they needed. One could argue that in the current startup environment of incubators and accelerators, entrepreneurs less frequently start without regard to resources. In fact, the first thing on their mind is what they have to do to raise money. So perhaps another definition is relevant to today's entrepreneur. This author would argue that entrepreneurs create opportunity from unmet needs or unsolved problems in the market and they gather the resources to exploit that opportunity, unusually through a new venture.

Entrepreneurship is not for everyone, no more than any other endeavor is. Table 2.1 presents an overview of the challenges and opportunities that come with choosing entrepreneurship as a career path. When reading the table, it is important to ask yourself if you would be able to deal with such a challenge and also if the opportunities of entrepreneurship are meaningful to you and compatible with your life goals. You may come up with even more challenges and opportunities than are presented in the table, but these are the most common.

The last challenge listed is "dealing with a sense of isolation and disillusionment." When Greg Allen left his corporate job to start a design and web development business out of his home, he quickly learned how lonely that could be. At his former job, he was surrounded by people who were always available to brainstorm ideas. Now, he had to plan his time to include opportunities to meet with people and to network. Eventually, as his business grew, he moved into office space so his team could more easily share ideas.

TABLE 2.1
Challenges and Opportunities with the Entrepreneur Career Path

Challenges	Opportunities
Finding the right business opportunity	Becoming independent—taking charge of a career
Needing to work, often without pay, for long hours	Creating wealth
Facing uncertainty and high risk	Doing well while doing good—the potential for social entrepreneurship
Needing to make major decisions, often that affect other people's lives	Working in a business environment that the entrepreneur creates
Relying on other people for expertise and resources	Doing something the entrepreneur is passionate about
Having no previous experience on which to rely	Making a difference
Facing failure at some point	Creating new jobs
Finding the right people to help grow the business	Supporting the community
Raising capital and other resources	
Dealing with a sense of isolation and disillusionment	

The lead-up to the launch of the business is a very exciting time. Everyone wants to see the entrepreneur succeed, so encouragement and support are never lacking. But beneath that excitement lurks a painful reality: Many entrepreneurs are surprised at what running a business day to day is really like. They have no comprehension of how difficult it is, and so often there is a feeling of being overwhelmed. This is one reason starting a business with a team makes sense; the difficulties and the work can be shared.

For all the challenges associated with entrepreneurship, the opportunities seem to outweigh them. To succeed at anything requires a higher-than-average amount of self-discipline and perseverance. Entrepreneurs don't give up easily, and they tend to stick doggedly to a concept until something or someone convinces them that it's time to move on to something else. That persistence is one important reason why entrepreneurs ultimately succeed. For example, Todd Stennett spoke with more than 450 people before he found the right person to guide him to the perfect business model for his now successful laser mapping business, Airborne 1. If entrepreneurs didn't have this kind of tenacity, there would be no great products and no great businesses, because every entrepreneur faces doubters and naysayers when a business concept is in its earliest stages. The ability to stick to the task and persevere against all odds is what wins the day for an entrepreneur.

One of the biggest problems that scientists and engineers face when they decide to consider entrepreneurship is the expectation that there are formulas for success and right and wrong answers to guide them. In short, they expect linear processes and predictability. Interestingly enough, in the current environment of "lean startups" and accelerators, more and more would-be entrepreneurs begin to believe that there's a formula they can follow to achieve success. If they only get accepted into an accelerator or incubator, some investor will hold their hand through the process to a huge acquisition or IPO at the end. If only it were that simple. But it's not. People who wish there were no surprises in life and who want an environment that is predictable and stable will find it very difficult to survive in the world of the entrepreneur. But those who embrace uncertainty and ambiguity will enjoy an endless stream of opportunity. One reason why entrepreneurship is such an interesting and exciting field is that it is constantly changing. It is well known that the greatest, most innovative ideas occur at the edge of chaos when things that aren't normally associated with each other are brought together in new ways. Opportunity is rarely found in stable, predictable settings, so potential entrepreneurs must learn to embrace change and uncertainty.

2.4   PREPARING TO BECOME AN ENTREPRENEUR

Starting any business, large or small, requires a tremendous amount of time, effort, and resources. Therefore, it usually makes sense to start a business that has the potential to grow large and provide a good return on that investment, rather than spend the same amount of effort on a very small business that yields only a single job. In fact, research supports that notion.[21] The probability of survival and success tends to go up with businesses that have more potential. Unfortunately, the vast majority of people who start businesses do not think like entrepreneurs. They think like small-business owners, wanting to keep everything under control, to grow slowly, and simply provide a job for the owner. Although there is nothing inherently wrong with looking at business from this perspective, it does, regrettably, expose you to significantly more risk. Because these small businesses typically do not create new value, innovate, or have a plan for growth, they tend to be undercapitalized, poorly managed, and unable to differentiate themselves from competitors. In a word, they are vulnerable.

How, then, does an entrepreneur increase the chances for success? Through preparation. There are a number of important steps that you can take to increase your chances of success in entrepreneurship. Figure 2.1 displays these steps, and we discuss them here.

2.4a   Find a Mentor

One very specific task that an aspiring entrepreneur can undertake to prepare for success is to find a mentor—that is, someone who is leading the type of life that you envision for your future and who can be your guide and sounding board as well as champion and gateway to contacts you would otherwise not have been able to meet. Vivek, an Indian entrepreneur, discovered that he had become so passionate about the product side of his computer hardware business that he had stopped listening to the good advice he was being given about the need to diversify his product line. It was not until his business was facing failure, something that is viewed very negatively in India, that he sought the guidance and wisdom of a *guruji* or mentor. The mentor helped Vivek understand that it was his own ego that was standing in the way of his success in finding the right path for his business.[22]

2.4b   Build a Professional Network

Networking is the exchange of information and resources among individuals, groups, or organizations whose common goals are to mutually benefit and create value for the members. Research in the field of entrepreneurship has

FIGURE 2.1   Preparing for Entrepreneurship

© Cengage Learning®

revealed much about the positive effects of effective networking. For instance, entrepreneurship has been found to be a relational process. Entrepreneurs do not act autonomously but, rather, are part of social networks with which they interact.[23] These social networks consist of strong and weak ties. *Strong ties* are your close friends and family members whom you know well whereas *weak ties* are your acquaintances and business contacts. In general, acquaintances are not socially involved; that is, entrepreneurs do not generally spend their nonbusiness hours with acquaintances.[24] Nevertheless, these weak ties play an important role in the entrepreneurial process because entrepreneurs typically move forward faster with the help and support of weak ties who are not biased by a prior history with the entrepreneur. Entrepreneurs rely on their weak ties for objective advice. Family and close friends, on the other hand, tend to restrict the entrepreneur's potential because they tend to look at the impact on them of the entrepreneur's business activities.

Building a large network with credible partners and maintaining the connections in that network will be important to your success. However, how do you achieve a large but meaningful network? You accomplish this by connecting with network brokers who serve as gateways to other networks. These brokers, or opinion leaders, exert influence between groups or networks rather than within groups.[25] Figure 2.2 depicts such brokering. The entrepreneur in this example initially has a network of family and friends as well as a network of professional engineers. Outside of these networks, the entrepreneur knows only two people: an angel investor and a production person. However, these two people are well connected into communities with which the entrepreneur has no experience. In effect, they are opinion leaders who serve as the gateways to those new communities and can make the appropriate introductions to provide the entrepreneur with instant credibility. Now it's easy to see why the adage "it's who you know" makes sense. Rather than spending an extraordinary amount of time trying to find all the required contacts, it would be more efficient and prudent for you to figure out who is the gateway to your community of interest and endeavor to meet and cultivate that relationship.

Entrepreneurs who successfully use their networks to build their businesses generally are committed to the success of the people in their network, are active listeners, and approach every contact with an open mind.[26] In that way, they derive the maximum value from their network ties. Networking is discussed in the context of building a startup team in Chapter 8.

2.4c   Learn About Entrepreneurs

One of the best ways to prepare for entrepreneurship is to learn as much about it as possible by reading magazine articles, books, blogs, and newspapers, and—most importantly—by talking to entrepreneurs. Today it's easier than ever to learn about entrepreneurs by simply scouring the Web. Some of the media that focus exclusively on entrepreneurs include *Fortune Small Business, Inc. Magazine, Business Insider,* and *Entrepreneur,* to name a few. University entrepreneur programs, local chambers of commerce, small business development corporations, and industry events are also great sources for meeting entrepreneurs.

FIGURE 2.2   Brokering across Networks

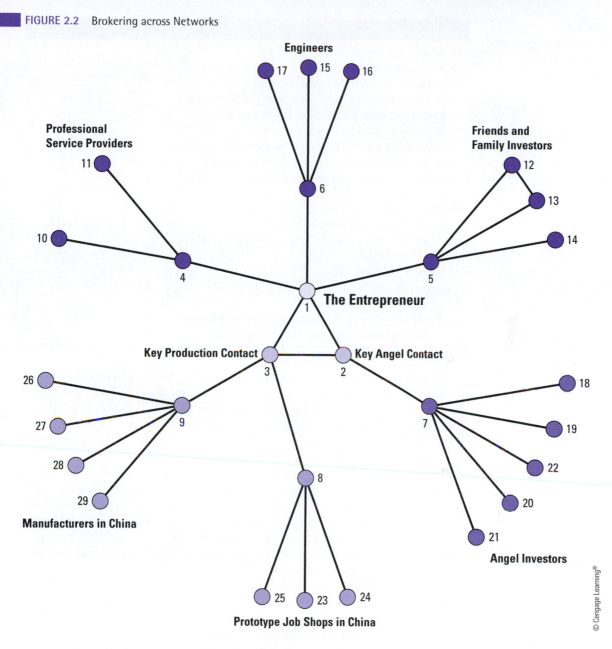

2.4d   Understand Personality and Business Preferences

Although we have dispelled many of the myths surrounding entrepreneurship in this chapter, it is a fact that there are barriers to becoming an entrepreneur that should not be ignored, and many of these barriers relate to the entrepreneur's personality and preferences—likes and dislikes. Research has uncovered six factors that serve as barriers to people becoming self-employed as entrepreneurs: (1) lack of

TABLE 2.2	Yes	No
Entrepreneur Personality and Preferences Questionnaire		

1. Are you a self-starter?
2. Are you able to work for up to a year with no income from the new business?
3. Do you stick with a project until it's finished?
4. Do you frequently abandon a project when you grow tired of it?
5. Do you enjoy working with other people on a regular basis?
6. Do you enjoy traveling for business purposes?
7. Are you comfortable with pressure (i.e., deadlines, fast-paced work environment)?
8. Do you enjoy working with people from other countries?
9. Are you comfortable hiring people you believe are smarter or more experienced than you are?
10. Do you enjoy being in an office at your desk for most of the day?
11. Are you comfortable in selling situations?
12. Are you comfortable asking for money or other resources?
13. Are you comfortable with debt?
14. Is security important to you?
15. Do you have time to devote to this new business?
16. Are you comfortable with unions?
17. Are you willing to work in a government-regulated environment?
18. Do you have the support of your family to start a business?

© Cengage Learning®

confidence, (2) financial needs, (3) startup logistics, (4) personal or family issues, (5) time constraints, and (6) lack of skills.[27] The questions in Table 2.2 reflect these factors and others that should be considered as well. They will help you understand more about what you like and dislike about business. The questions are posed as a definitive yes/no choice to force you to think about these questions independent of any particular opportunity being considered.

Launching a new business requires tremendous amounts of time and energy, as well as a great deal of support from family and friends. During the early stages of a new venture, resources are limited and you must wear many hats. This can be immensely stressful, so it is important that you be in good health and optimal physical and emotional condition. It is often said that entrepreneurs start businesses to be in charge of their lives. The reality is that after you start your own business, you might find yourself working more than you ever did for someone else. The major difference is that because you are building something you own, it doesn't feel like the work you are accustomed to; instead, you are bringing to life a new business that reflects *your* goals and values.

It is equally important for potential entrepreneurs to think about the kind of lifestyle they are striving to achieve. Not all businesses support the kind of lifestyle that some entrepreneurs want to lead. Is travel important? Is having a large home and all the things that go with it a requirement? Is achieving a balanced life with plenty of time for family and friends important? If so, starting a business that requires a lot of travel or puts you at the mercy of demanding clients probably won't provide that balanced lifestyle.

Most people spend the majority of the day at their work; therefore, the work environment should be an enjoyable place to be. Entrepreneurs who love the outdoors should probably not start businesses that require them to sit at a desk all day. Entrepreneurs who don't enjoy working with people should probably not start businesses that are labor-intensive or involve numerous daily interactions with the public. It is a good idea for future entrepreneurs to take a step back and contemplate their ideal work environment. What does this environment look like or "feel" like? What would spending a day in this environment entail?

2.4e   Improve or Acquire Critical Skills

Because entrepreneurs operate in a world of uncertainty, the ability to analyze a situation, extract the important and ignore the superfluous, compare potential outcomes, and extrapolate from other experiences to the current one is vital. Entrepreneurs also regularly have to weigh options in complex situations. Critical thinking skills can be improved through practice and by observing how others with well-developed skills work through a problem-solving situation. Many colleges and universities offer courses in critical thinking and there are a number of excellent books on the subject.

People who have a difficult time making decisions or who regularly find that they make poor decisions will probably not be successful as entrepreneurs. Making effective decisions is a critical part of the everyday life of an entrepreneur and is a skill that must be developed and exercised carefully. Poor decisions about hiring, business location, investors, and strategic partners can cost a company a great deal of money and prevent it from achieving its goals. Wise decisions, even in times of crisis, can provide an opportunity for growth.

Embracing uncertainty and ambiguity are essential to creating opportunity and to launching a new business. We live in uncertain times and it's likely that will not change. The world has become very complex and interconnected, so things that are out of our control can impact us. Entrepreneurs view uncertainty and ambiguity as an opportunity to discover a need or problem that no one else has seen. Therefore, anyone considering entrepreneurship would be wise to move out of their comfort zone and practice dealing with things they are not used to. For example, often the best ideas come from the juxtaposition of two unrelated fields or unrelated products. The robotics company iRobot made a connection between robots and vacuum cleaners to come up with the very successful Roomba. In fact, it created a platform on which they have now built all kinds of new products.

The saying "the devil is in the details" could not be more true in business. Entrepreneurs who proudly claim that they leave the details to others while they focus on the vision are telling the world that they don't participate in the inner workings of their business. Details matter, and although entrepreneurs should not be micromanagers as the business grows, they should be well aware of the status of critical numbers in their business, and they should make their presence known among employees on a regular basis. It is vitally important to the success of the business that you be detail-oriented. Table 2.3 lists some of the skills that you need to hone to be effective at starting and growing your business.

Note in Table 2.3 that storytelling is listed as a critical skill. Research tells us that entrepreneurial stories are a way to facilitate a new venture's identity

TABLE 2.3 Critical
Entrepreneurial Skills

Analysis and critical thinking	Written and oral communication
Calculated risk taking	Story telling
Embracing uncertainty and ambiguity	Vision
Opportunity creation	Persuasion and negotiation
Organizational and time management (details)	Decision making
Resource gathering	Leadership and people management

and legitimacy as well as create a competitive advantage that is difficult to replicate.[28] A compelling story about the founding of the business, how the need was identified, and why customers will choose to buy from your company over others will help you raise capital, find strategic partners, and build a board of directors. Entrepreneurs, therefore, must become skilled storytellers, crafting tales about who they are and how their new venture and its resources will benefit customers, investors, and society.

Entrepreneurial leaders have a distinct advantage over charismatic or heroic leaders. Being a hero is lonely; there are no peers to confide in or teammates with whom to share the load. More than ever before, entrepreneurs see themselves as part of a team, from the founding of the venture throughout all the various stages in the life of that venture. The days of the gunslinging solo entrepreneur seem to be gone. Today it takes a team to succeed and a leader who can inspire others to motivate and lead as well. Entrepreneurial leadership, like any effective leadership, is a balance of passion and pragmatism. It is the entrepreneur's passion that launches the business and keeps it going through the early days when survival is often in doubt. But a different kind of leadership is often required once the business has survived and has entered growth mode. A more pragmatic style of leadership that can deliver the right systems and controls to keep the venture on course is not often found in the same person who founded the venture. Unfortunately, in private companies it is often the entrepreneur/founder who is left to decide when it's time for him or her to hand the reins to a different type of leader, and only the rare entrepreneur recognizes when that moment is at hand. Sometimes, however, the entrepreneur remains as the visionary leader of the company but brings on a CEO with professional management skills. This topic is explored in more depth in Chapter 16.

2.4f   Study an Industry

One of the best ways to discover an opportunity is to study an industry in depth, perhaps even work in the industry for a time. An industry is a group of companies that are engaged in a similar or related field; for example, the computer industry consists of all the businesses that provide parts, assembly, manufacturing, and distribution for computers—essentially all of the businesses involved in the value chain for computers. The value chain is discussed in more depth in Chapter 4. The best opportunities come from your experience and knowledge of an industry, a market, or a type of business. Since opportunities are not limited to products and services, studying an industry offers the prospect of identifying opportunity anywhere in the value chain of that industry.

When all is said and done, business is about relationships—with partners, with customers, with investors, and with suppliers. Successfully building relationships requires honesty and integrity. It requires giving value and delivering on promises. Your core values are the foundation for the business and are always reflected in the business and in the way customers are treated. Integrity is something that you must guard more carefully than anything else because you cannot afford to taint or lose it. The next chapter explores how entrepreneurs cultivate ideas into business opportunities.

New Venture Action Plan

- Complete the personality and preferences questionnaire. (see Table 2.2)
- Do an inventory of your current skills and plan how to acquire the skills you're missing.
- Find a mentor and begin building a network.
- Pick an industry and begin studying it.

Questions on Key Issues

1. Why do myths emerge around phenomena such as entrepreneurship?
2. How do corporate entrepreneurs differ from other types of entrepreneurs?
3. What are the steps you should take to prepare yourself for entrepreneurship?
4. What might explain the rise in interest in social or nonprofit entrepreneurship?
5. Why are more ventures started by teams than by solo entrepreneurs?

Experiencing Entrepreneurship

1. Identify an entrepreneur who is leading the kind of personal and business life that you aspire to lead. Interview that person to find out more about how she or he achieved that lifestyle. During the interview, and only if the two of you have developed a rapport, approach the entrepreneur about the possibility of becoming your mentor.

2. Entrepreneurship is a journey, and many people contribute to that journey. Begin a contact portfolio that will contain the names of all the people you meet as you network. Record their contact information, how you met them, what they contributed to your journey and what you might do now or in the future to help them. Strive to meet three to five new contacts a week.

Relevant Case Studies

Case 5 Corporate Entrepreneurship and Innovation in Silicon Valley: The Case of Google Inc.

Case 7 Homerun.com

CHAPTER 3

Creating Opportunity

"The greater danger for most of us lies not in setting our aim too high and falling short; but in setting our aim too low, and achieving our mark."

—MICHELANGELO

CHAPTER OBJECTIVES

- Use design thinking to understand opportunity.
- Discuss creativity, its challenges, and how to develop creative skills.
- Understand ideation and its role in problem solving.
- Understand the innovation process.

A YOUNG ENTREPRENEUR WHO SOLVED A PROBLEM

British teen Nick D'Aloisio was always an intensely curious boy who spent his free time building things, not just any things, but computer programs and apps that solved problems. With no formal training in coding, D'Aloisio scoured the Internet for videos and other sources that would teach him how to code. He was 12 when the Apple App Store went live, too young to qualify for a developer's license, so he signed up using his father's name.

His first app was technically sound—it played sound bites from Steve Jobs's speeches—but he hadn't considered that he was violating any copyrights and the App Store rejected his app. But he later scored sales with an app that turned a smartphone screen into a finger treadmill, earning $120 the first day.

D'Aloisio was by no measure an average teenager. In his spare time he studied languages and began learning about natural language processing, a field that studies the relationship between human languages and computers. It was through the process of searching for information on linguistics that he uncovered an opportunity in the form of a problem that no one had adequately solved. The problem was this: When you're scanning through hundreds of articles, how do you know which ones are worth reading? This seemed particularly important to people who were time crunched like himself. D'Aloisio loved learning new things but didn't want to do a deep dive on something unless he was really interested.

Wouldn't it be great to have a tool that would provide a summary of an article in fewer than 400 characters? Historically, natural language processing had been accomplished in one of two ways: (1) semantic, where the program tries to figure out the meaning of a phrase; and (2) statistical, where the program calculates how to pick a few phrases that summarize the core meaning of the article by ranking and classifying. The statistical approach was the basis for D'Aloisio's first iteration of an app he called Trimit.

Trimit debuted in the App Store in July 2011 when D'Aloisio was just 15 years old. It was quickly noticed by Horizons Ventures, which, after some negotiation, provided him with a seed investment of $300,000. The investors saw in D'Aloisio someone who knew very clearly what the value proposition for Trimit was and could pitch it passionately and confidently. However, this was D'Aloisio's first experience being responsible to someone other than himself to make sure the job was done right. He was a designer more than a coder. Wisely, he decided to contract with a team of Israeli coders who had expertise in natural language processing. He also looked for a chief scientist in the field and found one in Thailand; he was added to the team. Other investors came on board, inspired by the then-15-year-old savant: Wendi Murdoch, Aston Kutcher, and Yoko Ono. D'Aloisio's strategy to refine the app ultimately worked, garnering more than one million users; and in March 2013, Summly, as the app was now called, was acquired by Yahoo! for a reported $30 million. At 17, D'Aloisio left formal school and went to work for Yahoo! where he now spends the bulk of his time improving on the Summly app, which has been integrated into Yahoo's! products. He's also looking at how an app like Summly could do for video what it did for text.

Meanwhile, D'Aloisio is also considering whether to go to college where he would study philosophy and political science, his two passions. "Language, algorithms, design and all that stuff, I have always loved learning—it's my favourite thing."

Sources: Stevenson, Seth (November 6, 2013). "How Teen Nick D'Aloisio Has Changed the Way We Read"; Brian Stelter (March 25, 2013). "He Has Millions and a New Job at Yahoo. Soon, He'll Be 18," *New York Times*, http://www.nytimes.com/2013/03/26/business/media /nick-daloisio-17-sells-summly-app-to-yahoo.html?_r=0; Jonathan Ford (January 24, 2014). "Lunch with the FT: Nick D'Aloisio," Financial Times, http://www.ft.com /intl/cms/s/2/dca46ecc-835d-11e3-86c9-00144feab7de .html#axzz2xULPinpr.

Ideas are a commodity; everyone has them, dozens of them every day. Entrepreneurs are no different in that regard, but what distinguishes entrepreneurs from others who have ideas is that entrepreneurs know how to extract value from those ideas and turn them into opportunities that have commercial potential. Fundamentally, that is the difference between an idea and an opportunity. An opportunity can turn into a business.

This chapter uses the principles of design thinking to frame a discussion around creativity, opportunity, and innovation. Design thinking is a process that was originally most associated with product design and architecture. Today, however, the benefits of design thinking have been incorporated into many fields, but particularly entrepreneurship. It is important to note that what we are calling a *process* does not suggest that design thinking is a step-by-step linear procedure. Instead, it can be thought of as groups of related activities that move from inspiration (creativity) to ideation (opportunity development) to implementation (innovation and commercialization). Figure 3.1 displays these activities. In its most simplistic definition, design thinking uses techniques and tools to define a problem, create and consider multiple options, refine those options through iteration, and then settle on a winning solution. But that definition leaves out the most important aspect of design thinking, "the human-centered design ethos," as IDEO founder Tim Brown refers to it.[1] At the heart of design thinking is a deep understanding or empathy with what people (customers) want. That level of empathy requires entrepreneurs to embed themselves in the world of the customers they are trying to serve so they can see needs from the customer's perspective.

Because it is people-centered, the design thinking process is not mechanical. It does, however, require some skills and capabilities that are not necessarily those you may have learned in school. Brown looks for the following characteristics in people to reveal potential design thinkers:

- **Empathy**: are you able to view the world from many different perspectives and do you notice things that others don't?
- **Integrative thinking**: are you able to recognize all the contradictory options there might be in solving a problem and come up with solutions that greatly improve existing solutions?
- **Optimism**: are you able to assume that there is always a better option than what is currently available and do you have the persistence to go after it?

Entrepreneurship
and the Elements of
Design Thinking

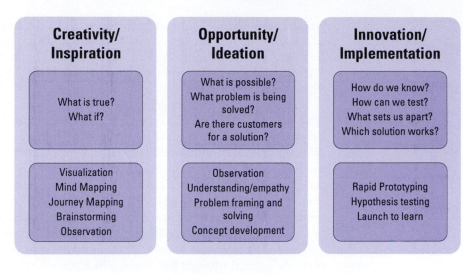

© 2016 Cengage Learning®

- **Experimentation**: are you willing to iterate on ideas hundreds of times in search of the best solution?
- **Collaboration**: are you an interdisciplinary thinker and are you knowledgeable in more than one field, for example, engineering and anthropology?

Let's look at the components of design thinking in more detail to see how they are used to turn an idea into an opportunity.

3.1   CREATIVITY AND INSPIRATION

What does creativity have to do with entrepreneurship? Everything! Creativity enables entrepreneurs to differentiate their businesses from competitors so that customers will notice them. Creativity is the basis for invention, which is discovering something that did not exist previously, and innovation, which is finding a new way to do something or improving on an existing product or service. Creativity is also fundamental to problem solving. Today, entrepreneurs face a rapidly changing environment brought about in large part by the speed of technological change and economic uncertainty. The combination of rapid change and the resulting uncertainty about what the future holds presents a fertile ground for new opportunities. Creativity, therefore, is a critical skill for recognizing or creating opportunity in a dynamic environment and for problem solving, which is necessary to satisfy customer needs.

What exactly is creativity? Many people have attempted to define creativity but always come up lacking because it's difficult to define something so intangible, so unquantifiable. Gryskiewicz defined creativity as useful, novel associations.[2] Noller developed a formula that suggests that creativity is a function of three dynamics: knowledge, imagination, and evaluation.[3]

Isaksen and others, recognizing the diversity of definitions and not wanting to subscribe to one single version, have adopted four general themes around creativity: (1) characteristics of creative people, (2) processes creative people perform, (3) products produced, and (4) the climate, culture, or context in which creativity occurs.[4]

The earliest research on creativity focused on the individual, in much the same way that early research on entrepreneurship focused on the entrepreneur. Researchers looked at personality factors and cognitive skills such as language, thinking processes, and intelligence to attempt to determine the profile of a creative person.[5] Then they examined the context in which people are creative and found that a number of environmental settings are conducive to creativity, among them the absence of constraints or freedom to do as one pleases, the presence of rewards or incentives to encourage creativity, and team effectiveness or the ability of people to collaborate and support each other's efforts.[6]

The creative process is difficult to study because it generally deals with a person's internal thought processes, which are often not apparent even to the person being studied. One of the earliest descriptions of the creative process came from Wallas, who had studied famous artists and scientists and from that identified four stages in the creative process: (1) preparation, or looking at a problem from a variety of perspectives; (2) incubation, or letting the problem lie in the subconscious for a time; (3) illumination, or the discovery of a solution; and (4) verification, or bringing the idea to an outcome.[7] Although one could certainly argue that not all creativity results in a predetermined outcome.

A more recent view of the creative process comes from photographer and documentary film producer Norman Seeff, who identified seven stages that individuals or teams go through as they move from the beginnings of an idea to the fulfillment or final outcome (see Figure 3.2).[8] This perspective does assume a desired outcome. In stage one, the honeymoon phase, the new idea is born and it brings with it all the possibilities for what it can become. However, that possibility stage is quickly followed by fear and resistance, typically precipitated by previous experience with failure that causes the individual to consider what might go wrong this time. Stage three is reached when an individual has reconciled the major fears associated with the idea and has answered enough of unknowns to feel comfortable moving forward. Stage four, the turning point, is when the

FIGURE 3.2
The Seven Stage Dynamic of the Creative Process

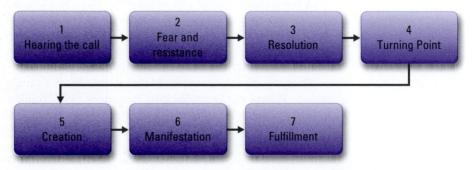

Source: Adapted from Norman Seeff Productions.

individual either makes the commitment to move forward despite not having all the answers, or he or she gives up on the dream. Stage five represents the implementation of the action plan to turn the idea into reality, while stage six is the outcome of the effort in the form of a new product, a new business, or whatever outcome has been defined. Seeff's process also has a stage seven, which represents the emotional fulfillment of the original dream. If Seeff's process is overlaid on the entrepreneurial process, which is typically a team effort, it is clear that stage seven represents the full emotional commitment of the team to each other as individuals and to the new venture as a whole. Seeff believes that this emotional commitment is essential to the successful completion of a creative endeavor. This belief was born out in his experience with teams at the Jet Propulsion Laboratory in Pasadena, California, working on the Mars Rover project (see the Social Entrepreneurship box). As Seeff's framework depicts, the creative process is fraught with many challenges that must be overcome before the dream can be realized.

SOCIAL ENTREPRENEURSHIP: MAKING MEANING

Tapping into Emotions to Understand the Act of Creation

Breakthroughs in understanding the creative process often come from people who are involved in an active way on a daily basis. Norman Seeff, a South African medical doctor turned photographer, has spent his life exploring the creative process, and through his work has managed to put a very human face on a highly technical project. Seeff is probably best known for his innovative and interactive photo sessions with actors, musicians, and artists that give a unique insight into the act of creation. It was this work that led him to be invited to work with NASA scientists at the Jet Propulsion Laboratory (JPL) in Pasadena, California, and to produce a documentary film about the Mars Exploration mission of 2004 called *Triumph of the Dream*.

In working with the JPL team, it would have been easy for Seeff to simply recount the events that led up to the successful mission, but Seeff knew that if he could tap into the team's emotions, he might figure out why this mission succeeded while the previous Mars Polar Lander mission had failed. As it turned out, the technical achievements of the mission served merely as the context or backdrop for the very real inner journey the team members experienced as they struggled to overcome the inertia of the previous failures. What Seeff discovered during this journey was that the imagination and emotional commitment the team had to each other and to the dream of successfully landing two Rovers on Mars made all the difference in their success. For the duration of the project, the team essentially became a family who believed in each other as much as they believed they could achieve the mission. And achieve the mission they did in just three and a half years from the date the idea was born. This experience cemented Seeff's belief that to achieve game-changing creativity, a team has to be emotionally connected with a vested interest in succeeding as individuals and as a team for the good of the whole.

3.1a   Challenges to Creativity

Creativity tends to occur naturally if one lets it, but entrepreneurs often unintentionally erect roadblocks that prevent them from following the creative path. These roadblocks are generally of three types: personal, problem solving, and environmental.

Entrepreneurs are often so busy that there is no time to think and contemplate, and this can keep them from exercising their creative skills. Today we are all bombarded by a constant stream of information pushed to us by our mobile devices. Some research has found that most U.S. workers complain that they are under a great deal of pressure in their jobs to get things done quickly. They report difficulty concentrating on a single task and they never feel that they have accomplished anything.[9] When the same study was conducted in 1994, researchers found that 82 percent of respondents claimed to accomplish at least half their planned work for the day, but in the current study that percentage had dropped to 50 percent. One of the biggest contributors to lowered productivity is multitasking. A study published in the *Proceedings of the National Academy of Sciences* surveyed 262 students about their media consumption habits. They then took the 19 students who multitasked the most and the 22 who multitasked the least and conducted additional tests. The findings were telling. In every test, those who spent the least amount of time simultaneously e-mailing, texting, talking on the phone, and surfing the Internet performed substantially better than those who spent the most time doing such activities.[10] The subconscious is the part of the brain responsible for discovery. If the thinking parts of the brain (left and right hemispheres) are constantly active, the subconscious is unable to supply the creative power it was designed for. Entrepreneurs need to set aside some time each day to let their brains free-associate or perhaps to do something creative that is unrelated to work. The simple act of turning off the e-mail notification button or turning off the phone can cut down on distractions and open the door to new ideas.

"Confidence is the expectation of success."[11] Those who expect to be successful generally are willing to exert the effort, spend the time, and expend the money to achieve it. Rosabeth Moss Kanter believes that confidence is composed of three elements: accountability, collaboration, and initiative.[12] Accountability is personal responsibility for actions taken and is a component of a person's integrity. Collaboration means working with others and being able to count on each other. Initiative is believing that the actions taken will make a difference. Taking the familiar, easiest, or shortest path usually happens when you lack confidence; you act out of fear of being criticized, and that often keeps you from fully realizing your potential. The need for their ideas to be acceptable or seem rational to others is a significant roadblock for some entrepreneurs; however, rationality is not a prerequisite either for innovative ways to seize opportunities or for receiving a patent on an invention. The inventor of patent number 2,608,083 probably thought he was being rational when he invented the Travel Washing Machine, a portable, mobile appliance that is mounted on the wheel of a vehicle and washes the driver's clothes as he or she motors down the road. Unfortunately, the motorist has to jack up the car first to install the device and, for optimum results, cannot travel faster than 25 miles an hour. Ridiculously irrational inventions notwithstanding, many of the products in use every day—the Internet and the mobile phone, to name two—would not have come about if the people who invented them hadn't had the courage to go against the general thinking of the time.

Setting manageable goals that create small wins when they're achieved can help entrepreneurs who lack confidence develop this important attribute. Conducting a feasibility analysis of a new business idea is an excellent way to reduce some of the risk of entrepreneurship and build confidence. For all the positives associated with creativity, it should not go unmentioned that creativity can also be an obstacle to achieving a goal. Creatives who don't know when to stop improving on an idea or planning their business and start moving into action mode face an uphill battle attempting to reach the outcome they seek.

All of the aforementioned roadblocks can stifle creativity, but individuals who believe they are not creative are doing themselves the greatest disservice. They are dismissing ideas before even trying them out and, at the very least, setting themselves up for failure. There are a number of things that can be done immediately to remove the roadblocks along the path to more creative thinking. The process starts with preparing an environment that makes it easier to think imaginatively and then moves to some techniques for enhancing creative skills. Table 3.1 provides an overview of some effective ways to develop creative skills. These are just a few of the many ways you can encourage creativity in your life. It is worth considering that creative skills will come

TABLE 3.1
Developing Creative Skills

Design a creative environment	Minimize distractions.
	Spend time in quiet contemplation—make thinking a habit.
	Pay attention to where you are when you feel creative.
	Move out of your comfort zone to try new things.
Log ideas	Maintain a journal of thoughts and ideas.
	Go back to your journal periodically for inspiration.
Put the familiar in a new context	Look for opportunity in the places you frequent.
	Pick a product and come up with new application for it.
	Identify a negative event (i.e. economic downturn) and brainstorm why it may be a positive.
Take advantage of your personal network	Who in your network can connect you with people doing very different things from what you're doing?
	Do you have a diverse network of people who can connect you to new communities of people? Entrepreneurs need networks for every aspect of their businesses.
Visualize something	Try visualizing what the world might look like in 50 years based on what you know today but not limiting what is possible.
	Visualize where a technology like mobile phone or social networking is going and what that might look like in the future.

© 2016 Cengage Learning®

in handy whether you're starting a business or going to work in a company. Those individuals who can tap into the creative part of their brains will be in high demand.

3.1b   Tools for Creativity and Inspiration

Idea generation, whether it be to find a significant problem or to generate solutions to a problem that has been defined, is an activity that benefits from few restrictions and no evaluation or criticism. The reason is that either praising or criticizing an idea at this point might shut off the flow of additional ideas or confine the direction of thought too early in the process. Instead, three rules of thumb apply:

- Go for quantity over quality of ideas initially.
- Capture every idea no matter how outlandish it may seem on the surface.
- Piggyback on ideas and create new combinations and modifications, but do this only after first generating ideas at the individual level.

Recent research conducted as a laboratory experiment has determined that where teams generate ideas first as individuals before coming together as a group to brainstorm (a hybrid approach), the number and quality of ideas improve, and the team is better able to discern which ideas are the best.[13] In fact, it appears that the best idea generated by the hybrid process is usually better than the best idea generated by the group approach. Why is this true? Group brainstorming often leads to situations where someone is unable to articulate an idea because others are speaking, an individual self-censors his or her idea before offering it based on evaluating other ideas already presented, or free riding takes place where some members contribute little or nothing because other members participate more actively.[14] The hybrid process, by contrast, produces about three times as many ideas per unit of time and these ideas are generally of much higher quality.[15] The bottom line is collaborative or team processes at the idea generation stage tend to lead to consensus and convergence, neither of which is useful to entrepreneurs looking for ideas that are innovative or game changing. A hybrid approach that involves working individually first to generate a set of ideas, then coming together as a group produces better results.

Brainwriting is a form of brainstorming that is often used to make sure that everyone on the team feels comfortable offering up ideas. There are a number of ways the exercise can be accomplished, but essentially it's about getting ideas down on paper and then organizing the ideas and creating themes. Each person is given a stack of Post-It® notes and asked to write three ideas, one on each of three Post-Its. As everyone finishes, they place their Post-Its in the center of the table. Then each one takes three Post-Its they didn't create, looks at the ideas and once again writes three new ideas on each of three new Post-Its. This continues for three to four rounds. Then all the Post-Its are placed on a white board or flip chart and the process of finding common themes and combining ideas begins.

One of the common sources of new inventions is the ability to connect things that don't normally go together. Leonardo da Vinci saw a connection between the branches of trees and the potential for a canal system in the city of Florence, Italy. He verbalized this connection as a metaphor: *canals are tree branches*. Nature has often served as the metaphor for an invention, including Velcro®, which was inspired by the sticky burr, and the entire field of nanotechnology. Review the "Make a Connection" box for an exercise in connecting things that are not normally associated.

Visualization is a technique that is used in all phases of the design thinking process and reflects the real creativity of the team. In the inspiration phase, it's used to make sense of things that you might observe or come up with as you're generating ideas. Being able to paint a picture of what you're seeing graphically or in words makes it easier to communicate to others with whom you might be working. Visualization is also important in identifying patterns in the masses of ideas you generate. It's not necessary to create works of art with your visualization. Lietdka and Ogilve, experts in design thinking, suggest keeping the visuals as simple as possible so that you don't spend too much time on them and lose the value of their purpose in the idea generation process.[16] Break ideas into

MAKE A CONNECTION

Try this exercise with a group of friends. It is sure to get everyone thinking outside the box. Give each person in the group a piece of paper. Then have each person write a noun on his or her paper—any noun. When all of the members have written a noun, everyone then passes his or her paper to the person on the right. Each person will now write an adjective on the paper—any adjective; do not consider the noun when writing it. Then the papers should be passed again to the right. Each person will then write a verb on the paper and pass it to the right. For the final round, each person will write an adverb on the paper. In each case, the word that is written does not have to relate to the previous words on the page.

Then the group should move into the next phase: connecting the words in a relationship so that a potential business opportunity appears. The group should decide on one page only and discard the others. Using the words provided, the group will come up with a business concept that includes product/service, customer, benefit, and distribution.

This exercise is based on the premise that many opportunities are created by going through a process that involves:

- Connecting dissimilar concepts
- Experimentation
- Inventing something new based on connections and experimentation
- Finding applications for the invention/opportunity created

FIGURE 3.3
The Journey Map

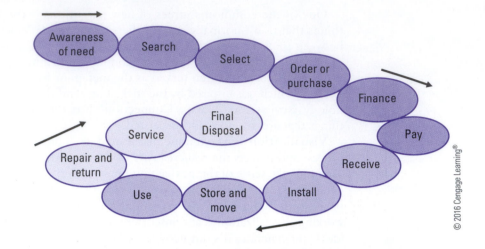

© 2016 Cengage Learning®

smaller parts and use storyboards to create sequences where appropriate. Mind-mapping is another effective way to visually lay out a lot of ideas and begin to organize them. The Internet is a rich source for mind-mapping tools, and some of them are free such as XMind.com. Apps like Mural.ly, an online whiteboarding tool, are good for working in groups when the members are not in the same room. Team members can share ideas using digital Post-it Notes.

Journey mapping is also an excellent way to understand customers' current experiences with a problem and existing solutions. Figure 3.3 presents an example of a simple journey map for a generic consumer product that depicts all of the touch points a company has with a customer from purchase to end of product life. Each point along the path is an opportunity to generate a new idea related to a problem the consumer could encounter.

3.2   OPPORTUNITY/IDEATION

Opportunity is the intersection of an idea and a customer. Research on entrepreneurial opportunity has identified two fundamental theories to explain how opportunities happen: discovery theory and creation theory. Discovery theory sees opportunity arising from shifts in external factors in the market or industry, such as regulation, technological changes, and changes in customer preferences.[17] These opportunities are out there waiting for entrepreneurs to discover them, so they require a more systematic approach to scanning the environment. If opportunities are out there for anyone to find, what explains why entrepreneurs tend to be better at discovering or recognizing opportunity when they see it? Research has learned that what distinguishes entrepreneurs from others is alertness or awareness. Alertness is a combination of a number of attributes such as risk preference, cognitive differences, and information asymmetries—what the entrepreneur knows that others do not.[18] Entrepreneurs often find themselves making decisions about opportunities without having all the required information needed to judge the risks and benefits associated with them. Therefore, a discovery type of opportunity requires decision making under high levels of risk.[19]

The second major theory of opportunity is creation theory where entrepreneurs are the actors; that is, entrepreneurs create opportunities via their actions, reactions, and experiments around new products, services, and business models.[20] This means that opportunities do not necessarily emerge out of existing industries or markets; therefore, search is not associated with creation theory. Entrepreneurs act and then monitor how customers respond to those actions. Creation theory allows for the fact that there are no "seeds" for opportunities in the industry/market environment.[21] If there are seeds, they lie within the entrepreneur, so these types of opportunities do not exist outside the mind of the entrepreneur. Consequently, a creation opportunity can emerge without any planning or foresight; the entrepreneur acts and then in a sense-and-respond fashion continues to move forward in a direction dictated by the responses he or she receives from the environment and the new information acquired from the experience. In practice this means that creation entrepreneurs, by their very nature, are willing to generalize from small samples, take more risk with less information, and rely on their own abilities to develop the opportunity.

One of the most effective ways entrepreneurs have of creating opportunity is to identify a problem in a market and seek a solution. Most people do this out of habit every day; they just don't realize it. They can't find a particular tool they need (say, a hammer), so they substitute something else (the handle of a screwdriver). That's using creative thinking to solve a problem. If the solution has commercial potential, then you may have turned the problem/solution into an opportunity.

Those who research and consult to large organizations on creative problem solving have developed complex processes by which teams can understand the problem or challenge, generate effective ideas, design a process, and prepare for action.[22] However, entrepreneurs need quick and flexible ways to creatively solve problems. Here we will introduce some techniques that may help entrepreneurs identify a problem or need and then focus on the best solution.

3.3   FIND AND FRAME THE PROBLEM

Once a bunch of ideas for needs or problems have been generated, there is a natural tendency to want to kill the "crazy" ideas quickly and rush to judgment on the best ideas. Both of these actions will ensure that the right problem gets lost in the scramble. To avoid this, use the principle of Affirmative Judgment, which is simply looking for the strengths or positive aspects of a problem first.[23] In other words, keep the criticism at bay until all the positives are articulated. Then when offering up criticisms, do it in a positive manner by focusing on how the problem might be restated or refocused. In fact, restating the problem and continually asking "why" is a proven method for getting at the root of the problem. This approach is discussed in the next section.

Using a set of predefined criteria is also helpful to establish some standards for the selection of the best problem definition. Alternatively, an evaluation matrix, often used to select product concepts for product development, can be used to select among several options against some critical benchmarks such as the following:

- An identifiable customer in a large market
- A significant pain or need
- An inexpensive prototype is possible

Many entrepreneurs make a number of common mistakes that prevent them from framing the problem correctly and then analyzing potential solutions.[24] They often define the problem incorrectly by asking, for example, "How can I fix this problem?" when the better question is "What is the source of the problem?" Answering the latter question opens the door to many more alternatives than are available with the first question. When we disregard the actual source of the problem, we may take mental shortcuts such as letting our personal biases interfere with the process, or relying simply on our intuition. Unfortunately, many of these mental shortcuts are subconscious; that is, we're not aware of them. For example, entrepreneurs frequently rely on patterns derived from previous experience, so when they face a new problem, they tend to consolidate all their previous biases based on experience and apply them to the new problem, which could be a huge mistake. Moreover, they sometimes draw conclusions before beginning their analysis or identify a solution before adequately framing the problem and analyzing it. Improperly or inadequately defining a problem means that the chances of ending up with the wrong solution increase substantially. There are a number of effective ways to overcome these challenges. A few of the more popular strategies include the following: restating the problem, attribute identification, and the decision tree.

3.3a   Restating the Problem

A problem stated as "we need to increase our revenues" appears to be an issue of how to generate more sales, but further investigation might conclude that the real problem is how to better serve the needs of the customer. If the value proposition for the customer has not been defined correctly, there is no realistic way to increase revenues and solve the actual problem. Two simple words, "how" and "why," can often break the logjam created by a problem statement that may be too narrow or too broad, giving the entrepreneur nothing meaningful to use. Look at Table 3.2 to see an example of how a problem statement can be reworked to get at the root problem that was not apparent from the original problem statement. In this case, it appears on the surface that the problem is not enough manufacturing space. One way to find the source of the problem is to consider the opposite of the original statement or put the statement into a broader or narrower context; for instance, if we had more manufacturing space, what could we do with it? The approach that gets at the root of the problem in this case is asking "why" and then restating the problem until the real cause of the problem emerges.

An effective problem statement has four components: (1) a "how" question, (2) an answer to who is responsible for dealing with the problem, (3) an action

TABLE 3.2
Restating the Problem

Original problem statement	We don't have enough manufacturing space
The opposite of the original statement	We have too much manufacturing space.
Broaden or narrow the focus. Put the statement into a larger or narrower context	What would we do with more manufacturing space?
Ask "why" to get to the root of the problem	**Original Statement:** We need more manufacturing space.
	Why? Because we don't have room for all our workers.
	Problem Restatement: How can we accommodate all the workers we need?
	Why? Because we have had to hire more workers to complete our contract on time.
	Problem Restatement: How can we get more workers without having to provide manufacturing space?
	Why? Because we don't have the funding to add more manufacturing space right now.
	Problem Restatement: How can we outsource some of the work to another manufacturer?
	Why? Because we need to finish the project on time or we'll lose our major customer.
	Problem Restatement: In what ways can we finish the project on time?
	(We have generated the root of the problem, which is time and an impending deadline.)

© Cengage Learning®

verb, which represents the positive course of action anticipated, and (4) the target or desired outcome. Notice that in Table 3.2, the final problem statement contains all these elements: *In what ways* (the how question) *can we* (the team) *finish the project* (action) *on time* (desired outcome).

3.3b Attribute Identification

This is a simple technique that has the entrepreneur breaking down a problem into its various elements and then generating new approaches or modifications for each of the elements. For example, suppose the problem being worked on is how to differentiate an apparel company from every other apparel company? You would first want to ask what the main attributes of this problem are. The attributes might include—among other things—the actual clothing line, the type of retail outlet, in-store service techniques, and customer acquisition strategies. Then you need to think about each attribute individually. Some questions to ask might be

1. What can we add or take away from this problem definition?

2. Can we combine this with something else?

3. What if we reverse the problem statement?

These questions and more can help you look at your initial problem definition in a different way. Looking at problem attributes will reveal numerous possibilities for how they might be configured to create a unique product/service differentiation.

3.3c   Force Fitting

Some of the best ideas come from connecting things that normally don't go together. In this case, you take a random object and create a relationship to the problem definition you're dealing with. For example, suppose you have come up with an alarm clock that you can talk to, solving the problem of having to reach over and shut off the alarm (Jonathan Nostrandt solved this very problem with "Moshi," an intelligent alarm clock). Now what if you wanted to test the possibility for further differentiation? You randomly bring a lamp into the discussion and brainstorm ways to connect the lamp to the alarm clock. Among many ideas, someone might suggest that your alarm clock could turn on the light in the morning to a level that would encourage you to wake up. This is an idea that might never have been discovered had you not forced yourself to associate two unrelated objects.

3.4   DEVELOP SOLUTIONS

Identifying the right problem is the most challenging aspect of the problem-solving process because it's important to get it right so that time and money won't be wasted on the wrong solution. Engineers know that product design represents about 8 percent of the new product budget, but it accounts for about 80 percent of the final cost. For example, every time an engineer has to go back and redesign a solution because the problem was not correctly identified, it adds to the cost and time lost getting to market. Once the problem statement is completed, it's time to turn that statement into action.

The same techniques used to generate and focus ideas related to the problem can now be employed to generate and focus potential solutions. Criteria often play a more critical role in the identification of solutions because there are constraints in the form of costs, skills, and timeframes associated with solutions that must be taken into consideration. Criteria can be explicit or more formal such as time limits, budget constraints, and the like. They can also be implicit: criteria that may not have been specifically identified but that are known to be part of what must be considered in any decision about a solution—such things as intuition, team culture, preferences, prejudices, and perspectives often based on previous experience.

For entrepreneurs, the closer the solution relates to the actual problem the customer is experiencing, the more likely that there will be immediate sales upon completion of product development. The issue of customers as problem identifiers and how to find out about customer needs is detailed in Chapter 4.

3.5   INNOVATION

Creativity and problem solving are important skills for entrepreneurs to acquire, but they don't in and of themselves solve the entrepreneur's dilemma of how to extract value from an idea, value that someone will pay for. Innovation has been defined in a number of ways, but the following definition reflects the concept that innovation is not simply about products and services but about other aspects of the entrepreneurial process as well.

Innovation is concerned with the process of commercializing or extracting value from ideas: this is in contrast with "invention," which need not be directly associated with commercialization.[25]

What this means is that unlike invention, which does not always result in products that see the market, innovation is all about creating marketable value. In the 1930s, economist Joseph Schumpeter identified five categories of innovation: (1) a new product or substantial change in an existing product, (2) a new process, (3) a new market, (4) new sources of supply, and (5) changes in industrial organization.[26] Strictly speaking, Schumpeter did not view incremental improvements as innovation even if they generated economic growth. Moreover, an innovation did not become an innovation until it was commercialized, that is, until it realized economic value. So, when we talk about innovation, we're really talking about the process that takes a novel idea and transforms it into a product or service that customers will pay for. *Commercialization* is the process that moves an innovation from the laboratory to the market by executing on a business strategy. Figure 3.4 depicts the innovation and commercialization process, the associated tasks, and the relationship of the various components. Research will have to be conducted on the opportunity, the business model, and the business design. Observe all of the activities that require research and validation to produce the financial outcomes listed. In effect, rather than a process, what you see is a complex system with multiple interactions, so that information uncovered in any one area has an impact on every other area in the chart. For example, if your research concludes that you have a patentable invention that also will require approval by a regulatory body before you can market it, that finding alone will impact timing, costs, the potential need for partners and investors, and so forth.

Innovations can be grouped into two broad groups—incremental and disruptive (or radical)—and each has ramifications for entrepreneurial strategy. The vast majority of innovations today are incremental, that is, they are built on existing technology. For example, the Apple iPad was a huge improvement over previous tablets but was actually an extension of the very popular iPhone. A number of important technologies had to be invented and available before Apple could develop either the iPad or the iPhone. Delivering an offline service over the Internet, such as distance learning, is an example of incremental innovation on a distribution channel. Incremental innovation improves on an existing technological or product base, often to create differentiation in the market.

By contrast, disruptive or radical innovations obsolete previous technology or ways of doing things, and in general can find no identifiable market in the earliest stages of development. Historically disruptive innovations have often

FIGURE 3.4   The Innovation and Commercialization Process

Phases	Environment, Discovery, & Opportunity	Business Model	Business Design
RESEARCH & VALIDATION	**Critical Industry Forces** Suppliers, Buyers, Competitive Rivalry, Barriers to Entry, Threat of Substitutes Trends: Technological, Political, and Social	**Solutions** Applications, Product/Service Offerings Benefits to Customer	**Benefits Process Flow** Customer Acquisition to Delivery Business Activities
RESEARCH & VALIDATION	**Market: Pains/Problems** Market Size and Growth Competition Trends	**Customer Segment Identification** Addressable Market Segments Benefits to Each Customer First Customer Customer Channels	**Key Resources Required & Timing** Physical–Plant and Equipment Capital–Working and Investment Human–Headcount
RESEARCH & VALIDATION	**Intellectual Property, Regulatory, & Prototype** Patent Decisions, Regulatory Impact Technology Platform Development Field Tests and pre-Clinical Tests Technology Validation	**Technology Application Validation** Field Tests with Customers Animal Trials Clinical Trials	**Operations** Manufacturing/Operations Plan Marketing Plan Management Plan Contingency Plan Execution Plan
OUTCOMES	**Revenue Sources and Drivers** Number of Sources Type Size Speed to Achieve		**Strategic Partners** Independent Contractors Strategic Alliances Investors
OUTCOMES	**Cost & Profitability Drivers** Type Size Importance		**Launch Strategy** License Start a Business Sell Joint Venture
OUTCOMES	**Startup Capital Requirements**		
EXECUTION	**Management Team** **Board of Directors/Advisors** Expertise, Experience, Network		**Market Timing** When to launch

been patented because achieving mass adoption in the market is a costly process taking many years to accomplish and the inventor wants to protect the time and effort he or she has put into the innovation. Some examples of disruptive innovations that have had enormous impact are the Internet, the birth control pill, and the transistor. On the other hand, today we see many examples of business model disruption that has nothing to do with products. For example Google Adwords had a huge impact on how many Internet companies monetized their businesses with advertising. We will take up the strategic issues that are related

TABLE 3.3   Some Sources of Innovation

Customers	Needs and suggestions for improvements or new products and services.
News Sources and Magazines	Reveal trends and needs in the market.
Observation	Sitting in an airport and observing the challenges people face.
Demographic shifts	The increasing Latino population or people moving to the sun belt states.
New government laws and regulations	The Affordable Care Act and the need for businesses and individuals to understand and comply with the requirements.
Emerging industries	Mobile and wearable devices.
Trends	Privacy and anonymity on the Internet.
Business operations	New processes that reduce costs.

© Cengage Learning®

to incremental and disruptive innovation in the chapters on marketing and growth. In the meantime, Table 3.3 provides some sources of inspiration for innovation.

Opportunity is everywhere, and much of it goes unnoticed. Entrepreneurs who make the effort to become more creative and opportunistic will have an unending supply of new ideas available to play with.

New Venture Action Plan

- Do the exercises suggested in Table 3.1, "Developing Creative Skills."

- Practice generating ideas and problems using the techniques provided in the chapter.

- Take one of the sources in Table 3.3 and come up with an innovation.

Questions on Key Issues

1. Give an example to demonstrate the difference between an idea and an opportunity.
2. Identify the challenges you face in becoming more creative. What three things will you do to address those challenges?
3. What is the value of early and excellent product definition?
4. Pick a business in the community, and find a creative way to change either the product/ service it offers or the way that product/service is delivered to customers. How does your innovation add value to the business, and how can that value be captured?
5. How is invention different from innovation? Which is more common today, and why?

Experiencing Entrepreneurship

1. Spend an afternoon walking around your community or your university or college campus. Don't look for anything in particular. Observe the things that you don't normally pay attention to when you're in a hurry. Watch people—what they do and don't do. At the end of the afternoon, write down all the thoughts that come to you on the basis of your afternoon of observation. Which of these ideas could possibly become a business opportunity and why?

2. Pick one of the sources of new product/service ideas discussed in Table 3.3. Using that source, come up with an opportunity that has business potential. Then, using the Internet or talking to people in that industry (always the best approach), develop a brief report that supports the viability of this opportunity.

Relevant Case Studies

Case 2 B2P: Micro-Bioinformatics Technology and Global Expansion
Case 3 CleanBee Baby

PART II

FEASIBILITY ANALYSIS

Startup Feasibility

Research

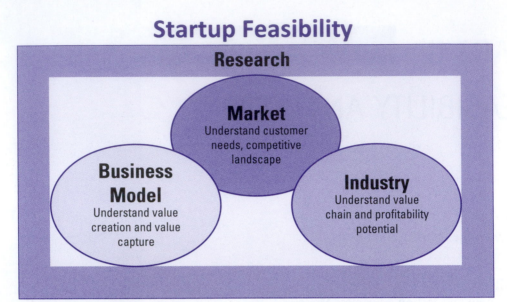

Market
Understand customer needs, competitive landscape

Business Model
Understand value creation and value capture

Industry
Understand value chain and profitability potential

Hypothesize, Test, and Pivot

Design and Execute

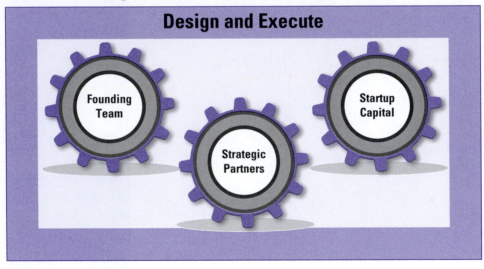

Founding Team

Strategic Partners

Startup Capital

CHAPTER 4

Analyzing the Industry and Market

"There is only one boss. The customer. And he can fire everybody in the company from the chairman on down, simply by spending his money somewhere else."

—SAM WALTON, FOUNDER, WAL-MART

CHAPTER OBJECTIVES

- Explain the difference between an industry and a market.
- Discover effective ways to research and analyze an industry.
- Determine first customer and the characteristics of the market.
- Use ethnographic techniques for understanding customers.
- Gather competitive intelligence.

PROFILE
4.1

GEMVARA FINDS A NICHE IN A TOUGH INDUSTRY AND A CROWDED MARKET

The jewelry industry is centuries old, so finding a new business model that stands out from the crowd is not an easy task. In 2006, Matt Lauzon and Jason Reuben were seniors at Babson College in Wellesley, Massachusetts, and very much involved in the world of startups, fully intending to start a business before they graduated. Jason's family had been in the diamond business for about 30 years, and the duo believed they could leverage that industry knowledge to find a novel way to enter the industry. In addition, the family's connections in the industry with suppliers would be invaluable. Their plan was to help the old-school jewelry businesses connect with consumers online through their company, Paragon Lake. The opportunity they saw was to take advantage of a trend at the time in mass customization with the creation of a network structure where an intermediary—Paragon Lake—brokered transactions among diverse jewelry retailers and manufacturers. The problem they were solving was to help smaller mom-and-pop jewelers boost sales through the Internet. Others seemed to like the concept as well because they went on to win Babson's annual Business Plan Competition and were featured in *Business Week* on a list of "America's Best Young Entrepreneurs."

Just before the two graduated, they received a call from Bob Davis, a general partner at Highland Capital Partners, a venture capital firm, who offered them a place in the firm's Summer@ Highland accelerator program for startups. They were given $7,500, office space, and the ability to get mentoring from Highland as they worked on their business. Lauzon and Reuben set up shop in Highland's Lexington, Massachusetts, office and began the development of a product they called

"virtual display case," essentially an online service for jewelry stores that let their customers customize their jewelry and see a 3D model of their design in advance.

To accelerate the startup process, Lauzon tried to raise a first round of funding but with no success. Davis, their venture capital mentor, thought they weren't ready. "The team wasn't well-rounded, and it wasn't totally clear who the customer was, how the market was segmented."[1] Eventually in December of 2007, the team signed a term sheet with Highland for $500,000 in seed capital and continued to work on the website and sign up jewelers. Before too long, Lauzon again believed they were ready for a much larger tranche of investment capital. This time his attempt was successful, and in July 2008, the company was able to raise $5.8 million in funding.

Unfortunately, Paragon Lake did not find the demand they had predicted from their target market of jewelry retailers, so it was time to change the business model and find the right customer. By February, 2010, Reuben was no longer with the company, and Lauzon had changed the company's name to Gemvara to reflect a new business model that involved selling directly to consumers over the Internet. The site, which targeted women aged 35 to 45, enabled consumers to choose custom jewelry from the comfort of their homes. Customers would get previews of the jewelry and pricing for various combinations of designs, metals, and jewels. Lauzon's goal was to give the customer an "awesome experience." To that end, many might argue that emotion mattered more than metrics.

By 2011, the company had raised $15 million in a Series C round led by Balderton Capital, a

European venture capital firm, with plans to open a New York office. Late in 2012, with by then $51 million in total capital raised and pressure from investors to grow faster, Matt Lauzon stepped down as CEO but remained as chairman. It was time for professional management—to go big or go home. As it turned out, the holiday season of 2013 produced a tripling of sales and the opening of Gemvara's flagship showroom in Boston. In 2014, the company hired former Gucci executive Matt Marcus to strengthen Gemvara's growing position in the luxury jewelry industry.

Sources: Huang, G.T. (November 27, 2012). "Gemvara CEO Matt Lauzon Steps Down," *Xconomy*, http://www.xconomy.com/boston/2012/11/27/gemvara-ceo-matt-lauzon-steps-down-thoughts-on-startup-culture-and-legacy/. Indvik, Lauren (March 27, 2011). "How Gemvara Is Changing the Way Fine Jewelry Is Bought," *Mashable*, http://mashable.com/2011/03/27/gemvara-funding/; Moore, G. (February 12, 2010). "Paragon Lake Now Named Gemvara, Targets Consumers," *MHT: The Journal of New England Technology*, www.masshightech.com/stories/2010/02/08/daily51-Paragon-Lake-now-named-Gemvara-targets-consumers.html; Ha, Anthony, "Paragon Lake Will Let You Customize Jewelry Online," *VentureBeat*, www.venturebeat.com, November 13, 2009; and Kirsner, S. (Jul 7 6, 2008). "Incubator Polishes Gem of an Idea," *The Boston Globe*. www.boston.com/business/articles/2008/07/06/incubator_polishes_gem_of_an_idea.

Unquestionably, an analysis of the industry in which a business will operate is critical to determining whether a new venture can be successful. From the broadest perspective, the industry is a grouping of businesses that interact in a common environment as part of a value chain or distribution channel for a particular good. The industry is essentially the environment in which a new business operates. There is enormous value in knowing an industry well. Ideas for new ventures frequently come from understanding and having experience with an industry. In addition, comprehending how an industry works can help entrepreneurs find strategic partners, customers, venture capital, and strategies for success as well as learn where the pitfalls and roadblocks might be. A strategic position in a growing, dynamic, healthy industry can go a long way toward ensuring a successful venture. For example, a relatively young, growing industry with many new entrants, like the social media industry, offers an opportunity to position a business to become a major player in the industry. By contrast, occupying a weak position in a mature industry, such as the PC industry, may sound a death knell for the business before it ever opens its doors. Understanding how an industry operates is fundamental to shaping effective entry and growth strategies and to determining the potential for profitability.

If an industry is defined by a product or service, a market is defined by customers. Identification of the primary market and the first customer is one of the most important tasks that needs to be undertaken during the feasibility analysis for a new business. What is meant by "first customer"? The customer is an individual or organization who pays for a product or service, so the first customer for the entrepreneur generally represents that segment of the marketplace that needs the product or service most—in other words, the customer in the most pain. The reason is that entrepreneurs have limited resources so they want to assure that their first sales come quickly, which will happen if they've targeted customers with real problems.

Entrepreneurs identify their primary customers by recognizing a need, or pain, in the market. One team of aspiring entrepreneurs wanted to solve the problem of identity protection when using credit cards. Initially, they were only thinking in terms of the consumer until they realized that it's not the consumer who will pay them but a credit card issuer who wants to differentiate its offering by including the new technology they had developed. Identifying a pain or need in the market is just the first step. Conducting in-depth market analysis to support the need you have recognized is equally important. This chapter helps you do efficient and effective industry and market research within the constraints of the limited resources available to you so that your new venture increases its chances for success.

4.1   AN OVERVIEW OF INDUSTRY ANALYSIS

There are two important reasons to study the industry in which your business will operate. First, it represents the business's external environment, and no business operates independent of its external environment. Second, you need to understand whether you can make a profit in the industry and if that profit will be significant enough to make the effort to start the business worthwhile. Return on investment (ROI) is a critical factor in any entrepreneur's planning. Some industries have strong forces working against them so ROI is relatively small, while others have more benign forces affecting them that enable higher returns. For example, the airlines and publishing industries have intense forces acting on them, so returns typically are not attractive. Return on invested capital for the airlines industry from 1992 through 2006 averaged 5.9 percent; publishing was 13.4 percent as compared to industries with weak forces acting on them such as software, which garnered an average of 37.6 percent and pharmaceuticals 31.7 percent in the same period.[2]

It's often not easy to identify where an industry begins and ends. If you define it too broadly, you may end up making assumptions that don't match your particular situation. For example, the social media industry is global; it's likely that you would want to define this industry more narrowly because the social media industry in the United States is probably different from the same industry in China due to cultural influences. It's also important to realize that your business may cross more than one industry. For example, one could argue that Amazon is in multiple industries: retail, consumer electronics, grocery, cloud computing, and most recently set-top boxes, to name a few. If your business is in more than one industry, you'll need to study every industry that is critical to your business's ability to make a profit.

Exploring an industry will involve gathering and synthesizing an enormous amount of information as well as talking to people who spend their days working in that industry. Starting with a clear understanding of what information needs to be gathered will increase the chances that the assessment is as accurate as possible.

The data collected should answer the following key questions:

■ *What does the industry look like?* Every industry possesses a particular character that may be described as hostile, collaborative, highly competitive, friendly, and so forth. It is also characterized by its demographics, such as size, number of active companies, revenues, and age.

■ *Is the industry growing?* Growth is measured by sales volume, number of employees, units produced, number of new companies entering the industry, and so forth. A growing industry means more opportunities for new ventures to enter and survive. The appropriate growth measure is determined by the type of industry. For example, the food services industry is typically labor intensive, so looking at growth in the number of employees makes sense. On the other hand, the import/export industry is not necessarily labor intensive, so growth in the number of employees is not a good measure of overall industry growth.

■ *Where are the opportunities?* Does the industry provide opportunities for new businesses with strategies involving new products and/or processes, novel business models, innovative distribution strategies, or new marketing approaches? Are there clear examples of new ventures that have succeeded in this industry?

■ *What is the status of any new technology?* How quickly does the industry adopt new technology, and does technology play a significant role in the competitive strategy of firms in the industry?

■ *How much do industry companies spend on research and development?* Expenditures on R&D indicate how important technology is, how rapid the product development cycle is, and whether technology is critical to industry success.

■ *Who are the opinion leaders in the industry?* Which firms dominate the industry and what impact do they have? How do they influence new firm strategy? Opinion leaders may or may not be a new firm's competitors in its markets depending on how you have defined your customers. Nevertheless, opinion leaders will affect the new venture's ability to access the supply chain and distribution channels.

■ *Are there young, successful firms in the industry?* This information will provide an indicator of how formidable the entry barriers are and whether the industry is growing rapidly.

■ *What does the future look like?* What appears likely to happen over the next five years? What are the trends and patterns of change? You need to prepare your new venture for success beyond the date of launch; you need to prepare for sustainability.

■ *Are there any threats to the industry?* Is there any chance that new technology will render obsolete either the industry or that segment of the industry in which you are doing business?

■ *What are the typical margins in the industry?* Looking at average gross margins in the industry provides an indication of how much room there is to make mistakes. A gross margin is derived by dividing gross profit by sales. It indicates how much money is left to pay overhead and make a profit. Both small and large gross margins have tradeoffs. If the industry typically has 2 percent gross margins or less, as the grocery industry does, making a profit will require selling in large volumes and keeping overhead costs to a minimum. Price, therefore, will be a driver of customer purchasing decisions. Where margins run at 70 percent or higher, there is a lot more room to play, but generally these industries (such as the software industry) have relatively short product life cycles, so R&D costs are high. Here customers are more interested in getting a solution to their problem and are willing to pay a premium to get that solution.

For all businesses, there are global trends that offer rich opportunities to innovate.[3]

- For the first time in 200 years, emerging-market countries will generate more growth than developing countries, which will provide a new market of middle class consumers.
- These developing economies need to become productive quickly so there are opportunities to offer innovations that increase productivity.
- Global interconnectedness in economies, markets, and social groups means more volatility and an acceleration of the rate of innovation.

Going into the analysis with a firm grip on which questions need to be answered is the first step. Figuring out where to find this information is the next step.

4.1a   Gathering Secondary Sources of Industry Information

It's generally wise to begin any research by looking at secondary sources of information to gather background data. Today, Google search engine or any other as well as Wikipedia.com are great places to get an introduction to an industry and pick up on some trends by noting what is being talked about. Journals, trade magazines, industry analysts, government publications, and annual reports of public corporations—normally available online in a university or community library—are also excellent starting points; they provide more targeted information and generally from experts. For example, a number of industry analysts offer excellent overviews of most of the major industries: Forrester, Gartner, IBISWorld, Standard & Poor's NetAdvantage, Passport (a Euromonitor international industry source), Thomson One, and Factiva. Any college or university will have several of these and more available online. Trade magazines provide a good sense of key firms and the direction the industry may be taking. LexisNexis and STAT-USA are also fine sources of industry statistics. The important thing to remember is to use multiple sources to draw conclusions because no one source is complete and it's important to get a variety of perspectives to look for patterns.

The North American Industry Classification System (NAICS), the classification system that the United States, Canada, and Mexico developed to identify industries and allow for common standards and statistics across North America has replaced the traditional U.S. Standard Industrial Classification system (SIC). NAICS covers 350 new industries that have never been coded before. Some of these industries reflect high-tech developments such as fiber optic cable manufacturing, satellite communications, and the reproduction of computer software. However, far more of these new categories are not technology-based: bed and breakfast inns, environmental consulting, warehouse clubs, pet supply stores, credit card issuing, diet and weight reduction centers, to name only a few. These codes can be found at www.census.gov/epcd/www/naics.html.

NAICS industries are identified by a six-digit code instead of the four-digit SIC code. The longer code accommodates a larger number of sectors and enables more flexibility in designating subsectors. NAICS is organized in a hierarchical structure much like the SIC. The first two digits designate a major economic sector (formerly division), such as agriculture or manufacturing. The third digit designates an economic subsector (formerly major group), such as crop production or apparel manufacturing. The fourth digit designates an industry group, such as grain and oil seed farming or fiber, yarn, and thread mills. The fifth digit designates the NAICS industry, such as wheat farming or broad-woven fabric mills. The international NAICS agreement fixes only the first five digits of the code. The sixth digit is used for industrial classifications in other countries where necessary. With the NAICS code, one can find statistics about size of the industry, sales, number of employees, and so forth.

It is easy to research common major industries like consumer goods and technology because they are frequently covered by the government, news sources, brokerage firms, and the financial press. More difficult are small industries, whose data may end up aggregated within a larger industry; new or emerging industries, which are not yet represented in the government classification system; business-to-business industries where information is kept proprietary; and those industries that are not yet perceived to be legitimate industries. However, there are some indirect ways to extrapolate valuable information to guide the analysis.

1. *Check the business press.* Often popular business publications and newspapers will write about an industry before it hits the radar of the more established sources.

2. *Talk to trade associations.* Since these organizations are comprised of industry companies, they tend to collect data that describes that industry. The *Encyclopedia of Associations* is a good way to find such a trade organization. Also consider searching online using the ".org" domain, which is typical of nonprofit organizations such as trade associations.

3. *Consult trade association journals.* These journals are often found online or through services like LexisNexis or Factiva.

4. *Check organizations that list government and agency resources.* For example, FedStats lists U.S. government sites that contain statistical information, and it can be searched by topic or agency.

5. *Look at blogs, wikis, websites, and social networking sites.* Find patterns of thought and support or disconfirming evidence for your conclusions.

The Internet is an exciting source of a vast amount of information, most of it for free. When using free sources such as wikis, websites, blogs, etc. it is important to remember that these are, for the most part, sources of opinion that may not have any evidence to support them. You should ask serious questions about who authored the information, what that person's credentials are, and what their motivation was for writing it. In addition, consider whether the author included citations to original sources and determine the currency of the information. Many significant events have occurred in the business environment in the past 10 years that will impact business strategy. Relying on outdated information could send you in the wrong direction.

4.1b   The Importance of Primary Industry Data

Secondary research paints a broad picture of the industry, but given the lead time from data gathering to print, it rarely yields the most current information available. Therefore, to access the timeliest information, it is extremely important to gather primary field data on the industry. Put more simply, you need to talk with people in the industry to validate what they have gathered with their secondary research. Some sources to tap are:

- *Industry observers and analysts*, who study particular industries and regularly report on them in newspapers or newsletters or through the media.
- *Suppliers and distributors*, who are in an excellent position to comment on the health of the industry in terms of demand for products and services, as well as on the financial strength and market practices of major firms in the industry.
- *Customers*, who can be a clue to satisfaction with the industry and the products or services supplied by firms in the industry.
- *Employees of key firms in the industry*, who are a good source of information about opinion leaders and competitors.
- *Professionals from service organizations*, such as lawyers and accountants, who regularly work with a particular industry.
- *Trade shows*, which give a good indication of who the opinion leaders are and who has the strongest market strategy.

4.1c   Understanding Industry Life Cycles

Industries do not remain static or stable over time; in fact, they are constantly evolving. Like people, industries and their products move through a life cycle that includes birth, growth, maturity, and ultimately decline. Today, many industry life cycles are accelerating with a corresponding speeding up of their product cycles; for example, the design cycle for automobiles has shrunk from 50 months to between 24 and 36 months, with similar patterns occurring across most industries. Consequently, many companies have been caught in the inertia of believing that their products would live forever. Like companies, industries decline when the story is no longer compelling. When companies in that industry stick to the old strategies while customers move on, the life cycle slows and eventually dies.

In some industries digital products have completely disrupted conventional products and services. Consider Skype or FaceTime in video-conferencing, Khan Academy in education, and Square in mobile credit-card processing.

These "big-bang disruptions," as they've been called, literally come out of the blue and often from a completely different industry. By combining several existing technologies, they offer a substantially better value proposition.[4]

The stages of the industry life cycle are identified by the different kinds of activities occurring at each stage. Figure 4.1 displays this life cycle, and we describe the stages and their strategic implications here.

Emerging Industry

A new industry emerges often with the introduction of a disruptive technology, such as the Internet, that displaces previous technology and creates opportunities that didn't exist before. In 2014, some of the top emerging industries were body-adapted wearable electronics, nanostructured carbon composites, predictive analytics, and brain-computer interfaces.[5] All of them are based on disruptive technologies that will change the way we do things. For entrepreneurs contemplating an industry entry at the earliest stage, it truly is the Wild West, with no rules and plenty of opportunities to try anything and everything. With sufficient resources, intellectual property, and a well-crafted strategy, an entrepreneurial firm can position its technology to potentially become the industry standard. If the new venture is unable to generate the momentum to become the standard, its strategy will be influenced and even dictated by the standards set by more dominant players.

Growth and Adaptation

A new industry typically goes through a volatile and rapid stage of growth as companies and their respective technologies jockey for position and the right to determine industry standards. This is an expensive period for most companies because they need to deploy extensive resources while developing critical partnerships to establish their position in the industry.

FIGURE 4.1   Industry Life Cycle

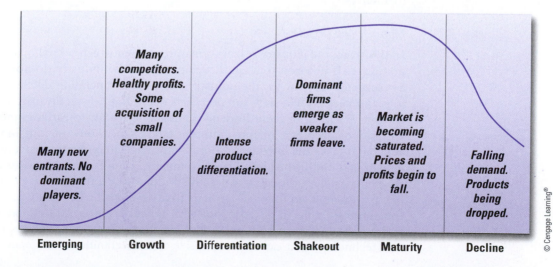

© Cengage Learning®

Differentiation and Competition

As more firms enter the industry, intense product differentiation occurs, because the industry's established standards and proprietary rights no longer provide the exclusivity they once did. Entrepreneurial ventures that enter the industry at this point must either identify niches that have not been served or differentiate themselves sufficiently in order to attract enough customers to be successful. One of the biggest threats at this stage is commoditization. It is commonly believed that all products eventually become commodities; however, recent research has revealed that this is not always the case. Take, for example, the humble toaster, which has gone through multiple iterations in its product life cycle and is still a prominent fixture in the home appliance industry. Today, the global marketplace in countertop toasting technology is demonstrably driven by differentiation, segmentation, and ongoing technical innovation.[6] When price becomes the most important differentiator, however, it signals to entrepreneurs that the time for innovation has already arrived and that new value must be created quickly.

Shakeout

When competition is the most intense, those companies that are unable to compete leave. The remaining firms then grow more rapidly as they pick up the slack. In fact, it is a curious truism that as the industry goes through its shakeout, the GDP (gross domestic product) actually increases, meaning that firms in the industry become more productive. Nevertheless, although shakeouts may lead to temporary efficiency gains, they also eliminate the possibility of competition and therefore contribute to a social loss from decreased market competition.[7] Entrepreneurial firms will not enter such an industry if they cannot survive the predatory tactics of the dominant players in the industry. The shakeout period moves the industry from many companies and high product costs, to a more stable and mature industry with only a few efficient firms. This is the period in the industry life cycle when the opinion leaders establish themselves.

Maturity and Decline

In this stage, the industry reaches a mature state in which several major players dominate. If new research and development in the industry do not produce a resurgence of growth, the industry could face impending decline as earnings and sales growth slow and prospects deteriorate. Typically, mature industries are described by high-dividend yields and low price-to-earnings ratios, and CEOs of companies in mature industries tend to focus on cost containment. In general, it takes the introduction of disruptive technology to turn a declining industry around. Broad industries like mining, manufacturing, and agriculture are all in decline, although some sectors within those industries have found new life. For example, in Iowa, soy farmers have developed a new soy flour that can substitute for eggs in baked goods with no cholesterol. And miners of mica in South Dakota are finding new applications for their minerals as a result of new technology that can reduce the size of mica granules to the nano level or less than 12 microns in size. Mica, traditionally used as an insulating material in electronics, is now used to dampen sound in automobiles and add shine to cosmetics.

For every industry, these life-cycle stages occur at different times and vary in their duration. The video rental industry presents a classic example of an industry in transition. In the early stages it was made up of small independent (mom-and-pop) owners. Wayne Huizenga sought to consolidate the industry by developing Blockbuster Video, a video megastore. In just a few years, independents were disappearing in favor of large-volume chain outlets. Then the megastores gave way to video on demand, available over cable television and even the Internet. And then Netflix made DVDs easily available through the mail at an even lower cost and more convenience and also streams its movies to the user's television or other playback device.

Recent research has identified four major industry trajectories that signal how fast change occurs in a particular industry.[8] Figure 4.2 depicts these trajectories from the most prevalent, progressive and intermediating, through radical and creative change. Progressive change takes place as companies in the industry grow geographically and increase profits through innovations in operations, processes, distribution, and technology. Examples are discount retailers like Wal-Mart and airlines like Jet Blue. Intermediating change, by contrast, is industry change that comes about when there are major shifts in the value chain in the form of forward and backward integration, strategic partnerships, and new ways to transact business with customers. A good example is the automobile industry, where dealers have moved onto the Internet in an effort to reach more customers and bring down costs.[9]

Radical change occurs in industries when an innovation results in the obsolescence of previous technology and drives old-line companies out of business. The Internet produced such a change for the automobile industry, and the PC drove typewriter manufacturers out of business. Radical change is transformative, but the transformation typically happens over decades. Finally, creative change is found in industries where resources turn over frequently and must continually be replaced. Companies in industries like the film production industry tend to undertake multiyear projects to develop new assets for customers (the moviegoers) who constantly seek new forms of entertainment.

FIGURE 4.2
Industry Trajectories

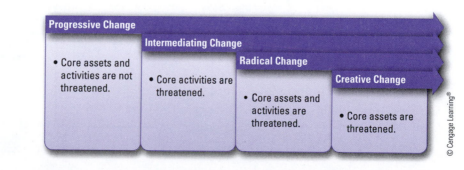

It is important to identify which stage of the life cycle an industry is in. Reading the analyses of industry watchers in trade magazines and talking with people who regularly work in that industry are good ways to learn where an industry is in the life cycle. Using a framework such as Porter's Five Forces, discussed in the next section, will assist you in determining the competitive characteristics of an industry or market as well as the industry's trajectory.

4.2   ANALYZING AN INDUSTRY

The industry is the context in which an entrepreneur's business will operate and every business operates within a value chain in that industry. The value chain consists of all of the companies that contribute to the development and distribution of products and service. If, for example, your company is a supplier or producer of raw materials, it will generally be at the top of the value chain and upstream from manufacturers. Intermediaries, such as distributors and retailers, will be downstream from manufacturers and assemblers. Where a company is located in the value chain normally reflects the entrepreneur's capabilities and risk-taking propensity.

Once the business is located on the value chain, it is easier to recognize who pays whom (who is the customer) and to determine costs and pricing. Figure 4.3 adds this information to a generic example of a complex indirect channel of distribution. The raw materials producer charges the manufacturer $4 per unit; the manufacturer turns the raw material into product and sells it to the distributor for $6. Alternatively, the manufacturer can use an independent sales representative (sales rep), who will find outlets and receive a commission on sales made. Note that the retailer, who buys from the distributor or sales rep, typically at least doubles its cost in setting the price to the consumer. This is known as keystoning. Also note that as a rule, markups increase as one moves down the channel. This occurs because the cost of doing business increases, as does the risk.

FIGURE 4.3
The Value Chain

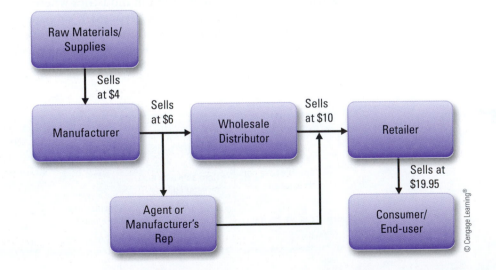

The value chain also illustrates the various markups, which is helpful in determining the lowest price possible for the product. The highest price possible is determined through market research with potential customers. The markups on the original cost reflect profit and overhead for the channel intermediary and are determined by what is typical in the industry. Every product or service has more than one channel option, so it's a good idea to depict distribution options graphically to compare their effectiveness. Graphing the value chain makes it possible to do the following:

1. Measure the time from manufacturing to customer on the basis of the lead time needed by each channel member.

2. Determine the ultimate retail price on the basis of the markups required by the intermediaries.

3. Figure the total costs of marketing the product. For example, manufacturers have to market to distributors, but to support their distributors, they may also market to retailers and even end users or consumers.

In addition to understanding how the industry value chain works, it is often helpful to attach a framework to the concept of an industry to organize all the data collected and to be able to effectively evaluate the industry. Many frameworks have been proposed, and several have been adopted successfully by entrepreneurs. Perhaps the most commonly used industry framework is Porter's Five Forces. Porter's work has been challenged on several levels, most notably, that a "sixth force," the government or public, should be included and that the attractiveness of an industry cannot be evaluated independent of the resources the company brings to the industry. Keeping these criticisms in mind, Porter's framework still provides an excellent exercise for entrepreneurs as they seek to characterize the industry in which they do business and the markets they will enter.

4.2a   Porter's Five Forces

For years, the work of Michael Porter has provided a way of effectively looking at the structure of an industry and a company's competitive strength and positioning relative to that industry and to the markets it serves. Porter's basic premise is that sustaining high performance levels requires a well-thought-out strategy and implementation plan based on knowledge of the way the industry works and the attractiveness of markets. Porter asserts that there are five forces in any industry that affect the ultimate profit potential of a venture in terms of long-run return on investment.[10] By contrast, such things as economic forces, changes in demand, material shortages, and technology shifts affect short-run profitability. Figure 4.4 depicts the Five Forces framework, which is discussed in more detail in the following sections.

Barriers to Entry

An entrepreneurial venture's success in a given industry or market is affected by the ability of new firms to enter the entrepreneur's market. If the costs

FIGURE 4.4
Porter's Five Forces
Framework

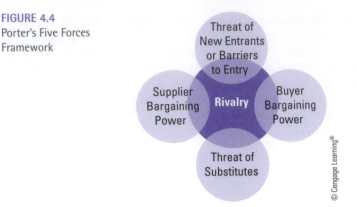

are low and few economies of scale exist, then competitors can easily enter and disrupt the entrepreneur's competitive strategy. In some industries and markets, however, barriers to entry are high and will discourage competitors from entering. Note that these factors may also present a challenge for entrepreneurs entering new markets or a new industry. These barriers may include the following:

Economies of Scale: Many industries have achieved economies of scale in marketing, production, and distribution. This means that their costs to produce have declined relative to the price of their goods and services. Typically, economies of scale are found in more mature industries. A new venture cannot easily achieve these same economies, so it is forced into a "Catch-22" situation. If it enters the industry on a large scale, it risks retaliation from those established firms in the industry. If it enters on a small scale, which is the more common strategy, it may not be able to compete because its costs are high relative to everyone else's. Another version of this dilemma occurs in an industry in which the major players are vertically integrated; that is, they own their suppliers and/or distribution channels, which effectively locks out the new venture. What most new ventures do when they must compete with companies that have achieved economies of scale is attempt to form alliances with other small firms to share resources and thus compete on a more level playing field. This type of collaboration is occurring more and more often as businesses realize that the industry is too complex for any one company to have all the resources and intellectual property required to control a portion of it. An example of this strategy is the grocery industry, where independent grocers have joined forces in consortia to achieve more buying power in their industry.

Brand Loyalty: New entrants to an industry face existing products and services with loyal customers who are not likely to switch easily to something new. A new firm will need to undertake an extensive marketing campaign focused on making the customer aware of the benefits of the new venture's products. The cost of undertaking this strategy can be a significant barrier to entry unless customers are dissatisfied with the competing brands. On the Internet, it has become clear that when incumbents like Gap and Barnes & Noble set up shop online, they retain the brand presence they have already established in their bricks-and-mortar stores—consequently, they can be profitable immediately. By contrast, it takes a company like Amazon.com (with the strongest online brand recognition), which had no bricks-and-mortar presence, years to become profitable in its retail operations. In Amazon's case, another factor in its slow pace to profit was that it was trying to grow the business into multiple areas—books, DVDs, music, and so forth—-simultaneously; and that kind of growth is very costly in terms of marketing and inventory. As of 2014, Amazon is highly profitable in its retail operations, but it's also investing heavily in fulfillment centers globally because it found that if it can provide cheap, fast shipping, its sales will go up.

Capital Requirements: The cost of entering many industries is prohibitive for a new venture. These costs may include up-front advertising, research and development (R&D), and expenditures for plant and equipment. Entrepreneurs often overcome this barrier by outsourcing to or partnering with established companies to leverage their resources and industry intelligence.

Switching Costs for the Buyer: Buyers in most industries don't readily switch from one supplier to another unless there is a compelling reason to do so. Switching costs the buyer money and time. For example, a manufacturing business that has spent a lot of time and money finding the best supplier for the raw materials it needs to produce its product will not easily change suppliers because that would mean going through the whole process again.

Access to Distribution Channels: The new venture must persuade established distribution channel members to accept its new product or service and must prove that it will be beneficial to distributors to do so. This persuasion process, like any sale, can be costly for a new venture in terms of time, personnel, and travel. One solution for some types of businesses is distributing via the Internet, which is a direct method of reaching the customer.

Proprietary Factors: Barriers to entry also include proprietary technology, products, and processes. Where established firms hold patents on products and processes that the new venture requires, they have the ability either to keep the new venture out of the industry or to make it very expensive to enter. Most favorable location is another form of proprietary barrier. Often entrepreneurs will discover that existing firms in the industry own the most advantageous business sites, forcing the new venture to locate elsewhere, perhaps in a less desirable location. The Internet diminishes such location advantages somewhat, but the ability of customers to find a Web address quickly through the major search engines also becomes a location advantage. Making sure the website is optimized so that the business name comes up near the top of the search list is important. Other proprietary factors include trade secret supplier and customer lists.

Government Regulations: The government can limit entry to an industry or market through strict regulation, licensing requirements, and by limiting access to raw materials via laws or high taxes and to certain locations by means of zoning restrictions. Food products and biochemicals must obtain FDA approval, which is a significant barrier to entry.

Threat from Substitutes

A new venture must compete not only with products and services in its own industry but also with logical substitutes that other industries bring to the market. Generally, these substitute products and services accomplish the same basic function in a different way or at a different price. For example, movie theaters regularly compete with other forms of entertainment for the consumer's disposable dollars. The threat from substitute products is more likely to occur where firms in other industries are earning high profits at better prices than can be achieved in the new venture's industry. It is also likely to happen where an incumbent firm has deep resources and technical talent so that it can move quickly into new markets.

Threat from Buyers' Bargaining Power

In industries where buyers (customers) have bargaining power, it is more difficult for a new entrant to gain a foothold and grow. Examples of buyers that have this type of bargaining power include Price/Costco, Barnes & Noble, and Wal-Mart. Buyers like these can force down prices in the industry through volume purchases. This is particularly true where industry products constitute a significant portion of the buyers' requirements—books for Barnes & Noble, toys for Wal-Mart. Under this scenario, the buyer is more likely to be able to achieve the lowest possible price, a price that entrepreneurs will find difficult to compete with. Buyers also gain bargaining power where they face few switching costs; where the industry's products are standardized or undifferentiated, so there are plenty of substitutes; or where the industry's products don't affect the buyer in a significant way. The largest buyers also pose a threat of backward integration; that is, they may actually purchase their suppliers, thus better controlling costs and affecting price throughout the industry.

Threat from Suppliers' Bargaining Power

In some industries, suppliers exert enormous power through the threat of raising prices, limiting the quality or quantity of goods they supply, or changing the quality of the products that they supply to manufacturers and distributors. If the number of these suppliers is few relative to the size of the industry, or the industry is not the primary customer of the suppliers, that power is magnified. A further threat from suppliers is that they will integrate forward—that is, they will purchase the outlets for their goods and services, thus controlling the prices at which their output is ultimately sold. And entrepreneurs must remember that where switching costs are high, it's difficult for firms to make the needed changes to increase their profitability.

Competitive Rivalry among Existing Firms

The four factors just discussed all work together to create competitive rivalry for the resources available in the industry. In general, a highly competitive industry serving highly competitive markets will drive down profits and ultimately the rate of return on investment. To position themselves in a competitive market, firms often resort to price wars and advertising skirmishes. Once one firm decides to make such a strategic move in the market, others will usually follow. The clearest example is the airline industry; when one airline discounts its prices significantly, most of the others immediately follow. The problem with this tactic is that it ultimately hurts everyone in the industry and may even force out some smaller firms because competitive prices drop below costs. Most new ventures can't compete on price and can't afford costly advertising battles to build an image. To compete in a market that is highly competitive, they must instead identify a niche that serves an unmet need for customers and that will enable them to enter quietly and gain a foothold. Southwest Airlines did that effectively by understanding an unmet need for customers to more directly fly to regional airports and pay less per ticket in exchange for giving up some nonessential services. Many entrepreneurs seeking entry into industries such as software, biomedical, biotech, and telecommunications deliberately position themselves to be acquired eventually by the larger rivals rather than try to compete against them.

In general, competitive rivalry in an industry will be the most intense where there are numerous competitors of generally similar size and power, where growth is stagnant and exit barriers are high, and where the competitive strategies among the rivals are very diverse.

Using the Framework to Draw Conclusions

You can quickly become overwhelmed by the amount of information and the inconsistencies you confront when you begin the search process. That is why it's important to understand how your information source defined the industry it is talking about, and to be careful of sources that define the industry in such a way as to make it appear larger than it actually is. The demographics in the industry are also difficult to get a handle on because if the industry is composed of a lot of private firms (and most are), then government data broken down into SIC or NAICS codes is valuable because it includes private and public companies. The extent of supplier power can be gauged by looking at a representative public company's income statements to determine what percentage of its direct costs were spent on suppliers. Economies of scale are a barrier to entry for entrepreneurs, so it's critical to examine government data from the census to calculate the percentage output of an average firm in the industry relative to the total output of the industry. If the firm's output is large relative to total output, it suggests that economies of scale are in play, so the entrepreneur's entry strategy must involve rapid scale up to survive.[11] When it comes to the issue of customer power, the general rule is that where the industry supplies many downstream markets, customers have little power. That means that if you have only one or two customers, those customers have significant power to affect your strategy.

Some additional things to watch out for include the following:

- A fast-growth industry may not be attractive because suppliers typically gain power and charge higher prices. Moreover, products reach commodity status much faster, which means that profit margins decline.

- A "sexy" industry that everyone is writing about will tend to attract more competition and will often have price-insensitive buyers, high switching costs, and high barriers to entry.

- The need for industry complements to enable a new venture to grow must be considered. For example, electric cars have been slow to take hold for a number of reasons, but the lack of an infrastructure (recharging stations) is a significant roadblock to mass adoption.

Using the Porter framework to characterize an entrepreneur's industry and target market is just the first step. To be able to use this information to refine a business model and entry strategy requires drawing some conclusions based on the information gathered. Figure 4.5 compares the general characteristics of attractive and unattractive industries.

Suppose you find that in the particular industry being considered, competitive rivalry is extremely high and there are few barriers to entry. Suppose also that buyer power is strong, signaling that buyers could exert downward pressure on prices, forcing a commodity pricing situation, and that there appear to be viable substitutes for what you are offering. This scenario is certainly not a very positive one for you because you must either figure out a way to change the conditions by perhaps modifying the business model or ultimately deciding that the business is not feasible under these circumstances.

When making decisions based on the Five Forces, it is important to consider the competencies and resources that your new venture brings to the equation. For entrepreneurial ventures, an industry has to enable the venture to access the supply chain and distribution channels and to make a profit; however, it does not mean that existing markets must be favorable. Entrepreneurs typically enter with a niche strategy serving an unmet need in the market, so by definition, there will be no competitive rivalry for a time. In the end, the Five Forces Model should be used as one of several tools to aid in the decision making that you must do when judging the feasibility of your new business concept.

FIGURE 4.5
Attractive versus
Unattractive Industries
Based on the Five Forces

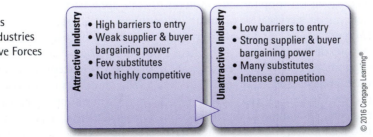

Attractive Industry
- High barriers to entry
- Weak supplier & buyer bargaining power
- Few substitutes
- Not highly competitive

Unattractive Industry
- Low barriers to entry
- Strong supplier & buyer bargaining power
- Many substitutes
- Intense competition

© 2016 Cengage Learning®

4.3   MARKET RESEARCH FOR CUSTOMER DISCOVERY

Starting a new business might be as relatively simple as launching a website, but securing enough customers to survive and make a profit is another matter entirely. Savvy entrepreneurs rely heavily on their market research to substantiate their intuitive belief that they have a winner, but the market research that entrepreneurs undertake doesn't resemble in any great degree the research conducted by large, established companies. In the first place, entrepreneurs are limited by a lack of sufficient resources, time, and high levels of uncertainty, so the data they collect is far from perfect and just enough to give some level of confidence that they should go forward with the new business. Entrepreneurs experiment by forming hypotheses about problems and needs and the customers who have them, and then test those hypotheses with real customers to validate their thinking. It is more frequent than not that first contact with customers will cause you to reformulate some hypotheses and test again. This iterative process many go through several cycles before you are satisfied that the problem being solved is the right problem and that it's matched to the right customer.

It is critically important that your first contact with customers be about understanding problems. Too often entrepreneurs head out to talk with customers with a preconceived idea for a solution in mind before they have even validated that a problem exists and is important to customers. If you take the time to understand the customer's problem in depth—it's called "customer empathy"—it will be much easier to come up with a solution that actually solves the right problem. Moreover, the chances are greater that the customer will pay a premium for your solution.

In a later section we'll talk more specifically about how to conduct this type of research with customers, but before you get out in the field, it's important to do some background work on the broader market just as you did with the industry analysis before heading out to talk with industry experts. Having a solid foundation in the demographics and characteristics of the market will insure that you ask better questions and get better results.

The previous discussion of frameworks for analysis of the industry also provides an effective way to describe the characteristics of the potential market you wish to serve. Recall that a market is defined by its customers. However, it is not until you get into the field and actually talk to potential customers about their problems and talk to those who deal with potential customers—distributors, retailers, and the like—that a clearer understanding of various customer segments and the first or entry customer is revealed.

In the beginning stages of customer discovery, the customer definition you use to conduct your secondary research will be fairly loose and may even change substantially once you get into the field with real customers. It is easy to become overwhelmed by the amount of information available about markets, so it's important to keep in mind the key questions that should be answered as you move from a broad group of potential customers (the market) to

SOCIAL ENTREPRENEURSHIP: *MAKING MEANING*

Medic Mobile: Customer Empathy in Africa

While an undergraduate student at Stanford University, Josh Nesbit had dreams of becoming a doctor until one day he took a trip to Malawi in southeastern Africa, and everything changed. He noticed that patients living in this rural area often had to walk as much as 50 miles for medical care, but he also noticed that his mobile phone actually worked better in Africa than it did in California. That insight led to his forming a nonprofit organization—www.medicmobile.org—that went far beyond simply supplying cheap cell phones to the poor. His organization has also developed tools to enable health care workers to explain symptoms and transmit medical records by using text messages. With these simple tools, Medic Mobile has connected more people with care, helped them maintain that care, and improved the quality of care. The organization continues to develop new solutions for health care in this emerging part of the world.

Sources: www.medicmobile.org; "Josh Nesbit: Forbes Impact 30," *Forbes*. http://www.forbes.com/impact-30/josh-nesbit.html

segmenting that market so that you can better understand customer needs and discover your first customer:

- What are the potential markets for the product or service? Are they clearly different from each other in terms of customer needs? How big is each market? How dynamic is the market? Is it growing?

- Of these potential markets, which customers are most likely to purchase the product or service at market introduction? In other words, which segment is in the most pain?

- How much do these customers typically buy, how do they buy, and how do they hear about the product or service?

- How often do they buy? What is their buying pattern throughout the year?

- How can your new venture meet these customers' needs?

Remember that for a new company, the goals of market research are to (1) identify and profile the first customer; (2) estimate potential demand from that customer; and (3) identify subsequent customer segments that can be tapped later on to grow the company. Growing markets generally experience two types of turbulence that any startup will need to deal with: market turbulence, which is the rate at which customer tastes and preferences change; and competitive turbulence, which is the rate at which competitors in the market change their strategies, such as introducing technological innovations.[12]

4.3a   Gathering Secondary Customer Data

Target market research provides critical data that is used to determine who the first customer is. Recall that the first customer is the one who has a significant problem you can solve. Therefore, the first customer may not be the biggest potential market but rather be an unserved niche that enables you to enter the market with no direct competition for a time.

The market data you collect is only as good as the research methods used to collect them. To ensure that useful and correct conclusions can be drawn from the data collected, sound research methods must be employed. Table 4.1 depicts a four-step process for ensuring that the right information is gathered and that it is used correctly.

As was true with the industry analysis, the Internet is a good starting point for gathering secondary data. Many of the traditional resources found in libraries are now available in online versions; for instance, U.S. census data can be found at www.census.gov. Using census data, for example, you can determine whether the geographic area you have defined for the business is growing or declining, whether its population is aging or getting younger, or whether the available work force is mostly skilled or unskilled, along with many other trends.

Some demographic data (data on age, income, race, occupation, and education) help identify the likelihood that a person will choose to buy a product. Demographic data also make it possible to segment the target market into subgroups that are different from one another. For example, suppose your target

TABLE 4.1   A Process for Gathering Market Data

Assess your information needs.	• How will the data be used?
	• What data need to be collected?
	• What methods of analysis will be used?
	• What are the potential business designs under consideration?
Research secondary sources first.	• What are the demographics of the target market?
	• What are the psychographics of the customer (i.e., buying habits)?
	• How large is the market?
	• Is the market growing?
	• Is the market affected by geography?
	• How can you reach your market?
	• How do competitors reach the market?
	• What market strategies have been successful with these customers?
Measure the target market with primary research.	• What are the demographics of the first customer?
	• Would they purchase your product or service? Why?
	• How much would they purchase?
	• When would they purchase?
	• How would they like to find the product or service?
	• What do they like about your competitors' products and services?
Forecast demand for the product or service.	• What do substitute products/services tell you about demand for your product/service?
	• What do customers, end users, and intermediaries predict the demand will be?
	• Can you do a limited production or test market for your product or service?

market is retired people over age 65. That's an enormous group of people who are not all alike. In fact, they can be further segmented by their buying habits (such as product requirements and quantity or frequency of purchase), the geographic region where they live, or by their income level, to name just a few variables that could differentiate them.

Finally, census data can be used to arrive at an estimate of how many target customers live within the geographic boundaries of the target market. Then, within any geographic area, those who meet the particular demographic requirements of the product or service can be segmented out. Furthermore, it is not only consumer markets that are described by demographic data. Business markets can also be described in terms of their size, revenue levels, the number of employees, and so forth.

Online sources are not the only sources of secondary market data. Most communities have economic development departments or chambers of commerce that keep statistics on local population trends and other economic issues. Some communities have Small Business Development Centers (SBDCs), branches of the Small Business Administration that offer a wealth of useful information, as well as services, for small and growing businesses.

4.3b   Customer Discovery Up Close

The most important data that entrepreneurs can collect on potential customers are primary data, in particular, data collected through direct observation or customer interviews. The general process for doing this involves collecting data based on the questions from Table 4.1, forming some hypotheses or educated guesses about the potential first customer, and then testing those hypotheses by conducting additional research with the customer. Customer discovery also involves identifying and engaging with a hierarchy of people who have different roles to play. Figure 4.6 displays this hierarchy.

Gatekeepers are those individuals or companies that hold the key to reaching particular customers; they control the flow of information. For example, if you want to sell to the U.S. government, you need to qualify as a government

FIGURE 4.6
The Customer Discovery Hierarchy

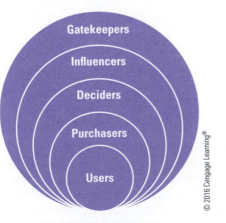

© 2016 Cengage Learning®

contractor through the appropriate agency, which is the gatekeeper. **Influencers** are people who want to affect the purchase decision and whose approval is often required before a decision to purchase is made. Physicians are often considered influencers in decisions about medical device purchases because they have direct contact with the beneficiary: the patient. **Deciders** are people who make the final decisions about purchases, usually for a company and usually based on a budget. **Purchasers** are those who have the actual authority to buy, and **users** are the ultimate beneficiaries of the purchase.

There are many ways to collect primary data on the target market, some more effective than others. We'll talk about them generally in the order of importance to the entrepreneur: observation using ethnographical techniques, interviews, informal focus groups, online or in-person surveys, and phone surveys. Notice we did not include mail surveys because entrepreneurs have neither the time nor the money to invest in this type of market research, particularly since it achieves a very low response rate and requires multiple reminders.

Ethnographical Techniques for Observing Customers

The problem with most market research is that entrepreneurs don't get at the heart of the customer's problem and, to make matters worse, they often lead the customer to a solution, which just happens to be theirs! Approaching the customer as an anthropologist would approach a family of gorillas being studied in the wild is actually a very effective approach. Ethnography, which is a way to explore the social culture of groups, is the basis for this approach. Some of the key features of this method are[13]:

- Studying customers in their everyday environment.
- Collecting data from a variety of sources, the most important and insightful of which are from observation and informal discussion.
- Analysis takes on the form of descriptions and explanations rather than statistical analysis.

Here is an ethnographic approach for entrepreneurs that consists of five steps, with step one arguably being the most important.

Step One: Learn from Observation. Observation requires inductive reasoning—studying customers in their natural habitat to gain insights into problems they face doing what they do. An example of pure observation is what Hewlett-Packard's medical division does when it wants to consider the development of new products. They embed their people in a hospital to observe how hospital personnel go about their day. Are there points where they may not have a tool or solution for something they need to do so they create a work-around? What do they struggle with most? The goal of these observers is to identify problems.

Where pure observation cannot not give the results needed or is just not possible, engaging customers in conversation is effective and can be another form of inductive reasoning. For example, suppose you wanted to improve on the standard alarm clock but weren't sure customers had any problems associated with alarm clocks. You might engage some random consumers in conversation about how they make sure they wake up in time to meet their obligations. You will hear everything from *I set an alarm clock*, or *I set my alarm clock and the clock on my cell phone*, to *My husband wakes me up*. That's the easy part of the conversation. What you really want to know is how customers would like to be awakened. Why? Because alarm clocks are essentially a commodity and you are trying to change the game. To develop a truly innovative product, you can't let customers be tethered to something they already know. They have to be free to think beyond what they know and focus on their problem. So the answer to the question *how would you like to be awakened* might be *I want to hear music. I would then say, 'OK, I'm up' and that would turn off the alarm.* The problem the customer has revealed is that they don't want to have to touch the alarm clock—they want a kinder, gentler way of waking up. The customer doesn't know how to solve this problem, but that's not the customer's job; it's the entrepreneur's job. And one entrepreneur, Jonathan Nostrandt, actually solved this very problem using artificial intelligence and creating an alarm clock the user can talk to—Moshi.

Step 2: Explain What Was Observed. Now you take what has been observed or gained from talking with customers and try to explain it in some logical fashion. In the case of the alarm clock example, the explanation might be that the customer is looking for a kinder, gentler way of waking up where they don't have to touch the clock. Essentially, you attempt to explain what you have observed objectively and without drawing any conclusions yet.

Step 3: Develop a Hypothesis. In this step you deduce or develop a hypothesis or theory from the explanations or premises generated in step 2. Your theory might be that the customer might want to talk to their alarm clock.

Step 4: Test the Theory. Armed with a hypothesis about the customer, you now go back into the field to test it with customers. *If we could provide an alarm clock that you could talk to, would that solve your problem?* Because this type of solution involves developing a prototype, it's important that you be confident that if the alarm clock were created and worked, there would be customers ready to buy before making the investment of time and money. That confidence comes from testing the solution with the customer.

Step 5: Conclusions. The final step involves drawing conclusions from the responses of customers. It is particularly important here not to bias the conclusions but to make them based on the preponderance of evidence provided by the customer and other sources, whether positive or negative. It's also important to distinguish between description and interpretation or judgment. Using our ongoing example, if the customer test indicates that talking to the alarm clock is considered the right solution, you would then move to prototyping the solution and taking that prototype back to customers for additional testing and refinement.

This observation technique takes time, but it's time well spent because the results will better ensure that the solution you develop is the right solution for the right customers. Figure 4.7 summarizes the principles behind an ethnographical approach to customer discovery and solution validation.

Structured Interviews

Although personal interviews are more costly and time-consuming than surveys, they have many advantages:

- They provide more opportunity for clarification and discussion.
- The interviewer has an opportunity to observe nonverbal communication and hence assess the veracity of what the interviewee is saying.
- The response rate is high.
- Interviews permit open-ended questions that can lead to more in-depth information.
- They provide an opportunity for you to network and develop valuable contacts in the industry.

Where time and money permit, structured interviews are an excellent source of valuable information from customers, suppliers, distributors, and anyone else who can help you determine the problem that needs to be solved, where the first customer is, and whether the proposed solution is the right solution. If you are interviewing a number of people, it would be important

FIGURE 4.7
An Ethnographical Approach to Customer Discovery and Solution Validation

OBSERVE   Record, Explain, Hypothesize, Test, Conclude
- Look for confusion, skipped steps, frustration, too much effort, and work arounds.
- Focus on understanding the problem.

QUESTION   Focus on the Problem
- Avoid leading to a conclusion.
- Avoid asking "will you buy?" or "How much will you pay?"

LISTEN   Remain Objective
- Develop a list of key questions.
- Rank them.
- Be prepared to scrap them if the customer takes you in a new direction.

DEMONSTRATE   Help Customers Experience the Solution
- Test for usability, compatibility with existing solutions, difficulty, ease of realizing the benefits
- Use storyboards, videos, prototypes

© 2016 Cengage Learning®

to have questions in common so that there is a basis for response comparison and the identification of useful patterns. It is critical to prepare for interviews by developing questions that focus on the information required to answer the market research questions, and by conducting some background research on the person being interviewed and the company. That way, more insightful questions can be asked rather than wasting the interviewee's time with questions that can be easily answered from material on the company website. During the interview, it's important to ask follow-up questions for clarification and to probe deeper on an issue but allow respondents to reply in their own terms.

Informal Focus Groups—The Group Interview

One efficient way to gain valuable information and feedback from customers and others is to conduct an informal focus group, in which a representative sample of potential customers is brought together for a presentation and discussion session. Group interviews are often used to elicit feedback on customer needs relative to a potential product or service or to compare products. It is essential to ensure that the person leading the focus group have some knowledge of group dynamics and be able to keep the group on track. Often these focus group sessions are videotaped so that you can spend more time later analyzing the nuances of what occurred. It is important to get the written permission of attendees before videotaping.

Survey Techniques

Survey techniques, whether online, in-person, or by phone require drawing a representative sample from the population of customers in which you are interested. The sample must be selected with great care because it determines the validity of the results. In general, to avoid bias, a sample should be random—that is, one in which you have as little control over the selection of respondents as possible. Most entrepreneurs, because of limitations of cost and time, use what is called a convenience sample. This means that not everyone in the defined target market has a chance of being chosen to participate. Instead, you may, for example, choose to select the sample from people who happen to be at the local airport on a particular day. Clearly, this method will not reach all possible customers at airports, but if the target customer is typically found at airports, there's a good chance of obtaining at least a representative sample from which results can be derived fairly confidently. Even if a convenience sample is used, there are ways to ensure the randomness of selection of the participants. Using the airport example, you can decide in advance to survey every fifth person who walks by. Thus the respondents are not chosen on the basis of attractiveness or lack of it—or for any other reason, for that matter. Whatever system is employed, the key point is to make an effort not to bias the selection so that the outcomes are more meaningful.

Conducting a survey, whether in person or online, entails designing a survey instrument, usually a questionnaire that, once filled out by the respondent, provides the desired information. Questionnaire design is not a simple matter of putting some questions on a piece of paper. There are, in fact, proven methods of questionnaire construction to help ensure unbiased responses. It is not within the scope of this text to present all the techniques for questionnaire construction; however, a few key points should be remembered:

- Keep the questionnaire short, with lots of white space, so that the respondent is not intimidated by the task.
- Be careful not to ask leading or biased questions.
- Ask easy, simple questions first, progressing gradually to the more complex ones.
- Ask demographic questions (questions about age, sex, income, and the like) last, when the respondent's attention may have waned. These questions can be answered very quickly.

The Internet has made it easy for small businesses to collect valuable data without having to enlist the help of costly market research firms.[14] Internet surveys such as SurveyMonkey and ZapSurvey are less expensive than traditional surveys, the response time is greatly reduced, and it's easier to include global respondents seamlessly. Posting surveys on the Internet is a convenient way to conduct research if the primary customer is an Internet user. The survey can be posted in user groups, social network sites, sent via email to target customers, or placed on a website (as long as the people who need to respond to the survey have a way of knowing that it's there). More information about this topic, including examples of question types, can be found at "Online Survey Design Guide," which is a project of the University of Maryland (http://lap.umd.edu/survey_design/).

Some entrepreneurs prefer to conduct their surveys in person at a location where their target customer can be found, for example, a shopping mall if the respondent is a consumer. Alternatively, a trade show is another popular source for these types of surveys. The advantage of this approach is an immediate and more targeted response as well as the opportunity to perhaps delve deeper into a particular response, not to mention the ability to observe nonverbal communication.

Each of the techniques discussed has advantages and disadvantages associated with it. In general, online surveys have a response rate of about 10–15 percent on average but that rate increases significantly to around 30–40 percent if the population being surveyed is motivated and the survey instrument is well crafted. At the same time, response rates can fall to as low as 2 percent if the population is not correctly targeted,[15] and several follow-ups are usually required to get a sufficient sample. You can improve your response rate for online surveys if you personalize your request, keep your survey to 5 minutes or less, make sure the questions are simple to answer, offer some type of incentive for completing the survey (a copy of the results is one example), and send no more than two reminders. Phone surveys are typically ineffective because in the past few years, people have been bombarded by telemarketers and now resist responding to a telephone survey. Whatever method is chosen, nothing beats feedback from the customer, whether it be at the discovery stage, the validation stage, or when testing possible solutions.

4.3c   Segmenting the Market with a Customer Matrix

Customer segmentation is critical to providing the right benefits to the right customer. Unfortunately, many entrepreneurs define their customer segments too broadly and then wonder why they are only capturing a small portion of the segment. One useful way to look at various customer segments is to construct a customer matrix that lays out the benefits, distribution channel, product/service, and potential competition for each of the identified customer segments. The matrix in Table 4.2 represents an initial hypothesis about three potential customers for a proprietary hand-held ultrasound device. This is an example where the primary customer (the one who pays) is not the primary beneficiary or end user of the device. To

TABLE 4.2   Initial Customer Matrix for a Portable Ultrasound Device[*]

Customers	Pain	Benefit	Distribution	Competition
Hospital Administration–customer who pays	Need to increase productivity and reduce risk in patient procedures	Save money and decrease potential for litigation	Medical equipment distributor	Siemens (Acuson), General Electric, SonoSite, Zonare, Pocketsonics, Signostics–Australia
End User Catheter Specialists	Guidance is difficult and causes patient discomfort; time consuming; reinsertion rate high	Guidance is easier, increased patient throughput to save time	Medical equipment distributor selling to hospital	Siemens (Acuson), General Electric, SonoSite, Zonare, Pocketsonics, Signostics–Australia
Rural practitioners in underdeveloped regions of various countries	Scarce imaging capability, travel for diagnosis is risky, for example, in rural India about 317 image centers service 742M people	Provide imaging capability at village level for basic diagnosis, so potential to save lives	Government agency or charitable relief agencies	International–Brazil, Russia, India, and China (BRIC) medical device manufacturers/suppliers likely have home-field advantage

© Cengage Learning®

[*]Example adapted from feasibility study conducted by Clifford Cousins, Masaru Nakagawa, and Ali Ziaee, University of Southern California, 2009.

give some context to the matrix, millions of ultrasound-guided catheter insertion procedures are performed annually, and a significant percentage of them fail because the doctor is forced to look away to view the images. As a result, the catheter must be reinserted, which is uncomfortable for the patient and wastes time. The product being introduced solves that problem because the probe and image display are integrated in a single miniaturized device.

Notice in the matrix how the benefit to the customer changes to meet the specific problem the customer is facing, so, for example, hospitals want to increase productivity and reduce cost and risk. This new procedure saves money and decreases the potential for litigation. Once the customer segments are identified, you have to make a choice. Which of these three customers should you go after first? The decision about where to enter the market first is affected by size of the market, customer demand, and resources, but the most important consideration is which customer is most likely to buy. Market research with customers may suggest, for instance, that the quickest early sales will come from rural practitioners because you are not dealing with the bureaucracy of a hospital. Note also that, in this example, the different benefits and distribution strategies for each of the three customers actually produce two distinct types of businesses: a manufacturer that sells to distributors and a company that manufactures, markets, and distributes to organizations in developing countries. The type of business you want to own then also influences the decision on first customer.

The Customer Profile

Out of the primary research will come a complete profile of the customer in great detail, that is, a description of the primary customer, be it a consumer or a business. The profile is critically important to the eventual marketing strategy, because it provides information vital to everything from product/service design to distribution channels and the strategy to attract the customer. Here is a list of some of the information that goes into the customer profile, whether that customer be a consumer or a business:

- Age
- Income level
- Education
- Buying habits—when, where, how much
- Where these customers typically find these types of products and services
- How they would like to purchase these products and services

If the customer is a business, it can be described in essentially the same way—for example, the first customer is a small to midsized construction company with annual revenues of $5 million that makes purchases quarterly, buys primarily over the Internet, and pays within 60 days. The customer profile will also play an important role in the development of the marketing plan, as we will see in Chapter 14.

Gathering Demand Data

It is no easy task to figure out what the demand for a new product or service might be. Even large, experienced companies have failed at it. For example, in 2013, one of the biggest failures was the HP Chromebook 11, a partnership of Hewlett-Packard and Google. Touted to be one of the product hits of the year, this lightweight, inexpensive laptop built on the Chrome operating system faced problems from the beginning, including capturing only one percent of the total PC and tablet market.[16] By November of the same year, the product was being pulled from the retailer's shelves.

If entrepreneurs are attempting to give customers what they need, something they will demand, the first thing they must understand is that customers can describe their problems and they can describe what they need to be able to do—their outcomes, but they are typically not effective at describing solutions to their problems.[17] For example, if you ask customers to identify what they like and don't like about your product or the competitor's product, customers will typically respond in the context of something they know. "I wish this smart phone had a scroll wheel on the right side." Customers are merely providing a missing feature that perhaps a competitor offers. By contrast, if you ask a question that seeks an outcome—"how do you want to use a communication device?" (or better yet, "how do you want to communicate?")—you have put no boundaries on the customer. Customers are free to think about how they want to communicate in various scenarios without describing features. With these outcomes understood, you can better design a solution to the customer's problem. More importantly, with this knowledge in hand, you are better prepared to gather demand data.

The question that you do not want to ask is "Would you buy this product?" The simple reason is that in many cases, the respondent will be reluctant to offend you and so will say "yes," knowing full well that they won't be asked to purchase it that day so there is no commitment on their part. A better approach is to identify a problem, confirm that the respondent is experiencing that problem, and then ask if your solution would interest them. This approach makes it easier for the customer to respond honestly.

Talking to customers to gauge demand is only the first step. It is also important to discuss demand with industry people such as suppliers and retailers. Getting estimates from at least three different sources enables you to derive a range of values and then triangulate to a best estimate. More detail about this process is found in Chapter 9.

4.3d   Drawing Conclusions from Market Research

Entrepreneurial decision making is more art than science, so the data gathered during the market research process must be analyzed, synthesized, and result in some conclusions about market feasibility. One of the first steps in working toward a conclusion is to organize the data into meaningful categories—-customer profile, market demographics, demand indicators, and so forth. This organization makes it possible to more easily analyze the data and seek patterns or trends that might provide vital information. A thorough review of all the data collected may also enable you to develop some sense of whether there are more positive aspects to the market than there are negative aspects. Furthermore, from the review, threats and challenges to the business goals can be identified and opportunities or courses of action that can include potential business models, customers, distribution channels, and business strategies can be taken. It is your job to interpret all the raw data and turn it into business intelligence. With a complete picture of the market in hand, you will be in an excellent position to draw a conclusion regarding the market feasibility of your venture.

4.4   GATHERING COMPETITIVE INTELLIGENCE

One of the weakest portions of any feasibility analysis or business plan is the competitive analysis. Why do entrepreneurs frequently underestimate or completely ignore the competition? For one thing, their information is incomplete because competitors don't reveal their most proprietary strategies and tactics. Entrepreneurs also tend to underestimate what it takes in the way of resources and skills to establish a presence in a market and they don't identify all the roadblocks along the way. The ability to identify roadblocks comes from experience in the industry and in running a business. Furthermore, it is difficult for entrepreneurs to know what they don't know! The competition generally possesses market share, brand recognition, management experience, customer knowledge, value chain relationships, industry knowledge, and resources. That is a formidable package of competitive strength. By contrast, many entrepreneurs take the naïve view that their concept is so new and innovative that they have no competition. Sadly, that is rarely the case. Even a niche strategy, probably the most effective strategy for a startup, will only leave an entrepreneur competitor-free for a very short time. Add to that the very real fact that entrepreneurial startups are short on resources and long on commitment and it is easy to see why it would be difficult for a small startup to respond effectively to a competitor attack.

In assessing the competition, the idea is not to benchmark the new venture against a competitor but rather to find ways to create new value that customers will pay for. To undertake effective competitor research, you have to first determine the target market that your venture is serving (which was discussed in the previous section), because entrepreneurs compete in markets. The next step is to identify the competition.

4.4a   Identifying the Competition

There are generally three types of competitors for a product or service: (1) direct, (2) indirect or substitute, and (3) emerging or potential. Identifying exactly who these companies are, including their strengths, weaknesses, and market strategies, will put your new venture in a better position to be a contender in the market.

The noteworthy research of M.I. Chen[18] on competitor analysis suggested that to correctly assess the competitive market, one must view it from two sides: the supply side, which includes resource capabilities such as R&D and production, and the demand side, which is represented by the customer and the customer's needs. Your direct competitors are those businesses that serve the same customer needs with the same types of resources. So, if you start a coffee house business, one direct competitor will be Starbucks because both businesses require the same types of resources (clearly Starbucks has more of those resources) and serve the same types of customers. Indirect competitors, by contrast, serve the same customer needs but with different resources as in substitute products, services, or distribution channels. For example, grocery stores are indirect competitors to your coffee house because they supply coffee and coffee makers so that customers can choose to make their own coffee. Potential competitors are those that are not currently serving the same customer needs but have the resources to quickly move into that space and compete.[19] In the example we have been using, Ralphs Grocers might open an in-store coffee house to directly compete with Starbucks and your business.

Because competition can come from multiple sources, it is important to look outside your immediate industry and market for competitors. You also need to look beyond existing competition to emerging competitors. In many industries today, technology and information are changing at such a rapid pace that the window of opportunity for successfully starting a new venture closes early and fast. Consequently, you must be vigilant in observing new trends and new technology that might portend new competitors.

Sometimes the most threatening aspect of a competitor is not readily visible in the typical facts that are reported, and frequently competitors come from outside your industry and market. For example, understanding a competitor's core competencies helps determine whether those competencies can ever be shifted to your niche market. Suppose your business is to train unskilled workers for well-paying jobs in industry. You look at all the competitors in the training industry and decide that you can compete because you have created a unique niche in the market. What you have failed to do is look outside your industry to companies that might have the same core competency and might have the deep resources required to shift to your niche very rapidly. Those companies are not always obvious. For example, one of Marriott's core competencies is training unskilled workers in the language and work skills they need to perform the various jobs in Marriott's hotel chain. It certainly has the resources to take this competency into any niche it desires. Another example is substitutes and new entrants to the market in the form of disruptive innovation coming from outside the market.[20] These "big-bang disruptions" can destroy the profitability of existing firms. That is why so many companies are continually innovating their products and processes, because of the strong competitive advantage it gives them. Therefore, to make certain that a potential threat like this one is not missed, you should:

- Determine what the competitor has to do to be successful in its own core business. Are there any core competencies that it must acquire?
- Determine whether the competitor has a competency in the same area as your business.
- Determine which of the competitor's core competencies are transferable to your business.

If the competitor is a large company, you may strategically position your company to be acquired eventually, because large companies typically acquire competencies rather than develop them.

Entrepreneurs also need to distinguish between good competition and bad competition. (See Figure 4.8.) Good competition comes in the form of companies that are doing what they do very badly; in other words, they aren't making customers happy. Ways to identify good competition include checking complaint levels at the Better Business Bureau, doing an online search, examining the archives of local newspapers for stories about the company, or checking the public records for financial or legal difficulties. It will be relatively easier to succeed against a good competitor than a bad one. Bad competitors are those companies that are doing everything right. Their customers are happy; they add value; and they're prosperous. In this case, identifying a niche that is currently not being served might be the most effective way to enter such a market and begin to build a brand.

FIGURE 4.8
Good Competition
Versus Bad Competition

© 2016 Cengage Learning®

4.4b   Finding Information about Competitors

Collecting information on competitors is one of the most difficult parts of researching a market. It is easy to gain superficial information from the competitor's advertising, website, or facilities, but the less obvious types of information, such as revenues and long-term strategies, are another matter. Information on publicly held competitors can be found in annual reports and other filings required by the U.S. Securities and Exchange Commission (SEC). Unfortunately, however, most startup companies are competing against other private companies that will not be willing to divulge these sensitive data. Data that are important to gather include current market strategies, management style and culture, pricing strategy, customer mix, and promotional mix.

The following are some suggestions on where to look for this information.

■ Visit competitors' websites or the outlets where their products are sold. Evaluate appearance, the number of customers coming and going, what they buy, how much, and how often. Talk to customers and employees.

■ Buy competitors' products to understand the differences in features and benefits and to learn about how they treat their customers.

■ Use Internet search engines such as Google.com and Amazon.com to read what customers are saying about the company.

■ Find information on public companies to serve as benchmarks for the industry. Public companies can be investigated through Hoover's Online (www.hoovers.com), the SEC (www.sec.gov), and OneSource (www.onesource.com), to name a few.

4.4c   Dealing with Competition

Undoubtedly the best way for you to stave off competition is to provide meaningful differentiation in your solutions to customer needs. One way to provide meaningful differentiation is to identify new market space—a niche that is not currently being served. That strategy gives you a temporary monopoly in which to establish your company before having to face competition.

You should also have a plan in place to maintain a market focus after launch. Market research does not end with the launch of the business. It's an ongoing process over the life of the business. The venture must constantly scan the environment for new competitors, trends, disruptions, and new opportunities. You should plan for a continual stream of disciplined experiments, always looking for ways to attract noncustomers and venture into new markets.

Finally, you need to quickly focus on developing relationships with key people in the supply chain as well as key customers. It creates a significant competitive advantage because business relationships take time to develop and once that trust is in place, it's difficult for a competitor to overcome it.

Studying the industry and market the new venture will serve is a difficult and time-consuming task, but it is perhaps the most important information you can collect because it helps you understand the business context or environment, and you will learn whether the business will have customers. Research and experimentation are at the heart of feasibility analysis and form the foundation for launching a successful business.

New Venture Action Plan

- Identify the NAICS codes for the industry in which the new venture will operate.
- Collect secondary data on the industry.
- Conduct field research by interviewing suppliers, distributors, customers, and others.
- Develop an industry profile that will indicate whether the industry is growing, who the major competitors are, and what the profit potential is.
- Define the target market, segment it, and identify the first customer for the product or service.
- Gather primary data on the target market to generate a customer profile and evidence of demand.
- Gather competitive intelligence and determine the impact on the new venture launch strategy.

Questions on Key Issues

1. Which primary and secondary information will tell you whether the industry is growing and favorable to new entrants?
2. What kinds of information can suppliers and distributors provide?
3. How should a market entry strategy be determined? What factors should be considered?
4. What is the value of defining a market niche?
5. Suppose you are introducing a new type of exercise equipment to the fitness industry. What would your strategy for research with the customer look like?
6. Given the definitions of direct and indirect competitors, provide an example of each for a product of your choosing.

Experiencing Entrepreneurship

1. Choose an industry that interests you. Create a status report using the Internet, LexisNexis, or other industry source, current periodicals, and interviews with people in the industry. In your estimation, does this industry have potential for new business opportunities? If so, where do those opportunities lie? Write your analysis in a two-page report, indicating sources you used to develop your conclusions.
2. Pick a product or service and formulate a plan for researching the customer. Identify what information needs to be collected (secondary and primary) and how to collect it. Justify the plan in a two-page report.

Relevant Case Studies

Case 1 AdRoll

Case 4 Command Audio

CHAPTER 5

Developing and Testing a Business Model

"I have come to recognize that getting the business model right is important to the innovation process and to business performance more generally"

(TEECE, 2006)

CHAPTER OBJECTIVES

- Explain what a business model is and what it accomplishes.
- Discuss the process for developing and testing a business model.
- Explore how to innovate a business model.

PROFILE
5.1

AMAZON: BUSINESS MODEL INNOVATOR

Now a global company based in Seattle, Washington, Amazon is arguably the finest example of a serial business model innovator. Building on its core retail business and highly efficient supply chain, it has gone on to introduce three new disruptive business models and is looking at a fourth. While no longer a startup by any means, the company does serve as an excellent example of how it is achieving long-term success where product innovators have not.

Amazon incorporated in 1994 and sold its first book in July of that year. In 1996, it became a public company to tap the public markets for capital to grow. And grow it did. After introducing "one-click" shopping in 1996, it began building fulfillment centers to support the sales of music, videos, and DVDs as well as software. Starting in 2001, each successive month saw the launch of a new product category: sports and outdoor goods, tools and building supplies, a baby store, apparel, apps for Windows, iOS, and Android platforms, toys and games, and more.

By the time it had launched the Kindle reader in 2006, it had an inventory of 300,000 books available and a personalized search engine to help customers find books that would interest them. In 2004, Amazon acquired Joyo, the Chinese version of Amazon, and just two years later, it became the largest online Chinese bookstore.

With the core retail business becoming profitable, Amazon continued to innovate on its business model in highly disruptive ways: (1) launching the Prime subscription model to link its customers even more to Amazon by providing guaranteed free shipping within two days and thousands of streaming films and Kindle books to borrow; (2) the Kindle e-reading

platform, a Gillette shaver model where the devices are sold at a relatively low price and Amazon makes money on the content; and (3) Amazon Web Services, which provides cloud-computing services to businesses. By 2014, it was ranked one of the top 10 search platforms in the world, along with Google and eBay and it was home to more than two million sellers for whom Amazon provides fulfillment services.

You can look at their strategy through the lens of the Kim and Marbourgne Eliminate-Raise-Create-Reduce framework. Amazon **eliminated** the traditional brick-and-mortar distribution channel and made it easier for customers to purchase books and other goods when and where they wanted with one click. Although Amazon was certainly not the first online store, it did **raise** the bar for those who followed by developing a next-generation platform that provided speed, convenience, and tremendous product scope. In **creating** the Amazon Web Service cloud platform, the company was a first mover with all the advantages of growth. Perhaps the most interesting aspect of its business model is that it incorporates **reducing** profits below those typical in the industry to pump those profits back into scaling the business globally. This can create enormous barriers to competitors and huge benefits to customers in terms of product scope and value pricing.

As of 2014, CEO Jeff Bezos was contemplating the use of small drones to deliver packages. This innovation is less about the drones themselves, which over time will become commodities, but more about another innovation in the business model. Here Amazon envisions making money from customers who want same-day deliveries right to their door.

Time will tell if Amazon's business model innovation can continue at the pace it has. Because its focus is on being the low-cost leader, Amazon's margins are small and that translates to lower earnings. It will also face challenges from global competitors as well as weak economies in some parts of the world. However, it has built a strong moat in the form of customer focus, which bodes well for its future.

Sources: Crawford, K. (January 21, 2014). "Amazon Innovates with Its Business Model, Not Drones," *Wired*, http://www.wired.com/2014/01/amazon-innovates -business-model-drones/; Anthony, S. (December 31, 2013). "The Three Most Innovative Companies of 2013," *Harvard Business Review*, http://blogs.hbr.org/2013/12 /the-three-most-innovative-companies-of-2013/; Faruk, I. (August 15, 2013). "Amazon: A SWOT Analysis," *The Motley Fool*. http://beta.fool.com/ishfaque/2013/08/15 /amazon-a-swot-analysis/34418/

In today's vibrant, fast-paced startup environment, it's easy to get the impression that all budding entrepreneurs have to do is get accepted into a venture accelerator with some seed funding and their success is assured. But even for Internet businesses, that exciting scenario is a stretch. Just because an entrepreneur builds a business does not mean that customers will come. In reality, a substantial amount of thought must take place and a great deal of effort must be put forth before a company's products or services ever successfully reach the market. That thought process includes developing a business concept that meets a real market need and creates value and a business model or way to capture that value.

Peter Drucker, often referred to as the greatest management thinker of the last century, understood as far back as the 1950s that there is no business without a customer. He regularly challenged entrepreneurs and corporate CEOs alike to answer five important questions about their business model:

- What is our mission?
- Who is our customer?
- What does our customer value?
- What are our results?
- What is our plan?[1]

In the field of entrepreneurship, no matter how many fancy names are given to what entrepreneurs do, no matter how many elaborate frameworks researchers use to explain who entrepreneurs are and why they succeed, it all comes down to these fundamental questions. If you don't have a firm grip on the answers to these questions, all the rest is a waste of time. You must be able to convince your stakeholders that your solution creates value that customers are willing to pay for and that will lead to a profitable business.

Drucker's five questions are the basis for the development of a business model. The mission is why you're in business—the big goal that your company is trying to achieve. The customer is the one who pays for the value being delivered, and that customer may be an individual or a business. What the customer values is the most difficult question to answer unless you have spent time in the market trying to understand the problems customers face. Solving those problems is the value or benefit customers are seeking. The results tell you if you're on the right path, but entrepreneurs also need to know what results they're working toward. Entrepreneurs don't predict the future—they create it and then find the means to achieve it. The plan for doing that is not the traditional business plan, a huge document that tends to cement ideas in place while the reality around those ideas keeps changing. For entrepreneurs, the plan is an action plan, a series of small experiments to provide feedback and help them test and rework the original ideas until they best meet the needs of the customer.

Today there are many tools and frameworks for depicting a startup's business model—this chapter will present a few—but as Chesbrough notes, "Tools, such as mapping, are useful to explicate business models, but cannot by themselves promote experimentation and innovation with those models"[2] Given that all technology products eventually become commodities, it is more important than ever that innovation not be solely product focused but also include business model innovation.

This chapter explains how to turn an idea into an effective concept for a new business through the development and testing of a business model that creates value for the customer and provides the new business a way to monetize that value.

5.1   UNDERSTANDING THE BUSINESS MODEL

The term *business model* has become quite popular in discussions about startups, but there still appears to be some confusion about what a business model actually is and how entrepreneurs use them throughout the life of their business.[3]

The term *business model* has been conceptualized in a number of different ways: as the activities or tasks that a business undertakes,[4] as an "analytical device for evaluation and action,"[5] or as a "blueprint" for running a business.[6] At its essence, the business model reflects the strategic decisions and trade-offs that entrepreneurs make to earn a profit.[7] A successful venture creates value by differentiating itself from competitors and/or by meeting an unserved need in the market. It then captures that value by monetizing its offering; in short, entrepreneurs find innovative ways to make money from what their businesses do. The creation and capture of value take place within what has been termed a *value network*, which is the community of partners, suppliers, and other members of the value chain with which the startup does business.[8]

Figure 5.1 depicts a framework for considering the key components of the business model. Notice that the top layer of the framework is all about the customer, the solution (value proposition) that is being provided, and the means by which the entrepreneur will reach the customer (distribution channel). The second layer deals with the functions of the business, the resources required to deliver the value proposition, and the strategic partners that the business will need to engage. The first two layers are all the activities employed to create value. The final layer represents the activities associated with capturing value by monetizing the business model. Here the sources of revenue for the business and the major factors that drive the costs for what is being offered are addressed. All of the components of the business model are interrelated; that is, a

The Components of the
Business Model

change in one component affects all the others to some degree. Furthermore, innovation is possible in every component. Once the business model is in place and validated, it's much easier to then determine the critical success factors for the business. An effective business model is difficult to copy because so much of the knowledge that is created by executing the business model is tacit, embedded in the model in a way that is not easily observed. Therefore, a well-crafted business model builds significant barriers for competitors. At the same time, it is also "grounded in reality ... based on accurate assumptions about customer behavior."[9] Let's review the various components of a business model in more detail.

5.1a   Value Proposition

The value proposition is the benefit that the customer derives from the product or service you are offering; in other words, the reason the customer will buy. It is "the unique mix of product, price, service, relation, and image that a company offers to a group of targeted clients. It must explain what the company thinks it is capable of doing for its clients better or differently from its competitors."[10] You can also think of the value proposition as the solution because if it is true that customers buy benefits, then the solution you're providing is really a bundle of benefits. To understand what the customer values, you need to identify a need or "pain" that customers are experiencing. When you first conceive of the concept for your business, you typically start with the value you believe customers will recognize and pay for. However, it is not until you do some actual market research and learn what customers value from their own words that you can be confident there will be someone to buy what you're selling. We talk about effective ways to understand customer needs in Chapter 4.

When designing their value proposition, entrepreneurs often confuse features with benefits. In general, benefits are intangibles such as better health, saving time and money, or reliability, whereas features reflect attributes of the product such as design and physical characteristics or functions. Table 5.1 offers an example of the distinction between features and benefits for a business

TABLE 5.1   Features versus Benefits for Premium Horse Feed for Thoroughbred Racehorses*

Features	Benefit to Retailer	Benefit to EndUser (horse owner)
2-foot length of hay	Revenue potential—this feature makes the product more attractive to endusers, leading to higher potential sales and customer loyalty	Save money because less of it is wasted than is wasted with regular hay
Packaged in plastic bags	Cost savings, because it leads to less waste in inventory	Save money because there is less waste in storage
Flash-baked for greater nutrition and to reduce dust and mold spores	Revenue potential, because of cost savings from longer shelf life	Can prevent common ailments that impede racing performance, so also save money
Made with molasses, giving it a good taste for the horse	More reliable revenue potential—this feature leads to more consistent use among horse owners because horses typically do not switch after trying it	Make more money—its good taste leads horses to eat this high-nutrition feed, which can improve racing performance

* Prepared by Sheryl Sacchitelli, Daniel Wang, and Jason White, MBA class of 2003, University of Southern California.

where the product is premium hay for thoroughbred racehorses. Note that the benefits for the customer—the retailer—and for the end user or beneficiary—the horse owner—are different.

5.1b   Customer Segments

Who is the customer? This vital question is deceptively simple. Many entrepreneurs cannot answer it accurately, because they simply assume that their customer is the user of the product or service they are offering. Although it is more common today than ever before for that to be the case, in many industries it is not. When Jordan NeuroScience first considered who the customer was for its ER-EEG technology designed to remotely monitor the brainwaves of trauma patients in emergency rooms, the founder immediately thought of the patients, the beneficiaries of the technology whose lives would be saved. But when faced with figuring out how to make money, he realized that the patients were not the customers; even the doctors were not the customers. Rather, the hospital administrators who made the purchasing decisions were the customers. This revelation changed everything about the business model. He had to decide what benefit his product was providing to the hospital administrators, which was quite different from the benefit to the patients and doctors. Although hospital administrators are interested in obtaining technologies to improve patients' quality of life, they are primarily focused on increasing revenues, reducing costs, and meeting compliance issues. In short, the immediate customer is always the one who pays for the solution. In this case, the doctors are the influencers and the patients are the beneficiaries.

If sufficient research has been conducted, you will find that you have many customers who will need to be segmented. Entrepreneurs frequently define their initial markets too broadly to include too many different kinds of customers. For example, offering a product or service to anyone between the ages of

FIGURE 5.2 Customer Segmentation Matrix*

	Diabetics			Health Care Professionals			Pregnant Women	Athletes
	Type 1	Type 2	Parents	Doctors	Nurses	Clinicians	Gestational Diabetes	High School/College
Description of Group	Compliant (e.g. children) Doctor-advised, motivated	Non-compliant (e.g. teens, less severe cases) Doctor-advised, non-motivated	Parents of Diabetics Doctor-advised, motivated		hospital workers		Doctor-advised, motivated	Could encompass athletes as well as coaches/trainers
Description of Problem/pain	Pain/inconvenience of finger prick	pain/inconvenience of finger prick	Guilt of pricking children	Compliance with patients	inconvenient to test patients/bio-waste		pain/inconvenience of finger prick	Poor performance due to low blood sugar levels, no current methods of testing blood sugar levels for athletes
Convenience	Non-invasive, increased convenience	Non-invasive, increased convenience	Non-invasive, increased convenience	N/A, may increase probability of patient compliance	Safer alternative than needles (less bodily fluids)	N/A, may increase probability of patient compliance	Non-invasive, increased convenience	Tool to be used in addition to current methods of assessing performance; not improving convenience
Reimbursement	Possible insurance reimbursement	Possible insurance reimbursement	Possible insurance reimbursement	Possible insurance reimbursement	Possible insurance reimbursement	Possible insurance reimbursement	Possible insurance reimbursement	Would not require reimbursement from insurance companies
Regulation	Would require FDA approval	Would require FDA approval	Would require FDA approval	Would require FDA approval	Would require FDA approval	Would require FDA approval	Would require FDA approval	May not require or at least less stringent FDA approval
Market Entry	Slow market entry due to FDA regulations	Slow market entry due to FDA regulations	Slow market entry due to FDA regulations	Slow market entry due to FDA regulations	Slow market entry due to FDA regulations	Slow market entry due to FDA regulations	slow market entry due to FDA regulations	Possible quick entry into the market
Market Size (TBD)	1.29 million (2011, CDC Fact Sheet)	24.51 million (2011, CDC Fact Sheet)	354,750				2-10% of pregnancies (2011, CDC Fact Sheet), ~ 80,000-395,000/yr	High School: 7.7 million (2013, nfhs.org)College: 420,000 (2012 NCAA partipation)
Ease of Customer Acquisition	Doctor referrals, direct advertising to consumer	Doctor referrals, direct advertising to consumer	Doctor referrals, direct advertising to consumer	Direct advertising	Direct advertising	Direct advertising	Doctor referrals, direct advertising to consumer	Sales
Customer Awareness of Problem	yes	no	yes	yes	yes	yes	yes	no
Customer search for alternatives	yes	no	yes	yes	yes	yes	yes	no

Blue = reason to target as customer Gray = reason to NOT target as customer

25 and 45 does not consider that people in different age groups have different needs and want to be reached in different ways. Segmenting a market is dividing it into meaningful and measurable segments based on needs, buyer behaviors, and demographics (age, education, income, ethnicity, etc.). One way to do that is to create a matrix that contains all the variables on which you want to compare your customers down the left side and your customer segments across the top as seen in Figure 5.2. Notice that this team went well beyond benefits and distribution channels to consider market size, key influencers, the significance of the problem, and the technological risk. The team also highlighted reasons to consider a segment as a target and reasons not to consider a segment. The categories you choose for comparison will depend on the unique characteristics of your business.

5.1c   Distribution Channels

The distribution channel answers the question "How do you deliver the benefit to the customer?" Many options exist, but in general, the best option is the one that fulfills the customer's expectations about where and how they want to purchase your product or service. Most services are delivered direct to customers, but products often go through channel intermediaries such as distributors and retailers. If you use an intermediary, then that intermediary is your direct customer and the end user or consumer is the beneficiary. That means you have to understand both very well, because you will need to convince the intermediary that there is sell-through to the end user or consumer who wants the product. There are a number of pros and cons involved in going direct to the customer versus selling through an intermediary or partner. Those advantages and disadvantages are depicted in Table 5.2. The distribution channel is addressed in more detail in Chapter 4, which deals with the new venture's marketing strategy.

TABLE 5.2
Direct to the Customer versus Indirect Through an Intermediary

Direct to Customer	Indirect Through Intermediary
Advantages	**Advantages**
• Entrepreneur has large upside potential. • Has control over branding, pricing, and relationship with customer. • Able to manage user data and experience.	• Partner does the build-out and capital investment. • Partner handles billing and customer service. • Cash flow is more predictable if the entrepreneur has a licensing agreement.
Disadvantages	**Disadvantages**
• Entrepreneur has greater risk. • Cash flow may be unpredictable. • Entrepreneur must do build-out and initial investment. • Responsible for billing and service.	• Partner gets the upside potential. • Partner controls branding, pricing, and customer relationship. • Partner owns the user data and manages the user experience.

5.1d   Strategic Partners

Today it is very common for startups to partner with existing companies to tap into expertise and resources the entrepreneur doesn't have. One of the most common types of partnerships is the buyer–supplier relationship, which is used to reduce costs or share facilities like manufacturing or warehousing. In some industries such as electronics, partnerships often involve competitors who may agree to share resources in one area while competing in another. One of the best examples was the collaboration that brought Blu-ray technology to the market, beating out HD-DVD. The partner companies then competed against each other in Blu-Ray-based products. Some partnerships involve licensing intellectual property instead of developing it in-house, which could be expensive and take a lot of time. The topic of strategic partners is taken up again in Chapter 11.

5.1e   Business Activities and Resource Requirements

Depending on the value proposition and where the entrepreneur's business is positioned on the value chain, business activities could involve manufacturing, distribution, R&D, or a network or technology platform. Each type of business has different functions and hence unique resource requirements that are critical to delivering the value proposition. Resources include human, physical, intellectual, and capital. Some businesses are more labor intensive than others, whereas some are more automated in nature—machines and software do the work. Chapter 12 addresses the issues of resources as they relate to the operations of the business.

5.1f   Revenue Sources

One of the most important components of the business model is identifying the revenue streams that will flow from the products and services being offered. A healthy business model always supports revenue streams from multiple types of customers and multiple products and services. Relying on one revenue stream from one type of customer is dangerous. What happens when the market shifts and that customer goes away? At launch it's not uncommon for new ventures to rely on one source of revenue from their primary product or service, but very quickly they need to move to multiple products and services and multiple markets to diversify their revenue streams and secure their sustainability.

The revenue model describes the various ways that you plan to make money. In general, the following categories of revenue models comprise the most common ways to monetize a product or service.

- **Subscription or membership**. Customers pay a fixed amount to belong or subscribe, generally monthly or annually.
- **Volume or unit-based**. Customers pay a fixed amount per unit and receive a discount for volume purchases.

- **Licensing and syndication**. Customers pay to use or resell, typically a product, technology, or brand.

- **Transaction fee**. Customers pay for services, generally hourly or on a project basis.

- **Advertising**. In this model, the customer is the advertiser, not the end user of the product or service. Many Internet businesses have advertising as one of their revenue models.

In the mid-1990s, Edmunds Inc., the 32-year-old publisher of automotive information, saw the Internet as just another marketing vehicle. Today, however, the Internet *is* the business. Edmunds's website provides independent ratings, reviews, and pricing data for every make and model of car, in addition to a variety of other interactive features. Edmunds.com's basic business model is to make its money through ads placed by manufacturers, parts dealers, and others in the automobile industry. Books now account for less than one percent of its revenues. Changing its business model with the changing times, Edmunds.com now has revenue streams from books, from advertising, and from selling and licensing information to other companies.[11]

The pricing model works in tandem with the revenue model. Both require significant market research and will be discussed in Chapter 9. Given the complexity of the interactive parts of the business model—a change in one part affects all the others—it is not surprising that business models fail.

5.1g Cost Drivers

Equally important as revenues, you need to understand the expenses and cost drivers of the business. The business that can keep its costs low enjoys a significant advantage and will bring more dollars to the bottom line. Every business has costs that produce the biggest impact on the cost structure; they are known as key cost drivers because they impact total costs.[12] These costs can be fixed (rent), variable (manufacturing), or nonrecurring, such as a onetime expense. In some businesses, there will also be semi-variable expenses, which are simply a combination of fixed and variable costs. For example, many retail outlets employ a base number of sales people as a fixed cost. During the holiday season, they may supplement with additional sales people to handle the increased volume, so the cost to the business goes up for that time but not proportionate to the volume as in a true variable cost.

Depending on the type of business, the cost structure may take on of the following forms:

- **Marketing or advertising cost structure**. The primary costs of the business come from customer acquisition and maintaining relationships with customers.

- **Inventory cost structure**. Here the biggest costs come from the maintenance of inventory, either goods for sale or raw materials.

- **Office or retail space cost structure**. In this type of business the primary cost driver is the cost per square foot of the space required to conduct business.

- **Support center cost structure**. Here the business has high fixed costs in personnel required to support the activities of the business.
- **Direct cost structure**. These businesses' costs are driven by the direct costs of producing the product or service.

The categories above represent the types of costs that affect the business model, but, in addition to these, you need to decide whether your business will be cost driven or value driven. In a cost-driven model, the emphasis will be on keeping costs as low as possible. This is because typically margins are narrow, so there's not much room to make mistakes and entrepreneurs in these businesses know that their customers are price conscious. By contrast, in value-driven models, entrepreneurs want to create premium experiences for their customers that typically involve personalized service and luxury facilities and products. Customers of these businesses are willing to pay more to solve whatever need they have, so they are value conscious, not price conscious.

Figure 5.8 at the end of the chapter offers a canvas version of the key business model components as a basis for considering the type of hypotheses and tests you will conduct to validate your business model.

5.1h   Why Business Models Fail

Research has determined that there appear to be four major problems associated with business models that may explain why many fail: (1) flawed logic, (2) limited strategic choices, (3) imperfect value creation and capture assumptions, and (4) incorrect assumptions about the value chain.[13] Here we will consider examples of each.

Flawed Logic

Business models are doomed to failure when the underlying logic about the future is incorrect. When entrepreneurs assume situations and conditions that do not currently exist, they face huge challenges in their ability to execute the model. Napster, the file-sharing music site that pioneered music downloads from the Internet, began with the flawed assumption that it was not going to be held accountable for copyright violations on the MP3 files that its users swapped and downloaded. Because the recording industry was slow to recognize the threat of the digitization of music, Napster presumed that it had a clear path to success, but its model was shut down by court order in 2001. If the story doesn't make sense, the business model will fail.

Limited Strategic Choices

The strategic choices that a business model addresses should reflect both the value creation and the value capture processes. Satisfying only one of these will often lead to problems. Many disruptive technologies fall into this category because by definition there is no market when the technology is first conceived. The innovators can identify potential value but there is no way to capture that value because customers don't yet know that they need the technology. Entrepreneurs in these situations are faced with a long exploration phase to find the right application whose perceived value is such that it can find a market. Axane, a subsidiary of the French Company Air Liquide, was in that exploration phase in 2002 when it was trying to find a killer app for its fuel cell technology. It explored a number of ideas around energy, deployable light, and continuous power for telephone relays when it hit upon the approach of identifying "useful effects," ways of improving the current way something is done. Shortly thereafter, the company figured out that the right hydrogen fuel application in a generator would enable firemen and construction workers to work in confined spaces without being asphyxiated and without the long cables that often got in the way.[14] This led the way to being able to capture economic value for the company.

Imperfect Value Creation and Capture Assumptions

One of the biggest challenges for business models is finding a way to make money from the value that has been created when that value is either weak or nonexistent. A poor assumption about the value will mean that there are fewer or even no customers to pay for that value. Similarly, even if there is a reasonable assumption of value created, it may not be the beneficiary of that value who has to pay for it. This is one of the biggest problems for entrepreneurs in the health care industry. An entrepreneur with a new medical device that can save patients' lives is not collecting revenue from the patient who immediately sees and benefits from the value but rather from the health care provider or worse yet an insurance company, whose mission is to contain costs, a completely different value proposition. When the numbers don't add up, the business model fails.

Incorrect Assumptions about the Value Chain

Entrepreneurs often assume that the value chain for their product or service is static, that is, that it will continue with the current players and with the current processes and information flow well into the future. This is a faulty assumption. Core competencies enable firms to move into new industries and new value chains unrelated to their current products and services. UPS did this when it examined Toshiba's lengthy and inefficient process for repairing laptops that involved shipping to UPS's hub, then to Japan, then back to UPS, and then to the customer. UPS cut out all the excess shipping for Toshiba and repaired their laptops in UPS's facilities.[15] UPS's core competency is designing effective and efficient systems, and it took that competency from the package delivery industry to the computer industry, serving new markets.

5.1i   When Business Models Change

An effective business model that takes into account customers' changing needs can be a recipe for enduring success. Using eBay as an example, the highly successful company had a very simple business model at launch. Its infrastructure enabled users to communicate with each other for a reasonable fee, and eBay removed itself from the responsibility for the items that were sold, for collecting payments or for shipping. It was merely responsible for making sure these transactions occurred. Its revenues came from seller fees;

its cost structure included the online infrastructure, marketing, product development, and general and administrative expenses. More importantly, it took only a few salaried employees and partners to implement the startup model. Much later, eBay acquired PayPal, which gave the company the ability to securely exchange online payments. That acquisition changed PayPal's business model, which ultimately enabled it to develop specialized marketplaces such as Stub-Hub, the global leader in event tickets. In 2014, eBay had a market cap of $71 billion.

It is a fact of business life that business models evolve and sometimes radically change over time due to circumstances often beyond the control of the entrepreneur. Change can occur in a number of ways. Businesses can: [16]

1. *Incrementally expand* the existing model geographically, enter new markets, modify pricing, or change product/service lines and distribution channels. An example would be Kiyonna, an apparel manufacturer that moved from physical boutiques to an online site that better served their young, plus-sized customers by providing a convenient and private way to buy clothing. (www.kiyonna.com)

2. *Revitalize an established model* to give it new life and stave off competition. This can be accomplished by introducing new products or services to existing customers as Starbucks did when it began selling CDs of the music it played in its stores as well as proprietary coffee makers.

3. *Take an existing model into new areas.* For example, Amazon.com, originally known as a highly effective Internet bookseller, began using its successful fulfillment process to market and sell everything from clothing to household goods and then moved to producing its own products such as the Kindle line of readers and Fire TV for streaming videos.

4. *Add new models via acquisition.* For example, Facebook acquired Instagram in 2012 to enhance its photo sharing capability and then Osmeta in 2013 to capture engineering talent in mobile platforms, where its presence was weak.

5. *Use existing core competencies to build new business models.* Canadian manufacturer Bombardier originally focused on snowmobiles. Because it sold its products through credit, it developed an expertise in financial services, which enabled the company to move into capital leasing. Its manufacturing expertise was leveraged into large-scale manufacturing for the aircraft industry.

Entrepreneurs who stay in touch with the changing environment in which they do business will find many opportunities to modify and even completely change their business models to stay competitive.

5.2   TESTING AND VALIDATING BUSINESS MODEL FEASIBILITY

Feasibility analysis involves the testing, evaluation, and validation of a proposed business model for a new venture. It is a tool that is used to assess and reduce risk at startup. All opportunities that entrepreneurs identify or create involve

TABLE 5.3   Feasibility Analysis

Areas to Be Analyzed and Some Questions to Ask

Industry and Market/Customer (Chapter 4)
1. What are the demographics, trends, patterns of change, and life-cycle stage of the industry?
2. What are the barriers to entry and are there any barriers you can set up?
3. What is the status of technology and R&D expenditures, and what is the level of innovation?
4. What are typical profit margins in the industry?
5. Who are the opinion leaders in the industry and how do they affect the industry?
6. What are distributors, competitors, retailers, and others saying about the industry?
7. What are the demographics of the target market?
8. What is the profile of the first customer? Are there other potential customers?
9. How have you approached customers to learn about their needs?
10. Who are your competitors, and how are you differentiated from them?

Product/Service (Chapter 6)
1. What are the features and benefits of the product or service?
2. What product development tasks must be undertaken to achieve a marketable product, and what is the timeline for completion and the associated costs?
3. What is the window of opportunity for this product?
4. Is there potential for intellectual property rights?
5. How is the product or service differentiated from others in the market?

Founding Team (Chapter 8)
1. What experience and expertise does the team have?
2. What are the gaps and how will you fill them?

Financial Needs Assessment (Chapter 9)
1. What are your startup capital requirements?
2. What are your working capital requirements?
3. What are your fixed cost requirements?
4. How long will it take to achieve a positive cash flow from the revenues generated?
5. What is the break-even point for the business?
6. What are your funding requirements? Timeline and milestones?

uncertainty—the unknown—and uncertainty is characterized by varying degrees of risk.[17] Risk serves as an incentive for entrepreneurs to achieve success, because with risk come rewards and, in general, the amount of reward the entrepreneur earns is proportionate to the risk taken. At the same time, there are levels of risk that entrepreneurs need to reduce (and investors expect them to reduce) so that the probability of a successful venture increases. Those risks are typically associated with the customer, the size of the market, the technical feasibility of the product, the feasibility of the business model, and the ability of the founding team to successfully execute the business model. Feasibility analysis is a way of dealing with the idiosyncratic risk of a new venture.

Uncertainty is also a natural part of the launch of any business. Uncertainty means that the outcomes are not known, so probabilities cannot be attached to them. For example, with startups, understanding the differences between the market conditions at the development of the original business model and the realities of the market at the time of launch is critical.[18] Many new businesses launch under assumptions about the market that were developed a year previously and are no longer valid. This is what happened to Command Audio after it had licensed its broadcast on-demand media software to industry leaders. Development delays on the part of the licensees caused them to postpone deploying Command Audio's technology for three years. This certainly was not part of the entrepreneur's original plan, and it caused Command Audio to rethink its business model.

So, how do entrepreneurs deal with uncertainty? Given that in uncertain situations there are choices that have to be made, entrepreneurs apply subjective probabilities (educated guesses) to the choices. Typically, someone who is naïve about starting a business will be more positive about the potential outcome of an effort, while someone who is experienced in startups will be more skeptical about potential success. But it's possible for quite the opposite to occur. In fact, research has found that entrepreneurs introducing pioneering products for which there was no precedent in the market tended to be overconfident about their ability to achieve success.[19] Whether that overconfidence came from underestimating the actual risk is not known, but it suggests that entrepreneurs introducing pioneering products need to be particularly mindful of correctly assessing the risks they face.

To more accurately assess the future for an opportunity, you must understand your capabilities, the capabilities and intentions of your competition, the needs and desires of customers, and the bargaining power that you have in the value chain.[20] Table 5.3 presents the various questions you need to ask yourself while conducting feasibility analysis. The bottom line is that the more information you acquire during the process of feasibility analysis, the higher the chance that your predictions will be close to the mark, risk will be reduced, and uncertainty managed. To accomplish this, you will need to develop hypotheses about the components of your business model and test them in the market.

5.2a   Developing and Testing Hypotheses

Refer to Figure 5.1 to review the components of a business model. In the beginning stages of developing the model, you will probably be filling in the blanks with information based on current knowledge. That information will be in the form of hypotheses about what you believe to be true. For example, one team wanted to create a mobile app that would solve the problem of standing in long lines waiting to order food. Figure 5.3 displays how the team initially thought about their business model. These thoughts are really hypotheses or educated guesses about what they believed to be true given their knowledge at the time. You should be prepared for the fact that, in all likelihood, most of your hypotheses will be proven wrong when you test them on real customers in the market, and that's a good thing. It's better to find out early in the process while changing the model does not incur any costs.

Once this team had their hypotheses in place, they then had to decide how they were going to test each of them to see if their judgment had been correct.

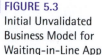

FIGURE 5.3

Initial Unvalidated Business Model for Waiting-in-Line App

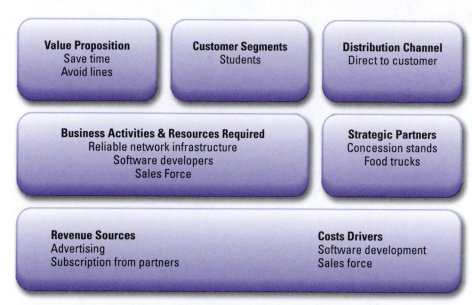

Value Proposition
Save time
Avoid lines

Customer Segments
Students

Distribution Channel
Direct to customer

Business Activities & Resources Required
Reliable network infrastructure
Software developers
Sales Force

Strategic Partners
Concession stands
Food trucks

Revenue Sources
Advertising
Subscription from partners

Costs Drivers
Software development
Sales force

So, for example, the team initially thought that their customer was the broad category of students who wanted to save time and avoid standing in line for food. There are actually two hypotheses embedded in that statement that need to be validated: the customer and the problem. The team designed a plan to talk not only to all types of students but also to non-students at a local shopping mall. It was important to find out if students were the right market, but also to learn if "students" really represented several markets; that is, not all students are alike. It was also important to validate the significance of the problem they had identified—waiting in lines. They planned to do this by getting their potential customers to talk about their experiences with concession stands and food trucks as well as standing in line for any other type of situation as a comparison. Recall that the methodology for doing field research with customers is discussed in Chapter 4. With the information from these field tests, the team went back and reconsidered how what they now knew about the problem and who it affected would impact other parts of the business model like strategic partners and distribution channels, which were as yet untested.

This iterative process of hypothesize, design an experiment, test the hypothesis, and make any changes to the business model as a result. It is an excellent way to make sure that what you are offering has a chance of being successful.

In addition to testing the business model components, feasibility analysis also addresses three critical success factors for any business. The questions you want to answer are:

1. *Is there a customer and market of sufficient size to make the concept viable and able to grow?* No business exists without customers, and even if you can determine that there are customers for your venture, it will be important to calculate whether there are *sufficient* customers to make the

FIGURE 5.4
Validating the Business
Model

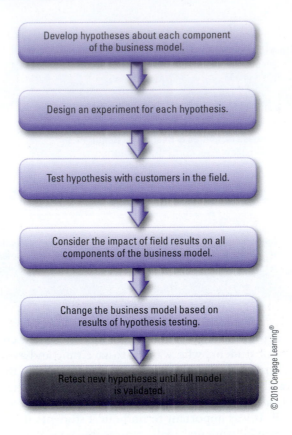

Develop hypotheses about each component
of the business model.

Design an experiment for each hypothesis.

Test hypothesis with customers in the field.

Consider the impact of field results on all
components of the business model.

Change the business model based on
results of hypothesis testing.

Retest new hypotheses until full model
is validated.

effort worthwhile. Some market niches are not large enough for entrepreneurs to make a suitable profit once competitors enter the market.
Knowing in advance that the market is too small enables you to make
adjustments in your business model to broaden the market niche or
decide not to go forward with the business before time and money have
been wasted.

2. *Do the capital requirements to start and operate to a positive cash flow make
sense?* Can this business be started with an amount of capital that you have or
will be able to raise? Are there ways to reduce startup costs through outsourcing or strategic partnering with another company? Too many entrepreneurs
underestimate the time it will take to establish a presence in the market,
acquire customers, and gain acceptance for what they're offering.

3. *Can an appropriate startup or founding team be assembled to effectively
execute the concept?* Recall that in today's complex, global environment,
most successful startups involve teams rather than solo entrepreneurs.
A team consists of the founders, advisory board, and any required strategic
partners, which can be people or other businesses with capabilities that
the business needs. The team is more important, in most cases, than the
idea, so assessing why the founding team is *the* team to execute this business is vital.

There are additional critical success factors that are unique to a particular business. For example, in a restaurant, the number of tables turned during the dinner timeframe is an important indicator of success. In a bed and breakfast inn, occupancy rate is a critical success factor. We look at key metrics for success further in Chapter 9.

Upon completion of feasibility analysis, you should be able to determine whether the conditions are right to go forward with the business concept. If conditions are not favorable, the areas tested, such as industry, market, product, pricing, and so forth, will need to be reviewed to discover whether another approach might make the business viable.

5.2b   Considering the Impact of the Macro Environment

Testing the hypotheses created during the development of the business model is essentially looking at the factors of the business that are somewhat in the control of the entrepreneur. But there are other factors outside the control of the entrepreneur that also impact the business model: (1) industry factors and trends, (2) market factors and trends, and (3) global economic factors. In Chapter 4 we look at industry and market factors and their associated trends and suggest that entrepreneurs have a clear understanding of these factors before they try to construct a business model. Figure 5.5 displays these factors and how they relate to the components of the business model.

FIGURE 5.5   Macro Environmental Factors and the Business Model

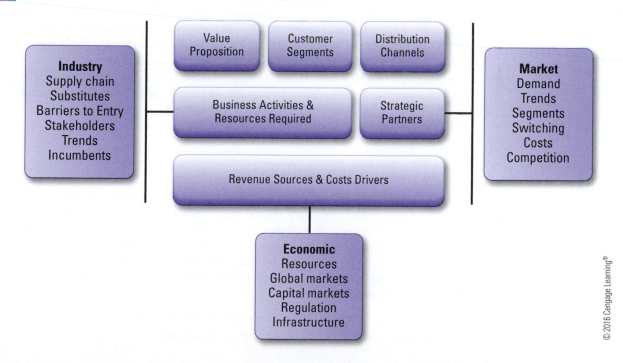

© 2016 Cengage Learning®

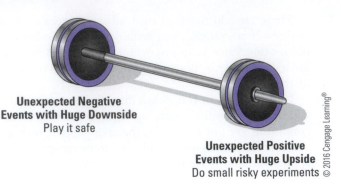

**Unexpected Negative
Events with Huge Downside**
Play it safe

**Unexpected Positive
Events with Huge Upside**
Do small risky experiments

© 2016 Cengage Learning®

No business model completely survives first contact with the market or the industry, and even effective models have to change over time to meet the pressures of the industry, market, and global economy. In fact, with success comes the fact that you now have more to lose than to gain. The key is not to wait until change happens before you rethink your business model. Making it a practice to visualize future scenarios and staying in touch with people who spend their time thinking about where things are going are ways to make sure your business doesn't get caught by surprise. Philosopher-mathematician Nassim Taleb, author of *Antifragile*, proposed that we think of businesses like barbells to represent the duality of playing it safe in some areas of the business to avoid high-impact negative events and taking small risks in others to be able to benefit from unexpected positive events.[21] (See Figure 5.6.) He calls businesses that guard what they cannot afford to lose (i.e., perhaps 90% of the business) and take risks with 10% of the business *antifragile*, meaning they benefit from the positive aspects of uncertainty without suffering from the negative side of uncertainty. The bottom line is every business needs to take risk to grow. Sometimes that risk is changing the business model to remain competitive; other times you change the business model because of events in the macro environment that threaten the sustainability of the model. Still other times, you will change your business model to opportunistically take advantage of change in the business environment. Figuring out how much risk your business can afford to take is part of designing an effective business model.

5.3   INNOVATING WITH BUSINESS MODELS

As entrepreneurs look into the future to predict how their business models might change over time, they should view the uncertainty of that future as an opportunity to find new places to compete. Kim and Marbourgne called this "blue ocean strategy," seeking the white spaces (blue ocean) where no one is playing, where opportunity is found at the intersection of value and cost.[22] They suggested four actions entrepreneurs could take to think about where those white spaces might lie.

1. Eliminate something that the industry has traditionally done.
2. Reduce something below the industry standard.

3. Raise something above the industry standard.

4. Create something the industry has never done.

The first two actions seek value creation by reducing costs. This approach is valuable in industries like health care and energy, which are highly regulated. The second two actions seek value creation in innovation. For example, the electronics industry relies on innovation for growth, but increasingly it also needs to find ways to reduce costs to keep prices in a competitive range.

The types of businesses models that entrepreneurs can generate are endless, but within specific contexts, some models are more appropriate than others. Here we consider two industries with challenging business models: where the customer doesn't want to pay and where the startup is facing dominant players.

5.3a   When the Customer Doesn't Want to Pay

Social networking sites like Facebook, Snapchat, YouTube, and Twitter provide a two-sided platform where users can upload and edit content, and share it with others. The platform is the intermediary, and the users become the content providers who contribute to the value of the platform provider, which depends on network effects—the increasing number of people using it. Because this content creation is contributed freely, entrepreneurs now have the problem of figuring out how to monetize the platform given that users do not expect to pay for something to which they freely contributed even if the platform reduced their personal costs for connecting with others.

Traditionally, advertising has been the model that most social networking sites have chosen; however, recently, this model has come under attack from both the advertisers and the users.[23] Advertisers have found that the ability to narrowly target discrete groups of consumers or businesses may actually work against them because they miss out on many customers who might be interested in their message but who are not part of the particular social network group they are targeting. Perhaps the bigger issue is the risk advertisers take with this targeting that they will actually offend their customers by posting ads based on the user's Facebook posts and suggesting products and services the user has no interest in.

Instead of advertising, some sites like LinkedIn, the social network for professionals, have used a freemium model where users can take advantage of the basic functionality of the site for free and pay a subscription fee for enhanced features and benefits.

Still others have sought sponsorships where an entity provides resources, both financial and other types, to the social network so that the network can offer its value proposition free to users. Sponsors do not sell directly to users, but their brand is present, expected, and not considered negative. Sponsorships have always been a part of sports so it isn't surprising that a social platform like Sportganizer, a French company that enables users to quickly organize sporting events, enjoys sponsorship from local and national companies who have products and services related to sports. These companies will sponsor an event, a team, or an individual in ways that avoid the intrusiveness of traditional online advertising.

5.3b   Facing Dominant Players

Startups that find themselves trying to compete for value with large, established firms that have strong negotiating power often struggle to correctly position themselves in the value chain. The most important decision they must make is how to capture value in the industry. For example, a startup producing a new patented medical device is faced with a complex value network that includes suppliers of parts, manufacturers, laboratories, regulatory bodies, hospitals, NGOs (nongovernmental organizations), and distributors, to name a few. Within the network, the startup can position itself along the value chain as one of the following (See Figure 5.7):

- An R&D company that would likely license its patents. This would be the lowest-risk model but produce the fewest rewards as well.

- An engineering design company that would develop customized solutions for its customers. However, there is risk to the intellectual property, and the value for the customer is much greater than that for the startup.

- A device manufacturing firm is an integrated position that would require the startup to control most of the points in the value chain as it sells finished product to its customers. In this position it could capture most of the value, but at high capital expenditures it may not be able to afford.

Each position has pluses and minuses as well as long-term ramifications for the startup. For example, if development of the technology requires complementary assets owned by another firm, a strategic partnership will be required or the stronger of the two firms will acquire the other. Given the limited resources of startups, it is highly likely that the company would start with one business model—for example, R&D—and as it gathered more resources to move to another model that would capture more value. However, where the industry has dominant players, it is equally possible that the startup could be acquired before it ever moved past the initial business model. Because of the power of dominant players, startups in these types of industries often focus on the acquisition of intellectual property and know-how that they can control and develop to where it is attractive to one of the dominant firms.

FIGURE 5.7
Simple Value
Chain for Devices

Research & Development   Parts Suppliers   Engineering & Design   Manufacture & Assembly   Distribution

GLOBAL INSIGHTS

Business Models For The Developing World

It may surprise many to learn that the "world's 4 billion poor people [are] the largest untapped consumer market on Earth."[24] As a group, they have more buying power than any other, with a total annual income of $1.7 trillion. Fortunately, today many organizations are beginning to address the needs of consumers in the developing world through products and services that meet their very unique requirements. Those organizations that have been successful have been able to transition from a nonprofit business model to a commercial business model.

KickStart (www.kickstart.org) is an East African nonprofit organization that worked with world-famous design company IDEO to develop a water pump that was suited to the needs, budget, and environmental conditions of Kenya. It was designed to employ manufacturing capabilities already available in Kenya; it cost less than $150, could survive the harsh Kenyan environment, and was easy to maintain. More than 24,000 pumps were sold in Tanzania and Kenya. Approximately 70 percent of those sales were to female entrepreneurs who used the pumps to produce $30 million per year in profits and wages. As of April 14, 2014, 155,000 new businesses generating over $130 million in new profits and wages were formed due to a compelling value proposition and a way for everyone involved to make money, an important incentive. KickStart employs a local supply chain from raw materials to manufacturing and distribution. Its execution plan involves five elements: (1) researching the market for small-business opportunities based on local resources; (2) designing new products and technologies as well as business models; (3) training local manufacturers in the production of the new technologies; (4) promoting the technologies to local entrepreneurs; and (5) monitoring the impact of the program to develop best practices.

Sources: www.kickstart.org/about-us, accessed April 14, 2014; and H. Chesbrough, S. Ahern, M. Finn, and S. Guerraz, (2006). "Business Models for Technology in the Developing World: The Role of Non-Governmental Organizations," *California Management Review*, 48(3): 54.

5.4   DRAWING CONCLUSIONS FROM FEASIBILITY ANALYSIS

Rejecting new ideas is an age-old practice. In the 1940s, von Neumann talked about self-replicating programmable manufacturing architectures, and in the 1960s Feynman revealed that atoms could be arranged in new ways, further supporting the notion that what we know today as nanotechnology was a feasible concept. But most products in common use today—airplanes, automobiles, smartphone—were originally thought to be infeasible.[25] Furthermore, even successful business concepts like eBay and Starbucks were initially considered to be infeasible. So how does an entrepreneur determine whether a new business concept is feasible once all the research is accomplished and the various aspects of the model tested?

Recall that the process of feasibility analysis is designed to convert an uncertain opportunity to one that has a specific level of risk associated with it. Uncertainty is reduced by acquiring more information and answering the questions that contributed to that uncertainty. At each point in the feasibility process, entrepreneurs are able to make a judgment about whether to proceed with the analysis. Each step in the analysis provides information about the conditions that are necessary to make the business feasible. The sum total of these conditions should give you a level of confidence about the risk associated with the concept and your ability to execute the concept given that risk. But there is another important decision that must be made, perhaps as important as whether or not the business is feasible. And that is whether this business, given the necessary conditions for success, satisfies your personal needs and goals. Feasibility analysis should provide you with significantly more information about how your business would work than was available when the concept was conceived. Sometimes, in learning more about the industry and how businesses operate in that industry, you may discover that you are not suited to this type of business. Perhaps the initial excitement over the business has waned and in its place is a reality that is no longer attractive to you. Maybe launching this business will be too difficult a task, more difficult than you first thought it would be.

Alternatively, the process of feasibility analysis might make you even more enthusiastic about the business and its potential, enough so that it compensates for any identified risk associated with it. What is generally certain in all of this is that the process of feasibility analysis will definitely help you draw an appropriate conclusion about the business, and therein lies its real value.

FIGURE 5.8:   Entrepreneur's Business Model Canvas

Problem	Solution	Unique Value Proposition	Unfair Advantage	Customer Segments
Top 3 problems you're addressing. Job to be done	Top 3 features and associated benefits that demonstrate the UVP	How are you different from everyone else?	What cannot be copied or bought?	First customer and secondary markets
	Key Metrics Key activities to measure.		**Channels & Strategic Partners** Path to the customer	
Cost Structure Customer acquisition Distribution People		**Revenue Streams** Life time value Gross margin		

© 2016 Cengage Learning®

Based on Alex Osterwalder's canvas licensed under Creative Commons and Lean Startup Canvas by Ash Maurya

New Venture Action Plan

- Develop your initial hypotheses about the components of the business model.

- Design experiments to test your hypotheses.

- Make changes in your business model to reflect what you learned.

Questions on Key Issues

1. What is the purpose of the business model, and why do business models typically fail?
2. What are the characteristics of an effective business model?
3. What is the purpose of feasibility analysis?
4. What are some ways to innovate in a business model?

Experiencing Entrepreneurship

1. Compare and contrast the business models of two early-stage companies. Here are their business models sources of innovation?
2. Suppose you intend to start a theme restaurant that can be replicated and franchised. Based on an analysis of some existing theme restaurants, what types of revenue streams could this business generate? What are its major cost drivers?

Relevant Case Studies

Case 4 Command Audio

Case 5 Corporate Entrepreneurship and Innovation in Silicon Valley: The Case of Google Inc.

CHAPTER 6

Prototyping and Validating a Solution

"If you are truly innovating, you don't have a prototype you can refer to."

—JONATHAN IVES, SENIOR VP DESIGN, APPLE, INC.

CHAPTER OBJECTIVES

- Discuss the current trends in new product design and development.
- Describe the product development cycle.
- Understand the requirements of a minimum viable product.
- Compare the advantages and disadvantages of outsourcing product development.

GROCKIT: ONLINE SOCIAL LEARNING

Farbood Nivi would be the first to tell you that the lean approach to product development is a significant reason for Grockit's success. A San Francisco–based company that is focused on social learning, Grockit began in 2007 as a tool that employed game mechanics to help students study in groups to take admission tests such as the SAT and the GMAT. It has since become much more with more than one million students now using it.

Nivi's early testing of what would become Grockit's platform was an innovative type of private tutoring via the Internet. Although he was generating revenues of about $15,000 per month with this platform, Nivi had a much bigger goal in mind—to use a collaborative approach to change the way students learn, in other words, to create a social learning service. Just a year into his company, he made the decision to adopt the lean process. Although customers were doing well using the program, he wanted to understand which features were most important so that his team could spend its time working on things that mattered. One of the first things he did was run an experiment with his team to convince them of the value of lean. He had them remove half of the features from the current Web application and run what's called a split test to check the performance of the scaled-down version against the original Web app. What Nivi learned was stunning. With only half the features, the site performed nearly as well as the full site did in the eyes of the customers.

Still, Nivi was not confident that he was measuring the right things. When Eric Ries, who popularized the notion of the lean startup, looked at the situation, he immediately saw that Grockit had been measuring its progress with "vanity metrics," the total number of customers and the total number of questions answered. Those metrics made the team seem like it was moving forward, but, in reality, they were not making progress. When Nivi changed the metrics from "gross metrics" to "cohort metrics," segmenting customers into smaller groups, he then conducted split-test experiments on every new feature the team planned to offer to determine exactly which feature mattered to which customer.

In addition to discovering the right metrics to measure progress, Nivi credits a simultaneous design and build approach to Grockit's ability to stay ahead of competitors. Grockit's subsequent growth trajectory led it to successfully raising a $20 million Series E round in 2012, bringing the total amount the company had raised to $44.7 million. With new money, the company broadened its scope from test preparation and Common Core standards to lifelong learning by launching Learnist, which has been dubbed the "Pinterest for education." For about a year, the team worked in stealth mode building out "a suite of Web and mobile apps for Learnist." Learnist was designed to enable teachers and students to post Web content to clipboards for comments and to share with others as well as to highlight experts in a variety of fields. Once the team had a working prototype, Nivi went to the Grockit board of directors to show them how it worked. The board, many of whom were investors, immediately saw Learnist as the bigger opportunity and embraced it. At that point, Grockit was in revenue, but everyone wanted to focus on the larger opportunity that Learnist presented. Fortunately, education giant Kaplan wanted to acquire the test prep assets and social learning platform that Grockit had developed. The lean startup team that Nivi had put together stayed with him to work on

Learnist and with the money from the sale, it appears that Nivi will not need to raise capital anytime soon.

Sources: Ries, E. (2011). "The Lean Startup: How Today's Entrepreneurs Use Continuous Innovation to Create Radically Successful Businesses," New York: Crown Business; Heussner, K.M. (December 18, 2012). "Social Learning Startup Grockit Raises $20M, Led by Discovery Communications," *Gigaom*, https://gigaom.com/2012/12/18/social-learning-startup -grockit-raises-20m-led-by-discovery-communications/; Farr, C. (August 2, 2013), "Cash Out, Pivot, Reboot: How Grockit's Team Jumped into a New Startup, Learnist," VB News, http://venturebeat.com/2013/08/02/cash-out -pivot-reboot-how-grockits-team-jumped-into-a-new-startup -learnist/.

Every business—large or small, product or service—is involved in design and development at every stage of its life cycle. Each time a new product or service or an improvement to an existing product or service is introduced, it will have gone through a complex design and development process. The goal of the product development process is to bring new products to market at the right time and for the right cost so that customers will pay a price that reflects value to them. However, accomplishing this is no simple task because most startups are limited by budgets, people, and time.[1] Moreover, in the midst of design and development, entrepreneurs also have to think about how to protect the investment in new products. The importance of intellectual property protections cannot be overstated and is covered in Chapter 7.

When Marc Cenedella started The Ladders in 2003, the Lean Startup movement had yet to take hold (that happened in 2011). The Ladders was founded to close the gap in online recruiting and employment seeking at the high end of salary scale. Their product development process involved defining a problem, reducing that problem to its source so that they were solving the real problem, not a symptom; talking, drawing, and prototyping to quickly get the proposed solution in front of customers; and getting feedback from customers, which they used to iterate the process again. When developing a new app, they always started with a hypothesis, the constraints under which they would need to work (e.g., the new app must integrate seamlessly into a recruiter's website), and some basic design principles.[2] They sketched out in detail a hypothetical user or "proto-persona" based on years of experience with customer outreach, and they then mentally put themselves inside that person to try to view their app from the customer's perspective. They also reflected on the advantages and disadvantages of the iPhone platform and how it affected the user experience (UX). With a well-developed hypothesis in place and a sketch of a solution, they would then head out to test the hypothesis with users. In one case, they found out to their chagrin that recruiters didn't have the problem they had originally hypothesized. That resulted in more conversations about the problem before they could ultimately return to the drawing board to rethink their solution. This early-stage testing before investment in an actual product is key to saving both time and money. Testing early and often is the hallmark of lean for software companies, but it also holds true in some form for all types of new product development.

6.1   ENTREPRENEURS AND NEW PRODUCT DESIGN AND DEVELOPMENT

Product design is defined as the activity that transforms a set of requirements into a format that brings all the elements into an integrated whole or system.[3] This system consists of form, texture, color, fit, user interfaces, production and assembly processes to manufacture the parts, and the methods for joining all the parts together. The design of a product is critical because it determines the features and performance, reliability, price, and appeal to the customer. More importantly, perhaps, design determines cost—in fact, as much as 80 percent of the final cost.[4]

Design is affected by the fact that technology has shorter product life cycles. A product life cycle is analogous to an industry life cycle, with periods of product development, market introduction, growth, maturity, and decline. A complete product life cycle can be as short as 90 days for fads or as long as 100 years as in the case of automobiles. Whereas 50 years ago a new tool product had a life cycle of 18 years and a new game or toy a life cycle of 16 years, today those life cycles have shrunk to 5 years or fewer. Consequently, companies must always be researching and developing new products and improving on existing ones to stay ahead of the competition.

The same can be said of service companies. New products often create the need for new services to support them. Even fundamental services such as advertising, consulting, and food services are affected by shrinking development life cycles. Customers now expect service entrepreneurs to provide new and innovative services much more rapidly and at significantly lower costs. As a result, for example, the fast-food industry continues to grow; even grocery stores have gotten into the game with an increasing number of convenience food offerings, such as packaged salads and reheatable meals. In addition, with email and the Internet ubiquitous throughout the professional services industry, customers now expect much shorter response times on correspondence and document preparation.

In a time of fast-paced new product development, entrepreneurs quickly discover that it's not just about producing one product or service and calling it a day. Rather, it's about managing an ongoing innovation pipeline that will keep their company competitive. A 2014 study found four key trends related to how companies characterize product development today: efficiency improvement, cost reduction, innovation, and robust products.[5] From this finding we see that the need to streamline the product development process and reduce costs while still innovating and producing superior products produces a complex set of tradeoffs that must be addressed if a company is to be competitive. The way that entrepreneurs deal with these tradeoffs is exemplified by the "lean startup" movement, a concept first proposed by Eric Ries but which is actually based on the original work of quality guru W. Edwards Deming. Deming's systemic view of quality—in other words, that it affects every part of the company—led to many of the product development principles employed today, such as lean manufacturing, agile software development, and the Theory of Constraints. Lean manufacturing focuses on the elimination of waste, while agile software development is based on iteration and incremental development. The Theory of Constraints proposes that every system has one major constraint around which everything else must be structured. It's most easily understood by the common idiom "A chain is no stronger than its weakest link." The constraint is that weakest link.

Ries translated the work of Deming and others into what he called the "build-measure-learn" concept, a way to quickly iterate through software development to achieve something good enough to test with customers. Ries promotes the idea that you don't need your hypotheses to be the best they can be; they just need to be good enough to get some meaningful feedback from customers. He advocates testing some ideas with a sign-up page on a website with promises to deliver a finished product, just to see how many people will actually sign up. Continual testing of the vision for the product will produce established customers when it is finally launched.[6] His mantra is "work smarter, not harder." We will discuss one of Ries's concepts—the minimum viable product—in a later section of the chapter.

While entrepreneurs rarely approach product development in the same systematic way that large companies do, they are still affected by the need to address the weakest link in their new product strategy to avoid failure. Given that new product failure is so prevalent for companies in general, it's important to spend some time looking at what causes failure.

6.1a   New Product Failure

Despite all the benefits that have accrued to new product development with the advent of information and systems technologies, the probability of success at launch is still about 60 percent.[7] Figure 6.1 depicts the typical percentage of new products that are successes, failures, or are killed during new product development. Notice that the kill rate during product development is higher for the best performing products; consequently, the failure rate is the lowest of the three categories.

A significant body of research has revealed that the principal reason for new product failure is lack of good market and industry analysis. Innovators can

FIGURE 6.1
New Product Successes, Failures, and Misses.

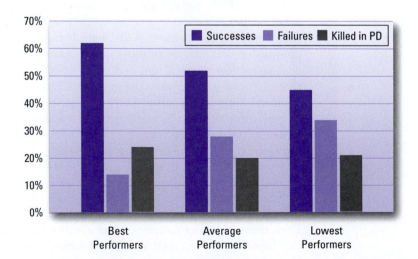

Source: Adapted from Edgett, S.J. (December 2010) Product Development Institute and APQC benchmarking study.

be successful at *creating* value but unless they have found a way to *capture* sufficient value, the returns from their innovation will be tapped by imitators, providers of complementary products, and others in the value chain.[8] When entrepreneurs consider the types of barriers they might erect to forestall the siphoning of innovation returns, they typically overlook the intellectual property environment (discussed in Chapter 7) and industry architecture because they believe there is no way to control these environments.[9] To capture the full value from innovation requires that entrepreneurs invest in complementary products, technologies, and services. In other words, if the product is 3D digital television, customers will expect original 3D content to support it. Electric cars require an infrastructure of charging stations. If entrepreneurs do not have control over these complements, then strong intellectual property rights or trade secrets will be critical to making a product difficult to copy.[10]

Industry architecture makes it easier or more difficult for entrepreneurs to succeed depending on whether they are producing a complete solution and control all the complements (a vertical architecture) or whether they are part of an industry where they are offering only part of the solution; that is, others in the industry produce parts that entrepreneurs need. For example, independent film studios are essentially system integrators. They gather the resources they need to produce a film from a variety of different companies. Their position as the integrator is weak if they don't control any intellectual property, which explains why frequently a film will make money, but the studio that produced it will not.

Another significant cause of new product failure is technical problems. The path from laboratory to production is fraught with challenges and obstacles, often because the product development team has not spent enough time correctly defining the problem they're solving. Consequently, the product definition may be incorrect, or worse, provide features and benefits that the customer does not value. Many of today's digital products offer almost limitless opportunities to add new features and make the product more complex; however, in most cases, customers prefer simplicity over complexity and only want those features that solve the real problem while at the same time providing a great user experience.

There are ways for entrepreneurial firms to compete effectively in the area of product development. In fact, the new lean environment for product development is uniquely suited to smaller companies, which are often better able to adapt to change and move quickly in new directions. Three fundamental strategies should be incorporated into any entrepreneur's product development program to enhance the chances of competing effectively: (1) design products right the first time, (2) shorten the time-to-market through the use of minimum viable product testing (discussed in a later section), and (3) outsource some product development tasks to create a lean structure. Strategies that support these outcomes will be discussed in the next section.

Most large corporations have separate departments responsible for research and development, engineering, and testing. In many cases, the budgets for these departments are astronomical, because new product development and the continual improvement of existing products and processes are among the most important and challenging, not to mention expensive, tasks of high-performing, world-class businesses. The high cost is due in large part to high-priced development staff, equipment, and, in some cases, regulatory requirements, such as those for medical devices. In the case of startup ventures, the task is equally challenging; however, most new ventures, unlike large corporations, have very limited or nonexistent budgets for product development. Investors frequently consider research and development, engineering, and testing to be the highest-risk stages for new companies, so funding for these activities is difficult, if not impossible, to secure. Entrepreneurs are left with a dilemma: how to perform the research and development (R&D) that will result in a high-quality, engineered prototype as quickly and as inexpensively as possible. A lack of sufficient new product development (NPD) resources has many unintended consequences. As illustrated in Figure 6.2, a lack of resources focused on NPD results in five common problems.[11]

1. *Poor execution.* The critical due diligence and market analysis required to ensure a successful product launch are often shortened or bypassed in favor of speed. Approximately 75 percent of NPD projects don't include vital market research.[12]

2. *Time-to-market increases.* When a new venture lacks sufficient resources, bottlenecks and backups tend to occur because there aren't enough people doing the work. When the work is completed, it must often be redone because it was done in haste. Overall execution is generally poor.

3. *First-to-market opportunities are missed.* Poor execution results in missed opportunities to enter the market at a quiet time without immediate competition. Also, because these "game changer" opportunities often require more resources than less risky initiatives, frequently they are bypassed in favor of incremental opportunities that are easier and can be done quickly at a much lower cost. Unfortunately, these kinds of opportunities provide little value or return to the company, and in fact, the returns continue to diminish until the company finally decides to change the game with a truly innovative project.

FIGURE 6.2   The Consequences of Resource Shortfalls for New Product Development

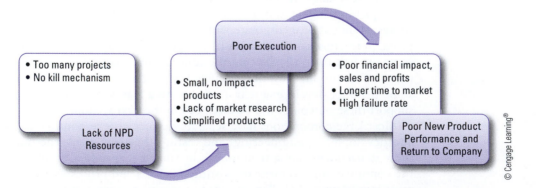

© Cengage Learning®

4. *Projects are made simpler so that more can be done with less.* The dumbing down of projects is another consequence of resource scarcity. Where resources are limited, product features and customer benefits are often sacrificed in order to get more products out.

5. *Team morale declines.* The combination of a lack of resources and increasing time pressure causes morale problems on product development teams and a sense that the team must accomplish the impossible.[13] Although members of the team are often willing to get the job done, more frequently the stressful environment saps their morale.

It is important to fully understand the product development cycle so that there will be no surprises about the complexity or timing of it.

6.2   OVERVIEW OF THE PRODUCT DEVELOPMENT CYCLE

Entrepreneurs who develop products usually go through a process much like that shown in Figure 6.3. The product development cycle consists of a series of tasks leading to introduction of the product in the marketplace. Although it appears from the graph to be a linear process, it is actually quite iterative with multiple feedback loops. Because new product success usually requires an ongoing dialogue with the customer, an iterative or sense-and-respond approach to the process is more appropriate.[14] All of the tasks displayed in Figure 6.3 will take place; however, they occur often in parallel or out of order.

The eight tasks are grouped into three main categories:

1. Customer Identification or Discovery. Who is the primary customer and what are their needs?

2. Customer Validation and Design. How can we design, develop, and test the product, market, and business model?

3. Business Creation. What should the launch strategy be?

6.2a   Customer Identification or Discovery

Before you can develop a product (a solution), you need to identify a problem that potential customers have. That problem may lead to a market niche that has not yet been served, a potential improvement in an existing product, or an opportunity for a breakthrough product or process. At this point, the problem is simply an opportunity that must be validated. However, this "front end" of product development is arguably the most impactful because research has shown that unclear or ill-defined product definitions result in higher costs and greater chances of product failure.[15] Moreover, if you don't spend sufficient time on product definition, you may end up with a mediocre product that does not add value for customers.

FIGURE 6.3   From Idea to Market

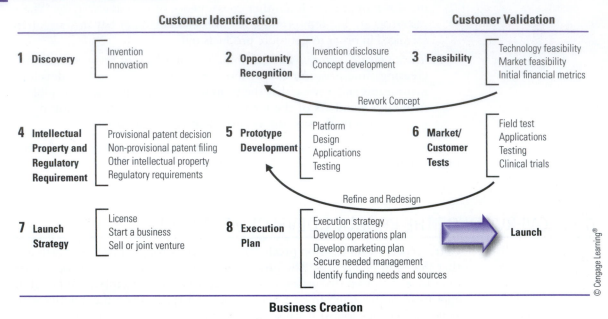

6.2b   Customer Validation and Design

When you validate a customer, you are conducting preliminary research to determine whether you have the right customer and the right solution. In looking at potential solutions, you will consider whether your solution currently exists, whether it is a way to actually solve the problem, whether your solution can be produced, whether it can be protected, how much it will cost to produce, and how much time it will take to bring it to market. Table 6.1 provides a checklist for broadly assessing the feasibility of new products.

Early in the development of your solution, you will need to determine the potential for intellectual property protections and to plan for filing for patent protection, if appropriate, at the optimal time. Regulatory requirements for many new technologies and products can be onerous, so it's also critical that you learn how your development process will be affected by any laws or regulations.

The first stages of design preparation go hand in hand with customer validation, because you will need some preliminary working drawings of the solution to estimate costs and manufacturing processes should those be needed. These preliminary drawings are also used to apply for a patent if you have a technology that is patentable. From the initial engineered drawings will come the prototype or model of the solution. Often the first prototype does not closely resemble the final product in appearance, but it usually does in function. Physical prototypes, whether they are three dimensional, a mockup of a mobile app, or a storyboard of a process, are helpful in communicating the form, fit, and function of the solution to customers; for providing an example to a vendor for quotation; for facilitating quick changes in a design; and for designing the

TABLE 6.1 New Product Checklist

	Yes	No	Needs More Study
THE MARKET			
Is there an existing need for this product in the marketplace? A first customer?	___	___	___
Will I be first in the marketplace with this product?	___	___	___
Will this product disrupt the market?			
Can the product be protected through intellectual-property rights?	___	___	___
Can market entry barriers be erected?	___	___	___
Is there a path to multiple customers?			
What specific and highly valued benefits will customers derive from this product? (validated by primary research with customers)			
Do customers have to change their behavior to adopt this product?			
SWOT ANALYSIS (STRENGTHS, WEAKNESSES, OPPORTUNITIES, AND THREATS)			
Do the strengths of this product exceed any weaknesses?	___	___	___
Are there various opportunities for commercializing this product?	___	___	___
Do any significant threats exist to the development of this product?	___	___	___
Does the product create network effects?			
DESIGN/DEVELOPMENT/MANUFACTURING			
Is the product innovative?	___	___	___
Can it be developed quickly to market-ready state?	___	___	___
Can it be easily manufactured?	___	___	___
Do I have the resources to manufacture the product?	___	___	___
Is it more practical to subcontract the manufacturing?	___	___	___
Are there ways to enhance the product over time?			
Is there a possibility for spin-off or complementary products?	___	___	___
FINANCIAL			
Is the return on this investment sufficient to justify the effort?	___	___	___
Are the development costs within reason?	___	___	___
Will it be possible to minimize the manufacturing investment through outsourcing, while still maintaining quality and control?	___	___	___
Is money available to produce the product?	___	___	___
Can the product achieve high gross margins?	___	___	___
Is there a viable business model for this product?	___	___	___

© Cengage Learning®

correct tooling—those devices that hold a product component in place during manufacturing and assembly. Entrepreneurs developing engineered products often use small engineering firms or solo engineers with small job shops and machine shops to complete the prototype. These sources are normally quicker and less expensive than the larger, better-known firms. When seeking an engineer or a model builder, it is important to be cautious and check out their qualifications, experience, and references relative to the task required of them. A major university engineering department is a good source of referrals, as are other engineers.

Businesses that do not manufacture products—service, retail, wholesale, and so forth—still need to design a prototype, but the prototype in this case will not always be physical in a three-dimensional form. Instead it will be a design, storyboard, or flowchart for how the business will provide a service or product to its customer. For example, a restaurant entrepreneur will design the layout of the restaurant and kitchen with an eye to how customers and servers move through the restaurant. The food preparation area will need to be laid out efficiently so that the chef and cooks can work quickly and not have to move great distances to retrieve cooking utensils and food items. Every activity the restaurant undertakes should be prototyped to ensure that there is no duplication of effort and that each task is performed as efficiently and effectively as possible.

Many software products and apps start with storyboards to walk the customer through the experience before the team starts to code the actual functional site. With a working prototype, it is possible to field-test it with potential users in environments where the product will typically be used. For example, it would be important to put a new construction tool in the hands of construction workers on real jobs in the field. In this way, you can collect feedback based on actual use in real-life situations. After conducting a small initial test production run in a limited market, you can go back and fine-tune the product and the process to completion and market-ready status. This is also the first opportunity to seriously test the manufacturing and assembly processes if your solution requires them, particularly if they are outsourced to partners. Testing will help determine accurate costs of production at varying levels of volume. For software products, giving a beta version to a limited group of early adopters to test functionality and usability will provide important feedback.

6.2c   Go-To-Market

The final phase is go-to-market or the launch strategy. From a business perspective, you need to determine the means by which you will commercialize your technology or product: whether to license the technology to another company to develop it into applications, start a business to make and distribute the product, sell the technology, or joint venture with another company that has the resources you need.

Many of the activities that have to take place to move the solution to market—the operations plan, the marketing plan, the funding plan, and so forth—have been taking place throughout the development process. It is at this stage that they all come together in a complete business model that has been tested. In fact, in many cases, you may already have acquired a few customers as part of a soft launch to validate the business model.

6.2d   Product Development Tradeoffs

Throughout the product development process, you will encounter tradeoffs that will have to be made among all the factors that affect development: product features, cost, capital expenditures, development costs, and timing.[16] A tradeoff by its very definition suggests that there will be some kind of compromise; something must be sacrificed to gain something else. Most tradeoffs involve the allocation of limited resources with the goal of finding the optimal balance among all the elements of the product development process. Tradeoffs can also be viewed as a set of contradictions. For example, building an app for an Apple iPhone has no contradictions because there is no contradiction between apps and the iPhone platform—we don't have to choose. Similarly, there are no contradictions in building a fast electric superbike that is blue. The color of the bike and its ability to go fast are not in conflict. However, there is a contradiction between the need for speed and the source of power. To achieve speed requires battery power; however, the more power required, the bigger the battery and the more weight it adds to the machine, essentially making it slower. How do you find the optimal balance between speed and weight?

Physical and technical tradeoffs are not the only types of tradeoffs you will encounter. You will also need to deal with all of the stakeholders who will have input into the product development process and who are affected by it. Those stakeholders may include your customers, retailers, distributors, partners, manufacturers, quality experts, and R&D. Their needs must be factored into the product and its associated business model.

Table 6.2 presents a list of many of the tradeoffs you will face when doing product development and some issues to consider. Before you can consider tradeoffs, you will need to have a tested and prioritized list of product features that you know your customers expect to see. It will be difficult to make informed tradeoff decisions if you don't know what matters to your customers in terms of their minimum requirements and the features/benefits that hold the most value for them. With that list, it will then be easier to answer questions about schedule, equipment costs, product development costs, and product costs. For example, consider the tradeoff between features and product cost. It may be easy to add on new features, but this will increase the cost of the product and the price the customer will have to pay. Features need to be prioritized according to what the customer values and resources put on those valued features while at the

TABLE 6.2
Some Product
Development Tradeoffs

Tradeoff	Issues to Consider
Features v. product cost	Put most of the product costs into the features that matter most to customers. Reduce costs for the customer by eliminating features that do not add value.
Features v. development costs	Make sure the features that take the most development talent also add the most value for customers.
Features v. schedule	What effect does seasonality have on your product launch? Are you trying to beat a window of opportunity to be first to market?
Product cost v. capital expenditures	Does it make sense to buy equipment and manufacture in-house or is it more cost effective to outsource or partner?
Product cost v. development costs	Your initial margins may be slim due to development costs. Will they improve with economies of scale?

© Cengage Learning®

same time deleting features that have little value. By allocating resources toward high-value features, the profit margin will go up. You will also need to look at which features are driving the cost of development. This tradeoff suggests that you might want to consider whether the most costly features can be modified to bring down their cost or whether it makes sense to acquire technology in this area rather than develop it in house to potentially save money.[17]

It should now be very apparent that managing tradeoffs effectively is a critical part of product development, and it's important that understanding tradeoffs be part of the design process. In addition to interviews and focus groups, statistical tools such as conjoint analysis are available to help entrepreneurs understand customer preferences. For example, one researcher was helping a company that was considering introducing a new type of functional beverage (one offering health benefits) as a hedge against downward price pressure for many categories of beverages. The researcher conducted a conjoint-based survey and was able to confirm what the company's qualitative research had found—that health benefits of beverages were not as important to consumers' purchasing decisions as they had always believed. Moreover, they learned that consumers made tradeoffs between health benefits and high price more often than not, although they did find out that consumers would prefer a medium-priced beverage with health benefits over a lower-priced one without those benefits.[18]

6.3   BUILDING A MINIMUM VIABLE PRODUCT

Coined by consultant Frank Robinson in 1987, the term *minimum viable product (MVP)* was made popular for Web development by Eric Ries. An MVP is that version of a product that contains just enough of the functionality and value proposition to attract early adopters who provide feedback and help you develop a final product for the mass market. The goal of the MVP is to attract those initial customers who can guide the direction of the product. The goal of the final product is to attract passionate users/customers who will refer your product to others. Achieving these goals is not as easy as it sounds. Early adopters may like your MVP and you might immediately consider that to be validation. The product is viable. But if early adopters don't like it, that doesn't necessarily mean that your product has not been validated or is not viable.[19] For example, in 2008, Drew Houston did a Digg video describing Dropbox to validate a not-yet-released Dropbox.com website. It drew 70,000 users, who signed up and helped confirm that Houston had a good product-market fit. However, what if this experiment had failed? If that had been the case, it would not necessarily mean that Dropbox as a concept was a failure. Failure to validate at this point could have been due to several reasons:

- Users expected much higher quality than they saw. Beta versions of products are often low quality.
- Digg users were not his initial customers.
- Something had distracted or prevented users from referring the site to their friends.

Running a series of MVP tests might not reveal any of those reasons. Testing the problem you're trying to solve might be more valuable. So, in this case, Houston would have come up with a way to test whether users needed a way to access their documents from any device. If you haven't focused on a real problem that customers find compelling enough that they want it solved, then it's fairly difficult to develop a validation experiment that will give you the information you need. It is far more effective to first validate the problem and then test a potential solution with an MVP.

In 1999, entrepreneur Bill Gross wanted to solve the problem of buying a car. Most people detest having to deal with salespeople and go through the back and forth of negotiation to arrive at a price that makes everyone happy. He decided to test an MVP of his concept by putting up a website where a customer could find a car and the various options desired and then pay for the car, all without a salesperson. Gross then bought the car from a dealer and delivered it to the customer. With a few satisfied customers under his belt, Gross felt confident enough to proceed with what became CarsDirect.com. In this example, the problem was well known, and the only way to understand whether he had the right solution was to test it with an MVP.

While an MVP can be an excellent way to gauge customer interest for many products, there are some types of products where this approach may not be optimal. As Cooper and Vlaskovits suggest in *The Lean Entrepreneur,* whether an MVP is the way to go depends on where the solution you're proposing lies on the innovation scale from incremental—building on existing technology—to disruptive—creating something new to the world.[20] Figure 6.4 displays the spectrum from products with known problems and solutions where solutions are incremental in nature to products with no identifiable markets and where the solutions are unknown. If your product concept falls closer to the incremental end of the spectrum, you are dealing with customers who have real problems and will quickly grasp whether a solution you propose will solve that problem. That also means that there is typically a lot of competition from major players in the market; therefore, you will need to build more than just a simple MVP to get the kind of feedback you need. In this case going out with a complete product actually might make more sense, since customers have alternatives.

FIGURE 6.4 The Innovation Spectrum

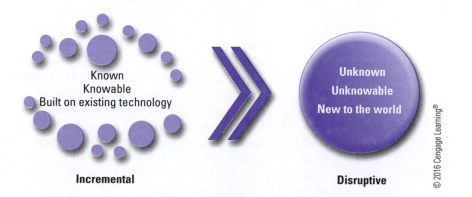

Known
Knowable
Built on existing technology

Unknown
Unknowable
New to the world

© 2016 Cengage Learning®

Incremental

Disruptive

By contrast, if your product concept lies closer to the disruptive end of the spectrum, building an MVP in stages based on customer feedback is more valuable because you don't have direct competition initially so you have time, and customers won't expect the MVP to be perfect since the solution is novel. PayPal is an excellent example of a product that changed the game in Internet payment processing. The initial version did not provide the best user experience, but it did demonstrate that customers wanted this type of solution.

Once you determine that your MVP solution fits the market you have targeted, it's time to finish the product so that it's a complete solution that reflects what you learned from your MVP testing. It's important to remember that it is not the number of times you iterate your MVP that produces a viable product; it's how well you recognize when the customer tells you that you have a viable product, and that could be after the first iteration. For disruptive products, you get many opportunities to fail because no customer yet is depending on you for a solution. New-to-the-world products are given a quality pass for a time because they are essentially experiments. Incremental products, which are most of the new products produced today, have only one chance to succeed because customers have many alternatives from which to choose.

6.3a   Customer Value Propositions

Validating the solution with customers is absolutely critical to startup success. In general, most teams think about their value propositions in terms of three different approaches: total benefits, points of differentiation, and focus on a key value. Many entrepreneurs choose to attribute benefits to all of the features their solution incorporates, and generally, these benefits are usually similar to the next best alternative that customers could choose. This approach is less than optimal because all your competitors are making essentially the same claims about their value, so customers have no particular reason to choose one solution over another. Worse yet, they are likely to remain with their current solution over subjecting themselves to the switching costs of moving to a new solution.

Entrepreneurs who choose to focus on favorable points of difference with competitors recognize that customers do have choices, so it's necessary to make the new solution stand out from the crowd. The problem comes when they haven't validated that their point of differentiation actually matters to customers. Again, with this approach customers have to weigh whether the cost of switching makes sense.

The third approach is perhaps the most optimal because to execute it, entrepreneurs need to understand the critical needs of their customers. With this unique value approach entrepreneurs focus on the unique difference they're offering that provides the most value for the customer. Achieving parity with competitors is only important to the extent that customers need a certain standard set of features and quality before they will even consider the new solution. If you remember that the value proposition is really your solution, it makes sense that providing a solution with unique and high value will be the best way to insure demand from customers.

6.3b   Outsourcing Product Development

It is becoming more and more common for entrepreneurs with both large and small companies to outsource all or part of their product development to third parties. The decision is due in large part to today's requirements for fast-paced innovation with shorter windows of opportunity. Most startup companies don't have the resources to do adequate product development in-house. And there is no reason why it should be done this way when it is possible to reduce risk, lower costs, and decrease cycle times by factors of 60 to 90 percent by outsourcing product development.[21] Outsourcing provides a young firm with a network of expertise that it couldn't afford to hire in-house. Some of the areas of product development that require engineering analysis, design, and expertise and are suitable for outsourcing are component design, materials specifications, machinery to process, ergonomic design, packaging design, assembly drawings and specifications, parts and material sourcing (suppliers), and operator's and owner's manuals.

Outsourcing domestically is very common to gain the capabilities just discussed. Offshore outsourcing to other countries for product development is generally about reducing costs or speeding the process of clinical trials in the case of medical products, both of which are relatively short-term objectives. Today, however, some experts in the global offshore product development space believe that companies are increasingly looking at offshoring (and this holds for domestic outsourcing as well) as part of a long-term strategy for several reasons:[22]

- **Improving the quality of software development.** Software startups have to be effective in many business functions—marketing, sales, operations, and product development. When entrepreneurs outsource domestically or offshore their product development, they are partnering with a company that focuses solely on product development and has skills and expertise that the startup team may not have.

- **Preserving the ability to be flexible to adapt to uncertainty.** Early-stage companies (and large ones as well) that carry too much overhead in the form of employees often find themselves in trouble when market needs or the competitive landscape changes. By contrast, companies that use a combination of full-time employees and outsourced staff are better able to downsize quickly if needed.

- **Enabling rapid scaling.** Startups and early-stage companies that enter a rapid growth stage are often caught unprepared for the human capital required to scale their offering. Developing a network of outsourced partners on a global level can enable the business to rapidly scale its product development to meet demand or take advantage of new opportunities.

Product development is such a critical issue for entrepreneurial ventures that a few entrepreneurs have actually started companies to help their fellow entrepreneurs get through the process more quickly and effectively. Steve Owens had 20 years of experience as an entrepreneur who struggled to put together winning product development teams and to fund the costs of the infrastructure he needed to develop a product. In 2002, he decided to offer a way to support startups with his service company, Finish Line Product Development Services.

Keeping costs low and charging by the hour, he is able to offer entrepreneurs who outsource their new product development to his company the ability to break even on their costs within a matter of months.[23] However, even when taking advantage of product development service firms, it's important to keep in mind a few simple rules of thumb.[24]

- Do not outsource the design and development of your product to the same firm. These tasks require very different skills that are not often present in one firm.

- Spend enough time on the design of your product before you begin to build or code. There is a temptation to quickly hand off a design idea to engineers only to later discover that the design had flaws. Engineers need fully developed designs.

- If you can break your product development into meaningful parts, you will be able to do early tests at low cost before incurring the expense of complete development.

When using other companies to do part or all of the product development, it is important to understand that these partners work with many other companies, so no single company will be a high priority for them. That's why

GLOBAL INSIGHTS

APOPO: How Rats Became the Unique Value Proposition

Any social venture, like any other business, must find a way to create value for the people it serves by solving a real problem with a product or service the "customer" wants. APOPO is a Dutch acronym that translates as "Anti-Personnel Landmine Detection Product Development," and that is the focus of this Belgian social enterprise. But it's the way that this innovative nonprofit tackles the problem of landmine detection in post-conflict countries that is so fascinating. It actually trains "giant African pouched rats in Tanzania" in a period of 12 months to detect explosives through their rather exceptional sense of smell. The most common type of animal used for this work is a dog, but training a dog takes at least 18 months. Moreover, rats are less expensive and they don't develop bonds with their handlers, so they can be moved around more easily. So successful was their "product development" effort that they decided to move their headquarters to a village in Tanzania where the rats could be trained in real conditions by local people. Like any new "technology," the mine action community was slow to adopt this new approach, but the success of this endeavor has led to looking at other ways to use the rats, tuberculosis detection for one. In the developing world, TB kills two million people every year while adding nine million new cases. The organization has now received funding to tackle this new screening approach.

Source: Verwimp, P. and Witmeur, O. (2012). The Social Entrepreneurial Process: Case Study on APOPO," *Solvay Brussels School, Universite Libre de Bruxelles.* http://www.positive-awards .be/IMG/pdf/7-The_social_entrepreneurial_process-_Aurore_FLAMENT.pdf

you must plan well in advance and allow extra time for delays that strategic partners might cause in the time-to-market plan. If time-to-market is the most critical factor in your business's success, you may want to consider doing tasks in-house that could delay the process rather than outsourcing them and being dependent on someone else's time schedule. It is also a good idea to help suppliers and original equipment manufacturers (OEMs) understand that the partnership will be a win-win relationship, so they have a vested interest in seeing it succeed. Contracts should be drawn up with every consultant, OEM, or vendor with whom the company does business so that there will be no confusion about what is expected and needed. During the process, it is vital to stay in touch with outsourced vendors and to be available to answer questions as they arise.

Outsourcing, whether domestically or offshore, can keep the costs of startup down, but you will need to make sure that it's right for your specific business. Keep in mind the following points:

- Never choose an outsourced partner based solely on price. Often the lowest prices carry the highest risk.

- Product development is fueled by customer needs and insights. Keeping your core R&D people close to the customer is essential to ultimately producing a product they will buy.

- Managing product development teams at a distance or, worse yet, scattered around the globe is certainly more difficult than managing a team onsite. Typically, your costs for managing those geographically dispersed team members will go up.

- If you have intellectual property to protect—patents, trade secrets, copyrights—it will be particularly difficult to do so if you have outsourced to regions of the world where piracy is rampant.

A recent study of 150 manufacturing firms by Massachusetts Institute of Technology (MIT) found that in the earliest stages of pre-commercial product development, doing product development close to home made sense as they tested the viability of their products through an iterative process. There was value in taking advantage of the tacit knowledge created by the ecosystem in Massachusetts around MIT. However, the significant demands for capital when it came time to scale up production meant that the majority of the firms needed to seek corporate and government partners because their needs went well beyond the capabilities of most venture capital firms. For example, one biomedical device company required high volumes of injection mold precision plastic, which it had been unsuccessful in acquiring in the United States. The government of Singapore succeeded in attracting the company with an investment of $30 million. The company subsequently moved its manufacturing to Singapore.[25]

Product development is one of the most important tasks that an entrepreneur faces; yet, most entrepreneurs do not give it the attention it deserves. Spending sufficient time on the front end in design and staying close to the product development team in the early stages is critical to producing a successful product with the potential to scale.

New Venture Action Plan

- Validate that your solution is solving a real and compelling problem for customers.

- Find ways to incorporate customer input into the design of your products, processes, and services.

- Lay out the tradeoffs you may have to make.

- Locate independent contractors who can help in the construction of a prototype.

- Determine whether your solution require MVP testing or a complete product.

Questions on Key Issues

1. How has the environment for product development changed in the last decade, and what does this mean to entrepreneurs starting new businesses?
2. What are the principal reasons why new products fail?

3. Suppose you are going to develop and market a new device for tracking calories consumed during the day. What will your product development strategy be, and why?

Experiencing Entrepreneurship

1. Visit an entrepreneurial company that is developing new products. What is the company's product development strategy, and how effective is that strategy? What criteria did you use to measure effectiveness? You may need to use outside sources to confirm what the company tells you.
2. Interview an entrepreneur who uses the lean approach to new product development. How did they test their MVP?

Relevant Case Studies

Case 2 B2P: Micro-Bioinformatics Technology

Case 3 Clean Bee Baby

CHAPTER 7

Protecting Startup Assets

"Every piece of software written today is likely going to infringe on someone else's patent."

—MIGUEL DE ICAZA, FOUNDER, GNOME AND MONO PROJECTS

CHAPTER OBJECTIVES

- Explain the role of intellectual property in a business.
- Discuss how to protect assets with trade secrets.
- Understand how copyrights and trademarks can be protected.
- Explain how to acquire and defend patents.

PROFILE
7.1

PINTEREST V. PINTRIPS: WHO GETS PINNED?

Trademarks are increasing the source of court cases as more and more companies seek to protect the valuable brands they have created. One ongoing case is that of Pinterest, the social media platform that enables users to post pictures on boards that they can share with others, against Pintrips, the tiny travel planning startup. It seems that Pinterest has accused Pintrips of infringing on its trademarked name by incorporating "Pin" in the travel company's name. In addition to infringement, Pinterest filed a claim for false designation of origin, unfair competition, and trademark dilution. As one of the largest social media sites on the Internet, Pinterest has a lot at stake. As a small startup, one might ask why of all the possible arbitrary names out there, Pintrips chose one very similar to a giant in the industry. They did start using it before Pinterest filed for trademarks in August 2012 (Pintrips was founded in 2011), but Pinterest had been using its name for several years (since 2010) under common law trademark rights. The Pin trademark is descriptive of the underlying service, and users seem to associate the "pin" term with the Pinterest site.

Undaunted by the $4 billion Pinterest, Pintrips is arguing that "pin" is a generic word that can't be trademarked; their attorney believes that the Pinterest trademark should be voided. Furthermore, the company claims that Pinterest is doing this solely to bully the smaller company just because they have the money to do it. Proof of that claim lies in the fact that huge companies like Microsoft, Facebook, and Google Maps all use the term "pin" and have not been stalked by Pinterest.

One of the primary arguments in cases like this is "likelihood of confusion." In this case, the two names are similar in some respects and it could appear that Pintrips is associated with Pinterest. Similarly, Pintrip's "Pin" button is arguably similar to Pinterest's highly recognized "Pin It" button. To add to the confusion, one of the biggest categories on Pinterest is travel, and Pinterest contends in its filing, "Pinterest has made a particularly big splash when it comes to travel… users have posted more than 550 million Pins in Pinterest's Travel category to date."

Pinterest is not new to going after infringers. In September 2013, it won a judgment of $7 million in a U.S. district court against a cybersquatter who had bought 100 domains that infringed on Pinterest's trademark: pinterests.com, pimterest.com, and so forth.

And, finally, in the category of "you can't make these things up," Pinterest is facing a European court that found that Pinterest does not hold a valid trademark on its name. That honor goes to a London-based startup called Premium Interest. Stay tuned.

Sources: Pinterest, Inc. v. Pintrips, Inc. *Justia Dockets and Filings*, October 3, 2013, http://dockets.justia.com/docket/california /candce/3:2013cv04608/270704; Gannes L. (September 30, 2013). "Pinterest Wins $7.2 Million and Injunction against Cybersquatter," All Things D. http://allthingsd.com/20130930 /pinterest-wins-7-2m-and-injunction-against-cybersquatter/; Lunden I. (Jan 9, 2014). "Pintrips Files a Motion to Dismiss Pinterest's Trademark Suit, Says Pin Is Too Generic," TechCrunch News. http://techcrunch.com/2014/01/09 /pintrips-pinterest-trademark/.

Whenever entrepreneurs develop a product or service and start a business, they are dealing with assets they will want to protect because those assets are an important part of their overall competitive advantage. Businesses create a lot of knowledge for their owners and that knowledge has value. There are three categories of knowledge as depicted in Figure 7.1. Intellectual capital is arguably the most common form of knowledge; it is essentially tacit knowledge or knowledge acquired in the daily activity of doing business. Tacit knowledge is not codified in any formal way. In fact, you can think of it as what you might learn around the water cooler. In the development of new products and services, tacit knowledge plays an important role because it is knowledge that is not easily transferred to someone else by simply writing it down. That is why when startups seek partners to develop applications off their technology, they often have to transfer the actual person who worked on the technology with the technology for a period of time. This is so that the partner can develop tacit knowledge from working with the technology under the guidance of the person who developed it. Other examples of tacit knowledge include leadership skills and intuition, both of which are difficult to teach and are generally acquired through trial and error, in other words, experience.

Intellectual assets, the second category, are explicit knowledge, that is, knowledge that is documented in a physical form and is easy to communicate and share. A user manual and a customer list are examples of intellectual assets. The last category, intellectual property (IP) is the highest form of protection and the most valuable. It carries exclusive legal rights that offer remedies through the courts for the protection of intangible assets. It is these intellectual property rights that are the focus of this chapter.

Any form of IP protection will require time and money, so it's important to understand the various types of intellectual property available and how they can be applied most effectively.

Product development and intellectual property development are closely intertwined. Chapter 6 looked at the product development process from an entrepreneur's perspective. Chapter 7 explores how to protect the various assets created from that product development process: patents, copyrights, trademarks, and trade secrets.

FIGURE 7.1
Categories of Knowledge

7.1   THE NATURE OF INTELLECTUAL PROPERTY RIGHTS

Developing a new product creates an asset that must be protected. If the product is a unique device, a novel process or service, or other type of proprietary item, it may qualify for intellectual property rights. These are the group of legal rights associated with patents, trademarks, copyrights, and trade secrets. Every business, no matter how small, has intellectual property rights associated with it: a trademark on the name of the business or a product brand, copyrights on advertising design, patents on a device the entrepreneur has invented, or trade secrets such as the company's customer list. In many respects, intellectual property (IP) is similar to personal property in that it can be bought, sold, donated, licensed, or exchanged for something of equal value. Moreover, the owner of IP has the right (and the duty) to defend that property against those who would infringe on the owner's rights or steal it. The most striking difference between IP and other types of physical property is that IP is intangible; that is, it is not described by a physical form.[1] It is, instead, a right under the law. However to exercise that right, you have to be able to put the IP into some physical form. We will discuss this idea further as we talk about specific types of IP.

In the growing knowledge economy, where intellectual assets are often more valuable than physical assets, the recognition and protection of IP rights are gaining increased importance. In 1975, about 83 percent of the S&P 500's market value was in tangible (physical) assets. By 2005, the ratio of tangible to intangible had flipped with intangible assets comprising fully 80 percent of their market value.[2] Given the importance of IP, entrepreneurs need to understand IP rights, not only to protect their property but also to avoid infringing on the rights of others. Strategically, IP rights can provide entrepreneurs a temporary monopoly enabling them to establish their asset in the market and perhaps even create a standard in their industry.

The next four sections provide a brief overview of the various rights under intellectual property law and how they can be used to protect the new venture's inventions and gain a competitive advantage. Figure 7.2 displays the intellectual

FIGURE 7.2
The Intellectual Property Pyramid

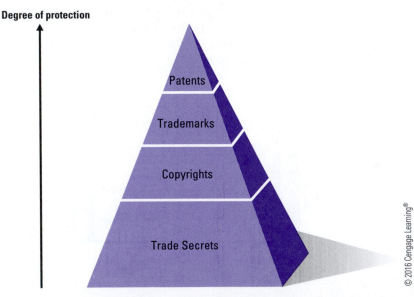

© 2016 Cengage Learning®

property pyramid with the types of protection from weakest to strongest. We start with the foundation for all intellectual property: trade secrets.

7.2 TRADE SECRETS

Under the Uniform Trade Secrets Act, a trade secret consists of a formula, device, idea, process, pattern, or compilation of information that gives the owner a competitive advantage in the marketplace, is novel in the sense that it is not common knowledge, and is kept in a reasonably confidential state. Some examples of trade secrets are survey methods used by professional pollsters, customer lists, source codes for computer chips, customer discounts, and inventions for which no patent will be applied.

Many companies, such as Hewlett-Packard (HP), choose not to patent some of their inventions but rather keep them for internal use only as trade secrets. The reason is that once a patent has been issued, anyone can look up the patent on the United States Patent and Trademark Office's (USPTO's) website and see how the device is made. Some of HP's inventions are devices and processes used in the manufacture of its computers and peripherals, and they give the firm a significant competitive advantage that it would lose if this information got into the hands of competitors. With the patent in hand, the competitor could build that device and use it to improve its own manufacturing processes. As long as the competitor is not selling the device in the market, however, it would require a court to decide whether the firm is actually infringing on HP's patent.

Protecting Trade Secrets

It is vitally important that entrepreneurs and their employees be careful about what they reveal through conversations in public places such as elevators, airports, and restaurants. If you disclose a trade secret during a conversation that is overheard by someone in the vicinity, you may lose your rights to claim that it was a trade secret if the person who heard it acts on the information. It is easy to forget when you're on your cell phone in an airport that others can hear you and some of those "others" could be competitors.

There are no legal means under patent and trademark law to protect trade secrets. The only way to protect them is through confidentiality agreements or contracts. But you do have to take reasonable steps to protect trade secrets. For example, an entrepreneur might have all employees sign an employment contract that specifically details what is considered trade secret information, both at the time the employee is hired and during his or her tenure as an employee. Then, should a current or former employee use or reveal a specified trade secret, the company can pursue legal remedies, such as an injunction or suing for damages.

Frequently, when entrepreneurs are speaking with potential partners or manufacturers, they will ask that those people sign a non-disclosure or confidentiality agreement to put them on notice that what they are about to hear is in fact confidential. However, many people that entrepreneurs deal with will not sign confidentiality agreements because doing so will put them in legal jeopardy. For example, investors and venture capitalists will generally not sign these agreements because they typically see hundreds of new ventures every year and the chances that what you're asking them to keep confidential is something they have never seen before is unlikely. By signing the agreement, they risk breaching it the next time they talk to an entrepreneur with a similar concept. In general, individuals who regularly work with entrepreneurs and inventors will not sign confidentiality agreements; however, they also would not be successful if they went around disclosing private information to others. Their work demands that they protect that information.

If you successfully prosecute someone who has misappropriated your trade secrets, you're entitled to several remedies:[3]

- **Injunctive Relief**. This means that the court will order that the defendant stop violating your trade secret rights.

- **Damages**. The court can order that the defendant pay damages to you for any economic harm you may have suffered. You can receive punitive damages if the court decides that the damage done was willful. Punitive damages can amount to twice actual damages.

- **Attorney's fees**. If the defendant is found to have acted maliciously or willfully, the court may order the defendant to pay the plaintiff's attorney fees. Similarly, if the plaintiff loses the case, the court could determine that the plaintiff acted in "bad faith" when filing the lawsuit; therefore, the plaintiff might have to pay the defendant's attorney fees.

Keep in mind that there is a statute of limitations for filing claims against someone for violating your trade secrets. It varies by state; in California, for example, it is three years. Trade secrets are an important part of your IP arsenal. The more steps you can take to protect them, the longer they will remain a competitive advantage for your company.

7.3   TRADEMARKS

Trademarks have become nearly as popular as patents as intellectual property assets. A trademark is a symbol, logo, word, sound, color, design, or other device that is used to identify a business or a product in commerce. The term *trademark* is regularly used to refer to both trademarks and service marks, which identify services or intangible activities "performed by one person for the benefit of a person or persons other than himself, either for pay or otherwise."[4] Other, less commonly used types of trademarks can be found at the USPTO website.

Here are some examples of trademarked items

Logo: FedEx (www.fedex.com)

Slogan: L'Oreal: "Because you're worth it." (www.loreal.com)

Container shape: Coca-Cola's classic beverage bottle (www.coca-cola.com)

Colors can be trademarked as well as long as they are not functional. In the 1995 Supreme Court case *Qualitex Co. v. Jacobson Products Co.*, 115 S.Ct. 1300 (1995), the Court held that the green-gold color of a dry-cleaning press pad could be trademarked. To protect a color, the applicant must be able to demonstrate that the color has a secondary meaning—that is, that people associate the color with a specific product. For example, pink has been associated with insulation, even though the color has nothing to do with the insulation's function. Colors that are functional in nature cannot be trademarked. For example, Ambrit, a frozen food company that used royal blue packaging, filed suit again Kraft Foods, which had used the same coloring on its frozen desserts. Ambrit believed that since it was the first to use the color royal blue on frozen foods, Kraft was infringing. U.S. courts denied the claim saying that royal blue used on frozen foods is functional, so it could not be monopolized.[5]

A trademark—with certain conditions—has a long life. A business has the exclusive right to a trademark for as long as it is actively using it and as long as it pays the renewal fees. However, if a trademark becomes part of the generic language, as have *aspirin* and *thermos*, it can no longer be trademarked. Furthermore, in the United States a trademark cannot be registered until it is actually in use. The symbol "®" means "registered trademark." Before a trademark is registered, the holder of the trademark should file an intent-to-use application with the USPTO and place ™ (or SM for services) after the name until the trademark has been registered. This is an important point, because trademarks cannot be stockpiled and then sold to potential users. They must be in use in the market to be protected.

Marks that cannot be trademarked include:

- Anything immoral or deceptive
- Anything that uses official symbols of the United States or any state or municipality, such as the flag
- Anything that uses a person's name or likeness without permission

Trademark Infringement

Like patents and trade secrets, trademarks can suffer from infringement, counterfeiting, or misappropriation. Infringement is found if a mark is likely to cause confusion with a trademark already existing in the marketplace. This is actually the most common reason that trademarks are denied. However, identical marks can exist where there is no relationship between the types of goods or services being offered. So, for example, Lynda is a popular software training service. Now suppose you wanted to open up a yoga studio with the name Lynda. You would probably be able to trademark your company's name because the services being provided are not likely to ever come into contact with the software training service.

One of the keys to protecting your trademark is to make sure that it is "inherently distinctive" and that it "identifies the source of goods that it is applied to." When it is distinctive and clearly associated with your brand, you will have an easier time getting the trademark and defending it against infringers. A New Jersey snack company, Princeton Vanguard LLC, introduced its product, Pretzel Crisps, to the market in 2004 in head-to-head competition with giant

Frito-Lay Inc. With many more resources than the tiny Princeton, Frito-Lay challenged the proposed trademark for pretzel crisps claiming that it was as common as "milk chocolate bar." In the end, the Trademark Trial and Appeal Board ruled that the name is generic and cannot be registered as a trademark, saying that "the law does not permit anyone to obtain a complete monopoly on the use of a descriptive or generic term simply by grabbing it first."[6]

Trademarks are also subject to dilution, which occurs when the value of the mark is substantially reduced through competition or through the likelihood of confusion from another mark. For example, American Express was able to prove that it suffered dilution when a limousine service used the American Express trademark for its business, even though the two companies were in different industries.[7] In 2006, the Trademark Dilution Revision Act was signed into law to provide relief to owners of famous trademarks whose marks had been tarnished by third-party marks. The act says that the injured party can seek injunctive relief and monetary damages against a third party that adopts a trademark that will cause dilution of the famous mark even though it is a non-competing use. It is difficult to say what the impact of the legislation will be until there are court rulings.

The deliberate copying of a mark (counterfeiting) is a particular form of infringement subject to civil and criminal penalties. An example would be a company producing the equivalent of your product and putting it in a box with your logo and branding on it. Counterfeiting is a growing problem, so you need to think about protecting your trademarks globally, and you need to register your marks very early in the development of your business and your brand. Even established companies such as Starbucks and Apple have made the mistake of waiting too long to seek trademark protection in China only to find that their trademarks had already been taken by other entities. In fact, the entities that owned the trademarks in China could actually claim that Starbucks or Apple was infringing on their trademarks.[8] First to file gets the trademark rights in China, so you need to file early and take advantage of the three years you have to actually use the mark in China.

Entrepreneurs also need to think about how to avoid infringing on trademarks internationally. For example, Amazon's U.K. subsidiary was found to have infringed on the trademark of Lush Retail Ltd, a cosmetic company that does not sell through Amazon, when it redirected customer searches for "lush" to other products. Amazon had also purchased Google AdWords that included the word *lush*, so when a Lush ad popped up on a consumer's search and they clicked on it thinking they were going to the Lush site, they were instead rerouted to competing products on the Amazon site.[9]

Registering a Trademark or Service Mark

Securing a trademark is a fairly complex process and not all applications result in a registration, so it is wise to employ the services of an attorney. Although registration is not required, entrepreneurs should register their trademarks and service marks to enjoy enhanced rights. Without registration you have what are known as "common-law" rights, which are limited, most often to specific geographic areas. Registering your mark gives you national scope to enforce your trademark for the goods and services you have identified. By registering your mark, it becomes part of the USPTO online database so that others can find it before they choose to employ a mark that is already in use. Registration also lets you record your mark with the U.S. Customs and Border Protection agency to prevent counterfeit reproductions of your products from entering the United States. Moreover, your U.S. registration is helpful when you apply for registration in a foreign country.

Before filing an application and to avoid the likelihood of confusion problem, you should conduct a search of existing trademarks. You can find the Trademark Electronic Search System (TESS) at the USPTO.gov site. Of course, this database covers only federally registered marks. Other sources you can check are the Internet and business name databases.

When choosing your mark, pick something that is not common or closely descriptive of your product or service. While that approach may run counter to the common notion that your brand ought to be related to what you're selling, these types of marks are relatively weak and costly to protect. Today companies often go for fanciful or arbitrary marks because they are distinctive and easier to protect. A fanciful mark is made up and probably can't be found in the dictionary, such as Cisco, Airbnb, and Microsoft. Arbitrary marks are words you can find in the dictionary but they're used in a different context than the word implies. The prime examples are Apple for the computer company and Gap for the clothing company.

Entrepreneurs do business in a global marketplace, so when choosing a mark, it's wise to test its translation in the languages of the countries where you want to protect that mark. A classic example of a poor mark happened when Kentucky Fried Chicken (now branded as KFC) expanded into China and wanted to use its trademarked phrase "Finger Lickin' Good." Unfortunately, that phrase translated into Chinese as "Eat your fingers off," which certainly provided a much less appealing image.

As part of your application, you'll be asked to choose the categories of products and services where you want to protect your mark. That means you should have developed a roadmap for the kinds of products and services you will add as your company grows. You will pay a fee for each category you choose, so it's important to have a plan.

Picking marks that define your company and your brand is one of the most critical decisions you make when you start a business. You will need to choose wisely because you will live with that decision for a long time.

7.4   COPYRIGHTS

Copyrights protect original works of authors, composers, screenwriters, and computer programmers. A copyright does not protect the idea itself but only the form in which it appears, which cannot be copied without the express permission of the copyright holder. For example, a computer programmer can copyright the written program for a particular type of productivity app, say, a calorie counter, but cannot copyright the idea of calorie counting. This is why several companies can produce similar apps without violating a copyright. What they really are protecting is the unique programming code of their software and the way it appears on a screen. The First Sale Doctrine [Section 106 of the 1976 Copyright Act] grants a copyright owner six rights: reproduction, preparation of derivative works, distribution, public performance, public display, and digital transmission performance.[10] Note that all of these rights protect ideas that are expressed in some tangible or physical form.

Under the Copyright Extension Act of 1998, a copyright lasts for the life of the holder plus 70 years, after which the copyrighted material goes into public domain. Works for hire and works published anonymously now have copyrights of 95 years from the date of publication.

There is no question that copyright law is undergoing its most strenuous test in the knowledge economy. With the proliferation of digital content comes the difficult task of finding ways to protect all the intellectual property that is being accessed, duplicated, transmitted, and published in digital form. One of the areas of contention is the Doctrine of Fair Use, which has been codified in Section 107 of the copyright law. This section asserts that reproduction of a copyrighted work is "fair" when it is done for purposes such as criticism, comment, news reporting, teaching, scholarship, and research. There is no clear distinction between fair use and infringement; even acknowledging the source may not be sufficient, so the safest course is to secure permission from the original copyright holder if you want to use the material for commercial purposes

7.4a   The Digital Millennium Copyright Act

One of the problems associated with delivering products over the Internet is the ease with which a person can infringe on another's rights. In October 1998, President Clinton signed into law the Digital Millennium Copyright Act (DMCA), which prohibits the falsification, alteration, or removal of copyright management data on digital copies. In other words, it made it a crime to circumvent an encrypted work without authorization. The law also made it illegal to manufacture and distribute products that facilitate the circumvention of encrypted work.

The DMCA does contain a safe harbor clause to protect Internet service providers from monetary damages if they unknowingly infringe on someone's rights, either by transmitting or storing infringing material or by linking users to websites containing infringing material. This law clears the way to licensing intellectual property for a fee over the Internet. However, some Internet retailers may find that they don't meet the qualifications for the safe haven. In 2014, CafePress (www.cafepress.com), an online retailer, found itself responsible for $6,320 of products posted on its site that infringed on others' copyrights. CafePress lets its customers upload their own images for printing on items such as T-shirts and mugs. They can then sell these items through a virtual store that they establish on the CafePress site. CafePress also prints these items in its own facility, and because CafePress actually determines the prices and pays a royalty to its customers, the courts determined that the company was not a service provider under the meaning of the law.[11] Thus, it was held liable for the infringing products.

7.4b   Obtaining Copyright Protection

To qualify for federal copyright protection, the work must be in a fixed and tangible form—that is, someone must be able to see or hear it. The law does not require that a copyright holder provide notice to a potential infringer; however, registering the copyright at the Copyright Office of the Library of Congress in Washington, DC, will ensure full protection under the law by creating a document trail. The notice on the copyrighted material should use the word *copyright* or the symbol © and should provide the year and the complete name of the person responsible for the work, as in © 2014 Stephen Barry.

Fortunately, copyright protection laws are fairly consistent across countries because of a number of international copyright treaties, the most important of which is the Berne Convention. Under this treaty, which includes more than 100 nations, a country must give copyright protection to authors who are nationals of any member country for at least the life of the author plus 50 years.

With the ease of digital distribution, entrepreneurs today are challenged in their efforts to protect their original creations. When you discover a case of infringement, it's important to put the party on notice with a cease and desist letter or take stronger action if the infringement will damage your company.

7.5   PATENTS

If a new venture opportunity relies on a product or device of some sort, it is especially important that entrepreneurs investigate applying for a patent, which is the primary means of protecting an original invention. A patent gives the patent holder the right to defend the patent against others who would attempt to manufacture, use, or sell the invention during the period of the patent, which for most patents is 20 years from the date of application. In other words, the right given by the Patent Office is exclusionary. The holder can "exclude others from making, using, offering for sale, or selling" the invention in the United States.[12] At the end of the patent life, the invention is placed in public domain, which means that anyone can use any aspect of the device the inventor created without paying royalties to the inventor.

Today, although most inventors work in the research departments of large corporations and 80 percent of all patents come from large companies, the basic legal tenets of patent law still protect the interests of the independent inventor. And in cases where large corporations have infringed on those interests, the courts have generally sided with the independent inventor. In a further effort to support the small inventor, the Patent Office created the Office of the Independent Inventor to handle the 20 percent of patents submitted by these inventors.

One of the most common questions entrepreneurs have is "how do I know whether or not to patent my invention?" Answering positively to the following questions may suggest a need for patents because the time and cost involved in bringing this type of invention to market means that you will need a temporary monopoly to recoup those costs and a patent may provide that:

- Does the invention solve a significant problem and change the way things are done?
- Does the invention fall under FDA regulations?
- Will the invention achieve revenues that exceed the potential cost of patent enforcement?
- Is there a plan to license?

On the other hand, if the field of use for the technology or product is changing rapidly, it may not make sense to spend the time and money to patent because the patent will outlive its economic life. Economic life (the ability to generate revenue) is a critical factor in the decision to patent. Today, patents on many inventions outlive their economic life because the pace of innovation results in new inventions that may obsolete or reduce the value of an existing invention long before its patent runs out. On the other hand, for inventions that require years of development and have regulatory hurdles to overcome, filing for patents is essential to protect the ultimate commercial opportunity.

7.5a   Is the Invention Patentable?

Before filing for a patent on an invention that you believe to be unique, you should consider the USPTO's four basic criteria that the invention must meet before it can be considered for a patent.

The invention must fit into one of five classes established by Congress:

1. Machine or something with moving parts or circuitry (fax, rocket, photocopier, laser, electronic circuit)
2. Process or method for producing a useful and tangible result (chemical reaction, method for producing products, business method)
3. Article of manufacture (furniture, transistor, diskette, toy)
4. Composition of matter (gasoline, food additive, drug, genetically altered life form)
5. A new use or improvement for one of the above that does not infringe on the patents associated with them.

The Supreme Court of the United States has stated that "anything under the sun that is made by man" falls into the statutory subject matter (*Diamond v. Chakrabarty*, 1980).[13] With this definition, it may appear that anything can receive a patent, but in fact, there are some exclusions. Laws and phenomena of nature, naturally occurring substances, abstract mathematical formulas, and mere ideas are not eligible to be patented. However, alterations to something found in nature, such as genetically enhanced corn, can be considered for a patent.

The invention must have utility; in other words, it must be useful:

Utility is not usually a problem unless the invention is an unsafe drug or something purely "whimsical," although the USPTO has been known to issue patents on some fairly strange inventions, such as a laser beam to motivate cats to exercise (Patent No. 5,443,036, August 22, 1995). However, the utility of the device must be a reality, not merely speculation, and it must be described in the patent application.

The invention must not contain prior art; that is, it must be new or novel in some important way:

Prior art is knowledge that is publicly available or was published prior to the date of the invention—that is, before the filing of the patent application. This means that an invention can't be patented if it was known or used by others, patented, or described in a printed publication before a patent was applied for. Accordingly, it is important to document everything that is done during the creation of the invention. In addition, the invention must not have become public or made available for sale more than one year prior to the inventor's filing the patent application. This rule is meant to ensure that the invention is still novel at the time of application. Many actions that entrepreneurs take with their inventions could actually create prior art and prevent them from receiving a patent. For example, if you demonstrate your invention in public so that people can identify specific features, it counts as a disclosure. If you do not file for a patent within a year or someone files ahead of you for the same patent, you may lose your right to file. Even works of fiction can be considered prior art if they are enabling; in other words, they permit someone to build the invention.

Novelty consists of physical differences, new combinations of components, or new uses. There are two levels of challenge to novelty: statutory and anticipatory. If the invention is published or used in an unconcealed manner either in the United States or in another country more than one year prior to the date of application, the inventor is statutorily barred from seeking a patent. Furthermore, if the patent is substantially similar to an existing patent, the inventor may not seek a patent because, in this case, the patent was anticipated.

The invention must not be obvious to someone with ordinary skills in the field:

This is a tricky criterion, but it has been further explained by the USPTO as meaning that the invention must contain "new and unexpected results." That is, the invention should not be the next logical step for someone knowledgeable in the field. Obviousness is one of the most common reasons why patent applications are rejected.

Obviousness, however, did not keep Ron Lando from securing a patent on his CliC eyewear (www.clicgoggles.com). The "unique" aspect of his eyewear is that instead of hooking over the ears, the glasses wrap around the wearer's head and snap together between the lenses with a tiny but powerful neodymium magnet. The benefit? When you unhook them, they simply drop around the your neck so they don't get lost. Lando knows that he will face copycats—it's a simple product, but he is counting on his brand and his strategy to supplement his patent protection.[14]

7.5b Patent Types

If all the requirements for patentability have been met, then the type of patent most appropriate for the invention should be considered. There are three major categories of patents: utility patents, design patents, and plant patents.

■ **Utility patents:** Utility patents are the most common type of patent. They protect the functional part of machines or processes. Some examples are toys, film processing, protective coatings, tools, and cleaning implements. Software qualifies for patent protection if it produces a useful and tangible result. For example, the USPTO will not issue a utility patent on a mathematical formula used in space navigation, but it may on software that translates equations and makes a rocket take off.[15] (Copyrights, discussed previously, are commonly used for software programs that don't qualify for a patent.) A utility patent is valid for 20 years from the date of application.

■ **Design patents:** Design patents protect new, original ornamental designs for manufactured articles. A design patent protects only the appearance of an article, not its structure or utilitarian features. The design must be nonfunctional and part of the tangible item for which it is designed. It cannot be hidden or offensive or simulate a well-known or naturally occurring object or person. Some examples of items that can receive design patents are gilding, an item of apparel, and jewelry. Inventors should be aware that although design patents are relatively easy to obtain, they are very hard to protect. It is not difficult to modify a design patent without infringing on the original patent. Design patents are valid for 14 years from the date of issuance.

■ **Plant Patents:** This patent is granted to someone who invents or asexually reproduces a new variety of plant. Recall that plants occurring naturally cannot be patented. A plant patent expires 20 years from the filing date of the application.

■ **Gene or Biological Patents**: You cannot patent naturally occurring DNA segments, that is, genes extracted from human, animal, and plant cells. However, you can patent edited forms of genes not found in nature.

Business method is actually a generic term to describe a variety of process claims, and as of this writing, the courts have not yet defined what differentiates a business method claim from a process claim. Thus business method claims are treated like any other process claim.[16] In general, business method applications are related to electronic commerce, graphical user interfaces, security, computer networks, and computer architecture. On March 29, 2000, the Patent Office issued a statement that the business method patent will cover only fundamentally different ways of doing business and that the embedded process must produce a useful, tangible, and concrete result.[17] The Supreme Court's most recent ruling in *Bilski v. Kappos* (Supreme Court 2010)(08-964) affirmed the unpatentability of "abstract ideas," but left open the possibility for the continuation of business method patents.

Provisional or Non-provisional?

A provisional patent is a way for inventors to undertake a first patent filing in the United States at a lower cost than a formal patent application. Legally, it permits the inventor to use the term *patent pending*, and is designed to protect small inventors while they speak with manufacturers about producing the invention. A provisional patent also puts U.S. applicants on par with international applicants under the General Agreement on Tariffs and Trade (GATT) Uruguay Round Agreements (see the discussion in the section on international patents). The provisional patent does not, however, take the place of a non-provisional patent application, which is discussed next.

The term of the provisional patent is 12 months from the date of filing, and it cannot be extended. This means that the inventor must file a non-provisional (formal) patent application during that period. The 12-month period does not count toward the 20-year term for a non-provisional patent. Because the 20-year clock starts with the filing of the formal patent application, the provisional patent effectively extends patent protection by 1 year. The invention disclosure in the provisional patent application should clearly and completely describe the invention so that someone with knowledge of the invention could make and use it. If an earlier provisional date of application-provisional application is not filed within the 12-month period, the provisional application is considered abandoned, and the entrepreneur loses the ability to claim the earlier provisional date of application as the date of invention.

The primary advantages of filing a provisional patent application are the lower initial cost of filing, postponing expensive examination costs, and adding one year to the legal life of the patent. The America Invents Act (AIA) has given provisional patents another advantage: It is a quick and inexpensive way to disclose an invention early to meet the first-to-file requirements of the AIA, which is discussed in a later section. A provisional patent does have some disadvantages, however. First and foremost, it does not result in a patent and it does start the one-year clock on filing for a non-provisional patent. Second, it also starts the one-year clock on filing foreign applications.

The *non-provisional patent application* is required for any patent to issue, and it lasts for 20 years from the date of filing. The patent application contains a complete description of the invention, what it does, how it is uniquely different from anything currently existing (including prior art), and its scope. It also includes detailed drawings, explanations, and engineering specifications such that a person of ordinary skill in the same field could build the invention from the information provided.

The claims section of the application specifies the novel parts of the invention on which the inventor wants patents and must include at least one claim that attests to its novelty, utility, and nonobviousness. The claim serves to define the scope of patent protection; whether the USPTO grants the patent is largely determined by the wording of the claims. The claims must be specific enough to demonstrate the invention's uniqueness but broad enough to make it difficult for others to circumvent the patent—that is, to modify the invention slightly without violating the patent and then duplicate the product.

For example, suppose you attempt to patent a new type of rapid prototyping device. If the patent application defines the invention for use in prototyping of machine components, that would be a narrow definition. Another inventor could conceivably patent the same invention for a new use, such as creating artificial bone, for example. That's why it is important to define the claims as broadly as possible to include as many potential applications as can be identified. Drafting a claim is an art, so it's a good idea to hire an intellectual property attorney to craft the patent application.

The patent process also requires that the invention be reduced to practice to prove that it actually works in the way it was intended. This does not mean that you must actually construct the invention in a physical form. For purposes of the patent application, the detailed description of the invention such that someone could build it is considered "constructive" reduction to practice.

The process for applying for any of these patents is well defined by the USPTO and is discussed briefly in the next section.

7.5c   The Patent Process

Although the USPTO has described the process clearly on its website (www.uspto .gov), it is always a good idea to seek the counsel of an intellectual property attorney when considering filing a patent. An attorney who specializes in intellectual property can increase the chances of moving successfully through the USPTO application process. Figure 7.3 depicts the patent process for a utility patent. It is very similar for other types of patents. What is important to note is that communicating effectively with the patent examiner assigned to your application is critical to successfully traversing the hurdles in the process. Most patent applications are denied on the first pass. A good patent attorney can help reduce the number of times you have to interact with the patent office and increase your chances of actually securing a patent.

Once it has received the application, the USPTO will conduct a search of its patent records for prior art. The Patent Office then contacts the inventor to either accept or deny the application claims and, in the case of denial, gives the inventor a period of time to appeal or modify the claim. It is not uncommon for the original claims to be rejected in their entirety by the USPTO, usually due to the existence of prior art, but often because of lack of non-obviousness. It will then be the job of the inventor's attorney to rewrite the claims and resubmit the revised application for another review.

If and when the Patent Office accepts the modified claims, it issues a notice of allowance. Then all the inventor has to do is pay the required fees and wait for the patent to be issued. The inventor may market and sell the product during this period but must clearly label it "patent pending." Most patent applications will be published 18 months after the filing date of the application, but entrepreneurs should always be prepared for it to take longer. The USPTO maintains all patent applications in the strictest confidence until the patent is issued or the application is published. Once the patent has been issued, the original application and the patent itself become public record.

If the patent examiner rejects the modified claims again, the inventor has the right to appeal to a Board of Patent Appeals within the Patent Office. Failing to find agreement at this point, the inventor may appeal to the U.S. Court of Appeals for the Federal Circuit. This appeals process may take years.

One thing that many inventors fail to realize is that there are maintenance fees on patents to keep them in force. These fees are paid to the USPTO 3½, 7½, and 11½ years from the date the patent is granted. Failure to pay these fees can result in expiration of the patent. Entrepreneurs should check with the USPTO to determine if their company qualifies for Small Entity Status, which may lower their maintenance fees.

In addition, under the AIA there are many processes that can take place after your patent has been issued. These include the following[18]:

- **Ex Parte Reexamination**: Any individual can request that a patent be reexamined in light of new evidence to suggest that it may be invalid. Unfortunately, infringers often use these reexaminations as tactics to delay costly court proceedings when they've been accused of infringing on a patent.

- **Supplementary Examination**: If you receive a patent, you can request this type of examination for specific cases where you want to make sure that, for example, prior art not documented in the patent will not affect any sales of your product.

- **Inter Partes Review and Post-Grant Review**: These reviews come from third parties with an interest in challenging the validity of the patent and, like the ex parte reexamination, they are frequently used as a tactic to delay lawsuits. The patent office has been known to make mistakes such as not documenting all the prior art either because it didn't have enough information or simply making a bad decision.

Effects of the America Invents Act

Historically, there were important differences between international and U.S. procedures in the areas of first-to-file and novelty.[19] The European Patent Convention (EPC) grants patent rights to the first person to file for the patent, whether or not that person is the original inventor. By contrast, in the United States, only the original inventor had the first right to file an application. However, as of March 2013, the United States changed its filing system from first-to-invent to first-to-file to bring it into line with the rest of world. This means that rather than emphasizing the date of invention, it emphasizes the date the application was filed by the inventor. So, if two people unbeknownst to each other were working on the same invention, the inventor who filed first would have priority whether or not his invention was the earlier of the two. Furthermore, it means that it's now critical to disclose and file much earlier in the development process or risk losing out to another inventor. This could have ramifications for independent inventors who typically don't have the resources to file for a patent at the time of their discovery. Many other changes could affect the potential for infringement and invalidation of your patent, so it's important to work closely with a good patent attorney.

FIGURE 7.3
The Utility Patent Process

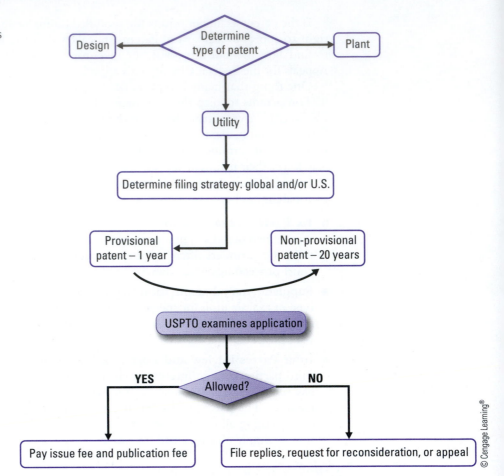

Filing for Foreign Patents

After determining which type of patent to file, you must determine the *filing strategy*, which means that you must decide if you need international patents or simply a U.S. patent. It is important to remember that the patent rights granted to an individual in the United States extend only to the borders of the United States. They have no effect in any foreign country, which means that someone could manufacture and sell your product in another country and you won't be able to do anything about it. However, if you file an application overseas within one year of filing in the United States, your application will be treated as if it had been in force from the original date of filing in the United States. Because every country has different laws regarding intellectual property, patent attorneys face a real challenge when helping their clients apply for or defend foreign patents. Furthermore, most countries require that the invention be manufactured in the country within three years of the issuance of the foreign patent. In 1983, the Trilateral Co-operation was established between the European Patent Office (EPO), the Japan Patent Office (JPO), and the

USPTO to process patent applications filed worldwide. The Patent Cooperation Treaty (PCT) allows inventors in any nation that signed on to the treaty
to file a single international patent application covering all the countries under
the treaty. That application is then subjected to an international search to determine the probability of a patent being issued. Subsequent to a positive finding,
the applicant can begin to pursue the grant of patents directly from the countries or regions desired.

When considering foreign patents, be sure to consult an intellectual property
attorney who specializes in this area. Because of the high cost and effort involved in obtaining foreign patents, it is important to determine whether a reasonable profit can be made from them. Often, it's more valuable to seek solid
strategic alliances in other countries, thus obtaining good distribution channels
through which to export products, than to spend the time and money seeking
patents in every country in which the entrepreneur will do business. Advice
from a knowledgeable attorney can make this decision easier.

7.5d   Patent Infringement

On a sleepless night in 1957, Gordon Gould conceived the idea for the laser.
He wrote down all his thoughts, sketched the design and its components, and
forecasted future uses. He had a notary witness, sign, and date his notebook
in anticipation of applying for intellectual property protection in the form of
a patent. But then he made a critical mistake. Thinking that he had to build
a working model of the laser before filing for a patent, he went to work for
Technical Research Group Inc. (TRG) to begin the development of laser applications. In the meantime, a pair of scientists, Charles Townes and Arthur
Schawlow, filed for a patent on the optical maser (it used microwave energy
instead of light, as Gould's did), and it would come to be considered the true
laser patent for many years. Gould spent the next 30 years of his life battling the
USPTO before he could finally lay claim to one of the most important inventions of all time. His laser applications are used in 80 percent of the industrial,
commercial, and medical applications of lasers. Had Gordon Gould understood
the patent process and secured an intellectual property attorney early on, he
might have saved himself years of struggle.

Once issued, a patent is a powerful document that gives the holder the right
to enforce the patent in federal court against any infringers. If such a lawsuit
is successful, the court may issue an injunction preventing the infringer from
making any further use of the invention and award the patent holder a reasonable royalty from the infringer; if the infringer refuses to pay, the patent holder
can enjoin or close down the infringer's operation. Alternatively, the court may
mediate an agreement between the parties under which the infringing party
will pay royalties to the patent holder in exchange for permission to use the
patented invention.

Infringement of patent rights occurs when someone other than the inventor (patent holder) or licensee makes and sells a product that contains every
one of the elements of a claim. The Patent Office also protects inventors from
infringers who would violate a patent by making small, insignificant changes in

the claims. This policy is called the *doctrine of equivalents*. If, for example, an inventor had a patent on a three-legged wooden chair, and the infringer produced and distributed the exact same chair but gave it three metal legs, that person would be violating the inventor's patent under the doctrine of equivalents. Patent infringement actions are costly and difficult to prosecute. Many times, the alleged infringer will defend himself or herself by attempting to prove that the patent is invalid—that is, that the USPTO mistakenly issued the patent.

With infringement cases, the courts tend to favor the inventor and may issue injunctions against alleged infringers even before the case goes to trial. If the courts determine that infringement was willful, they can triple the damages.

Patent Trolls

While it is clear that patents are important to operating companies, they are also of interest to investors and others who see value in the asset and the ability to create an arbitrage situation. Some of those interested in patents as an asset class are non-practicing entities (NPEs) or "patent trolls." NPEs are companies established for the sole purpose of finding infringers and extracting payments under the threat of litigation. Many large companies are now creating separate entities to hold patents and force companies to license their technology.

Of the 6,092 patents lawsuits filed in 2013, the majority were filed by a small number of entities, most of whom were patent trolls. That was an increase of 12.4 percent over 2012.[20] Sometimes companies don't fight the trolls; they simply sell their patents to them. For example Digimarc Corp., a digital watermarking company, sold to Intellectual Ventures, an NPE, the right to license and market its patents in exchange for $36 million and 20 percent of the profits.[21] The trolls see their role as "leveling the playing field" for the small companies that can't protect themselves from lawsuits. However, for entrepreneurs with limited resources, the lawsuits that these NPEs file can quickly drain a company's bank account. The biggest patent trolls include Acacia Technologies, whose business model is to encourage inventors and patent holders to hire them to license those patents and then split the royalties; Round Rock Research LLC, founded by a successful patent litigator; and Intellectual Ventures, the largest NPE by far with nearly 60,000 patents.

7.5e   Intellectual Property Strategy

Understanding what you need to protect and with what type of protection is half the battle: knowing *when* to protect and enforce IP is critical to creating an effective long-term strategy for your business. In general, patents are the most time sensitive of all the forms of IP, especially now that the United States has adopted the first-to-file convention. The longer an entrepreneur waits to file for protection, the greater the chance that his or her invention will no longer be considered novel. In some countries, the EU is one example, if you publicly

GLOBAL INSIGHTS

Intellectual Property Is on China's Radar

While not yet close to the United States in its protection of intellectual property rights, Chinese officials are beginning to recognize that if they want their own inventions protected, they will need to protect all inventions from infringement. The 2008 National IPR Strategy was designed to "improve the legal frameworks and channels through which companies can protect their IPR." With that in mind, the government established administrative channels to help businesses keep costs down and speed up the process of filing and adjudicating infringement claims. Businesses can bypass the painfully slow court system and choose among several agencies depending on the nature of their IP. Where criminality is involved, the company can go to the public security bureau, which carries out an investigation. Once the investigation is complete, the agency issues a ruling. If it finds infringement, the infringer is forced to stop producing the infringing goods, those goods are confiscated, and a fine is levied. If either of the parties is unhappy with the verdict of the administrator, they can take their case to the Supreme People's Court, which has the final say.

For all these improvements in defending intellectual property against infringers, the path is still not smooth. Counterfeiting networks in China are large and complex involving "local protectionism," which makes it difficult for investigators to get information. Nevertheless, many people in China understand that innovation is important to their economy and must be protected if it is to thrive. In 2014, China's largest search platform, Baidu, was labeled a violator of copyrighted videos and fined for infringement, one of several such cases that will slowly change the IP landscape in the country.

Source: Brzeski P. (January 1, 2014). "Chinese Search Giant Baidu Fined for Copyright Infringement," *The Hollywood Reporter*. http://www.hollywoodreporter.com/news/chinese -search-giant-baidu-fined-668155; Ong, Ryan. (March 1, 2009). "Tackling Intellectual Property Infringement in China," *China Business Review*. http://www.chinabusinessreview .com/tackling-intellectual-property-infringement-in-china/.

disclose your invention, you cannot file for a patent. There is no grace period as there is in the United States.

A similar situation exists with trademarks where the first person to file for a trademark holds the presumptive legal right to keep others from using a mark that would be confusing. In fact, with "intent-to-use" applications, individuals or companies can file to register a trademark before they have actually begun to use it in the marketplace. That means that where disputes arise, the party with the earliest filing date on their intent-to-use application will likely see the dispute resolved in their favor.

It is not just at filing for IP protection that timing plays a critical role. Timing comes into play in paying the required renewal fees in every country in which you have protection; it also affects how much time you have to defend your patent claims when competitors challenge them. In fact, if you delay taking action too long, you may lose your rights to enforce your IP.[22]

For entrepreneurs, securing IP is only part of what needs to be done during product development and beyond. Aligning your IP strategy with your business strategy is critical because filing for IP protection is generally not a onetime event. It is usually part of an ongoing competitive strategy, particularly in industries that spend a lot of money on product development. In addition, it is far more common today that the products entrepreneurs produce will involve not only their own inventions but inventions from other companies. For example, in the mobile device industry it is rare that one company will hold the patents on all the components of the device. It is far more common that an entrepreneur will have to execute license agreements with several companies to enable their technology.

In the world of patents, research has found that there are three major patent strategies that align well with particular business models: proprietary, defensive, and leveraging strategies.[23] In the proprietary strategy, your principal goal is to defend your market position by acquiring the patents you need to cover the opportunity and be able to defend your rights. In this strategy, licensing another company's patents would only happen if there were no other choice. This is an expensive strategy because it requires owning all the proprietary technology around a solution and defending it.

The defensive strategy gives you the freedom to use design rather than patents to achieve a competitive advantage. So you may design around existing patents or develop a portfolio of patents to employ as bargaining chips with other companies in cross-licensing agreements.

The leveraging strategy is useful when you don't seek freedom to operate (freedom from infringement on others, usually outside the geographical jurisdiction of an existing patent) or when having proprietary protections are not critical. In this case, patents are typically licensed for cash or to extract needed concessions from other companies.

The bottom line is that you must think strategically about why you need IP and how you can use it most effectively to create a competitive advantage over the life of your company.

New Venture Action Plan

- Identify intellectual property rights appropriate to your business concept.
- Get referrals for IP attorneys.
- Develop a product/technology roadmap and IP strategy.

Questions on Key Issues

1. What type of knowledge has legal rights associated with it and what are those rights?
2. What are three ways you can maintain your trade secrets confidential?
3. What actions can you take that will cause you to infringe another company's trademarks?
4. What types of assets in your business might you want to protect with copyrights?
5. Under what circumstances would you decide to patent your new technology?

Experiencing Entrepreneurship

1. Visit the U.S. Patent Office at www.uspto.gov .Pick a patented product that interests you and contact the inventor to determine whether the patent has ever been commercialized. If so, in what ways? If not, can the inventor provide a reason? What can you conclude about the potential for this patent?
2. Interview an entrepreneur who is producing a product. What is their IP strategy? What forms of IP are they using to protect their assets?

Relevant Case Studies

Case 2 B2P: Micro-Bioinformatics Technology

Case 4 Command Audio

CHAPTER 8

Building the Founding Team

"Coming together is a beginning. Keeping together is progress. Working together is success."

—HENRY FORD

CHAPTER OBJECTIVES

- Explain how to effectively build a founding team.
- Understand what causes teams to fail.
- Discuss the importance of roles, responsibilities, and rewards.
- Explain how boards of directors work in a private company.
- Compare and contrast the pros and cons of outsourcing with independent contractors versus hiring employees.

PROFILE
8.1

FANDEAVOR

Who said you can't move from management positions at an online retailer of shoes to founding a company dedicated to satisfying the cravings of die-hard sports fans? While there isn't a clear connection between the two, there actually is a similarity in the types of people who make up the customer base. You see Tom Ellingson and Dean Curtis are former employees of online shoe giant Zappos who left their full-time jobs in management to launch Fandeavor, a startup dedicated to providing sports fans with the types of sports experiences that only corporate sponsors typically get. Zappos caters to women who love shoes and are impulsive buyers; Fandeavor caters to sports fans who will do anything to get closer to their favorite teams and athletes.

Fandeavor launched in 2012 with $575,000 in seed funding from the co-founders' former boss and Zappos founder, Tony Hsieh, through his investment fund: VegasTechFund. The launch strategy was to partner with colleges and sports teams to create, package, and sell unique experiences for fans. Fans could peruse the Fandeavor site to see what was available and then either bid on experiences, much like eBay's auction, or purchase the experiences at preset prices. Initially the experiences ranged in price from $179 for a pregame tour for two to $500 for a pick-up game at a team's arena with locker room passes and an autographed basketball. The value proposition for the schools and their teams was that they could focus on the sports and Fandeavor would take care of their fans.

Naturally, Ellingson and Curtis are die-hard sports fans themselves. During their time at Zappos, Ellingson worked as the Head of Business Development and Curtis was an Engineering Manager. Zappos is a company that is obsessed with the customer experience, providing the best customer service possible at all the touch points in the buying process. Their primary mission is to make buying shoes as easy, convenient, and fun as possible. So it's no wonder that Ellingson and Curtis were able to recognize an opportunity to take that obsession with the customer experience to rabid sports fans like themselves. They believed that the combination of their passion for sports and their experience working together to create customer experiences at Zappos was a winning formula for a founding team.

Before leaving Zappos, the duo decided to test their concept for Fandeavor at the University of Nevada, Las Vegas (UNLV), where they had a basketball connection. They managed to set up a basic website with information about the experiences they were offering, which included signed basketballs, sports gear, box suites, and the opportunity to present the game ball at mid court. UNLV promoted the site through its fan page on Facebook, and the fan experiences sold out almost immediately. Then they started tracking what fans were most interested in so they could offer more of those types of experiences. But tracking interest also told them that fans also wanted to have them manage the logistics around those game experiences. For example, if Fandeavor was offering a unique experience at the World Cup, fans wanted the company to also suggest deals on hotels and travel to complete the package. Ellingson and Curtis began curating existing travel packages and offering the best alongside their sports experiences. Eventually, they became a one-stop shop for a complete sports experience. In 2014, they promoted the World Cup in Brazil and fans were able to customize their experience by choosing which matches they wanted to attend, selecting among 3-, 4-, and 5-star hotel packages as well as discounted travel and day trips to other venues.

Sources: Fandeavor, www.fandeavor.com; Empson, R. (August 14, 2012). "Funded by Tony Hsieh, Ex-Zappos Managers Launch Fandeavor to Turn Everyday Sports Fans into VIPs," *TechCrunch*, http://techcrunch.com/2012/08/14/funded-by-tony-hsieh-ex-zappos-managers-launch-fandeavor-to-turn-everyday-sports-fans-into-vips//

Throughout history, entrepreneurs were known for starting businesses as soloists. In this way they could retain individual ownership, make all the key decisions, and not have to share the profits. This approach to starting a business is still relatively common, but mostly in small lifestyle businesses and among craftspeople and artisans. Founders who wish to go it alone usually do so for several reasons:

- They want total control of the startup effort.
- They have the resources they need to launch the venture.
- The startup is not expected to grow large enough to support more than one founder.
- The founder may simply want to avoid the difficulties associated with founding teams.

Of course, there are short-term and long-term ramifications of the decision to go it alone. In the short term, going solo may work quite well; it's easy, decisions are quick, and there is no argument over who controls the profits. However, as the company grows and more diverse skills are required, growth may be stunted by the lack of those skills in the founder. Larger businesses tend to become complex with too many tasks for one person to manage.

On the flip side of the coin, with the proliferation of accelerators and incubators run by venture capitalists who prefer to invest in teams, one would naturally assume that a team approach to startup is the only way to go. And that would not be a bad assumption because a growing body of research supports a team approach for a variety of reasons.[1]

- The intense effort required of a startup can be shared.
- Should any one team member leave, it is less likely to result in the abandonment of the startup.
- With a founding team whose expertise covers major functional areas—marketing, finance, operations—the new venture can proceed further before it will need to hire additional personnel.

■ A skilled founding team lends legitimacy to the new venture in the eyes of lenders, investors, and others.

■ The entrepreneur's ability to analyze information and make decisions is improved because he or she benefits from the diverse expertise of the team, and ideas may be viewed and analyzed from several perspectives.

When the startup effort is collective, with a team that displays diverse capabilities, the new venture is more likely to be innovative and carve out a unique niche for itself.[2] Furthermore, one body of empirical research has provided evidence that firms founded by heterogeneous teams are generally more successful than those founded by individuals.[3]

Despite the research and investment support for team-based entrepreneurship, there is also evidence to support the role and importance of a lead entrepreneur—that is, a person who displays a higher level of entrepreneurial vision and self-efficacy than other members of the team.[4] Lead entrepreneurs drive the development of new ventures and serve as the guardians of the vision. They have the ability to see what others cannot see and to identify ways to change the marketplace rather than simply recognize an opportunity. While the team approach is still a sacred cow in places like Silicon Valley, it matters how you define the word *team*. Most ventures are born when an individual with passion for an idea—a problem he or she wants to solve—starts to think about how to make that solution a reality. That individual is the one willing to give up everything to make this venture happen. Does it make sense to share the ownership of your new venture with "co-founders" that you might have spent a few days with at a hackathon or startup weekend or met through referrals? The best teams develop over time, so unless you begin with people you know well and have worked with, it might make more sense initially to be the sole owner and pay for the people you need until you get to know them better. Investors are even willing sometimes to bet on a solo entrepreneur with the right credentials. In fact, in 2012, Atlanta Ventures Accelerator produced a reported exit of $300 million for the solo founder of Vitrue, Reggie Bradford.[5] Of course, this is not the norm, but it is possible.

The reality is that entrepreneurs never really start businesses all on their own; rather, they are "embedded in a social context, channeled and facilitated, or constrained and inhibited, by their positions in social networks."[6] Successful entrepreneurs take advantage of social networks to grow and maintain loyal customers, seek and acquire resources and talent, and eventually sell their companies. The extended networks of entrepreneurs are critical to the entire entrepreneurial process.[7] When an entrepreneurial firm interacts with other firms in its industry, it creates additional extended networks. At the hub of these networks is the founding team that has the vision and dedication to coordinate the efforts of all the partners toward a common goal. See Figure 8.1 for a view of an entrepreneur's network.

This chapter explores the fascinating world of founding teams—what we know from research about what makes them effective or ineffective, how entrepreneurs can choose the right people, and how they can make the team changes needed to scale the venture over time.

FIGURE 8.1
The Entrepreneur's
Network

8.1   THE SCIENCE OF FOUNDING TEAMS

Given that so much of the work of business involves teams, it is not surprising that a huge body of research exists to study the dynamics and performance of teams in all sorts of settings and all types of industries. One study at MIT's Human Dynamics Laboratory sought to find out why seemingly identical teams delivered very different levels of performance. Using 2,500 subjects wearing electronic sensors that collected social behavior data over a period of weeks, they were able to determine with consistency that "the most important predictor of a team's success was its communication patterns."[8] In fact, communication is "as significant as all the other factors—individual intelligence, personality, skill, and the substance of discussions—combined."[9]

It turns out that communication patterns can predict who will receive funding and which team will likely win a competition. The MIT study found several characteristics of communication that seem to define effective teams:

- Each team member spends about the same amount of time talking and listening. No one dominates, and no one drones on and on.
- The conversations take place face to face and tend to be energetic and alive.
- Conversations occur among all the members, not just from the members to the leader.
- Back-channel or sidebar conversations are typical.
- Team members often go outside the team to seek information and bring it back to share with the team.

One of the most surprising findings was that 35 percent of a team's performance is accounted for by the number of face-to-face conversations they had. And social time as a team explains about "50 percent of positive changes in communication patterns."[10] So communication is perhaps the most critical factor in effective startup teams, but it's also important to understand some factors that may work against a team succeeding.

8.1a   Why Startup Teams Fail

Sometimes even great leaders can't make their team deliver a successful outcome. That is particularly the case when the team is new to working together. Research by the National Transportation Safety Board discovered that 73 percent of the near misses and other incidents that occurred with commercial airplanes happened on the first day the crew flew as a team.[11] Newness is a liability when it comes to performance. A new founding team has to learn and execute new roles, develop a trusting relationship, and negotiate how ownership will be distributed.[12] This is no easy task, so it's no wonder that so many startups fail.

It is interesting that a number of studies have attributed the failure of startups to problems within the founding team. For example, one study looked at the portfolios of 49 successful venture capitalists that contained a total of 96 companies that had failed or were heading toward failure. The researchers found that 95 percent of the failures could be attributed to problems with the team.[13] Another study, which looked at 67 companies, found that 61 percent had internal weaknesses in the management team.[14]

What are some of the weaknesses that founding teams exhibit that can slow or derail startup and early growth processes? Some of these issues are the following:[15]

- **Putting structure on the organization before it's time**. Things never happen fast enough for entrepreneurs, but taking time to do sufficient market and competitor research may prevent entrepreneurs from creating the wrong type of organization for what they want to achieve. What this means is that entrepreneurial teams should operate as teams, rather than formal hierarchies, as long as possible to avoid the weight of company bureaucracy and to assess whether the team is the right team to take this opportunity to market.

- **Pretending there are sales from beta customers**. While it's true that entrepreneurs often need to secure beta customers, those who try the product in its earliest stage at no cost, you should not confuse these beta customers with actual customers. For beta customers, the value is "free." These individuals or companies enjoy trying new things and typically like to be the first to have the latest and greatest of anything they buy. However, that value proposition is not going to build a company. The only bona fide customers are those who pay for your products and services at a market price.

- **Suffocating under opportunity overload**. Entrepreneurs rarely suffer from a lack of opportunities. In fact, quite the opposite is generally true: They have more opportunities than their resources can support once they've established their businesses. That's why you must focus efforts and stick to your strategy for growth so that the opportunities you do take advantage of are aligned with those goals and have a greater chance for success.

- **Believing that engineers can do marketing**. Engineering and science entrepreneurs must bring in critical business skills as early as possible to avoid slowing progress for lack of expertise. It takes both technical people and business people to successfully ramp up a startup, and it's rare to find an entrepreneur who is equally effective at both skills.

- **Licensing the technology too soon**. In an effort to speed a technology to market, entrepreneurs sometimes elect to enter into license agreements too soon and thereby give away significant upside potential or worse have to rely on a licensee that has chosen the wrong market or done a poor job of developing the market application. An alternative is to pay a strategic partner to develop the applications and retain the technology rights in-house.

New ventures in the high-tech arena are frequently funded by "angel," or venture capital, and these startups face different issues in the formation of their founding teams. Very often, the founding team consists of scientists and engineers with little market or business experience. Investors understand clearly that these kinds of teams are not the most effective for overseeing the rapid and successful execution of the business strategy. A technology venture with significant up-front funding and the potential for exponential growth early on requires a professional management team with experience and an excellent track record in the industry. Usually, investors will help entrepreneurs locate the right people for the job. Bringing on professional management as soon after startup as possible ensures that there will be no glitches when rapid growth begins, and it also leaves the creative founders the time they need to continue to develop and improve the product and/or service.

Technology has made it possible for geographically dispersed teams to form and collaborate through synchronous and/or asynchronous communication media, relieving team members of the need to juggle global and local priorities.[16] Virtual teams are distinctly different from face-to-face teams in both spatial distance and communication. It is not the actual distance that matters but the effect that this distance has on how the team interacts. For example, suppose a startup team is located in Los Angeles and one team member lives in Pasadena, approximately 10 miles away. The spatial distance is not great, but given traffic and other challenges, the time distance may be 40 minutes or more. Therefore, technologies such as videoconferencing, phone, and email are used to mediate the distance. In addition, appropriate routines keep everyone connected and on track.[17]

Recall from an earlier section that communication patterns predict team performance more than any other factor and that face-to-face communication is a big contributor to team success. Clearly, virtual teams work at some disadvantage; however, despite the disadvantages caused by distance, virtual teams have several advantages. They enable you to access the most qualified individuals for a particular position, regardless of location, and to create a more flexible organization.[18] Depending on the type of business you start, the benefits of bringing on the unique skills of a team member who is geographically distant may outweigh the disadvantage of not having that member physically present.

SOCIAL ENTREPRENEURSHIP: *MAKING MEANING*

Vera Solutions: Data for Social Enterprises

One of the best ways to find co-founders is to meet while working together on a project because you can gain insights into that person's values and work ethic in a way you could never achieve through a résumé or interview. Zak Kaufman, Taylor Downs, and Karti Subramanian met in 2008 in South Africa, where they were all working on an HIV-prevention project. They quickly discovered that one of the biggest time wasters for the organization was the paperwork required to provide the regular donor reports. They were drowning in data and no one had the time to keep it updated. The trio decided to solve the problem by building an application that would track the hundreds of thousands of people the project served, logging outcomes and tracking every step of the prevention process. The application was so successful in reducing the reporting burden that Zak, Taylor, and Karti figured it might also help other organizations. They decided to launch Vera Solutions to provide "simple, cost-effective technology to help social impact organizations ask and answer increasingly targeted and relevant questions about their operations and performance." As of 2014, they had supplied the technology to more than 80 organizations in more than 30 countries. In 2012, this successful founding team was selected as one of the Forbes "30 Under 30 in Social Entrepreneurship."

Sources: Vera Solutions, www.versolutions.org/our-story/; "30 Under 30: Social Entrepreneurs," *Forbes*, 2012.

8.2   BUILDING THE FOUNDING TEAM

Choosing partners to start a new venture is one of the most critically important tasks that an entrepreneur must undertake. It is a difficult task because it's often not possible to understand a person's character until that person has spent some time working with you in the company. The stressful environment of a startup often reveals traits and responses that were not apparent when the person was originally selected. Everyone from investors to bankers to potential customers looks at the founding team to determine whether its members have the ability to execute their plans. Therefore, it is vital to choose partners who have complementary skills and experience and who do not have a history that might be detrimental to the company.

Noam Wasserman's longitudinal study of 10,000 founders over a decade sheds new light on the dynamics of founding teams and the challenges they face working together to create a successful startup.[19] These challenges or dilemmas can be divided into three big buckets: (1) relationships—who is on the team; (2) roles—what their responsibilities are; and (3) rewards—why they want to be on the team.

8.2a   Who Should Be on the Team?

It is an unfortunate fact that too many entrepreneurs do not take the time to consider whom they should team with to launch their venture. Two of the many important questions that should be asked before that process begins are:

- Do I want a highly diverse team very different from me or a team that is more like me in terms of values and skills?
- Should I bring on family and friends with whom I have trust or should I stay away from family and friends?

Wasserman's work proved that we tend to want to work with people just like us more often than not. That means overall you're more likely to see all-male or all-female teams and ethnically similar teams.[20] Homogeneity has benefits in the short term because it's easier to find people quickly and to build trust if those people are like you, but, over the long term, homogeneous teams can underperform if you have sacrificed the best talent for someone more like you. Founding teams composed of friends face unique challenges. Because the friendship is important, the team may avoid tough conversations or confrontations and instead make sub-optimal choices to maintain a stable relationship and keep everyone happy. Wasserman found that "each additional social relationship [that did not involve a professional working relationship] increased … the likelihood of cofounder departure by 28.6 percent." Surprisingly, socially familiar teams are actually less stable than teams composed of strangers. This is likely due to high levels of affective conflict that can occur among people who are socially familiar. By contrast, teams where the members had been coworkers were far more stable. By coworkers we do not mean classmates in a university setting. Students as coworkers are more similar to friends in terms of their effectiveness as team members. Evan Williams, co-founder of Blogger, learned firsthand how familiarity breeds contempt. His co-founder was his girlfriend, and the rest of the team consisted of good friends. When the business started falling apart, so did his relationship with his girlfriend who left, and eventually several of his friends quit as well. When it comes to friends and startups, you might want to ask how important the friendship is. Would you mind losing it?

In general, heterogeneity will provide better results in the long term. Research supports this argument saying that teams with diverse skills make better strategic choices that lead to higher performance.[21] In fact, some research has found team heterogeneity to be a significant predictor of long-term performance.[22] In terms of skill sets, heterogeneous teams also tend to handle the complexity of new ventures better than homogeneous teams.[23] Diversity in experience and professional networks can enable a startup to grow more quickly and find more innovative ways to be competitive. However, heterogeneous teams are more likely to face conflicts in values and ways of doing things. This could be problematic if the team has different communication and decision-making styles. Table 8.1 presents five factors that are significant in team composition: (1) homophily (similarity); (2) functionality (skill diversity); (3) status expectations (cultural bias); (4) network constraints (social contacts); and (5) ecological constraints (geographic distribution).

It's relatively easy to figure out whether your team is diverse or homogeneous on factors such as experience, networks, and expertise. It is much more

TABLE 8.1 Significant Factors for Founding Team Composition

Homophily (similarity)	The extent to which the characteristics of founding team members, such as gender, race, age, values, and beliefs, are similar. The benefit is that a high degree of similarity predisposes the team toward interpersonal attraction, trust, and understanding.
Functionality (skill diversity)	The degree of diversity among team members with respect to leadership skills and task expertise. Diversity of work experience and occupational background has been found to be linked to functional performance* and to communication and innovation.[†]
Status Expectations (cultural bias)	Widely held cultural biases regarding status (such as men having higher status than women) frequently affect the process of task group formation (although, in the case of gender, less so today). Those who perceive themselves to be in a higher-status group will tend to choose team members of the same status, however they define that status. Therefore, the entrepreneur who has lower status typically starts a venture as a soloist.
Network Constraint (social contacts)	The ability to choose members of a team is constrained by structural opportunities for social contact. For example, starting a business with only family members makes it more difficult to create a diverse team, because family members tend to be linked by strong ties and are in many respects an undesirably homogeneous group.[‡]
Ecological Constraint (geographic distribution)	The size of the population of potential team members and their geographic proximity is critical in the formation of founding teams.[§] The likelihood that different team members will associate is a function of their relative proportions in the population and their proximity to each other.[‖]

Source: Based on Martin Ruef, Howard E. Aldrich, and Nancy M. Carter, "The Structure of Founding Teams: Homophily, Strong Ties, and Isolation among U.S. Entrepreneurs," *American Sociological Review* (2003), 68(2): 195

*Eisenhardt, K., and C.B. Schoonhoven. (1990). "Organizational Growth: Linking Founding Team, Strategy, Environment, and Growth among U.S. Semiconductor Ventures, 1978–1988." *Administrative Science Quarterly*, 35: 504–529.

†Ancona, D., and D. Caldwell. (1992). "Demography and Design: Predictors of New Product Team Performance," *Organization Science*, 3: 321–341.

‡Aldrich, H.E., A. Elam, and P.R. Reese. (1996). "Strong Ties, Weak Ties, and Strangers: Do Women Business Owners Differ from Men in Their Use of Networking to Obtain Assistance?" in S. Birley and I. MacMillan (eds.), *Entrepreneurship in a Global Context*. London: Routledge, pp. 1–25.

§Carroll, G., and M. Hannan. (2000). *The Demography of Corporations and Industries*. Princeton, NJ: Princeton University Press.

‖Blau, P. (1980). "A Fable about Social Structure," *Social Forces*, 58: 777–788.

difficult to make that determination on more intangible factors such as work ethic, values, risk preference, and communication style. The more a team differs on these factors, the more conflict there will be and the greater the chance the team will blow up when faced with a significant challenge.

Of course, it isn't always possible or necessary to put together the "perfect" team from the start. The right person to fill a particular need may not have been determined, or the right person may be too expensive to bring on board during startup. In the latter situation, it is important to talk to that person about potentially joining the team at a later date and to keep him or her apprised of the company's progress. Many an aggressive startup company has eventually wooed an experienced person away from a major corporation when it becomes apparent that the startup has a serious future.

Although there are no perfect founding teams and no fail-safe rules for forming them, effective founding teams tend to display the following characteristics:

- The lead entrepreneur and the team share the same vision for the new venture.
- The team members are passionate about the business concept and will work as hard as the lead entrepreneur to make it happen.

- One or more members of the founding team have experience in the industry in which the venture is being launched.
- The team has solid industry contacts with sources of capital.
- The team's expertise covers the key functional areas of the business: finance, marketing, and operations.
- The team members have good credit ratings; this will be important when the team seeks financing.
- The team is free to spend the time a startup demands and can endure the financial constraints of a typical startup.

Despite knowing a potential business partner as a friend or colleague for many years, the new venture scenario presents a different set of challenges that may reveal some negatives that were not apparent before.

When considering who to bring to the team, it's also important to think about how big that team should be. One study of the top startups in 2012 found that the average number of founders in the top 50 companies for that year was 2.4, with the most frequent size being 2.[24] The greater the size of the team, the more likely it is that you will have affective conflict, which is conflict that is personal and emotional, rather than substantive. Every person you add to your team increases the communication issues and that increases the risk the new venture is facing. That is why it's important to add founding team members for what they bring to the business—their value to the bottom line.

When You Absolutely Must Work with Friends and Family

As we said in the previous section, turning to friends and family members is certainly the easiest and quickest way to find partners to start a new venture, but it may not be the best decision for the business. If a small business has no intentions of seeking outside financing, having a founding team that consists entirely of family members may not be a problem if they are all compatible. But if the plan is to grow the venture significantly, seek outside investors, or potentially do a public offering when the company reaches the appropriate size, a founding team consisting of only family members may not be an attractive asset. Here are some things to think about before making the decision to take on a family member or close friend as a partner in a new venture:

- Friends or family members should possess real skills and expertise that the business needs to be successful.
- They should have the same work ethic as the entrepreneur. If you are a workaholic and love it and a family member is a slacker, there will be problems.
- Consider using a trusted third party to referee disagreements.
- If there are family members on the startup team, there should be outsiders on the advisory board and/or board of directors so that the company will have the benefit of objective input to the business.
- The relationship with family and friends should be treated as a business relationship. The responsibilities and duties of all should be clearly spelled out in writing, and everyone should understand how disagreements will be settled. As much as possible, the activities of the business should not be brought home at night.

The founding team will need to agree on a number of important issues before launching a business together. One of the most effective ways to determine whether your team has the potential to work together successfully is to individually take a quiz that uncovers each person's values, goals, and expectations. Table 8.2 presents such a quiz. After each team member has taken the quiz independently of the others, the team should review the responses to learn if your team appears to be rowing the same boat, heading in the same direction. It is not uncommon to find that one or more members of an otherwise cohesive team have different expectations for the outcomes of the business or their role in it. These differences must be discussed and agreed upon before moving further as a team. It will be far more costly in time and money, not to mention friendships, if these differences are ignored and cause problems later when the business is growing.

TABLE 8.2
A Founding Team Quiz

1. What are your core values?
2. What is your goal for this business?
3. What do you see as your role in the business? Why?
4. What roles do you see the other team members playing and why?
5. How should ownership of the business be divided?
6. How should decisions be made?
7. Do you enjoy business travel?
8. What kinds of hours will you keep?
9. What is your preferred mode of communication?
10. What is your credit rating?
11. How do you spend money?
12. What is your lifestyle goal?

© Cengage Learning®

8.2b   Who Does What: Deciding on Roles and Responsibilities

If each individual on the founding team brings important expertise and experience, then each individual should have a specific role to play with the appropriate responsibilities. The discussion around who does what is one of the most critical discussions the founding team will have because it directly impacts ownership. Many startups choose to avoid more formal corporate titles such as CEO, CFO, and COO in the early stages of the venture because it seems out of place when the company doesn't yet have customers and the environment is more team-based than hierarchical. Nevertheless, identifying functional titles with defined duties will go a long way toward avoiding conflicts as the company grows.

In two-person teams, particularly where ownership is evenly divided, it's especially important to designate areas of responsibility and give the final say-so in that area to the designated founder. Even in a two-person team, someone must assume the leadership or CEO role, which is the "face" of the company. As the CEO is often the person out raising money for the company, he or she will typically be the one who is most comfortable and effective at conveying the startup's story to investors, partners, and other stakeholders.

It is not uncommon for several people on the team to want to be the CEO. After all, that title carries with it a great deal of prestige and authority. The reality is, however, that in startups, being CEO is arguably the worst job of all. Not only are you responsible for raising capital to keep the startup afloat, but it's your job to make sure that you're supporting the people on the team who are developing the product. That is why the critical development people—the scientists, the Web developers, the engineers—should not be the CEO. Instead, they should be focused on getting the product ready for market. Wasserman's study found that typically "idea people" attempt to secure the CEO position in an effort to be the leader and drive the direction of the company. Other founders are given C-level titles as consolation prizes. This pattern of inflating the titles of co-founders is prevalent and can present a problem as the company grows and more people are brought on board, especially when professional management is needed. If all the co-founders hold all the C-level titles, then they have to be demoted when a professional CFO or CTO is brought on board to take the company to the next level.

Of all the C-level titles, CEO is probably the one that makes most sense in a startup because someone has to be the face of the company and drive the execution strategy. Startups that attempt to be completely flat in structure and consensus driven in their decision making will tend to move too slowly for most startup environments. Moreover, consensus-based decisions by their very nature tend to be mediocre compromises rather than the best decisions to generate growth and competitive advantage for the company.

8.2c   What's in It for Me: Rewarding Co-Founders

The tendency for founders to want equality in terms of roles and responsibilities naturally leads to wanting equality when it comes to an ownership stake in the company. For many founders, the reward for all their hard work and risk taking is in the appreciation of the stock that they hold in the company, and they often don't believe that any co-founder should hold more stock than any other. Choosing equal splits is rarely the best idea because on no team does everyone start equal or contribute equally to the startup. Furthermore, founders often have trouble navigating the fine line between deciding equity splits too early and waiting too long. Both can result in agreements that won't hold up for the long term. Most startups agree on equity splits within the first month of founding.[25] The problem with that is the team is making a critical decision with very little information. Unless the team has had experience working together in similar types of situations, they really won't know in the first month if everyone is going to carry their share of the load. Waiting even a few months and giving everyone tasks to complete in that timeframe can go a long way toward finding out who is committed to the venture and who is bringing the right skills to the effort.

However, every situation is different. Sometimes by waiting too long to make the decision you risk losing a member of the team who gets a better offer elsewhere. The other risk you take is that someone you've decided is not a good fit creates something the team actually needs during the test period and now that person is claiming "squatter's rights" to own shares in the company. Do you give him shares that will tie him to the company for the long term or fight off his efforts to remain part of the team? In any event, you must have the negotiation about equity splits before the startup is worth anything. Once people starting thinking in terms of how much the company is worth, all bets are off that you will get rid of anyone you don't want on the team without a fight.

Many of these potential challenges can be resolved by taking action from the beginning to make sure the negotiations, when they happen, go smoothly. Teams that experience the fewest problems consider the following four questions before the negotiations begin:

- What did each founder bring to the table? The idea for the business? Seed funding? A patent?
- What did each founder give up to work on this venture? Leave a job? Mortgage a house?
- When did each founder come on board? Did the team start together or did someone join the team later?
- What is each founder expected to contribute in the future? Needed connections to money? Product development?

In general, founders who bring the idea or seed capital to the venture will receive a premium on the share of stock they receive, typically between 10 and 15 percent. The site Foundrs.com provides a co-founder equity calculator for a startup that helps you begin the discussion about equity splits. After you answer a number of questions about the role of the co-founders, it calculates the suggested percentage equity. Of course, it would be important to get professional advice, and ultimately each situation is different. You might also consider using a dynamic agreement about equity splits with your co-founders. This approach lets you adjust how equity is split to reflect changes in conditions.

For example, what if one of the co-founders drops out for whatever reason? The other co-founders must have the ability to adjust that person's split to reflect his leaving and the others taking on larger roles. What a dynamic agreement does is lessen the potential for conflicts when unexpected change happens. One way to do this is to have the equity percentages vest over time, which means that each co-founder doesn't actually own their stake completely until they reach whatever vesting milestone has been established. Usually these milestones are associated with major events in the life of the startup: completing a working prototype, getting the product to market, raising a round of capital, and so forth. In this way, the stock vesting serves as an incentive to work hard. So, for example, whatever total percentage of equity the co-founder was granted is spread out over time, maybe two to three years, so that you're not giving equity to someone who is no longer with the company or who fails to perform as expected. Note that we're talking about relative shares of equity; no dollar value is assigned because at the point at which you're negotiating equity splits, the company has little or no value. But at whatever future value the company achieves, the co-founders know the precise percentage of that valuation that belongs to them. Of course, if the team raises any outside capital, their percentage will get diluted, which means their percentage of ownership will decline.

Suppose that you've determined that your startup's pre-money valuation is $1,000,000 based on one of the generally accepted methods (discussed in Chapter 15) and that the co-founders collectively hold 100 percent of the equity. Now suppose you raise $200,000 in seed capital. That means your post-money valuation is $1,200,000. The new investor now holds 17 percent of the stock in the company ($200,000/1,200,000) and the founders have had their shares diluted by 17 percent; they now own 83 percent of the company. Again, whenever you're talking about equity splits, it's always in terms of relative percentages because the percentage change as the company takes on investment or adds employees to whom they grant stock as incentives.

How your team will be rewarded for its efforts is one of the most important discussions you will have. Bringing in objective advisors who have earned the respect of the team will help make the discussion go more smoothly.

8.3   WHEN ENTREPRENEURS DON'T SCALE

As many as many as four out of five founders are asked to step out of the position of CEO at some point in the life of their company. Moreover, fewer than 25 percent of founders are still the CEO when their company goes public.[26] Those are the findings of a number of studies on the longevity of founders. It turns out that the skills required to conceive and launch a venture are very different skills from those required to grow and maintain a business. Not surprisingly, entrepreneurs typically hit a wall not long after launch where, whether they recognize it or not (and they usually don't), they reach the limits of their capabilities as leaders. If they don't modify their way of thinking about the business, the business will suffer. In the rare cases like Amazon CEO Jeff Bezos, their leadership style and view of the business evolves as the business grows, and they are able to remain in the CEO position through several rounds of capital and perhaps even an IPO.

Research has found four approaches that entrepreneurs take in the early stages of the company that are not effective when the company is larger and more complex[27]. The first approach is near **blind loyalty to the founding team** that came through the challenges of startup together. Where their talents were valued in a scrappy entrepreneurial environment, some of the team may not have the professional skills to lead a larger organization. Often the entrepreneur CEO will keep an original team member well beyond their usefulness, even to the detriment of the company. Recall the mistake of giving all the co-founders C-level titles. Unless they have the professional skills to manage others in a larger organization, they should not be given titles that suggest that they do have those capabilities.

The second approach is a **dedicated focus on a task**, which at startup is essential to get the company off the ground quickly. But entrepreneurial leaders need to be able to see the big picture to stay on a growth target, and many are unable to move away from micro-managing the organization to do that. Instead of setting clear strategic goals for everyone and keeping an eye on the overall strategy, entrepreneurs of growing companies often stay in the weeds too long in a reactionary position rather than proactively guiding the bigger plan.

The third approach is **sticking to a single-minded purpose**—usually to change the world—and without expanding that view to grow the company with a more defined and staged strategy. Unfortunately, you can't really learn to lead people, persuade investors, or think strategically in school. These capabilities are learned from experience, and, regrettably, most entrepreneurs have not had that type of experience before launching their first venture. Effective entrepreneurs who can scale know how to create a simple, achievable strategy, set some targets, and then regularly revisit the strategy to make sure they're still on track or to change direction should circumstances call for it.

Finally, the fourth approach, and this is typical of startups run by scientists and engineers, is **focusing solely on the technology**. Even after the company is in the market with their product, this type of entrepreneur CEO still cares more about the technology than anything else and is vulnerable to being blind-sided by external forces that threaten the business, forces that he or she could have foreseen. The leader of a growing entrepreneurial venture is the face of the company and needs to be out in the marketplace interacting with stakeholders like customer, partners, and investors. If the entrepreneur CEO is also the chief technology person, then it's time to step out of the position of CEO and assume a CTO-type position.

For entrepreneurs to scale effectively, they need to be open to coaching, learning, and experimenting. It is possible for founding CEOs to continue to lead their companies to a substantial size, but they have to reinvent themselves and their key people to do it.

8.4   EXPANDING THE TEAM

To this point we have focused on the founding team. But growing businesses requires expertise and connections that are rarely found in the founding team alone. Here we look at how you can use professional advisors to expand your team.

8.4a   Seeking Professional Advisors

When a new venture is in its infancy, it generally doesn't have the resources to hire in-house professional help such as an attorney or accountant. Instead, it must rely on building relationships with professionals on an "as-needed" basis. These professionals provide information and services not normally within the scope of expertise of most entrepreneurs, and they can play devil's advocate for the entrepreneur, pointing out potential flaws in the business concept. They provide the new venture—and the entrepreneurial team in love with its own concept—an invaluable reality check. There are a number of these professional advisers that entrepreneurs rely on at various times in their venture's life. We will consider attorneys, accountants, bankers, and insurance agents:

Attorneys

There is hardly any aspect of starting a new venture that is not touched by the law. Unfortunately, entrepreneurs who have never had any education in the legal aspects of business often don't recognize that they need legal help until their business gets into trouble. Attorneys are professionals who typically specialize in one area of the law (such as taxes, real estate, business, or intellectual property) and can provide a wealth of support for the new venture. Within their particular area of expertise, attorneys can

- Advise you in selecting the correct organizational structure: sole proprietorship, partnership, LLC, or corporation.
- Advise about and prepare documents for the acquisition of intellectual property rights and for licensing agreements.
- Negotiate and prepare contracts.
- Advise you on compliance with regulations related to financing and credit.
- Keep you apprised of the latest tax reform legislation and help minimize the venture's tax burden.
- Assist the entrepreneur in complying with federal, state, or local laws.
- Represent the entrepreneur in any legal actions as advocates.

Choosing a good attorney is a time-consuming but vital task that should be accomplished prior to startup. Decisions about such things as the legal form of the business or contracts made at inception may affect the venture for years to come—hence the need for good legal advice. To find the best attorney for the situation, you should

- Ask accountants, bankers, and other business people to recommend attorneys who are familiar with the challenges facing startup, particularly those in the entrepreneur's industry.

- Look for an attorney who is willing to listen, has time, and will be flexible about fees while the business is in the startup phase.
- Confirm that the attorney carries malpractice insurance.

Accountants

A lawyer is an advocate, but an accountant is bound by rules and ethics that do not permit advocacy. Whereas an attorney is bound to represent his or her client no matter what the client does, an accountant cannot defend a client who does something that violates the accounting industry's Generally Accepted Accounting Principles (GAAP).

Accounting is a complex field that entrepreneurs need to understand at least at a basic level in order to communicate with accountants, auditors, lenders, bankers, and investors, in addition to internal and external stakeholders. In the beginning, an accountant may set up your company's books and maintain them on a periodic basis, or, as is often the case, you may hire a bookkeeper to perform the day-to-day recording of transactions. The accountant will also set up control systems for operations, as well as payroll. You then visit the accountant during the tax season to review everything. Once your new venture is beyond the startup phase and is growing consistently, it's a good idea to do an annual audit to determine whether the company's accounting and control procedures are adequate. The auditors may also require a physical inventory. If everything is in order, they will issue a certified statement, which is important should you ever decide to take the company public.

Accountants are also a rich networking source in your search for additional members of your team. Like attorneys, accountants tend to specialize, so it is wise to find one who is used to working with young, growing businesses. Indeed, the accountant who takes your business through startup and early growth will probably not be the best person to take care of the company's needs when it reaches the next level of growth. As the financial and record-keeping needs of the business increase and become more complex, you may have to consider a larger firm with expertise in several areas.

Bankers

There is a saying that all banks are alike until you need a loan. Today this is as true as ever, so having a qualified banker on the advisory team will put your startup in a better position to seek a line of credit for operating capital or a loan to purchase equipment once your business has a track record.

To narrow the search for a banker, you should prepare a list of criteria that defines the banking needs of your business. You should also talk with other entrepreneurs in your industry to identify a bank that works well with the type of venture you plan to launch. Another approach is to ask an accountant or attorney to suggest the best bank for your particular type of business.

When choosing a banker, seek out an officer with a rank of assistant vice president or higher, because these officers are trained to work with new and growing businesses and have enough authority to make decisions quickly. In particular, it is important to ensure that the lending officer can approve loans and lines of credit in the amounts needed. Today many of the largest banks have moved their lending facilities to a central location, so it is difficult to establish a relationship with the person who has responsibility for approving a request. That's why many entrepreneurs seek out community banks that have a vested interest in supporting local businesses.

Insurance Agents

Many entrepreneurs overlook the value of a relationship with a competent insurance agent, but a growing venture will require several types of insurance:

- Property and casualty
- Medical
- Errors and omissions
- Life (on key people)
- Workers' compensation
- Directors and officers
- Unemployment
- Auto (on the firm's vehicles)
- Liability (product and personal)
- Bonding

Major insurance firms can handle all types of insurance vehicles, but specialists will be required for certain kinds of protection, such as bonding (which is common in the construction industry to protect against a contractor not completing a project), product liability insurance, and errors and omissions (which protects the business against liability from unintentional mistakes in advertising). Your company's insurance needs will change over its life, and a good insurance agent will help you determine the needed coverage at the appropriate times.

8.5   SEEKING PERSONAL ADVISORS

In addition to professional advisors, entrepreneurs seek the advice and support of personal advisors. Personal advisors take on several forms, but they have the common purpose of supporting the founding team in their efforts to launch and grow the business. Here we discuss boards of directors, boards of advisors, and the mentor board.

8.5a   Building a Board of Directors

Although the decision to have a board of directors is influenced by the legal form of the business, it is a long-held belief that establishing governance early in the organization of a startup will enhance the quality of the company as it grows. If a new venture is a corporation, a board of directors is required and is elected by the shareholders. If the business needs venture capital, a board will be necessary, and the venture capitalist will probably demand a seat on it. Boards of directors serve a valuable purpose; if chosen correctly, they provide expertise that fills gaps in the founding team's knowledge. In that capacity they act as advisers. They also assist in establishing corporate strategy and philosophy. They do not have the power to sign contracts or commit the corporation legally; instead, they elect the officers of the corporation, who are responsible for its day-to-day operations. Board members assist with business development, act as arbitrators for dispute resolution, and give credibility to the new company's image.

It is important to distinguish between boards of privately owned corporations and those of publicly owned corporations. In a privately owned corporation, the entrepreneurial team owns all or the majority of the stock, so directors serve at the pleasure of the entrepreneur, who has effective control of the company until several rounds of investment capital dilute that control. On the other hand, directors of publicly traded companies have legitimate power to control the activities of the company and liability for what they do or fail to do. They are elected by the shareholders and represent the shareholders' interests in the company.

Private boards can be composed of inside or outside members or a combination of the two. An inside board member is one who is a founder, employee, family member, or retired manager of the firm, whereas an outside board member is someone with no direct connection to the business. Which type of board member is better is a matter of opinion and circumstance; research has not provided any clear results on this issue. In general, however, outside directors are beneficial for succession planning and for raising capital. They can often bring a fresh point of view to the strategic planning process, along with expertise that the founders may not possess. Insiders have the advantage of complete knowledge about the business; they are generally more available and have demonstrated their effectiveness in the particular positions they occupy in the business. Typically where the entrepreneur/CEO has power to configure the board, the board will be small and composed primarily of insiders, particularly family members and co-founders.[28] But there are political ramifications when the board members report to the CEO; insiders may not always be objective and independent. They also may not have the broad expertise from outside the company that is necessary to effectively guide the growth of the business.

Consider carefully whether your startup requires a working board—that is, one that directs the strategy of the business. Most working boards are used for their expertise, for strategic planning, for auditing the actions of the firm, and for arbitrating differences. These activities are not as crucial in the startup phase, when the entrepreneurial team is gathering resources and raising capital. However, a board of directors can assist the entrepreneurial team in those functions and can network with key people who can help the new venture. Some stakeholders will ask to be included on the board so that they can monitor their investment in the company. This is common among significant private investors, venture capitalists, bankers, and even accountants. To be sure of getting only the best people on the board, you should set standards for membership in advance and should strictly adhere to them.

The size and complexity of an entrepreneur's business, as well as the legal requirements of the state in which the company operates, will determine how many directors serve on the board. There is no research consensus on the relationship between the size of the board and the performance of the company, although some research has found that a large board encourages laziness on the part of some members[29] and thus may undermine the board's ability to initiate strategic actions.[30] Moreover, larger boards tend to develop factions and coalitions that often lead to conflict. The general recommendation is to have no fewer than 5 and no more than 15 board members. In the earliest stages of a new venture, the board will often consist of the founders, though that should quickly change as the company begins to grow and needs to tap the expertise of people who have managed growth in their own companies.

When choosing people to serve on the board of directors, you should consider those who have

- The necessary technical skill related to the business.
- Significant, successful experience in the industry.
- Experience running a company at the level the entrepreneur wants to grow to next.
- Important contacts in the industry.
- Expertise in finance, capital acquisition, and possibly IPOs.
- A personality compatible with the rest of the board.
- Good problem-solving skills.
- Honesty and integrity, to engender a sense of mutual trust.

In addition, it is critically important to choose the right board members for the stage the company is in. Figure 8.2 displays the various stages of a company's growth, the status of the business during that stage, and the type of board member that may be most appropriate for the needs of the business at that point in time. You must align your objectives with the venture's life cycle stage and then select the board members and advisers so that they are congruent with these objectives.

As CEO you have a responsibility to educate your board about your business so that they can advise you more effectively. This is particularly important when your board members are investors in the company. Rather than putting yourself in an adversarial role by only telling them what you want them to know, it's better to be open and transparent in your dealings with them as they are taking on some liability by being on your board. It's also important to communicate frequently with your board to keep them in the loop in-between more formal board meetings and conference calls. Be prepared to accept the feedback you receive without becoming defensive; your board wants you to succeed and their suggestions are offered in that spirit.

Send any relevant materials to your board several days in advance of a meeting so they have time to prepare. Boards are metrics driven; that is, they want to know if you achieved the goals you set at the previous meeting. Use their time wisely, be prepared, and follow up on their suggestions.

FIGURE 8.2   Board Members and the Business Life Stage

Board Needs	*Need: Advice on feasibility*	*Need: Resource expertise*	*Need: Strategic advice*	*Need: Access to capital markets and growth expertise*	*Need: Catalyst for innovation*	*Need: Turnaround specialist*
Status	**Concept Development** Feasibility analysis undertaken	**Startup Resources** Management team First customer acquired	**Early Growth** Develop operational and sales capabilities	**Rapid Growth** Spurs need for capital and controls	**Growth Slows** Innovation required	**Crisis** Cash flow, market, leadership are the focus
Stage	**Conception**	**Startup**	**Early Growth**	**Rapid Growth**	**Maturity**	**Decline**

© Cengage Learning®

The board is headed by the chairperson, who, in a new, private venture, is typically the lead entrepreneur. The entrepreneur is also likely to be the president and CEO. The current trend is for the CEO and perhaps the chief operating officer (COO) or CFO to be the only inside members on the board. Depending on the type of business, boards normally meet face to face an average of five times a year and through teleconferences as necessary. How often the board meets will be largely a function of how active it is at any given time. Directors typically spend about 9 to 10 days a year on duties related to the business and are usually paid a retainer plus a per-meeting fee. Their expenses are also reimbursed. The compensation can take the form of cash, stock, or other perquisites.

Today it is more difficult to get people to serve as directors because in some cases they can be held personally liable for the actions of the firm, and the frequency with which boards are being sued is increasing. For this reason, potential directors will require that the business carry directors' and officers' (D&O) liability insurance to indemnify them. The expense of this insurance is often prohibitive for a growing company, but it is essential in getting good people to serve. Additional expenses related to the development of a board of directors include meeting rooms, travel, and food. Because of the expense of maintaining a formal board of directors, many entrepreneurs with new ventures maintain a small insider board of directors and rely heavily on their informal advisory board for objective perspectives.

8.5b   Advisory Board

The advisory board is an informal panel of experts and other people who are interested in seeing your new venture succeed. They are a useful and less costly alternative to a formal board of directors. Advisory boards can range from those that meet once or twice a year and do not get paid to those that meet more regularly and are provided an equity stake in the company.

Advisory boards are often used when a board of directors is not required or in the startup phase when the board of directors consists of the founders only. Often first-time entrepreneurs seek advisory boards to demonstrate an association with industry experts and to benefit from their advice. An effective advisory board can provide the new venture with needed expertise without the significant costs and loss of control associated with a board of directors. In a wholly owned or closely held corporation (in which you and your team hold all the stock), there really is no distinction between the functions of a board of directors and those of a board of advisers, because in either case, control remains in the hands of the entrepreneurial team. However, the advisory board is not subject to the same scrutiny as the board of directors, because its actions are not binding on the company.

Advisory boards don't come without problems. In general, the people who serve on them are very busy with their own responsibilities and will not necessarily be proactive in providing help. The main reason is they generally are given a tiny percentage of equity that over time will become highly diluted. Therefore, the time they give to you is essentially pro bono. In addition, because they don't spend a lot of time with the company, they don't know enough detail about it to be as helpful as you would like.

As your company resources grow, you might benefit more from a well-constructed board of directors and a mentor board, which is discussed next.

8.5c   The Mentor Board

In addition to an advisory board and a board of directors, you should have a personal mentor board of individuals whom you respect and trust. They will serve as a sounding board for ideas, act as coaches to raise your spirits, and warn you when you are heading down a wrong path. The members of a personal mentor board are usually role models and people who have businesses and lifestyles like the one you want to create. Because they have no financial interest in your business, mentors also provide a safe place for you to air your fears and concerns and express your hopes and dreams.

In general, it takes time to develop a mentor board because you first have to establish a relationship with potential mentors before asking them to mentor you. Mentoring has become big business in the new world of incubators and accelerators, so you will need to be careful that you're not taken in by potential mentors who promise you things that will never happen. But, you do need to be willing to listen to what they have to say, good or bad, without becoming defensive. That is not easy to do, but it's essential if you intend to benefit fully from your mentor's advice. A mentor board might typically consist of one to four people you can go to for personal advice on an ad hoc basis. As a group they may never meet each other, so the advice they give you will be independent and objective with no personal agenda.

8.5d   Outsourcing with Independent Contractors

A new business typically does not have the resources to pay for all the management and operational staff that may be necessary to get it up and running. In fact, most entrepreneurs avoid hiring employees as long as possible, because employees are the single biggest expense in the business. But how does a new venture survive with as few employees as possible and still grow?

The solution lies in outsourcing, which means using independent contractors (ICs) to undertake functions that you don't want to handle. ICs own their own businesses and are hired by you to do a specific job. They are under your control but only for the results of the work they do, not for the means by which those results are accomplished. The independent contractors that entrepreneurs use on a regular basis include consultants, manufacturers, distributors, and employee leasing firms (note that professional advisers are also independent contractors). Entrepreneurs seek out independent contractors for their expertise in specific areas. Using an independent contractor means that you don't have to supply medical and retirement benefits, provide unemployment insurance, or withhold payroll taxes. These are costly benefits that can amount to more than 32 percent of an employee's base salary. But there are hidden costs to outsourcing whether domestically or globally that you should be aware of:[31]

- *The cost of searching for and contracting with an independent contractor (IC).* The best way to reduce this cost is for you to secure referrals from people you know who have had a successful experience with the IC.

- *Transferring activities to the IC.* Getting the IC "up to speed" on the business takes time and human resources. Transfer costs can be reduced if you identify up front what you want the IC to handle and lay out a plan for preparing the IC to do the work.

- *Managing the independent contractor.* This is one of those cases where experience counts. The first IC contract takes the longest and costs the most. The best IC relationships occur when communication is an ongoing process so that the IC becomes a real part of the business.

- *Bringing the activity in-house.* Many companies eventually bring in-house activities that they once outsourced. This may occur because the company has grown to the point where it needs and can afford in-house staff for the activity or because the company wants more control over the activity. One way to reduce the transition cost is to have the person who manages the IC relationship learn enough about the activity to be able to ease the company through the transition.

To reduce the hidden costs of using independent contractors, you should retain in house critical activities and core competencies that are idiosyncratic or unique to the business. You should also research vendors carefully and seek referrals. Above all, you must work with legal advisers who have experience with independent contractor law to draft binding contracts.

The IRS has very strict rules for the use of independent contractors. The Law of Agency defines the terms *employee* and *independent contractor.* It states, "While an employee acts under the direction and control of the employer, an independent contractor contracts to produce a certain result and has full control over the means and methods that shall be used in producing the result."[32] If an employer doesn't follow the rules regulating classification of workers as independent contractors, they can be considered employees for tax purposes, and the employer can be held liable for all back taxes plus penalties and interest, which can amount to a substantial sum.

To ensure compliance with IRS regulations, you should

- Consult an attorney.
- Draw up a contract with each independent contractor, specifying that the contractor will not be treated as an employee for state and federal tax purposes.
- Be careful not to indicate the means or methods of accomplishing the work, only the desired result.
- Verify that the independent contractor carries workers' compensation insurance.
- Verify that the independent contractor possesses the necessary licenses.

More specifically, the IRS uses a 20-point test for classifying workers (see Table 8.3). Even if an employer follows all the IRS rules, however, there is no guarantee that the IRS won't challenge its position. Therefore, it is important to document the relationship with an independent contractor through a legal agreement that explicitly demonstrates that the independent contractor owns his or her own business. The IRS can decide that an IC is an employee even if only one of the 20 points is true!

On the positive side, independent contractors can make the very small startup venture look like an established corporation to anyone on the outside. A large corporation will generally have vice presidents for departments of operations, sales, marketing, and finance. It is possible to replicate these functions by using independent contractors, thereby lowering costs and remaining more flexible.

Many types of independent contractors operate behind the scenes of the new venture but make a valuable contribution nonetheless. These include consultants, professional employer organizations (PEOs), manufacturing support, sales support, and government agencies.

TABLE 8.3
The 20-Point Test for
Independent Contractors

A worker is an employee if he or she

1. Must follow the employer's instructions about how to do the work.
2. Receives training from the employer.
3. Provides services that are integrated into the business.
4. Provides services that must be rendered personally.
5. Cannot hire, supervise, and pay his or her own assistants.
6. Has a continuing relationship with the employer.
7. Must follow set hours of work.
8. Works full time for an employer.
9. Does the work on the employer's premises.
10. Must do the work in a sequence set by the employer.
11. Must submit regular reports to the employer.
12. Is paid regularly for time worked.
13. Receives reimbursements for expenses.
14. Relies on the tools and materials of the employer.
15. Has no major investment in facilities to perform the service.
16. Cannot make a profit or suffer a loss.
17. Works for one employer at a time.
18. Does not offer his or her services to the general public.
19. Can be fired at will by the employer.
20. May quit work at any time without incurring liability.

Consultants

The consulting industry is one of the fastest-growing industries in the United States, and it can provide a variety of services for a new venture. Consultants can

- Train the sales staff and/or management.
- Conduct market research.
- Prepare policy manuals.
- Solve problems.
- Act as temporary key management.
- Recommend market strategy.
- Design and engineer products.
- Design a plant layout and equipment.
- Conduct research and development.
- Recommend operational and financial controls.

Because they tend to be fairly expensive, consultants are best used for critical onetime advising or problem-solving assignments. In that capacity, they are typically more cost-effective than employees because they are accustomed to working quickly within the constraints of a fixed budget. Consultants are generally paid in one of three ways: monthly retainer, which pays for a specified amount of time per month, hourly rate, or project fee. More recently, consultants have also been known to ask for some form of equity stake in the companies for which they consult. Some entrepreneurs have chosen to go this route when cash is in short supply. However, you should consult an attorney before giving up any equity in your company. It is much harder to dismiss an IC who is a shareholder in the company.

Professional Employer Organization (PEO)

Leasing staff is a way for a new business to enjoy the advantages of major corporations without incurring many of the expenses. A professional employer organization assumes the payroll and human resource functions for the business for a fee that generally ranges from 3 to 5 percent of gross payroll. Each pay period, you pay the PEO a lump sum to cover payroll plus the fee. In addition to payroll processing and taxes, the services they provide include safety and risk management, benefits administration, and human resource management. PEOs and human resource business process outsourcing are growing rapidly as more companies take advantage of their services.

Manufacturing Support

Even those new ventures that involve manufacturing a product can avail themselves of the benefits of independent contractors. Because the cost of building and equipping a new manufacturing plant is immense by any standard, many entrepreneurs choose to contract the work with an established manufacturer domestically or in another country. In fact, it is possible for an entrepreneur who has a new product idea to subcontract the design of the product to an engineering firm, the production of components to various manufacturing firms, the assembly of the product to another firm, and the distribution to yet another. With the rapid rate of technological innovation, it is difficult for any one company to keep up, so remaining focused and profitable is critical to success.

Cooperative purchasing has become an important way for companies to be globally competitive and keep costs down. In addition to being able to take advantage of significant quantity discounts, companies who collaborate also reduce transaction costs with bundled orders.[33]

Sales Support

Hiring sales staff can be an expensive proposition for any new venture, not only from the standpoint of benefits but also because salespeople must be trained. As new high-growth ventures seek a geographically broad market, even a global one, it is vital to consider enlisting the aid of manufacturer's representatives (reps) and foreign reps who know those markets. Using distributors enables you to reach your target market without having to deal with the complex retail market. In addition, sales agencies can provide you with fully trained salespeople—in much the same manner as temporary services supply clerical help. Some can also provide advertising and public relations.

For any business, people mean the difference between success and failure. Starting a business with a carefully chosen founding team and expanding that team with professional and personal advisors will take you a long way before you have to take on the expense of employees.

New Venture Action Plan

- Identify the members of the founding team or at least the expertise needed to start the venture.
- Determine what expertise is missing from the founding team and how you will supply it.
- Begin asking questions about potential professional advisers, such as an attorney or accountant.
- Determine whether you will need a board of directors, an advisory board, or a mentor board.
- Identify at least one type of independent contractor that your new venture could use.

Questions on Key Issues

1. For what kinds of businesses is starting as a solo entrepreneur sufficient? Are there advantages to starting even these types of businesses with a team?
2. What strategy should an entrepreneur employ when selecting a personal board, an advisory board, or a board of directors?
3. How might the need for an attorney differ for a service business and a high-technology company?
4. How can you ensure that you are using independent contractors correctly and in accordance with the law?
5. Suppose you are starting an apparel company where you will design and manufacture a unique line of clothing. What kinds of independent contractors can help you start this venture?

Experiencing Entrepreneurship

1. Interview an entrepreneur who started a venture as a soloist, and then visit an entrepreneurial venture started by a team (two or more people). Based on your interviews, write a two-page report discussing the advantages and disadvantages of each approach.
2. Choose a lawyer, accountant, or banker to interview as a potential professional adviser to your business. What information will you need to secure from him or her to make your decision?

Relevant Case Studies

Case 1 AdRoll

Case 8 Vision to Learn

CHAPTER 9

Calculating Startup Capital Requirements

"Money never starts an idea; it is the idea that starts the money."

—WILLIAM J. CAMERON, (1878 –1955), JOURNALIST AND PR REPRESENTATIVE
FOR THE FORD MOTOR COMPANY

CHAPTER OBJECTIVES

- Discuss how entrepreneurs acquire the resources they need to launch a business.
- Identify typical startup financial metrics.
- Explain the role of financial assumptions.
- Discuss how entrepreneurs should assess risk when calculating financial needs.

PROFILE
9.1

BAREFOOT: WHAT DOES IT COST TO START A WINE BUSINESS?

How do you go from knowing next to nothing about the wine industry in 1986 to becoming the top-selling brand in the United States and changing the entire culture of the wine industry? That is what Michael Houlihan and Bonnie Harvey did, but the journey was not a walk in the park.

In the 1980s, the wine industry was cloaked in a culture about as staid and dull as it could be. The average person was intimidated by the language and the snobbery associated with fine wine versus table or jug wine. It was at that time that Mark Lyon, a respected winemaker, was having trouble collecting on 300 tons of grapes he had sold to Souverain, a Napa Valley winery that was experiencing financial troubles. His employee Bonnie Harvey, who managed his books, and her boyfriend, Michael Houlihan, decided they wanted to help and they contrived a way to barter with Souverain to get Lyon's money back. They would use the vintner's bottling facility to bottle and sell 18,000 cases of wine. The hitch was that Lyon had no interest in running the new business they would need to form. That's when Houlihan and Harvey stepped in and said that they would own the business and do that end of the work and Lyon could work for them. With a deal struck, they were on their way—or so they thought.

From the beginning the goal was to create a friendly, approachable wine at a low price. After much brainstorming, they decided to call the wine Barefoot and use a bare foot as a logo. Little did they know how much difficulty that one decision would cause them because in the wine industry distributors and retailers generally are reluctant to take on new labels. That fact alone predicted all the necessary costs they would incur to launch the business. In the first year, they had to factor in the cost of providing free bottles as samples to anyone they wanted to sell to and providing those samples meant that Houlihan had to be on the road in California calling on all the distributors and retailers. He quickly realized that he would have to clone himself five times to accomplish everything that needed to be done. Meanwhile, Harvey took care of the office and the reorders that eventually began to come in.

Pricing was one of the biggest challenges they had to tackle. In retail there is the concept of Velocity Price Point, which is based on the fact that some things sell faster at one price point than at another. To arrive at their price, Houlihan and Harvey worked backward from the price that needed to be on the shelves for the customers; they subtracted the store's and distributor's cuts and also taxes to arrive at that number. They ended up pricing most of their bottles at $4.99, but that gave them a tiny margin, which meant they had to go back and see where they could fine-tune their understanding of all the costs involved in making and selling wine. They bootstrapped their salesforce by using college interns, but they were surprised by the impact of sales incentives and commissions, which added a high degree of uncertainty to the business. For example, if a store wanted to put the wine on sale for $3.99, Barefoot and the distributor would have to eat the discount. Often the distributor would bill the entire discount to Barefoot. It was at this point that Houlihan finally realized that he wasn't so much in the wine business as he was in the merchandising business and the costs associated with keeping the right amount of wine on the retailers' shelves were extraordinarily high.

As the company grew, Houlihan and Harvey faced some new contradictions. The stores they had been selling to now complained that their price was too high, but when they dropped the prices, those same stores accused them of selling "cheap" wine. Moreover, the small outlets that initially didn't want to carry the Barefoot brand because it was unknown now thought it was too big to carry. Houlihan and Harvey would never stop learning new things about this fascinating industry. Yet eventually the company reached the magical 500,000 cases a year in sales to get noticed by the giant winemaker Gallo, which acquired the company in 2005. The Barefoot brand had become known as "your personal house wine," and it had changed the entire landscape of the wine industry.

Sources: Houlihan, M. and Harvey, B. with R. Kushman. (2013). *The Barefoot Spirit*, Evolve Publishing, Inc.; Burke, A. (May 24, 2013). "Rags-to-Riches Beach Reading: The Barefoot Wine Story," *Yahoo! News*, http://news.yahoo .com/blogs/profit-minded/rags-riches-beach-reading -barefoot-wine-story-211559420.html

Every business requires resources to start and grow. Resource gathering is one area where entrepreneurs demonstrate their unique capabilities to maximize the use of minimal resources, whether in the form of people, equipment, inventory, or cash. Up to this point, you have focused on testing a business model in the market to ensure that there are customers and sufficient demand, and on testing the solution—the product or service—to gauge whether it can be produced at a cost that leaves room to pay overhead and make a profit. With a positive response from the market and a feasible product/service, it now becomes important to consider the financial conditions required for a successful launch and operation of the business to a positive cash flow generated through sales. No matter how many financial tools entrepreneurs use or how many complex analyses they construct, the bottom line for any new venture is cash. Income statements and balance sheets can make a company look good on paper—these are accounting tools—but cash pays the bills and enables the company to grow. A new venture's health is measured by its cash flow and the business metrics that inform that cash flow serve to keep you on track.

It makes no sense at the feasibility analysis stage to create a full set of pro forma financial statements. In the first place, because the business exists only on paper, there is no reliable way to forecast sales and expenses until you conduct proof-of-concept experiments in the field; therefore, any projections for sales and expenses will likely not begin to approach reality. Nevertheless, you are still faced with having to paint a financial picture of your startup that is sufficiently supported by real data. You need this information so that you can achieve legitimacy in the eyes of investors, bankers, and others you will need to tap to make your business a success, and, more importantly, to convince yourself that the venture has potential that can be achieved. Realistically, the only financing early stage companies without proof of concept are going to secure is seed capital from strategic investors who are not expecting to see detailed financial statements (and wouldn't believe them anyway), particularly when chances are the new venture is still in product development.

Second, investors will confirm that what is more important than the financial statements are the assumptions behind the numbers. For instance, how much money will it take for the company to support itself from its cash flows? And how long will that take? Generally speaking, investors focus on the first 18 months to 2 years of a startup because during that time, you are continually adjusting the business model as you respond to the market. The information you gain from this process will help you make decisions about how to grow the business from that point on. Third, absolutely no set of financial projections, no matter how elegant or detailed, survives first contact with customers. It's a simple fact that entrepreneurs do not control their customers' behaviors, and customers are fickle—they can change like chameleons based on new information. Therefore, at the feasibility stage, it is best to simply get a handle on whether this new business can make money (i.e., customers want what is being offered), whether overhead can be kept to a minimum for survival, and how long it will take for the company to be self-sustaining. Once you have determined that the business appears to be feasible, pro forma financials will be built as part of a complete business plan to support the requirements of investors, bankers, or other potential stakeholders. By then, you will have already launched the business and will have more real-life numbers to work with. It's important to keep in mind that at startup, you are testing and revising the business model to refine it based on customer feedback. Startup is an experimental stage, so focusing on a set of financial statements that portray numbers that are fluid is probably not very useful and certainly not the best use of your time. Venture capitalist Steve Blank reminds entrepreneurs that they have to be actively involved not only in customer discovery but also in customer validation. This is too important a task to simply delegate to sales people.[1] Customer validation is the process of determining whether your business has a repeatable sales model; that is, can you demonstrate that multiple customers will buy the solution? The answer to this question will tell you when you can successfully execute the business model.

This chapter is structured to walk you through the process of determining the startup capital and other resource requirements you will need to support your business model. It starts with an understanding of how your business works.

9.1 IDENTIFYING STARTUP RESOURCE REQUIREMENTS

Determining what resources are needed, when they are needed, and how to acquire them is a critical piece of the startup feasibility puzzle. Startup resources include (1) people, such as the founding team, employees, advisors, and independent contractors; (2) physical assets, such as equipment, inventory, and office or plant space; (3) financial resources, such as cash, equity, and debt; and (4) intellectual resources, such as a brand, patents and copyrights, licenses, and proprietary knowledge. At startup the goal is to create a mix of resources that will enable the new venture to start and operate until sales of the product or service produce a positive cash flow, that is, enough cash to cover all the cash outflows without investment capital.

The decisions about resources are related to the four key activities of the business:

1. **The value proposition or solution**: What activities are associated with creating the solution to meet the needs of the customer?
2. **Distribution channels**: What activities do we have to do because of our channel partners?
3. **Customer relationships**: What activities do we have to undertake to maintain good relationships with our customers?
4. **Revenue generation**: What activities do we have to do to produce sufficient revenue?

All of these activities require resources, whether human, financial, intellectual, or physical. One of the secrets to success in constructing this resource mix is to maintain flexibility by acquiring and owning only those resources that cannot be obtained by any other means because ownership reduces flexibility and mobility, two critical needs of a startup venture, and it increases startup capital requirements. A dynamic marketplace, coupled with the natural chaos inherent in startup ventures, requires that startups remain lean as long as possible so that their products, services, and strategies can be tested and modified quickly in response to customers' feedback. Consider the case of a software-as-service startup whose entrepreneur let his ego get the better of him. After signing a long-term lease on prime office space in an expensive section of Los Angeles, he expected potential customers to meet there, be impressed by his success, and decide to do business with him. Instead, he quickly discovered that his customers preferred that he meet them at their businesses or in restaurants, not in his office. Moreover, his software programmers did not require fancy offices; they preferred to work from home. As a result, this entrepreneur soon found himself saddled with expensive overhead that neither his customers nor his employees needed.

It is important to fully understand the key activities of your business because, generally, they are the functions that you may want to keep in house. If a core function of your business is not able to be controlled, then you may not experience a successful launch. One team of young entrepreneurs was trying to solve the problem of credit card fraud and they had devised a microprocessor that would randomly generate new account numbers when the card was used. While the technology itself was feasible, the business model required the team to get banks and credit card companies to sign on to the system, not an easy task when those companies have so much invested in their current technology. The team was unable to validate their customer and so could not control one of four critical activities of the business: customer relationships. Figure 9.1 presents a suggested plan for approaching the capital needs assessment for a new venture. The next sections will walk through those steps you need to take to have a clear picture of your resource needs.

FIGURE 9.1 Steps for Calculating Startup Capital Requirements

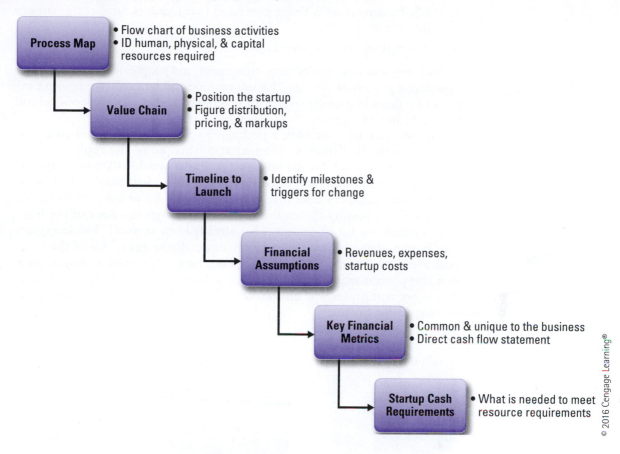

© 2016 Cengage Learning®

9.1a Construct a Business Process Map

Recall that resources can be divided into four categories: human, intellectual, financial, and physical. To identify accurately the resources required to start the venture, it's important to understand all the activities and processes in the business—in other words, to know exactly how the business works. This is best accomplished by creating a process map that details how information flows through the business. Having such a map on hand makes it much easier to define the operations, information flow, and resource requirements of the business. To create a process map, take a virtual tour of your business during a single day, listing all the functions, activities, people, equipment, supplies, and space required to run the business. Figuratively, begin at the front door of the business and ask the following questions:

1. Who does the work in this business?
2. Where do these people work?

3. What do they need to do the work (equipment, major supplies, space, etc.)?

4. What information is being generated (work orders, invoices, customer lists, etc.)?

5. Where does that information go?

Then begin making lists of tasks, equipment, and people needed to complete a particular process or activity. This information will be useful for figuring expenses for financial projections and for determining what kind of personnel will have to be hired to perform those tasks.

Suppose you are launching a packaging solutions business as an example, what is the first thing a customer sees when he or she approaches the business site? The sign for the business? A display window? When customers enter, is there a counter attended by someone who will answer their questions? What equipment does that person use to do his or her job? Note that without going beyond the customer's entry through the door of the business, a significant list of resources has already been amassed. The imaginary tour is one of the best ways to begin to detail the processes in the business. Figure 9.2 traces one such imaginary tour of a service business. Note that this process map also indicates outsourced functions—those activities that other companies will undertake; outsourcing is another resource the company must pay for.

FIGURE 9.2

A Virtual Tour of a Service Business

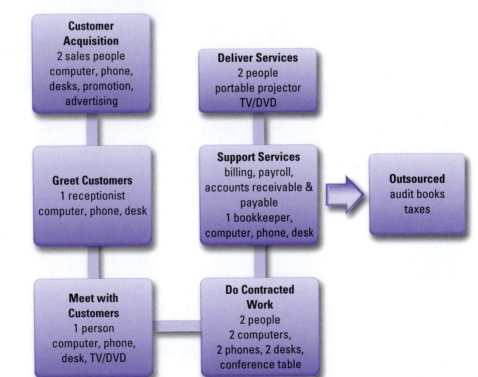

© Cengage Learning®

A product business may involve production and assembly processes in addition to packaging and shipping. Alternatively, you may try to reduce overhead costs by outsourcing production. In this instance, the outsourced capability could be shown on the graphic outside of the workflow of the new venture because it does not require any resources on your part beyond coordination with the company that is managing production and paying for their services.

Returning to Figure 9.2, once all the activities of the business have been identified and the people and equipment recorded, you can go back over the map to see whether the people required for various tasks need to be full-time or part-time employees. A preliminary pass through the example might suggest that 10 people are needed (entrepreneur, two sales people, receptionist, two partners, a bookkeeper, and two delivery/service people) but upon further reflection, a case could be made for reducing that number to the essentials. For example, you and one of your partners might be able to deliver services to the customer in the early stages of the business. Bookkeeping can be outsourced on a part-time or as-needed basis and you and your partners can perform several of the other tasks to bring the total number of full-time employees down to four. Looking at the equipment required is also important. Capital expenditures, which are equipment expenses, can eat up a lot of startup resources, so it would make sense to consider whether any of this equipment could be leased rather than purchased. A process map is a great tool for looking at how your business works so that you can better estimate the resources you will absolutely need and those that can potentially wait until the company is on firmer ground.

9.1b   Position the Venture in the Value Chain

Where your new venture lies in the value chain will determine what its margins are, who its customer is, and how much it can charge for its products and services—in short, what business you are in. In the case of a service business, the task is easy because services are delivered direct to the customer. But the case is much different with a product company. Where the company is positioned determines whether it is a manufacturer or producer, a wholesaler or distributor, or a retailer dealing directly with consumers. Each position produces different margins, different ways of pricing, and different logistics requirements. The value chain was discussed more fully in Chapter 4, but it bears repeating that if done correctly, it gives you a good picture of the environment in which you will be doing business and a better handle on the value your company creates and the price you can charge for that value.

9.1c   Create a Timeline and Milestones for Resource Requirements

The next step in preparing to calculate how much capital will be required to launch the business involves creating a timeline that notes key milestones that you expect to achieve from idea conception to the launch of the business and beyond. Figure 9.3 depicts a timeline to launch for a hypothetical product business (note that due to space constraints we have presented a very aggressive timeline that does not necessarily reflect what is typical). At each monthly milestone the management team expects to complete a specific goal. Notice also that the initial funding requirements have been identified and associated with a milestone. It is also valuable to extend this timeline through at least the first year. This is because the first year is typically a series of ups and downs and it's important to understand what triggers those changes. For example, suppose you project that you will secure a major customer in month 6, but it will take until month 9 to see the benefits of that acquisition in terms of sales revenue. If you didn't know that, you might mistakenly project revenue for those three months that you wouldn't actually have in hand. Now suppose that about month 9, the company needs to plan for a seasonal downswing of revenues. Every company experiences seasonality, which may match the seasons of the year or, as in the case of restaurants, may be a weekly event, with certain days of the week being low revenue days and others being high revenue days. Understanding the market and when customers purchase is important to determining when your company will experience downswings or upswings in its revenues. Going back to the example, in month 10, the company plans to hire an additional salesperson to prepare for the busy season that begins about month 12 and for which they have prepared a vital marketing campaign. There is always a lead time with respect to milestones. These lead times are known as triggers that indicate a change in the current revenue pattern. For example, acquiring a major customer was a trigger for an upswing in revenues. Likewise, bringing on a new salesperson does not mean that he or she will hit the ground running, racking up sales immediately. It can actually take months for a sales person to

FIGURE 9.3   Timeline and Milestone to Launch

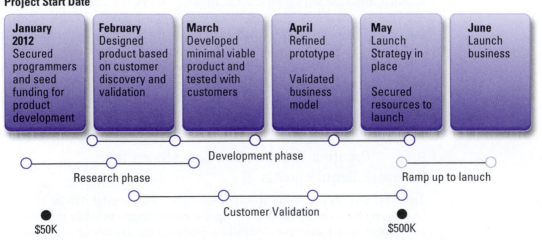

earn more for the company than his or her salary, so you need to allow for some ramp-up time in your calculations.

The bottom line is you need to think carefully about your needs versus your company's ability to generate revenue, and developing a detailed timeline with realistic milestones will help you do that.

9.1d Define Your Launch Strategy to Reduce Risk

The best launch strategy will have identified as many potential risks as possible and eliminated them. But it's not just about eliminating risk; it's about eliminating the right risks in the right order employing the right amount of resources.[2] Gilbert and Eyring wrote in *Harvard Business Review* that risk can be divided into three broad categories that are compatible with former Secretary of Defense Donald Rumsfeld's oft quoted "known, unknowns and unknown unknowns." The four categories are as follows:

- **Deal-killer risks**. It is unfortunate that many entrepreneurs never attempt to kill their businesses in the early stages of their development. What that means is they don't seek out those existential risks that might prevent the business from even launching in the first place. Gilbert and Eyring talk about an entrepreneurial venture in satellite radio that assumed a large latent need in the developing world and signed broadcasting licenses in several countries. Unfortunately, the founders also assumed that customers would be able to access their satellite radio by means of low-cost radio receivers. As it turned out, it was impossible because the required receiver was too complex and therefore costly for people to afford. As a result, the company ultimately went bankrupt.[3] Of course, many of these deal-killer risks fall into the "unknown unknowns" category and are completely unpredictable.

- **Path-dependent risks**. These are risks that arise from a decision to take what turns out to be the wrong path. With sunk costs in that path, do you continue or regroup and move down a better path? This type of risk also happens when a startup needs to hit several markets simultaneously, which is common in a strategy to create a technology standard in the industry. In this case, the startup reduces path-dependent risk by partnering and outsourcing non-core functions like production and application development and focusing on controlling the core technology that serves as the platform on which all the market applications will be built.

- **Low-hanging fruit with high ROI**. These are risks that are easy and cheap to resolve, and it's important to take them on because left unmitigated, they could turn into deal killers or at a minimum waste time and money. Gilbert and Eyring worked with a startup in the early days of the medical tourism industry where patients would fly to countries like India for high-quality care at significantly lower cost than in the United States. Well into the development of their business, they finally decided to do something very inexpensive but vital—talk to patients who were their prospective customers. What they learned told them that their business as designed was doomed to failure because patients were only interested in a small number of procedures and for those particular procedures U.S. hospitals were willing to lower their prices.

Taking the time to consider the risks your business faces is time well spent. It is much easier to figure out ways to mitigate a risk before you face the risk and have to move quickly to deal with it.

In Chapter 6 we talked about the minimum viable product and the value of seeking feedback early and often when failure is at its least expensive. With that in mind, your launch strategy should have several goals.

- To reflect the needs of your customers with respect to the solution, the price, and how it is delivered.

- To reach the best first customers—the ones who need their problem solved the most.

- To have in place the funding needed to reach positive cash flow.

- To reduce as much risk as possible.

In the next section we look at some of the critical financial metrics that startups need to track.

9.2   STARTUP FINANCIAL METRICS

The financial metrics that entrepreneurs employ at startup are different from the metrics that established companies use to monitor their progress toward whatever goals they've set. Startup financial metrics must give entrepreneurs feedback on whether their business model is working and whether it's the business model the startup should retain as it grows. Some of the common metrics that all types of startups use are:

- Sales forecast

- Headcount

- Expenses (fixed and variable)

- Break-even cash flow

In addition, specific types of businesses have unique metrics appropriate to measuring their financial success. Some examples are:

- **Gross margin** (product businesses). This is gross profit divided by gross sales.

- **Inventory turns** (businesses that hold inventory). For many businesses like retail, the frequency with which their inventory turns over provides important information about the success of their marketing strategy and their product mix.

- **Occupancy** (hotels, apartments, commercial). This metric is critical to businesses with assets like hotels that require a certain level of income to break even and begin to make a profit. If vacancy rates reach a particular level, the business is not sustainable.

- **Qualified leads** (Internet businesses). Lead generation processes are designed to produce qualified leads, which are users that fit the image of a qualified buyer and who provide a certain level of activity and response to the company's marketing campaigns.

Let's discuss in more detail some metrics that speak specifically to the creation and capture of value:

- **Customer acquisition costs (CAC)**. In real dollars, how much did it cost the startup to acquire a customer? In figuring CAC, you must convert time to dollars, but the time it takes to secure a customer is time that could have been spent elsewhere, so there's also an opportunity cost that must be considered. Advertising expenses and promotional expenses must also be factored in as well as travel, food, trade shows, conferences, and so forth. Depending on the type of business, the CAC will be different, but there will always be a cost associated with securing customers.

- **Average order size, time to reorder, and lifetime value per customer**. These metrics entail tracking what each customer spends, how often they spend, and based on that data, projecting what the potential lifetime value of that customer is. At startup, with no customers, this metric will be based on market research on similar companies and be discounted to reflect the startup's inexperience in the market.

- **Revenues per salesperson and time to revenue for direct sales**. Entrepreneurs with businesses that sell directly to their customers may employ salespeople. The critical mistake that most entrepreneurs make is not factoring in the amount of time it takes for a new salesperson to get up to speed and begin generating revenue that exceeds their costs and their portion of the contribution margin or overhead. A salesperson selling a better, faster, and cheaper-type product or service will ramp up to revenue fairly quickly, but a salesperson who is selling something brand new or is developing new customer relationships is going to have a much longer ramp-up period, sometimes up to a year.

- **For Internet ventures: acquisition, retention, revenue, viral coefficient**. Internet ventures have unique metrics because they typically start with three types of "customers": (1) visitors or end users, (2) contributors, and (3) distributors, or people who share or refer content to others helping to drive traffic to the site. Today many Internet ventures suffer from some of the same flaws in thinking that plagued the dotcom ventures. Much like Munjal Shah, founder of Riya, a visual search photo service, they think that if they can get coverage by TechCrunch and benefit from a crush of users as a result, their site will go viral—that is, take on a life of its own. Shah succeeded in getting the TechCrunch effect from the blogging community, but his company's servers weren't prepared for the onslaught of users uploading photos to his site. Consequently, the user experience was unsatisfactory, and the initial benefit was lost. Ultimately, the company shut down.[4] This example speaks to the importance of understanding the viral coefficient, which is a measure of how many new users come to the site on referrals by existing users. It's used to track site growth, popularity, and level of engagement by users. As a formula, it is simply

Viral Coefficient = X (invited friends) × Y % (acceptance or conversion rate)

Practically speaking, if the coefficient is greater than 1.0, the site is growing, meaning that each user is bringing in at least one more user; if it's 1, the site is stagnant; and if it's less than 1, growth is slowing. The viral coefficient is simply one metric and it is hampered by the fact that it doesn't incorporate cycle time into the equation. Cycle time affects growth for more than the viral coefficient. The shorter the cycle time (visitor sees the application, tries it, invites friends, friends try application), the more dramatic the growth. Table 9.1 presents some Internet metrics in each of the categories of visitor, contributor, and distributor. In addition, there are many metrics around Internet control, security, infrastructure, and access as well as additional sources for measuring online activity that may be appropriate for certain types of ventures. An excellent summary of these metrics can be found in a research publication by Robert Faris and Rebekah Heacock.[5]

- **Contribution margin**. This figure, expressed as a percentage, is found by subtracting variable costs from revenues and dividing the difference by revenues to yield a percentage. That percentage expresses how much money remains to pay overhead and make a profit after the costs of producing the product are considered. This figure is important because it tells you how much room you have to make errors. If the contribution margin is very small, say 5 percent, there is very little room for error and you will need to plan for volume sales to generate enough money to cover overhead and make a profit.

- **Monthly burn rate**. This figure represents how the startup uses its cash to cover its overhead before it generates a positive cash flow from operations. Burn rate signals to investors whether the company can sustain itself and how quickly it will need another infusion of capital.

TABLE 9.1   Metrics for Web 2.0 Ventures

	Visitor	Contributor	Distributor
	Total unique visitors Total page views Total visits		Shares content with others
Acquisition (Registrations and activations)	Watch a video	Submit a video or other content	Shares a video with other users and other sites
Retention	Visit once a week for 3 months	Submits content once a month	Shares video that drives X visits a month for 3 months
Revenue	Click on an ad (qualified lead)	Pays for subscription or premium membership	Drives X number of premium users

© Cengage Learning®

9.3   DEVELOP FINANCIAL ASSUMPTIONS

With a good handle on how your business works and what specific resources are needed and when, you can attach some numbers to the timeline. To accomplish this, narrative assumptions about the numbers for demand, revenues, expenses, and startup costs must be developed.

One of the biggest problems that many entrepreneurs have when trying to present a case for the financial feasibility of their business models is that they can't justify the numbers they have put into their projections. Unfortunately, the business education courses they may have taken typically haven't prepared them to do this. Although they are wizards at creating spreadsheets with all sorts of what-if scenarios, they are rarely asked to explain where they found the actual numbers they entered into those spreadsheets. When asked, the response is typically, "Well, I did best-case, worst-case, and most-likely-case scenarios and took the average." Or, worse yet, "I assumed we would capture 2 percent of the market." It is not likely that an investor or banker would accept that explanation because there is no justification for how you would capture that 2 percent.

Therefore, the most important part of any analysis of financial feasibility is the assumptions on which the analysis is based. Here is an example of how one entrepreneur explained his customer acquisition costs.

> **Customer acquisition costs**—The company will sell via a direct sales model, which requires regular client contact. In addition, the product plan calls for launching both the core product and the ancillaries at well-attended industry conferences to maximize the value of the presentations. We estimate the associated costs to be as follows:
>
> 1. Customer site visits: 3–4 trips per month beginning July 7 @ $800 each for travel expenses.
>
> 2. Booth price for Gartner-sponsored data mining conference: $3,000 as provided by Gartner representative.
>
> 3. Travel to/from conference for two attendees: 3 conferences, 2 people @ $2,200 each to include transportation, hotel, and meal allowance. [9]

The narrative assumptions play a vital role in helping to explain the entrepreneur's rationale and establish his or her credibility. Therefore, the first step is to find good numbers and then justify them.

9.3a   Estimate New Product/Service Demand

One of the most difficult tasks facing any entrepreneur is estimating the demand for a new product or service, particularly if that product or service has never existed previously in the marketplace. Much of this difficulty is due to a lack of historical data and to issues of seasonality and price discounts. Because entrepreneurs often overestimate the level of sales they will achieve in the early stages of the company, it is important to triangulate demand from at least three different points of view: (1) historical analogy with similar products/services; (2) customer feedback, end-user and intermediary feedback; and

(3) the entrepreneur's own perspective, gleaned from previous experience and from going into limited production or doing a test market. Calculating total demand is only part of the challenge, because every product or service is subject to adoption patterns and rates. Total demand is never achieved all at once but rather accumulates over time. Understanding the adoption patterns of similar products or services will be critical to forecasting sales revenues over the first couple years. Adoption patterns are discussed in Chapter 14.

Use Historical Analogy or Substitute Products

If the new product is an extension of a previously existing product, it may be possible to extrapolate from the existing product's adoption rate and demand to the new product. For example, the demand and adoption rate for compact disks was derived from the historical demand for cassette tapes and records. The adoption patterns did not match exactly, but they certainly landed the entrepreneur in the ballpark. In other cases, it may be possible to turn to another product in the same industry for an indication of demand potential and the rate at which customers will purchase, assuming that the target markets are the same. Channel partners such as distributors and retailers can help you gauge the adoption rate for products in the same category as your product.

Talk to Customers and Intermediaries

When attempting to gauge levels of demand, the customer is certainly the prime source of information, but many entrepreneurs fail to ask the right questions so that customers will give them honest answers. Asking "would you buy this product?" or "how much would you pay for this product?" is going about it the wrong way. This approach will overestimate the level of demand because customers have no reason to say no—no one is asking them to pay for anything, so they have nothing to lose by saying "yes." A better approach is to gauge demand from the customers' responses to your solution to their problem. In other words, presenting potential customers with a solution in the form of a product or service and then monitoring the feedback and response to it will give you an honest estimate of whether this customer would purchase or not. Better yet is developing your solution with customers, in effect, building the solution to meet a specific demand.

For example, suppose when you do demonstrate your complete solution to customers that 7 out of 10 potential customers respond positively to the solution. Given that these responses might be optimistic, you should consider reducing the ratio. The amount of reduction is purely arbitrary and is based on how confident you are in the responses received from research with the customer. Suppose you decide to reduce the estimate of demand to 6 out of 10, or 60 percent. Applying this percentage to the size of the niche market that you intend to enter can give a rough estimate of how many total customers might purchase. Then comparing these results with feedback from value chain partners might confirm the numbers or cause you to modify the estimate. Results of research on adoption patterns for similar products or services would then be applied to determine sales on a month-by-month basis. Of course it will also be important to factor in how quickly you can produce certain quantities of product or provide a particular service.

No one knows the market better than the men and women who work in it every day. They are typically very astute at predicting trends and patterns of buyer behavior. Spending time in the field talking with intermediaries (distributors or wholesalers, sometimes referred to as "middlemen"), retailers, and the like can provide a fairly good estimate of demand or at least a range that would validate what you found when talking with customers. With a consumer product, observing the buying patterns of consumers for a similar product could be useful.

Use Your Knowledge and Experience

The knowledge and experience you bring to the business will be helpful in forecasting sales, particularly if you have worked in the industry in which the business will be operating. However, it is important to remember that your experience is anecdotal and should always be confirmed by other sources.

Go into Limited Production

The best way, and sometimes the only way, to accurately gauge customer demand is to go into business in a limited way—produce a small number of products and get them into the hands of people to use. If you have an Internet business, put up a functional website with the core features to get feedback. Going into limited production is also an appropriate next step if the other techniques have produced positive results. Limited testing of a product will not only gauge customer satisfaction in a very real way, but it may also suggest possible modifications to improve the product. This technique also works for service businesses and is excellent for testing procedures and for gauging the actual time it takes to provide a service, something that is difficult to do when you are not working with an actual customer.

9.3b   Pricing Assumptions

Pricing a product or service is as much a part of a launch strategy as it is of the financial strategy. Unfortunately, entrepreneurs typically have to price their products and services long before they know the exact costs of producing the product and before they have a good handle on the price the customer will pay. Pricing is one of the many features associated with a product or service; it becomes the central selling point when the product or service is a commodity—that is, when the only feature differentiating the product or service from those offered by competitors is price. Some examples of commodities are basic food products, such as milk, and most electronics categories that have been in the market for some time, such as desktop computers and printers. Wherever there is competitive rivalry, prices will be driven down. Entrepreneurs can price new technology at a premium because it offers features and benefits not currently in the market, but technology quickly becomes a commodity as competitors introduce their versions, driving prices down.

Here we discuss pricing as it relates to your attempt to calculate startup capital requirements. Pricing is addressed as part of the marketing mix in Chapter 14. Innovation expert Clayton Christensen once said that customers do not buy products; they hire products to do a job.[6] What he meant is that in conventional marketing we tend to segment markets by customer attributes rather than by customer needs, which is how customers really make their buying decisions. Christensen believes that it's important to understand what job a customer needs done and to create a solution that the customer can "hire" to get the job done. In other words, pricing is really about cost and value in use.[7] Let's look at this idea in more detail.

When you ask entrepreneurs how they are going to price their offerings, they often respond based on cost to produce. One mistake many entrepreneurs make is to set their prices so that they cover total costs plus a margin the entrepreneur is expecting to achieve. The problem with this approach is that pricing is not designed to cover *total* costs but "to maximize total contribution (i.e., unit price minus unit variable costs)."[8] What this means is that fixed costs (overhead) should not be apportioned within the price because these costs do not come into play when generating additional sales. It is the contribution margin that affects profitability. For example,

Unit price = $49.95

Variable costs (material costs, direct and indirect labor, factory overhead) = $35

Contribution margin = $49.95 − $35.00 = $14.95 or 30% of unit price

The contribution margin represents the amount available to pay for fixed costs and provide a profit to the business.

You need to be aware that every industry has discounts associated with its various products and services. These include such things as cash and quantity discounts. You should factor these discounts into your pricing models and into your cash needs for the business.

While cost is one important factor to consider, there are other equally important factors. For example, how a product or service is priced is a function of a company's goals. If the goal is to *increase sales* or *market share*, prices may need to be lowered to raise the volume sold. If the goal is to *maximize cash flow*, raising prices and reducing direct costs and overhead may be the answer. *Maximizing profit* can be accomplished by raising prices, lowering prices and increasing volume, or decreasing overhead. If the goal is to *define an image*, setting a higher price based on higher perceived and/or actual quality is one way of establishing a particular image in a market. To *control demand* when a company doesn't have the resources to meet it may mean temporarily setting prices at a level that discourages sales to a particular degree. This approach also enables the company to recuperate its initial development costs through higher margins.

These are all important considerations but for startups perhaps the most important factor to consider is the value the customer perceives in using the product or service. Some of that value will be based on utility—getting the job done. Additional value will come from reducing opportunity costs for the next best alternative. Today, customers often perceive great value in experiences, which means what the entire customer journey was like—was it satisfying from beginning to end?

Customer goals influence entrepreneurs' pricing strategies. Figure 9.4 depicts two scenarios for an entrepreneur who is offering a customer management software solution. In the first scenario, Customer A's goal is to keep operational costs low because their margins are thin. This type of customer focuses on price and makes purchasing decisions accordingly; consequently, the entrepreneur's margins will be small. This is a typical commodity situation. By contrast, the second scenario depicts a customer whose goal is to improve the way the company manages its customers; in other words, this customer has a real problem that the entrepreneur can solve, so the entrepreneur's margins can be greater because a higher price can be charged. Entrepreneurs must decide which customer to target first so their company can enter the market and survive until it has a chance to grow. To accomplish that, it makes sense to target the customer who is in the most pain—who has a problem that the entrepreneur's product or service can solve. In this way, the entrepreneur can charge a premium and recoup development costs before competition enters the market and causes prices to decline.

There is a lot of evidence that customers will pay more for perceived superior benefits. Look no further than private labeled consumer products where the private label is always cheaper than the branded label for the same product; yet, customers are willing to pay more for the perceived benefit of getting a branded product.

Knowing what a pricing strategy is supposed to accomplish in advance of setting a price will ensure compatibility with company goals, both yours and the customer's. Table 9.2 presents the most common general pricing strategies. For entrepreneurs, a combination of cost-based pricing and demand-based pricing with consideration for a premium based on the novelty of what

FIGURE 9.4
Customer Goals and Price

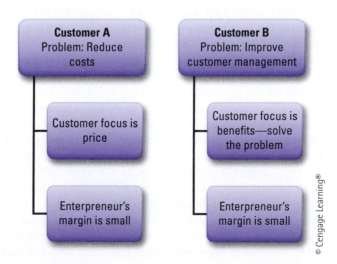

© Cengage Learning®

TABLE 9.2
Common Pricing
Strategies at Startup

Premium Pricing	Uses a high price to reflect a unique product/service and a significant competitive advantage.
Price Skimming	Starts with a high price to capture uniqueness and competitive advantage. Then as new competitors enter the market, drops the price to stay ahead of competition.
Demand-Based Pricing	Find out what customers are willing to pay for the product and price it accordingly.
Captive Product Pricing	Where the entrepreneur's product has complements, charge a low price for source product (i.e., a printer) and a premium for consumables (i.e., ink cartridges).
Psychological Pricing	To create a complex pricing structure by combining multiple products and services into one package.
Product Bundle Pricing	In a channel with many intermediaries (distributors, retailers), the final price to the consumer or end-user must be tolerable, given all the markups along the value chain. Compare what the market will bear with the cost of getting a product to market.
Geographical Pricing	Used where there are price variations in different geographical locations where the product is sold.

© Cengage Learning®

is being offered can work well. For new products or services with no direct comparison, this approach is often used to arrive at a satisfactory price. In general, customers recognize several prices for any one product: the standard price, which is the price normally paid for the item; the sale price; the price paid for specials; and the relative price, which is the price of the item compared to the price of a substitute product. For some products, customers may have to add the normal cost of shipping, handling, or installation to their comparison with other like products.

The Internet and search engines like Google have had a major impact on companies' pricing models because it is easy for customers to compare pricing across all competitors. Simple products, those whose price is transparent, or easily identified, are most subject to downward pricing pressure. Complex products (those that are bundled or modular) are more difficult to compare directly across companies, so they typically command a higher price.[9] An example is cell phone rates when they include a fixed monthly fee and a per-minute charge for options.

In Chapter 5, the freemium model was discussed as a potential revenue source as it is a common model for many Internet ventures. It is based on offering your product or service with minimal features and benefits for free in the hopes that those users will convert to paying customers to secure better benefits. But the fact is that only about one to two percent of users upgrade over two years, so you need millions of users to cover your costs. Chargify, a 2009 startup, offers billing management software. At launch they offered the software free to merchants who were billing fewer than 50 customers per month. None of those merchants converted to the paid version and Chargify was on the road to bankruptcy. However, the company took a risk and changed to a subscription business model with a $65 per month starter plan and by July 2012 they were profitable. The lesson learned was that you must incentivize conversion; in other words, the value for converting must be obvious to the customer and there must be a natural progression from free to paid. Dropbox, the cloud storage company, understood this when they limited the amount of storage you could have for free in the belief that users would begin to store much more than they originally thought and would need to upgrade to a paid version to acquire more space.

Converging on a Price

There are no formulas that will give your new venture with no track record a solution to the problem of pricing. Furthermore, getting answers from industry will not be an easy task; most companies do not want to talk about pricing because it is the cornerstone of their competitive strategy.[10] However, given the considerations discussed previously and triangulating by taking into account (1) costs, (2) any competitor pricing, and (3) feedback from customers and value chain partners, you can reach a number that can be tested in the market. The importance of understanding customer behavior cannot be stressed enough. If, for example, a product is complex and it is difficult for customers to judge quality, they will rely on price as a proxy for quality and therefore choose the higher-priced item. On the other hand, if the product bears a known brand, they might be willing to purchase the lower-priced item. Likewise, if the customer savings are small and the price is close to the best alternative, the customer will incur switching costs that may influence their willingness to buy. Keep in mind that the reference value of the product/service (the price as compared to competing products—the expected price) plus the differentiation value (the customer's perception) equals the maximum price you can charge.

9.3c   Estimate Revenues, Expenses, and Startup Costs

Estimating revenues, expenses, and startup costs at the feasibility stage is a daunting task at best for entrepreneurs. At the nascent stage everything is fluid, so most of the numbers collected will change after the business is launched and factors you didn't consider come into play. There are many reasons why feasibility estimates of sales, expenses, and startup costs will probably change by the time you're actually in business.

1. If your business involves manufacturing or outsourcing to a manufacturer, it will be nearly impossible to estimate parts and manufacturing costs accurately without a production-quality product in place. For this reason, it is important to get to a physical prototype early, so as to have a better idea of the parts, components, and types of materials that will be needed, as well as what provision to make for labor.

2. For many new product companies, product development may take several months to several years, depending on the nature of the product—and the costs for prototyping are always substantially higher than the ultimate production costs will be. Therefore, it is difficult to determine true feasibility from an economic perspective before there is a physical prototype.

GLOBAL INSIGHTS

Migration Still a Strong Source of Entrepreneurship

The Global Entrepreneurship Monitor 2012, which included 69 countries, reports that there are more than 210 million international immigrants worldwide. And there is increasing evidence that the growth in migration will continue. For the countries that are at the receiving end of immigration, challenges arise around integrating these newcomers economically and socially. Often, however, the benefits of immigration outweigh the associated difficulties as the GEM report found that in innovation and factor-driven economies like the United States and Egypt respectively, migrants participated more frequently in entrepreneurship than non-migrants, and they tended to market their products to international customers. In innovation or developed economies, greater than 10 percent of new businesses have first-generation immigrants as founders. Some examples in the United States are Google and Sun Microsystems. The countries from which people are emigrating also derive benefits and suffer challenges. Benefits arise from emigrants returning to their country of origin with additional knowledge and resources to add to the economic development of the country. On the negative side, these countries often face the challenge of brain drain, with young people leaving to seek opportunities in countries where the economy is growing. Despite challenges with migration, the bottom line is that migration has a net positive impact on economic growth and global competitiveness.

Source: *Global Entrepreneurship Monitor,* 2012 Global Report, http://www.babson.edu /Academics/centers/blank-center/global-research/gem/Documents/GEM%202012%20 Global%20Report.pdf

Source: Bosma, N. and Levie, J. (2009). *Global Entrepreneurship Monitor, 2009* Executive Report , www.gemconsortium.org/about.aspx?page=pub_gem_global_reports.

3. For service companies, the actual costs to deliver a service must be based initially on information gathered from other companies in the industry. This is tricky to achieve without "inside information"—that is, without knowing someone who works in that type of company. Estimates for the cost of delivery of the service will be more accurate if the service is prototyped under a variety of the most common scenarios. For example, a restaurant owner might want to calculate how long it takes to completely serve a customer, from arrival to departure. The owner needs to look at the number of tables planned, hours of operation, and the number of servers and cooks needed. Peak and slow periods and other aspects of serving customers are also factored in. The more variables that can be accounted for, the better the estimates will be.

4. As you grow in knowledge of your industry by being in business, you naturally gather better information because you know whom to talk with and where to find the best industry intelligence. Because getting inside an industry is difficult and time-consuming, many entrepreneurs choose to start ventures in industries with which they're familiar or in which they have experience.

Let's now focus on how to estimate revenues, expenses, and total startup costs.

Sales Forecast

Revenue is the accounting term for the business' sources of income. For startups, the primary sources are sales of products, services, or subscriptions. In Chapter 5, we discuss various sources of revenue to consider when developing your business model. Here we look at how to forecast sales off your revenue model.

The sales forecast should be calculated first because the volume of sales you project affects many business expenditures. For example, the cost of producing a product is usually tied to how many products you can sell — it's called *economies of scale*. The higher the volume, the lower the cost. Using the timeline, milestones, and triggers developed previously, and the demand and adoption rate estimates, the sales revenues can be laid out. An example of a forecast can be found in Figure 9.5 in the next section. In this example of a mobile peer-to-peer payment company, the 7,500 users per financial institution is an industry average number for online banking and bill pay usage for a bank with more than 12,000 total customers.[11] It is necessary to remember that any increase in sales will be influenced by the following factors:

- Growth rates in the market segment of the product or service
- The innovations offered that will make the product/service more attractive to the consumer, even at a higher price
- The technological innovations employed that enable the entrepreneur to produce the product or service at a lower cost than competitors, thus making it more accessible and enticing to the consumer

Net sales are the result of subtracting customer acquisition costs as well as channel and associated costs. Sales are rarely consistent over a year. What your sales cycle looks like will depend on your customers' buying patterns and the type of product or service you're offering. For example, for consumer retail companies, it is typical that the biggest surge in sales comes in the fourth quarter. It is important that you understand at what points during the year the sales will likely increase or decrease and why that will happen. Most entrepreneurs cannot effectively predict sales, so you will need to prepare for scenarios of lower-than-projected sales or demand greater than expected. How do these scenarios impact your bottom line?

Expenses

Once sales have been forecast, predicting some expenditures becomes much easier, particularly for those expenditures that vary with the volume of sales, such as the direct costs of producing the product or service. In wholesale businesses, for example, after the sales forecast has been determined, the figures for inventory purchases can be applied as a percentage of sales and forecast from that. Therefore, if inventory cost is 25 percent of sales, you can apply that percentage to sales as they increase to forecast increases in the volume of inventory. Be aware, however, that in some industries, volume discounts on raw materials or inventory may actually reduce costs over time and should be factored into the expenditure forecast. Whether volume discounts will be available is an important piece of information that is gathered during field research.

In manufacturing businesses, forecasting expenditures is a bit more complex because cost of goods sold (COGS) must be derived first. COGS consists of direct labor, cost of materials, and direct factory overhead. Applying COGS as a percentage of sales will probably suffice for purposes of pro forma statements for the feasibility stage. Month-by-month analysis of outcomes and use of a cost accounting model that considers raw materials inventory, work-in-process inventory, finished-goods inventory, total inventory, factory overhead, work-in-process flow in units, and weighted-average cost per unit will give a more accurate estimate as the business grows.

In service businesses, the COGS is equivalent to the time expended to produce and deliver the service. The rate at which the service is billed, say $100 an hour, comprises the actual expenses incurred in providing the service, a contribution to overhead, and a reasonable profit. The actual expenses incurred are equivalent to the cost of goods sold.

In addition to the costs associated directly with producing your product or service you will have sales, general and administrative expenses (SG&A). Direct selling expenses include advertising costs, travel expenses, sales salaries, commissions, and the cost of promotional supplies, while indirect selling expenses, which are not linked to the sale of a specific product, are proportionally distributed to all products sold during a particular period of time (telephone, interest, and postal charges). General and administrative expenses will include the salaries of nonsales personnel and overhead such as rent, utilities, and equipment expenses. In general, entrepreneurs tend to underestimate their costs, so it is important to get your cost estimates from reliable sources so the discrepancy between what you projected at startup is not substantially different than what you actually encounter when the business is in operation.

Startup Costs

The bulk of expenses in the first year of a new business are probably incurred prior to the business opening its doors for the first time. Startup costs are all those expenses you incur prior to the business being in operation. The costs of purchasing furniture, equipment, startup inventory, and supplies can quickly add up to a substantial amount—and that doesn't include deposits for leases and utilities. A manufacturing startup might also include product development costs, a deposit on the lease for production facility, and raw materials costs. Startups with new products typically accrue heavy pre–startup development costs that include engineering, programming, prototyping, and patent assessment and application. These are onetime expenses to get the business started. In addition, you must remember that employees may need training before the business opens, so that becomes part of the startup costs as well.

Keeping the Numbers Real

It's important for entrepreneurs to keep in mind that all of the numbers they come up with in their forecasts will be challenged and they must be prepared to defend them. It's difficult to do that if the estimate was simply pulled out of the air. "We assumed…." will not justify a number. There is a 100 percent chance that the numbers from the feasibility analysis will be wrong, but effort should be put into getting as close to the right number as possible. The founders of Redfin, an online real estate broker, shared their startup numbers against their numbers two years later and the difference was telling. Table 9.3 presents a summary of some of their expenses. It is instructive to note that many numbers worked in favor of the startup. This was due to the fact that the founders, while building their financial model, assumed the worst-case scenario each month. Their goal was to outperform their estimates, and in most cases they did. Founder Glenn Kelman had seen too many cases of venture-funded Internet businesses that had burned through their money because they hadn't correctly or conservatively estimated their expenses.

Entrepreneurs need to remember that employee costs are the biggest costs the business will bear because of all the associated taxes and any benefits offered, so it's vital to track the number of employees needed and all costs associated with that employee and to keep in mind that employee costs go up every year.

Finally, it's important for entrepreneurs to compare their estimates to what other similar companies in the industry spend. It's not easy to get private company figures, but even public company numbers at least provide a sense of the upper limit of possibility. No startup is going to achieve anything close to the numbers for a public company, so those numbers are an important reality check.

TABLE 9.3
Redfin: How Startup Expense Estimates Change

Type of Expense	Redfin's Model	Actual Expenditures
Rent per employee per month	$250	$336
Initial per-employee equipment cost	$6,500	$5,700
Annual payroll tax	12.5%	8.5%
Monthly travel costs	$300	$369
Monthly telephone costs per field employee	$125	$261
Annual accounting costs	$45,000	$32,912

Source: Kelman, G. (October 1, 2007). "Financial Models for Underachievers: Two Years of the Real Numbers of a Startup," *How to Change the World,* http://blog.guykawasaki.com/2007/10/financial-model.html#axzz0uM3rRMgX.

9.4   CALCULATING A STARTUP'S CASH REQUIREMENTS

Developing the cash flow statement is the first step in arriving at startup cash requirements. For feasibility purposes a direct cash flow statement, essentially a cash budget or sources and uses statement, is used so that cash inflows and outflows are easy to identify and examine. Figure 9.5 displays a direct cash flow statement (also known as sources and uses) through month 14 for a mobile payment product company. The entrepreneur would support these numbers with narrative assumptions to explain how the figures were derived. The first section of the statement displays key milestones for the first 14 months of the business that will affect sales forecasts and expenses. The next section is cash inflows, which records all the inflows of cash into the business *when they are received*. Therefore, if a sale is made in March, for example, but payment is not received until April, the sale is counted in April on the cash flow statement because that's when it was received. Note that an income statement (also known as a profit and loss statement) differs from a cash flow statement in this regard. Income is recorded when the transaction accrues, which may not be when the money is received, resulting in a receivable on the income statement.

The next section records cash outflows or disbursements. These are the expenses of the business and they are recorded when the company actually pays the bill. The final section of the cash flow statement provides crucial information about the net change in cash flow—in other words, whether the business had a positive or a negative cash flow in that month. Note that in each month, the net cash flow reflects only the cash inflows and outflows for that month, assuming no startup capital. Recall that the goal is to figure out how much startup capital is required. In the example in Figure 9.5, an additional line, the net cumulative cash flow, provides a critical piece of the cash needs requirements, which is the highest cumulative negative cash flow number. This figure ($564,374, which occurs in month 14), plus startup costs, is the minimum amount the entrepreneur needs to survive until a positive cash flow is generated from sales, which for this company occurs in month 18, supposing no investment capital.

Because this figure is an estimate based on a whole series of estimates, there is a very good chance that it is not entirely accurate, so entrepreneurs typically add a safety margin or contingency factor. The safety margin is an amount of cash that is often based on the sales and collection cycle of the business. If, for example, customers typically pay on a 60-day cycle, it will be important to be able to cover at least 60 days of fixed costs. The business used in this example is typical of most startup businesses in that it takes time to generate enough sales and other sources of cash to cover the costs of doing business, but it is important to calculate how much money is needed to start and operate the business to a positive cash flow, meaning the business is self-sustaining, so that you can make a wise assessment of how much capital to raise.

Table 9.4 presents a breakout of the startup capital requirements for the mobile payment company. Note that the cash needs are separated into types of

FIGURE 9.5 Sample Direct Cash Flow Statement for Mobile Payment Product Company

Milestones	Mo. 1	2	3	4	5	6	7	8	9	10	11	12	13	14
New Financial Institutions (FI) on System	0	0	0	0	0	1	0	1	0	1	0	1	1	0
Cumulative Financial Institutions	0	0	0	0	0	1	1	2	2	3	3	4	5	5
Consumer Transactions	500	575	656	747	852	971	1,107	1,262	1,439	1,640	1,870	2,132	2,430	2,770
Salaried FTE	2	2	2	2	2	2	2	2	2	3	3	3	4	4
Lease Office Space	0	0	0	0	0	0	0	0	0	0	0	0	1	1
Cash Inflows	**Mo. 1**	**2**	**3**	**4**	**5**	**6**	**7**	**8**	**9**	**10**	**11**	**12**	**13**	**14**
Financial Institution (FI) Revenue														
FI Users (Net 30)	0	0	0	0	0	0	7,500	7,500	15,000	15,000	22,500	22,500	30,000	37,500
FI User Churn	0	0	0	0	0	0	0	0	−75	−75	−150	−150	−225	−225
Integration Fees (Net 30)	0	0	0	0	0	40,000	0	40,000	0	40,000	0	40,000	40,000	0
Total FI Revenue	0	0	0	0	0	40,000	7,500	47,500	14,925	54,925	22,350	62,350	69,775	37,275
Consumer Revenue														
Transactions (Net 30)	0	100	115	131	149	170	194	221	252	288	328	374	426	486
Total Consumer Revenue	0	100	115	131	149	170	194	221	252	288	328	374	426	486
Total Cash Inflows	0	100	115	131	149	40,170	7,694	47,721	15,177	55,213	22,678	62,724	70,201	37,761
Cash Outflows	**Mo. 1**	**2**	**3**	**4**	**5**	**6**	**7**	**8**	**9**	**10**	**11**	**12**	**13**	**14**
Fixed Costs														
Capex Equipment	50,000													
Salaries	10,000	10,000	10,000	10,000	10,000	10,000	10,000	10,000	10,000	15,000	15,000	15,000	20,000	20,000
Commissions	0	0	0	0	0	4,000	750	4,750	1,493	5,493	2,235	6,235	6,978	3,728
FTE Workstations	5,000	0	0	0	0	0	0	0	0	2,500	0	0	2,500	0
R&D Costs	250,000	0	0	0	0	0	0	0	0	0	0	0	100,000	0

(continued)

FIGURE 9.5 Sample Direct Cash Flow Statement for Mobile Payment Product Company *(continued)*

Cash Outflows	Mo. 1	2	3	4	5	6	7	8	9	10	11	12	13	14
Office Space w/ Utilities	0	0	0	0	0	0	0	0	0	0	0	0	5,000	5,000
Office Equipment	500	500	500	500	500	500	500	500	500	500	500	500	750	750
Advertising	750	750	750	750	750	750	750	750	750	750	750	750	1,000	1,000
Travel & Entertainment	1,000	1,000	1,000	1,000	1,000	1,000	2,000	2,000	2,000	2,000	2,000	2,000	2,000	2,000
Accounting	1,000	1,000	1,000	1,000	1,000	1,000	1,000	1,000	1,000	1,000	1,000	1,000	1,000	1,000
Legal	1,500	1,500	1,500	1,500	1,500	1,500	1,500	1,500	1,500	1,500	1,500	1,500	1,500	1,500
Insurance	1,000	1,000	1,000	1,000	1,000	1,000	1,000	1,000	1,000	1,000	1,000	1,000	1,000	1,000
FTE Load	3,500	3,500	3,500	3,500	3,500	3,500	3,500	3,500	3,500	5,250	5,250	5,250	7,000	7,000
Total Fixed Costs	324,250	19,250	19,250	19,250	19,250	23,250	21,000	25,000	21,743	34,993	29,235	33,235	148,728	42,978
Variable Costs														
Server Lease	1,200	1,200	1,200	1,200	1,200	2,700	2,700	4,200	4,200	5,700	5,700	7,200	8,700	8,700
Transportation	1,500	1,500	1,500	1,500	1,500	3,000	3,000	4,500	4,500	6,000	6,000	7,500	9,000	9,000
Installation Costs	500	500	500	500	500	1,000	500	1,000	500	1,000	500	1,000	1,000	500
Cell Phones	500	500	500	500	500	500	500	500	500	750	750	750	1,000	1,000
Internet	500	500	500	500	500	500	500	500	500	750	750	750	1,000	1,000
Total Variable Costs	4,200	4,200	4,200	4,200	4,200	7,700	7,200	10,700	10,200	14,200	13,700	17,200	20,700	20,200
Total Cash Outflows	328,450	23,450	23,450	23,450	23,450	30,950	28,200	35,700	31,943	49,193	42,935	50,435	169,428	63,178
Net Cash In/Outflow	−328,450	−23,350	−23,335	−23,319	−23,301	9,220	−20,506	12,021	−16,765	6,020	−20,257	12,289	−99,226	−25,416
Cumulative Cash Flow	−328,450	−351,800	−375,135	−398,454	−421,754	−412,534	−433,040	−421,018	−437,783	−431,763	−452,020	−439,731	−538,957	−564,374

Capital Expenditures (CE)	In Dollars	
Equipment	50,000	
Pre-Operating Startup Costs (POSU)		
R&D Costs	250,000	
Salaries	10,000	
FTE Workstations	5,000	
Office Equipment	500	
Advertising	750	
Travel & entertainment	1,000	
Accounting	1,000	
Legal	1,000	
Insurance	1,000	
FTE Load	3,500	
Server Lease	1,200	
Transportation	1,500	
Installation Costs	500	
Cell Phones	500	
Internet	500	
Total Pre-Op SU	277,950	
Working Capital (WC)		
Working Capital Needs	236,424	Difference between highest cumulative negative CF and CAPEX + Pre-Op SU
Highest Cumulative Negative CF	564,374	
Safety Factor (SF)		
Safety Factor	77,000	120 days of fixed expenses
Total Startup Capital	641,374	

capital resources that will be required: capital expenditures, startup expenses, working capital, and a safety margin, which is a contingency amount based on the probability that the entrepreneur's estimates might be off (a fairly safe assumption). Breaking out the total funding requirements by types of capital helps an entrepreneur make decisions that might bring down the cost of starting the business. For example, it appears that this entrepreneur requires a $50,000 piece of equipment. That is a significant expenditure at startup; the entrepreneur might want to investigate whether leasing the equipment might make sense. From this capital requirements analysis, it is clear that the entrepreneur will need a minimum of $641,374, including the safety margin, to start and operate this business until it generates a positive cash flow in month 18.

9.4a Assessing Risk

Many entrepreneurs make the mistake of thinking they have done a complete analysis of their startup financial requirements because they have generated pages of spreadsheets with numbers that, on the surface, appear to work. And if they have developed assumptions that justify their numbers, it is not irrational on their part to believe their work is done. But this would be a mistake. The true test of financial feasibility is whether the key financial figures are in line with the company's goals and are achievable. What would be the effect on the financials of a change in price, a decline in sales, or unexpected demand? What would be the effect on cash flow if the company grew at a more rapid pace than the predicted percentage a year? What if it grew more slowly? How sensitive to change are the cash flow numbers? And how will the company deal with these changes? Creating scenarios to consider the impact of these kinds of changes is called sensitivity analysis.

At the feasibility stage, it is important to consider the potential changes to the forecasts with the highest probability of occurrence and to factor in how the impact of these changes will be dealt with. Analyzing the financial risks and benefits of a new venture is a difficult and challenging exercise, but it must be done so that two fundamental questions can be answered: (1) Do the startup capital requirements make sense? In other words, is the business financially feasible? and (2) looking at the capital investment and the profit possibilities, is there enough money in this opportunity to make the effort worthwhile?

Unfortunately, many businesses are financially feasible—they can make a profit—but the return on the initial investment is so low that an entrepreneur would be better off putting that investment into real estate or some other vehicle. New businesses take an extraordinary amount of work, which entrepreneurs often fail to put a value on. All too often, the business is running and making a profit, but the entrepreneur is making less than he or she would have made working for someone else. The feasibility stage, when the investment has still been minimal, is the time to look seriously at financial feasibility and quantify the risks and potential benefits. Once the venture has been deemed feasible in all respects, a business plan with a full set of financial statements can be developed. That process will further reduce the uncertainty inherent in the startup process.

Figuring out how much money will be needed to launch and operate a new venture can be a daunting task for any entrepreneur, even one with a finance background, because there are so many unknowns and unknowables. Startup finances are based on best-guess projections for what the future might look like. That is why your assumptions are so important; they serve to justify the numbers and provide a rationale for the thought process you followed to reach those numbers. A well-conceived financial plan will go a long way toward ensuring that the business is started with the appropriate amount of capital and for the right reasons.

New Venture Action Plan

- Determine the startup metrics for your company.

- Gather the numbers you need for performing your financial analysis.

- Gather sales forecast data through triangulation.

- Create a cash flow statement from startup until a positive cash flow is achieved.

- Perform a cash requirements assessment to determine how much capital you will need to start the business.

- Determine whether this venture is financially feasible.

Questions on Key Issues

1. Describe the typical metrics for a startup business.
2. What are the types of resources that entrepreneurs need to gather to start a new venture?
3. Why is the cash flow statement the most important statement for the entrepreneur?
4. What are some ways to forecast sales effectively for a retail business? For a manufacturer? For a service business?

5. What are the three categories of funds in the cash needs assessment, and how are they used to calculate how much money is needed to start the business?

Experiencing Entrepreneurship

1. Interview a banker and an investor about the key financial statements that entrepreneurs need to understand to launch their businesses. Ask about the biggest mistakes business owners make in preparing their financial models. Compare and contrast the responses of the banker and the investor. Are their views of the financials different? Why? Prepare your responses in a two-page report.

2. Interview an entrepreneur who has been in business no longer than five years to find out how he or she calculated how much money was needed to start the venture. Did it turn out to be enough? Why or why not? In a brief PowerPoint presentation, present what you would have advised the entrepreneur to do differently.

Relevant Case Studies

Appendix Currency13

PART III

BUSINESS DESIGN

The Customer Journey

From the moment the customer is aware of us, what are the touch points with our company where we can create value?

Touch Points for Marketing Strategy & Value Creation

- Awareness of need
- Search
- Select
- Order or purchase
- Finance
- Pay
- Receive
- Install
- Store and move
- Use
- Repair and return
- Service
- Final disposal

- How do customers view us?
- Where are we not using valuable data?
- What are the most critical points in the journey?
- What do our customers need at each point in the journey?

CHAPTER 10

Preparing a Business Plan

"When all is said and done, the journey is the reward. There is nothing else."

—RANDY KOMISAR, THE MONK AND THE RIDDLE

CHAPTER OBJECTIVES

- Describe how to prepare to construct a business plan.
- Identify stakeholder interests.
- Explain how to demonstrate proof of concept.
- List the components of a compelling executive summary.
- Discuss the elements of an effective business plan.
- Describe how to successfully pitch a new business.

PROFILE
10.1

ANATOMY OF A NEW BUSINESS FAILURE IN SOUTH AFRICA

"Airborne wiped out every cent I had in the world, and I think it aged me rather rapidly. It also taught me a butt-load about raising money, hiring people, and evangelizing a cause. It was my life, my identity for so many years… and now it's gone.… I will tackle this tiger one day, but that day is not today.… It's time to recharge and rebuild." These were the words of Airborne founder Justin Melville posted on Reddit after he had just announced the closing of his startup after only two years.

Melville, a designer, has always loved to solve big problems; in 2008 he decided to focus his thinking on the music industry where there seemed to be a lot of big problems, especially the problem that artists have getting heard and connecting with their fan base. Taking a page from the Medici approach to the patronage of artists, a practice prevalent during the Renaissance, he came up with a business model that overcomes the music licensing problems that plague music lovers and artists around the world. From his perspective, artists want to get their creations out to as many people as possible and do that by getting to the fans' hearts, minds, and wallets. According to Melville, it's the job of the artist to win the loyalty of his or her fans (called "carriers") so they will want to support that artist with just $1 per month for the right to freely receive and share that artist's music. For the artists, it can mean a regular income that enables them to go on creating.

Initially self-funded, Airborne was built by five Ukrainian contract developers, one developer in Switzerland, and seven more in Cape Town, South Africa. Melville had no trouble signing up bands and it was quickly apparent that the super fans were willing to pay to support their favorite artists, with the average user supporting one to two bands per month and about 15 percent of users paying more than $1 per month to the artists they supported. However, like most Internet companies with bold ideas, getting the business model to go viral was essential to sustainability, and growing quickly required money and the right people on the team, neither of which they had. South Africa has produced some notable successes when it comes to entrepreneurship—Elon Musk and Mark Shuttleworth to name two. But it has been the pattern that these big successes tend to leave the country to go where they can access a larger pool of talent and capital. With hindsight, Melville believes that one big mistake he made was not moving the business to San Francisco, where there is a culture that would support his type of business. In October 2013, with no money in the bank, he abruptly shut the business down and moved on. His fan base tweeted their condolences and support.

Failure in the startup world is not rare; in fact, within about five years, more than half of all startups fail.[1] Even if Justin had achieved venture capital funding, it would have been no guarantee of success as about 75 percent of venture-backed companies fail to provide a return to their investors.[2] But unlike most startups that simply shut their doors, Melville's venture was an emotional journey from the start and its end was no less emotional. The team put a memorial on the site for their users to remember their accomplishments and acknowledge the vision for the music industry that they still hope to realize some day.

Sources: "Rethinking the Music Industry: Justin R. Melville at TEDxCapeTown," https://www.youtube.com /watch?v=oDiWA6b_5CE, accessed June 17, 2014; Granger, L. "Anatomy of a Startup Failure: The Airborne Story," *Ventureburn*, February 17, 2014, http://ventureburn.com/2014/02 /anatomy-of-startup-failure-the-airborne-story/print/

t is an unfortunate fact that many universities and other institutions are perpetuating the myth that entrepreneurs must create business plans before they start businesses. Potential entrepreneurs are spending up to 200 hours of their valuable time in pursuit of the perfect plan to present at a competition or to an investor, only to discover that investors are more impressed by a founding team that has gotten the business up and running, even in a minimal way, to prove the concept.

Recall that Part Two of this book was about feasibility analysis, which involves customer discovery and validation—testing the business model in the market with real customers to determine the conditions you must have in place to insure the chance of a successful launch. Going through the feasibility process helps you learn about your business, reduce some of the risk, and prepare to launch. However, today most investors and experienced entrepreneurs would advise to start the business then spend time on a plan. Of course, that doesn't mean "just do it" in the sense that you don't think before you do. What it does mean is that there is no way to answer all the questions about the problem you're solving or the business you're creating without actually getting into business. There is something about running your business that gives you insights no research could have revealed. Therefore, it is reasonable to assert that a business plan depends on your having achieved a validated business model that has been market-tested and is reliable, repeatable, and scalable because a business plan is about building and growing a company, not starting it. Business plans must be based on reality. For years, the traditional model of business planning involved carefully crafting a business plan and then sending it out to potential funders for consideration. Of course, much like a slush pile of manuscripts at a publishing house, those business plans sat stacked on the investor's desk, rarely seeing the light of day. Today, submitting a professionally crafted business plan is less important than demonstrating what you have accomplished in the way of securing sales from real customers.[3] Potential investors want to see that the venture has customers and a track record, however brief. They want to see that the business model actually works. The new environment for business planning actually makes the case for the importance of a feasibility analysis and validation experiments to prove the concept.

Chapters 1 through 9 focused on helping you design and analyze a business opportunity to determine if there was a market of sufficient size with customers who had a need your startup could fill. This chapter explores the business planning process as a way to build on the results of customer discovery and business model validation, which were the outputs of feasibility analysis.

10.1   PREPARING TO WRITE THE BUSINESS PLAN

Writing a business plan is a huge undertaking that should be planned in terms of tasks and a timeline. If you have launched your new venture in limited form to achieve proof of concept, as suggested previously, the writing of the business plan must now be sandwiched among all the day-to-day activities associated with an operating business. Even if your startup has not yet launched, an action plan for completing a business plan in a relatively short period of time will help accelerate the process. The following tasks are a guide to the founding team in preparing to write the business plan.

- *Identify who is responsible for what.* Updating information about the industry, the market, the customer, and costs is an ongoing process. Even though you gathered this data when you conducted your business model validation, some time may have elapsed before you undertake the writing of the business plan, so it is important to make sure that all your information is current. Make a list of everything that must be collected and how it needs to be collected (secondary research, talking to customers, etc.). Decide who will do what and by when it must be accomplished.

- *Develop a timeline based on tasks identified.* It is important to be realistic about how much time it will take to complete all the tasks associated with the business plan. The timeline is very likely to be long, especially if you're doing the work on evenings and weekends, so the next job will be to determine whether all of the tasks are critical to the business plan and to prune any that are not essential to conveying a convincing argument.

- *Hold the team to the timeline and work diligently to get the plan done.* Once the business plan is complete, it's a good idea to get a trusted third party to review the plan to catch anything the team may have missed. Keep in mind that this process continues after you complete the plan because a business plan is a living document that needs to be kept current so it's ready when you need it.

10.1a   Stakeholder Interests

Every new venture has stakeholders external to the founding team. These stakeholders view the new venture from different perspectives; consequently, you need to develop your executive summary, pitch, and business plan to address the needs of particular stakeholders. Here we discuss the interests of investors, bankers and lenders, and strategic partners.

Investor Interests

Anyone investing in a new venture has four principal concerns: rate of growth, return on investment, degree of risk, and protection. Investors are generally betting that the value of their ownership interest in the business will increase over time at a rate greater than that of another type of investment or of a bank account. They want to know how fast the business is projected to grow, when that growth will take place, and what will ensure that the growth actually occurs as predicted. For this reason, they tend to look for market-driven companies rather than product- or technology-driven companies. They expect that predictions will be based on solid evidence in the marketplace and on thorough knowledge of the target market.[4] Investors are naturally concerned about when and how the principal portion of their investment will be repaid and how much gain on that investment will accrue over the time they are invested in the company. The answers to these concerns are largely a function of the structure of the investment deal: whether it involves a limited or general partnership, or preferred or common stock, and so forth. Investors want to understand thoroughly the risks they face in investing in the new venture; principally, they want to know how their original equity will be protected. They expect you to present the potential challenges facing your new venture, along with a plan for mitigating or dealing with them to protect the investors against loss.

Although the business plan is vital to investment decision making, it is not the only piece of information considered. In one survey of 42 venture capitalists, 43 percent claimed to have invested in a venture in the previous three years without the benefit of a business plan.[5] Only 36 percent reported that the business plan was "very important" in their evaluation. And perhaps the most revealing statistic of all was that 96 percent preferred to learn about a potential investment through a referral from someone they trusted. Furthermore, investors found that the primary flaws in most business plans were overly optimistic financial projections, too much hype, poor explanation of the business model, and no demonstration of customer demand.

Lenders' Interests

Lenders, whether they are banks or private lenders, are primarily interested in the company's margins and cash flow projections, because they are concerned about how their loans or credit lines to the business will be repaid. The margins indicate how much room there is for error between the cost to produce the product (or deliver the service) and the selling price. If margins are tight and your business has to lower prices to compete, it may not be able to pay off its loans as consistently and quickly as the lender would like. Similarly, lenders look at cash flow projections to see whether your business can pay all its expenses and still have money left over at the end of each month. They also look at the qualifications and track record of the management team and may require personal guarantees of the principals. When considering a business plan and an entrepreneur for a loan, lenders have several concerns:

- *The amount of money the entrepreneur needs.* Lenders are looking for a specific amount that can be justified with accurate calculations and data.

- *The kind of positive impact the loan will have on the business.* Lenders would like to know that the money they are lending is not going to pay off old debt or to pay salaries, but rather will improve the business's financial position, particularly with regard to cash flow. This is the same perspective that investors have.

- *The kinds of assets the business has for collateral.* Not all assets are created equal. Some assets have no value outside the business, because they are custom-made or specific to that business and therefore cannot be sold on the open market. Lenders prefer to see industry-standard equipment and facilities that can easily be converted to another use.

- *How the business will repay the loan.* Lenders are interested in the earnings potential of the business over the life of the loan, but even more important, they want to know that the business generates sufficient cash flow to service the debt. Fixed expenses are fairly easy to predict, but variable expenses—those related to the production of the product or service—present a more difficult problem. In an attempt to avoid any long-term issues, lenders pay close attention to the market research section of the business plan, which highlights the demand for the product/service. They also focus on the marketing plan, which tells them how you intend to reach the customer.

- *How the lender will be protected if the business doesn't meet its projections.* Lenders want to know that you have a contingency plan for situations where major assumptions prove to be wrong. They want to ensure that they are paid out of cash flow, not by liquidating the assets of the business, which generally would only give them a small percentage of the value of the assets.

- *The entrepreneur's stake in the business.* Like investors, lenders feel more confident about lending to a business in which the entrepreneur has a substantial monetary investment. Such an investment reduces the likelihood that the entrepreneur will walk away from the business, leaving the lender stranded.

Strategic Partners' Interests

If you intend to manufacture a product or bring a new drug or medical device to market, you will likely choose to form a strategic alliance with a larger company so that you don't have to incur the tremendous costs of purchasing equipment for a manufacturing plant or funding expensive clinical trials required by the FDA (Food and Drug Administration). You may, for example, grant a license to another firm to manufacture and assemble the product and supply it to you to market and distribute. Alternatively, you may enter into an agreement with a supplier to provide necessary raw materials in exchange for an equity interest in the startup venture.

Strategic alliances may take the form of formal partnership agreements with major corporations or may consist simply of an informal agreement such as a large purchase contract. In either case, the larger company that is allying itself with the new venture is usually looking for new products, processes, or technologies that complement its current line of products or services. Accordingly, it will seek a new venture management team that has some previous corporate experience so that the relationship will be smoother. Larger companies are also interested in strategic issues such as the marketing and growth strategies of the new venture.

Knowing in advance what these third parties are looking for will help you address their specific needs in the business plan, enhancing the partnership's ability to achieve the goals of your business.

10.1b   Proof of Concept Demonstration

As part of the preparation for writing a business plan, you will want to insure that you have a way to demonstrate that you have proved your business concept, that is, that you can provide evidence that customers in sufficient numbers want what you're offering. Figure 10.1 depicts various types of proofs of

FIGURE 10.1   The Proof of Concept Pyramid

concept (POCs) and the strength of the evidence they provide. Clearly having actual customer sales is the strongest proof. It is important to note that these POC tests all involve fieldwork with the customer that should have been accomplished during feasibility analysis. Supporting evidence from secondary sources such as industry analysts and third-party statistics providers are not POC, strictly speaking, because they don't directly address the specific product or technology you are offering.

The environment for entrepreneurs going forward will be characterized by an increase in uncertainty, fewer available resources, and a need for more innovation.[6] This type of environment calls for startups that can move and adapt quickly as they implement smaller strategies to accomplish near-term outcomes on the path to bigger, longer-term goals. Logan and Fischer-Wright have called this type of business planning *micro strategies*, and it is adapted from military science.[7] This approach works well for entrepreneurs who need to prove a concept for a new venture quickly while avoiding the inertia of planning.

Figure 10.2 depicts the Entrepreneur's Micro Strategies for Achieving Proof of Concept. Like the Logan-Fischer-Wright model, it consists of three primary elements: (1) outcomes, which are the near-term goals that you are attempting to achieve; (2) assets, which are the human, social, physical, and financial assets needed to achieve the outcomes desired; and (3) actions, which are the tasks you must undertake to achieve the necessary outcomes.

The three elements interact and take you forward through much the same type of effectual process that was used to conduct feasibility analysis. What that means is you set a specific outcome and then consider the assets currently available to achieve the outcome. If you don't have the right assets or enough assets, the process doesn't stop; it simply shifts to an interim strategy designed to secure the needed assets. For example, the founders of one Internet company had set an outcome of proving their business model in two months. Unfortunately,

FIGURE 10.2

Entrepreneur's Micro Strategy for Proof of Concept

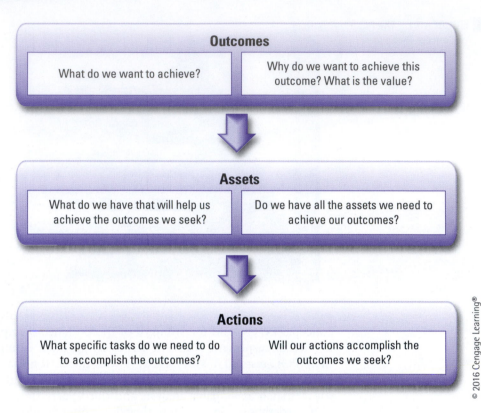

along the way they discovered that their users were not willing to become customers and pay for the services they were being offered. Instead of giving up, the founders devised an interim strategy to determine exactly what their users valued so they would have a better understanding of what those users were willing to pay for. Once they had acquired that knowledge (the missing asset), they could go back to working on the original outcome of validating the business model with a new target date for completion.

The micro strategy process repeats itself over and over again and with each successful outcome, you move the business toward a complete proof of concept. During the process, you launch the business in a small, controlled way, so that feedback from the micro strategy process is real and meaningful. Assets are gathered, outcomes are determined, and when assets and outcomes are congruent, you can come up with an action plan to achieve the outcome.

The Role of Intuitive Decision Making

The micro strategy approach to planning a business enables more flexibility and makes it possible for a startup to adapt and change quickly as new information is gathered. The problem with the traditional business planning process is that it was always focused on the document, often a 50-page monstrosity that solidified the plan and made it more likely that you would not modify it in the face of new information. You were expected to have everything resolved before you ever launched the business. In today's environment, no one is able to predict with any degree of certainty what the future holds. More and more, entrepreneurs have to rely on intuitive decision making, and the traditional business planning process is not conducive to this approach. Nobel Prize–winning psychologist Daniel Kahneman believes that there are some circumstances where intuition plays an important role in decision making. For example, when entrepreneurs are pressured by time, as occurs when there is a brief window of opportunity to launch, they may need to follow their intuition. This is particularly true where they have been able to create a clear and simple story around the business that gives them a high degree of confidence in their intuition that the story is based in reality.[8] Intuition also works when a situation is defined by a certain structure or predictability; it is less reliable in a very uncertain environment or where the problem is unique with no precedent.

Entrepreneurs are typically very confident individuals, so they inspire confidence in others, even when there is no basis for that confidence. Entrepreneurs who are aware of this potential flaw in their objectivity would be well advised to consider undertaking a premortem.[9] The premortem involves the entrepreneurial team assuming that the new venture has failed. Their job then is to identify all the reasons the business failed. This exercise is not designed to kill a new venture but to force the team to modify its thinking so as to avoid potential failure points. Identifying those failure points in advance is a way to overcome any confirmatory bias they may have had when they did their validation research in the first place.

Business planning entails a series of decisions, many of which are intuitive. Each decision involves data gathering and analysis, conclusions and insights. In other words, business planning is a process, not an event or end-stage document. There are a number of ways to demonstrate proof of concept and we discuss those next.

Achieving Proof of Concept with a Prototype

One of the biggest problems that technology or product entrepreneurs have is that until they actually build a POC prototype of what they're offering, it's difficult to gauge customer interest or demand. Even if you are solving a real problem customers have, they still will not make the commitment to purchase without the ability to try the product. As you learned in Chapter 6, most start-ups initially test a minimum viable product or MVP. The MVP is usually developed quickly and it contains only the key functionality, usually the main features that solve the customer's problem. Demonstrating proof of concept with a prototype has a number of important benefits:

- You develop a clear understanding of customer needs when you put the prototype in their hands and watch how they use it.
- Changes in the prototype can be made early in the process when they are less costly.
- Doing a prototype reduces the risk of failure.

Achieving Proof of Concept with a Website

Today when people hear about a new business or a new product or service, the first place they go for more information is the Internet. This makes sense, because the Internet is the perfect place to communicate a new venture's message and to get feedback. However, many new businesses make the mistake of simply slapping up a single page marked "under construction" or "coming soon" until they finish their due diligence and start the business. Worse yet, they put up a teaser page to gauge interest and track how many people landed on the page and spent any time, or maybe registered for more information. The problem with this approach is that it can give a false sense of the level of actual interest in the market. There is a huge chasm between spending a few minutes on a dummy page and actually purchasing a product or service. It might make more sense to wait to put up a website until you have something valuable for customers to see. At that point your new business can look as successful and established as any large company for relatively few dollars invested in development of the site. A quick online demonstration can communicate to visitors what the business does, who its customers are, and what its value proposition is. The site can inform users about the founding team, the company's mission and goals, and disclose to potential investors, customers, and other interested parties how to contact the business. It can also communicate to customers/ users the look and feel of the site without demonstrating the full functionality. But most importantly, this enhanced beta site will tell you whether people are interested, how much time they spend on the site, how often they come back, and whether they communicate with the company. In other words, it will prove that it's worth the time and money for you to build out a more elaborate site.

One word of caution about websites, particularly in the beta phase: Proprietary information that is not protected by patents or trademarks should not be put on the site, because companies regularly peruse the Internet for information on their competitors. In fact, you should definitely study the websites of your competitors for important clues about what features you should build into your own site and how you might improve on what your competitors are doing. As with every promotional or informational piece about the business, differentiation is critical. It is not within the scope of this text to discuss website development; however, information on building an effective website is ubiquitous on the Internet and in every bookstore.

Achieving Proof of Concept with Purchase Orders and Customer Sales

Today most investors are seeking ventures that have the most powerful POC: a customer. For some types of products, securing a purchase order or actual sale is very possible. For example, Nordic Track, the successful supplier of workout equipment, started its business by getting customers to pay upfront to order one of its original skier machines. In this way, the company didn't have huge inventory costs and its customers were funding the manufacturing costs.

Proof of concept can take many forms, from the simple prototype to an actual sale. Figure 10.1 at the beginning of this section depicts the spectrum of POC approaches from weakest to strongest. The point is not to settle on one but to move through the entire spectrum with one POC building on the next until critical mass is achieved and the entrepreneur is confident that the business can survive.

10.2 STARTING WITH A COMPELLING STORY

Today most investors want to see a well-written executive summary that tells a compelling story and grabs their interest. An important argument for developing an executive summary and pitch is that it forces entrepreneurs to identify and focus on the most persuasive aspects of the business. One of the biggest problems entrepreneurs have is developing and honing a convincing story about their new venture that creates excitement and interest and encourages the listener to want to know more. An effective executive summary and its associated pitch, which may be in the form of a PowerPoint deck or Prezi presentation, will do the following:

- Convey the compelling story quickly and memorably.
- Highlight the critical elements of the business that provide a competitive advantage.
- Highlight the various proofs of concept that have been achieved.
- Present a coherent path to profitability and success that makes sense.
- Demonstrate that the team can successfully execute the plan.

The traditional view is that you write the executive summary after completing a full business plan, but over the years we have found that entrepreneurs struggle with condensing their business into a few key points that drive home the value proposition, the customer, the competitive advantage, and the business model in a clear, concise, and compelling way. The executive summary tells a story; the business plan provides the supporting evidence and the strategy for executing the story. With a highly focused executive summary and pitch presentation in hand, it will be easier to develop a full business plan, if required, without deviating from the essentials. In the next sections, essential questions that must be answered by the executive summary are discussed. The questions are organized in an order that builds the compelling story.

10.2a   How Will You Grab My Attention?

It is vital to lead with the most persuasive reason for the existence of the business. Leading with the compelling reason solves the problem of grabbing attention in the first 15 seconds and makes sure that what investors and others need to hear is up front and obvious. For example, do you have a unique solution to a very big problem? Or, does the founding team include recognized people who have had previous successes? The compelling story needs to be the attention grabber so the listener will want to hear more. One easy way to develop a quick elevator pitch is to fill in the blanks in the following list of words.

The Leading Word	What You're Addressing
FOR	The specific customer
WHO	What the customer needs
THE	Name of the product
IS A	Product niche
THAT	Reason to buy, the benefit, what problem it solves
UNLIKE	Competitive option
WE (THE COMPANY)	Primary difference between you and your competitors

An example of what this might look like is the following:

For socially oriented people living in areas where communication is monitored and **whose** primary form of communication is text messaging, **WhatsApp Messenger is a** cross-platform mobile messaging app **that** lets you exchange messages privately without paying for SMS. **Unlike** other text plans that charge separately for text messaging, **WhatsApp** charges a nominal annual subscription, does not employ ads, and uses the same Internet data plan that users have for email and Web browsing.

There are a number of ways to effectively "pitch" the essence of your business in 15 seconds. In addition to the example above, another simple approach is to answer three questions:

1. What do you do? (What problem are you solving and how are you solving it?)
2. Why should we care? (Why is this a compelling idea?)
3. How will you win? (What's your competitive advantage?)

Grabbing attention at the start of the executive summary means that your readers will likely not tune out when you start to get into the details.

10.2b   What Pain Is Being Addressed and Who Has It?

Entrepreneurs need to emphasize that they are going to solve very big and very important problems because big problems translate to large markets. If you did your customer discovery and validation work effectively, you discovered a total available market (TAM), a serviceable available market (SAM), and a serviceable obtainable market (SOM). (See Figure 10.3). Entrepreneurs always start with the TAM because it's the easiest to calculate being simply the total size of the market for whatever you're selling. Suppose you're starting a themed restaurant concept. Theoretically, your TAM is the worldwide market for themed restaurants, but you have a startup and are not able to address the total market (nor would you want to). It is more likely that your product or service falls within a portion of that market (SAM). Perhaps you've decided to launch in Austin, Texas, so now your SAM becomes the total market available in Austin. But, again, you have competition and your one initial restaurant is not going to

SOCIAL ENTREPRENEURSHIP: *MAKING MEANING*

The Little Schoolhouse That Could

Gifford Pinchot is best known for his classic 1985 book, *Intrapreneuring: Why You Don't Have to Leave the Corporation to Become an Entrepreneur*, but largely thanks to the influence of his grandfather, who founded the forest service in 1905, Pinchot has become an avid conservationist. In that capacity, he founded the Bainbridge Island Graduate Institute (BGI) near Seattle, Washington, in 2002. There, students are immersed in studies of environmental sustainability and social responsibility in the context of entrepreneurship and innovation.

BGI was launched in just six months with $120,000 of Pinchot's own money. Thereafter, he raised another $300,000 from Ben Cohen (Ben & Jerry's co-founder) and Wayne Silby (founder of the Calvert Fund). He recruited a president and together they worked to gain state authorization to award an MBA. The first class of 18 students enrolled in the fall of 2002. BGI is one of the first graduate schools in the United States to focus on sustainable business, to "create profit in ways that contribute to taking care of people and the planet." Pinchot is determined to make a mark on society by educating more people in how to be entrepreneurial while also being socially responsible. Today the school also prides itself on teaching its students how to find their "internal compass," which helps them figure out what they really want to do with their lives. Betsy Blaisdell, a senior manager at Timberland, an outdoor apparel company, attended BGI to learn how to better help her company achieve its sustainability goals. While at BGI, she worked with industry people to develop the Higg Index, which is now used by the apparel industry to measure and improve environmental impact.

Sources: BGI, www.bgi.edu, www.bgiedu.org "Green Curriculum," *Washington CEO* (January 12, 2006); BGI, http://www.bgiedu.org/index.htm; and E. Winninghoff, "The Little Green Schoolhouse," *Inc. Magazine* (July 2003), www.inc.com.

capture all of Austin, so your SOM represents realistically the people near your restaurant who will give it a try. Initial markets (first customers or SOMs) are always those for which the pain is greatest. That first customer is your foot in the door. Later customers will have the benefit of seeing how well you solved the problem for the first customers, and they will pass that knowledge on to other customers. It's easy to find the numbers for your TAM and SAM and forecast based on historical data for those markets. However, the SOM is another story. It will require a bottom-up forecast that includes how you will use your startup's resources to reach your sales goals. So it's not enough to simply say that you're going to capture a certain percentage of your SOM, you need to explain how you will get there.

FIGURE 10.3 Types of
Market Evaluation

TAM	Total Available Market

- Total market size
- This is your potential at scale
- Example: Total market for text message applications

SAM	Serviceable Available Market

- Your segment of the market — the portion your business is focused on
- Example: Messaging over IP

SOM	Serviceable Obtainable Market

- What share of the SAM can you achieve?
- This is the short-term sales potential. (SOM/SAM = market share)
- Example: Focus on countries where communication is monitored

© 2016 Cengage Learning®

10.2c   How Is Your Venture Solving the Problem?

Here you should demonstrate a clear link between the problem or pain and the solution you're offering. What are you providing and how does it specifically solve the problem? What kind of business is this? Where does it fit in the value chain? If you currently have customers or any proof of concept, now is the time to emphasize these facts. It's important to be specific about who your first customer is and how you know that they will buy what you're offering. Getting the customer wrong means there is no business.

10.2d   What Is Your Venture's Competitive Advantage?

No venture can succeed in the long term without a sustainable competitive advantage—not a single competitive advantage but a bundle of them encompassing every aspect of the business. The executive summary needs to address which advantages will enable this venture to create a unique unserved niche and to enter the market and secure customers with little or no competition in the beginning. The reality is that every new venture has competition, so it's important to recognize where competitive threats might occur. In the executive summary, you should be very specific about comparing your offering with a significant competitor. Given the competitor's established brand and position in the market, why would customers choose your company?

10.2e   Can Your Venture Make Money?

Most executive summaries do not adequately address the business model. How will the business create and capture value that will enable it to make money over the long term? In general, value is created when the business is adequately capitalized and has highly regarded investors, an experienced management team, customers, a unique technology, product, or service, the ability to continually innovate, and a rapidly expanding market.[10] Once your new venture has passed the startup stage, additional value is created by its position in the market, significant customers, effective operating systems, a strong gross margin, positive cash flow, and a high return on equity. You need to be able to identify the critical metrics on which the business will be judged and demonstrate that the business model is repeatable, can be leveraged to develop new revenue streams, and is scalable as the market grows or new markets are added.

Because executive summaries are most often used to raise capital, the questions they answer are frequently of great interest to an investor or lender. How much money is needed to address this opportunity? How will capital be allocated (i.e., to increase sales, to boost profits, or to enhance the value of the company) and at which milestones? How will the business provide a superior return on investment (ROI)? Which exit strategies are possible?

In addition to explaining the business model, you need to present a well-thought-out summary financial plan with three to five years of projected revenues, expenses, cash flow, and headcount or personnel requirements at various milestones. When will the company break even on cash? When will it make a profit? These numbers must be backed up with solid assumptions. In the executive summary, only the key numbers and their assumptions are presented. You also need to identify the critical success factors for the business as well as the critical risk factors and how they will mitigate them.

10.2f   Can the Founding Team Execute the Plan?

Why is this founding team the best team to execute this concept? Can it be demonstrated that the founding team has the experience and skills required by the various areas of the business? If the team has someone who accomplished something significant in the industry, it should be highlighted. Do the founders have their own money invested in this concept? It is easy to spend other people's money or to consider "sweat" equity as equivalent to cash—but it isn't equivalent in the eyes of investors, who figure that the founding team won't give up easily if they have invested their own money in the deal. Does the team have the passion and the drive to make this business a success? Passion and drive are difficult to measure but are reflected in the level of work that was put into the market research. How many people did the team talk to—industry experts, customers, and so forth? The bottom line is that you must prove that your team has relevant expertise and experience.

10.2g   Why Is Now the Right Time to Launch This Venture?

What makes this concept so valuable right now? If this business is the only one of its kind, why is that so? Has anyone tried this before and failed? If so, why? What makes the current environment right for this venture? Timing is critical in the launch of any new venture, so it is important to explain why *now* is the right time and how long the window of opportunity will remain open.

10.2h   What Is the Team Seeking from Investors?

A finely honed executive summary is needed whether or not you are seeking investor capital. If your new venture is self-funded (that's admirable), this section of the business plan will discuss the funding plan going forward. What will be the various sources of capital? If you are seeking investor capital, this section will specify the minimum amount of capital required to meet the next major milestone. If you expect to need several rounds of investment, the associated milestones and funding amounts should be projected. Do not include any language about equity stakes or return on investment for the investors. That will come later as part of a negotiation.

10.2i   Guidelines for Executive Summaries

Pulling the executive summary into a coherent story is critical to persuading others to give your business a chance. Here are some guidelines to consider when developing the executive summary. These guidelines are also relevant to the pitch you will develop, which is discussed in a later section.

- Keep the executive summary to no more than three to five pages, single-spaced with white space and headers for easy reading.
- Read each sentence multiple times to prune unnecessary words and to make sure that the summary is focusing on the critical points. Each sentence should be clear and compelling.
- Include recognizable names if there is an established relationship with the person or company. Do not include any names of people or companies with whom you have not spoken. Do not make claims about unnamed "key employees" who will join after funding or a large company that will sign a contract "next week." Unless something has already been accomplished, it's simply wishful thinking.
- Avoid puff words and phrases such as "no one else is doing this" or "our financial projections are conservative." These types of words suggest that you haven't done your homework and you're naïve.
- Avoid jargon and acronyms that might be foreign to the reader or listener. (See Table 10.1)
- Explain the business, no matter how technical or complex, in words that anyone can understand.
- Use analogies if they help the reader or listener to quickly understand your business. For example, "We are the eBay for the auto parts industry." Be careful not to sound like you're simply cloning an existing business.
- Keep the pitch deck to about 10 slides that contain only the key points in large fonts. Graphics and high quality photos are generally more effective than text.

Entrepreneurs should keep in mind that the purpose for doing an executive summary is to sell the business. That means that you should not go deep into any one topic; you should hit only the most critical points. The problem or compelling pain statement should take no more than two sentences. If readers can't understand the pain immediately, then it's not a compelling pain.

TABLE 10.1 Business Jargon to Avoid

Think outside the box	Scalable
Lots of moving parts	Best practice
Ducks in a row	Empower
Core competency	Drinking the Kool-Aid
Leverage	Move the needle
Buy-In	Drill down
Core Values	Vertical
Unpack	Synergize

© 2016 Cengage Learning®

Explaining in excruciating detail how the product or technology works is not needed to sell the business. What is needed is an understanding of how the product or technology solves a real and compelling problem.

10.3 PREPARING THE FULL BUSINESS PLAN: STRATEGY AND STRUCTURE

You will most likely write a business plan if a banker or investor has asked for one. You can find many templates online and even software products that claim to automate the process. However, the most effective plans focus on telling a story about the business in a clear and compelling manner, providing evidence to support claims made, and giving the reader a rich picture of the strategy the company is taking as it grows.

Here we discuss the components of the full business plan and some important points to remember.

10.3a Components of the Business Plan

All business plans have some major sections in common. The outline in Table 10.2 is a guide to the sections that are typically included and some of the areas that need to be covered in those sections. It is important that you customize you business plan to meet your specific needs and the needs of those who will read them. Table 10.2 also notes the various chapters in this book where a particular section is discussed in detail. Here we will briefly summarize what each section discusses.

The Business

This section provides the key information a reader would want to know about the business so that the rest of the business plan makes sense. Starting this section with the elevator pitch as you did in the executive summary gets readers set up for more detail. Painting a picture of a significant problem is always persuasive; unfortunately, too many businesses are not solving significant problems—in fact, they're not solving problems at all. Instead they are selling fads or trendy products and services that are vulnerable to being knocked off or left behind when customers discover the next shiny item. For this type of business, showing a huge market opportunity and a plan for quickly capturing a large share of that market is the way to go. This section also introduces the business model, which is the heart of the business. It will be important to provide evidence that your business model works.

TABLE 10.2   Outline for the Business Plan

Executive Summary

Table of Contents

The Business—Chapter 5
What business are you in?
What are the mission and goals of the business?
What is the pain or problem you are addressing?
Who is the customer and what is the value proposition (solution) being delivered?
How will the value be delivered?
How will you differentiate the business?
What is the business model and how did you validate it?

Industry/Market Analysis—Chapter 4
Demographics, major players (opinion leaders), trends
Market segmentation, first customer profile
Demand estimates
Competitor analysis and competitive advantages
Distribution channels
Entry strategy (initial market penetration, first customer)

Product/Service Development Plan—Chapter 6
Detailed description, unique features/benefits of product/service
Technology assessment (if applicable)
Plan for prototyping and testing
Tasks and timeline to completion of product/service prototype
Acquisition of intellectual property

Founding or Management Team—Chapter 8
Qualifications of the founding team
How critical tasks will be covered
Gap analysis—what's missing? Professional advisors, board of directors, independent contractors

Operations Plan—Chapter 12
Facilities and location
Business process flow chart including all functions (inventory, warehousing, etc.)
Plan for outsourcing (if applicable)
Plan for manufacturing and distribution

Organization Plan—Chapter 11
Statement of management philosophy and company culture
Legal structure of the company—Chapter 12
Organizational chart and key management
Personnel required (headcount)
Strategic Partners

Marketing Plan—Chapter 13
Purpose for the plan, business identity and branding
Target market (SOM) and unique market niche
Customer acquisition plan
Pricing model
Distribution channels
Marketing strategy

Financial Plan—Chapters 8 and 17
Summary of key financial metrics and capital requirements
Risk factors and mediation
Sales forecast
Break-even analysis and payback period
Narrative assumptions for financial statements
Full set of pro forma financial statements (cash flow, income, balance sheet) for 2–3 years
Plan for ongoing funding

Growth Plan—Chapter 16
Strategy for growth
Resources required (personnel, facilities, equipment, capital)
Organizational changes resulting from growth

Contingency Plan and Harvest Strategy—Chapter 16
Strategies for dealing with deviations from the plan

Timeline to Launch—Chapter 10
Graphic that details task needed to be accomplished up to the date of launch

Endnotes
Appendices (A, B, C, etc.)
Questionnaires, maps, forms, résumés, etc.

Industry/Market Analysis

The industry is the environmental context for your business; it determines whether the business can be profitable. Presenting the demographics of the industry, the major trends, the possibilities for disruption, and the potential impact of industry opinion leaders should demonstrate your ability to be successful in this industry. The market is defined by customers. Again you would want to lay out the demographics of the broad market you're targeting and then show how you segmented that market to arrive at a first customer. You also need to explain how you calculated demand, what the competitive landscape looks like for that market, which distribution channels you'll use, and what your overall entry strategy will be.

Product/Service Development Plan

This section provides a detailed description of your product or service and the timeline for completion of the prototype and final product or service. If you have a technology business, you should provide a technology assessment with a Technology Readiness Level (TRL). The TRL is a measurement system originally developed by NASA to assess the maturity level of a technology. It ranges from 1, where scientific research is just beginning, to 9, which is a proven technology. It is useful to measure the development of your technology or product against the TRL as many investors will not consider an investment until a technology has reached at least TRL 6 or 7. Readers should understand your plan and timeline for building a prototype and acquiring intellectual property rights if applicable. Figure 10.4 presents an example of technology readiness levels for a generic product.

Founding or Management Team

The team is arguably one of the most important components of the business plan because the successful execution of the plan rests in the hands of the team. This section should present the qualifications of the team (experience, expertise,

FIGURE 10.4
Technology Readiness Levels

1	New concept proposed
2	Academic research to validate concept
3	Laboratory proof of concept research
4	Proof of concept validation in relevent environment
5	Breadboard demonstration - primitive prototype
6	Prototype demonstration
7	Demonstration of pre-production hardware in operational environment
8	Extended operation - system completed
9	Commercialization

© 2016 Cengage Learning®

resources), how they will cover the critical tasks, and what gaps, if any, there are in the team. Significant people who will participate as advisors or on the board of directors should be noted.

Organization Plan

This section discusses the legal form of organization that the venture will take, whether that be sole proprietorship, partnership, LLC, or corporation. It also deals with the entrepreneur's philosophy of management and company culture as these are significant competitive advantages if developed well. The section includes an organization chart showing key management, talks about personnel required for specific duties and employee incentives, and discusses the use of strategic partners.

Operations Plan

This section of the business plan contains a detailed description of the business operations, including those processes that the new venture will own and undertake in-house, such as assembly, and those that will be outsourced to a strategic partner, such as manufacturing. A major portion of this section explains how the business will operate, where it will get its raw materials, how a product will be manufactured and/or assembled, and what type and quantity of labor will be required to operate the business. The location strategy for the business is also included in this section.

Marketing Plan

The marketing plan is something quite distinct from market analysis. Market analysis gives you the information about the customer and market that will be used to create a marketing plan. The marketing plan, by contrast, is the strategy for communicating the company's message, developing awareness of the product or service (brand equity), and enticing the customer to purchase. The marketing plan includes a discussion of the plan's purpose, the market niche, the business's identity, tools that will be used to reach the customer, a media plan for specific marketing tools, and a marketing budget.

Financial Plan

This section demonstrates the financial viability of the venture and explains the assumptions you made in doing the forecasts. It is designed to show that all the claims about the product, sales, marketing strategy, and operational strategy can work financially to create a business that can survive and grow over the long term. The financial plan begins with a summary of the key metrics for the business: time to positive cash flow, break-even, sales volume, and capital requirements to launch the business. Fundamentally, it presents a snapshot of the entrepreneur's predictions for the immediate future of the business. Generally, these forecasts are in the form of a complete set of pro forma financial statements broken out by month in the first year or two, and then annually for the next two to three years.

Statement of Cash Flows: Many CEOs use a statement of cash flows from operations, which is a bit more complex than the simple direct cash flow statement used for feasibility analysis. It provides information on changes in the company's cash account through inflows and outflows of cash and cash equivalents associated with the daily operations of the business. Operating cash inflows include sales and accounts receivable that have been collected, whereas nonoperating cash inflows are comprised of loans, investments, or the sale of assets. Cash outflows consist of inventory payments, accounts payable payments, and payments associated with payroll taxes, rent, utilities, and so forth. Nonoperating cash outflows include such items as payments of principal or interest on debt, dividend distribution, and asset purchase. A financially healthy company will see its major source of cash inflows coming from operating sources, such as sales. In preparing this type of cash flow statement, the income statement items are linked with changes from normal operations in the balance sheet from one period to the next. These include sales, cost of sales, and operating expenses. It is not within the scope of this book to go into further detail on this statement.

Income Statement: The income statement, also known as a profit and loss statement, gives information about the projected profit or loss status of the business for a specified period of time. It depicts when the new venture will cover its costs and begin to make a profit. It is important to note that revenues and expenses are recorded in the income statement when a transaction occurs in the case of sales, or when a debt is incurred in the case of expenses, whether or not money has been received or expended. The income statement is also important in determining the tax liability the company will have.

Balance Sheet: The balance sheet, called a "statement of financial position," is different from the other financial statements in that it looks at the financial health of the business at a single point in time—a given date—whereas the cash flow and income statements review a period of time: month, quarter, or year. The balance sheet is divided into two parts that must balance; that is, be equal to each other based on the following formula:

$$\text{Assets} = \text{Liabilities} + \text{Shareholders' Equity}$$

In small businesses, shareholders' equity is often called "owners' equity." Decisions you make have a direct effect on the balance sheet. For example, an increase in sales typically results in an increase on the asset side of the balance sheet because you have had to increase inventory or purchase equipment to meet demand. Likewise, your decision to retain earnings for growth will increase the equity portion of the balance sheet. The balance sheet is an important tool for answering questions about the health of the business. For example,

- Did debt financing increase or decrease from period to period? It is important to match any changes in debt financing to a particular decision or event.
- Did the amounts of accounts receivable and inventory increase or decrease relative to sales in the same period? This is an important measure of how well the business is managing these items.

Examining changes from period to period on the balance sheet is one way to gauge business performance. Ratios are another.

Ratios Entrepreneurs have a number of ratios that can be used as gauges to analyze a company's performance. Ratios compare items in the financial statements and convert them to relative terms so they can be compared to the same ratios in other periods or in other companies. It is not within the scope of this text to present all of the possible ratios available, so we discuss here five of the most common ratios used to measure liquidity, debt, and profitability.

Current ratio The current ratio provides information on the company's ability to meet short-term obligations. It is found by

Current ratio = Total current assets/Total current liabilities

The higher the number, the more liquid the company is and the more easily these assets can be converted to cash to pay off short-term obligations.

Profit margin This is a profitability ratio that uses net income and net sales from the income statement to give the percentage of each dollar of sales remaining after all costs of normal operations are accounted for. It is found by

Profit margin = Net income/Net sales

The inverse of this percentage (100% − PM) equals the expense ratio, that is, the percentage of each sales dollar accounted for by operating expenses.

Return on Investment This ratio provides a measure of the amount of return on the shareholders' investment based on the earnings of the company. It is found by

Return on investment (ROI) = Net income/Shareholders' equity

Inventory turnover This ratio is a measure of the liquidity of inventory or the number of times it turns over in a year. It is found by

Inventory turnover = Cost of goods sold/Average inventory

This ratio helps you judge whether the business has too much capital tied up in inventory.

One other tool that is valuable to know is break-even analysis, which tells you how many units must be sold before your company can achieve a profit or the sales volume required to be profitable. The break-even point is that point at which the total variable and fixed expenses are covered and beyond which the company makes a profit. The formula to calculate breakeven is as follows:

$$BEQ = \frac{TFC}{SP - VC \ (unit)}$$

Where
TFC = total fixed costs
SP = selling price
VC = variable costs

As an example, assume that total fixed costs for your business are $300,000; selling price per unit is $95.00; and variable costs per unit are $45.00. Then the number of units that must be produced and sold to break even is found by

$$\text{B/E} = \frac{\$300,000}{\$95 - \$45} = 6,000 \text{ units}$$

The dynamic nature of markets today makes it almost impossible to project out three to five years with any degree of certainty—hence, the need and importance of having detailed financial assumptions that explain the rationale for the numbers. Also important is sensitivity analysis to identify triggers that may change the financial forecasts and affect the business negatively. Finally, the financial plan should include a funding plan with a timeline and milestones to indicate when the new venture will need an infusion of investor or other capital.

Growth Plan

The growth plan discusses how you plan to take your business from startup through the various stages of growth and outlines the strategy that will be used to ensure that the business model is sustainable and continues to scale over its life. This may mean looking at new products and services or acquiring other businesses. It is important that this section reassure an investor or lender that the company has a future.

Contingency Plan and Harvest Strategy

The contingency plan is simply a way of recognizing that sometimes, even "the best laid plans" don't work the way they were intended to work. It presents potential risk scenarios, usually dealing with situations such as unexpected high or low growth or changing economic conditions, and then, for each situation, suggests a plan to minimize the impact on the new business. By contrast, the harvest or exit strategy is the plan for capturing the wealth of the business for the founders and any investors. It typically involves a liquidity event, such as an initial public offering, a merger, or a sale, among other options.

It is not normally a good idea to discuss deal structure in a business plan. Entrepreneurs rarely value their businesses correctly—typically, they are far too optimistic. Putting such optimistic statements into the business plan only alerts an investor or other interested party that you are naïve. Entrepreneurs who seek investment capital will find that it is a long process that evolves over many meetings with potential investors; the eventual deal structure will be reflected in a term sheet. Deal structure is discussed further in Chapter 16.

Timeline to Launch

The business plan should contain a graphic that depicts the timeline to launch and the critical milestones that take the business from its current status to first customer. Figure 10.5 presents one type of timeline; however, you can easily find many different types of timelines online, some with much more detail. The key point to remember is that you are trying to give the reader of your business plan a clear sense of when the business will launch. If your business already launched before you undertook a business plan (arguably the preferred approach), then your timeline would begin at launch and depict major milestones over a period of one to two years. In Figure 10.6, you see a business that had a soft launch of its minimum viable product to acquire its first customer and followed that with the launch of a mobile app and later the targeting of a new customer segment.

Appendices

Appendices are the appropriate place to put items that support your claims in the main body of the report—things like résumés, calculations, surveys, spreadsheets, and so forth. A good rule of thumb is not to put in the appendix anything that is vital for a reader to see. If the plan does have appendix items, a reference to those items should be made at the points in the body of the report where they are relevant.

Endnotes

Endnotes are simply the linked citations to material in the main body of the report that were gathered from sources other than the entrepreneur. You must remember that when you are attempting to build a strong case for a new venture

FIGURE 10.5   Timeline to Launch

| Planning & Design | Testing & Validation | Launch Preparation | Launch Business |

© 2016 Cengage Learning®

FIGURE 10.6   Timeline for a Business That Has Launched

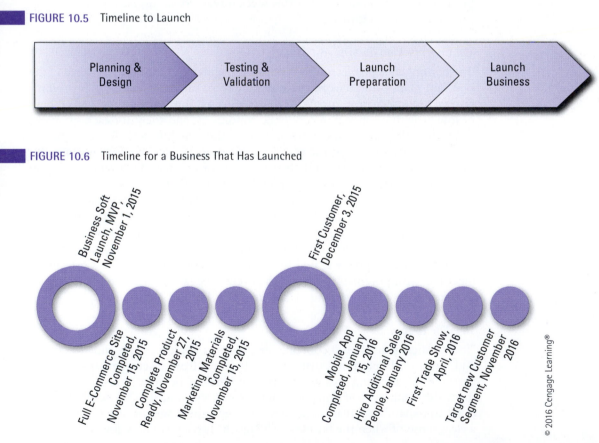

Business Soft Launch, MVP, November 1, 2015

First Customer, December 3, 2015

Full E-Commerce Site Completed, November 15, 2015

Complete Product Ready, November 27, 2015

Marketing Materials Completed, November 15, 2015

Mobile App Completed, January 15, 2016

Hire Additional Sales People, January 2016

First Trade Show, April, 2016

Target new Customer Segment, November 2016

© 2016 Cengage Learning®

concept, you can't rely solely on you own opinions; you must support those opinions and arguments with solid evidence gathered from reliable sources.

10.3b   Mistakes in Developing the Business Plan

Developing an effective business plan involves more than merely inserting information or data into the plan in an organized fashion. A persuasive plan requires that you weave a compelling story with supporting evidence so that readers can reasonably conclude that the business is viable. Unfortunately, many entrepreneurs make some common mistakes that could potentially cost them an investor or other interested party. The following sections present some of the common mistakes entrepreneurs make.

Boring Your Readers to Death

If you don't excite your readers in the first 15 seconds, you may never recapture their interest. If your business is not wrapped in a compelling and realistic story, then why would investors, customers, and partners waste their time with you? There are too many other opportunities out there. Review the earlier section on how to create a compelling and memorable story about your business.

Trying to Do Too Much Too Soon

It's easy to be swept away by all the possibilities for your business: this market, that market, doing multiple versions of your product. Avoid trying to be all things to all people. Focus is what will win the day—a strong first customer, a solid solution that solves that customer's problem, and a coherent strategy to deliver that solution to the customer.

Drowning Your Plan in Jargon

Every industry has its own jargon, that is, its own specialized language that people use to speed up communication. Be aware that most investors and others who will read your plan are not always familiar with the specific jargon you use on a daily basis in your industry. Here are some examples of jargon that will frustrate your readers.

"After unpacking the most urgent action items, we will have the bandwidth to address the mission-critical deliverable."

"The best way to leverage our resources is to incentivize all relevant constituencies and pick off the most optimal low-hanging fruit."

To avoid excessive jargon and being accused of intellectual laziness, scour your plan for highly technical language and replace it with language even your grandmother would understand. Check Table 10.2 for a list of the jargon you might want to avoid.

Rapid Growth That Requires Capabilities beyond Those of the Founding Team

Examples of rapid growth include rapidly increasing demand, or sales doubling or tripling on an annual basis in the first few years. Entrepreneurs believe this will be very attractive to investors, but what they don't realize is that if there is no evidence in the business plan that the founding team can manage and control this type of growth, investors will back away. They have too frequently seen a business fail during rapid growth because management didn't have the systems in place to deal with it. It is far better to project controlled growth and exceed it with a plan for bringing on the necessary personnel when the company is ready for more rapid growth. The other danger in projecting too high a level of success is that doing so increases the chances that your new venture will not be able to live up to the projections; consequently, it is better to project more conservatively and try to exceed those projections.

One Ringleader in a Three-Ring Circus

Many entrepreneurs pride themselves on being generalists, claiming to have expertise in all the functional areas of the new venture. What they really have is general knowledge of all the functional areas and a real expertise in perhaps only one area. Investors are very nervous about relying on solo entrepreneurs to lead world-class ventures. They much prefer a team of founders with at least one person specializing in each of the functional areas.[11]

Performance That Exceeds Industry Averages

Entrepreneurs who predict performance that is better than that of existing companies in the industry in some or all areas of the business is a serious red flag for investors. Although it is possible for a new venture to exceed industry averages in a particular area, it is not likely. Most averages, such as those for receivables turnover, manufacturing costs, and bad debt losses, have come about as a result of economies of scale, which a new business is not likely to achieve for some time. You should instead report performance measures at or slightly below industry averages, with a credible plan for exceeding those averages at some time in the future.

Price as a Market Strategy

Using price as a strategy for a product or service suffers from the same problem as projecting performance above industry averages. It is rarely possible for a new venture with a product or service that currently exists in the marketplace to enter on the basis of a lower price than that of its competitors. Established companies have achieved economies of scale that the new venture usually cannot duplicate; moreover, they can no doubt easily match the price set by a new entrant into the market.

Not Investing Capital in Your Own Business

Investors are more comfortable investing in a new venture where the entrepreneur has contributed a reasonable amount of the startup capital. That signals to the investors a level of commitment necessary to achieve the goals of the company and gives them confidence that you will not easily walk away from the venture. After all, if you won't invest cash in your business, why should anyone else?

10.4   SUCCESSFULLY PITCHING THE BUSINESS

For entrepreneurs seeking outside investment capital, it is not uncommon to be asked to do a pitch or presentation designed to persuade or sell the value of the business. Usually the pitch occurs after potential funders have reviewed the executive summary and determine that it is worth their time to hear from the entrepreneur and the founding team to judge whether they measure up to expectations.

The pitch should answer the fundamental questions discussed in the section on creating a compelling executive summary. The pitch itself should take less than half an hour—usually about 15 to 20 minutes, though questions and discussion will probably follow. The pitch should catch the audience's attention in the first 15 to 30 seconds. This is usually accomplished by conveying the compelling story of the pain or problem in the market, the magnitude of the pain, and how the new venture will cure or solve that pain for the customer. Here are some additional guidelines to consider to ensure an effective pitch.

- Stand without using a podium. This enables a better command of the situation, enhances rapport with the audience, and makes it easier to use gestures and visual aids.

- Move around (but no pacing), because moving helps reduce stress and livens up the presentation.

- Maintain eye contact with everyone and talk to the audience. Do not talk over their heads to the back of the room—that technique only works in large auditoriums.

- Visual aids, such as colorful PowerPoint slides with high-resolution photos and minimal text, help keep the pitch on track and focused on key points. You should avoid using too many slides and complex animations, or listeners may find themselves more interested in the rhythm of the slides' motion than in what you are attempting to convey. The point is do not make your audience have to choose between you and your slides. It's likely you will lose.

- Slides should be kept simple (no more than three lines per slide), be big enough to read from a distance, and be professional-looking.

- If there is a service or product involved, a live demonstration helps to generate excitement about the business, but ensure in advance that the demonstration is flawless.

- Typically, the CEO and chief technical person will do the pitch, although other members of the team may be drawn in during the question and answer period. Most important, your team should practice the pitch in advance for a small group of friends or colleagues who can critique it. Alternatively, a practice session can be videotaped so that the founding team can critique themselves.

10.4a   Answering Questions

When the founding team has successfully made it through the pitch, it has cleared the first hurdle. The second hurdle, however, is harder: answering questions from investors. One thing to remember about investors is that they generally like to ask questions to which they already know the answers; this is a test to see whether the founding team knows what it's talking about or whether the team is making up answers spontaneously. Investors often ask questions that either require an impossibly precise answer or are so broad that it's hard to tell what they are looking for. In this instance, the presenter should repeat the question to ensure that it has been understood or ask for clarification.

The type of question that poses the most problems for the founding team is the inordinately complex one that contains several underlying assumptions. For example, "If I were to analyze your new venture in terms of its market share before and after this potential investment, how would the market strategy have changed and how much of the budget should be allotted to changing that strategy?" The first thing you should do when faced with such a question is to ask that the question be repeated, to ensure that you haven't missed anything or made an incorrect assumption. Alternatively, you can restate the question and confirm that you have understood it correctly. You can then take a few seconds to formulate an answer. With the more complicated question, you may feel comfortable answering only part of it; for example, you may have evidence that could be presented to support a change in market share as a result of the capital infusion. On the other hand, it is critical not to commit the venture to any change in course of action or any budget amount without having had time to consider it further and gather more facts. Saying this to investors in response to the question will no doubt gain you a measure of respect for having demonstrated that you don't make important decisions precipitously, without considering all the facts.

If investors ask a factual question to which you do not know the answer (usually, such queries are tangential to the business plan and are asked to see how you will respond), you should admit that you don't have that answer off the top of his head but will be happy to find it after the meeting is over and get back to the questioner. Finally, if the pitch or anything the team has proposed is criticized by investors (a likely possibility), you should be careful not to be defensive or to turn the criticism in any way on the audience.

10.5   FINAL THOUGHTS ON BUSINESS PLANS

Preparing and pitching a business plan are the culmination of months of work and represent the heart and soul of a new venture. If the business idea has been researched thoroughly and you have proven the business model in the market, the chances of starting a successful venture are enhanced. A well-conceived plan enables the benchmarking of progress toward the company's goals. It establishes the purpose, values, and goals of the company that will guide its decision making throughout its life. No entrepreneur plans to fail, but many fail to plan and thus end up reacting spontaneously to situations in the business environment instead of proactively dealing with change.

Even successful entrepreneurs who have started businesses without a written plan have had to write business plans when they needed growth capital, a government grant, or a credit line from the bank. The important thing to remember is that a business plan is a living document that will no doubt undergo numerous changes over the life of the business.

New Venture Action Plan

- Develop a micro strategy approach to achieving proof of concept.
- Identify the stakeholders in the business and their interests.
- Create a compelling executive summary and pitch.
- Plan and execute the development of a full business plan.

Questions on Key Issues

1. What is the difference between a feasibility study and a business plan?
2. Why might it be better to start the business after completing the feasibility study and before completing a business plan?
3. What are the principles behind the micro-strategy approach to proof of concept?
4. How might the business plan change if the reader were an investor versus a potential management hire?
5. What are three key elements of a successful business plan pitch?

Experiencing Entrepreneurship

1. Interview someone who invests in small businesses about what he or she looks for in a business plan. On the basis of your discussion, what will you need to remember when you write your business plan?
2. Go to www.bplans.com and select a business plan to review. Using the guidelines for an effective plan given in this chapter, evaluate the plan in three to five pages. What are its strengths and weaknesses? How can it be improved?

Relevant Case Studies

Case 6 Andrew Mason and Groupon, Inc.

Case 8 Vision to Learn

CHAPTER 11

Designing an Entrepreneurial Company

"You can design and create, and build the most wonderful place in the world. But it takes people to make the dream a reality."

—WALT DISNEY

CHAPTER OBJECTIVES

- Explain how your business works.
- Discuss how entrepreneurs make the decision about the design of their company.
- Explain how to identify the appropriate business site.
- Discuss the most critical issues related to organizing people.

CULTURE IS THE COMPETITIVE ADVANTAGE

The pizza business is nothing new; in fact, it's a very crowded industry with about 75,000 establishments in the United States alone. It's hard to find a town that doesn't have a pizza parlor and most have more than one. It's one of those businesses that haven't seen a lot of innovation or creative thought since Dominos started the pizza delivery business, so it's ripe for something new and exciting.

Enter Nick Sarillo who grew up around pizza. His father owned a pizza restaurant in Carpentersville, Illinois, so it wasn't surprising when Nick opened his first restaurant in Crystal Lake in 1995. Although he did use his father's recipe, he decided early on that he was going to build a culture in his company that would set him apart from his competitors. One of the biggest problems in the pizza industry (and the fast-food restaurant industry in general) is high employee turnover—about 200 percent annually. That means higher costs and time spent in training new workers. The industry also averages 6.6 percent net profit and most establishments find themselves competing on price. Sarillo was determined not to play that game.

Sarillo adopted a form of management known as "trust and track," which is essentially the opposite of command and control. In the typical pizza restaurant, the boss takes responsibility for success, tells the employees what to do, and then checks to make sure they did it. Sarillo wanted his employees to understand what had to happen for the business to be successful, and then he would trust them to do what was necessary. That way the system would operate nearly flawlessly even if he weren't there. It seemed to have worked because Sarillo's turnover rate became a mere 20 percent and his profit margins reached 18 percent. One of the secrets to his success is his ability to understand the pain his community

is experiencing. With an 11 percent unemployment rate in his community, he decided that people would pay half price in the dining room on Mondays and half price for carryouts on Tuesdays until the unemployment rate returned to normal. This approach benefited the community and the business because the two slowest days of the week now became the most popular. Sarillo is also known for surprising his guests by picking up the check and hosting community fundraisers nearly every week where his company donates 5 percent of net sales to a particular cause.

The journey has not been uneventful. For one thing, Sarillo over built his second store in Elgin, a $5 million project that was more than twice the size of his first store, based on projections of 80,000 people moving into new housing developments. That never happened and the troubles began early in 2011. That's when he learned the importance of watching the liabilities side of his balance sheet. But by September of that year, he finally had to write a letter to his customers telling them that the business was about to fail. It was then that he learned the benefit of having been customer oriented for so many years. In the first week after he sent the letter, sales in the Elgin store increased 105 percent, with a 110 percent increase in Crystal Lake. For approximately 5 weeks, sales remained above normal, just enough time for the business to recover and for Nick to work with the bank to restructure the loan.

Sarillo has always made it a practice to hire only the best and those employees know that while they work for the company, they will have many opportunities to grow, learn, and increase their wages. The company now tracks financial and behavioral metrics that support company goals. For example, how many times does a guest request a particular server or bartender? How often does a carryout cashier develop a conversation with a customer? Nick's Pizza & Pub has grown to two locations, and he has added catering and banquet services. He believes that it's important to make sure that he has the right people managing his current restaurants—people who believe in "trust and track." Sarillo's internal leadership training program has been so successful that he has decided to share it with the public, creating Nick's University, which now teaches leadership

skills and the employee training methods he and his team developed over the years.

Sources: Nick's Pizza & Pub, www.nickspizzapub.com/home, accessed June 25, 2014; Mount, I. (October 24, 2012) "A Pizzeria Owner Learns the Value of Watching the Books," *NY Times,* http://www.nytimes.com/2012/10/25/business /smallbusiness/at-pizzerias-an-owner-learned-the-importance -of-accounting.html?_r=0;Burlingham, B. (February 2010), "Lessons from a Blue-Collar Millionaire," *Inc,* p. 57; and Detwiler, M.W. (May 2006), "Field of Dreams," *Pizza Today,* www .pizzatoday.com.

Organizational design is a critical component of any business plan both at launch and as the company grows and faces challenges from an increasingly complex external environment. As the sources of competitive advantage at startup lose their power, while at the same time competition is intensifying, organizational design and capabilities become increasingly vital to long-term success. Superior company design begins with an understanding of how the business works—how information flows through the business. This understanding is critical to making decisions about business location, number of employees, management expertise required, and technology needed to facilitate business goals.

The principles that designers use to solve problems and create successful products can also be applied to the creation of exceptional businesses.[1] In this chapter we deal with business design as we look at the various aspects of the company and the people who manage and work in it. A design thinking approach means that you consider the entire organization and how the various components and activities are interconnected. Liedtka and Ogilvie[2] assert that design thinking is essential in a high-velocity, highly unpredictable global marketplace and it is an asset to entrepreneurs for several reasons. First, design thinking is more about doing than talking, which is important when you consider that the track record for results promised by businesses has not been exceptional. Most businesses do not achieve the outcomes they say they will achieve.[3] A "doing" approach results in a company that is designed to allow for taking risk and being customer focused, which means that you have to be accepting of failure and your budget needs to factor in the costs of staying close to customers. For example, bringing marketers and programmers into meetings about the design of an interface for a website or including manufacturing personnel in a discussion about the development of a new product are "doing" activities.

Second, design thinking is about telling stories—making your strategy real and tangible. Too often when entrepreneurs talk about their businesses they simply parade a series of facts or reiterate talking points about their company mission and culture. However, the design of a company should be the result of a compelling story about solving a significant problem for customers. The way the company looks and feels should be aligned with that story. Third, design thinking is about flexibility and adaptability to uncertainty so your company needs to be organized to adapt quickly to change, to allow for experimentation within reasonable constraints, and to manage the unpredictability of the future. And fourth, design thinking is very much about people—their behaviors and emotions—rather than objective target markets or employees who simply perform a function. It's easy to understand the economic value of superior design on new products and services, but arguably the greatest value lies in applying design thinking to the business model and to the business itself. Apple is a clear example of how a company designs its business to follow customers to new opportunities rather than stubbornly sticking with the original business model. Three broad components make up the design of an entrepreneurial company: processes, people, and culture. Formal processes include the planning system, control mechanisms, compensation and reward policies, and other human resource and task-oriented processes that make the organization run more efficiently and effectively. These processes are not independent but, rather, are linked to all functions of the company that require them. For example, quality control mechanisms are not solely the purview of a single department, but flow from product development through manufacturing, to distribution, and throughout all the support functions needed to get a product to the customer.

Because teams are a common phenomenon in entrepreneurial companies, people who work in startups must have team-building skills as well as the ability to make decisions and implement them with very little input from top management or the CEO. In new ventures, those teams often consist of independent contractors whose skills are "rented" on an as-needed basis, so the startup must be designed to facilitate collaboration both internally and externally. This chapter focuses on strategies for organizing the business and its many processes, finding a superior location, and putting together a team or work force that will implement the company's processes and build the company's culture. Operations related to the production of goods and services are discussed in Chapter 12.

11.1   DESIGN: UNDERSTANDING THE WAY THE BUSINESS WORKS

Today's entrepreneurs need to design their companies to adapt continually to an ever-changing global environment that has presented the business world with complex problems. These new types of problems must be solved in innovative and interesting ways using new heuristics—ways of understanding or quick solutions for learning and discovery—rather than algorithms or formulaic approaches. To accomplish this adaptability and to be able to innovate quickly, entrepreneurs should think about business design from the perspective of project workflows rather than permanent departments and personnel assignments. Roger Martin of the Rothman School of Design argues, "This new world into which we are delving will require us to tackle mysteries and develop heuristics, and that will require a substantial change in some of the fundamental ways we work. Traditional firms will have to start looking much more like design shops on a number of important dimensions."[4]

There probably is no single best organizational structure for all types of ventures in all situations. Rather, entrepreneurs must find the best fit, given the existing contextual factors (environment, technology, market), design factors (strategy and models), and structural factors (complexity, formalization).[3] A misalignment or misfit among these factors could result in an organizational structure that does not suit the particular market you wish to serve. For example, if you choose a low-cost strategy to compete but do not implement tight control systems, minimize overhead, and focus on achieving economies of scale, your strategy will probably not succeed. Given that entrepreneurs at startup don't typically have the resources to implement control systems, minimize inventory, or achieve economies of scale, a low-cost entry strategy is rarely viable.

Firms in different industries tend also to differ in their administrative mechanisms and structures, so it's important that you consider how the firms in your value chain are organized. You may decide to organize similarly or you may identify a competitive advantage in organizing differently. Several studies have found that the design of the organizational structure—how business activities are grouped, divided, and coordinated—is a critical factor in business performance and as such a startup must continually modify its structure to meet the demands of growth.[5] These findings are very compatible with the previous discussion about design and the business. They also reinforce the argument presented in Chapter 4 on the importance of conducting thorough industry and market analyses to understand the external conditions that will affect the business. So, to design your business more effectively, it's important to identify the key success factors (KSF) for the business—what the business has to do to be successful—and then check that those KSF and your goals as a founder are congruent.[6] For example, you may want your business to have a relaxed and casual environment where creativity is fostered. But, if the external environment for your business requires that you adhere to certain regulations, that requirement may turn out to be in conflict with your personal goals for the company and you will have to make a choice or, at a minimum, compromise. To achieve your goals, you will also want to hire people with skills and values that match your objectives and the KSF for the business. In the end, your company's performance will be measured against how well you achieved the KSF.

Information systems technology has facilitated various kinds of organizational structures that enable new businesses to compete more effectively in rapidly changing environments.[7] For example, the move from centralized structures to more decentralized or distributed structures is highly compatible with the mindset of the entrepreneur. Today, companies are increasingly operating at a global level, involving multiple partners on different continents working together. This more distributed form of organization requires new ways to coordinate activities, manage documents, and communicate. Companies are typically distributed on four levels: (1) geographically, whether it be locally or across continents; (2) organizationally by department or project group; (3) temporally by time zone; and (4) by stakeholder groups, which can include such stakeholders as customers, project managers, sales staff, and so forth[8] (see Figure 11.1). Software companies are classic examples of distributed

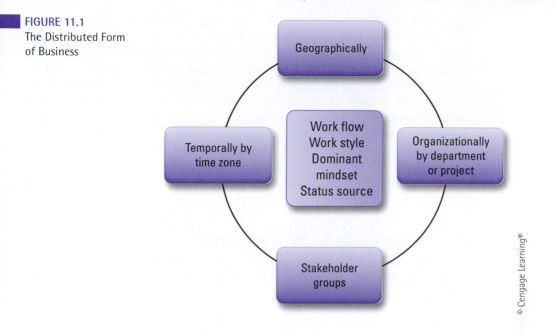

© Cengage Learning®

organizations where developers may be located in India, designers in Pakistan, corporate management and sales in the United States, and users around the globe. Despite geographic and organizational distances, the team must find a way to interact effectively to produce the best products and services it can. This is often accomplished through collaborative online work environments and videoconferencing. Chances are that you will choose a distributed form of organization in whole or in part. Whichever the case, it is important to employ the elements of design thinking to enable the company to respond quickly to both opportunities and threats.[9] Workflow should emphasize projects assigned to multidisciplinary teams rather than jobs and tasks assigned to functional departments or individuals as a permanent assignment. The style of work and the reward for that work is not individually based but team based. The team comes up with ideas and solutions and the team is rewarded for its efforts collaboratively. In more traditional businesses, by contrast, the source of status is being in charge of a large budget or having the desired corporate title. Clearly, startups are unable to operate in that manner and so their bootstrapping approach with small budgets is looked upon as a badge of courage and a source of pride. The reward or status in a startup can come from solving a big problem that no one else could solve. The dominant mindset in a design thinking approach is "there is nothing we can't accomplish." Entrepreneurs revel in challenges and figuring out ways around seemingly insurmountable constraints. Contrast this perspective with the dominant thinking in more traditional organizations, which is "we can't work under these constraints and this small budget."

Because they work with limited resources and a creative and opportunistic mindset, entrepreneurs are naturals at improvisation—they are the jazz musicians of the business world—they can find ways to work around even the most rigid structures imposed on them by their industry. As a result, startups and early-stage companies reflect a fine balance between structure and chaos, clarity and ambiguity. If left to their own devices, most entrepreneurs would embed design principles into their businesses quite naturally. They tend to retain internally what the company does best and outsource the rest of the activities for which it doesn't have expertise. Constraints and limited resources also demand that entrepreneurs look for ways to keep overhead (non-revenue-producing plant and equipment) to a minimum, while spending precious capital on revenue-generating areas of the business like marketing and sales.

To design your business around its natural workflow, you need to have a solid understanding of what workflow entails, which is the subject of the next section.

11.1a   Identifying Business Processes

One of the most eye-opening experiences you can have is identifying all the processes (activities, tasks, etc.) that occur in your business. Even more revealing of how the business works is a process map or flowchart that traces how information from those processes and activities flows through the business. Recall that in Chapter 9, you developed a process flowchart to understand the capital and other resource requirements of your startup as well as to figure out how many people to hire, how much equipment to purchase, and what kind of facility will be needed. To create such a map of the business processes, take an imaginary tour of the business during a single day, listing all the tasks, people, equipment, supplies, and space required to run the business. Understanding how the business works makes it easier to determine how to organize the business. Refer to Chapter 9 for an example of a process map. With a clear picture of how your business works, you're in a better position to make some important decisions.

11.1b   Making Decisions: Doing It All or Outsourcing

Today it is much more difficult for a new venture to achieve total in-house control of its value chain. The global marketplace is more complex, time-to-market has decreased, and it is difficult for any one company to have the broad expertise necessary to master all the functions of the supply chain (the inputs to your business) and the distribution channel (how you deliver your product or service to the customer). At present, a growing company is more likely to increase its flexibility by choosing one function to concentrate on—what it does best—and subcontracting functions it does not want to handle. The general rule is that if the resources to manufacture, assemble, and distribute your product already exist efficiently in the market in which you want to do business, the process should be outsourced. If your business's competitive advantage lies in proprietary rights to its product, you will likely choose to maintain control of strategic functions related to that product and outsource such things as warehousing, transportation, and some aspects of marketing. Startup entrepreneurs often choose to outsource administrative functions such as payroll, accounting, and inventory management and may even lease some of their employees from an employee-leasing company so they can focus on getting their product or service to the customer. Today many companies outsource aspects of their business processes; by contrast, virtual enterprises outsource most of the functions of the business. To their customers, they look like any other company, but behind the public image is an entrepreneur who is basically a ringmaster in a three-ring circus.

The Virtual Enterprise: Getting Traction Quickly

The term *virtual enterprise* was borrowed from the science of virtual reality, which enables a person to become an integral part of a computer-generated, three-dimensional world. In business, a "virtual enterprise" has much the same purpose. You build a company that to the rest of the world looks like any other company, but it's a business without walls where you do not incur the risk of acquiring employees, costly equipment, and enormous overhead. A virtual company makes it possible to operate the business from practically anywhere—a home, car, or vacation cabin. Research defines the virtual corporation as "a temporary network of independent companies, suppliers, customers, even erstwhile rivals—linked by information technology to share skills, cost, and access to one another's markets."[10] Today cloud computing has spawned a resurgence in virtual companies. Cloud computing is simply moving computing tasks and storage from local desktop computers and business servers to remote servers across the Internet. It is analogous to the electricity grid: resources, software, and information are provided to the user on demand, saving them a significant amount of money.

The goal of the virtual enterprise is to deliver to the customer the highest-quality product at the lowest possible cost in a timely manner. To do this requires the participation and management of the entire value chain, from producer to customer, through a series of strategic alliances. Once the goal is achieved or a predetermined period of time is met, the virtual organization dissolves itself, or it grows to the point where it can afford to integrate its suppliers and/or distributors, giving the company more control over quality and delivery and becoming a more traditional company.[11] This strategy is known as vertical integration. Today, in a global business environment, this same goal can also be accomplished through strategic partnerships with other companies in the value chain, which is discussed in the next section.

Strategic Alliances

Another way in which startups become more flexible and responsive, as well as grow more rapidly, is by forming strategic alliances, or teams of businesses, to share resources and reduce costs. These alliances are more than sources of capability for the entrepreneurial venture; they are the glue that holds the venture together. Strategic alliances are more like true partnerships, but they take many forms. The partnering companies may purchase major equipment jointly or share the costs of research and development and of training. Particularly in the area of R&D, it is very difficult for any one small company to manage the expense alone. Networking and alliances enable smaller businesses to bid successfully against large companies. They offer the convenience and savings of access to one source for everything, shared quality standards, and coordination of vendors. The key to managing a small business alliance successfully is being willing to share internal information such as manufacturing processes, quality control practices, and product information for the good of all.

Dealing with strategic alliances (something virtual companies must do) is not without problems. If you want to maintain control of every aspect of your growing venture, it is frustrating to have to give up some of that control to

GLOBAL INSIGHTS

When the Global Startup Community Inspires Change at Home

Innovation is not created from the top down; it bubbles up from the creativeness of people who are free to innovate. It is clear that China is beginning to understand that. In 1978, when the Chinese initiated economic reforms, government represented 90 percent of GDP: today that figure has dropped to less than 50 percent. Self-employment, which didn't exist until 1994, is now increasing thanks to Chinese university graduates educated abroad who return to China to find opportunity. Communities of entrepreneurs in cities like Shanghai, Beijing, and Guangzhou have formed networks with each other and with investors. They write about entrepreneurship in news platforms like TechNode, the partner of U.S.-based TechCrunch. As in other parts of the developed world, accelerators and incubators are forming to coach these new entrepreneurs to success. In 2014, for example, online education site TutorGroup managed to raise $100 million in venture funding, while Alibaba, the giant search engine, went public in the United States. In fact, the Chinese government has acknowledged that 75 percent of new jobs have come from entrepreneurial ventures. Nevertheless, many challenges remain for those wanting to start businesses in China. Intellectual property rights are still a problem and there are huge regulatory hurdles to overcome. The World Bank reported that China ranks 158th out of 183 economies for having an unfavorable business environment for startups with no significant reforms over the past five years that will help small businesses develop and grow. However, this grass roots effort is gaining steam and party leaders are finally recognizing the power of entrepreneurship.

Sources: Ortmans, J. (June 23, 2014). "What's Ahead for China's Entrepreneurs? Entrepreneurship.org, The Kauffman Foundation, http://entrepreneurship.org/Blogs /Policy-Forum-Blog/2014/June/Whats-Ahead-for-Chinas-Entrepreneurs.aspx?utm _source=Newsletter&utm_medium=Email&utm_campaign=Policy_06_23_2014; "Doing Business," The World Bank, accessed June 25, 2014, http://www.doingbusiness.org/data /exploreeconomies/china

other companies. Getting virtual partners to meet your demands for quality, timeliness, and efficiency can also be a long and difficult process. Shifts in economic conditions or customer demand can negatively affect one or more of the partners, making it difficult to achieve stated outcomes. Perhaps the biggest problem is the fact that startups don't have the experience or depth of resources to effectively manage their alliances. Unfortunately, large company partners know this and often take advantage by exerting their power to their own ends.

Consequently, it is important that you and your strategic partner come to written agreement on your duties and responsibilities and that you both enjoy the benefits of the relationship. Your company should be represented by an attorney who can protect its interests and make sure that it can't be held hostage by its partner. Strategic partnerships do have some challenges, namely, higher administrative costs, potential organizational culture differences among the partners, and ethical issues.[12] Many entrepreneurs have found, however, that the benefits of strategic partners far outweigh the problems and that they are the most efficient and effective way to give the startup traction.

Keeping Distributed Employees and Strategic Partners Linked

One of the important challenges that distributed organizations with strategic partners or distributed organizations with employees at a distance face is keeping everyone connected and in touch even though they are geographically separated. A distributed company may be a great way to keep overhead down and flexibility up, but it is no substitute for human contact and face-to-face communication. Even in a virtual environment, it's important to conduct a face-to-face meeting at least once every three to six months and arrange for employees and partners in specific geographic regions to meet regularly in between company-wide meetings. It is also essential to create a collaborative workspace online and to encourage everyone to share important information and discussion points. A regular conference call should be set up once a week to stay in touch. With distributed companies growing by leaps and bounds, online companies have sprung up to provide services and products that these businesses may need. Here are some examples:

- *Management team:* Many websites aggregate independent professional service providers and help small businesses find experienced financial management and other services on a limited budget.

- *Marketing:* At several online sites, a company can accomplish its public relations, marketing, direct mail, customer relationship management, and even market research for far less than it would cost to hire a marketing firm. Check out www.marketingprofs.com, one of the best sources for marketing help on the Internet.

- *Supply chain management:* Online companies will do everything from order management to assembly, configuration, packaging, and e-commerce fulfillment and collaboration.

■ *Virtual meetings:* Collaboration services such as Citrix, Google Groups, and Go to Meeting help keep distributed organizations connected at a relatively low cost.

How you organize your business determines what type of physical location, if any, you will need. We take up the topic of location strategy in the next section.

11.2   LOCATION STRATEGY: FINDING THE APPROPRIATE BUSINESS SITE

If your new venture cannot be operated as a distributed or virtual enterprise, a significant part of the organizing process will be finding an appropriate physical site for doing business. Most people are familiar with the three key factors for determining value in real estate: "location, location, location." Similarly, your business' location significantly affects its success. Location determines who will see the business, how easily customers can find it and access it (Is the business at ground-floor level and easily seen? Or is it out of sight in a multistory building?), and whether or not they will want to access it (Is the neighborhood safe? Is parking available?). Even businesses such as manufacturing, where the customer doesn't come to the site, benefit from a location near major sources of transportation or supply. Because many business owners view their business site as permanent, selecting the best site becomes a crucial decision that will need to be justified to investors, lenders, and others. Site decisions generally begin at a macro level, considering first the state or region of the country, next the city, and then the parcel on which the facility will be located. Starting your business in the town in which you currently live may not always be the best choice. There are a number of factors you should consider and we'll discuss those next.

11.2a   Choosing the Region, State, and Community

Locating a site for a new business normally begins with identifying the area of the country that seems best suited to the type of business you are starting. "Best suited" may mean that firms in a particular industry tend to congregate in a particular region, such as the high-tech firms that gravitate to Route 128 in Massachusetts or to the Silicon Valley in California. For some businesses, "best suited" may mean that a state is offering special financial and other incentives for businesses to locate there as states like Texas and South Dakota do. In other cases, "best suited" means being located near major suppliers. Often entrepreneurs start businesses where they happen to live. This may be fine during the incubation period, but soon, what the area contributes to the potential success of the business over the long term must be considered.

The economic base of a region or community is simply the major source of income for the area. Communities are viewed as primarily industrial, agricultural, or service-oriented. In general, industrial communities export more goods than they import. For example, suppose the community's principal income is derived from farming and the associated products that it ships to other communities. This activity brings money into the community. Now suppose the citizens of the community must travel to another community to do major shopping. This activity takes money out of the community. An important thing to learn about any community being considered as the home base for your business is whether the money brought in from farming or some other activity exceeds the money that leaves through shopping. If it does, the community appears to have a growing economic base, which is a favorable factor for new businesses. Entrepreneurs can learn more about the economic base of any community by contacting the state or regional economic development agency in the area. These organizations exist to bring new business into the region, so they have to stay on top of what is going on. They can provide all the statistics on the economic health of the region, as well as estimate the cost of doing business there. Another helpful site is the U.S. Department of Commerce website (www.commerce.gov).

Most community governments are faced with cash needs that go well beyond the tax tolerance level of their citizens; consequently, they work diligently with economic development agencies to attract new businesses—and the accompanying tax revenues—into the community. One of the ways they attract businesses is by offering incentives such as lower taxes, cheaper land, and employee training programs. Some communities have enterprise zones, which give the businesses that locate in them favorable tax treatment from the state on the basis of the number of jobs created, as well as lower land costs and rental rates. They also expedite permit processes and help in any way they can to make the move easier. It is important, however, to be wary of communities that offer upfront cash in compensation for the community's lack of up-to-date infrastructure. The community may be hiding a high corporate tax rate or some other disincentive that could hurt the new business's chances of success. In general, the larger the incentives, the more exacting your homework must be.

Consider also that you want a community that has other businesses in your industry so that your chances of tapping a skilled pool of talent are greater. You also want to see amenities such as restaurants, theatres, and other cultural venues that make it an attractive place for employees to live and work.

11.2b Population Demographics

In addition to studying the economic base and the community's attitude toward new business, entrepreneurs, particularly those whose businesses deal with consumers, should carefully examine the population base. Is it growing or shrinking? Is it aging or getting younger? Is it culturally diverse? The level and quantity of disposable income in the community will indicate whether there is enough money to purchase what you are offering, and the skill level of workers in the community you will need to meet the needs of your new venture.

Demographic information in the United States is usually based on the U.S. census, which tracks changes in population size and characteristics. The United States is divided into Standard Metropolitan Statistical Areas (SMSAs), which are geographic areas that include a major metropolitan area such as Los Angeles or Houston. These are further divided into census tracts, which contain approximately 4,000–5,000 people, and into neighborhood blocks. With this information, it is possible to determine, for example, whether the city in which you want to locate a new software development firm has enough people with sufficient technical and educational skills to support it. Population data also indicate the number of people available to work. Demographic data are easily obtained from the local economic development agency, the public library, the Internet, or the post office, which tracks populations by zip code. Population demographics for global communities can be found at a number of sites, such as GeoHive (www.geohive.com).

11.2c   Choosing a Retail Site

With a retail business, you are dealing directly with the consumer, so naturally, one of the first considerations is locating near consumers who have disposable income. Because a retail business is unlikely to survive if not enough consumers have easy access to the business, it is imperative to locate where there are suitable concentrations of consumers. Understanding a trade area is one way to calculate the potential demand from consumers. The trade area is the region from which you expect to draw customers. The type of business will largely determine the size of the trade area. For example, if your business sells general merchandise that can be found almost anywhere, the trade area is much smaller; customers will not travel great distances to purchase common goods. Yet a specialty outlet—for example, a clothing boutique with unusual apparel—may draw people from other communities as well.

Once the location within the community is identified, the trade area can be calculated. With a map of the community, the business site is identified; then, the point of a compass can be placed on the proposed site and a circle can be drawn whose radius represents the distance people are willing to drive to reach the site. Within the circle is the trade area, which can now be studied in more detail. Using a census tract map, census tracts can be identified within the trade area, and the number of people who reside within the boundaries of the trade area can be calculated (see Figure 11.2). The demographic information will also describe these people in terms of level of education, income level, average number of children, and so forth.

Once the trade area is established, the competition can also be identified. One way to do this is to drive or walk through the area (assuming it is not too large) and spot competing businesses. Note their size and number, and gauge how busy they are at various times of the day by observing their parking lots or actually entering the business. If competitors are located in shopping malls or strip centers, look for clusters of stores that are similar to the new venture and have low vacancy rates. Then look at the stores near the proposed site to check for compatibility. Often, locating near a competitor is a wise choice because it encourages comparison shopping, which is a good thing if your business has a competitive advantage. Observe the character of the area. Does it appear to be successful and well maintained? Remember that the character of the area will have an important impact on the business. Online tools such as Google Earth

FIGURE 11.2
Sample of a Trade Area

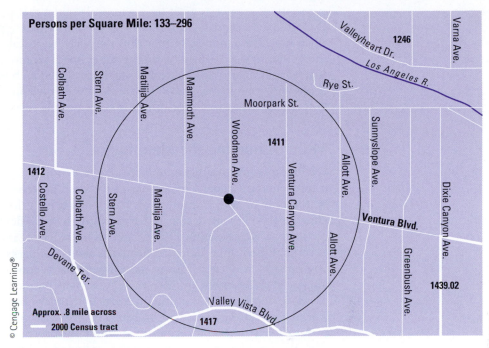

(http://earth.google.com) are helpful for initial evaluation of a site that is not within driving distance.

It is important to identify the routes customers might take to reach a proposed site: highways, streets, and public transportation routes. If a site is difficult to locate and hard to reach, potential customers will not expend the effort to find it. The parking situation should also be checked. Most communities require provision of a sufficient amount of parking space for new construction, through either parking lots or garages; however, in some older areas, street parking is the only available option. If parking is hard to find or too expensive, customers will avoid going to that business. A foot and car traffic count for the proposed site will determine how busy the area is. Remember, retail businesses typically rely heavily on traffic for customers. A traffic count is easily accomplished by observing and tallying the customers going by and into the business. City planning departments and transportation departments maintain auto traffic counts for major arterials in the city.

11.2d   Choosing a Service/Wholesale Site

If you have a service or wholesale business that has customers who come to your place of business, you will need to find a site that offers some of the same attributes that a retailer looks for. Accessibility, attractiveness, and a trade area of sufficient size are all key factors in the selection of a site. There is no need to choose from among the more expensive commercial sites because customer expectations are not as great for a wholesale outlet that sells to the public, such as Costco for example. Customers who patronize these types of businesses usually want to save money, so they don't expect the upscale version of a business site. Some service businesses, on the other hand, require attractive office space that is easily accessible. These are usually professional businesses—lawyers, accountants, consultants, and so forth. The image they present through the location and appearance of their offices is crucial to the success of the business.

11.2e   Choosing the Manufacturing Site

Setting up a manufacturing operation is not something that most startup entrepreneurs will undertake because of the cost; however, in some cases, it may be the only option. Communities have zoning laws that limit manufacturing companies to certain designated areas away from residential, retail, and office commercial sites to reduce the chance of noise, odor, and pollutants affecting citizens. Often these areas are known as industrial parks, and they are usually equipped with electrical power and sewage plants appropriate to manufacturing. By locating in one of these parks, your new business may benefit from the presence of other manufacturing nearby, which may offer opportunities for networking and sharing resources to keep costs under control.

Another common location for manufacturing is within enterprise zones, which are public–private partnerships designed to bring jobs to inner cities, downtown areas, and rural areas suffering from the shift of jobs and population to the suburbs. The draw for businesses is tax incentives, regulatory relief, and employee training programs. Empowerment zones in any state can be found by going to the U.S. Housing and Urban Development Agency website (www .hud.gov). Entrepreneurs seeking manufacturing sites are concerned with four key factors: access to suppliers, cost of labor, access to transportation, and cost of utilities. These factors may not be weighted equally. Depending on the type of manufacturer, one or more factors may have greater importance in evaluating a site.

Land and location are only part of the equation. If the site contains an existing building, the question becomes whether to lease or to buy. If the site is bare land, building a facility is the only option. Because the facility accounts for a significant portion of a new venture's startup costs, it is important to consider these scenarios in more detail. See Table 11.1 for an overview of the broad criteria for the lease-build-buy decision and some of the important questions to ask.

11.2f   Alternatives to Conventional Facilities

Today entrepreneurs have a variety of alternatives to conventional business locations. These alternatives lower the cost of overhead and make it easier for you to change your mind should the location not work out. We'll consider four of these alternative sites: incubators, shared space, mobile locations, and temporary tenant agreements.

TABLE 11.1   The Lease-Build-Buy Decision

Stage of Business	Lease	Build	Buy	Temporary Space
Questions to Ask	Also ask the "buy" questions. Do you need to conserve capital for growth? Do you expect the company to grow rapidly and need to move? Can you include clauses that permit the option to renew the lease? Can you remodel to suit your needs? Which type of lease works best for the business: gross, net, or percentage? Do you have a choice?	Do you have the time to build? Is it important to show an asset on your balance sheet? Are your facility needs unique? Do you intend to remain in the facility for a long time?	Is the building of sufficient size to meet future needs? Is there sufficient parking? Is there space for customers, storage, inventory, offices, and restrooms? Is there curbside appeal and compatibility with surroundings? Is there sufficient lighting fixtures and outlets and power to run equipment?	Do you need to keep overhead costs very low? Are you willing to share space? Is your product or service suitable to a mobile location such as a kiosk or pushcart? Do you need to test the product on customers in a real situation before committing to a building? Do you have a product that can be demonstrated?
Startup	A short-term lease gives the business the option to move and to gauge its long-term requirements.	At startup, use this approach only when there is no facility available to meet the needs of the business. It requires large amounts of capital and time.	Not recommended at startup unless it is the only option and the company is sufficiently capitalized.	Excellent for testing new products, services, and locations on customers. Low overhead.
Rapid Growth	A short-term lease will enable the business to move to larger facilities to meet growing demand without tying up a lot of precious capital.	Resist building during rapid growth as it will use up limited cash needed for growth. It is also a time-consuming process, and time is precious during rapid growth.	Rapid growth is not the time to buy a facility unless the company has received, from investors, a large infusion of cash that more than meets its operational needs.	During rapid growth, temporary locations make sense. This approach keeps the overhead low so that more cash can be directed toward satisfying demand.
Stable Growth	If the location is appropriate to the growth needs of the company, a long-term lease will provide more stability in cash flows.	With stable growth and positive cash flow, the company can afford to spend the time, effort, and capital to build a facility that specifically meets its needs.	Buying a building that allows for expansion is appropriate when company growth stabilizes and the company has a loyal customer base. It is also appropriate when the company needs to show a sizable asset on its balance sheet. If the company subsequently needs cash for a new period of growth, it can sell the building to an investor and lease it back, providing an instant infusion of capital.	Temporary space will typically be used to test new products and services before making a commitment.

Incubators

Some entrepreneurs find it helpful to start their new venture's life in a business incubator, which has the same purpose as an incubator for an infant—to create a controlled environment that will enhance the chances that the business will survive the startup phase. Private and state-sponsored incubators can be found in nearly every region of the country for almost any type of business. Incubators offer space at a lower-than-market rate to several businesses, which may then share common support functions, such as receptionist, copy machine, and conference room. The incubator may even offer business courses and training to help new entrepreneurs with the myriad details involved in running the business. After about three to five years, depending on the incubator, the young business is helped to move into its own site elsewhere in the community.

You should be aware that some incubators cater only to high-tech firms or to service firms. The National Business Incubation Association is a good place to start to learn more about incubators in your area. When considering an incubator, it is imperative to look at its track record and make sure it provides critical higher-order needs, such as a network of contacts, access to expertise and capital, professional resources, and access to customers.

Shared Space

Another choice is to locate the company within the facilities of a larger company. As the largest of the chain stores continue to downsize, opportunities to take excess space arise. A variation on this theme is to lease a location that has enough space to sublet to a complementary business. For example, a copy service might lease excess space to a new computer graphics company or one that is seeking a new location. A shared arrangement is an effective way to secure the best location at a reasonable price.

Mobile Locations

One of the more interesting ways to introduce new businesses and new products/services to the marketplace is through the use of pushcarts and kiosks. Pushcarts and their more fixed alternative, the kiosk (a small booth), also enable your company to expand so that you can acquire new locations without the high overhead of a conventional retail storefront. Mobile locations like these are often found in airports, malls, and other areas where consumers gather. Of the various areas where these types of mobile businesses can be found, airports pose perhaps the most difficult challenge to secure. They typically want an experienced business and you will often have to compete against companies that focus on airport locations.

Temporary Tenant Agreements

Some landlords have found that, rather than sitting on an empty space until the new tenant moves in, they can rent the space on a temporary basis so that their cash flow is not interrupted. In fact, the concept of the temporary tenant has grown so rapidly that there are now leasing agents who specialize in this area. The most successful of these temporary tenants possess the following characteristics that seem to draw customers to them: personalized merchandise, opportunities to sample the product, products that can be demonstrated, and products that can be used for entertaining the customers. For the temporary concept to work, significant foot traffic and high customer turnover are required. This is an excellent alternative for retail businesses that want to test a location before making a major commitment. Whichever choice is made, the location and type of facility need to be compatible with the business and its strategic goals.

11.3   PEOPLE STRATEGY: ORGANIZING HUMAN RESOURCES

The organization of the business processes and the business location are critical aspects of the business design, but it is people who implement those processes and use the company facility on a daily basis. The roles and responsibilities of people in the organization are typically displayed in a traditional organizational chart like the one depicted in Figure 11.3. However, at startup, the organization chart is more likely to be flat, reflecting the fact that the entrepreneur and the founding team often perform all the functions when the business is starting, and much of the work is accomplished through an informal organization or network of relationships. Informal networks are social links that constitute the real power base in the organization. Metaphorically speaking, the organizational chart is the skeleton of the body, while the informal networks are the arteries and veins that push information and activity throughout the organization—in other words, they are the lifeblood of the organization.

Entrepreneurs seem to recognize intuitively the value of informal networks in the organizational structure, and often the most successful new ventures adopt a team-based approach with a flatter structure. The lead entrepreneur is the driving force for the entrepreneurial team, which normally consists of people with expertise in at least one of the three functional areas of a new venture: marketing, operations, and finance.

FIGURE 11.3   Traditional Organizational Chart for a Growing Business

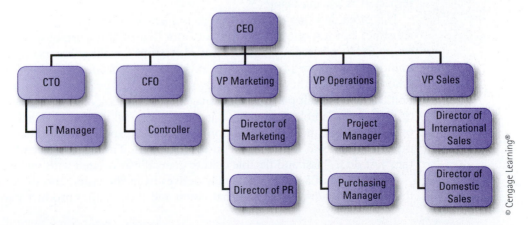

© Cengage Learning®

At no time is the entrepreneur's role as leader of the organization more critical or more vulnerable than in the first year of the business. If you are not able to gain traction and build momentum to propel your new venture forward, it will remain in a constant state of struggle. To build an effective organization, you must avoid some common leadership traps:[13]

- Isolating yourself from the rest of the startup team and failing to keep the lines of communication open
- Always having the one "right" answer instead of looking for the best solution
- Keeping people on board who are not up to the needs of the company
- Taking on too much too soon
- Setting unrealistic expectations based on inadequate information
- Not building support networks

11.3a Creating the Company Culture

Researchers actually disagree as to exactly what culture is. Some believe it is the reflection of the core values of the company, which stem from the firm's history.[14] Others believe culture is changeable, that it really reflects the behaviors and attitudes of those in the company at the time.[15] In their 1982 book *Corporate Cultures: The Rites and Rituals of Corporate Life*, Terrence Deal and Allan Kennedy coined the term *corporate culture* to describe the organization's tendency to develop its own characteristic way of doing things.[16] In very simplistic terms, organizational culture is the personality of the company, that intangible set of values that determines how and why the people in the organization respond to their business environment as they do.[17] It is the part of the company that is invisible—it is sensed rather than seen. A description of the company culture may be spelled out in the company handbook, but the real culture is found within the attitudes and actions of the organization's people as they interact on a daily basis. If you look at culture from a design perspective, you think of it as how people interact with each other so as to produce a sense of "energy, reassurance, and a sense of calm that comes from being deeply respected as a living being."[18]

It is often said that entrepreneurial companies—startups in particular—have a distinct culture, one much different from that of large, established corporations. This is misleading, because not all startups are alike. For example, if the founders came from a big corporate environment or from a traditional business school education, they are very likely to think in terms of elaborate organization charts and multiple levels of management that look much like those of GE or Procter & Gamble. You see that in teams where all the founders have C-level titles. However, most founders don't have these experiences, so they tend to organize as a team to make the business happen. These startups end up with the "just do it," fast and flexible culture generally associated with startups.

The culture of a startup generally derives from the vision and values of the founder or founding team and that vision and those values produce particular behaviors or ways of doing things. The advantage of startups is that as a founder, you have the opportunity to hire only people who fit with the culture you want to create; this is a much easier task than trying to re-engineer the ingrained culture of an existing company. For culture to create a competitive advantage for a startup, however, the values, practices, and behaviors need to align with the goals, processes, and tasks that the business engages in.[19] Figure 11.4 depicts this relationship. For example, the processes and activities a company undertakes are reflected in the practices or the way those processes are implemented. In the figure, the right side of the circle reflects people while the left side represents organizational issues.

In organizing the business to reflect its culture, the founding team would identify its core values and the overriding mission of the company. Then the team would specify the outcomes it's trying to achieve. Suppose an outcome is developing a loyal customer base. It would be important to do significant market research with customers to determine what matters to them. The results of this research would tell the team what they would have to do to get the result they want. This would lead to practices such as giving customers an easy way to provide feedback to the company and behaviors such as always being honest with customers.

Aligning the operational and organizational performance of the company with its beliefs and behaviors is only the start. In some manner, this all has to be conveyed to the market in the form of a story—not a dry, factual statement of facts, but a story that gives customers a sense of what this culture feels like. Stories are much stickier than business statements because they contain people

FIGURE 11.4
Aligning Culture and Strategy

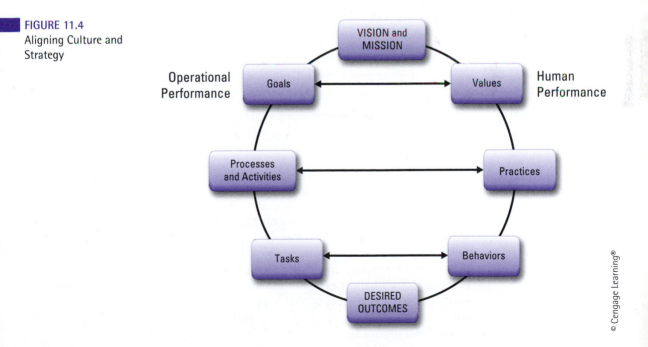

© Cengage Learning®

that customers can relate to and they provide rich context that gives customers a lot of information.[20] Saying "We help people find the best prices" is less effective than telling a story about a customer who was able to save a lot of money using the company's product. A great story will provide context, characters, content, and takeaway lessons that the customer can extrapolate to their own situation.

Some of the questions that lead to a definition of a company's culture and values are the following:

1. Do the organization's people work in teams or individually?
2. How does the organization deal with change?
3. How does the company deal with failure?
4. How are decisions made? Who makes the critical decisions?
5. How is work prioritized?
6. How is information shared within and outside the organization?
7. Does the company take a long-term or short-term focus on decision making?
8. How does the company ensure employee competence?
9. Does the company encourage diversity?
10. How are employees treated, and what is their role in the company's vision?

One company that takes its core values very seriously is online shoe retailer Zappos. Founder Tony Hsieh has identified 10 core values that define the company's culture. They are[21]

1. Deliver WOW through service.
2. Embrace and drive change.
3. Create fun and a little weirdness.
4. Be adventurous, creative, and open-minded.
5. Pursue growth and learning.
6. Build open and honest relationships with communication.
7. Build a positive team and family spirit.
8. Do more with less.
9. Be passionate and determined.
10. Be humble.

Like other companies with company culture as their best competitive advantage—Starbucks, Amazon, and 3M—Zappos believes that everything the company does and every decision it makes stems from its culture. That culture has given the company a lower turnover rate than its peers and an extremely high happiness quotient for its employees and its customers. To successfully create a culture that supports your KSF and enables you to serve your customers in the most effective and meaningful way possible, you need to do three things.

1. Be definitive about the kind of culture you want to create in your company.

2. Be clear on the core values and communicate them constantly.

3. Be consistent about reinforcing your company's values and don't accept any behavior that contradicts your culture.

With a firm sense of your company's core values and the culture you want to create, you need to hire the right people and get rid of those who do not share the company's values.

11.3b   Hiring the Right People

Today, with more and more employees suing their bosses for wrongful termination, sexual harassment, and racial/gender/age discrimination, it is increasingly important that entrepreneurs understand how to hire. Hiring is not a simple matter of placing a help-wanted ad in the newspaper or on a website, receiving résumés, and then holding interviews to select the best candidate. The bulk of the work of hiring comes before the person is actually needed.

Part of organizing the business is determining what positions are needed for the required tasks of the business. This is a wise practice, because employees are generally the largest expense of the business and therefore should be hired only when necessary. Nevertheless, it is important to develop job descriptions to prepare for the eventuality of hiring employees. Typically, when entrepreneurs (and managers) develop job descriptions, they focus entirely on the duties and responsibilities of a particular job. Although this is important, it is equally important to develop behavioral profiles of these jobs. Even though a job candidate may have the education and experience required by the job description and may display some of the behavioral traits necessary for success in the position, the candidate's personality and values may not fit in well with the culture of the organization. This is an important distinction, because education and experience can be acquired and behaviors can in most cases be taught, but the right values—which enable compatibility with the company culture—must already be present. In today's business environment, a company's culture is a competitive advantage, so hiring people whose attitudes and values are consistent with it becomes an important goal in hiring.

The first and best place to look for an employee is among current employees, subcontractors, or professional advisers. Referrals from trusted people who know the business have a greater likelihood of yielding a successful hire. Even during startup, it is important to be constantly on the lookout for good people who might come on board as the business grows. Executive search firms are excellent sources for management positions, and online resources have become an effective starting place for hiring, particularly with technically oriented positions. Companies such as Monster (www.monster.com), Guru.com (www.guru .com), and Craigslist (www.craigslist.com) are places where qualified people post their résumés, and it's easy for an employer to search for the particular skills required. But to save time and avoid interviewing the wrong people, it's always wise to follow up with references before calling the candidate in for an interview.

Most entrepreneurs dread interviewing job candidates, primarily because they don't know what to say and don't understand that their questions should be designed to reveal the individual's personality and behavior—how he or she might react in certain situations. This is because a résumé simply reveals what the candidate sees as their relevant experience and that's only part of the total picture. How the candidate behaves during the interview and particularly what their nonverbal communication tells the interviewer is far more revealing of the candidate's character. Understanding who the candidate is can be effectively accomplished in part by asking open-ended questions, questions that call for more than "yes–no" answers. For example, ask, "What is your greatest strength?" or "How would you handle the following hypothetical situation?" While the person is answering the questions, you should be careful to note the nonverbal communication being expressed through body language.

You must be aware that certain questions should never be asked in an interview situation because they are illegal and leave you open to potential lawsuits. Under the laws administered by the Equal Employment Opportunity Commission (EEOC), before the point of hire a person may *not* be asked about religion or religious background, nation of origin, living arrangements or lifestyle choices, plans for pregnancy, age (to avoid discrimination against people over 40 or under 21), criminal arrest record ("Have you ever been convicted of a crime?" may be asked), or military record.

Human Resource Leasing

Entrepreneurs who are not ready to hire permanent employees or who need to remain flexible because the business environment is volatile and unpredictable may want to consider leasing employees or employing temporary services. A leased employee is not legally your employee but is, rather, the employee of the lessor organization. That firm is responsible for all employment taxes and benefits. You simply receive a bill for the person's services. Employee leasing is a rapidly growing industry now known as the professional employer organization (PEO) industry (www.peo.com). More and more business owners are finding it advantageous to have a third party manage their human resources. In effect, the PEO becomes a co-employer, taking on the responsibility of payroll, taxes, benefits, workers' compensation insurance, labor law compliance, and risk management. Elizabeth Bradt is an accomplished veterinarian, but like many professional service providers, she did not have the skills or the patience to handle human resource issues, such as hiring interviews, regulatory compliance, and benefits. She couldn't offer the types of benefits that large employers offer, such as 401(k) plans and dental insurance. As a result, her business, All Creatures Veterinary Hospital in Salem, Massachusetts, lost half its employees in the first year. Bradt had not realized how much she would have to deal with when it came to hiring and supporting her staff. To solve the problem, she made Integrated Staffing, a professional employer organization, the legal employer of her staff. The PEO gave her peace of mind and provided her employees with benefits that she alone could not have provided. As a result, beginning in 2006, she had zero turnover and since that time her business has thrived.[20]

11.3c   Managing Employee Risk

Risk management is a set of policies and their associated decision-making processes that reduce or eliminate risks associated with having employees. For example, one entrepreneurial service company with 120 employees was suffering from a high turnover rate of new hires during the first 90 days of employment. Although the company's overall turnover rate was in line with the industry average, its turnover rate for new hires was about double that of its competitors. This turnover was costing the company more than $10,000 per employee, which posed a significant financial risk for the company and raised its cost of doing business substantially. To solve the problem and reduce the risk, the company realized that it needed to implement some new procedures, so it improved its interviewing skills and instituted an orientation program for new employees.

Financial risks are one type of employee risk. In Chapter 13 the legal issues related to the formation of the business are discussed, but the law affects every aspect of business operations as well, especially the way employees are treated. The federal government and state governments have enacted a number of laws and regulations to protect employees from unhygienic or dangerous work environments, discrimination during hiring, and payment of substandard wages. One of the critical tasks of the person in charge of human resources is to make certain that the business is obeying all the laws and regulations to which it is subject. Failure to do so could result in severe penalties for the business and its owners. It is not within the scope of this text to address these laws in depth; however, Table 11.2 presents some of the major employment laws that affect small businesses. More information about these laws can be found on the Internet and through the federal and state agencies.

11.3d   Planning for Ownership and Compensation

Two of the most perplexing management issues faced by an entrepreneur heading a new company are how much of the company to sell to potential stockholders and how much to pay key managers. Whatever route is ultimately chosen, it should reflect the goals of the company and reward the contributions of the participants. There is a tendency on the part of small, privately held companies to use minority shares as an incentive to entice investors and to pay key managers, primarily because new companies generally do not have the cash flow to provide attractive compensation packages. The prevailing wisdom is that providing stock in the new company will increase commitment, cause management to be more cost-conscious, reduce cash outlay for salaries, and induce loyalty to the company in the long term. But studies have found that this is not always the case.[22] More often than not, the person who has been given stock in good faith will ultimately leave the company, possibly taking the stock with her or him (absent an agreement prohibiting this), and this action creates the potential for future harm to the business.

In the initial growth stage of a new venture, it is difficult to determine with any degree of accuracy what long-term role a particular person may play in the organization. Entrepreneurs typically are not able to attract the best people to

TABLE 11.2   Important Employment Laws

Law	Type of Business It Applies To
Age Discrimination in Employment Act Prohibits discrimination against people age 40 to 70, including discrimination in advertising for jobs	All companies with 20 or more employees
Americans with Disabilities Act Prohibits discrimination on the basis of disability	All companies with 15 or more employees
Civil Rights Act Guarantees the rights of all citizens to freedom from discrimination on the basis of race, religion, color, national origin, and sex	All companies with 15 or more employees
Equal Pay Act Requires equal pay for equal work	All companies with 15 or more employees
Family and Medical Leave Act Provides for up to 12 weeks of unpaid leave for employees who are dealing with family issues	Companies with 50 or more employees
Immigration Reform and Control Act and the Immigration Act of 1990 Designed to prevent undocumented aliens from working in the United States. Companies must complete an Employment Eligibility Verification Form (I-9) for each employee.	All companies of any size
National Labor Relations Act and Taft-Hartley Act Requires employers to bargain in good faith with union representatives and forbids unfair labor practices by unions	All companies of any size
Occupational Safety and Health Act (OSHA) Designed to ensure safety and health in the work environment	All companies of any size
Title VII of the Civil Rights Act The original was amended to include discrimination against pregnant women; people with AIDS, cancer, or physical and mental disabilities; and people who are recovering from, or being treated for, substance abuse. Victims of discrimination may sue for punitive damages and back pay.	Companies with 15 or more employees for 20 weeks in the current or preceding year
Workers' Compensation Each state has enacted a law to compensate employees for medical costs and lost wages due to job-related injuries.	Requirements vary by state

© Cengage Learning®

take the company beyond the startup phase, so they often hire a person with lesser qualifications for little salary plus a minority ownership in the company. In this scenario, you are literally betting on the potential contribution of this person—and it's a gamble that frequently doesn't pay off. Later, when the company can afford to hire the person it needs, it will have to deal with a minority shareholder who has developed territorial "rights." Therefore, when minority ownership is an important issue to a potential employee, it is imperative to make clear to that person exactly what it means. There are few legal and managerial rights associated with a minority position; thus, for all practical purposes, minority ownership is simply the unmarketable right to appreciated stock value that has no defined payoff period and certainly no guarantee of value. Using a stock-vesting agreement is one way to make sure that only stock that has been earned will be distributed. With a stock-vesting agreement, stock purchased by the team is placed in escrow and released over a three- to five-year period. A buyback provision in the stockholders agreement is another way to ensure that stock remains in the company even if a member of the team leaves in the early days of the new venture.

Worse than giving stock to an employee who is new to the company with no track record is giving an equity stake to an independent contractor who is providing a service. For example, one entrepreneur who was short on cash wanted to give a programmer equity in lieu of paying him for building a website. The amount agreed upon was 3 percent of the company for a job that would have cost $3,000. The problem with this scenario is that if at some point the company is worth $1 million, the entrepreneur would now have paid that programmer $30,000 for a $3,000 website. Giving someone owner-ship rights in the company is a serious decision that should receive very careful consideration. There are several things to contemplate before taking on an equity partner, be it an investor, independent contractor, or key employee. Anyone brought in as an investor/shareholder or partner with the entrepre-neur does not have to be an equal partner. Investors will hold whatever share of stock is negotiated on the basis of what they contributed to the business. In general, you should never bring someone in as a partner/investor if that person can be hired to provide the same service, no matter how urgent the situation. In addition, the company should not be locked into future compen-sation promises such as stock options, and cash for bonuses should be used whenever possible. It is important that the company be established as your company before any partners are taken on—unless, of course, the company was founded by a team.

11.3e Founder's Stock and Dilution

Founder's stock (144 stock) is stock issued to the first shareholders of the cor-poration or assigned to key managers as part of a compensation package at startup. The payoff on this stock comes when the company experiences a li-quidity event such as an IPO or an acquisition by another company. Assuming that the company is successful, founder's stock at issuance is valued at probably the lowest it will ever be, relative to an investor's stock value. Consequently, a tax problem can arise when private investors provide seed capital to the new venture. Often the value of the stock the investors hold makes it very obvious that the founder's stock was a bargain and that its price did not represent the true value of the stock. According to Internal Revenue Code (IRC) §83, the amount of the difference between the founder's price and the investor's price is taxable as compensation income. One way to avoid this problem is to issue common stock to founders and key managers and to issue convertible preferred stock to investors. The preference upon liquidation should be high enough to cover the book value of the corporation, so the common stockholders would essentially receive nothing. This action would effectively decrease the value of the common stock so that it would no longer appear to be a bargain for tax purposes and subject the founders to an immediate tax liability.

Founder's stock is restricted, and the SEC rules (Rule 144) state that the restriction refers to stock that has not been registered with the SEC (private placement) and stock owned by the controlling officers and shareholders of the company (those with at least 10 percent ownership). If a stockholder has owned the stock for at least three years and public information about the company exists, Rule 144 can be avoided in the sale of the stock. If the stockholder has held the stock for less than three years, the rules must be strictly complied with. It is not the intent of this chapter to discuss the details of Rule 144. Suffice it to say that the rule is complex and that the appropriate attorney or tax specialist should be consulted.

Issuing Stock When the Company Is Capitalized

The number of shares authorized when a corporation is formed is purely arbitrary. Suppose a new venture, NewCorp, authorizes one million shares of stock. This means that NewCorp has one million shares available to be issued to potential stockholders. If each share of stock is valued at $1 and $100,000 is capitalized, the company will have 100,000 issued shares; if each share is valued at $10, the company will have 10,000 issued shares. The value placed on each share is arbitrary. For psychological reasons, however, it is customary to value a share at $1, so a shareholder who contributes $10,000 to the business can say that he or she owns 10,000 shares of stock (as opposed to 1,000 shares at $10/share). In short, the number of shares issued depends on the initial capitalization and the price per share.

Now suppose that the founder of NewCorp initially contributes $250,000 in cash and $300,000 in assets (equipment, furniture, etc.) to fund the company. At $1 a share, the company issues the founder 550,000 shares of stock; this constitutes a 100 percent interest in the company, because only 550,000 shares have been issued. At a later date, the company issues 29,000 additional shares at $5 a share to an investor. This minority shareholder has therefore contributed $145,000 (29,000 shares at $5/share) to the company and owns a 5 percent (29,000/579,000) interest in the company (that is, 29,000 of the 579,000 shares of stock that have been issued). The investor will require that the current value or future additional income of the company be sufficient to justify the increase in price per share. As additional shares are issued, the original investor's percentage ownership in the company declines or is diluted. However, the founder's shares will not go below 55 percent (550,000/1,000,000) unless the company authorizes additional shares and issues a portion or all of those additional shares.

The type of stock issued is common stock, which is a basic ownership interest in the company. This means that holders of common stock share in both the successes and the failures of the business and benefit through dividends and the appreciating value of the company. Once common stock is issued, a company can then issue preferred stock to holders who are paid first if the company is liquidated. Preferred stockholders must accept a fixed dividend amount, no matter how much profit the company makes. Recall that if the company were a sub-chapter S-corporation, it could issue only one class of stock.

11.3f Alternatives to Equity Incentives

There are other ways to compensate key managers that do not require you to give up equity in the company. The following are a few of these alternatives. In choosing among them, consider the advice of an accountant, who can recommend the most appropriate structure for the business.

Deferred Compensation Plans

In a deferred compensation plan, you can specify that awards and bonuses be linked to profits and performance of both the individual and the company, with the lion's share depending on the individual's performance. The employee does not pay taxes on this award until it is actually paid out at some specified date.

Bonus Plans

With a bonus plan, a series of goals are set by the company with input from the employee, and as the employee reaches each goal, the bonus is given. This method is often used with sales personnel and others who have a direct impact on the profitability of the company. The key to success with bonus plans is to specify measurable objectives.

Capital Appreciation Rights

Capital appreciation rights give employees the right to participate in the profits of the company at a specified percentage, even though they are not full shareholders with voting rights. Capital appreciation rights, or "phantom stock," provide long-term compensation incentives whose value is based on the increase in the value of the business. The phantom stock will look, act, and reward like real stock, but it will have no voting rights and will limit the employee's obligation should the business fail. Typically, the employee has to be with the company for a period of three to five years to be considered vested in capital appreciation rights, but otherwise employees do not have to pay for these rights.

Profit-Sharing Plans

Profit-sharing plans are distinct from the previously discussed plans in that they are subject to the ERISA rules for employee retirement programs. These plans must include all employees, without regard to individual contribution to profit or performance. They are different from pensions in that owners are not required to contribute in any year and employees are not "entitled" to them.

Organizing business processes, location, and people into the most effective business design is an important and difficult task that requires considerable thought and planning. Decisions made in the earliest stages of the new venture can seriously—and often negatively—affect the new firm's ability to grow and be successful in the future. This chapter highlighted many critical organizational considerations and offered suggestions for addressing them. However, it is important to consult with people who specialize in these functions to be sure that the right decisions are made.

New Venture Action Plan

- Identify the processes and information flow in your business.

- Identify potential ways to operate like a virtual enterprise or at least to outsource some aspects of the business.

- Locate a site for the business, if required.

- Decide whether to lease, buy, or build a facility.

- Determine the personnel required to run the business at startup and over the next three to five years.

- Create job profiles for positions in the business.

- Determine the ownership and compensation requirements of the business. Formulate a plan to find the best candidates for positions in the company.

Questions on Key Issues

1. How can design thinking principles be employed to organize your business?
2. What are the advantages and the disadvantages of a virtual company?
3. What is the purpose of the imaginary tour of the business?
4. Which factors important in choosing a retail site would not be relevant to a manufacturing site—and vice versa?
5. What are the advantages and disadvantages of using stock as compensation and incentives?
6. How can the entrepreneur improve the chances of choosing the best job candidate?
7. List three alternatives to equity incentives for key managers.

Experiencing Entrepreneurship

1. Choose an industry in which you have an interest. Find a business in that industry; arrange to visit the site and talk with key personnel, and do a flowchart of the business processes that reflects what you learned about it on your visit.

Did you find any inefficiencies that if corrected could improve the process flow?
2. Interview an entrepreneur about his or her hiring practices. How successful have those practices been in getting and retaining good employees?

Relevant Case Studies

Case 5 The Case of Google, Inc.

Case 7 Homerun.com

CHAPTER 12

Planning Startup Operations

"One way to increase productivity is to do whatever we are doing now, but faster. . . . There is a second way. We can change the nature of the work we do, not how fast we do it."

—ANDREW S. GROVE, CEO, INTEL CORPORATION

CHAPTER OBJECTIVES

■ Identify the components of the production process for products and services.

■ Explain the critical aspects of supply-chain management.

■ Discuss how to manage quality.

■ Explain how outsourcing can benefit an entrepreneurial venture.

PROFILE

12.1

GIVING CUSTOMERS A TASTE WITHOUT SACRIFICING QUALITY

It's not every day that a tech guru and serial entrepreneur becomes a vintner and online retailer of wine samples. It only happens when your two passions happen to come together in a great opportunity. Tim Bucher (pronounced bu-CARE) was raised in the wine country of California on a farm in Healdsburg. He loved the land and by the time he was 16, he and his siblings managed to pool all their resources and buy a two-acre vineyard. But it was while he was in college at UC Davis that he found his second passion—technology—and so upon graduation he went to work for Sun Microsystems. Over the next 25 years he designed hardware for companies like Dell, Microsoft, and Apple but on the side he was developing his own technology solutions, one of which was a data access device that he sold to Seagate for a reported $30 million.

About 2010, while a VP of consumer and entertainment software at Dell in Austin, Texas, he finally grew tired of flying back and forth to California to maintain the online olive oil business he was running on the side in addition to the vineyards. However, he had used his flying time productively. Since he had experience selling olive oil samples online, he wondered if it would be possible to do the same with wine. After all, most people would like to know if they will like a particular wine before they spend a lot of money to buy a full bottle. He decided to call the venture The Tasting Room. The problem with his idea was that wine begins to oxidize when it's rebottled and it would be very important to maintain that quality if he were ever going to get vintners to partner with him. This was the moment when his two passions came together. Using his technical expertise, he designed a system (and later patented it) that consisted of a pressurized chamber for "total anaerobic sample transfer" that would move a 759-ml bottle to where a robotic arm would open and decant the wine and pour it into 50-ml bottles and cap them.

Bucher realized that with this device, his idea had the potential to scale to a very large operation, but it required more wine than his tiny vineyard could produce. At the same time, he began to learn more about the supply chain for wine and realized that there were a lot of complex problems to solve. For one thing, the vintners were skeptical that the quality of their wine could be maintained; however, taste tests eventually convinced Seghezio to become the first winery to come on board. For another, he learned that every label for every one of his projected 900 varietals would have to be approved by the Alcohol and Tobacco Tax and Trade Bureau and he had to meet the requirements to ship to 33 states. He also had to secure the appropriate packaging that would protect the sample bottles.

If the supply chain issues were daunting, raising money was not—at least for the first round where he was able to raise $10 million from several VCs while retaining about 10 percent of the company. However, burning $300,000 a month meant that he would quickly run out of cash and need to go for another round. As it turned out, the success of the taste tests convinced more than 1,000 vintners to sign up by 2012. In 2013, Lot18, an online retailer of fine wines, acquired most of the assets of Tasting Room.com, which meant that Bucher could now focus on the technology side of the business and leave the marketing to Lot18.

Sources: Adams, A. (January 24, 2013). "TastingRoom .com Partners with Lot18," Wines & Vines, http://www .winesandvines.com/template.cfm?section=news&content=110 726.Adams, A. (January 24, 2013). "TastingRoom.com Partners with Lot18," Wines & Vines, http://www.winesandvines.com /template.cfm?section=news&content=110726. Casserly, M. (April 23, 2012). "Try Before You Buy," Forbes, p. 53.

In today's fast-moving, uncertain global environment, effective management of operations has become a critical success factor for any business wanting to increase profits and particularly startups that need to get up to speed quickly or risk losing customers. It is important to remember that startups are not simply smaller versions of large companies. For one thing, entrepreneurs don't generally operate their startups with a well-tested and proven business model, so they're constantly sensing and responding to their customers and then revising and refining the business model. Large companies typically have a proven business model in place that they execute with experienced management through the formal operations of their company. By their very nature, startups don't have these formal systems and controls in place and they often rely on partnerships or outsourced capability to fill the gaps in their operations expertise and experience. When it comes to operations management, large companies are chiefly dealing with variables that are known and predictable while startups are dealing with unknowns and uncertainty. And that is precisely why so many large, established companies have missed game-changing transformations in industries from computers (mainframes to PCs) to journalism (newspapers to digital news to user-generated content), and telephone (landline to mobile).[1] The inertia of their hierarchical operational and product development structures have made it difficult to spot opportunities that didn't fit those structures. Bringing these same corporate types into a startup will burden the new venture with structure that it can neither afford nor needs. Although the formal operations of a large company can be a competitive advantage in terms of achieving economies of scale efficiencies, startups need to create operational competitive advantages in very different ways.

Operations management covers activities and processes such as new product development, purchasing, inventory, production, manufacturing, distribution, and logistics that are necessary to produce and distribute products and services. The manner in which operations are managed is dependent on the type of business, whether that be retail, wholesale, manufacturing, or service. Moreover, whatever the business, the ability to innovate in the operations of the business can be a superior competitive advantage for any startup. Operational innovation entails "fundamentally changing how [the] work gets accomplished."[2] This means finding new ways to fill customer orders, create new products and services, and deal with customer service. Wal-Mart is the largest company in the world because of operational innovation. Its cross-docking strategy for moving goods from the supplier directly to its trucks going to the various Wal-Mart stores has resulted in substantially lower operating costs that it has passed on to its customers in the form of lower prices. Zappos.com, the highly successful online shoe company, now owned by Amazon.com, has turned the entire notion of customer service on its head to create a game-changing opportunity and competitive advantage. Where most companies think of customer service as a cost center, Zappos CEO Tony Hsieh understands that his customers are taking a huge risk buying online something as difficult to fit as shoes. So Zappos decided to take a risk and make customer service an investment rather than an expense. Not only were they going to spend more on customer service than the average company, they would make it easy for customers to "try on" shoes by offering free shipping and returns. In fact, Zappos has built its entire company culture around understanding the mind of the customer and being viewed as a customer service company.

Very few business owners think about the cost of operations until their products and services have become commoditized—that is, they find themselves competing on price rather than on value. It is only then that they begin to look for ways to improve operations and cut costs to maintain or improve their profit margins. Entrepreneurs with startup ventures have an advantage in this regard, because they can more easily implement process innovations without having to overcome the challenge of existing structures. In this chapter we look at the major areas of operations that you need to understand and which areas offer opportunities for both process innovation and operational excellence.

12.1   PRODUCING PRODUCTS AND SERVICES

In simple terms, production is managing the flow of material and information from raw materials to finished goods. Think of manufacturing equipment as hardware, and of the people and information needed to run the machines as software, and it's easy to see why it's possible for two companies to have the same equipment and yet produce significantly different products. The difference lies in the software driving the machinery—in other words, information and people.

Any new venture that is offering innovative new products will need an operational plan that consists of a fairly complex product development analysis that includes prototyping, production processes, supply chain, distribution, and inventory control mechanisms. The depth of analysis is a function of the type of product offered, the technological newness of the product, and the number of different ways the product can be produced. The more complex the product, the deeper the analysis needs to be to keep costs down and avoid making time-consuming, expensive mistakes.

Let's make an important point clear at the outset. Building a complex production system while the company is in startup or even later when it is rapidly growing is a recipe for disaster. Not having a reliable fulfillment process in place prior to launch has cost many a company customer loyalty and significant revenues because the company was unable to produce and deliver products to customers in a timely fashion. Once lost, that customer base is nearly impossible to regain in time to fend off competing firms and save the company from failure. As noted in Chapter 11, the virtual enterprise, consisting of strategic alliances among all links in the value chain, is one way to achieve control of the entire process from raw materials to distribution, while still keeping the firm small and flexible enough to meet changing needs and demands. With the exception of ownership, this model is similar to the Japanese *keiretsu* in the automobile industry, which links banks, suppliers, electronics firms, and auto companies through a series of cross-ownerships. The U.S. model leaves ownership in the hands of the individual owners but links the organizations into a virtual entity that acts as a team with a common goal. Wal-Mart is probably the best example of this type of partnership and integration in the United States. It has established point-of-sale linkups with its suppliers and has given its manufacturers the responsibility for handling inventory. The ultimate goal is to construct one organization with a common purpose that encompasses the entire supply chain from raw materials supplier to retailer, with each link along the chain performing the task that it does best. Establishing this type of network takes time. A startup can't expect to achieve quickly the level of integration and control that a Wal-Mart has taken years to accomplish. Instead, startup companies need to build relationships slowly, beginning with key independent contractors to whom they may be outsourcing some tasks.

One of the best ways to understand how the production process touches customers and affects the bottom line is to follow an order through the company and document where the order flow gets bogged down, is duplicated, or is hindered in some manner. Any slowdown or duplication of effort means higher production costs and slower response to the customer, leading to dissatisfaction. If you believe that only product companies have to think about this, you would be wrong. Consider a market research firm that provides customized reports to companies to enable them to judge their markets for new products and services. This is an example of what would typically be called a service firm, yet note that this service firm produces a product—a market research report. Now suppose that in the process of gathering the research and analyzing it, there is no plan for who should do a particular aspect of the research. Duplication of effort could easily occur, and it's possible that something important, such as an emerging competitor, might be overlooked. Both duplication of effort and the need to go back and cover something that has been overlooked are costly and delay the production process, potentially causing the company to miss a customer deadline.

Every startup is involved in a supply chain that is either large or tiny, so it's important to understand supply chain management because it can make or break your company.

12.2 SUPPLY CHAIN MANAGEMENT

A supply chain consists up upstream and downstream business activities that move a product through the stages of designing, making, sourcing, and delivering to the final customer. By contrast, a value chain is a cooperative effort among all the participants to add value at each point in the value chain thereby creating benefits for the entire value chain. In an increasingly complex and global environment where outsourcing, offshoring, and insourcing are common activities, supply chain management (SCM) has become a mission-critical activity for most companies.[3] The earthquake and tsunami that hit Japan in 2011 pulled into focus how interconnected businesses are through their supply chains. For example, Ford Motor Co. was forced to slow manufacturing in its Belgium plant because a supplier in Tokyo was unable to secure raw materials to make the parts that Ford needed.[4]

Good SCM enables your company to forecast demand, match supply with demand, and fulfill that demand through the optimal distribution channels and logistics. It also enables you to create backups in case of any supply chain disruptions. You find supply chains in both product and service businesses, but the complexity of those supply chains varies tremendously from industry to industry and within types of businesses in the same industry. Today, companies within a particular supply chain work together to increase the value and reduce the costs at every step, so it's not surprising that now entire supply chains compete against other supply chains.

Victor Fung and his brother William turned their grandfather's small export company, Li & Fung, the first such company in China, into a multinational company with expertise in SCM. The two brothers started as regional sourcing agents for supplies and components, extending the reach of their Hong-Kong based company to Taiwan, Korea, and Singapore. It wasn't long before they had developed a unique understanding of the complexity of the each industry they worked with. The next iteration of their business saw them bundling manufacturing capability with their expertise. For example, one of their customers might come to them with an idea for a line of clothing and request a production program design. Li & Fung would develop a prototype, iterate on the design with the customer, and then contract all the resources required to deliver the finished goods. As Hong Kong became more expensive and competitive, the duo eventually began assembling all the components for production and then shipping "kits" to an assembler in China to keep costs down. By then they had also diversified in the type of customers they served to include electronics manufacturers. Today Li & Fung is sourcing its supplies all over the globe and the volumes it has achieved enable the company to secure the best prices for its customers all along the supply chain.[5] The key lesson for entrepreneurs is that there is huge opportunity in understanding and managing a supply chain well. However, that is not the only lesson. Li & Fung, whose profits had tripled from 2005 through 2011, suddenly began to see them decline. The reasons? In addition to increased competitiveness, the company had strayed from what it did best—SCM—and had begun opportunistically acquiring brands that ended up providing historically low returns for the company. When you deviate too much from a winning strategy, you do risk the health of your overall business.

Because effective supply chain performance is now critical to any company's success, you must have ways to manage and measure the performance of your supply chain, especially in terms of customer satisfaction. You must have a clear understanding of what is important to your customers—what is the level of service they are expecting and what performance level are they willing to pay a premium for. For example, one company judged its performance by the percentage of orders received in any one day that were filled on time. This metric indicated that the company was performing at over 98 percent effectiveness. However, when the company tracked how long it took for a customer to receive their order from the time they had placed it, the company's performance level dropped dramatically. In examining what was causing the delay, the company found that their system for tracking orders once they left the warehouse was often sending orders to the wrong distribution center.

The goal in supply chain management is to provide the exact service the customer wants at minimal cost. In SCM terms, it's the *efficient frontier* and it's not easy to achieve. To do so, you need to use current technology that provides superior data analysis, ensure that the warehouses and distribution centers you use are efficiently located, and you should look at every aspect of the supply chain to see if there are ways to reduce costs.

Companies that are recognized for their superior SCM, like Spanish apparel manufacturer and retailer Zara, maintain total control of the entire supply chain so they can set the pace of product and information flow. In the case of Zara, their retailers around the globe have strict deadlines for placing orders twice weekly and because Zara produces approximately half of all it products in house, it can control the front end of the supply chain. To be clear, Zara has achieved optimization of every step in the supply chain, something that a startup cannot hope to do for some time. However, depending on the type of business you have, it may be a worthy objective because it creates a very strong long-term competitive advantage. The key principles that Zara follows are adaptable to any enterprise, even a startup, especially when you're in revenue.[6]

1. Plan for an information system that enables you to track materials, products, and information through each step from raw materials to the store shelf. You need to do this whether you are producing in house or outsourcing —especially if you're outsourcing.

2. Plan to spend money on ways to improve the speed and responsiveness of your supply chain. It's in everyone's best interests to reduce costs.

3. Plan to invest in capital assets so you can produce complex products in house and outsource simple ones.

If you have a business that purchases raw materials or parts for production of goods for resale, you must carefully consider the quality, quantity, and timing of those purchases. Quality goods are those that meet specific needs. Quality varies considerably among vendors, so if you have established certain quality standards for your products, you must find vendors who will consistently supply that precise level of quality, because customers will expect it. The quantity of raw materials or parts that are purchased is a function of (1) demand by the customer, (2) manufacturing capability, and (3) a company's storage capability; consequently, timing of purchases is very important. Purchases must be planned so that capital and warehouse space are not tied up any longer than necessary. Because materials account for approximately 50 percent of total production cost, it is crucial to balance these three factors carefully.

Figure 12.1 depicts a generic supply chain for a product that is being produced and transferred through the supply chain to the consumer. Within the major supply chain functions as displayed are many activities that must be planned for and coordinated. They include such things as:

- purchasing for profitability
- reducing inventories
- tighter supplier integration
- more frequent and smaller customer orders and receipts
- faster time from source to stock in the wholesale or retail outlet

FIGURE 12.1   Example of a Supply Chain

© Cengage Learning®

FIGURE 12.2   The Production Process

© Cengage Learning®

Figure 12.2 depicts the supply chain for an apparel manufacturer. Some entrepreneurs have been creative in forming their own supply chains consisting of other entrepreneurial companies. For example, the tourism industry's supply chain relies on location-based assets. In upstate New York, the Finger Lakes Wine Trails area is organized to draw customers to the region and its activities. Wineries, vineyards, restaurants, B&Bs, tour organizers, and event planners all work together, sharing resources, for the good of the entire supply chain.

Next we look at some of the important functions of the supply chain.

12.2a Purchasing

Locating vendors to provide raw materials or goods for resale is not difficult, but finding the best vendors is another matter entirely. The issue of vendor relationships has become increasingly important in markets that demand that companies reduce costs and maintain effective relationships. Research has found that these vendor relationships reflect factors such as trust or commitment,[7] uncertainty and dependence, and how these factors affect performance.[8]

Furthermore, buyers and sellers are connected in an increasing number of ways: through information sharing that improves the quality of the product produced or brings about new product development; operational linkages such as computerized inventory, order replenishment systems, and just-in-time delivery; legal bonds such as binding contractual agreements; cooperative norms; and relationship adaptations wherein vendors modify their products to meet the needs of the customer.

Given the importance of the vendor–customer relationship, should a startup buy from one vendor or from more than one? Obviously, if a single vendor cannot supply all the startup's needs, that decision is made. However, there are several advantages to using a single vendor where possible. First, a single vendor will probably offer more individual attention and better service. Second, orders will be consolidated, so a discount based on quantity purchased may be possible. On the other hand, the principal disadvantage of using just one vendor is that if that vendor suffers a catastrophe, it may be difficult or impossible to find an alternative source in a short time. To guard against this contingency, it is wise for a startup to use one supplier for about 70 to 80 percent of its needs and one or more additional suppliers for the rest.

When considering a specific vendor as a source, you should ask several questions:

- Can the vendor deliver enough of what is needed *when* it's needed?
- What is the cost of transportation using a particular vendor? If the vendor is located far away, costs will be higher and it may be more difficult to get the service required.
- What services is the vendor offering? For example, how often will sales representatives call?
- Is the vendor knowledgeable about the product line?
- What are the vendor's maintenance and return policies?

It is also important to "shop around," compare vendors' prices, and check for trade discounts and quantity discounts that may make a particular vendor's deal more enticing. Computer technology has made materials planning more of a science than ever before. Information systems can now provide a purchaser with detailed feedback on supplier performance, reliability of delivery, and quality control results. Comparing results across suppliers provides more leverage when it's time to renegotiate the annual contracts with suppliers. It is, however, important to keep in mind that sourcing materials and supplies is a time-consuming process that can often slow your ability to launch on schedule.

12.2b Inventory Management

Inventory is defined as the stocks of items used to support production, associated activities, and customer service. Whether entrepreneurs start small manufacturing enterprises, retail businesses, or restaurants, they will frequently hold an inventory of materials or goods. Today, businesses that hold inventories of raw materials or goods for resale have found that they must reduce these inventories significantly to remain competitive. Instead of purchasing large quantities and receiving them on a monthly basis, businesses are purchasing daily or weekly in an effort to avoid costly inventories. Of course, some inventory of finished goods must be maintained to meet delivery deadlines; therefore, a delicate balance must be achieved among goods coming into the business, work in progress, and goods leaving the business to be sold.

The problem that entrepreneurs face relative to inventories is that once they get beyond early startup and begin growing, most still do not have the resources to purchase raw materials and goods for sale in sufficient quantities to trigger significant industry discounts, often ranging from 30 to 50 percent. Even if you could purchase the required quantities, you typically don't have the space to store the inventory. As a result, today many entrepreneurs are taking advantage of inventory management companies that oversee storage, track inventory numbers, and fill and ship orders, among many other services. There are many advantages to this approach. It saves you time and the cost of hiring employees to manage the inventory. It frees up space at your place of business and the need to purchase special equipment. In addition, because most inventory management companies have information technology for tracking and providing detailed data on the inventory, you can inspect and control your inventory from any computer with Internet access.

In general, you order the goods or raw materials direct from the manufacturer and they are delivered to the inventory management company, which immediately pays you under due-on-receipt terms. This means that you now have cash flow to use until the OEM (original equipment manufacturer) must be paid, typically in three to six weeks. Meanwhile, you can access the raw materials or goods as needed, paying the inventory management company as they're purchased, depending on the terms of the agreement.

Businesses such as UPS help startups that need to ship to retailers. They stock merchandise in their warehouses, process orders, make deliveries, and handle billing. In that way, retailers don't incur the costs associated with maintaining a backup supply of items from the entrepreneur. Avoiding too much inventory is a trend that is expected to continue for the foreseeable future, but it requires careful coordination and cooperation of all members of the supply chain.

12.3 PRODUCTION AND MANUFACTURING

Production is the actual manufacturing and assembly of a product. Today manufacturers tend to produce one unit at a time serially in manufacturing cells—also called flexible manufacturing cells (FMCs) or work cells. What that means is that the product moves from raw materials through a series of tasks and processes in a continuous flow to complete the product while remaining inside the manufacturing cell. The benefits of cell manufacturing are reduced lead times, improved costs, quality, and timing in addition to giving employees more involvement in the production of the entire product rather than simply one component of a product. This means that workers need to be cross-trained in all the required tasks to produce the product, but it also means that when a worker is out sick, another is there to immediately fill the gap.

The production process—as depicted in Figure 12.3—consists of a series of inputs, such as raw materials, labor, and machinery, which are then transformed through a series of processes into new products and services. Each component of the process must be managed, measured, and tested for efficiency and effectiveness.

In general, manufacturing and production firms are organized as product-focused or process-focused organizations. Product- or project-focused organizations normally are highly decentralized or distributed so that they can respond better to market demands. Each product or project group acts essentially as a separate company or profit center. This type of organization is well suited to products and projects that don't require huge economies of scale or capital-intensive technologies. Process-focused organizations, on the other hand, are common among manufacturers with capital-intensive processes (such as those in the semiconductor industry) and among service companies (such as advertising firms). These organizations are highly centralized in order to control all the functions of the organization.

Identifying all the tasks in the production process makes it easier to determine what equipment and supplies are needed for completing the tasks. If, for example, the equipment necessary to produce the product is beyond a start-up's resources, it may be necessary to outsource part or all of production to a manufacturer that has excess capacity with the needed equipment and workers. This topic is discussed in a later section in this chapter. After the production tasks have been identified, a preliminary layout of the plant can be undertaken to estimate floor space requirements for production, offices, and services. It may be beneficial to consult an expert in plant layout to ensure that the layout makes the most efficient use of available space.

FIGURE 12.3   The Production Process

Inputs
Raw materials
Labor
Machinery
Facility

Transformation
Materials management
Production scheduling
Manufacturing
Assembly
Quality control
Packaging

Output
New products
and services

© Cengage Learning®

12.3a Quality

Quality control is the process of reconciling product or project output with the standards set for that product or project. More specifically, it is "an effective system for integrating the quality-development, quality-maintenance, and quality- improvement efforts of the various groups in an organization so as to enable marketing, engineering, production, and service at the most economical levels, which allow for full customer satisfaction."[9] In this sense, quality does not necessarily mean "best"; rather, it means "best for certain customer requirements," which consist of the features and benefits of the product or service and its selling price.[10]

Quality is a strategic issue that is designed to bring about business profitability and positive cash flow. Effective total quality programs result in customer satisfaction, lower operating costs, and better utilization of company resources. There are three major processes in any company that must be aligned if quality is going to be the outcome. They are management processes, business processes, and support processes.[11] Management processes are the source of strategic direction and organizational governance, so they usually affect or shape all the other processes of the business. Business processes are "mission-critical" processes and generally relate to the core competencies of the company, such as manufacturing, distribution, and product development. Business processes are critical because they are typically viewed by the customer and include marketing, fulfillment, and service. Support processes are common functions in any business; these include payroll and human resources management and are viewed by the internal stakeholders of the company—the employees.

Today thousands of manufacturers and producers have embraced the philosophy of quality first but have focused principally on equipment and processes rather than on the human element. Both must be considered for total quality control to permeate every aspect of the organization. Over the past twenty years, manufacturers have invested heavily in quality improvements. Concepts such as lean manufacturing, which views manufacturing from the customer's perspective, and Six Sigma, which relies on statistical tools and specific processes to achieve the measurable goals of fewer defects, increased productivity, reduced waste, and superior products and processes,[12] have helped companies lower production costs, produce less scrap, allow fewer defects, and reduce warranty expense.[13] Even though the highest probability is that entrepreneurs will not manufacture their own products, they still need to select a quality manufacturer that practices these concepts.

The real success or failure of the quality control effort is dependent on the human element in the process: customers, employees, and management. Quality begins with satisfying the needs of the customers, and that cannot be accomplished unless those needs and requirements are communicated to managers and employees. An entrepreneur with a new venture has a unique opportunity to create a philosophy of quality from the very birth of the business, in the way the business is run and in the employees hired. Startups have the advantage of creating new habits and patterns of behavior instead of having to change old ones.

Many quality programs exist to help companies better meet the needs of their customers. Table 12.1 lists several of them.

TABLE 12.1 Quality Management Programs

Benchmarking	Involves the use of criteria or standards that can be employed to compare one company with another to better understand organizational performance
Continuous Improvement	A program that focuses on undertaking incremental improvements in processes to increase customer satisfaction
Failure Mode and Effects Analysis	A way to identify and rank potential equipment and process failures
ISO 9001	An internationally recognized quality set of standards with a certification process
Total Quality Improvement	A set of management practices designed to meet customer requirements through process measurement and controls
Six Sigma	A data-driven approach to eliminating defects with a goal of 3.4 defects per million

© Cengage Learning®

12.3b Logistics

Logistics is the management and control of the flow of goods and resources from the source of production to the marketplace. Every business is affected by logistics to some degree, even service businesses that rely on logistics to receive their supplies. Logistics is a fundamental part of supply chain management and can make the difference between success and failure, profit and loss in a growing company. South West Trading (http://soysilk.com) had the pleasant problem of more demand for its yarns made from bamboo, corn, and soy fibers than it could handle. The problem was not with its manufacturing operation in China, which churned out 800 metric tons of yarn every month, but rather with the logistics of getting the yarn from China to the warehouse in Phoenix, Arizona. Because founder Jonelle Raffing was concerned about meeting the needs of her customers, she maintained a $1 million excess inventory, which increased her operating costs. She was unable to combine orders from different factories into one container, so she incurred a charge of $1,000 to $2,000 for each separate shipment. She also paid a customs agent $17,000 a year to move the products through the various ports. In all, her annual logistics costs amounted to over $100,000.[14] Raffing was able to reduce her costs by turning to UPS and its Shanghai facility, which combines orders into one container, handles the paperwork, and delivers the products all the way to Phoenix, Arizona. Raffing's logistical problems are not solely because her business is small; even multinational companies experience them.

Small companies that sell to large discount retailers like Wal-Mart are subject to strict requirements for packing, shipping, and tagging for RFID tracking. Most small companies don't have the people resources to meet these requirements, so they outsource to third-party logistics providers who can move packages by air, land, and sea from the factory to the customer without stopping at the entrepreneur's business. Although a majority of the major logistics providers service large companies, today many of those providers have begun offering services to entrepreneurs. Among the most aggressive is UPS Supply Chain Solutions, which uses its own aircraft to handle shipping of products that meet the weight requirement and do not need to go by sea.

SOCIAL ENTREPRENEURSHIP: MAKING MEANING

Five Socially Responsible, For-profit Startups

Increasingly, entrepreneurs today are looking at how to create a for-profit business that gives back in a socially responsible manner as part of their business model. Here are five startups that subscribe to the socially responsible business model.

Accessibility Partners decided that it wanted to provide jobs for people with disabilities and make sure that companies that produce devices are thinking about the disabled when they design their products. It tests and reviews products for accessibility, and 70 percent of its employees are disabled.

Children Inspire Design is the creation of artist Rebecca Peragine who creates wall art, posters, and cards to provide environment education to children. All of her raw materials are eco-friendly, and her paper ornaments are made by a women's cooperative in Mexico.

Juntos Shoes sells shoes inspired by traditional Ecuadorian canvas shoes. For each pair it sells, the company donates a backpack filled with school supplies to an at-risk Ecuadorian child.

Prime Five Homes hits both the environmental and the charitable sides of being socially responsible. Their homes are sustainable, so eco-friendly, and they have a nonprofit branch of their company that donates a portion of all sales to charities.

Zady is part of a growing trend of retailers that sell "ethical" clothing made by responsible American manufacturers or boutique craftsmakers overseas rather than low-wage factories. They are hoping that consumers are willing to pay a bit more to know that their clothes were made under good conditions.

Sources: Accessibility Partners, http://www.accessibilitypartners.com/; Children Inspire Design, http://www.childreninspiredesign.com/; Juntos Shoes http://www.childreninspiredesign.com/; Juntos Shoes, http://www.juntosproject.com/; Prime Five Homes, http://www.primefivehomes .com/; Zady, https://zady.com/

12.3c Warranting the Product

Entrepreneurs who subscribe to total quality management will probably wish to provide warranties with products and services, both in order to protect their companies from potential liability and to demonstrate that they stand behind what they produce and the work that they do. Today, product/service warranties have also become a competitive marketing tool.

A number of decisions must be made about warranties. Although the length of the warranty depends on industry standards, the components of the product, or what aspects of the service to cover, depend on the situation. Some components may come from other manufacturers who have their own warranties. In this case, it is important to have use of that component on the product certified by the original equipment manufacturers (OEM) so that the warranty isn't inadvertently invalidated. Then, if a warranted component from that manufacturer becomes defective, it can be returned to the OEM. However, it is probably good business practice to have customers return the product directly to the company or its distributors for service, repair, or exchange under the warranty, which covers the whole product. Warranties on services cover satisfaction with work completed. The product/process scope should also be considered. Will the warranty cover one or all products in a line or will there be separate warranties? Generally, for services, a warranty covers the service as a whole, unless there are products involved as well. In addition to the product scope, the market scope is a factor. Will the same warranty apply in all markets? This will depend on local laws. Another consideration involves the conditions of the warranty that the customer must fulfill. Is there anything the customer must do to keep the warranty in force, such as servicing or replacing disposable parts? These conditions should not include registering the product via a postcard. Today a product is covered by warranty from the moment it is purchased, whether or not the purchaser returns a postcard stating when and where it was purchased and answering a short, informational questionnaire. What many companies now do is offer update notification and potential discounts on future products in exchange for the information the postcard solicits or the option to register online.

Yet another consideration is who executes the warranty. You must decide who will handle warranty claims (manufacturer, dealers, distributors, the entrepreneur's company), recognizing that customers do not like to mail products back to the manufacturer. It is also necessary to decide how the public will be educated about the warranty. What are the plans for advertising and promotion relative to the warranty? Finally, the policies for refunds and returns, and who will pay shipping and handling costs, need to be considered. A return policy is a function of your philosophy about doing business. A customer-oriented company is likely to offer a generous return policy and pay for the cost of returns.

The manufacturer who provides a warranty incurs a cost, but that cost must be weighed against the potential loss of business if no warranty is provided. In the case of a new business with a new product or service, it is difficult to anticipate the number of problems that might occur as the product or service gets into the marketplace. Careful and adequate field-testing prior to market entry will go a long way toward eliminating many potential problems and the possibility of a recall (in the case of a product), which is very costly for any firm, let alone a growing new business.

12.4 OUTSOURCING TO REDUCE COSTS

Calculation of the up-front investment in plant, office, and equipment, coupled with the high per-unit cost of production, has convinced many entrepreneurs to outsource manufacturing to an established manufacturing firm, particularly one overseas, where labor costs are much less. Some products that consist of off-the-shelf components from original equipment manufacturers can give you the option to set up an assembly operation, which is far less costly than a manufacturing plant. In any case, the process of outlining all the costs of setting up a product company is invaluable in making the final decisions about how your business will operate.

Entrepreneurs who wish to manufacture products have many options today. It is still possible, in many industries, to manufacture domestically and to compete successfully if processes are refined and quality is built into every step. If it is too costly to do all the manufacturing in-house, outsourcing non-core capabilities is one possibility; another is outsourcing everything and playing the role of coordinator until the company is producing a healthy cash flow.

12.4a Manufacturing Overseas

In some industries, particularly labor-intensive ones, the only way to achieve competitive costs is to manufacture in a country where labor costs are low; Mexico, India, and China are examples. You should look at what other firms in your industry are doing. Crimson Consulting Group of Palo Alto, California, now competes with the likes of market research firms McKinsey and Bain for work from Fortune 500 companies by sourcing some of its research from companies in China, the Czech Republic, and South Africa. However, outsourcing is not always the wisest choice. One Tampa, Florida, manufacturing company moved some of its manufacturing operations to China several years ago and achieved real cost savings by doing so. Today, however, it is re-evaluating that decision for several of its products. These products are too heavy to ship by air, and shipping by sea is costly because the company loses the advantage it has in schedule flexibility. Schedule flexibility is an example of an opportunity cost—that is, forgoing an important competitive advantage in order to save on production costs.

The truth is that many companies have not been able to leverage the benefits of outsourcing to create real impact in their companies in the areas of pricing at a premium, entering new markets, and creating entry barriers for competition. That is why you need to work backward from customer needs and align your workflows appropriately. Not all products are appropriate for offshore manufacturing. For example, a business that uses expensive equipment to produce its products may not achieve enough cost savings to overcome the problems associated with offshore manufacturing, such as difficulties in communication and degradation in quality control. By contrast, a manual-labor-intensive business such as apparel manufacture can often achieve significant cost savings by moving overseas.

The weight of the product is also a factor in the decision whether to manufacture overseas. Heavy products with large "footprints" must be shipped by sea, which typically takes four to six weeks. That represents an inventory issue for you and added cost for the customer. Some entrepreneurs have calculated that it takes a 15 to 20 percent cost savings to justify manufacturing offshore and to balance the added costs of freight, customs, security, logistics, and inventory carrying cost. It is also important to remember that customers are not always looking for the lowest price; rather, they're looking for the highest quality at a competitive price. If products are innovative and meet the specific needs of target customers, you may be able to manufacture domestically in a successful way.

Deciding to move some operations offshore is an important decision that will affect your business in ways you may not have considered. Look at Figure 12.4 to see some questions you should ask yourself as you start to think about this decision. Here are some additional considerations that you should look at before deciding to leap offshore:

1. Go offshore when all efforts to boost efficiency and innovation at home have been exhausted. Don't do it just because everyone else is doing it.

2. Consider whether to set up a captive operation (you own it) or to contract with a local specialist.

3. Management and employees must both believe in going offshore and must be in the loop during transition.

4. Don't do it if management does not have the time and willingness to put a lot of effort into the process. Savings are in direct proportion to the effort exerted to train and prepare offshore workers in the company's processes.

5. You must be willing to treat your outsourcing partners as equals, not as subservient workers, and make them part of the project design process.

6. The supply chain needs to be flexible to avoid disruption, particularly through natural and man-made disasters.

FIGURE 12.4 The Outsourcing Decision

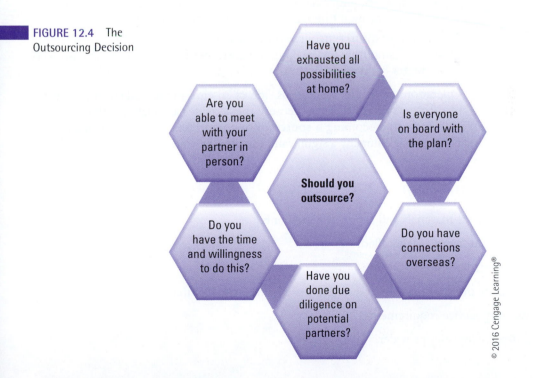

© 2016 Cengage Learning®

12.4b Lessons from Outsourcing Overseas

Whether you are looking to ship manufacturing overseas or outsource your back office functions to firms in China and India, successful outsourcers point to several critical lessons they have learned from the experience.

1. Start by doing some serious research. Talk to entrepreneurs, consultants, lawyers, and others who have successfully outsourced or advised companies on manufacturing overseas.

2. It is important to start small and gradually build the overseas capability because there will always be problems in the beginning that will slow the process. The most common problem is a technical workforce that doesn't understand the industry in which you are doing business. Therefore, it is important to meet your overseas partner in person so you know with whom you're dealing.

3. Communicating by email and fax is not enough. Most projects require a company expert who can guide the technical workers in person.

4. Often it is best to use a combination of an offshore captive operation and a local contract firm to supplement critical needs. In this way you have more control over outcomes.

5. Outsourced staff typically have a high turnover rate because the average age is 25 and they are constantly looking to move up. Therefore, it is important that you create a culture that encourages the staff to stay with the business long term.

6. Make sure you understand the regulatory requirements of your industry and how they might impact your ability to manufacture overseas.

7. It is important to outsource only those tasks that have a high probability of going smoothly and making the customer happy. Problematic projects are better handled domestically.

Operations is not the glamorous side of an entrepreneurial startup, but it *is* a critical aspect of any business because the activities associated with operations are increasingly becoming a source of opportunities for innovation that will give a growing company a significant competitive edge.

New Venture Action Plan

- Source suppliers for your materials and supply requirements.
- Determine how inventory will be handled.
- Develop quality control metrics.
- Itemize and calculate production costs and determine whether to outsource.
- Determine warranty service requirements.
- Identify a third-party logistics provider.

Questions on Key Issues

1. Why is it important to consider your manufacturing plan in the earliest stages of a new venture?
2. What are three factors that you must take into consideration when choosing vendors to meet materials requirements?
3. Suppose you had a new advertising firm. How could you schedule activities to create more efficiencies in your operations?
4. What are some of the key factors that must be considered when setting up a quality control system?
5. Characterize the critical aspects of an effective supply chain for any business.

Experiencing Entrepreneurship

1. Visit a manufacturing facility that is using technology to facilitate its processes. Develop a flowchart of the manufacturing process. Can you see any ways to improve the process?
2. Interview an entrepreneur with a product company about his or her views on quality. How is this entrepreneur implementing quality control in his or her organization?
3. Choose a young company that has a global supply chain. Develop a process flowchart depicting the supply chain and analyze it for efficiency and flexibility based on information provided in the chapter.

Relevant Case Studies

Case 2: B2P:Micro-Bioinformatics Technology and Global Expansion
Case 4: Command Audio

CHAPTER 13

Choosing the Legal Form of Organization

"It will not injure you to know enough of law to keep out of it."

—THE OLD FARMER'S ALMANAC (1851)

CHAPTER OBJECTIVES

- Distinguish between sole proprietorships and partnerships.
- Discuss the corporate form and its advantages and disadvantages.
- Explain the limited liability company.
- Define the nonprofit corporation.
- Make a decision about which legal form to use for which purpose.
- Discuss how a business entity can evolve from one legal form to another.

PROFILE
13.1

LIVING WELL IS THE BEST REVENGE

What do you do when your partners, who share equal equity with you in the business, decide to shut you out and take over the business? This may not appear to be a common occurrence but, unfortunately, it is more common that most people think. Partnerships are difficult at best and all too often they end up ruining life-long friendships.

Kathleen King started baking at 11 years old and quickly began selling her chocolate chip cookies to help pay for her school clothes. Almost 23 years later, after creating hundreds of recipes for the bakery she had opened in 1980 as a sole proprietor in Southampton, New York, she was enjoying huge success. She decided it was time to get some help with the business side of the business. King found two brothers with the skills she needed, brought them on board, and agreed to split the ownership of the company into three equal shares. The year was 1999. Six months later in January 2000, she arrived at work to find the brothers blocking the entrance to the business and holding an eviction notice. They were claiming that she was not in her right mind and would not cooperate with them. She was not allowed to enter her store.

Stunned by this turn of events, King filed a lawsuit, but the only thing she recovered after 8 months of fighting was the building. She had lost her name, Kathleen's Bakery, and all her recipes and was left with $200,000 in debt. But she still had the building and she firmly believed that the brothers would not be able to carry on the business without her. To help get herself out of the debt from the lawsuit, she refinanced the building and started a new bakery, which she called Tate's Bake Shop after her father. Meanwhile, her customers boycotted the old Kathleen's Bakery and that, coupled with the fact that the duo did not maintain quality control, resulted in the original bakery eventually shutting down.

King's new business quickly became a huge success and once again her chocolate chip cookies were rated by Consumer Reports as the number one cookie in America. By 2009, she was producing one million cookies a week and sending them to 42 states with a profit of about $6 million. By 2013, the volume of cookies had increased to over two million per week in 50 states and she had added additional products to her line of baked goods that were now in many well-known stores around the country. She also willingly shared her ideas and recipes in four cookbooks. What started as a lifestyle business had become a bakery empire.

It goes without saying that King advises that entrepreneurs need to be very cautious about bringing on partners and to never do it without the firm guidance of a good attorney. As for King, this time around she decided to hire a competent manager rather than bring on another partner and says that she will never have a partner again.

Sources: Witchel, A. (August 2, 2013). "One Tough Cookie," *The New York Times,* http://www.nytimes.com/2013/08/02/nyregion/how-kathleen-king-built-her-chocolate-chip-empire.html?pagewanted=all&_r=0&pagewanted=print; Cortez, S. (September 25, 2012), "How to Come Back from a Failed Partnership," *Business Insider,* http://www.businessinsider.com/how-to-come-back-from-a-failed-partnership-2012-9

The choice of legal structure is one of the most important decisions that entrepreneurs have to make because it will affect every aspect of the business, including tax planning, the amount of paperwork you have to do, the cost of maintaining the legal structure, whether you can raise capital, and the level of personal liability you will have. For example, if a business entails any degree of risk, such as product liability, then choosing a legal form that protects your personal assets from being attached as the result of a lawsuit is just as important as carrying the appropriate insurance. The decision about the legal form of the business should reflect careful consideration about the type of business and your personal goals for that business, and it should always be made under the guidance of a qualified attorney. To make an educated decision about the legal form of the business, it is imperative to understand all the risks and benefits associated with a chosen form. Table 13.1 provides an overview of the various legal forms available to entrepreneurs according to the level of risk, with the sole proprietorship carrying the most risk. We will discuss each form and several more later in the chapter.

13.1 MAKING THE DECISION ABOUT LEGAL FORM

The traditional view of legal forms was that you started your business as a sole proprietor and then changed to a partnership or corporation as your business grew and you required more protection. A study done by the SBA Office of Advocacy found that this view is now out of date. Results showed that only one in three businesses actually started as a sole proprietorship, that is, with one owner. Fewer than one in ten firms changed their legal form in the first four years but when they did, it was generally to a more complex form such as a corporation.[1] The study also learned that entrepreneurs who start their businesses as LLCs or as one of the corporate forms tend to do so because they have several employees, the venture is highly levered, or the founder is more educated. By contrast, entrepreneurs tend to start with less complex forms when the founder is female, the founder achieves profit quickly, the venture has many tangible assets, and it is financed with personal loans.

Prior to making the decision on which type of legal form to choose, you should ask yourself seven very important questions.

1. Does the founding team have all the skills needed to operate this venture?
2. Do the founders have the capital required to start the business alone or must they raise it through equity capital or debt?
3. Will the founders be able to run the business and cover living expenses for the first year?
4. Are the founders willing and able to assume personal liability for any claims against the business?

TABLE 13.1   Comparison of Common Legal Forms

Issues	Business Form				
	Sole Proprietorship	Partnership	Limited Liability Company	Subchapter S-Corporation	C-Corporation
Number of Owners	One	No limit	No limit. Most states require a minimum of two members.	100 shareholders or fewer	No limit on shareholders
Startup Costs	Filing fees for DBA and business license	Filing fees for DBA; attorney fees for partnership agreement	Attorney fees for organization, documents; filing fees	Attorney fees for incorporation documents; filing fees	Attorney fees for incorporation documents; filing fees
Liability	Owner liable for all claims against business but with insurance can overcome liability	General partners liable for all claims; limited partners liable only to amount of investment	Members liable as in partnerships	Shareholders liable to amount invested	Shareholders liable to amount invested; officers may be personally liable
Taxation	Pass-through; taxed at individual level	Pass-through; taxed at individual level	Pass-through; taxed at individual level	Pass-through; taxed at individual level	Tax-paying entity; taxed on corporate income
Continuity of Life of Business	Dissolution on the death of the owner	Dissolution on the death or separation of a partner, unless otherwise specified in the agreement; not so in the case of limited partners	Most states allow perpetual existence. Unless otherwise stated in the Articles of Organization, existence terminates on death or withdrawal of any member.	Perpetual existence	Continuity of Life
Transferability of Interest	Owner free to sell; assets transferred to estate upon death with valid will	General partner requires consent of other generals to sell interest; limited partners' ability to transfer is subject to agreement	Permission of majority of members is required for any member to transfer interest	Shareholders free to sell unless restricted by agreement	Shareholders free to sell unless restricted by agreement
Distribution of Profits	Profits go to owner	Profits shared based on partnership agreement	Profits shared based on member agreement	Paid to shareholders as dividends according to agreement and shareholder status	Paid to shareholders as dividends according to agreement and shareholder status
Management Control	Owner has full control	Absent an agreement to the contrary, partners have equal voting rights	Rests with management committee	Rests with the board of directors appointed by the shareholders	Rests with the board of directors appointed by the shareholders

© Cengage Learning®

5. Do the founders wish to have complete control over the operations of the business?

6. Do the founders expect to have initial losses or will the business be profitable almost from the beginning?

7. Do the founders expect to sell the business some day?

The answers to these questions will narrow the choices by eliminating legal forms that do not facilitate the achievement of the outcomes in these seven questions, but it is always wise to get the advice of an attorney and/or accountant. For example, if a new venture is expected to have initial losses in the first year due to product development or other large startup costs (question 6), a form that enables those losses to pass through to the owners to be applied against other personal taxable income would be advantageous. Since the company is not yet generating income, you will be able to shelter other personal income from a tax liability. Sole proprietorships, partnerships, S-corporations, and limited liability companies all permit pass-through earnings and losses, but S-corporations and LLCs offer more protection from liability. The next sections review the various legal forms of organization and their advantages and disadvantages.

13.2   SIMPLE FORMS: SOLE PROPRIETORSHIPS AND PARTNERSHIPS

All businesses operate under one of four broad legal structures—sole proprietorship, partnership, limited liability company, or corporation. Because the legal structure of a new venture has both liability and tax ramifications for you and any investors, you must carefully consider the advantages and disadvantages of each form. It is also quite possible that you may decide to change the legal form sometime during your business's lifetime, usually for financial, tax, or liability reasons. These situations are discussed as each legal form is examined. Table 13.1 presents a summary comparison chart of all the structures.

13.2a   Sole Proprietorship

More than 76 percent of all businesses in the United States are sole proprietorships, probably because the sole proprietorship is the easiest form to create. For the tax year 2008, the most current year for which numbers are reported in the Statistical Abstract, there were just over 22 million tax returns that reported sole proprietor income that was nonfarm in nature.[2] In a sole proprietorship, the owner is the only person responsible for the activities of the business and, therefore, is the only one to enjoy the profits and suffer the losses.

To operate as a sole proprietor requires very little—only a DBA, and not even that if the you use your name as the name for the business. In other words, a sole proprietorship called Jennifer Brooks Corporate Consultants does not require a DBA if the entrepreneur's name is Jennifer Brooks, but a sole proprietorship called Corporate Consultants does. A DBA, or Certificate of Doing Business under an Assumed Name, can be obtained by filing an application with the appropriate local government agency. The certificate, sometimes referred to as a "fictitious business name statement," ensures that this is the only business in the area (usually a county) that is using the name you have chosen and provides a public record of business ownership for liability purposes.

Advantages

A sole proprietorship enjoys several advantages. First, it is easy and inexpensive to create. It gives the owner 100 percent of the company and 100 percent of the profits and losses. The owner also has complete authority to make decisions about the direction of the business. In addition, the income from the business is taxed only once, at the owner's personal income tax rate, and there are no major reporting requirements such as those imposed on corporations.

Disadvantages

There are, however, some distinct disadvantages that deserve serious consideration. The sole proprietor has unlimited liability for all claims against the business; that is, any debts incurred or judgments must be paid from the owner's assets. Therefore, the sole proprietor puts at risk his or her home, bank accounts, and any other assets. In today's litigious environment, exposure to lawsuits is substantial. To help mitigate this liability, a sole proprietor should obtain business liability insurance, including "errors and omissions coverage," which protects against unintentional negligence such as disseminating incorrect information in a company advertisement. Another disadvantage is that it is more difficult for sole proprietors to raise debt capital, because very often the owner's financial statement does not qualify for the amount needed. Sole proprietors are definitely not attractive candidates for investor capital for the obvious reason that they control 100 percent of the business. To take investment capital, they would have to change their legal form. Another complication associated with a sole proprietorship is that the business's ability to survive is dependent on the owner; therefore, the death or incapacitation of the owner can be catastrophic for the business if the owner did not transfer ownership through a will.

Often small businesses such as restaurants, boutiques, and consulting firms are run as sole proprietorships. This is not to say that a high-growth venture cannot be started as a sole proprietorship—many are—but it will in all likelihood not remain a sole proprietorship for long, because you will typically want the protections and prestige that organizing as a corporation affords.

Jennifer Overholt, Anne Murguia, and A.C. Ross sought the freedom to work when they wanted and not have to worry about overhead and assets. They essentially wanted to be sole proprietors who partnered when it was expedient to do so. Indigo Partners (www.indigohq.com), as their venture is called, is a loose association of six partners who take on projects on their own or as a team. They all have the common bond of wanting to do what they want and spend a lot of time with family, friends, and traveling. As soloists, they partner to give themselves the freedom to control their time.

13.2b   Partnership

When two or more people agree to share the assets, liabilities, and profits of a business, the legal structure is termed a partnership. The partnership form is an improvement over the sole proprietorship from the standpoint that the business can draw on the skills, knowledge, and financial resources of more than one person. This is an advantage not only in operating the business but also in seeking bank loans. Like the sole proprietorship, however, the partnership requires a DBA when the last names of the partners are not used in naming the business. Professionals such as lawyers, doctors, and accountants frequently employ this legal structure.

In terms of its treatment of income, expenses, and taxes, a general partnership is essentially a sole proprietorship consisting of more than one person so each partner pays taxes and receives income based on their proportionate interest in the partnership. However, where liability is concerned, there is a significant difference. In a partnership, each partner is liable for the obligations that any other partner incurs in the course of doing business. For example, if one partner signs a contract with a supplier in the name of the partnership, the other partners are also bound by the terms of the contract. This is known as the doctrine of ostensible authority. Creditors of an individual partner, on the other hand, can attach only the assets of that individual partner, including his or her interest in the partnership.

Partners also have specific property rights. For example, unless otherwise stated in the partnership agreement, each partner owns and has use of the property acquired by the partnership. Each partner has a right to share in the profits and losses, and each may participate in the management of the partnership. Furthermore, all choices related to elections such as depreciation and accounting method are made at the partnership level and apply to all partners.

Types of Partnerships

There are two types of partnerships: general and limited. In a general partnership, all the partners assume unlimited personal liability and responsibility for management of the business. In a limited partnership, by contrast, the general partners have unlimited liability, and they seek investors whose liability is limited to their monetary investment; that is, if such a limited partner invests $25,000 in the business, the most he or she can lose if the business fails is $25,000. It is important to note, however, that limited partners have no say in the management of the business. In fact, they are restricted by law from imposing their will on the business. The penalty for participating in the management of the business is the loss of their limited liability status. Other types of partnerships include (1) secret partners, who are active but not publicly known; (2) silent partners, who typically provide capital but do not actively participate in the management of the business; and (3) dormant partners, who are generally not known publicly and are not active, but still share in the profits and losses of the partnership.

Advantages

Partnerships have all the advantages of sole proprietorships plus the added advantage of sharing the risk of doing business. Partnerships enjoy the clout of more than one partner and, therefore, more than one financial statement. Partners can also share ideas, expertise, and decision making. Financially, partnerships enjoy pass-through earnings and losses to the individual partners, to be taxed at their personal tax rates.

Disadvantages

Partnerships also suffer from several disadvantages that you should consider carefully before choosing this form. Partners are personally liable for all business debts and obligations of the partnership, even when individual partners bind the partnership to a contract or other business deal. Unless otherwise stated in the partnership agreement, the partnership dissolves when a partner either leaves or dies. And finally, individual partners can be sued for the full amount of any partnership debt. If that happens, the partner who is sued, and loses, must then sue the other partners to recover their shares of the debt. It is important to understand that partnership litigation is expensive and time consuming, so having a solid partnership agreement that calls for arbitration may be the preferred way to go.

Partnership Agreement

Although the law does not require it, it is extremely wise for a partnership to draw up a written partnership agreement, based on the Uniform Partnership Act, which spells out business responsibilities, profit sharing, and transfer of interest. This is advisable because partnerships are inherently fraught with problems that arise from the different personalities and goals of the people involved. A written document executed at the beginning of the partnership will mitigate eventual disagreements and provide for an orderly dissolution should irreconcilable differences arise. Many partnerships have minimized conflict by assigning specific responsibilities to each of the partners and detailing them in the partnership agreement. Additional issues arise when one or more of the partners in a partnership leaves, either voluntarily or through death. To protect the remaining partners, the partnership should have in place a buy-sell agreement and "key-person" life insurance.

GLOBAL INSIGHTS

Legal Forms of Organization in the UK

We often forget that other countries don't necessarily operate with the same legal forms of organization that are employed in the United States, even if those countries have English as their principal language. The UK presents a good example of differences with the United States, sometimes solely in the name applied to the form and other times differences in what the rules are for forming a particular type of organization. In the UK, a sole proprietor is known as a "sole trader," but in all other respects, the two terms mean the same thing. In both countries the term *partnership* is used in the same manner to refer to legal arrangements between two or more people to do business. In the UK, however, when a company incorporates, it becomes a "Limited Company," (not to be confused with Limited Liability Company in the United States), which is owned by its members who invested in the business. Those members' personal assets are not at risk. Most companies in the UK are Companies Limited by Shares where each member holds one or more shares in the company with voting rights and is only liable for the amount invested in the company. Companies Limited by Shares are either private (Ltd) or public (PLC), where the public companies can sell shares in the public markets. Just like in the United States, the Limited Company has to deal with stricter regulations than its non-incorporated counterpart. The next time you see Ltd after a company's name, you'll know that it's the equivalent of a private corporation in the United States.

Source: "A Guide to Legal Forms for Business," Department for Business Innovation and Skills, November 2011, https://www.gov.uk/government/uploads/system/uploads/attachment _data/file/31676/11-1399-guide-legal-forms-for-business.pdf

A buy-sell agreement is a binding contract between the partners. It contains three primary clauses that govern the following issues:[3]

1. Who is entitled to purchase a departing partner's share of the business? May only another partner do so, or is an outsider permitted to buy in?

2. What events can trigger a buyout? Typically, those events include a death, disability, or other form of incapacity; a divorce; or an offer from the outside to buy the partner out.

3. What price will be paid for the partner's interest?

Having these issues decided from the beginning prevents disagreements and legal battles with the departing partner or with the estate of a deceased partner.

It is unfortunate that many entrepreneurs fail to take the precaution of creating a partnership agreement with a buy-sell clause. The consequences can be critical for the business. For example, say one partner dies, and the partnership, absent a buy-sell agreement, is forced to work with the spouse or a family member of the deceased who may not be qualified to run the business. Yet another

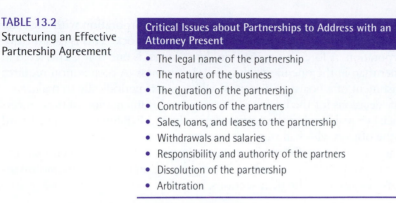

TABLE 13.2
Structuring an Effective
Partnership Agreement

Critical Issues about Partnerships to Address with an Attorney Present
• The legal name of the partnership
• The nature of the business
• The duration of the partnership
• Contributions of the partners
• Sales, loans, and leases to the partnership
• Withdrawals and salaries
• Responsibility and authority of the partners
• Dissolution of the partnership
• Arbitration

© Cengage Learning®

example is without a partnership agreement, one partner can potentially sell his or her interest to a stranger without the consent of the other partners, so it is critically important to have such an agreement. For more protection from liability than a partnership affords, organizing the business as a corporation or a limited liability company should be considered.

Any partnership should have an agreement to describe the structure of the partnership, who is entitled to what, and what happens if the partners disagree or leave the partnership. Table 13.2 presents some of the critical issues that should be addressed in the agreement and discussed with your attorney. Because this is a legally binding contract, it should always be reviewed by a qualified attorney.

13.3   CORPORATE FORMS

Only about 25 percent of all U.S. businesses are corporations, but they account for about 67 percent of all business receipts.[4] A corporation is different from the preceding two forms in that it is a legal entity in and of itself. The U.S. Supreme Court has defined the corporation as "an artificial being, invisible, intangible, and existing only in contemplation of the law." It is chartered or registered by a state and can survive the death of the owner(s) or the owner's separation from the business. Therefore, it can sue, be sued, acquire and sell real property, and lend money. The owners of the corporation are its shareholders, who invest capital in the corporation in exchange for shares of ownership. Like limited partners, shareholders are not liable for the debts of the corporation and can lose only the money they have invested.

Most new businesses form what is known as a closely held corporation; that is, the corporate stock is owned privately by a few individuals and is not traded publicly on a securities exchange such as the New York Stock Exchange. This chapter will focus on such private corporations. The issue of "going public" typically arises after your business is established and you want to raise substantial capital for growth by issuing stock (shares of ownership in the corporation) through an initial public offering (IPO). The IPO and public corporations in general are the subject of Chapter 16.

A corporation is created by filing a certificate of incorporation with the state in which the company will do business and by issuing stock. This is called a domestic corporation. A foreign corporation, by contrast, is one that is chartered in a state other than in the one in which it will do business. A corporation requires the establishment of a board of directors, which meets periodically to make strategic policy decisions for the business. The regular documentation of these meetings is crucial to maintaining the corporation's limited liability status. The board also hires the officers who will run the business on a day-to-day basis.

There are two primary for-profit corporate forms from which to choose: the C-corporation and the S-corporation. Their purpose and advantages and disadvantages are discussed in the next sections.

13.3a   C-Corporation

It would be difficult to claim that the Pennsylvania Railroad Corporation of the 1950s resembles in any way the General Electric Corporation of today, let alone the Business.com Corporation operating on the Internet. Even the most traditional of legal forms—the corporation—has evolved over time. Yet it remains the most commonly chosen legal structure for a growing company that seeks outside capital in the form of equity or debt.

Because it is a legal entity, the corporation can enter into contracts, sue, and be sued without the signature of the owners. In a startup or young company, however, bankers, creditors, and the like generally require that majority shareholders or officers personally guarantee loans to ensure that the lender is protected against the potential failure of the corporation by having the ability to pursue the assets of the owners. Personal guarantees should be avoided wherever possible, but the reality is that a young corporation has few assets, so you may not be able to avoid having to personally guarantee loans.

Advantages

The C-corporation offers several important advantages. It enjoys limited liability in that its owners are liable for its debts and obligations only to the limit of their investment. The only exception to this protection is payroll taxes that may have been withheld from employees' paychecks but not paid to the Internal Revenue Service. Capital can be raised through the sale of stock up to the amount authorized in the corporate charter; however, the sale of stock is heavily regulated by federal and state governments. A corporation can create different classes of stock to meet the various needs of its investors. For example, it may issue nonvoting preferred stock to conservative investors who, in the event that the corporation must liquidate its assets, will be first in line to recoup their investment. Common stock is more risky, because its holders are paid only after the preferred stockholders. Common stockholders are, however, entitled to vote at shareholders' meetings and to divide the profits remaining after the preferred holders are paid their dividends, assuming that these profits are not retained by the corporation to fund growth. Startups and early-stage companies rarely pay dividends; rather, they retain that capital pay for growth.

Ownership in a corporation is easily transferred. This is at once an advantage and a disadvantage, because you will want to be careful, particularly in the startup phase, to ensure that stock does not land in the hands of undesirable parties such as competitors. This problem is easily handled through a buy-sell clause in the shareholder's agreement that states that stock must first be offered to the corporation at a specified price before being offered to someone outside the corporation. Most entrepreneurs restrict the sale of their stock so that they can control who holds an ownership interest in the company.

Corporations typically enjoy more status and deference in business circles than do other legal forms, principally because they are a legal entity that cannot be destroyed by the death of one—or even all—of the principal shareholders. Moreover, to enter the public equity markets, a business must be incorporated, so it will be subjected to greater scrutiny from governmental agencies. The reason for this scrutiny is the fact that the assets of the corporation are separate from the assets of the individual owner/shareholders. Therefore, the owners may take risks that they wouldn't take with their personal assets. Corporations can also take advantage of the benefits of retirement funds, Keogh and defined-contribution plans, profit-sharing arrangements, and stock option plans for their employees. These fringe benefits are deductible to the corporation as expenses and not taxable to the employee. Finally, you can hold certain assets (such as real estate) in your own name, lease the use of the assets to the corporation, and collect a lease fee.

Disadvantages

Corporations do, however, have disadvantages that must be carefully considered. They are certainly more complex to organize, are subject to more governmental regulation, and cost more to create than sole proprietorships or partnerships. Although it is possible to incorporate without the aid of an attorney, doing so is not recommended. In too many cases, businesses have failed or endured significant financial hardship because they did not incorporate properly at the start of the business or did not maintain the corporation according to the legal requirements.

A more cumbersome disadvantage derives from the fact that the corporation is literally a person for tax purposes. Consequently, if it makes a profit, it must pay a tax, whether or not those profits were distributed as dividends to the shareholders. And, unlike partners or sole proprietors, shareholders of C-corporations do not receive the pass-through benefit of losses (the S-corporation does enjoy these benefits). In a C-corporation, if losses can't be applied in the year they are incurred, they must be saved and applied against future profits. Accordingly, C-corporations pay taxes on the profits they earn, and their owners (shareholders) pay taxes on the dividends they receive; hence, the drawback of "double taxation." It is principally for this reason that many entrepreneurs who operate alone or with a partner do not employ this form. However, if you draw a salary from your corporation, that salary is expensed by the corporation, effectively reducing the company's net income subject to taxes. You will then be taxed at your personal income tax rate. However, you should understand what the IRS classifies as reasonable compensation. If you exceed that number, your compensation can be reclassified as a dividend distribution subject to the corporate tax in addition to associated penalties.

By creating a corporation and issuing stock, you are giving up a measure of control to a board of directors. Realistically however, in privately held corporations, the entrepreneur largely determines who will be on the board and will certainly seek people who support his or her vision. Entrepreneurs who seek outside venture funding in the very early stages of their venture where the risk is highest may find that they have to give up the majority of the stock to the investors. The choice is either to hang on to the equity and watch the business stall because funding can't be secured or to give up control so that you can own a smaller piece of something successful. It is not always necessary, however, that the founder retain 51 percent of the stock to maintain effective control. As long as the founder's skills and vision are vital to the success of the venture, and as long as the shareholders share that vision, the founder will have effective control of the organization, no matter how much stock she or he has given up. In fact, if you own a tech company, by the time you go public, you will own a very small percentage. For example, Aaron Levie, the founder of Box.com, is projected to own approximately 6 percent of his company after its impending IPO. Mark Benioff, co-founder of Salesforce.com, holds about 7 percent of the company's shares.[5] With a corporate form, unlike the sole proprietorship or partnership, you are accountable principally to the shareholders and secondarily to anyone else. If the corporation is privately held, the board usually serves at the pleasure of the entrepreneur, who is accountable to himself or herself and to any investors.

A corporation must endeavor in all ways to act as an entity separate from its owners. You must keep personal finances completely separate from corporate finances, hold directors' meetings, maintain minutes, and not take on any financial liability without having sufficient resources to back it up. Failing to do any of these things can result in what is known as "piercing the corporate veil," which leaves the officers and owners open to personal liability.

Where to Incorporate

Apart from legal considerations, where to incorporate is also an important issue. Some states have corporate income tax rates higher than individual tax rates, so a C-Corporation may pay higher state taxes than it would have being organized as an S-Corporation (discussed later). It is normally advantageous to incorporate in the state in which you intend to locate the business, so that it will not be under the regulatory powers of two states (the state in which it is incorporated and the state in which it must file an application to do business as an out-of-state corporation). Normally, however, a corporation will not have to qualify as a "foreign" corporation doing business in another state if it is simply holding directors' or shareholders' meetings in the state, or holding bank accounts, using independent contractors, or marketing to potential customers whose transactions will be completed in the corporation's home state. It has often been said that incorporating in Delaware is wise because it has a large body of case law that makes it easier for a company to plan to avoid lawsuits; furthermore,

Delaware's Chancery Court, which oversees corporate law, is reputed to be one of the finest in the United States. If neither seeking venture capital nor doing a substantial amount of business in Delaware is a goal of your company, however, the cost and hassle of qualifying in another state as well may outweigh the benefits of incorporating in Delaware. Moreover, today most states have modified their corporate laws to be in alignment with those in Delaware. You should also consider the favorableness of the tax laws governing corporations in the state chosen. Some states, such as California, levy a required, minimum annual corporate income tax, whether the business has a taxable income or not.

13.3b   S-Corporation

An S-corporation, unlike the C-corporation, is not a tax-paying entity. It is merely a financial vehicle that passes the profits and losses of the corporation to the shareholders. It is treated much like a sole proprietorship or a partnership in the sense that if the business earns a profit, that profit becomes the income of the owners/shareholders, and it is the owners who pay the tax on that profit at their individual tax rates. In this way, it avoids the double taxation found in the C-corporate structure. However, in all other respects it operates under the same requirements as the C-corporation. You will need to file articles of incorporation, have a board of directors, hold an annual shareholders' meeting, keep corporate minutes, and hold shareholder votes on major decisions. Approximately six states tax S-corporations like regular corporations, so it is important to check with the tax division of the state in which you will do business to find out if a tax will be imposed. S-corporation shareholders are not required to pay self-employment taxes (Social Security and Medicare), which can amount to more than 15.3 percent of income, if they receive compensation that is reasonable for the services they provide. Additional profit is then distributed as non-wage dividends so they are not subject to self-employment tax. It is very important to work with an attorney who specializes in these forms of organization so that you don't make a decision without considering all the ramifications. In recent times, the S-corporation has largely been replaced by the limited liability company (LLC), which is a more flexible form.

Some of the key rules for election of the S-corporation option include the following: The S-corporation may have no more than 100 shareholders. These shareholders must be U.S. citizens or residents (partnerships and corporations cannot be shareholders). Profits and losses must be allocated in proportion to each shareholder's interest. An S-corporation shareholder may not deduct losses in an amount greater than the original investment. In addition, it is always wise to check with an attorney to make certain that the election of S-corporation status is valid. If a C-corporation elects to become an S-corporation and then reverts to C-corporation status, it cannot re-elect S-corporation status for five years.

Advantages

The S-corporation permits business losses to be passed through and taxed at the owner's personal tax rate. This offers a significant benefit to people who need to offset income from other sources. The businesses that benefit most from an S-corporation structure are those that don't have a need to retain earnings. In an S-corporation, if you decide to retain, say, $100,000 of profit to later invest in new equipment, your company must still pay taxes on that profit as though it had been distributed. The S-corporation is a valuable financial tool when personal tax rates are significantly lower than corporate rates. However, as top personal rates increase, a C-corporation might be preferable at higher profit levels. For some small businesses, however, the S-corporation may still be less costly in the long run because it avoids double taxation of income. A good tax attorney or certified public accountant (CPA) should advise you on the best course of action. Ventures that typically benefit from S-corporation status include service businesses with low capital asset requirements, real estate investment firms during times when property values are increasing, and startups that are projecting a loss in the early years.

Disadvantages

You should probably not elect the S-corporation option if you want to retain earnings for expansion or diversification, or if there are significant passive losses from investments such as real estate. This is because unless the business has regular positive cash flow, it could face a situation in which profit is passed through to the owners to be taxed at their personal rate, but the firm has generated insufficient cash to pay those taxes, so they must come out of the pockets of the shareholders. Furthermore, although most deductions and expenses are allowed, S-corporations cannot take advantage of deductions based on medical reimbursements or health insurance plans.

13.3c   The B Corporation

The B Corporation is also known as a benefit corporation, a for-profit entity with a social mission. Presently, as of 2014, it was recognized in 26 states and the District of Columbia, with an additional 12 states and the territory of Puerto Rico having introduced legislation to recognize the form. While these organizations are very similar to other for-profit organizations, they do differ in a number of important ways: purpose, accountability, and transparency.[6] In the statement of purpose in the Articles of Incorporation, you will need to identify the positive impact on society and the environment that your company intends to have. Some examples of this benefit are promoting economic opportunity and improving public health. Entrepreneurs choose this form over the C-Corporation because it emphasizes and clarifies their social purpose and even presents a branding opportunity. Each state has its own requirements relative to purpose, accountability, and transparency, so you should investigate and consult with counsel that has expertise in this particular form.

13.3d   The Nonprofit Corporation

It is not outside the realm of possibility for a nonprofit corporation to be a high-growth, world-class company; however, it is not generally started with that goal in mind. A nonprofit corporation is a corporation established for charitable, public (scientific, literary, or educational), or religious purposes, or for mutual benefit (such as trade associations, tennis clubs), as recognized by federal and state laws. Some additional examples of nonprofits are child-care centers, schools, religious organizations, hospitals, museums, shelters, and community health care facilities. Like the C-corporation, the nonprofit corporation is a legal entity and offers its shareholders and officers the benefit of limited liability. There is a common misconception that nonprofit corporations are not allowed to make a profit. As long as the business is not set up to benefit a single person and is organized for a nonprofit purpose, it can still make a profit on which it is not taxed if it has also met the IRS test for tax-exempt status. However, income derived from for-profit activities is subject to income tax.

Before starting a nonprofit venture, there are a few questions you need to answer so that you will understand if this is the appropriate vehicle for what you want to accomplish. The National Council of Nonprofits (a nonprofit itself!) suggests these questions.[7]

1. Do you have a clear idea of what you want to do and have you considered whether it's feasible? Even nonprofits need to operate like businesses, so it's important to have a plan.

2. Who will you involve in your nonprofit? Do you know people who can help you or who can serve on your board and connect you to the resources you need?

3. Do you know what paperwork you need to file and when and where it needs to be filed? You will have paperwork for filing as a nonprofit corporation at the state level and paperwork at the federal level to apply for tax-exempt status. Do you know where to get help in filing the required documents?

4. Is forming a new organization the best way to accomplish your mission? Nonprofits have lots of competition for resources. If you can accomplish your goal in three years or less, it might make more sense to operate under the auspices of another nonprofit. In this approach, your sponsoring nonprofit would be the recipient and administrator of donations for your organization.

There are two distinct hurdles that you must overcome if you want to operate as a nonprofit corporation and enjoy tax-exempt status so that your donors can benefit from tax-deductible donations: The first is to meet the state requirements for being designated a nonprofit corporation and operating as such in a given state. The second is to meet the federal and state requirements for exemption from paying taxes [IRS 501(c)(3)] by forming a corporation that falls within the IRS's narrowly defined categories.

Advantages

Nonprofit organizations offer many advantages to entrepreneurs seeking to be socially responsible or just to start a business doing something they love that helps others. The nonprofit with tax-exempt status is attractive to corporate donors, who can deduct their donations as a business expense. The nonprofit can seek cash and in-kind contributions of equipment, supplies, and personnel.

It can apply for grants from government agencies and private foundations. The nonprofit may qualify for tax-exempt status, which means that it is free from paying taxes on income generated from nonprofit activities.

Disadvantages

There are a few disadvantages to a nonprofit organization. For example, profits earned by the corporation cannot be distributed as dividends, and corporate money cannot be contributed to political campaigns or used to engage in lobbying. In forming the nonprofit corporation, the entrepreneur gives up proprietary interest in the corporation and dedicates all the assets and resources of the corporation to tax-exempt activities. If a nonprofit corporation is ever dissolved, its assets must be distributed to another tax-exempt organization. This means that the nonprofit form is not suitable for ventures that need to access the capital markets either public or private. Finally, the nonprofit cannot make substantial profits from unrelated activities, and it must pay taxes on the profits it does make.

N2TEC Institute was formed as a nonprofit organization in 2004 with the purpose of serving rural communities in the Midwest with guidance on building entrepreneurial ecosystems. When it completed its mission in 2012, it dissolved the corporation and distributed the remaining capital to other nonprofit organizations as required by law.

It is not uncommon for tax-exempt organizations to engage in activities that generate unrelated business income (UBI)—that is, income that is not related to the nonprofit's exempt purpose. For example, if a research institute were to operate a café on a regular basis, this would be considered a UBI activity. The institute would have to report it to the IRS and pay taxes on the income. If and when their UBI activities start to become significant, nonprofits often establish for-profit entities to run their UBI activities to protect the tax-exempt status of the parent organization.

13.4 LIMITED LIABILITY COMPANY

The limited liability company (LLC), like the S-corporation, enjoys the pass-through tax benefits of partnerships in addition to the limited liability of a C-corporation. It is, however, far more flexible in its treatment of certain ownership issues. It is not recognized by the IRS as a legal form of organization because it is a hybrid of a partnership and an S-Corporation. Only privately held companies can become LLCs, and they must be formed in accordance with very strict guidelines. LLC statutes vary from state to state, so in addition to meeting the partnership requirements of the Internal Revenue Code, applicants must file with the state in which they intend to do business and follow its requirements as well.

An LLC is formed by filing articles of organization, which resemble articles of incorporation. There is no minimum number of people required to form an LLC, but if you are the only member, you must be very careful in how the activities of the LLC are documented so that the IRS or the state does not consider the LLC a sole proprietorship. The owners of an LLC are called members, and their shares of ownership are known as interests. The members can undertake the management of the company or hire other people to manage it. Managers, officers, and members are not personally liable for the company's debts or liabilities, except where they have personally guaranteed these debts or liabilities. The members create an "operating agreement," which is very similar to a partnership agreement that spells out rights and obligations of the members.

13.4a Advantages

Most LLCs will be organized for tax purposes like partnerships, so that income tax benefits and liabilities will pass through to the members. In New York and California, however, the LLCs will also be subject to state franchise taxes or fees. Under the Internal Revenue Code, an LLC exhibits all four characteristics of a corporation—limited liability, continuity of life, centralized management, and free transferability of interests—but it can still be treated as a partnership for tax purposes without fear of being reclassified as a corporation. This enhances the attractiveness of the LLC, already the most rapidly growing legal form.

The LLC is often thought of as a combination of a limited partnership and an S-corporation. However, there are differences. In a limited partnership, one or more people (the general partners) agree to assume personal liability for the actions of the partnership, whereas the limited partners may not take part in the management of the partnership without losing their limited liability status. In an LLC, by contrast, a member does not have to forfeit the right to participate in the management of the organization in order to retain his or her limited liability status. Moreover, in an LLC, unlike in an S-corporation, there are no limitations on the number of members or on their status. Corporations, pension plans, and nonresident aliens can be members. Also, whereas S-corporations can't own 80 percent or more of the stock of another corporation, an LLC may actually possess wholly owned subsidiary corporations. LLCs are not limited to one class of stock, and in some ways they receive more favorable tax treatment. For example, unlike an S-corporation shareholder, the LLC member can deduct losses in amounts that reflect the member's allocable share of the debt of the company. If at a later date the entrepreneur decides to go public, the LLC can become a C-corporation by transferring the LLC assets to the new corporation. It is, however, a bit more difficult to go in the other direction, and capital gains tax must be paid on the appreciation.

13.4b Disadvantages

Clearly, the LLC offers more flexibility than other forms, but it does have a few disadvantages that should be considered. In contrast to the creation of a partnership or sole proprietorship, a filing fee must be paid when the LLC is formed. It is probably not a good form to choose if there will be a large number of members, because it will be difficult to reach consensus among the owners, who might also be the managers of the LLC. It is not a separate tax-paying entity. Earnings and losses are passed through to the members to be taxed at their individual tax rate, so members must make quarterly estimated tax payments to the IRS. If all the members do not elect to actively manage the LLC, the LLC ownership interests may be treated like securities by the state and the Securities and Exchange Commission (SEC). This means that if the company does not qualify for an exemption (most small LLCs do), it must register the sale of its member interests with the SEC.

LLCs are becoming a popular vehicle for companies that may have global investors because the S-corporation does not permit foreign ownership by non-legal residents. An attorney should be consulted to find out whether this form is available in a particular state. One ambitious entrepreneur knew that she wanted her furniture-importing business to be global in all respects. She even intended to bring in investors from among her business acquaintances around the world, because that would help her find the important contacts she needed to be successful. As an importer, she needed liability protection but did not want the high tax rates she would have with a corporation. Friends had told her that the S-corporation would solve the tax problem, but her attorney advised her to consider the LLC as her choice of legal form because it would allow her to have foreign investors.

13.5 CHOOSING THE RIGHT LEGAL FORM AT EACH MILESTONE

Having a strategic plan in place for your venture enables you to choose a legal form that won't have to be changed or one that can easily be shifted to when the time is right. For example, suppose you plan to offer shares of stock in the company at some point in the future to raise additional capital. To accomplish that, the company will need to become a corporation or LLC; so if the company began as a sole proprietorship, it would need to file incorporation or LLC papers in the state in which it would be doing business. Consider the following example of a married entrepreneur, Cheryl Kastner. Kastner's spouse is a highly paid executive for a major corporation, making it possible for her to devote herself full-time to developing a technology product she has been designing for some time. Kastner decides to set up a small business with a workshop near their home. She is not worried about medical insurance because she is already covered by her spouse's company. However, she needs to limit liability, because they have acquired a number of valuable assets, such as their house and cars, and she doesn't want those assets to be in danger should things go badly. She realizes that in any business dealing with products, some liability issues might crop up and she wants to make sure they're covered. She also wants to ensure that she and her husband are protected from personal liability for things that happen at the business.

At startup, it is typical to experience losses as equipment is purchased, and prototypes are built and tested in the market. Once the product is launched, continuing losses will come from promoting the business, finding space outside the home to lease, and hiring new employees. Kastner has big plans for her business; in fact, within a year of introducing the product, she expects to need venture capital to be able to grow as fast as the market demands. She also sees an acquisition in the future that will be the liquidity event that enables investors to cash out. Given these circumstances, she needs to consider which organization form is best at each milestone.

During product development, before the business is actually launched, it often doesn't make sense to use a more formal form such as a corporation, especially in a state where you have to pay minimum state franchise taxes. A simple sole proprietorship or partnership (if there's more than one person involved) will suffice. At this stage, the liability to family assets is negligible because only Kastner is involved with the technology. But the minute Kastner's business grows out of the home environment and takes on the responsibilities of a lease and employees, she must consider either being heavily insured or moving to a legal form with limited liability. Kastner plans to move the business to a leased location and hire employees. Since there would still be losses from product development and she would want to use them to shelter other income, she is also advised to consider either the S-corporation or the LLC, depending on the degree of flexibility she needs. She is also advised by her attorney that at the point at which she decides to seek venture capital and/or an IPO, she will need to convert to a C-corporation.

It is clear from this example that the legal form of an organization is not a static decision, but rather one based on the needs of the company at the time of formation and into the future. Choosing the legal structure of the new venture is one of the most important decisions you can make, because it affects the tax strategy of your company for years to come. The correct selection depends on the type of venture you are starting, the profits the venture generates, your personal tax bracket, the assets used by the business, the risk factors in the business, its potential for growth, and state laws. Again, particularly in the case of corporations and LLCs, it is important that an attorney who specializes in this area review your documents to ensure that all the rules have been followed and that you will receive all of the benefits to which the business is entitled.

New Venture Action Plan

- Answer the questions on page 227 before considering which legal form to choose.
- Consult with an appropriately qualified attorney to determine the best form to meet your business goals.
- Complete the necessary agreements for the legal form you have chosen (partnership agreement, articles of incorporation, etc.).
- Determine if you meet the test for tax exemptions under IRC 501(c)(3) if you are founding a nonprofit corporation.
- Meet with a qualified attorney to determine what other legal issues might arise with your particular type of business.

Questions on Key Issues

1. Assuming that you were running a successful consulting practice as a sole proprietorship, what would induce you to change the legal form to a corporation?
2. Why would you choose an LLC form over a partnership or an S-corporation?
3. What kinds of businesses are well suited to the nonprofit legal structure?
4. What key factors determine the strategic plan for the legal organization of the business?

Experiencing Entrepreneurship

1. Employing this text and additional research on the Internet, acquire a basic understanding of the different legal forms of organization. Then, using a business that you are considering launching, discuss your initial strategic plan for the business with a qualified attorney to get his or her advice about the best form to use for that type of business. Write a two-page summary of your findings to justify the choice of legal form.

2. Visit an entrepreneur whose business is set up as a partnership. How do the partners describe the experience of setting up the business? How have they divided the duties and responsibilities? What key issues have they covered in their partnership agreement? Summarize your findings in a two- or three-page paper.

Relevant Case Studies

Case 2 B2P:Micro-Bioinformatics Technology and Global Expansion
Case 8 Vision to Learn

CHAPTER 14

Developing a Startup Marketing Plan

"Don't forget that it [your product or service] is not differentiated until the customer understands the difference."

—TOM PETERS, THRIVING ON CHAOS

CHAPTER OBJECTIVES

- Discuss the role of the product adoption/diffusion curve for marketing strategy.
- Explain how to create an effective marketing plan.
- Discuss the forms of advertising and promotion that entrepreneurs can tap.
- Describe the role of publicity in a marketing strategy.
- Explain how entrepreneurs can employ social media to their advantage.
- Discuss the role of personal selling in a marketing strategy.

THE STARTUP EXPERIMENT IN MARKETING

On an otherwise normal Tuesday afternoon, Nashville-based author Jon Acuff posted an entry on his blog and linked it to Facebook and Twitter. The post read:

> Adventurers Wanted.
> For dangerous journey.
> 24 people, 24 days, 1 awesome result.
> Success difficult.
> Risk guaranteed.[1]

Within seconds, comments were flying. Many people were nervous, including one man who sent in his information and commented, "I made a choice to do something that scares the crap out of me. I need a change. Just a start. A crazy — and possibly impetuous — start." Others responded as if they had been expecting the invitation all along. Out of the 100 or so comments that appeared on the blog within the first 12 hours, only one person outwardly expressed concern about sending sensitive information to an unverified Gmail address. Everyone else seemed to believe that sharing personal information was just part of the deal.

The response to Acuff's post was overwhelmingly positive; it seemed he was hitting on a secret desire held by many of his fans—the desire to be picked from the many— to be the special "chosen" few. In total, Acuff received almost 3,000 responses from eager fans, many who chattered about the possibilities on Twitter, some even saying they might leave jobs or move to take part. *Never mind that Acuff had yet to define the adventure or share what it entailed.*

You might describe Jon Acuff as "mildly famous" or "sort of known." He has written two best-selling books, *Quitter* (2011) and *Start: Punch Fear in the Face, Escape Average and Do Work That Matters* (2013). He also created the very-popular "Stuff Christians Like" blog, which was turned into a book of the same name. He works for the much-better-known financial guru Dave Ramsey, who often mentions Acuff on his show and in his written media. In fact, if Acuff were to walk through a grocery store in many parts of the country, odds are he'd make it out unrecognized. Yet for whatever reason, this group of people was willing to make life-altering decisions based on trusting Acuff as an authority.

As it turned out, no one had to make those leaps. Since Acuff received applications from more than 3,000 hopefuls, he decided to open the project to all entrants. Instead of choosing one team of 24 as he had initially stipulated, he created multiple teams of 24 and invited everyone to join his private Facebook group. Within days of adding all the new members, people began disappearing from the group. Some claimed they were too busy; others decided the experiment was not for them. Only one person took the time to ask the question that was likely on many people's minds: "I thought you were only picking 24 people?"

Surprisingly, a large number of people stayed and continued following Acuff's direction, despite the fact that he failed to deliver on his initial promise. One by one, they introduced themselves to the group, offering up personal information that made them more vulnerable than the nature of the group warranted. Posts about life regrets and personal failures littered the page, making the experience feel more like a 24-hour confessional than an adventure.

However, Acuff had ignited an entire community focused on marketing his ideas. External fan-supported websites launched to support his Start

Experiment, along with YouTube campaigns and local meetups. So great is the desire by many consumers to be picked that clever entrepreneurs like Acuff have found ways to harness that desire to promote their businesses.

Sources: Ford, J.C., Brand Voice Expert and Storyteller, Interview, July 1, 2014; Clark, Corrie (June 2013) "The Start Experiment," CorieClark.com, http://corieclark .com/2013/07/10/the-start-experiment/; Casey, Nicholas (July 8, 2013) "A New Start," NicholasCasey.blogspot.com http://nicholasccasey.blogspot.com/2013/07/a-new-start .html

In today's digital world, launching a business can be as easy as putting up a simple website, but that doesn't guarantee that the business will be sustainable. To create a sustainable business requires a plan for winning loyal customers; to accomplish that, you need to understand thoroughly customer needs, preferences, channel demands, and competition. Marketing includes all the strategies, tactics, and techniques used to raise customer awareness; to promote a brand, product, service, or business; and to build and manage long-term customer relationships. Marketing can be thought of as a bundle of intangible benefits a company is providing to its customers, and these benefits reflect the company's core values. Traditionally, marketing has been described in terms of the "5 Ps"—people, or customers; product or what is being offered to the customer; price or what the customer is willing to pay; place, which is the channel through which customers can find the product or service; and promotion, which involves the strategies for creating awareness and reaching the customer. Pushing a marketing strategy on potential customers—a very costly approach—does not make sense to entrepreneurs, who typically have limited resources at startup. Rather, they prefer to invest in building long-term relationships with customers and designing their products or services with the customers' needs in mind. In that way, much of the "selling" that would otherwise have to be done has been taken care of by giving customers what they want, when they want it, and in the way they want it.

Marketing in a global, digital economy means responding to speed and connectivity. Indeed, given much shorter competitive and economic lives for products and services and the impact of Internet search on price transparency, price dispersion, market entry, and product variety, the real challenge is how to quickly rise above the crowd and build a competitive brand that is sustainable. The challenges to product development are greater than they have ever been due to increasing costs, global competition, and rising supply chain complexity with increased costs of trade promotions. The IRI/Symphony Group, which supplies data to the consumer products industry, created a standard for measuring the success of a new product. It is called the New Product Pacemaker and it refers to a product that can garner $7.5 million in sales in the first year in the U.S. market. In 2012, for example, 1900 new products were launched into the U.S. market. Of those only 77 achieved Pacesetter status at an average cost of $71 million each.[2] Statistics like this can be daunting for entrepreneurs who do not have those kinds of resources. Too many entrepreneurs make the mistake of thinking they can compete against these resource-heavy new-product companies; they discount the impact of the global market; and they develop products for a broad market rather than a specific and unique niche market that is currently not served.

Fortunately for startups, marketing strategy has also been affected greatly by social technologies. A 24/7 on-demand connection is now the norm, and it has changed the way people communicate, organize, collaborate, and create or break social bonds. As a result, social technologies have had a significant impact on the way businesses think about their marketing strategies; in other words, how businesses operate is changing as entrepreneurs discover that social technologies are a rich source of insight on customers at a much lower cost than more traditional methods. We devote a section later in the chapter to social media to understand its associated technologies and the analytics that are used to measure the effectiveness of those technologies.

If we look to the future of marketing, it's clear that the coming trends all relate to the customer experience. Mobile connectivity, more user-friendly online spaces built on the HTML5 language, and the Internet of Things, which is a network of sensors and actuators embedded in physical objects that can communicate with each other, are trends that will shape the customer experience of the future. Technology is on the verge of enabling consumers to search for things they want to buy by means of image, voice, and gesture and to augment their reality with devices such as Google Glass. What this means is that consumers' expectations will rise in four primary ways:[3]

- Consumers will want to interact with anyone, anytime, and anywhere.
- They will want to be able to do new things with new information in new ways.
- They will expect everything to be targeted to their precise needs, so they can have the unique experience they want.
- They want this all to happen easily with no learning curve.

Moreover, we're finding that customers care more about use than ownership. Think about Zipcar, a way to borrow a car rather than own one. Consumer services now account for nearly 50 percent of consumer purchases. Demographic changes, such as the enormous growth of the teenage market, and customer demand for more specific goods are all driving changes in customer expectations.

Understanding the new environment for marketing is critical because as one study found, customer experiences now influence two-thirds of the decisions they make and the other third is mostly driven by price.[4] Today marketing must consider all the touch points with the customer from brand awareness to product evaluation, purchase, and after purchase experience. If you did the type of ethnographic market research that was suggested in Chapter 4, you will have a much deeper understanding of this customer journey when it comes time to build out your marketing strategy.

The intent of this chapter is not to review marketing fundamentals, which are best left to textbooks focused on this subject or to excellent websites like www.marketingprofs.com where professionals gather to discuss the subject. The purpose is to explore marketing from an entrepreneurial perspective in an age of social media and to look at how to create a marketing plan that will enable a startup to develop a successful brand and build long-term relationships with its customers. This chapter builds on the feasibility analysis and market research strategies and tactics discussed in Chapter 4. The market/customer information gathered during market research can now be applied to a marketing plan that reflects the customer journey.

14.1 PRODUCT ADOPTION AND THE CUSTOMER JOURNEY

Understanding the product life cycle and how customers adopt new products is critical to any marketing strategy because it enables you to plan for which customer segment to target first and the rate at which sales can potentially occur. To the extent that you can predict the points of takeoff (optimism) and slowdown (pessimism) in the cycle, you can better manage demand. If you can manage demand, you can more effectively plan for varying levels of production, inventory, sales personnel, distribution, marketing, and advertising. Finally, if you can more effectively plan for changes in sales patterns, you can adapt your strategy to remain competitive.[5]

The adoption/diffusion curve, which describes how customers adopt new products, was developed at the Agricultural Extension Service at Iowa State College in 1957 to monitor patterns of hybrid seed corn adoption by farmers. What they learned was explained in a book, *Diffusion of Innovations*, written by Everett Rogers six years later. The study grouped customers into categories based on how quickly they adopted a new product, ranging from those who adopted immediately to those who were the last to adopt.[6] What the Iowa agricultural agency found over time was that not all farmers would adopt new technology at the same time; only those most comfortable with new methods would adopt in the earliest stages. Everyone else would wait to see what the outcome of the first trials would be before taking on the risk or wait until they had no choice but to adopt.

Critics of Rogers's model claim that it is simplistic and doesn't take into account the evolution of the product in terms of improvements as it moves from the first customer to the last customer. Another criticism is that disruptive technologies, those that make previous technology in the area obsolete, tend to follow a different diffusion pattern from the one Rogers described; this pattern will be explained later in the chapter. Despite these challenges, the adoption/diffusion curve is still employed to explain customer adoption behavior. Figure 14.1 presents a depiction of the new product adoption/diffusion curve. The innovators are the visionaries; they are a very tiny customer base that is always interested in trying the latest, greatest thing. Innovators, who are typically younger in age, represent the gatekeepers, the group that is instrumental in deciding whether a new product will go forward to ultimately achieve mass adoption. They will typically follow the development of the technology or product over a long period and often become beta version testers. The early adopters, by contrast, are the true first customers because they pay for the product. They are eager to adopt new products to solve problems and create a competitive advantage for themselves.

FIGURE 14.1   New
Product Adoption/
Diffusion Curve

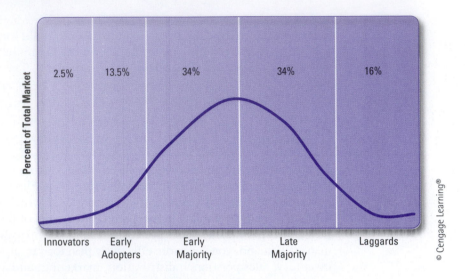

An optimistic group, they usually have money to spend, and they only require that the product be able to solve about 80 percent of their problem. For that reason, they are not good reference points for the mass market because they tend to understand the need for the product better, and they don't expect productivity improvements and ease of use like the early majority does.

The early majority comprises the more pragmatic customers who tend to wait until a new product is proven and plenty of people are using it. They need to know that a product actually works before they adopt it because they don't want to make bad decisions. They tend to watch the early adopters to see how they fare before leaping into a purchase. The late majority tends to be an older group who typically buys only proven products with good price points. This group waits for the price to come down, which means that for the product has become a commodity. The final group is the laggards who tend to purchase the product only if they absolutely have to; in other words, they are skeptical that the product is necessary to solve their problem at any price. This group is the non-customers. To entice them to buy will mean making the product signifi-cantly cheaper, easier to use, and with no switching costs.

For technology products, the adoption/diffusion cycle has a twist. Figure 14.2 presents a modification of the adoption/diffusion curve showing what Geoffrey Moore has called the "chasm."[7] The chasm is a period when the early adopters have been exhausted and the technology stops selling. The reason is that innovators and early adopters are the only ones with an interest in the technology, while the rest of the potential market, which is far more pragmatic, is not experiencing any "pain" or problem that the technology can solve. Moore believes that to cross the chasm, the customer has to have a compelling reason to buy. To achieve that means identifying niche markets where the technology can produce a pragmatic application that solves a real problem. For example, GPS (global positioning system) technology was available long before there was an actual pain in the market that it could alleviate. When GPS began to be used

FIGURE 14.2   The Technology Adoption–Diffusion Curve

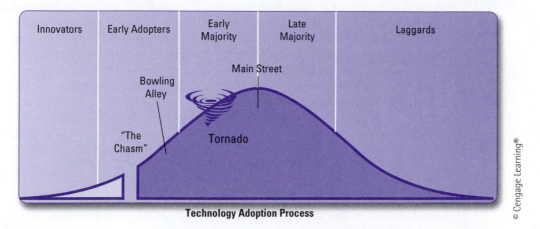

© Cengage Learning®

in luxury automobiles, early-adopter customers liked that it could help them find where they needed to go. Eventually, as the price came down and the technology became more user-friendly, it was adopted by the early majority in less expensive automobiles. Moore suggests that to cross the chasm, you must find multiple niche market applications that get the technology into many different customer sectors (called the Bowling Alley). Once a critical mass of niches is acquired, there may be a flashpoint where the market *en masse* adopts the technology. That throws the technology into what Moore calls a "tornado," with year-over-year growth of 100 percent or more and where your most important job is to focus on producing and distributing the product. Customer demand is not an issue in this situation because there is actually more demand than your company can manage. That is why having good systems and controls in place prior to attempting to achieve a tornado is critical. A recent example was the market share battle between high-definition DVD formats Sony Blu-ray and Toshiba's HD DVD. After a protracted battle, Toshiba abandoned its format, paving the way for Blu-ray to cross the chasm and become the standard. Once the tornado has passed, the entrepreneurial venture has arrived at "Main Street," which is a period of aftermarket development where the company is attempting to sell more to its current customers. This can be a very difficult period for a young venture because it must now learn how to be a large company with operational excellence and how to maintain the customer relationships it built. Crossing the chasm is a critical achievement for technology companies that want to set a new standard in the industry and keep competitors from doing the same.

What is important to take away from the discussion of adoption/diffusion cycles is that the rate at which a new product is adopted across the various customer segments is a function of several factors that include perceived benefit, price and total product costs, usability, acceptance of promotional efforts, distribution intensity, switching costs, learning curve, and the ability to test the product before purchase. Not all customers will respond the same way to a new product introduction.

The adoption pattern of customers is not the only thing you need to understand before preparing a marketing plan. You also need to identify the points at which you interact with your customers from the moment you create awareness for your product or service to the end of the life cycle for that product/service. Table 14.1 presents the components of a complete customer journey that you will need to comprehend if you are going to create value for your customers at every point in that journey. Note that some of the components are essential and others are optional and depend on the type of business you have and the kinds of customers you serve. The essential items are processes, needs, and perceptions, in other words, the stages at which customers interact with your company and how that happens; what customers require at each of those interaction points; and how customers perceive these interactions. Are they satisfied? Are the interactions valuable?[8]

When you are journey-mapping your customer's experience, it's important to get everyone on the startup team involved and it's also vital to include some customers. Chances are you will uncover areas where you don't score well, but that is the value of doing the journey map in the first place. It puts you in the shoes of your customers and lets you view your business from their perspective.

TABLE 14.1 Components of a Customer Journey Map

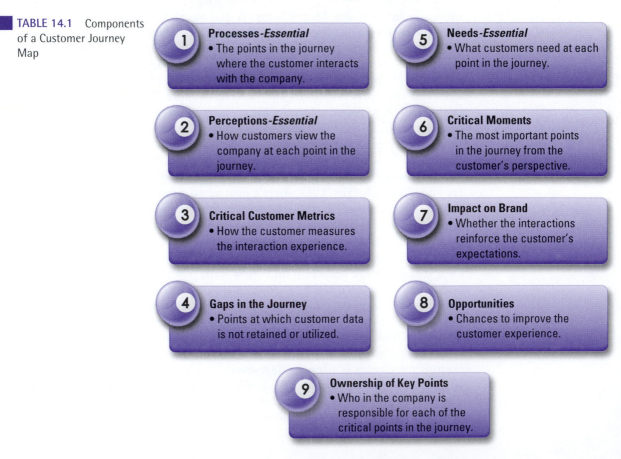

1 Processes-*Essential*
• The points in the journey where the customer interacts with the company.

2 Perceptions-*Essential*
• How customers view the company at each point in the journey.

3 Critical Customer Metrics
• How the customer measures the interaction experience.

4 Gaps in the Journey
• Points at which customer data is not retained or utilized.

5 Needs-*Essential*
• What customers need at each point in the journey.

6 Critical Moments
• The most important points in the journey from the customer's perspective.

7 Impact on Brand
• Whether the interactions reinforce the customer's expectations.

8 Opportunities
• Chances to improve the customer experience.

9 Ownership of Key Points
• Who in the company is responsible for each of the critical points in the journey.

© Cengage Learning®

14.2 THE MARKETING PLAN

For any company, an effective marketing strategy incorporates a marketing plan. The marketing plan for a startup is a living guide to how the company plans to build customer relationships over its life in order to fulfill the company's mission statement. It details the strategies and tactics that will create awareness on the part of the customer and build a brand and a loyal customer base. Furthermore, an effective marketing plan develops a consistent message to the customer and creates an opportunity for you to make a sale. Marketing plans are written at many points in the ongoing life of a business. The original plan will contain a strategy for introducing the company and its products and services to the marketplace. Later a marketing plan may be used to launch new products and services and/or to grow the business, perhaps in a new direction.

A few important steps taken before the actual writing of the marketing plan ensure that the plan is on target and is one your company can live with for a long time. Living with a plan for a long time may sound inconsistent with your need to remain flexible and adapt to change in the marketplace, but one of the biggest problems with most marketing plans is that they are not followed long enough to achieve the desired results. Typically, when business owners do not see immediate results from their marketing effort, they decide that it must not be working—so they change it and start the cycle all over again. Changing the plan on impulse is the wrong thing to do. It takes time to make customers aware of a product or service. Furthermore, it takes time for a particular marketing strategy to take hold and secure customers' trust. Consider this: From the first time a customer sees an ad to the point at which the customer actually buys the product, weeks or even months may pass. In fact, on average, a customer will see an ad 15 to 20 times before actually purchasing the product. This pattern speaks to the importance of providing a product or service that meets a compelling need so that the time to purchase can be shortened. Just like a successful stock market investor, you must think of the marketing plan as an investment in the future of the business and you must remember that any investment takes time to mature. Reaping the benefits of a well-structured marketing plan requires persistence and unwavering dedication until the plan has an opportunity to perform.

14.2a Creating Customer Value

A company's mission and core values will set the tone for the marketing plan and inform the initial steps in writing the plan. First, the approach to the market, or the bridge between strategy and execution, must be defined. The approach to the market includes such things as the message, differentiation tactics, channel strategies, and performance goals. Choosing the wrong approach can result in customers not understanding the benefits being provided. Choosing the same approach for all customers will ensure that not everyone will be satisfied. Selecting an approach is based on a thorough understanding of customers—what they need, when they need it, and where they want to find it. That understanding should have been acquired during the market research phase of the feasibility analysis. Next, it is important to identify a niche that you can dominate. Typically, this is a segment of the market that is not being served. To capture customers, you need to create value, which is a central aspect of marketing activity.[9] It is the principal way that you differentiate your business[10] and is essential for customer satisfaction.[11] Customer value has been defined as "a customer's perceived preference for, and evaluation of, those product attributes, attribute performances, and consequences arising from use that facilitates (or blocks) achieving the customer's goals and purposes in use situations."[12] More simply, it is seen as intangible benefits, such as quality, worth, and utility, that customers receive from the product as measured against what they paid for it.[13] Recall the discussion of the development of the business model in Chapter 5. Intangible benefits that customers appreciate include such things as access, saving money, saving time, convenience, health, and so forth.

14.2b   Setting Marketing Goals

Once the value proposition for the customer has been defined, it's time to consider all the marketing options or means to communicate the company's message. To begin to understand which options should be considered, you should talk to other business owners, customers, and suppliers and read books and articles on marketing strategies for entrepreneurs such as those found at MarketingProfs.com. It's also important to learn which approaches are typically used by other businesses in your industry because that will give you an idea of customer preferences and expectations. This process will generate a list of possibilities to consider, which may range from sponsoring a business conference to advertising in a national trade publication to developing a social media approach. Determining which strategies are the most effective, or even feasible, can be left for later. It is important for you to think like a customer and imagine the business from the customer's point of view. What would entice a customer to enter that store, buy that product online, or avail himself or herself of that service? You should study the competition to determine what makes them successful or unsuccessful. What marketing strategies do competitors seem to employ, and are they effective? What improvements could be made on what competitors are doing? Finally, you must analyze the marketing options and rank them by first eliminating those that either don't meet the needs of the target market or simply are not feasible at the time (usually for budgetary reasons). A ranking of the top ten choices should suffice. Once the options for creating awareness and reaching the customer have been determined, sales and marketing goals should be established. These goals should follow the SMART rule; they must be sensible, measurable, achievable, realistic, and time specific.[14] Measurable means that there must be financial metrics associated with the goals, such as gross profit, sales revenue, and amount of sales per salesperson, as well as customer acquisition costs and number of customers acquired. These metrics are discussed further in a later section.

Many experienced marketers suggest that an important step in creating the marketing plan is to condense all the ideas about marketing strategy into a single paragraph. Impossible? Not at all. Crafting a single well-written paragraph forces you to focus carefully on the central point of the overall marketing strategy. This paragraph should include the purpose of the marketing plan (*What will the marketing plan accomplish?*), the benefits of the product/service (*How will the product/service help the customer or satisfy a need?*), the target market (*Who is the primary buyer or first customer?*), the market niche (*Where does the concept fit in the industry or market? How does the company differentiate itself?*), the marketing tactics to be used (*What specific marketing tools will be employed?*), the company's convictions and identity (*How will the customers define the company?*), and the percentage of sales that the marketing budget will represent (*How much money will be allocated to the marketing plan?*). Here is an example of an effective one-paragraph statement of the marketing plan for a product/service business.

> TradePartners enables qualified importers and exporters from a variety of countries to find trading partners through an Internet-based, business-to-business network. The purpose of the marketing plan is to create awareness and name recognition for TradePartners in the market space. The target customer or first customer is the small exporter who needs to find buyers for excess inventory in another country; the secondary customer is the importer who wants to find new sources for products to import to the United States. Customers will enjoy the benefits of reduced time and risk in finding new customers or suppliers. TradePartners has defined a niche targeting small companies that want access to the same opportunities as large companies worldwide. Customers will view TradePartners as a professional, innovative, and customer-focused company. Initial marketing tactics include personal selling at industry events, strategic alliances with complementary companies, and providing free workshops on import/export. TradePartners will spend an average of 40 percent of sales to implement the marketing strategy in the initial stages.

With a clear and compelling one-paragraph marketing plan, you need to establish your launch objectives, which are the key goals for the marketing campaign. What needs to be accomplished, when, and how does the company intend to do it? For a startup venture, two important objectives are (1) to create awareness for the company and its brand and (2) to reach target customers to produce sales quickly. As the company begins to grow, it will add other objectives such as reaching out to non-customers in the current market or diversifying the product line to attract a new market. Objectives need to be matched to a timeline for achieving them. Marking on a timeline the major milestones for advertising and promotional events, trade shows, and social media events gives some direction to the marketing plan.

14.2c   Brand Strategy

Brand building is a critical part of any marketing strategy, but what is a brand? The American Marketing Association defines the term as a "name, term, design, symbol, or any other feature that identifies one seller's good or service as distinct" from other sellers. This definition is distinguished from "brand image," which is how the customer perceives the brand.[15] Brand strategy is "a set of decisions about the brand's positioning in a marketplace."[16] These decisions can include developing the brand concept (BMW's "the ultimate driving machine"), building brand extensions to take the brand into new product areas, licensing the brand to third parties to expand opportunities, or co-branding with another company, such as Godiva chocolate did when it partnered with SlimFast to co-brand a new diet drink. "Brand equity," another often-used term, conveys the effectiveness of the brand in the market, often in terms of financial metrics such as return on marketing costs. These metrics are important because entrepreneurs are typically dealing with limited resources and they want to ensure that the dollars they spend will produce the results they want.

Building brand equity requires that customers form an emotional attachment to the brand. To accomplish that, everything associated with your company—products, services, signage, web design, location, and so forth—must convey the overall value message that you want to project. So, if your company is in the educational software business with a focus on children, for example, it may need to create a brand image that suggests expertise, integrity, fun, perhaps a sense of adventure, and trust. The company's location, color scheme, product packaging, and advertising must all be aligned in a consistent message. Customers should have no doubt about what the brand stands for because that clarity and consistency serve to engender trust on the part of the customer.

To ensure that a new brand and the branding strategies used to build the brand image have a chance to achieve a high level of brand equity, you should test your brand against the following three questions:[17]

1. Is everyone in the company in agreement as to what the brand stands for?
2. Is there consistency between the brand image the company is projecting and the perceptions of customers?
3. Do customers describe the brand in ways that could inspire loyalty and evangelism?

It's also important to understand that branding strategies that take advantage of "word-of-mouth endorsements" through social networks, enabling endorsers to gain recognition by their peers is a powerful way to sustain the brand. Consumers also enjoy bragging about their achievements relative to what you are offering. For example, Bodybuilding.com finds that members like to tell the world when they achieve their target weight and this serves as essentially no-cost promotion for the company.[18] Connecting the company website to Facebook and Twitter enables these endorsements for your brand to reach a much wider audience.

14.2d Assessing Effectiveness

Measuring the effectiveness of marketing efforts is critical to avoid wasting precious company resources. For example, matching sales forecasts to specific marketing tactics and assigning a specific person responsible for measuring the outcome is important to assessing the effectiveness of the marketing plan. Another way you can measure success in a marketing effort is to ask customers how they heard about your company or the product/service. Tracking specific marketing efforts, advertising, and promotion, and matching specific performance outcomes to each effort are vital to understanding where to focus resources. Sales reports alone will not provide the required information to make a decision about customer value.[19] For example, consider a situation where annual sales are increasing, the number of orders is increasing, and the number of customers is increasing. This all sounds promising; however, looking closer reveals that the number of orders per customer is declining significantly, which means that more customers are ordering less frequently. That translates to higher marketing costs (to keep attracting more customers) and reduced lifetime customer value (the goal is to sell more to existing customers because new customer acquisition is expensive).

It is not within the scope of this text to go into detail on marketing metrics, but Figure 14.3 provides some key performance indicators that should help entrepreneurs understand how successful they are in acquiring customers, maintaining customers, and building brand equity. It is important to note that you should also consider any additional metrics that might be appropriate to your specific business. We will talk about metrics used in Internet businesses in a later section.

14.2e   Advertising and Promotion

Advertising and promotion are both used to create awareness for a company's products and services and influence customers to buy; but they are not interchangeable terms because they have different objectives. Advertising generally focuses on non-price benefits and targets end-users. It can also have some influence on the channels of distribution through which the customer will seek a product or service. In that sense, advertising is employed to pull the product

FIGURE 14.3 Some Marketing Metrics for Entrepreneurs

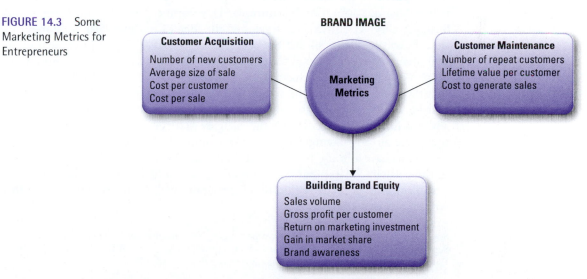

© Cengage Learning®

through the distribution channel—called a pull strategy. By contrast, promotion tends to be more price-focused or incentive-focused and therefore is usually considered a push strategy. Table 14.2 depicts a matrix of factors that affect whether a push or a pull strategy should be used and under what conditions.

TABLE 14.2   Push or Pull Strategy?

Factors to Consider	Use Advertising (Pull)	Use Promotion (Push)
Price sensitivity	Not effective	Effective
Brand loyalty	High loyalty	Low loyalty
Need for information	High need	Low need
Risk—switching costs, learning curve	High risk for customer	Low risk for customer
Product life cycle stage	Growing or mature	New product or declining product
Market status	High market share	Low market share
Purchasing pattern	Predictable	Unpredictable
Contribution to profit	Above average	Below average
Differentiation	Strong differentiation	Little differentiation

© Cengage Learning®

SOCIAL ENTREPRENEURSHIP: *MAKING MEANING*

Fabio Rosa: Bringing Energy to Rural Brazil

To the people in Encruzihada do Sul, Brazil, part of the two billion people who have no access to electricity, Fabio Rosa is a hero. The remoteness of their village made it very unlikely they would ever be connected to the electricity grid because companies in the energy business typically have no experience with supplying power to the developing world. However, through Rosa's nonprofit organization, The Institute for Development of Natural Energy and Sustainability (IDEAAS), he developed the idea of renting solar equipment to rural Brazilian villages so that the people could avoid having to purchase expensive solar panels and also avoid paying Brazil's harsh sales taxes of more than 50 percent. The biggest challenge he had to overcome was the villagers' belief that they couldn't afford the system and that it was unreliable. For more than a year he worked with community leaders to understand the needs of the people and was finally able to convince the villagers that they would pay no more than they were already paying for candles and lamp oil. Where it might cost at least $3,000 to have a house hooked up to the grid, Rosa could rent his solar energy to the villagers for less than $24 a month. In 2010 he had more than 600 families in the Encruzihada region on his program, well on his way to serving this community of 1,000.

Sources: "The New Heroes," PBS, www.pbs.org/opb/thenewheroes/meet/rosa.html, accessed September 27, 2010; and "Fabio Rosa—Making the Sun Shine for All," MercyCorps, Global Envision, February 7, 2006, www.globalenvision.org/library/10/954.

For many entrepreneurs, putting a great deal of money into advertising and promotion doesn't make sense. They simply don't have the resources and budgets of a Starbucks, so their money is better spent on more effective ways of reaching very specific customers. Today you can sometimes achieve phenomenal velocity in awareness for a new product by turning it into a fad through the speed and reach of social networking.

As of August 2014, YouTube, an Internet platform for uploading and sharing videos, had more than one billion unique users worldwide per month who watched more than 6 billion hours of video—a statistic that doesn't even include videos that are embedded or watched on mobile devices. According to Nielsen, YouTube reaches more U.S. adults aged 18–34 years than any cable network. [20] It is estimated that only one-third of one percent of YouTube videos get more than a million views while about 50 percent receive fewer than 500 views.[21]

In 2013, the business that reaped the most attention on YouTube, landing in the Top Ten list, was Volvo Trucks for "The Epic Split Feat" featuring actor Jean Claude Van Damme doing above-the-ground splits between two moving trucks (it was accomplished in one take). The video went viral with more than 68 million views—a win for Volvo, although it remains to be seen how many trucks it sold as a result.

You don't have to control the resources of Volvo to achieve success. Small businesses that take the time to plan a well-crafted video can also score big. In March 2012, DollarShaveClub.com made waves with a hilarious and innovative company video: "Our Blades Are F***ing Great." Using sarcasm, random bits of humor, and direct messaging, the company managed to attract more than 11 million eyeballs. The company's business model is simple: a subscription service that delivers razors to your door monthly at a cheaper price than a drugstore or grocer could offer. Within two days of launching the video, Dollar Shave Club received 12,000 orders. Over the next year, Dollar Shave Club attracted more than 200,000 subscribers and raised $9.8 million in funding. The company has since added shave butter and disposable wipes for men. CEO Michael Dubin's goal? "To own the entire bathroom."[22]

From all appearances, Dollar Shave Club became a success due to its initial YouTube spike. But is YouTube the sole reason for the company's runaway success? Or was YouTube just a launch pad to give a boost of traffic to a company that was already destined for success? Let's take a quick look:

Dollar Shave Club solves a real problem. Razors are known for being extraordinarily expensive relative to the cost of making them. Creating an inexpensive, off-label product that is delivered (literally to your door) solves a problem for those who hate spending $15 to $16 for refills.

The company is run by someone with business experience. CEO Michael Dubin has a well-respected marketing background that includes companies like MSNBC, *Time*, and *Sports Illustrated*. He also created online brand assets for companies such as Gillette, Ford, and LG. He led teams at many of the companies and also did time as an associate and as an intern. Dubin teamed up with co-founder Mark Levine, who has a deep background in manufacturing.

The team didn't depend on the video for success. Dubin invested $35,000 of his own money to create the website. He signed up his first 1,000 users through conversation, not acquisitions. Dubin and Levine worked out the kinks in their manufacturing process and figured out their initial strategy. Then they created the video as a way for investors to learn about their company. They never intended the video to go viral. Instead, they thought of it as a visual business card.

The video brilliantly sells the product. Most viral videos focus on the audience more than on the product. For Dollar Shave Club, the reverse is true. Despite being funny, intelligent, and paced well, the video also clearly lays out the vision of the product and why it's important.

Ultimately, the long-term success of Dollar Shave Club will be determined not by YouTube views or social media, but by the quality of its products and services. For example, Crocs, the plastic shoes that are a combination of clog and sandal, achieved explosive growth from 2005 to 2007, when consumers were seeing them everywhere. But then the fad was over, sales dropped precipitously, and the company had to scramble to sustain itself as a much smaller company.[23] So, the cautionary note is that entrepreneurs who want to use the Internet to create a viral effect and speed the adoption of their products need to have a plan for what they will do when the fad dies.

14.3   ENTREPRENEURIAL MARKET STRATEGIES

Entrepreneurs approach marketing from a point of view distinctly different from that of the traditional marketer. Because they don't have the time or money for elaborate, high-profile marketing strategies, entrepreneurs often mimic what the big companies do, but they do it for much less money, in more creative ways, and for a shorter period of time. There are many ways to promote a company and its products and services effectively. The next sections consider a variety of entrepreneurial marketing tactics.

14.3a   Traditional Advertising

Traditional advertising—a pull strategy—consists of print and broadcast media. It is not the purpose of this book to provide all the information you need to use each medium presented, but only to create awareness of how and when each is used. Table 14.3 presents some of the traditional print and broadcast media options available to entrepreneurs with some hints for how to use them most effectively. Most entrepreneurs today shy away from traditional media because it is not only much more expensive but it may not reach their target audience as effectively as digital media and social technologies might. These will be the subject of a later section.

14.3b   Publicity and Referrals

Publicity and word-of-mouth (referrals) are two of the most effective marketing tools around because they don't cost your company any money. What they do require is a compelling story that will attract attention. If your business or

TABLE 14.3   Traditional Media Comparison Chart

Media	Advantages	Disadvantages	Hints
Print Media			
Newspapers	Broad coverage in a selected geographic area Flexibility and speed in bringing to print and modifying Generates sales quickly Costs relatively little	May reach more than target market Difficult to attract reader attention Short life	Look for specialized newspapers for better targeting Include a coupon or 800 number Locate ad on right-hand page above the fold
Magazines	Can target special interests More credible than newspapers	Expensive to design, produce, and place	Look for regional editions Use a media-buying service Use color effectively Check on "remnant space," leftover space that must be filled before magazine goes to print
Direct marketing (direct mail, mail order, coupons, telemarketing)	Lets you close the sale when the advertising takes place Coverage of wide geographic area Targets specific customers More sales with fewer dollars More information provided Highest response rate	Not all products suitable Need consumable products for repeat orders Response rate on new catalogs is very low, about 2%	Create a personalized mailing list and database from responses Use several repeat mailings to increase the response rate Entice customers to open the envelope
Yellow pages	Good in the early stages for awareness Good for retail/service	Relatively expensive Targets only local market	Create ad that stands out on the page
Signs	Inexpensive Encourage impulse buying	Outlive their usefulness fairly quickly	Don't leave sale signs in windows too long; people will no longer see them
Broadcast Media			
Radio	Good for local or regional advertising	Can't be a one-shot ad, must do several	Advertise on more than one station to saturate market Sponsor a national radio program Provide the station with finished recorded commercials Stick to 30-second ads with music
Television	Second most popular form of advertising People can see and hear about product/service Can target at national, regional, or local level	Very expensive for both production and on-air time Must be repeated frequently	Time based on GRP (gross rating points). Range is $5–$500 per GRP. Use only if you can purchase 150 GRPs per month for three months. Seek help of media-buying service
Cable TV shopping	Good for new customer products Targets the consumer Good products sell out in minutes	Not a long-term strategy Good only for products between $15 and $50 Product must be demonstrable	Call network for vendor information kit Contact buyer for your product category Be prepared to fill an initial order of between 1,000 and 5,000 units

© Cengage Learning®

(continued)

TABLE 14.3   *(continued)*

Media	Advantages	Disadvantages	Hints
Infomercial	Good for consumer items that can't be explained quickly	Very expensive to produce Hit rate is about 10%	Most profitable times are late nights, mornings, and Saturday and Sunday during the day Test time slots and markets to confirm effectiveness
Miscellaneous Affinity items (T-shirts, caps, mugs), Searchlights, Couponing, In-store demonstrations, Videotapes, Free seminars	Good for grabbing consumer's attention Effective, yet inexpensive, way to showcase the company	Value varies significantly with type of business and product or service	Every company should make use of affinity items to create free publicity

product is newsworthy, there are several ways to get some publicity. Contacting newspapers, magazines, or online reporters, editors, and bloggers to pitch them with an idea and then following up with a phone call often works. Whenever possible, it's a good idea to get to know people in the media on a first-name basis. Taking a reporter to lunch before there is a need for free publicity will help cement a relationship that can be accessed when the time is right. When it comes time to seek publicity, entrepreneurs who already have a contact can simply issue a press release answering the who, what, where, when, and why of the business.

It is also important to understand that seasonality affects publicity just like it does sales in a business. New stories or product introductions receive the most notice when they are placed near an event that normally gets a lot of attention, such as a presidential election or tax season. Summertime is when many journalists are looking for interesting stories because not much is happening, so summer is a better time to get out a story about your company in general. When contacting the press, a good approach is to include a press kit containing the press release, bios, and photos of the key people in the story, any necessary background information, and copies of any other articles written about your company. The idea is to make it as easy as possible for the reporter to write or tell the story. The media are always looking for news and appreciate the effort to give them something newsworthy. When an article is written about your business, reprints can be used in future advertising and brochures, and thus you gain even more value for the effort.

Constructing an Effective Press Release

Although some have argued that the traditional press release is dead in the age of social media, the fact is that it is alive and well. Press releases are certainly important for investor relations and they help tell the marketplace the ongoing story of a company. An effective news release should contain the date, the name of the person to contact for more information, and a phone number; the release date (for immediate release or for release after a certain date); an appropriate, descriptive headline; the release information typed double-spaced with wide margins; the who, what, where, when, and why at the very beginning of the press release; a photo, if appropriate; and a note explaining briefly why the release was sent. There are also several publishing services that can be used to gather and distribute information about the business. For example, PR Newswire is a leading source for press releases on companies (www.prnewswire.com).

Getting Customer Referrals

The best customers are those acquired through referrals from current satisfied customers. A study conducted over 3 years by a team at Goethe-University in Frankfurt, Germany, looked at the customer referral program of a leading German Bank. The researchers wanted to learn if social capital converts to economic capital. What they found was very encouraging. Referred customers generate higher profit margins than other customers, are 18 percent more likely to stay with the bank, and to produce a significantly higher customer lifetime value.[24] And research supports the fact that offline referrals carry more weight than online referrals because when you're receiving a referral from someone you know rather than relying on a "like" or rating, you tend to trust the recommender more.

Trust requires mutual empathy and a history of personal interactions; and to the extent that we spend more of our relationship time online, trust can be eroded, particularly where those long-term face-to-face relationships have never been developed. Today we are being asked to trust that a review we read online is honest and not paid for. We are being asked to believe that our programmer in India is a capable and respectful employee, even though we've never met. Sites such as LinkedIn, the professional social network, attempt to build trust by letting you meet new people through referrals from people you already know and maybe have worked with in the past. But even LinkedIn is not getting you the return on referrals that you might get offline. If you ask the average person what percentage of word-of-mouth referrals originate online, that person will likely guess somewhere around 50 percent or more. Given that so much of business today occurs online, that number seems to make a lot of sense. But it's not even close. Recent research finds that only 7 percent of word-of-mouth-type referrals happen online—the rest are all from face-to-face relationships where there is a much higher level of trust.[25] Even though it may seem counter intuitive, Internet entrepreneurs should really consider how they're going to reach their customers when they're not online.

Unfortunately, most entrepreneurs don't understand how to get customers to refer others to their business and become their company evangelists. The process is actually quite simple. You should begin by getting critical information that will clarify customers' motivations for buying and referring. Talking with current customers who have provided referrals is an excellent way to find out what they really like about the company, how they describe it to others, and what they value most about it. Specific ways to gather this information include taking a customer to lunch at least once a week and encouraging him or her to do the talking. Another approach is doing a global Internet search on a search engine like Google to find out what is being said about the company. Companies frequently don't know that some customers set up personal websites to either praise or criticize a company they have strong feelings about. Other options include having a qualified third party conduct in-depth interviews with customers, administering an open-ended online survey that's easy to complete, and hosting an online discussion. Finally, another great way to gather customer feedback is to create a customer advisory board to advise your company on everything from what products to carry to how best to market them.[26]

14.3c   When It Makes Sense to Give It Away

Although it seems contrary to what is taught in business schools, more and more entrepreneurs are using the tactic that Netscape and Microsoft used when they gave their browsers away in order to grow their markets rapidly. Giving customers something for nothing makes sense in an environment where it's hard to get the customer's attention. But it is important to know whether giving something away will help your business or simply cost money that it can't afford to lose. You should consider giving away information, consulting, or samples of a product when the customer is likely to return; when the cost for each additional item is low and margins are high; when customers need to try the product or service in order to risk the money to buy it, especially if it's unproven technology (consider offering the product or service to a well-known customer who will testify to his or her satisfaction with it); or when samples of the product or service can be offered at a large event such as a conference or trade show. On the other hand, it's important not to give away a service such as financial expertise that relies on credibility, because doing so may cause customers to question its value. Similarly, expensive items and commodity items, which customers buy on the basis of price, should not be given away, especially when the probability of retaining those customers is low.

14.3d   Internet Marketing and Social Media

In 2013, Internet ad revenues hit an all-time high of $42.8 billion, a 17 percent increase over 2012. And, for the first time, online ad revenues exceeded broadcast television.[27] Industry experts see traditional media boundaries disappearing while information floods markets, producing commodity pricing. Information erupting from a multitude of sources and not controlled by any one organization has the potential to overwhelm decision makers or at the very least distract them or prevent them from making effective decisions. Moreover, with everyone having access to the means to produce highly targeted messages to reach customer niches, the competitive advantage of Internet marketing disappears. With video and content production technology now priced within the reach of individuals and small businesses, the barriers to content creation have been breached so that anyone can produce a broadcast-quality commercial or magazine-quality advertisement and distribute it to a very targeted audience. Customers, who are being deluged with these targeted ads, however, have become jaded and can now use the same technologies the marketers use to opt out of receiving promotions and advertising. Customers also find themselves with the power to control when, where, and how they view ads. These and other media trends discussed later in this section present huge challenges to entrepreneurs but also new opportunities for those seeking to market their products and services.

Any marketing strategy should be anticipated, personal, and relevant. Potential customers don't want to be surprised by marketing tactics. They want to know that marketing is about them, and they want to know that it's about things they're interested in. The reason why most online marketing campaigns (and offline ones, as well) are unsuccessful is that they are unanticipated, impersonal, and irrelevant. Today you must find ways to give your customers more control over the purchase experience and engage them using new media tools, a topic for discussion in the next section.

In addition, there must be an effective way to measure advertising performance that is interactive, capable of being updated quickly, and minimally intrusive, so that customers don't opt out. There is a misconception that advertising on the Internet is cheap and/or free. Actually, any method of acquiring new customers on the Internet carries an acquisition cost that can often be quite high. For example, suppose a company spends $150 on pay-per-click Google ads to attract 25 people to its site, which equates to $6 per lead. Now suppose that three of these people actually buy something. That means that the conversion rate is 12 percent and the cost of acquiring those three customers is $50 per customer ($150/3 conversions). If each customer only spends $25 on the site, the company has a problem. Metrics matter; they will tell you the truth about how effective your marketing efforts are.

Social Media

Social media marketing is the direct result of the emergence of online communities and social networking sites like Facebook, LinkedIn, and Pinterest. Estimates suggest that today close to 2 billion people are registered on a social network. In fact, McKinsey & Co found that the rate of adoption for social technologies by consumers is faster than for any previous technology.[28] If we consider how long it takes to reach the 50 million mark for technology adopters, television took more than 15 years, the Internet took 3 years, but Facebook reached its 50 millionth user in just one year. On the business side, however, it's a different story. Businesses are just beginning to understand how to use these technologies to create value. Figure 14.4 depicts some of the ways that social technologies can benefit all areas of a business.

McKinsey & Co. found that across all types of industries, the companies that will most benefit from social media and the associated technologies have at least one of the following characteristics:[29]

- Knowledge workers comprise most of the company's employees.
- The company relies on its brand and how customers view the company.
- The company's primary goal is a great reputation and consumer trust.

Product Development

Gain customer insights and involve customers in the development of the product or service

Operations

Use social technologies to forecast, monitor progress and quality, and distribute results

Marketing and Sales

Gain customer insights, generate leads, promote, communicate with customers

Customer Service and Support

Provide ongoing customer care
Better match company's talent to the job

© Cengage Learning®

- The company distributes digital products or services.
- The company provides experiential or inspirational products and services.

From the above list, it is clear that consumer product companies have a lot to gain from adopting social media technologies.

Viral marketing and crowdsourcing are two social media marketing techniques that emerged as a direct result of the Internet's ability to replicate and distribute information quickly and efficiently. Its offline counterparts are the traditional "word-of-mouth" and "network marketing." Even though the term *viral marketing* has negative connotations, it is widely used to describe a marketing strategy that entices customers to pass on the marketing message to others. For example, Adobe, the successful software company, gives away its proprietary software that lets people share documents across multiple platforms in a form called PDF, which retains the original formatting and can't be manipulated. Adobe puts a link in the document that sends the person to the Adobe website to download the required Adobe Reader. That gives Adobe an opportunity to let the user know about its other software products available for sale. The strategy has been so successful that Adobe is now the de facto standard for sending corporate documents. Dell, the computer manufacturer, used crowdsourcing to improve its customer service reputation by developing user forums so that users could help each other as well as interact with Dell technical people.

Today, social media tools have taken the concept of viral marketing to a new level. See Table 14.4 for a summary of key social technology applications. Categories of social media applications include social networking sites like Facebook and YouTube, blogs, podcasts, RSS Readers, and wikis. Each has a specific purpose and each is more or less effective depending on what you

© Cengage Learning®

TABLE 14.4 Major Types of Social Media Applications

Social Media Application	What It Does
Media and file sharing	Upload, share, comment: photos, videos, audio
Social networks	Connect using personal business profiles
Blogs	Publish and comment: opinions and experiences
Ratings and reviews	Evaluating products, services and experiences
E-Commerce	Group purchasing and sharing experiences
Wikis	Search, create, edit articles as shared knowledge
Discussion forums	Open communities on specific topics
Shared workspace online	Collaboration on content for projects
Crowdsourcing	Source of collective knowledge for problem solving
Gaming	Play video games with others online

are attempting to promote and to whom. Here we provide a short summary of each of these categories.

- **Blogs, Twitter, email, and e-newsletters** are generally a way for you to communicate the expertise of your company or opinions on relevant issues of the day and to generate interest and excitement. In the case of blogs, the communication is typically bi-directional so that customers can respond or add to the discussion. Email opt-in subscriptions, such as newsletters, can be an effective way to keep the company's message in front of the customer. Giving customers the ability to receive a targeted message on their mobile device or place the message on their Facebook page or LinkedIn site, send a tweet, or forward the email to their network increases your company's reach dramatically and also increases your subscriber list.

- **Podcasts and vodcasts** are ways to bring the human element into communications with customers by adding voice and video. They are often used for "how to" information on new products or to provide advice. Podcasts, which can be either video or audio, can be downloaded from your company's site as well as from iTunes, where you can achieve a broader reach. YouTube has become a huge source of viral videos on the Internet. Entrepreneurs can use YouTube as a hosting platform to embed or link content to other sites, to build and support the company's brand by creating a profile or channel, and to create a group and invite others to join and participate.

- **RSS Readers (Really Simple Syndication)** provide a way to find out what others are saying about your company by enabling you to subscribe to blogs and podcasts. RSS is also used to add targeted news, blogs, or podcasts to your website, usually by using an RSS aggregator, a software that locates all the news of interest to you.

- **Wikis** are editable websites that enable multiple users to create content and then edit it. Typically they provide information, such as the most popular wiki, Wikipedia, does.

- **Facebook, Pinterest, and YouTube** are examples of social networking sites that are effective at reaching a broad market, particularly if the target demographic is young consumers who respond to new types of social advertising.

Although there is no single best way to craft a viral strategy using social media, most successful marketers incorporate the following:

- **Provide free products and services**. Good marketers know that "free" is the most powerful word in any language, and online marketers know that if they generate enough "eyeballs" through an effective viral marketing campaign, somewhere down the road, they will also achieve their desired level of revenues.

- **Make it easy to pass on the message**. There is nothing easier than clicking on a button and forwarding an email to someone. For example, online magazines and newspapers have made it easy to forward an article to someone by simply clicking on a button that brings up an email message into which the person's address is entered.

- **Make sure that your mail server can handle the traffic**. There is nothing worse than starting a viral campaign that ultimately annihilates its host. Viral marketing spreads a message extremely rapidly, so it is important to plan ahead for additional server capacity.

- **Take advantage of existing social networks**. Just as in the offline world, people online create networks of people and information that they tap into regularly. Placing an interesting message into one of those networks can accelerate its diffusion exponentially.

- **Use other people's websites.** Finding compatible websites and arranging to place a message on them works because the company is tapping into another network and increasing the scope of its own.

Social Media Metrics

For any business, if you're going to use social media to reach customers, you need to track your effectiveness. Fortunately, small businesses have a wealth of metrics available online. For example, one of the common metrics for social media effectiveness is the activity level of your followers. It serves to identify whether you or your company is an influencer; in other words, it's a measure of your authenticity. In a world where one million Twitter followers can be purchased for about $1,700, more and more customers are becoming skeptical when they see huge numbers associated with an individual or a company that a good share of those followers might be fake. And they ought to be skeptical. An app from Status Group can now diagnose the percentage of Twitter followers someone has that are fake and inactive and makes them publicly available.[30] For example, as of 2012, Twitter co-founder Jack Dorsey had over two million followers, of which 15 percent were fake and 45 percent were inactive. Dick Costolo, the CEO of Twitter, had just under a million followers, of which 24 percent were fake and 48 percent were inactive. The big winner was the president of the United States with over 18 million followers, 41 percent of which were fake and 35 percent inactive.

By contrast, Steve Farnsworth is a social media marketing expert who can claim over 115,000 active followers, 95 percent of which are authentic. He credits his success to tweeting out things that may start a conversation; he also attends real events and meets people that way —they eventually end up a follower. Relationships are not fostered online, even when they begin there. They actually develop offline and Twitter is an extension of that—a way to keep an interesting conversation going. He also advises that it's important to stay on point. If your business is related to import-export, for example, you shouldn't be tweeting about the latest TV show. It's important to focus.

Over time, those who use social media tools have developed ways to measure the effectiveness of those tools. In general, there are four major categories of metrics you should be aware of that work across all social platforms.[31]

1. **Conversation Rate**. This measures the number of conversations per post, so a reply to a tweet, or comment on a pin, post, or photo on Pinterest, Facebook, or Instagram. Conversation rate will help you understand where your users' interests lie and how they're relating to your brand.

2. **Amplification Rate**. Whenever your post is shared or retweeted, the conversation is being amplified. This is an important indication of whether or not your brand is growing. Recall that referrals are the best path to new customers. Amplification rate is a measure of that.

3. **Applause Rate**. All social platforms have easy ways for you to say "atta boy." Facebook uses "likes" and Google+ has pluses, while other sites use a thumbs up or down. This metric helps you understand the relative quality of various content you're putting out to customers.

4. **Economic Value**. This is the sum of your short- and long-term revenues and cost savings across all your media channels: email, display, search, and social. It's not easy to measure but it can be done using tools like Google Analytics or Omniture that will give you detailed feedback on all your social media activity.

Over time you will learn which tools will do the best job of helping you achieve whatever goals you have, whether you want to increase site traffic or improve customer engagement. Or if at startup you don't have time to manage all these numbers, you could sign up for a platform like TrueSocialMetrics that will pull all your social networks into one dashboard for you to analyze.

Search Engine Marketing

Search engine marketing (SEM) and search engine optimization (SEO) are simply tools for increasing the level of visibility of your website when customers search for your company online. Visibility is critical for businesses that sell products and services online or generate leads from their websites. Today, branding a company online means that you must be aware of your company's positioning in the Google search engine. Although there are a number of search engines available, when customers hear about a company, they immediately Google the name. Therefore, it is critical to have a website that conveys what you want the customer to learn about your company. Optimizing a site with appropriate keywords can help customers find a company much faster, but it is important to note that major search engines such as Google have very specific rules regarding how keywords are used. Failing to follow those rules could get a website "Google-sacked," which means that the site is not assigned a PageRank (used for parsing sites) and therefore simply disappears from a user's search. If you don't have the talent in house to do your SEO, you should get referrals for third-party optimization specialists because there are many such companies and some do not deliver what they promise.

A number of new terms have emerged out of keyword search marketing, and they represent ways to capture value for an advertiser and measure how effective that advertising is. They also serve as a means for you to create revenue streams on your site. Here are a few of them.

- *Conversion rate:* The number of customers who take a particular action such as register on the site, subscribe to a newsletter, download software, or purchase a product.
- *Cost-per-action:* A payment model where the advertiser pays based on some manner of conversion such as a sale or site registration. In this model, the entrepreneur, or publisher, is taking the risk because they receive a commission based on leads generated.
- *Cost-per-click:* The cost of a paid click-through.
- *Cost-per-impression:* Cost per 1,000 advertising impressions, with an impression being a single instance of an online advertisement being displayed. This form of advertising is not dependent on a click-through type of activity.
- *Pay per lead:* A model where payment is based on qualified leads.

Affiliate Programs

One way to increase the traffic on a website is to use affiliate programs, which are basically strategic partnerships with other companies that offer complementary products and services. Banner exchange programs are one example of an affiliate program. The banner company posts your banner on other compatible Internet sites. Costs may be associated with posting a banner, or it may be possible to negotiate a barter exchange if your company's website is compatible with the website on which you want to place a banner. Getting a banner on a website may be the easiest part of the challenge. Convincing people to click through and buy a product or service is quite another thing. There are many effective ways to attract customers to a website. These include assuring them that their private information will not be sold; giving them something free to entice them to discover more; offering them more, beyond the free information, that they will have to pay for; using electronic gift certificates as a way of getting customers to try products or services; providing a toll-free number for people who need to hear a human voice to overcome resistance; and offering to accept payment for items in as many ways as possible: credit cards, checks, debit cards, and so on.

Lobster Gram, the creation of Chicago-based Dan Zawacki, who sends out fresh lobsters through overnight mail services, relies on more than 2,000 affiliate sites that in 2006 generated about 6 percent of its online sales. To set up the program, Zawacki paid a onetime fee of $1,800 plus a 13 percent commission on every sale to affiliate marketer Commission Junction, which found and negotiated the appropriate affiliates for Lobster Gram. In addition to the affiliate program, Zawacki spent money on radio ads to drive customers directly to his site without going through an affiliate. However, because affiliate marketing works, many customers hit the affiliate's site first, which generated a commission for Commission Junction that Zawacki had to pay on top of his regular marketing costs. Nevertheless, according to Zawacki, his customer acquisition costs have actually gone down as a direct result of affiliate marketing.[32] Like everything else, it's important to get a recommendation from a satisfied user of an affiliate marketing program. Banner ads on affiliate sites should never be the primary source of advertising for any company; rather, they should be one tool in an arsenal of tools designed to create awareness and give customers a reason to think of the brand the next time they want to purchase something.

Content Strategy

One of the effective ways that entrepreneurs generate leads for their businesses is through a well-conceived content strategy that addresses the needs of customers at every stage of the buying process. Content tactics typically include research, eBooks, Webinars, white papers, and social media. Through an effective content strategy targeted to the various touch points with customers, you have an opportunity to secure a competitive advantage by addressing the needs of business customers at every stage of the buying process.

At the awareness stage, the goal is to capture attention and demonstrate that what is being offered meets the precise needs of the potential customer. Seeds of awareness can be planted in social media sites such as Facebook and YouTube or even by speaking at conferences or to targeted organizations. In the search stage, customers are seeking more information about your offering and other similar offerings from competitors. At this stage it's important that customers see a sufficient amount of informational and positive content around what is being offered so they will be incentivized to move to the evaluation stage. The evaluation stage is where the unique value proposition you have created by meeting specific customer needs should be apparent because the customer will be comparing your product with competitors. The ability to provide user testimonials, supporting research, and other relevant information through a variety of media will serve to strengthen your case. Offering something for free (a report, white paper, or video) or a limited time discount may be the incentive that gets the customer to decide to purchase. Once the purchase has been completed, maintaining contact and developing the customer relationship should be an important part of the ongoing content strategy.

Privacy Issues and Other Risks of Social Technologies

For all the benefits of social media, there are some serious risks that should not be ignored. The most obvious is that many of these technologies are addictive and you risk the fact that your employees may spend too much of their workday chatting online or posting negative attacks about other employees or the company. Moreover, social technologies tend to increase the chances that confidential information will be leaked and that disgruntled customers will take to the Internet, reaching a global audience with their complaints.

Although companies have collected consumer information for years and used it to target customers and sell more products and services, the advent of online commerce has made consumers more aware of privacy issues. When Jane Consumer goes online to investigate possibilities for her next vacation, she soon finds that she is inundated with advertisements for cruises, hotels, and anything else remotely related to her the trip she plans to take. This is the power of the Internet at work, as it magnifies anything done in the offline world. Amazon.com ran afoul of the Federal Trade Commission (FTC), which claimed that the company's practices were deceptive. Amazon did not make it clear to customers that it was selling their information to other companies. In fact, an FTC survey estimates that 97 percent of all e-commerce websites collect information that is personally identifiable. Therefore, companies must now do more to ensure that their customers' privacy is respected. Customer-focused companies inform their customers how the information collected will be used. The most successful companies maintain policies against selling customer information. Other firms seek seals of approval from online auditing companies such as TrustE and PricewaterhouseCoopers LLP, but these audits can cost up to tens of thousands of dollars. The best practice is to get a customer's permission before using his or her information for any purpose. Any effective marketing strategy, whether online or offline, should target the appropriate customers and address their specific needs, including their need for privacy.

One other area of potential risk comes from how social technologies are disrupting many business models, particularly in industries that have content intermediaries—journalism, entertainment, and music, to name a few. Social media platforms deliver the content direct to the public without the need to go through a producer, publisher, or other expert.

While there are risks to employing social technologies, they must be weighed against the benefit of developing better relationships with customers and getting valuable feedback to inform your product and service offerings.

14.4 PERSONAL SELLING

Traditional selling techniques don't always meet the needs of today's customers, who expect a quality product at a fair price with good service. Today, a business distinguishes itself in the marketplace by identifying and meeting specific customer needs. Therefore, even if you are selling a commodity, you need to figure out some way to add value to the product, and one way is through personal selling. A good example of a company that adds value to a commodity product is Danny O'Neill, who owns The Roasterie, a coffee roaster company in a very crowded market. He recognized that Africa is now the "in" place for growing high quality coffee beans. He buys his beans from small agricultural cooperatives and is helping the African farmers improve their production capability. "We get involved in the community; we have long-term relationships."[33] In this way he can distinguish his brand from others in the market and command a premium to serve the ever-increasing upscale coffee market.

Becoming a value-added company by tailoring products to meet customers' needs requires that everyone in the company become service-oriented, a time-consuming task that necessitates training and educating employees. It also demands an opportunity mindset, rather than a selling mindset. It is a lengthier process, but the returns are potentially greater. Working more closely with customers can translate into reduced selling and marketing costs.

14.4a   Improving Personal Selling Skills

Personal selling is an important talent that entrepreneurs should possess and continue to hone throughout their careers. To improve upon personal selling skills, you need to do some research before attempting to sell. It is important to learn what customers want from the sale and give them what they want. The following are some suggestions:

- The first meeting with the customer is typically designed to gather as much information as possible about the customer's needs and build credibility with the customer before trying to sell anything.

- Next, you must position your company as a solution provider in the mind of the customer, making sure to grab the customer's interest immediately. Whenever possible, the customer should be able to actually use the product in order to understand and appreciate it. During demonstrations and conversations, the entrepreneur should stand in front of the customer, not to the side, paying close attention to the customer's facial expressions as the benefits are being explained. The major benefits of the product or service should be explained to facilitate speedy decision making.

- If the customer declines the offer, you should maintain a sense of composure, then inquire why, and follow up by repeating the value the company is providing.

- As a final touch, you could invite the prospect to contact two existing customers and ask them about their experience working with you.

14.4b   Selling at Trade Shows and Exhibits

For entrepreneurs in many industries—electronics, industrial equipment, and gift items, for example—trade shows, fairs, and exhibits are a primary way to expose their products and do some personal selling. Attending trade shows is an effective way to find out who the competitors are and what marketing techniques they are using. A trade show is one of the best places to meet and negotiate with sales representatives and to gather contact information for a mailing list. But the primary reason to display products at a trade show is to eventually sell more products. To accomplish this, you should consider renting booth space and hiring a display designer to produce a quality display booth that will attract attention. Visiting several trade shows before setting up a booth will clarify what works and what doesn't. It may also be possible to work out a deal with a company that has compatible products to share a booth and combine resources. You should save the expensive brochures to hand out to potential customers who actually come to the booth and provide their business cards. It is important to have enough knowledgeable, personable people in the booth at all times so that potential customers are not kept waiting to talk with someone. Another good idea is to offer something free at the booth, such as a sample or a raffle. Finally, it is vital to follow up with anyone whose business card was collected and to call all serious prospects.

14.5 MANAGING CUSTOMER RELATIONSHIPS (CRM)

One of the most rapidly growing areas of marketing is customer relationship management, or CRM. Customer relationship management (CRM) is a combination of technology, training, and business strategy that results in a system for gathering and using information on current and prospective customers, with the goal of increasing profitability. This critical component of any successful marketing strategy has long been a mainstay of large corporations, but until only a few years ago it was too costly for smaller companies. Today, however, affordable database software with sample templates makes it easy to set up a CRM system in a relatively short period of time. A good CRM system can generate better sales leads, allow rapid responses to changing customer needs, and ensure that all employees who need customer information have it when they need it in the form they need. A well-constructed CRM system contains the names, addresses, and attributes of people who are likely to purchase what the company has to offer. It will help you define a trading area, reach new customers in the marketplace, select specific target audiences, and survey current customers.

CRM is not merely a way to reach customers by mail more easily. Today, retaining and maintaining current customers is more important than spending money to find new customers. It has been reported that 65 percent of a company's business comes from current customers. In fact, it costs five to ten times more to go after a new customer than to serve an existing one. Furthermore, with good customer profiles, you can match demographic information about current customers with demographic data in the geographic area of interest to find prospects more effectively. Information contained in the database can be used in advertising, sales promotion, public relations, direct mail, and personal selling.

One huge benefit to building relationships with customers is that if a problem occurs, a customer who has a relationship with the company won't automatically shift their loyalty to a competitor. Often their loyalty is actually *strengthened* when a problem-solving session with the company results in a satisfying conclusion. All too often, however, customers have had negative experiences with companies, where the problem has not been resolved satisfactorily. In those situations, the customer never forgets. Today, customers have a multitude of platforms from which to publicize their grievances, and one problem aired on national television or on YouTube or Facebook can cause a public relations nightmare from which the company may not recover. In 2007, Sara Russo, a huge fan of the Nutella spread, created a website dedicated to her passion. In fact, she created a World Nutella Day in honor of the popular hazelnut spread. The company, in what could only be described as a moment of insanity, sent her a cease and desist letter demanding that she take down the site. However, after complaints from customers, Nutella recanted, realizing the ridiculousness of shutting down positive free publicity. Perhaps the most important benefit of establishing lifelong customer relationships is that over time, the full value of customers is revealed. Customers are no longer viewed as a series of transactions but as bona fide, contributing members of the team who bring value to the bottom line. The more your company learns from its customers, the better it will become, and the more difficult it will be for a competitor to attract these customers.

14.5a   Identifying and Rewarding Lifetime Customer Value

It is not uncommon for a company to find that as few as 24 percent of its customers account for 95 percent of its revenues. Those 24 percent are the customers the company needs to know well and to keep happy, because these are the customers who will readily try new products and services and refer the company to others.

It is relatively easy to predict who will make a purchase and what that customer will buy. But for a company to grow, it needs those customers to talk about their experience with others who might then become new customers. In a world of new social technologies, it's easy for customers to have this conversation. What you must do is make sure that what they say will result in new customers. Calculating a customer's lifetime value to your company will entail estimating future purchases based on past purchases, adding in the value of referrals (again based on previous experience), and subtracting the cost of maintaining the relationship. But the reality is that most companies do not actually measure the real value of referrals. Instead, they measure the *willingness* of a customer to make referrals as demonstrated by checking the box in a post-sale survey indicating that they would likely tell others about the company. One large study of about 17,000 customers found that although the intention to recommend was very high, the percentage that actually did recommend the company to others was only about 32 percent. Among the recommenders, only about 13 percent of their recommendations converted to customers, and only a very small percentage of these customers were profitable for the company.[34] You might believe that customers who purchase the most will also be the ones with the most referrals, but, in fact, that is not always the case. A high CLV does not necessarily predict a customer's lifetime referral value (CRV). And, as the authors of the study note, CRV is not a relevant metric in every type of business. For example, where you might be able to entice consumers to respond to incentives to bring referrals to your company, it's not likely that would happen in a B2B situation where the companies compete with each other. Customers also refrain from making referrals if they're not emotionally invested in the product.

14.5b   Complaint Marketing

A dissatisfied customer will probably tell at least nine other people about the problem he or she faced with your company. (And those nine people will tell their friends as well!) It's easy to see how quickly even one unhappy customer can damage a company's reputation. Consequently, complaints should be viewed as opportunities for continual improvement. Making it easy for a customer to register a complaint and carry on a dialogue with a human being who listens and attempts to understand is an important way to learn from the customer. Nothing is more frustrating than to have to leave a complaint on a voice mail message. Some companies have used bulletin board type services on the Internet to let customers communicate complaints, but this method, though effective, attracts more complaints than any other method. Companies using these methods have found, in fact, that this system works almost too well, because customers feel free to vent their frustrations more angrily online than when they are hearing a soothing, caring voice at the other end of a phone line. Moreover, because anyone with access to the Internet can read the angry messages, a strong complaint can build momentum and create more problems than necessary.

One way to stem complaints at the source is to provide satisfaction surveys at every point of contact with the customer so that problems can be coped with quickly, at the outset, before the customer becomes so angry that resolution and satisfaction are nearly impossible. Effective handling of complaints can be accomplished by understanding that the customer is a human being and should be treated as such—never as a number or as someone without a name or feelings. A customer should be allowed to explain a complaint completely, without interruption. Extending this courtesy acknowledges that the complaint is important and worthy of attention. Customers should always be asked this question: "What is one thing we can do to make this better?" A customer's anger should be defused by sincerely taking his or her side on the issue; then the customer should be moved from a problem focus to a solution focus. Finally, the customer should be contacted one week after the complaint to find out whether he or she is still satisfied with the solution and to express the company's desire for a continued relationship.

The most important message that can be sent to customers through a company's marketing effort is that the customer is the most important part of the organization and the company will do whatever it takes to keep good customers satisfied. While it's certainly true that a young, growing company needs to build a customer base by continually adding new customers, it will reap the greatest returns from investing in the customers it currently has.

New Venture Action Plan

- Determine your business's compelling story.
- Analyze your marketing options and rank them.
- Write a clear, concise, one-paragraph statement of the marketing plan.
- Develop an advertising, publicity, and promotion strategy incorporating social media.

Questions on Key Issues

1. What are the differences between an entrepreneurial marketing strategy and a large corporation's marketing strategy?
2. Is it important to stick with your marketing plan even if it isn't returning immediate results? Why or why not?
3. What role should social media play in your marketing strategy?
4. What are the critical factors that should be considered in building a brand?
5. How can personal selling be used to build long-term customer relationships?

Experiencing Entrepreneurship

1. Compare and contrast the marketing strategies of two companies in the same industry in terms of the points in the marketing plan on page 321.
2. Find an Internet company that interests you. Contact the entrepreneur or the person in charge of implementing their marketing strategy to discuss their plan for building a brand. Are they undertaking any of the strategies or tactics discussed in this chapter? What is working and what is not? Present your findings in a brief PowerPoint presentation.

Relevant Case Studies

Case 4 Command Audio

Case 7 HomeRun.com

CHAPTER 15

Incorporating Ethics and Social Responsibility into the Business

"Ethics is knowing the difference between what you have a right to do and what is right to do."

—POTTER STEWART, U.S. SUPREME COURT JUSTICE, 1915–1985

CHAPTER OBJECTIVES

- Explain the role of ethics in entrepreneurship.

- List the types of ethical situations entrepreneurs may face.

- Discuss how entrepreneurs can demonstrate social responsibility.

- Describe how an entrepreneur's vision and values contribute to the culture of the new venture.

- Discuss the relationship of core values to success.

PROFILE
15.1

BUILDING HEARSAY SOCIAL ON CORE VALUES

You can be socially responsible as a business and still have a for-profit business model. At least that is the perspective of Clara Shih, co-founder and CEO of San Francisco–based Hearsay Social, a social media platform. Founded in 2009, the company provides social media tools to insurance companies and banks so they can reach and interact with their customers at a local level. Shih and her partner Steve Garrity met while students in the Computer Science Department at Stanford where they developed a strong working relationship and friendship. Shih went on to gain experience in web applications at Google and then Salesforce while Garrity honed his mobile, cloud, and enterprise capabilities at Fortify Software and then Microsoft. In 2007, Clara created a Facebook app that, to her surprise, went viral and led to her identifying an opportunity to help businesses drive sales and loyalty in the social media environment. She texted Garrity to see if he would join her and the concept for Hearsay Social was born.

Shih is the first to tell you that although they have raised over $51 million in venture funding from Sequoia Capital, NEA (New Enterprise Associates), and from executives at Facebook, Twitter, LinkedIn, and Google, they are resource constrained compared to the much larger companies with which they compete, so they have to move quickly and stay lean. From the very beginning, Shih was determined that the business would be designed around three core values or principles: (1) the customer is first, (2) company before self, and (3) rapid execution. It was those values that guided the development of her team, which includes an eclectic group of 110, including former insurance agents and government officials, a medical doctor, and a former employee of an Egyptian cruise line. Shih believes that her company has found a good balance among values, a great culture, and a viable business model. That isn't always the case with some startups where the business model overshadows the company culture (the culture becomes toxic or nonexistent) and others where the culture is dominant but there's no way to make money.

Hearsay Social can now claim customers like Raymond James, Mutual of Omaha, the Penn Mutual Life Insurance Company, and more recently RBC Wealth Management. In 2014, the company partnered with LinkedIn Corporation to facilitate the social media management of compliance for financial services firms. For example, whenever a banker wants to change his or her profile on LinkedIn or communicate on behalf of the bank to customers, it has to meet stringent regulatory requirements. The new platform makes it easy to stay compliant while still connecting with customers, prospects, and peers.

Shih believes strongly that "You can run a very successful business through a lens of humanity and strong values." So far, she has been absolutely right about that.

Sources: Sheridan, K. (February 13, 2014). "Hearsay Social and LinkedIn Introduce Social Business Platform," *Insurance & Technology*, http://www.insurancetech .com/management-strategies/hearsay-social-and-linkedin -introduce-so/240166120; Hearsaysocial.com, accessed July 14, 2014; Hunnicutt, T. (February 14, 2014). "Hearsay Social Adds RBC to Its Client List," *Investment News*, http://www .investmentnews.com/article/20140214/FREE/140219928

In a dynamic, global marketplace that places a premium on speed and quick returns, shareholder value is often considered more important than basic human values. The pressure to achieve unattainable goals and sustain a business in such a chaotic environment causes stress, and when people suffer stress, they don't always make wise decisions. Moreover, given that we do business in a global economy easily navigated via the Internet, businesses are regularly colliding with cultures that may define morality in terms of very different contexts, values, and codes of ethics. Yet we expect our employees to navigate this environment through the lens of the company's ethics. Most entrepreneurs, executives, and employees are not inherently unethical; however, they are often placed in situations that ignore or even reward unethical behavior. In a 2011 article in the *Harvard Business Review*, Max Bazerman and Ann Tenbrunsel pointed to the some of the things we regularly do in business that actually encourage unethical behavior. They are summarized here:[1]

- We set goals and incentivize employees based on those goals, but this often encourages bad behavior. For example, in law firms where employees are rewarded based on achieving a certain number of billable hours, employees may pad their numbers when under stress to meet their required hours.

- We pretend there is no unethical behavior if it serves our interests. For example, you might ignore the fact that your employee bribed an official to speed things up if it meant your project would finish on time.

- We don't see unethical behavior if it comes on gradually. For example, you are less likely to question unethical behavior if you have overlooked small violations of the rules along the way.

- We tend to ignore unethical behavior when the outcome is positive. For example, if no one dies or sues the company over shoddy workmanship in its products, the company will likely think that its actions were ethical.

Yes, it's a challenging environment, but those entrepreneurs who understand their value systems and create a code of ethics for their businesses can successfully maneuver through these challenges without forsaking their principles.

This chapter looks at three key issues for entrepreneurial companies, issues that will become increasingly important as companies interact more frequently in the global marketplace: ethics, social responsibility, and values. The chapter closes with a discussion of the components of success and how to make sure that your company's success is aligned with its vision and values.

15.1 ETHICS

Ethics, or the moral code by which we live and conduct business—essentially the concept of right and wrong—derives from the cultural, social, political, and ethnic norms with which we were raised as children. People don't often pause to reflect on their value system; instead, they merely act instinctively on the basis of it. It's only when they are faced with a dilemma that raises obvious moral or ethical issues that they may consciously ask themselves what is the correct thing to do. Many people believe that if they follow the Golden Rule, the

Judeo/Christian ethic that says "Do unto others as you would have them do unto you," they're safe from ethical dilemmas. Nothing could be further from the truth. Most ethical dilemmas do not come packaged in huge scandals like Enron or the more recent McKinsey consulting firm scandal where in 2010, a managing director pleaded guilty to insider trading and supplying corporate secrets to the founder of a hedge fund in return for cash.[2] In reality, most ethical issues are not criminal acts but rather small dilemmas that present themselves with great regularity every day. However, avoiding criminal acts does not equate to being ethical in business. Being ethical is about doing the right thing all the time—being proud of acting honorably.

Unfortunately, most ethical dilemmas in the business environment are subject to "gray areas" that are troubling when one attempts to apply an ethical principle. For example, one Oregon construction company hired a subcontractor to do a $15,000 concrete job. That particular subcontractor did not have solid bookkeeping practices and never submitted an invoice to the construction company for the work it did. The construction company could have kept quiet, but instead it sent the subcontractor a copy of the plans, specifications, and names of workers on the job, and told the subcontractor how much to bill it. The gray area here is the decision point—whether to notify the subcontractor of its failure to invoice. The construction company demonstrated its ethical values by contacting the subcontractor to ask for the invoice.

Another ethical decision had to be made by a marketing company that received two checks from a client for the same $50,000 project. There was no way the client would have easily discovered it, yet the marketing firm immediately sent the second check back. These kinds of ethical dilemmas occur every day in business. Although these two entrepreneurs did what they believed to be ethically correct, not everyone operates under the same standards of ethics. The employee who steals notepads, pens, and flash drives because "the employer won't miss them," the executive who abuses his or her expense account, and the business owner who evades taxes by not reporting employee income demonstrate their lack of clear ethical standards. This kind of behavior is accepted too widely and costs entrepreneurs both time and money.

Entrepreneurs face special problems when it comes to ethical issues. Their small companies generally are more informal and often lack systems and controls. They frequently don't have the time or resources to focus on ethics while they're struggling to keep their businesses alive, and they often take for granted that everyone in their organization and everyone with whom they do business shares their values. This is a mistake, because unethical behavior left undetected can contaminate a business for as long as it exists. Another very practical reason why small firms should pay attention to the ethics of employees concerns their ability to defend themselves against criminal action in a court of law. The U.S. Sentencing Commission's guidelines assert that a company needs an effective ethics program to protect it or lessen the impact of potential criminal penalties if an employee violates federal law.[3]

Recent research has identified four categories of ethical decision making that entrepreneurs face on a daily basis: (1) individual values, such as integrity and honesty, (2) organization values concerning employee well-being, (3) customer satisfaction, as reflected in the value provided to the customer, and (4) external accountability, or how the company relates to the community and the environment. The research further determined that in these four areas entrepreneurs do not differ in their ethical values from general societal norms.

The work of Paul Adler has determined that awareness is a critical first step in identifying and assessing an ethical dilemma.[4] There are four components of awareness. The first component is identifying the issues. You need to ask yourself if your conscience is bothered by the activity; does it violate any known laws or regulations; would you be OK if the activity were published on the front page of the newspaper? Does the activity harm anyone in some way? The second component of awareness is identifying the stakeholders affected by what you are proposing to do. Who exactly is affected by your action or inaction? Third, how will the stakeholders perceive the action or inaction? Do these parties have any rights or legitimate concerns? Finally, what options are available to you? Is there anyone from whom you can seek advice?

Once the analysis of awareness of an ethical issue is complete, you have to make a decision and that decision is affected by your perspective.

Most ethical dilemmas require balancing conflict among three perspectives: ideals (what ought to be true), obligations or duty, and utility or cost/benefit. This is no easy task; therefore, according to Alder, many people resort to avoiding ethical issues through one of four approaches, none of which is completely satisfactory:[5]

1. Dogmatism: "I simply will never lie or cheat or steal."
2. Egoism: "Everyone needs to look out for himself."
3. Relativism or situational: "When in Rome, do what the Romans do."
4. Subjectivism: "Ethics is simply a point of view."

Figure 15.1 depicts the relationship of these elements. When faced with an ethical dilemma, it's important to understand what's at stake. What are the issues that will need to be resolved? Who will be affected by the decisions you

FIGURE 15.1
The Elements of Ethical Action

© Cengage Learning®

make and what will the impact be? What options do you have to resolve this dilemma? In answering these questions, you will need to figure out if there is an ideal action that is possible, whether this situation involves an obligation, and whether a cost-benefit analysis is warranted. All of these considerations will be viewed through the lens of your view of ethics—typically, one of the four perspectives noted previously. Unfortunately, resolving ethical dilemmas is never simple. It takes courage to do the right thing. We will take an in-depth and pragmatic look at ethical dilemmas in business by considering the five most common types: conflicts of interest, survival tactics, responding to incentives, stakeholder pressure, and pushing the legal limit.

15.1a Conflicts of Interest

Conflict of interest is a universal problem in business today. A conflict of interest occurs when a person's private or personal interests clash with his or her professional obligations such that an independent observer might reasonably question whether the individual's professional actions or decisions are influenced by personal gain, financial or otherwise. For example, a company may want to continue an important manufacturing process that provides many jobs and profit, even when the community claims that this same process is not good for the environment. Entrepreneurs have vested interests in many areas of their lives: careers, business, family, community, and their financial investments, to name just a few. It is rare for all these interests to be in complete harmony with one another at any point in time.

Conflict of interest has also found its way into our dealings online. Today an online company can use its website to gather information about customers, profile them, and send the right message to the customer at the right moment. Through "cookie" technology, a company can track customers' movements online. Over time, a company will have compiled an enormous amount of data that it can use to better target its marketing messages. An ethical company that uses cookie technology will usually offer a notice of privacy to its customers, promising not to sell the information it gathers to other companies. Unfortunately, many Internet companies have gone back on their promises to protect customers' privacy in the interest of making easy money. In 2014, Facebook came under fire when an "emotional contagion" experiment it had conducted on 700,000 users without their knowledge was published in the *Proceedings of the National Academy of Sciences*. Co-authored by researchers at Cornell University and UC San Francisco, it confirmed what sociologists have been saying for decades—that people tend to behave like the people around them. So if your Facebook news feed is full of posts about something sad, you're not likely to post something upbeat and look like you're not in touch. Bioethicist Robert Klitzman asserts that although Facebook did not apparently break the law, because it does not receive federal funding for its research (which would make it subject to federal regulations regarding human subject research), what it did was unethical and a conflict of interest because its research partners are subject to the law and the journal in which the study was published also claims to follow the law.[6] Furthermore, Facebook's terms of use were not particularly clear that users could become part of its "scientific" research effort.

The healthcare community is not immune from conflict of interest issues. A recent study by the University of Michigan's Comprehensive Cancer Center found that a significant number of clinical cancer studies that have been published in highly regarded journals failed to disclose financial connections to major pharmaceutical companies, and that many of the results were biased to the benefit of big pharmas.[7]

As a business owner, you have an obligation to your customers to do what is best for them. Putting your own interests first is a costly strategy that will certainly negatively affect your brand.

15.1b   Survival Tactics

Many are the stories of entrepreneurs who did whatever it took to survive, even violating their own standards to do so. Survival is an area where most people's ethics really face a test. It's easy to be ethical when things are going your way, but what about the entrepreneur who is facing bankruptcy or can't make payroll? What does the entrepreneur's ethics look like at that point? Small firms, especially in the early years, are vulnerable to setbacks that would not significantly affect a large organization. The loss of a major customer or supplier could put a small business out of business pretty quickly. In these types of life-or-death situations, your commitment to ethical practices can force you to make some difficult decisions. Again, the importance of sticking to an ethical code is critical, because what you do today out of desperation will follow you for the rest of your business career.

15.1c   Responding to Incentives

Sometimes entrepreneurs inadvertently make it easy for their employees to participate in unethical behavior as the unintended consequence of badly designed incentives. One entrepreneur learned the hard way that you can't assume that everyone operates with the same value system and ethical code. This entrepreneur owns two successful bed and breakfast inns and, believing that she had reached the point where she could afford to cut back the time she spent managing them, she decided to rely on her general manager to run them while she took a two-year break to relax and travel; she even got married. She had the utmost confidence in her manager with whom she had been working for some time, but she continued to check with him while she was on her self-imposed sabbatical. About 18 months into her retreat, she began to learn of problems at the B&Bs from the head housekeeper—reports of dishonesty on the part of the front-desk people, paying employees in cash, and not keeping records of guests' stays. In the end, she did an audit and discovered, to her dismay, that she was losing about $50,000 a year to internal theft. After firing her general manager, she returned to the B&Bs full-time, only to discover that the losses were much higher than expected. Not only did she not have solid procedures in place, but she also didn't have an effective way to monitor what was going on. Her general manager had actually been teaching employees how to cheat the company.[8] It is important to have high ethical standards in business, but it is also important to put procedures in place that make it difficult for employees to act in an unethical manner. Having more than one person sign checks and making sure that each person matches the check to an invoice or purchase order is one way to put a lid on those who might take more than they deserve.

You should also keep in mind that what is considered ethical versus unethical behavior is perceived differently by Western and Eastern cultures and by people who work in the private sector versus the public sector. Today with more entrepreneurial ventures operating in a distributed fashion with team members located in various parts of the globe, understanding the value systems that will impact the company is important. In the West, we tend to describe ethical behavior in terms of appropriate behavior, moral standards, and compliance.[9] It is more transactional in nature. In Eastern culture, ethical leaders are viewed as being modest and open to others' ideas; they are humble and seek to follow their inner calling or purpose rather than material wealth. There are differences related to unethical behavior as well. For example, in many Eastern cultures, corruption and bribery are endemic and entrepreneurs face the ethical dilemma of playing the game so they can move their business forward or sticking to their ethical values and possibly losing out. In Western cultures, entrepreneurs consider discrimination to be a problem.[10] However, at their foundations, both cultures share basic moral values of honesty and integrity.

Survival is not an excuse for poor ethical decisions. If you do pull your business back from the brink, those unethical actions you used to do so will no doubt come back to bite.

15.1d   Stakeholder Pressure

One area of research has focused on what the business ought to do in terms of the "ends it pursues and the means it utilizes."[11] There are many stakeholders in a business, and they all want what is owed them when it's owed them. Stakeholders include any person or organization that has an interest in seeing the company succeed—investors, shareholders, suppliers, customers, and employees, to name a few. Every business, no matter how small, has stakeholders. For many entrepreneurs, there are times when managing the demands of stakeholders becomes a real juggling act. For example, to grow a company to the next level, you may decide that you will need to access the capital markets through an initial public offering to secure the money to fund that growth. Once that issue is raised, you will find lots of stakeholders pressuring you to move forward, even when you are not sure it's the best thing to do. These stakeholders include investment bankers who get a fee for doing the deal, business partners who may be able to cash out of some of their holdings in the company, and lawyers who want the additional business. All these stakeholders want to be served, but research has revealed that the most healthy outcome is realized when you hold to your code of ethics and base decisions on it, not on the personal agendas of stakeholders who may not have the best interests of your company at heart.

15.1e   Pushing the Legal Limit

Some entrepreneurs look for ways to bend the law as much as possible without actually breaking it. They proudly claim, "We're entrepreneurs; we're supposed to break the rules." Entrepreneurs who regularly play too close to the edge of legality eventually get caught, and the price is high—often their businesses and their reputations. Ethical entrepreneurs don't play those games, but they're always on the alert for companies that might use quasi-legal practices against them to gain an edge in the market. These types of tactics must be dealt with decisively. For example, a large water-meter repair company that operated within the law was attacked by a competitor in collusion with a newspaper reporter. The competitor accused the repair company of bribing public officials. It was a false accusation, clearly unethical, but perhaps not illegal. It caused the innocent utility company a great many problems and cost it a lot of money defending itself, but the company had no choice because its reputation was at stake. Your reputation and that of your business must be protected at all costs, because without it, chances are there will be no business.

15.1f   Learning from Real-Life Dilemmas

There is no better way to understand the role of ethics in any business than to encounter real-world dilemmas and to think about how you might deal with them. Here are some examples of real-life ethical dilemmas. What would you do?

1. A struggling Internet company is not producing revenues at the rate originally projected. At the same time, the burn rate (the rate at which cash is spent) is increasing as the company continually seeks new customers. The website claims to protect the privacy of visitors who purchase its products and services, and this is something the company takes pride in. However, the entrepreneur is concerned that if she doesn't find a quick source of income, the company may not survive. The entrepreneur learns that she can sell customer information lists to companies that will pay a lot of money for them. She has also heard that if she starts tracking which websites her customers visit, she can sell that information to major advertising firms for use in targeted advertising, another source of revenue. These tactics will violate customers' privacy, but if she doesn't do something quickly, she may have no business to offer them. What should she do?

2. Duncan is an analyst at a major consulting firm that serves Wall Street investment banks. While working late one night, he realizes that he needs some transaction data that he had sent to Eva earlier in the day. Duncan had accidentally seen what appeared to be Eva's computer password written on a tablet on her desk. He decides to log into her computer to retrieve the data he needs. While in the computer, he notices an open email to one of Eva's friends detailing the top secret transaction that Duncan is working on. He realizes that the person receiving this information can act on it and potentially make a lot of money. Duncan finds himself between a rock and a hard

place. He should report this violation of confidentiality but then he would have to reveal that he had logged into Eva's computer without permission. What should he do?

3. An employee confides to the CEO that another employee is planning to leave the company in two months to start her own company as a competitor. Armed with this knowledge, the CEO is tempted to fire this employee immediately, but she is in the middle of a major project that is critical to the company, and it will be completed within two weeks. What should the CEO do?

4. A retail company has hired a design firm as an independent contractor to design and build an e-commerce website. It paid a large portion of the fee, $25,000, up front to begin the work. The owner of the design company assures the customer that the work is on schedule to be completed on time; but as of a week before the due date, the client has yet to see any designs. A meeting is scheduled at the design office to check on the status of the project. While waiting at the office, the customer overhears employees talking about the impending closure of the design business. She also hears that the programmer assigned to her project has not been paid and there is no money to pay him. The owner of the design firm says nothing about this during the meeting and instead assures his client that the project will be completed as planned. The client suspects that the owner is not being truthful and worries that if the business closes and she has not received the designs and software for the project, her company will be out $25,000 and will have to file a lawsuit. Should the client talk to the programmer and reveal what she has heard? Should she confront the owner? Should she approach the disgruntled employees to find a way to gather the data she needs to win a lawsuit?

5. A company is about to begin doing business in another country where it is well known that paying cash to officials makes business transactions move more quickly. The entrepreneur knows that paying bribes is illegal in the United States, the home base for the business, but this contract will ensure that the company establishes a foothold in the global market before its competitors do. What should the entrepreneur do?

Small businesses are as guilty as multinational corporations when it comes to ethical missteps. Paying personal expenses out of business funds and writing them off, not reporting all cash receipts, cheating customers on price, using misleading advertising, failing to pay bills on time, and lying to customers, employees, and suppliers are all examples of poor ethics. Aristotle, the Greek philosopher, said that courage is the first of the human virtues because without it, the others are not possible. How we make these difficult and courageous choices is the subject of the next section.

15.1g   The Importance of Developing a Code of Ethics

Most of the research on ethics has been conducted in large organizations, so we have very little information about ethics in small businesses. Some studies have suggested that entrepreneurs are subject to compulsive behavior such as the need to be right and the need for an instant response. This tendency to make decisions under circumstances where there is little time for reflection and no one to advise can lead to ethical problems. However, we caution that it is simply impossible to stereotype entrepreneurs when it comes to decision making in ethical dilemmas.

GLOBAL INSIGHTS

Think Small to Grow Big in Istanbul

In 2003, Bulent Celebi had just left his Silicon Valley CEO position with Ubicom, a microprocessor company. He had dreams of starting a global business in his native Turkey, but with a twist—it would operate like an American company. The company, AirTies, would manufacture wireless routers in Asia using American chips and sell into developing countries where broadband was still emerging. The big problem he was able to solve was enabling wireless signals through the typically Turkish concrete floors and walls. Celebi figured that in Istanbul he could bootstrap the operation and take advantage of the many new incentives being offered by the Turkish government as a component of its bid to become part of the European Union. For example, his company did not have to pay corporate income tax for 10 years because it developed a product inside one of the many "technoparks" set up by the Turkish government as economic zones. However, there were some negatives to Celebi's plan. Turkey is still trying to overcome problems with bribery and corruption, and it suffers from oppressive regulations that make it difficult to launch a business there. Celebi deals with the red tape, but he refuses to pay bribes, so things sometimes take longer. For example, at one point he had $400,000 worth of inventory that remained in customs for six months because he didn't bribe the officials. Nevertheless, for AirTies, Istanbul was ideally located to sell into Europe, Africa, and the Middle East, so with $300,000 that he raised from Silicon Valley investors, Celebi and his family made the decision to change their life and settle in Istanbul. Immediately he began laying the groundwork for an American-style culture in his company; he encouraged his employees to take initiative and to set their own goals and deadlines, and he hired as many Turkish citizens who had been educated in the United States as possible. However, when he and his employees went outside the office, they did business Turkish style, which was actually an advantage because most U.S. companies in his industry had very poor customer service, especially when dealing in the Balkans and the Middle East. Celebi decided to add great customer service to his competitive advantage, becoming the dominant company in the wireless router market in that part of the world.

Sources: Bayrasli, E. (2012). "Entrepreneurs Save the World," World Policy Institute, http://www.airties.com/_press/Press_20120613152727.pdf; AirTies, Rated in Top Four Fastest Growing Communications and Networking Vendors in Deloitte Technology Fast 500 EMEA," (December 9, 2009), IT Backbones Innovation News, www.itbinnovation.com/pr/34476; AirTies, www.airties.com; and S. Clifford, "Fully Committed," *Inc.* Magazine (April 2007).

The ethical behavior of employees is very much influenced by the code of ethics of the company.[12] When a code of ethics is spelled out and written down, people in the organization take it more seriously, so it's important for you to develop a formal code. After all, the best way to handle ethical dilemmas is to have in place a mechanism for avoiding them to begin with.

The Process of Developing a Code of Ethics

The process of developing a code of ethics begins with a company's self-examination to identify values held by individuals and alert everyone to inconsistencies in how people deal with particular issues. For a new company, this means getting the founding team together to discuss how certain issues should be dealt with. For a larger company, forming a committee to oversee the process may be appropriate.

The Josephson Institute of Ethics has developed a list of ethical values that should be considered in any code of ethics,[13] and Table 15.1 presents a worksheet for employing these values to gauge how to respond in a particular ethical dilemma.

A code of ethics should also outline behaviors that would enable your business to display these characteristics. This can be accomplished by using a Kantian[14] approach and asking four questions about any ethical decision to be made:[15]

1. Will the actions taken result in the "greatest good for all parties involved"?
2. Will the actions respect the rights of all parties?
3. Are the actions just? Will anyone be hurt by the actions?
4. Would I be proud if my actions were announced in my local newspaper?

The last question, in particular, gets to the heart of how you determine what is ethical in any situation, and most people can immediately and intuitively answer it.

Characteristics of an Effective Code

The most effective code of ethics will have the following characteristics. The code and its associated policies will be clear and easy to understand. Details about special situations that need further explanation will be included (e.g., political factors in particular countries). In cases where employee judgment may be required, descriptions and examples will make it easier for the employee to make the decision.

You should make sure that all employees are aware of and understand the code as well as the values and culture of the company. The following are some guidelines for ensuring that the code of ethics is implemented and maintained over time.

1. You should model the behavior expected of others in your company. In some companies, the ethical behavior exhibited by managers and employees in tough situations can become legendary—a part of the company culture that people remember and speak about with pride over and over again.

TABLE 15.1   Character
Counts Inventory

Michael Josephson, President of the Josephson Institute for Ethics, believes that entrepreneurs should consider how they incorporate the six pillars of character in their business and in their relationships with employees and others. List what you do to display each trait in your business environment.

Trustworthiness: Loyalty, honesty, integrity
Example: I always do what I say I will do.

_____

_____

_____

Respect: Privacy, dignity, courtesy
Example: I am courteous to everyone I meet.

_____

_____

_____

Responsibility: Accountability, pursuit of excellence
Example: I do not blame others for my failures.

_____

_____

_____

Fairness: Impartiality, consistency, equity, due process, equality
Example: I consider all the relevant facts carefully before making judgments.

_____

_____

_____

Caring: Compassion, kindness, giving, consideration
Example: I forgive the mistakes of my employees and guide them to do better.

_____

_____

_____

Citizenship: Abiding by laws, community service, protection of the environment
Example: I give my employees time off from work to do service in the community.

_____

_____

_____

Source: Based on Character Counts! National Office, www.josephsoninstitute.org.

2. Employees should be educated about ethics through workshops that put employees in hypothetical situations. For example, "What would you do if you found out that your best customer was harassing your administrative assistant?"

3. You should demonstrate commitment to the ethics program by mentioning it on a regular basis and providing examples of appropriate behavior that employees display during the course of their work.

The code of ethics should be shared with customers so that they understand the company's commitment and are assured of its integrity. A clear channel for reporting and dealing with unethical behavior must exist, and there should be a means of rewarding ethical behavior through recognition, bonuses, raises, and so forth. There is no way to avoid the ethical problems that business brings. But developing a strong ethical code and enlisting the cooperation of everyone in the business will go a long way toward making those challenges easier to deal with.

AN ETHICAL DILEMMA

Superior Machine Works had developed a new type of generator that was environmentally friendly and could be controlled from a distance. Superior's research had determined that the market for the generator was quite large and had the potential to be very profitable. Superior was marketing two models: a small, lightweight version for people who would use it to power small tools, and a bigger, heavier version used generally as backup power for an office or home, in addition to supplying power for a variety of electrical tools. The smaller version retailed for $895, and the larger version sold for $1,500. The larger version had a patented noise reduction feature that significantly reduced the sound the machine produced. Studies on similar equipment had shown that over a long period of time, the noise level of the small machine could actually produce hearing loss in the user.

At the same time, Superior's main competitor was also developing a generator very much like Superior's small version, and that company was also aware of the noise problem and the potential for deafness over time. Still, it was going ahead with the product. Superior was faced with a real dilemma. If it didn't move quickly to get its smaller version to the market, it would lose its first-mover advantage to its competitor. At the same time, did Superior want to market a product that was known to cause deafness over time? If it marketed only the larger machine, it would quickly lose market share to its competitor's smaller, lighter machine. If Superior could not introduce a successful product quickly, it would have to lay off many of its workers. Considering the downward trend in its current sales, the company might fail if it didn't introduce its product quickly.

1. What options does Superior have and what are the consequences of each?
2. What should Superior do and why?

15.2 SOCIAL RESPONSIBILITY

Where business ethics is the foundation for good corporate governance, social responsibility is really the link between a company as an ethical entity and a socially responsible citizen.[16] Today it's not enough to have a successful business and make a profit. Many would argue that the business must hold itself to a higher standard of social responsibility by giving something back to the community or communities in which it does business and, through them, to society as a whole. Social responsibility is operating a business in a way that exceeds the ethical, legal, commercial, and public expectations that society has of the business. This means obeying the law, respecting the environment, and being mindful of the impact the business has on its stakeholders, the industry, and the community in general. The benefits to businesses that seek to become socially responsible are many. They include improved financial performance, reduced operating costs by cutting waste and inefficiencies, enhanced brand image and reputation, increased sales and customer loyalty, increased productivity and quality, increased ability to attract and retain employees, and reduced regulatory oversight.

All entrepreneurs should practice social responsibility when it comes to running their businesses; however, some entrepreneurs have chosen to make social responsibility the reason for their business's existence. Socially responsible entrepreneurs generally start their businesses with a social mission, and they are faced with different challenges as they seek the resources to fund and sustain their businesses.[17] Their rewards derive not only from profits but also from the social value they create by being change agents for the betterment of society. This has been called a triple bottom line strategy: people, planet, profit.

There are many types of social ventures serving a variety of purposes. For example, Fenugreen is solving the problem of lack of access to refrigeration causing spoilage of food. The company has created FreshPaper, which is a low-cost compostable paper that keeps produce fresh two to five times longer than current methods.[18] After graduating from high school, Maggie Doyne completed a trek through the Himalayas where she met hundreds of Nepalese orphans. Upon returning to New Jersey, she raised the money to build them a home and school that now serves 300 children.[19] The majority of social ventures are nonprofits that must seek their funding from philanthropists or grants. Jordan Kassalow, who is a practicing optometrist, founded VisionSpring to provide glasses to people in Asia, Latin America, and Africa. He also trains locals in how to sell the glasses, producing a new crop of entrepreneurs.[20]

Social entrepreneurs need to choose a mission that is achievable. Paul Brainerd founded The Brainerd Foundation, in Seattle, Washington, for the purpose of helping entrepreneurs "give back" strategically to protect the region's air, land, and water. He suggests that entrepreneurs follow two simple rules:

1. Don't wait until later in life to begin giving back. Start when the business is young and giving can become part of the culture.

2. Don't go for something huge. Start at the grassroots level, where help is needed the most.

Three types of ventures typically engage in social entrepreneurship.[21] For-profit ventures in the private sector can have a socially oriented purpose, such as Cooperative Home Care Associates (CHCA), which is a worker-owned co-operative in the Bronx. It provides opportunities for low-income, minority women to have jobs and get off government assistance. The second type is social entrepreneurship ventures in the nonprofit sector conceived with a so-cial purpose in mind and not constrained by the need to make and distribute a profit. The Brainerd Foundation and the Grameen Bank are two such ventures. The final type is social entrepreneurship ventures in the public sector, which includes governmental agencies such as the Small Business Administration and community organizations like the Castleford Community Learning Centre of West Yorkshire in the United Kingdom, which works with adults with learning disorders.[22]

15.2a   Effective Ways to Become Socially Responsible

You do not need to have a large, multimillion-dollar firm to begin to give something back to society. Even a very small company can have an impact on its community if it does a few things by way of preparation. First, you should set goals. What do you want to achieve with your social responsibility efforts? You should pick a single cause to focus on, rather than trying to support many dif-ferent causes, and consider partnering with a nonprofit organization to make a greater impact. The nonprofit contributes its expertise in the social issue, while your company contributes its expertise and the time of its employees to the nonprofit. Next, it is vital that everyone in your company be incentivized to get involved. There really is strength in numbers. Whether you choose the for-profit or the nonprofit route, you can create a successful social venture in a number of important ways:

■ *Target disadvantaged markets.* KickStart (www.kickstart.org) is an example of a nonprofit that is focused on lifting people out of poverty by developing products with local resources and creating businesses.

■ *Employ disadvantaged individuals.* Cooperative Home Care Associates, mentioned previously, creates jobs for low-income women to get them off public assistance.

■ *Procure products and supplies.* You can add a social component to the pur-chasing function of your business by purchasing from emerging economies and buying supplies and products that come from ethical and environmen-tally conscious sources.

■ *Create products or services that have social value.* MindWare focuses on toys, games, and other products that help develop children's brains by engaging, educating, and entertaining.

■ *Donate products, services, or revenues.* Any company can donate the products or services it produces. However, Laura Scher takes it one step further and donates a portion of all the revenues of her company, Working Assets—a provider of long-distance, credit card, and wireless services—to nonprofit organizations to encourage "ordinary people to become activists." Since her company was founded in 1985, its members (customers) have donated over $75 million to nonprofit groups.[23]

- *Donate expertise.* Room to Read (see the "Social Entrepreneurship" box) donated its expertise in raising funding and starting libraries to teach students in Sri Lanka how to raise funding to rebuild the schools lost in the tsunami of 2004. They raised more than $400,000 and inspired a new student-led initiative to provide Room to Read programs around the world.

- *Produce for social good.* Some entrepreneurs use production methods for a social purpose. For example, Green Mountain Energy Company provides clean electricity from wind, solar, water, and natural gas sources.

Whether you choose to start a dedicated social business or simply commit to being socially responsible in the for-profit business you are launching, it is clear that ethics and social responsibility should be key foundations for any successful business.

15.3   VISION AND VALUES

Every great company begins with the entrepreneur's vision of what that company will become. Just as top professional athletes envision every play of an upcoming game before they ever set foot on the playing field, so do entrepreneurs envision the kind of company they want to build. The company's "true north" acts like a beacon, guiding it and keeping it from straying when opportunities try to pull the company in a different direction. Although it is possible for a company to be successful without a vision, it is difficult, if not impossible, to become a *great* company without a vision. Researchers Jim Collins and Jerry Porras, authors of *Built to Last: Successful Habits of Visionary Companies* and *Good to Great*, back up this assertion.[24] These books are two of the most influential books in recent times. In their research, Collins and Porras found that the number-one company in every industry it studied outperformed its number-two competitor by a significant amount in terms of revenues, profits, and return on investment. The primary reason was that each number-one company had a strong vision comprised of core values that it regarded as inviolable. It has been more than 20 years since Collins and Porras identified their visionary businesses. It is interesting to note that while all are still in business, by 2004, nearly half of them had seen declines in both performance and reputation.[25] In most cases, it was because they had strayed from their core values.

Before delving deeper into the components of vision, consider Figure 15.2, which presents a broad view of the components of a complete vision and their relationship to each other. To review, the vision for your company stems from your core value system, which is the foundation for all the decisions you will make as your business grows. You then must identify your company's purpose, and you need a compelling mission that is congruent with your core values and goals or operating objectives, which are milestones along the way to achieving the mission. Finally, you will develop strategies to achieve the goals and choose tactics to execute those strategies.

15.3a Core Values

Core values are the fundamental beliefs that a company holds about what is important in business and in life in general. They are based on the personal values and beliefs of the founder or the founding team; therefore, they are not something that can be created or invented for the company out of thin air. A company's core values tell the world who it is and what it stands for. Because they are so fundamental to the existence of a company, core values rarely change over time, and they endure beyond the tenure of the founder. For example, Whole Foods Market's core values are:[26]

- We sell the highest quality natural and organic products available
- We satisfy, delight and nourish our customers
- We support team member excellence and happiness
- We create wealth through profits and growth
- We serve and support our local and global communities
- We practice and advance environmental stewardship.
- We create ongoing win-win partnerships with our suppliers
- We promote the health of our stakeholders through healthy eating education

One way to test whether a value (e.g., "The customer is always right") is a core value or not is to ask yourself whether you would ever relinquish that value if there were a penalty for holding it. If your company is willing to let go of the value, then it's not a core value.

15.3b Purpose

Purpose is your company's fundamental reason to be in business. It is the answer to the question "Why does the business exist?" It is not necessarily a unique characteristic of the business; in fact, more than one business may share the same purpose. What is crucial is that the purpose be authentic; that is, the company must mean what it says. "We are in the business of helping people" might be the purpose of a socially responsible business. Jordan NeuroScience, a company that provides patented brain nets to monitor a patient's brainwaves in the emergency room, is in the business of "saving brains." A properly conceived purpose will be broad, enduring, and inspiring, and it will allow the company to grow and diversify.

15.3c Mission

A company's mission is what brings everyone together to achieve a common objective and is closely related to the company's purpose. According to Collins and Porras, a mission is a "Big Hairy Audacious Goal" (BHAG), designed to stimulate progress. All companies have goals, but a mission, or BHAG, is a daunting challenge, an overriding objective that mobilizes everyone to achieve it. The natural metaphor for a mission is mountain climbing. The mission is *to scale Mt. Everest,* a major challenge to be sure. To get there, however, will require smaller goals, such as *reaching base camp in one week.* The smaller wins motivate the team to achieve the more bold and compelling mission.

A company's mission is communicated through a mission statement. A mission statement precisely identifies the environment in which the company operates and communicates the company's fundamental philosophy.[27] Management guru Peter Drucker always asserted that a company's mission should "fit on a t-shirt."[28] The best mission statements are simple, precise, and use clear words.

Here are three examples of mission statements:

Starbucks: "Our mission: to inspire and nurture the human spirit – one person, one cup and one neighborhood at a time." (Source: www.starbucks .com/about-us/company-information/mission-statement.)

Facebook: "Giving people the power to share and make the world more open and connected." (Source: www.facebook.com/facebook.)

Leader to Leader Institute: "To strengthen the leadership of the social sector." (Source: www.leadertoleader.org/about/index.html.)

The mission statement should convey what the company wants to be remembered for; therefore, in writing a mission statement, it is important to gather the thoughts of everyone in the organization. The initial drafts should be evaluated against a set of criteria and should explain why the organization exists, indicate what the company wants to be remembered for, and be sufficiently broad in its scope. It should not prescribe means but should provide direction for doing the right things. Finally, the mission statement should address your company's opportunities, match your company's competence, and inspire your company's commitment.

FIGURE 15.2
The Components of
Company Vision

© Cengage Learning®

15.3d Strategies and Tactics

Once goals have been set, strategies should be developed. These are the plans for achieving those goals and, ultimately, accomplishing the mission. Tactics, which are the means to execute the strategies, should also be put in place. An example will make these points clearer. Suppose your company's mission is to be number one in its market. Two goals or milestones you could set to help you accomplish the mission might be (1) to create an online presence and (2) to achieve brand recognition. Strategies for achieving these goals might include building a website that includes a social networking platform and e-commerce capability to meet goal 1 and developing a social media marketing campaign to build the brand, goal 2. Then you will need to choose a variety of tactics, or ways to implement the strategies. For example, to implement the strategy of building a website, you might determine the purpose and focus of the website, hire a Web designer and developer, purchase a server, and plan the content.

Merely setting a goal is not enough. A plan for achieving the goal must be in place, and that is the role of strategy. But even strategy is not enough to achieve a company's goals; tactics, or action plans, will also be required.

15.4 CORE VALUES AND SUCCESS

Why are we talking about success in a chapter on ethics and social responsibility? Because your personal definition of success—what it means to be successful—is really a function of the core values and vision that you have for your life. A business's success is easily measured in terms of total revenues, earnings, return on investment, and so forth, but you don't typically measure your personal success solely in these terms. In fact, research has shown that the personal rewards that motivate entrepreneurs to start businesses are independence and freedom.[29] Entrepreneurs tend to be goal-oriented, so being one's own boss, being in control of one's destiny, and having ultimate control of the success of the venture are reasons for going into business. They measure their personal success by their achievement of those goals.

15.4a Constants of Success

No matter how success is defined, there are four constants that seem to permeate everyone's definition. These constants are 1) your purpose, 2) failure, 3) a sense of satisfaction with what was accomplished, and 4) having to pay for, or earn, success.

- *Purpose.* To feel successful, you need to know that what you are doing is taking you in the direction of a meaningful goal you want to achieve. True success is a journey, not a destination—even the achievement of a goal will be just one step on the way to the achievement of yet another goal.

■ *Failure.* The second constant is that life has its ups and downs. Failure is the other half of success, and most entrepreneurs have experienced several failures of one sort or another along the way. Still, they typically do not fear failure, because they know intuitively that those who obsessively avoid failure are doomed to mediocrity. To avoid failing, you have to virtually retreat from life, to never try anything that has any risk attached to it. Most entrepreneurs are calculated risk-takers, so they make sure that every time they come up to bat they give it their best; then, win or lose, they strive to learn from the experience and go on. Entrepreneurs are generally optimists who believe that failure is a normal part of the entrepreneurial process.

■ *Sense of satisfaction with work.* The most successful entrepreneurs are doing what they love, so their satisfaction level is usually very high. Does satisfaction with the work result in success, or does success bring satisfaction? Probably a little of both, so it's important to know what kinds of tasks and activities will give you the most satisfaction in your business. If you enjoy developing new products, then hire someone who is more interested in running the day-to-day operations of the business so you will be doing the work that you want to do.

■ *No free lunch.* Success rarely comes without work. Entrepreneurs do not have the luxury of a nine-to-five workday; they are usually married to their businesses 24 hours a day, at least in the beginning. It is not just the number of hours of work that distinguishes entrepreneurs, of course, but also the way they use their time. Entrepreneurs make productive use of odd moments in their day—while they're driving, on hold on the telephone, in the shower, or walking to a meeting. Because they love what they're doing, it doesn't feel like work, and that's probably why, wherever entrepreneurs are, they're always working on their businesses in one way or another.

Firm core values and ethics plus a socially responsible business can lead to the kind of success that is meaningful to most entrepreneurs: satisfaction in creating something and seeing it thrive. Today, more than ever before, the world is watching the way entrepreneurs run their businesses, so it is more critical than ever to design a new business on the basis of sound values and ethical practices.

New Venture Action Plan

■ Identify the core values held by the founding team.

■ Develop an initial code of ethics for the business.

■ List possible ways your business can be socially responsible.

■ Define what success means to you.

Questions on Key Issues

1. Do you believe that your code of ethics should remain firm in any situation? Why or why not?
2. Suppose you are doing business in a country where paying fees (bribes) to get through the process more quickly is standard practice. In the United States, bribery is against the law. How will you deal with this conflict taking into account your ethical standards when you're doing business in that country?
3. In addition to the suggestions given in the chapter, name two ways your company can demonstrate its social responsibility.
4. Would you require your employees to give back to the community as part of their work contract with your company? Why or why not? If yes, how could you implement this policy?
5. How do you define your personal success? How can your definition be applied to your business?

Experiencing Entrepreneurship

1. Choose an industry that interests you and interview a manufacturer, a distributor, and a retailer about the code of ethics in that industry. In a two-page report, discuss whether the industry has ethical problems. If so, what are they and how are people responding? If not, how have they been avoided?
2. Choose two companies in different industries. Interview a manager in each company about how the company practices social responsibility. In a two-page paper, compare these managers' answers and account for any basic differences.

Relevant Case Studies

Case 6 Andrew Mason and Groupon, Inc.

Case 8 Vision to Learn

PART IV

PLANNING FOR GROWTH AND CHANGE

IPOs
Report
2013

Number of IPOs from 2009 to 2013

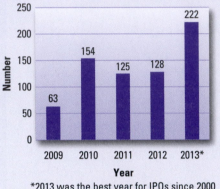

*2013 was the best year for IPOs since 2000

Funding from IPOs in 2013
$55B

81 VC-Backed Deals

Median deal Size	Proceeds Raised	Average U.S. IPO Return
$ 126.3M	$ 54.9 B	40.8%

CHAPTER 16

Funding Startup and Growth

"While money can't buy happiness, it certainly lets you choose your own form of misery."

—GROUCHO MARX

CHAPTER OBJECTIVES

- Understand the importance of a financial plan.
- Explain methods of funding with equity.
- Discuss how to finance with debt.
- Explore non-dilutive funding sources.
- Describe the valuation process for pre-revenue companies.
- Understand the IPO process.

PROFILE
16.1

REACHING $100 MILLION WITHOUT SPENDING YOUR VENTURE CAPITAL

Many entrepreneurs treat raising a round of funding as if it were equivalent to being in revenue. While it certainly is a measure of success and validation by investors, it does not mean that your business is actually *in business*. Christian Chabot would argue that starting and growing a business without venture capital is more motivating and satisfying. Chabot and his partners, Chris Stolte and Pat Hanrahan, founded Tableau in January 2003 out of the ruins of the dot-com bust. Chabot, who had studied entrepreneurship, spent two years as an associate at SoftBank Capital where he was able to see firsthand how startups responded to receiving venture capital and it often wasn't a pretty picture. Either the founders would blow through the money too fast or the (VCs) would exert too much control. Either way, Chabot believed there had to be a better approach.

Chris Stolte was a PhD candidate who was doing research on visualization techniques for analyzing relational databases and looking to solve a big problem and change the world. The big problem was giving anybody direct access to data in a way that they could understand it, analyze it, and apply it. His research advisor Pat Hanrahan, who had been a founding member of Pixar, the wildly successful animation studio, worked with Stolte to bring together computer graphics and databases with an invention called VizQL Chabot saw the promise of this invention from a business perspective and the three conceptualized a software company that would bring their ideas to life.

Choosing to bootstrap the startup was an easy decision. Naturally wary of investors, the two scientists agreed that bootstrapping the startup was the way to go. Each brought small amounts of money to the business and they worked for free. That meant they had to live fairly frugally. Chabot shrank his lifestyle, cutting out anything that wasn't essential. Stolte was a PhD student, so he was already in bootstrap mode, and Hanrahan, a tenured professor, by nature led a rather modest lifestyle.

One of the most critical insights they drew from their early experiences was that you need to start selling your product or service as soon as possible. Don't wait until it's perfect. The only way you will really learn if customers want what you have is to try to sell it—and that's what they did. They were honest with customers about the state of their product, offered them discounts to try it, and worked with them to gather more insights and make it better.

In the second year of bootstrapping, they hired their first employee, making sure they chose someone who bought into the mission of the company and the bootstrapped way of life. They wanted someone who wanted to work on something cool more than they wanted to earn a salary. "Our first employees reported to work in my bedroom, which was our first Seattle space. Our second Seattle space was my basement." By their third office space, they were in a low-rent office building. The focus was on raising customers, not money, and not investing in fancy work spaces.

Eventually the team did take a Series A round of $5 million in 2004 and later a $10 million Series B in 2008, but every dime they raised is sitting in the bank to protect the company from anything going wrong. In 2013, the company went public on the New York Stock Exchange, giving it a new status and a level of visibility that it hadn't previously experienced. With 24 percent of its revenues now being invested in R&D, the company is investing in the future and making a strong statement about R&D as a critical competitive advantage.

Sources: Tableau, www.tableau.com; Swallow, E. (December 27, 2012). "How One Startup Grew a $100M Business without Spending Venture Capital," *Forbes*. http://www.forbes.com/sites/ericaswallow/2012/12/27/bootstrapping-startup-venture-capital/; Tse, A. (February 12, 2014). "Tableau's Building the 'Google for Data,'" *The Street*, http://www.thestreet.com/story/12330709/1/tableau-builds-google-for-data-ceo-exclusive.html

"How can I fund my new business?" Probably no question is more on the minds of first-time entrepreneurs with new venture ideas; and it's no wonder when they hear about huge transactions like Facebook's acquisition of WhatsApp for $19 billion in February 2014, or Amazon's acquisition of online shoe company Zappos.com for $928 million. Money seems to be the topic that always draws a crowd, whether it's for a university course on venture capital investment or a conference hosted by venture capitalists talking about their deals. Budding entrepreneurs suppose that if they have enough money they can make any business concept a success. Unfortunately, that reasoning is faulty. In fact, throwing money at a bad idea won't change it into a good idea; it just delays the inevitable failure. Putting a lot of money into the hands of an inept team is essentially throwing it away. Moreover, a team that has more money than it needs often makes poor decisions because there's plenty of money to pay for mistakes. The truth is that it is much more challenging (and rewarding) to figure out how to launch without outside capital than it is to raise money. However, while we would argue that finding the right problem to solve and making sure there are customers who will buy should be the principal concern of entrepreneurs in the earliest stages, it is a fact that one of the contributing factors to new venture failure is lack of adequate capital to sustain the startup until it secures sufficient revenue.[1]

In addition to placing too much value on money as a critical success factor, inexperienced entrepreneurs typically identify venture capital as their first and primary source of funding at startup, but this mistake springs from a misconception about the needs of startup ventures, the requirements of venture capitalists (VCs), and the nature of financial markets. It is a fact that VCs typically seek startups with protectable concepts (the secret sauce) and a huge potential for growth.[2] Recent research has shown that of the top funding sources that entrepreneurs tap, by far the biggest are personal savings and credit, and friends and family money. Figure 16.1 displays how the funding pie is typically divided.

The reality is that money is only one of the resources needed to start a successful business, and it may not even be the most important resource at startup. Moreover, you don't want to make the mistake of seeking investment capital when you're not really ready to do so. Before beginning the hunt for capital, ask yourself the following questions:

- Can I take time away from the business to spend it on fund raising?
- Is your business on a firm footing through its own resources? Yes, you can grow faster with investor capital, but have you gotten your business to the point where it's about to take off?

FIGURE 16.1

Funding Sources for
Entrepreneurs

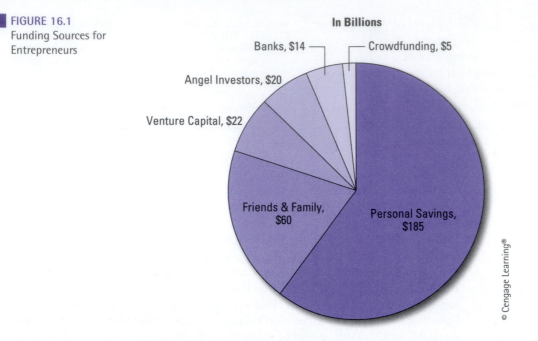

In Billions

Banks, $14 — ⌐ Crowdfunding, $5

Angel Investors, $20

Venture Capital, $22

Friends & Family,
$60

Personal Savings,
$185

© Cengage Learning®

Sources: Center for Venture Research, US Small Business Administration, Angel Resource Institute, Angel Capital
Education Foundation, Fundable, and Empact.

- What have you accomplished on your own? What have you invested in the business in terms of money, time, and resources?

- Do you have a validated business model—one that you tested in the market with real customers?

- Do you have a financial plan for growth? Do you understand the milestones you will need to hit and how much funding will be required to get you there?

- Have you put together a compelling story that investors will buy?

Securing funding for a new venture is a time-consuming and difficult process made more challenging by the issue of information asymmetry; that is, entrepreneurs have more information about themselves and their ventures than do the people from whom they seek resources.[3] In other words, the value proposition may be very clear to the entrepreneur but if it can't successfully be conveyed to a potential investor, supplier, customer, or partner, that value is lost. How do you improve your chances of securing required resources from sources available at startup? Research points to the importance of your social network and reputation in increasing the chances of securing funding. But that is only the beginning. This chapter will discuss the financial resources that startups require and strategies for securing the right resources from the right sources at the appropriate time. Not all of the sources and strategies discussed in this chapter will be suitable for every business, but it's important that you understand a variety of options so you can make wiser choices.

16.1 THE FINANCIAL PLAN

Knowing whom to tap for startup capital is only half the battle. The other half is having a strategic plan for funding the startup and growth of your company with the right kind of money from the right sources at the right milestones. You should raise only what is actually needed, not whatever is possible in the prevailing economic environment. At the same time, planning carefully will avoid the need to seek financing too often, which can be costly both in time and money. It is important at the outset to approach the search for money armed with accurate information. The fact is that for startup companies in the earliest stages, relatively few investment sources exist outside of the three Fs: friends, family, and fools. For this reason, you need a plan, and the following sections review three important considerations in developing that plan.

16.1a The Cost and Process of Raising Capital

Make no mistake about it, raising capital of any type is a time-consuming and costly process. For this reason, many entrepreneurs choose to grow slowly instead, depending exclusively on internal cash flows to fund growth (See Profile 16.1 for an example). They have a basic fear of debt and of giving up to investors any control of equity in the company. Unfortunately, sometimes they may act so conservatively that they actually stifle any potential growth. You must understand the process of raising money so that your expectations will not be unreasonable. The first thing to understand about raising capital is that it will invariably take at least twice as long as expected before the money is actually in your company's bank account. Consider the task of raising a substantial amount of money—$500,000, for instance. It can take several months to find the financing, several more months for the potential investor or lender to do "due diligence" and say yes, and then up to six more months to receive the money. In other words, if you don't look for funding until it's needed, it will be too late. Moreover, because this search for capital takes you away from your business just when you're needed most, it is helpful to use financial advisers who have experience in raising money, and it is vital to have a good management team in place. The second thing to understand about raising capital is that your chosen funding source may not materialize, even after months of courting and negotiations. It's essential, therefore, to continue to look for backup investors in case the original investor backs out.

16.1b It Takes Money to Make Money

It is a fact of life that it takes money to make money. The costs incurred before investor or bank money is received must be paid by the entrepreneur, whereas the costs of maintaining the capital (accounting and legal expenses) can often be paid from the proceeds of the loan or (in the case of investment capital) from the proceeds of a sale or internally generated cash flow. If you have kept your business plan and financial statements up to date since the start of the business, a lot of money can be saved during the search for growth capital, which can be quite expensive. When large amounts of capital are sought, however, growth capital funding sources prefer that financials have the approval of a financial consultant or investment banker, someone who regularly works with investors. This person is an expert in preparing loan and investment packages that are attractive to potential funding sources. A CPA (Certified Public Accountant) will prepare the business's financial statements and work closely with the financial consultant. All these activities result in costs to your company. In addition, when you seek equity capital, you will need a prospectus or offering document, and preparing that calls for legal expertise and often significant printing costs. Then there are the expenses of marketing the offering; such things as advertising, travel, and brochures can become quite costly.

In addition to the up-front costs of seeking growth capital, there are "back-end" costs when you seek capital by selling securities (shares of stock in the corporation). These costs can include investment banking fees, legal fees, marketing costs, brokerage fees, and various other fees charged by state and federal authorities. The cost of raising equity capital can go as high as 25 percent of the total amount of money sought. Add to that the interest or return on investment paid to the funding source(s), and it's easy to see why it costs money to raise money.

16.1c   Growth Stage Identification

The starting point for planning for funding is identifying the stages of growth that your business will experience. Every business is different, but in general, each will reach certain milestones that suggest the time has come to grow to the next level and that will require an infusion of capital. Figure 16.2 indicates the typical funding stages. In the first stage, where the business model is being developed and tested with the first customers, seed funding is usually needed. This type of funding will normally come from the founders and other sources of "friendly money." In general, these "investors" are individuals who believe in you and want to support the earliest stages of startup.

By the second stage, transition, your business is requiring capital to grow on the basis of a proven business model. In fact, customer demand may require that your company grow, but internal cash flows at the time may not be sufficient to fund that growth. You may require outside capital from a private investor, early-stage venture capitalist (VC), or debt source. Taking on formal investment capital means that you must also plan for some type of liquidity event so that investors can cash out of the business and receive a return on their investment at some defined point in the future. That liquidity event may be in the form of an initial public offering (IPO) or an acquisition. The second stage offers more types of capital to access than at startup because your venture has survived and appears to be growing.

If your new venture has been successful moving through the first two stages, it is likely that it will begin to experience rapid growth that calls for larger sums of capital and perhaps a different type of money, termed *mezzanine financing*

FIGURE 16.2
Funding Stages and Risk

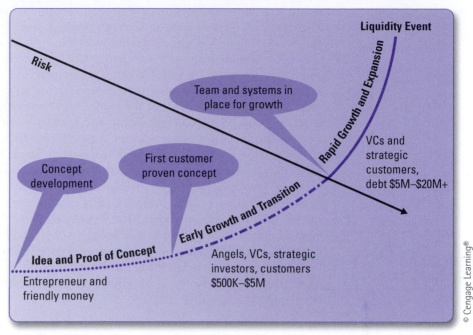

© Cengage Learning®

or *bridge financing,* to provide you with the funds required to get through an initial public offering. This phase of rapid growth can come relatively early in a startup's life cycle or very late depending on the type of business and the industry in which your company operates. For some businesses, particularly lifestyle businesses, rapid growth may never be part of their evolution. They may instead enjoy slow, steady, organic growth. If your business thrives over the long term, it will probably reach a relatively mature phase in which it ideally maintains a stable revenue stream with a loyal customer base. In today's dynamic environment, however, stability is rarely an enduring state. To continue to be profitable, a mature business must punctuate its equilibrium with new products and services and new markets so that it can remain competitive.

What is clear from this discussion is that there are different types of money for different stages of your venture. In general, each milestone your business achieves creates more value for the company and enables you to seek greater amounts of capital in the form of equity or debt.

16.1d   The Unique Funding Issues of High-Tech Ventures

High-tech ventures that introduce breakthrough or disruptive technologies, such as a new drug, device, or process that changes the way we do things, tend to follow a pattern discussed in the works of Geoffrey Moore.[4] Recall that the adoption/diffusion curve was discussed at length in Chapter 14. In technology ventures, early seed funding and grants support a long period of product development. Often this early-stage money comes from government grants or foundations. It is a rare venture capital firm that will invest during the earliest product development phase of a high-tech venture because the risk is too high. The time from idea generation through product development, market testing, and product launch is often referred to as the "valley of death," because the failure rate is high due to the lack of identifiable markets, poor product design, and lack of funding. The valley of death is similar to the "chasm" referred to by Moore where a new technology languishes because no practical or useful applications have been found. Once the technology approaches market readiness—in other words, it has successfully traversed the valley of death—it moves into a phase known as the "early adopter" stage where technically oriented users, who regularly purchase leading-edge technology, begin to use it. At this point, the company will require marketing dollars to create awareness on the part of potential customers and enough demand to capture sufficient niches in the market to develop critical mass. A critical mass of users in a variety of niches can shift the product into what Moore refers to as the "tornado," a period of mass adoption that enables the technology to potentially become the standard in the industry. High-technology ventures have longer development times but generally move through the product and business evolution cycle much more rapidly than other types of businesses, often becoming commodities relatively quickly.

16.1e　The Unique Funding Issues for Social Ventures

Social ventures, those that are structured with a focus on providing a benefit to society, are rarely attractive to traditional types of investors because they don't typically produce a significant return on investment; moreover, in most cases, they're structured as nonprofits so legally they can't offer true ownership stakes.

VisionSpring, a nonprofit based in New York that sells affordable reading glasses to the poor in Asia, Latin America, and Africa, faced the problem that all social ventures face: how to scale the venture so that it can achieve its goals in a big way. Founder Dr. Jordan Kassalow decided to try the "Business in a Bag" approach by providing entrepreneurs in the communities he wanted to serve with a kit containing all the products and materials they would need to sell eyeglasses in their community. They would pay the company back as the eyeglasses sold.[5] The creative approach enabled the company to grow much more rapidly.

A new type of investment vehicle for social ventures is emerging; it is called "impact investing." For example, major insurance companies and pension funds make equity investments and cash deposits into community banks that then lend to social ventures to help them grow. The investors are able to receive a return on their investment in the bank and do good at the same time.[6] The social entrepreneurs then get access to capital they need to scale. Alternatively, groups like GrayGhost Ventures, invest in for-profit companies that have social impact potential.[7]

Social investment funds are another example of creative ways to finance social ventures. These funds pool various sources of funding (donations, foundations, financial institutions, and corporations) and then lend to social ventures for lower-than-market rates of return, but significant social impact. An example of such a fund is the Nonprofit Finance Fund with offices in a number of U.S. cities (www.nonprofitfinancefund.org).[8]

In addition, several foundations, such as Ashoka Foundation and Skoll Foundation, offer seed-stage and growth-stage grants to social ventures, and these grants do not need to be repaid. As an increasing number of entrepreneurs choose to start social ventures, more creative ways to fund those ventures are emerging to meet the need.

16.2 FUNDING STARTUPS THROUGH BOOTSTRAPPING

Most startup ventures begin with a patchwork of funding sources that include credit cards, savings, friends, family members, borrowing, and bartering or trading products and services. The term *bootstrapping* refers to techniques for getting by on as few resources as possible and using other people's resources whenever feasible. It involves begging, borrowing, or leasing everything needed to start a venture and is the antithesis of the "big-money model" espoused by many when they talk about entrepreneurial ventures.[9] More often than not, bootstrapping is a model for starting a business without money—or at least without any money beyond that provided by the entrepreneur's personal resources.

The capital structure of startup ventures depends heavily on the entrepreneur's personal resources: savings, credit cards, mortgages, stock market accounts, vendor credit, customer financing, and loans. According to a Wells Fargo/Gallup study,[10] most new ventures are started with less than $10,000. RightNow Technologies was started in a spare bedroom of Greg Gianforte's home in Montana. In 2011 it was acquired by Oracle for $1.5 billion. Gianforte started by getting customers to pay him to finish the software he would ultimately sell them to solve the problem of responding to email inquiries. San Francisco–based TechCrunch, the highly regarded technology blog, was started in 2005 by Michael Arrington, who set up a simple, inexpensive blog site to satisfy his need to talk about technology ventures and Internet startups. In 2010, AOL acquired TechCrunch for a reported $25 million, a relatively small amount in Silicon Valley terms, but for Arrington, it was a nice return on his investment.

These entrepreneurs are the rule, not the exception; typically, personal resources are the most reliable, and sometimes the only, source of startup funding. This is because startups suffer from the liability of newness. By definition they have no track record, so all their estimates of sales and profits are pure speculation. A large number of new ventures fail, so the risk for an outside investor is usually high. Many have no proprietary rights that would give them a competitive advantage and a temporary monopoly in the market they enter. The founders often do not have a significant track record of success. And too many new ventures are "me too" versions of something that already exists, so they have no real competitive advantages. Consequently, prelaunch preparation in the form of feasibility analysis and business planning is critical to optimizing the firm's use of the options available at startup. Poor planning can result in less than advantageous financial choices and a poor return on investment.

SOCIAL ENTREPRENEURSHIP: *MAKING MEANING*

Room to Read

Social entrepreneurs are on a mission. Their ventures often start as the result of an unusual experience that inspires them or simply as a passion to change the world. John Wood knew that being an executive at Microsoft was not going to be his life's work. He was successful, financially secure, and reasonably happy, but there was something missing, and he needed to get away from the rat race to find it. Wood found what was to be his life's mission while on a trek through the Himalayas. He discovered that in the villages of Nepal there were no libraries, and the schools had no books. He sent out an email to his friends back in the United States, telling about his adventure and the need for books. The next morning, his inbox was filled with 100 messages from people wanting to know how they could help. That told him that he could do this. After many bumps in the road (which he recounts in his 2013 book, *Creating Room to Read: A Story of Hope in the Battle for Global Literacy*), in 2000 he made the decision to leave Microsoft and launch Room to Read as a nonprofit organization dedicated to promoting literacy. Today his organization, one of the most successful social ventures in the world, has established more than 16,549 libraries and 1,824 schools in 10 countries in the developing world and improved the lives of more than 8.8 million children. It has grown to more than 600 employees and 10,000 volunteers who do fundraising in 44 cities around the globe.

Sources: Whiting, S. (April 1, 2010), "Room to Read Sends Books Worldwide," *SFGate*, http:// articles.sfgate.com/2010-04-01/entertainment/20830272_1_book-drive-empty-library-read; John Wood, Leaving Microsoft to Change the World (New York: HarperCollins, 2006); and www. roomtoread.org, accessed July 15, 2014.

Although there are thousands of ways you can bootstrap, the following are some of the most common tried-and-true methods.

Get Traction as Quickly as Possible

Getting traction, or getting into business in some form, is a step that many entrepreneurs overlook, yet it is one of the most important steps you can take if you want to build credibility so you can eventually raise outside capital. Getting traction means launching the business in the quickest manner possible to start receiving real feedback from customers and to test the business model. This may mean putting up a website, opening a kiosk location, or putting the product in an existing store on consignment to test the retail potential for a new product. Potential investors, and that includes friendly money, will be much more likely to consider an investment if they can see your business in operation and attracting customers.

Hire as Few Employees as Possible

Hiring as few employees as possible runs counter to the economic development efforts of most communities that are looking at job creation, but your goal at startup is survival. Typically, the greatest single expense a business has is its payroll (including taxes and benefits). Subcontracting work to other firms domestically or offshore, using temporary help, and hiring independent contractors can keep the number of employees and their associated costs down. However, it is important to follow IRS regulations carefully. One California company, a maker of heart catheters, found out the hard way that failing to follow the rules can cost the company a lot. Several of this company's "independent contractors" were working 40 hours a week exclusively for the high-tech company and were being paid by the hour, all of which suggested to the IRS that they were really employees. This misclassification cost the company $25,000 in penalties and interest. The rules for using independent contractors and leasing employees were discussed in Chapter 8.

Lease or Share Everything

At some point, virtually all new ventures need to acquire equipment, furnishings, and facilities. By leasing rather than purchasing major equipment and facilities, you can avoid tying up precious capital at a time when it is badly needed to keep your venture afloat. With a lease, there usually is no down payment, and the payments are spread over time. A word of caution, however. Be careful about leasing new, rapidly changing technology for long periods of time to avoid saddling your company with obsolete equipment. Some entrepreneurs have also shared space with established companies not only to save money on overhead but also to give their fledgling ventures the aura of a successful, established company.

Use Other People's Money

Another key to bootstrapping success is getting customers to pay quickly and suppliers to allow more time for payment. To accomplish this, you must be willing to continually manage receivables. Sometimes that means walking an invoice through the channels of a major corporation in person or locating the individual who can adjust the computer code that determines when a government agency pays its bills.

Suppliers are an important asset of the business and should be taken care of. Establishing a good relationship with major suppliers can result in more favorable payment terms. After all, the supplier has an interest in seeing your new venture succeed as well. Often a young company can't get sufficient credit from one supplier, so it is a good idea to seek smaller amounts of credit from several reputable suppliers. In this way, you can establish your company's creditworthiness, and when you qualify for a larger credit line, you will know which supplier is the best source. Where possible, it's preferable to sell wholesale rather than retail. Dealing with wholesale distributors makes life easier because they are the experts at working with customers. They have already set up the consumer and industrial channels needed to expand a company's markets. Nevertheless,

© Cengage Learning®

TABLE 16.1

Some Great Bootstrapping Techniques

- Use student interns, who will often work for free just to get the experience.
- Barter for media time.
- Seek ways to motivate employees without money.
- Manage receivables weekly.
- Leverage purchasing discounts.
- Put resources into things that make money rather than use money.
- Work from home as long as possible.
- Seek referrals from loyal customers.
- Use independent contractors whenever possible.
- Seek vendor credit.
- Get customers involved in the business.
- Keep operating expenses as low as possible.
- Use email, Twitter, and social networks; they're essentially free.
- Network to find complementary resources that can be shared or leveraged.

using a wholesaler (the entrepreneur's customer) does not alleviate you of the responsibility for understanding the needs of the end-user—the wholesaler's customer. No one knows the product better than you do, and the relationship with a wholesaler must be a coordinated team effort. More bootstrapping techniques can be found in Table 16.1.

16.3 FUNDING WITH EQUITY

When someone invests money in a venture, it is normally done to gain an ownership share in the business and to see that share appreciate. This ownership share is termed *equity*. It is distinguished from debt in that equity investors put their capital at risk; typically there is no guaranteed return and no absolute protection against loss. There are a variety of sources of equity financing, including informal capital, such as personal resources and "angels" or private investors, and formal sources such as venture capital.

16.3a Friends and Family

You need to think very carefully about accepting money in the form of loans or equity investment from family members and friends. This type of money is often called the most expensive money around because you pay for it for the rest of your life. Chris Baggott knows that all too well. In 1992, he quit his job and bought a local dry-cleaning business, eventually building it into a seven-store chain. To fund the business, Baggott borrowed $45,000 from his father-in-law, who also co-signed on a $600,000 bank loan. Things were going well until the "business casual" trend happened, and people stopped wearing suits and clothes that needed dry cleaning. The unfortunate end to the story was that Baggott had to sell the business, pay his debts, and live with the very uncomfortable knowledge that his father-in-law had lost tens of thousands of dollars on the deal.[11] Because friendly money often is the only money available at startup, it is important to treat the deal as a business deal and put everything in writing so there is no question about who gets what and what happens if there's a disagreement or the business fails.

Many investors suggest structuring a convertible debt deal for friends and family because this tactic avoids having to place a valuation on the company that is likely to be wrong. If you overvalue the company, friends and family will see their shares diluted in the next round of financing. With convertible debt, the issue of valuation is deferred and you essentially get a loan that can be exchanged for equity in the next round of financing.

16.3b   Private Investors—Angels

The most popular follow-up source of capital for new ventures is private investors, typically people you know or have met through business acquaintances. These investors, who are called "angels," are part of the informal risk-capital market, the largest pool of risk capital in the United States. They can't be found in a phone book, and they don't advertise. In fact, their intentions as investors are often well hidden until they decide to make themselves known. They do, however, have several definable characteristics. Angels normally invest between $25,000 and $100,000 individually, or join forces to collectively invest between $250,000 and $1 million for about 20 to 40 percent of the equity. For that investment, they are typically seeking a return of approximately 20–30 times the original amount of the investment over a period of about 5 years. Angels usually focus on first-stage financing—that is, startup funding or funding of firms younger than five years. They are generally well educated, are often entrepreneurs themselves, and tend to invest within a relatively short distance from home because they like to be actively involved in their investments. They tend to prefer technology ventures, manufacturing, energy and resources, and service businesses. Retail ventures are less desirable because of their inordinately high rate of failure, but angels with restaurant experience can often be found. They typically look to reap the rewards of their investment within three to seven years, but the risk/reward ratio is a function of the age of the firm at the time of investment. They find their deals principally through referrals from business associates and tend to make investment decisions more quickly than other sources of capital. Their requirements in terms of documentation, business plan, and due diligence may be lower than venture capitalists, but they are still onerous.

Today, many angels have joined forces to create larger pools of capital. These "bands" of angels have strict rules about how much their members must invest each year and how much time they must spend in exercising due diligence over other members' deals. In some cases, these angel groups look and act like professional venture capitalists. As venture capital pools have grown in size to the point where the deals they engage in are much larger, angels have stepped in to take the deals formerly funded by VCs. In general, angels are an excellent source of seed or startup capital. The secret to finding these elusive investors is networking—getting involved in the business community and speaking with those who regularly come into contact with sources of private capital: lawyers, bankers, accountants, and other businesspeople. Developing these contacts takes time, so it is important not to wait until the capital is needed before beginning to look for them. The bottom line on an angel investment is that the angel is investing in the founding team and it's a very personal investment. Angels often want to experience again the excitement of starting a new venture, but they want to do it vicariously through the entrepreneur. That is why they often fund young entrepreneurs with a lot of enthusiasm, a great idea, and the energy to make it happen. They want to be involved and to mentor the entrepreneur. Like the venture capitalist, they want to make money, but the real payback is in doing good and helping a novice entrepreneur get his or her start.

16.3c   Venture Capital

Private venture capital companies have been the bedrock of many high-growth ventures, particularly in the computer, software, mobile, and biotechnology industries. Venture capital is, quite simply, a pool of money managed by professionals. These professionals usually assume the role of general partner and are paid a management fee plus a percentage of the gain from any investments. The venture capital (VC) firm takes an equity position through ownership of stock in the company, normally requires a seat on the board of directors, and often brings their professional management skills to the new venture in an advisory capacity. Because venture capitalists rarely invest in startup ventures outside the high-tech arena (with the exception of startups such as Uber), the growth stage of a new venture is where most entrepreneurs consider approaching them. Waiting until this stage is advantageous to you, because using venture capital in the startup phase can mean giving up significant control. Today we are seeing changes in the VC industry that will have ramifications for entrepreneurs and the ventures they start. Four trends seem to be in play and they are interrelated.[12]

- Smaller funds now account for about 67 percent of the new funds raised in 2014, although they still represent only about 6 percent of the total amount of VC capital raised.
- Capital is now concentrated in about 10 big VC firms representing about 67 percent of VC capital.
- Only 18 percent of funds are in the $100–$500 million bracket.
- Startups seems to be remaining private longer, seeking larger amounts of capital before going public.

What is behind these trends? It has been argued that it's much less costly to start a technology venture today. Moreover, social networking enables many startups to experiment with customers at nearly zero cost. That explains why there are so many small funds. The larger funds then supply the growth capital that is required to win in a global market. Therefore, when a private company reaches late stage, it can tap traditional VC, corporate VC, and public investment such as hedge funds and mutual funds.

The ability to secure classic venture capital funding depends not only on what you bring to the table but also on the climate in the venture capital industry. The PricewaterhouseCoopers and Venture Capital Association *MoneyTree Report* finds that at the historical peak of investment in 2000, the height of the dot-com/technology boom, VC investing was at $105 billion for the year 2000. By the end of 2004, that amount had plunged to approximately $22 billion for the year. (see Figure 16.3). Then, in 2013 there was a big gain in investment, with 3,995 deals worth $29.4 billion. And the first quarter of 2014 alone saw over $9 billion in venture capital deals. The types of ventures that received funding were not surprising. In 2013, Internet ventures received about 24 percent of all investor capital, the highest level since the dot-com bust.[13] An even greater percentage (37 percent) flowed into the software industry, the highest percentage since the *MoneyTree Report* began in 1995. Although seed-stage ventures saw a 14 percent increase in the dollars invested, those dollars went to 26 percent fewer ventures, the smallest number of seed deals since 2003.[14] However, entrepreneurs with early-stage ventures captured 33 percent of all the investment dollars and 50 percent of the deals in 2013. The average deal was worth $4.9 million, up slightly from the previous year. Silicon Valley was by far the biggest recipient of venture capital, snagging 41 percent of the dollars and 31 percent of the deals. The next closest region was New England with 11 percent of the dollars and 10 percent of the deals.

The Sequence of Events in Securing Venture Capital

To determine whether venture capital is the right type of funding for a growing venture, you must understand the goals and motivations of venture capitalists, for they dictate the potential success or failure of your attempt. VCs process hundreds of business plans every month, so their first priority is to quickly eliminate those that don't meet their most important criteria. They do this by looking for flaws in the business plan that would suggest that a venture is not a good investment opportunity. This is an important point, because a business plan may present a viable and lucrative investment for the entrepreneur,

FIGURE 16.3
Venture Capital
Investment Q1
2004–Q1 2014

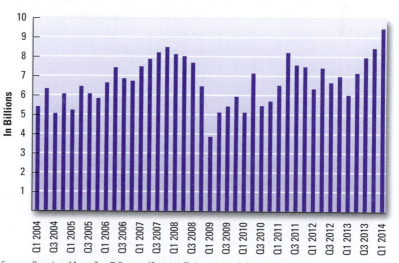

Source: Based on MoneyTree™ Report, (Q4 2013/Full-year 2013). Pricewaterhouse Coopers/National Venture Capital Association.

but if it can't achieve the size and returns that the VC needs to be successful, it will not be deemed a good investment opportunity. VCs are fundamentally risk averse, so it is your job to reduce risk in the three key areas where VCs find it: management risk, technology risk, and business-model risk. A sound business plan demonstrating market research with customers can help, but proving the concept in the market is even more important. Refer back to Figure 16.2, which depicts the three major stages during which entrepreneurs receive funding: (1) idea and proof of concept stage, which includes startup and initial survival; (2) early growth; and (3) rapid growth and expansion. The first stage, which involves identification and validation of the first customer and testing the business model, is the riskiest stage because uncertainty is at its highest with many questions about the business model and the market remaining unanswered until the second stage. VCs rarely invest at this stage even though the returns will be higher because the probability of not achieving those returns is also at its highest. The early growth stage finds the business in operation, having proven the business model in the market, so a significant amount of risk has been reduced. VCs will enter at this stage if the potential to move into rapid growth is imminent. The third stage, rapid growth, is where most VCs invest because this stage is more likely to bring them to the liquidity event they need in three to five years to make the investment worthwhile. Most of the critical questions have been answered, the team has been proven, and now it's a matter of funding rapid growth and preparing the venture for an IPO, acquisition, or other liquidity event. At this point, funding is used to finance several stages: scale-up of manufacturing and sales; working capital for expanding inventories, receivables, and payables; funding for new products; and bridge financing to prepare for an initial public offering.

When venture capitalists scrutinize a new opportunity, they typically evaluate the market, management, and technology, in that order. Market is usually first because it serves to weed out opportunities that don't solve a serious problem or don't have large enough markets in a fast-growing industry sector that will enable the business to grow to at least $50 million in three to five years. If the market is great (year-over-year growth of at least 25 percent and no domination by other companies), the management team does not have to be complete at the time the VC considers investing in the venture. The team does need to have technical skills, industry experience, and a track record that suggests that they could take the company to the next level of growth.[15] In addition to experience, VCs are looking for founding team commitment to the company and to growth because they recognize that growing a company requires an enormous amount of time and effort on the part of the management team.[16] Once they have determined that the management team is solid or that the missing pieces can easily be found, they look at the product to determine whether it enjoys a unique or innovative position in the marketplace. Product uniqueness or "secret sauce," especially if protected through intellectual-property rights, helps create entry barriers in the market, commands higher prices, and adds value to the business. All of these characteristics are important because it is from the consequent appreciation in the value of the business that the VCs will derive the required return on investment.

A venture capital firm invests in a growing business through the use of debt and equity instruments to achieve long-term appreciation on the investment within a specified period of time, typically three to five years. By definition, this goal is often different from your goals as an entrepreneur, because you usually look at your business from a much longer frame of reference. The venture capitalist also seeks varying rates of return, depending on the risk involved. An early-stage investment, for example, characteristically demands a higher rate of return, as much as 50 percent or more annual cash-on-cash return, whereas a later-stage investment calls for a lower rate of return, perhaps 30 percent annually. Depending on the timeframe for cash-out, the VC will expect capital gains multiples of 5 to 20 times the initial investment. Very simply, as the level of risk increases, so does the demand for a higher rate of return. This relationship is not surprising. Older, more established companies have a longer track record on which to base predictions about the future, so normal business cycles and sales patterns have been identified, and the company is usually in a better position to respond to a dynamic environment through experience. Consequently, investing in a mature firm does not command the high rate of return that investing in a high-growth startup does.

Armed with an understanding of what VCs are looking for, you are prepared to begin the search for a company that meets your needs. Because the venture capital community is fairly close-knit, at least within regions of the country, it is wise not to "shop" the business plan around looking for the best deal. It is important to do some research on the local venture capital firms to determine whether any specialize in the particular industry or type of business that you are growing. Getting recommendations from attorneys and accountants who regularly deal with business investments is an excellent way to find these VC firms. In fact, the best way to approach venture capitalists is through a referral from someone who knows the VC. Because VC funding is usually later-stage funding, it is likely that entrepreneurs seeking this type of funding have already tapped the angel investor network. In fact, entrepreneurs who have successfully navigated through angel investor screenings and mentoring are typically in a more valuable position when they are introduced to a VC firm that can provide them their next round of capital. Angel networks work closely with the VC firms in their region, so they understand their strict requirements and can help prepare a new venture to meet those requirements.

The process of venture funding can vary from firm to firm, but, in general, it proceeds as follows. If your business came to the VC's attention through a referral, the VC may ask for a copy of your brief business plan with an executive summary or a pitch deck. The executive summary or pitch deck is a screening device. If it can't be immediately determined that your team's qualifications are outstanding, the product concept innovative, and the projections for growth realistic, the VCs will not bother to read a business plan or talk with you. On the other hand, if they like what they see in the plan, they will probably request a meeting to determine whether your management team can deliver what they project and whether the team seems to be coachable, in other words, you can take advice without becoming defensive. This meeting may or may not call for you to do a formal presentation or pitch, if you haven't already been asked to do so. During this meeting, the initial terms of an agreement may be discussed in a general sense, but it will probably take several meetings before a term sheet is delivered. The term sheet is essentially a letter of intent and it spells out the terms that the VC is prepared to accept. Term sheets are discussed in the next section. If the meeting goes well, the next step is due diligence—that is, the VC firm will have its own team of experts check out your team and the business thoroughly. If after exhaustive due diligence the VCs are still sold on the business, they draw up the term sheet, which signals the start of a negotiation. You should not expect to receive funding immediately, however. Some venture capitalists wait until they know they have a satisfactory investment before putting out a call to their investors to fund the investment. Others just have a lengthy process for releasing money from the firm. The money is typically released in stages linked to agreed-upon milestones. Also, the venture capital firm will continue to monitor the progress of your venture and probably will want a seat or several seats on the board of directors, depending on its equity stake in the company, to ensure that it has a say in the direction you take.

Getting to a Term Sheet

Getting to a term sheet is a sign that the VC firm is serious, but it does not guarantee a "done deal." The term sheet lays out the amount of investment the VC firm is willing to consider and the conditions under which it is willing to consider the funding. You are not required to accept the term sheet as is; it simply represents the start of a negotiating process. At the top of the term sheet will be the actual dollar amount the firm is offering and the form that those funds will take, whether that be common stock, preferred stock, a bond, promissory note, or some combination of the aforementioned. It will also set a price, usually per $1,000 unit of debt or share of stock, which represents the cost basis for investors to get into the deal. The term sheet will also refer to the "post-closing capitalization" or post-money valuation, which is the projected value of the company on the day the terms are agreed upon and accepted by all parties. For example, the VCs might offer $3 million in Series B preferred stock at $.50/share (6 million shares with a post-closing capitalization of $16 million, the VC's estimate of value; see the section on valuation). The VC firm then owns 18.7 percent of the company ($3 million divided by $16 million). The rest of the term sheet outlines the capital structure for the company and is discussed in the next section.

Capital Structure

It may seem that entrepreneurs are totally at the mercy of venture capitalists when it comes to the negotiation of a deal. That, unfortunately, is true if they enter a negotiation from a weak position, desperately needing the money to keep the business alive. A better approach is to go into the negotiation from a position of strength. True, VCs have hundreds of deals presented to them on a regular basis, but most of those deals are not big hits; in other words, the return on the investment is not worth their effort. VCs are always looking for that one business that will achieve high growth and will return enough on their investment to make up for all the average or mediocre-performing investments in their portfolio. If you enter a negotiation with a business that has a solid record of growth and performance, you are in a good position to call at least some of the shots.

Any investment deal comprises four components:

1. The amount of money to be invested
2. The timing and use of the investment moneys
3. The return on investment to investors
4. The level of risk involved

The way these components are defined will affect your venture for a long time, not only in constructing your growth strategy but also in formulating an exit strategy for the investors. VCs often want both equity and debt—equity because it gives them an ownership interest in the business, and debt because they will be repaid more quickly. Consequently, they tend to want redeemable preferred stock or debentures so that if your company does well, they can convert to common stock, usually at a 1:1 ratio at the investor's option. Alternatively, if the company does poorly or fails, they will be the first to be repaid their investment. In another scenario, the VCs may want a combination of debentures (debt) and warrants, which enables them to purchase common stock at a nominal rate later on. If this strategy is implemented correctly, they may be able to get their entire investment back when the debt portion is repaid and still enjoy the appreciation in the value of the business as stockholders.

There are several other provisions that venture capitalists often request to protect their investment. One is an antidilution provision, which ensures that the selling of stock at a later date will not decrease the economic value of the VC's investment. In other words, the price of stock sold at a later date must be equal to or greater than the price at which the VC could buy the common stock on a conversion from a warrant or debenture. In addition, to guard against having paid too much for an interest in the company, the VC may request a forfeiture provision. This means that if your company does not achieve its projected performance goals, the founders may be required to give up some of their stock to the VC as a penalty. The forfeited stock increases the VC's equity in the company and may even be given to new management that the VC brings on board to steer your company in a new direction. You should never accept these terms unless you are confident of your abilities and commitment to the venture. One way to mitigate this situation is to request stock bonuses as a reward for meeting or exceeding performance projections.

Venture capital is certainly an important source of funding for an entrepreneur with a high-growth venture. It is, however, only one source, and with the advice of experts, you should consider all other possible avenues. Clearly, the best choice is one that gives your new venture the chance to reach its potential and the investors or financial backers an excellent return on investment.

16.3d Small Business Investment Companies

Small business investment companies (SBICs) are actually privately managed VC firms licensed by the Small Business Administration. They receive financing at very favorable rates, in partnership with the federal government, to invest in small and growing businesses through equity (generally preferred stock or debt with warrants) and long-term debt. Companies that qualify for SBIC financing must have a net worth under $18 million and have had an average after-tax earnings of less than $6 million during the previous two years. In addition, at least 51 percent of assets and employees must reside in the United States. The typical deal involves a loan with options to buy equity, that is, a convertible debenture (debt that can be converted to equity). Preferred stock, which pays the investor back first in the event of a failure, is sometimes used for first-round financing.

16.4 FINANCING WITH DEBT

When entrepreneurs choose a debt instrument to finance a portion of startup expenses, they typically provide a business or personal asset as collateral in exchange for a loan bearing a market rate of interest. The asset could be equipment, inventory, real estate, or the entrepreneur's house or car. Although it is best to avoid pledging personal assets as collateral for a loan, it's sometimes unavoidable, because banks generally require first-time entrepreneurs to guarantee loans personally. There are several sources of debt financing.

16.4a Commercial Banks

Banks are not normally a readily available source of either working capital or seed capital to fund a startup venture. Because they are highly regulated, their loan portfolios are scrutinized carefully, so they generally do not make loans that have any significant degree of risk. To mitigate risk, banks like to see a track record of positive cash flow, because it is out of this cash flow that their loan will be repaid. Unfortunately, new ventures don't *have* a track record, so an unsecured loan is probably not possible.

Generally, banks make loans on the basis of what are termed the five Cs: character, capacity, capital, collateral, and condition. In the case of entrepreneurs, the first two—character and capacity—become the leading consideration, because the new business's performance estimates are based purely on forecasts. Therefore, the bank will probably consider your personal history carefully. However difficult, it is important for you to establish a lending relationship with a bank. This may mean starting with a very small, secured loan and demonstrating the ability to repay in a timely fashion. Bankers also look more favorably on ventures with hard assets that are readily convertible to cash.

16.4b Commercial Finance Companies

As banks have tightened their lending requirements, commercial finance companies have stepped in to fill the gap. Often called "hard asset" lenders, they are able to do this because they are not so heavily regulated, and they base their decisions on the quality of the assets of the business. They do, however, charge more than banks, as much as 5 percent or more over prime, at rates more similar to those charged by credit card companies. Therefore, you must weigh the costs and benefits of taking on such an expensive loan. Of course, in cases where starting the business or not starting it, or surviving in the short term or failing to survive, depends on that loan, the cost may not seem so great.

Factoring, one of the oldest forms of banking, accounts for more than $1 trillion a year in credit. Factoring is a particular type of receivable financing wherein the lender, called the factor, takes ownership of a receivable at a discount and then collects against it. When the U.S. military needed machinery to create the infrastructure in Afghanistan after the initial invasion, it turned to one of its major contractors, IAP Worldwide Services, which specializes in logistics. But IAP had to purchase the goods the government needed and meet payroll before it would be paid from the order. IAP turned to a factor to get the cash it needed to serve its customer.[17] Factoring has become a popular form of cash management in smaller businesses that sell to big companies. Large companies are notorious for paying extremely slowly, which can wreak havoc with an entrepreneur's cash flow. Small businesses that sell to Walmart, for example, must be patient with the giant. Frequently, you may need to sell some of your receivables to a factor so as to not disrupt your cash flow. Factors know that Walmart will eventually pay, so there is little risk to them of taking on the receivable. In fact, Walmart has helped to grow the factor industry significantly. You should make sure that any factor you use is a member of the Commercial Finance Association, which is the major trade group for the industry. You should also have an attorney verify the authenticity and background of the factor. In general, taking out a bank loan is less expensive than using a factor, but in hard times, bank loans for startups are difficult to secure.

16.4c Small Business Administration Loan

When a conventional bank loan does not appear to be a viable option, you may want to consider an SBA-guaranteed loan. With an SBA-guaranteed loan, you can apply for a loan of up to $2 million from your bank, and the SBA guarantees that it will repay up to 90 percent of the loan to the commercial lender (generally a bank) should the business default. This guarantee increases the borrower's chances of getting a loan. A further incentive to banks is that SBA-funded ventures tend to be growth-oriented and have a higher survival rate than other startups. Of course, because the government backs these loans, the documentation and paperwork are extensive, and interest rates are usually no different from those paid on a conventional loan. You should be aware that it's difficult to secure an SBA loan at startup. The SBA requires a track record of at least a couple of years before they're willing to step in.

The SBA also has a program called the micro loan that makes it easier for entrepreneurs with limited access to capital to borrow small amounts (up to $35,000) with the average loan being about $13,000. Instead of using banks, as in the guarantee program, the SBA uses nonprofit community development corporations. In addition to the money, you are usually required to participate in business training and technical assistance.

16.5   OTHER NON-DILUTIVE FUNDING SOURCES

Entrepreneurs who need funding but don't want to dilute their ownership in their company choose debt if it's available and other sources where the return is not based on ownership. Some examples are crowdfunding, strategic alliances, grants, state-funded incentives, and incubators, which are discussed in the next sections.

16.5a   Crowdfunding

Crowdfunding is a rapidly growing, new approach to raising capital at the seed stage where more traditional forms of funding tend to shy away. The term derives from crowdsourcing, an approach that has long been used to tap creative expertise to solve problems or design anything from a logo to a complete product. It has been defined as "A collective effort by consumers who network and pool their money together, usually via the Internet, in order to invest in and support efforts initiated by other people or organizations." [18] Budding entrepreneurs and inventors use sites such as Kickstarter and Indiegogo to pitch a project to the general public seeking "donations" to reach a targeted level of funding. In return, the "backers" receive discounts, free services, an early version of the product once the goal has been met, and the finished product is ready to ship.[19] In this way, the process not only raises money for product development, but it's a way to validate whether the problem you are solving is real enough that customers will pay for a solution. Sites like Kickstarter use an all or nothing approach where the pledges are not collected until the project reaches its goal. If the startup exceeds its goal before the end of the solicitation period, it can add stretch goals to secure even more funding. As of July 2014, Kickstarter claimed over $1.2 billion in dollars pledged to projects and 65,881 successfully funded projects. They also reported over 87,000 unsuccessfully funded projects and the fact that 80 percent of projects that had exceeded 20 percent of their goals were successfully funded.[20]

The advantages to crowdfunding are many, not the least of which is that you receive the money without having to give up a stake in your company. It is also excellent validation that you're doing the right product. However, there are limitations to the use of crowdfunding, principally, the cap on the amount of money you can raise. In the United States, the maximum amount is $1 million as specified by the JOBS Act, 2012. Also, like any other fund raising, you will need to spend a lot of time promoting your product and company and thinking about how to get strangers to be interested in what you're doing.

One of the great success stories on Kickstarter was GoldieBlox. Debbie Sterling, a Stanford-educated design engineer, developed a product that would develop spatial awareness skills in girls. She had completed design and feasibility studies, and had found a Chinese manufacturer that could produce the product; however, the manufacturer required a minimum 5,000 lot purchase. Having drained her own resources, she decided to give Kickstarter a try and sought $150,000 for her first production run. She actually exceeded her goal within five days, gaining 3,200 backers. Many of the backers had contributed the minimum $30 to preorder the products, but she also received donations as high as $5,000. At the end of the solicitation period, she had 5,519 backers and $285,881, which gave her enough funding to begin work on new products. Her Kickstarter success earned a listing on Amazon.com[21]

You should be cautious about exceeding your Kickstarter goal by too much, especially if you don't have the resources to handle the demand. According to Wharton Professor Ethan Mollick who, with Jeanne Pi, did an analysis of more than 471 fundraising projects on Kickstarter, only about 25 percent of funded projects deliver on time; those that exceeded their goal by the most were the least likely to ship on time. Moreover, they found that when a project does succeed, it typically does so by a small margin, with 50 percent of projects raising only 10 percent more than their goal.[22]

Some of the important things to remember when you consider doing a crowdfunding campaign are the following:

- Set a realistic goal for the amount of money you need.
- Have a plan in place for manufacturing before you start the campaign.
- Keep the timeframe for the campaign short to avoid attracting more backers than you can serve.
- Have a real business in place before you market your product.

16.5b   Strategic Alliances

A partnership with another business—whether formal or informal—is a strategic alliance. Through strategic alliances, you can structure deals with suppliers, manufacturers, distributors, or customers that will help reduce expenditures for marketing, raw materials, production, or research and development (R&D). Reducing expenditures increases cash flow, providing capital that wouldn't otherwise have been available. One type of strategic alliance is the R&D limited partnership. This vehicle is useful for entrepreneurs starting high-tech ventures that carry significant risk due to the expense of research and development. Through a limited partnership agreement, the strategic partner contracts with you to provide funding for the development of a technology that will ultimately be profitable to the partnership. This is advantageous for both the limited partner and the new venture. Limited partners are able to deduct their investment in the R&D contract and enjoy the tax advantages of losses in the early years on their personal tax returns; they also share in any future profits. In the R&D limited partnership, the startup acts as a general partner to develop the technology and then structures a license agreement with the R&D partner whereby you can use the technology to develop other products. Often the limited partnership's interest becomes stock in a new corporation formed to commercialize the new technology. An alternative to this arrangement is an agreement to pay royalties to the partnership.

Yet another vehicle to secure resources for a startup is the formation of a joint venture, which enables you to buy back the joint venture interest after a specific period of time or when the company reaches a certain volume in sales. Your startup may incur significant costs in creating a partnership, a process that could take up to a year. In addition, giving up sole ownership of the technology may be too high a price to pay if the partnership does not survive. Many entrepreneurs neglect to consider one of the largest and most accessible sources of funding—their customers and suppliers. The reason why these two groups are more accessible than many other types of financing is that they are colleagues in the same industry; they understand your business and have a vested interest in seeing you succeed. Suppliers and customers can grant extended payment terms or offer special terms favorable to your business. In return, your business can provide such things as faster delivery, price breaks, and other benefits. Customer financing is not easy to achieve, but definitely possible under the right circumstances. In general, those circumstances include such things as offering higher returns than more traditional investments or getting in on the ground floor of a potentially high-growth business. Recall the example of GoldieBlox from our discussion of crowdfunding. Getting customers to pay for preorders is an excellent way to finance the production of your product.

16.5c   Grants

The Small Business Innovation Development Act of 1982 was designed to stimulate technological innovation by small businesses in the United States. It requires that all federal agencies with research and development budgets in excess of $100 million give a portion of their budgets to technology-based small businesses in the form of Small Business Innovative Research (SBIR) grants. Small businesses find out about these grants by checking the published solicitations by the agencies to see whether they can qualify by providing what the agency needs. Grants have three phases. Phase I is the concept stage and feasibility phase, which provides up to $150,000 for an initial feasibility study to determine the scientific and technical merit of your proposed idea. This amount is made available for six months. If results are promising, your company is eligible for Phase II funding. Phase II provides up to an additional $1 million for two years for the firm to pursue the innovation and develop a well-defined product or process. Phase III requires you to access private sector funds to commercialize the new technology but may also include government contracts for products, processes, or services that might be used by the U.S. government.

To qualify for an SBIR grant, your company must employ fewer than 500 people, be at least 51 percent independently owned by a U.S. citizen, be technology-based, be organized for profit, and not be dominant in its field. If you receive a grant, you must perform two-thirds of the Phase I effort and one-half of the Phase II effort. At least half of the principal investigator's time must be spent working in the small business.

The STTR (Small Business Technology Transfer) program fosters partnerships between small businesses and universities or research labs. Unlike the SBIR program, a small business must conduct only 40 percent of the grant activities. STTR Phase I provides $100,000 total costs for 12 months and $750,000 total costs for Phase II.

16.6   VALUING A PRE-REVENUE OR VERY EARLY-STAGE COMPANY

Whenever you seek investment capital, the issue of your company's valuation will come up because, quite simply, it is the means by which investors calculate the return on their investment. In Chapter 10 about the business plan, we cautioned that you should not attempt to place a value on your company when pitching to investors. There are several reasons why this is so. First, you will always overvalue the business because you have an emotional attachment to it. Furthermore, your perspective on the business is likely very different from the investors who take into consideration a variety of factors that you probably do not. Not all of these factors are straightforward calculations; some involve terms such as board seats, preferred stock, warrants, and antidilution. We will discuss some of those factors here, but let's begin by defining some important terms.

- **Post-money valuation**. This is quite simply the amount being invested divided by the investor's ownership percentage. So if you are receiving $50,000 in investment for 20 percent of the company, the company is now valued at $250,000.

- **Pre-money valuation**. This is the value of your company prior to the investment; so in this case, we subtract the amount of investment from the post-money valuation ($250,000 − $50,000) making the pre-money valuation at $200,000.

- **Fully diluted shares**. This is the total number of shares outstanding after accounting for all possible conversions such as stock options or convertible bonds that could be exercised at some point in the future.

- **Investors' initial percentage of ownership**. This is the percentage of full-dilution shares that investors own at the time of investment.

- **Liquidation preferences**. This defines the distribution of preferred and common stock after company obligations have been satisfied.

In any valuation scenario, it is the market that ultimately determines the value; it serves as a starting point for negotiations. In other words, investors will look at the typical range of valuations for, say, seed capital. The Kauffman Foundation has reported that since 2002, venture-backed seed-stage startups have ranged in value from $1.7 million to $2.5 million.[23] Therefore, it is not likely that you will have much success trying to negotiate a higher valuation unless your venture is not typical. And, given that investors expect you to grow your venture to at least $50 million, a precise valuation in the earliest stages is not necessary. Follow-on funding has a much wider range of values and is a function of whether you're in the product development phase, the shipping product phase, or your company is profitable.

At seed stage, it's important to remember that the risk for investors is extraordinarily high; they will likely achieve their required return from only

10 percent of their portfolio. A study of 117 investments by four angel investors produced the following takeaways:[24]

- Angel investors want scalable businesses that can grow to at least $50 to $100 million in five to eight years.
- Early-stage investors take on great risk and their ownership percentage gets severely diluted by later-stage investment. This must be factored in to their original valuation of the company and into the terms of the deal.
- Putting a high valuation on a seed-stage startup increases the chances that there will be a down round (investment at a lower valuation) as the company grows.
- Depending on the quality of the founding team, seed-stage investment should be between $1 million and $3 million.

When investors look at early-stage companies, they look at a number of factors before they begin to calculate a valuation. Most of these factors not only focus on the management team that will drive the strategy, but they also look at the size of the opportunity, the competitive landscape, and the current status of the business. Figure 16.4 summarizes these factors with the key questions that are asked.

There are many ways to value a business However, valuation of early-stage private companies is typically a very subjective process fraught with the challenge of predicting future earnings in a highly uncertain environment and with no track record on which to base those projections. Moreover, the already difficult task of valuation is exacerbated by the fact that most of the valuable assets that startups and early-stage companies hold are intangible. That is, they consist of patents, knowledge, and people instead of plant and equipment. Calculating value is fundamentally challenging because *value* is a subjective term with many meanings. In fact, at least six different definitions of value are in common use. They can be summarized as follows:

- *Fair market value*—the price at which a willing seller would sell and a willing buyer would buy in an arm's-length transaction. By this definition, every sale would ultimately constitute a fair market value sale.
- *Intrinsic value*—the perceived value arrived at by interpreting balance sheet and income statements through the use of ratios, discounting cash flow projections, and calculating liquidated asset value.
- *Investment value*—the worth of the business to an investor based on his or her individual requirements in terms of risk, return, tax benefits, and so forth.
- *Going-concern value*—the current financial status of the business as measured by financial statements, debt load, and economic environmental factors (such as government regulation) that may affect its long-term continuation.
- *Liquidation value*—the amount that could be recovered by selling off all the company's assets.
- *Book value*—an accounting measure of value that reflects the difference between total assets and total liability. It is essentially equivalent to shareholders' or owners' equity.

Most of the financial measures for business valuation, including discounted cash flow (DCF), market multiples, and real options methods all rely on the analysis of the future market for the company's products. Market multiples, such as price/earnings (P/E) ratios, are often used by venture capitalists, but their use is speculative because they are based on public companies in the industry and on the bet that the new company will go public in three to five years. The DCF method is probably the technique most commonly used to account for the going-concern value of a business, but it has problems as well. Clearly, the quality of the outcome depends on the analyst's ability to accurately forecast future market conditions and future cash flow, an almost impossible task with a venture that has no track record. Moreover, it is also difficult to arrive at an appropriate discount rate, which reflects the risk in the investment. A higher discount rate means higher risk.

Here we discuss two commonly used methods that take into account the lack of history on the part of startups and attempt to offer a more realistic estimation of value.

FIGURE 16.4 Summary of Factors That Enter into the Valuation of Pre-revenue Companies

Founding Team Experience

- Previous startup or business experience
- Product or sales experience

Coachability of Founder

- Is the founder willing to listen to guidance?
- Is the founder willing to assume a role other than CEO if necessary?

Completeness of Management Team

- Are all the functional bases covered?
- Does the team have experience working together?

Size of the Opportunity

- How big is the target market?
- How big can the company become in five years?

Competitive Landscape

- How strong are the competitors?
- How large are the barriers to entry?
- What sales channels are established?
- Does the company have intellectual property?

Status of Business and Funding Requirements

- At what stage of development is the business?
- How much funding is required and what will that funding achieve?

© Cengage Learning®

16.6a Two Venture Capital Models

In this section we look at two models frequently used to value entrepreneurial ventures seeking venture capital. A simple version of the venture capital method involves estimating the terminal value (TV), the expected return in the harvest year, the post-money valuation, and the pre-money valuation. We will use a simple example where the TV—the startup's predicted worth at the end of the valuation period—is estimated to be $50 million and the investors expect a 30x return on investment (ROI) on their $500,000 investment in the harvest year. Note that these are all predictions based on the VC's experience with similar ventures. Using this example, the formulas are the following.

Post-money Valuation = Terminal Value in the nth year/Anticipated ROI in the nth year

$50 million/30x = $1.6 million (Post-money valuation)

Pre-money = Post-money Valuation − Investment

$1.6 million − $0.5 million = **$1.1 million**

To arrive at the post-money valuation, divide the terminal value predicted in the harvest year by the anticipated or desired return on investment. In this case, the post-money valuation is $1.6 million. Subtracting the amount of the investment from the post-money gives the pre-money valuation of $1.1 million.

Another method, employed in the private equity arena to value investments with negative cash flows and earnings but with future promise, involves the VC firm determining what (ROI) is required during the holding period it desires. It then applies a P/E ratio or multiple of earnings to the estimated future value of the venture at the end of that period, which is equivalent to its TV. The TV is then discounted based on the targeted rate of return the investor is seeking.

Discounted TV = TV/(1 + Target Return)$^{\text{\# years}}$

Percentage ownership is then calculated using the following formula:

Required Ownership Percent = Investment Amount/Discounted TV

For example, suppose a company required an investment of $5 million over three years. Considering the high risk of an early-stage venture, the VC wants a 50 percent return on the initial investment and forecasts that the company's after-tax earnings in the third year will be $10 million. The investor sets the P/E ratio at 8 on the basis of comparables in the public market and experience with similar ventures and multiplies that times the $10 million to get the TV in Year Three. Using the formulas shown previously, the investor would expect to receive a 21 percent ownership stake in the company assuming no additional capital was raised during that time that might dilute the VC's interest:

Discounted TV = ($10 million × 8)/(1 + 0.50)^3 = $23.7 million

Required Percent of Ownership = $5 million/$23.7 million = 21%

Keep in mind that formulas like these are merely tools to give guidance in determining the final valuation. As mentioned previously, many other factors must also be taken into consideration to arrive at an appropriate valuation.

16.6b Divergence and Dilution

For all investments, investors are seeking returns based on the appreciation of the value of the shares they bought. However, it can be shown that as the value of a venture increases, the value of its shares does not always achieve a corresponding increase. In his research, Villalobos has referred to this discrepancy as "valuation divergence."[25] Entrepreneurs need to be aware of this phenomenon so they can be more realistic in their expectations of valuation. To illustrate the concept, Villalobos recounted an investment he made in Gadzoox, a network technology company. Table 16.2 presents the series of investments in the company that led to an IPO and Villalobos's discovery of the valuation divergence phenomenon.

Notice that there are five funding rounds beginning with an angel investment of $2 million for 30.3 percent of the company. At that time, the shares were valued at $0.74 a share. By the time of the IPO, the company was valued at $1,876 billion, which was an increase of $284x$ and the price per share was $74.8125, an increase of only $101x$. The divergence is found by the ratio of the increase in the value of the venture versus the investor shares ($284x/101x$) or 2.8, meaning that the valuation of the venture increased at 2.8 times the value of the investors' shares. Both of these numbers were based on the post-money valuations of the angel round.

How does divergence relate to dilution, which is the decrease in the percentage ownership of the company as new rounds of funding are secured? Villalobos found that the angels' equity stake was diluted to 10.8 percent from its original 30.3 percent ($30.3/10.8 = 2.8$) by the additional rounds of funding. The same is true for founding team shares, which explains how a founder who begins a venture holding 100 percent of the equity can reach an IPO holding only 10 percent.

Valuation is by its very nature an incremental process of bringing together key pieces of information that give some insight into the health and future of the business. In all discussions of value, you should be clear about whose

TABLE 16.2
Valuation Divergence

Round	Angels	Venture Capital	Strategic #1	Strategic #2	IPO
Date	Jan 1996	Sept 1996	May 1997	Sept 1998	July 1999
$ per Share	0.74	1.80	4.78	7.65	74.81
Pre-money in Millions	4.60	17.00	69.40	135.10	1,802.70
Post-money in Millions	6.60	25.00	79.50	156.10	1,876.20
Investment in Millions	2.00	8.00	10.10	21.00	73.50
Angel Equity %	30.30%	19.50%	16.30%	13.20%	10.80%

Source: Based on Villalobos, L. (2007). "Valuation Divergence," in *Valuing Pre-revenue Companies*, Kauffman Foundation, p. 21.

definition of value is being used. In general, what a willing buyer and seller can agree on under normal market conditions is the real value of the company at a particular point in time. With a new venture, there are many financing options. However, creating a capital structure that works depends in large part on creativity and persistence in securing, at the right price, the capital needed to launch the venture successfully. Growing a venture requires substantial resources, but if a company has established a healthy track record and has good potential for growth, the number of resources available to it increases substantially. Preparing for growth and change is the subject of Chapter 17.

16.7   ACCESSING THE PUBLIC MARKETS

Undertaking the initial public offering, or "going public," is the goal of many companies because it is an exciting way to raise large amounts of money for growth that probably couldn't be raised from other sources. However, deciding whether to do a public offering is difficult at best, because doing so sets in motion a series of events that will change the business and the relationship of the entrepreneur to that business forever. Moreover, returning to private status once the company has been a public company is an almost insurmountable task. An IPO is just a more complex version of a private offering, in which the founders and equity shareholders of the company agree to sell a portion of the company (via previously unissued stocks and bonds) to the public by filing with the Securities and Exchange Commission and listing their stock on one of the stock exchanges. All the proceeds of the IPO go to the company in a primary offering. If the owners of the company subsequently sell their shares of stock, the proceeds go to the owners in what is termed a secondary distribution. Often the two events occur in combination, but an offering is far less attractive when a large percentage of the proceeds is destined for the owners, because that clearly signals a lack of commitment on the part of the owners to the future success of the business. For IPOs, market timing is critical because not every year or portion of a year is favorable for an IPO. Research suggests that the value of the stock at the time of issuance is an important determinant in the ultimate decision to issue stock.[26] The bottom line is that an IPO is never a sure thing, either for the entrepreneur or the investor. Recall what happened to Vonage, the voice-over-IP company, which debuted on the New York Stock Exchange on May 24, 2006, and within the first seven days lost approximately 30 percent of its value, precipitating a class-action lawsuit claiming that shareholders were misled.[27] This is not an uncommon occurrence, however, because historically IPOs have underperformed the broader market. One exception in recent times was the class of 2004, which performed better than any group of IPOs since 1999, with the first day jump averaging 11 percent and a total return to shareholders of 34 percent from 216 companies.[28]

Since about 2005, many smaller companies that have not found the U.S. IPO market very inviting have looked to the European and Asian markets to find money. These markets have less stringent capitalization requirements and reporting rules, and investors there are eagerly looking for technology companies in which to invest.[29] With small valuations of $10 to $60 million, these companies are very attractive to Japanese investors, for example, who typically only see later-stage Japanese companies on the Nikkei exchange. They would prefer to get in at an earlier stage where there is greater potential for larger gains. The trend of companies looking for money in foreign markets will only increase due to the global economy and the relative ease with which these markets can be tapped.

16.7a   Advantages and Disadvantages of Going Public

The principal advantage of a public offering is that it provides the offering company with a tremendous source of interest-free capital for growth and expansion, paying off debt, or product development. With the IPO comes the future option of additional offerings once the company is well known and has a positive track record. A public company has more prestige and clout in the marketplace, so it becomes easier to form alliances and negotiate deals with suppliers, customers, and creditors. In addition, restricted stock and stock options can be used to attract new employees and reward existing employees. It is also easier for the founders to harvest the rewards of their efforts by selling off a portion of their stock or borrowing against it.

Public offerings do offer some serious disadvantages, however. From 1980 to 2013, 7,857 companies completed initial public offerings, raising a total of $763 billion. Nevertheless, about $143 billion was "left on the table," which refers to the closing market price on the first trading day on Amex, NYSE, and NASDAQ minus the offer price and multiplied by the number of shares offered globally.[30] A 2010 study by the Center for Effective Organizations at the University of Southern California found that investment in human resources is the most positive predictor of 90-day, 1-year, 3-year, and 5-year stock price and earnings growth for companies that survive the IPO past 5 years.[31] Those firms that scored highest on human resource factors had a 92 percent chance of survival five years after the IPO, while those firms that scored low had only a 34 percent chance of survival. What this means is that those companies that value their employees and create team cohesion in a risk-taking environment will generally outperform their less employee-oriented counterparts by a significant amount.

A public offering is a very expensive process. Whereas a private offering can cost about $100,000, a public offering can average over $3.7 million, a figure that does not include a 5 to 7 percent commission to the underwriter, which compensates the investment bank that sells the securities.[32] Other one-time costs such as drafting new articles of incorporation, can add another $1 million to the costs. It is easy to see why an IPO failure can be a financial disaster for a young company. Because failures do happen, one way to prevent such a disaster is to ask for stop-loss statements from lawyers, accountants, consultants, and investment bankers. The stop-loss statement is essentially a promise not to charge the full fee if the offering fails.

In addition to the expense, going public is enormously time-consuming. Entrepreneurs report that they spend the better part of every week on issues related to the offering over a four- to six-month period. Part of this time is devoted to learning about the process, which is much more complex than this chapter can express. One way many entrepreneurs deal with the knowledge gap about the process is by spending the year prior to the offering preparing for it by talking with others who have gone through the process, reading, and putting together the team that will see the company through it. Another way to speed up the process is to start running the private corporation like a public corporation from the beginning—that is, doing audited financial statements and keeping good records.

A public offering means that everything the company does or has becomes public information subject to the scrutiny of anyone interested in the company. A shift in company control makes the CEO of a public company responsible primarily to the shareholders and only secondarily to anyone else. The entrepreneur/CEO, who before the offering probably owned the lion's share of the stock, may no longer have a controlling portion of the outstanding stock (if he or she agreed to an offering that resulted in the loss of control), and the stock that he or she does own can lose value if the company's value on the stock exchange drops, an event that can occur through no fault of the company's performance. Macroeconomic conditions, such as world events and domestic economic policy, can adversely (or positively) affect a company's stock, regardless of what the company does.

Public companies are also subject to the stringent disclosure rules under the Sarbanes-Oxley Act (SOX). This act was passed in response to accounting scandals that started with Enron Corporation and to improve the accuracy and reliability of corporate disclosures. Sarbanes-Oxley covers such issues as establishing a public company accounting oversight board, auditor independence, corporate responsibility, and enhanced financial disclosure.[33] Most public companies (about 61 percent) report annual SOX compliance costs at $500,000 or less.[34]

Finally, a public company faces intense pressure to perform in the short term. An entrepreneur in a wholly owned corporation can afford the luxury of long-term goals and controlled growth, but the CEO of a public company is pressured by shareholders and analysts to show gains in revenues and earnings per share on a quarterly basis that will translate into higher stock prices and dividends to the stockholders.

16.7b   The Public Offering Process

There are several steps in the IPO process, as depicted in Figure 16.5. The first is to choose an underwriter, or investment banker, which is the firm that sells the securities and guides the corporation through the IPO process. Often called "the beauty contest," investment banking firms parade before the company's board of directors proclaiming their strengths after which the entrepreneur chooses one or more to comanage the IPO. Some of the most prestigious investment banking firms handle only well-established companies because they believe that smaller companies will not attract sufficient attention among major institutional investors. Getting a referral to a competent investment banking firm is a first step in the process. Investment banks underwrite the IPO based

FIGURE 16.5
The IPO Process Simplified

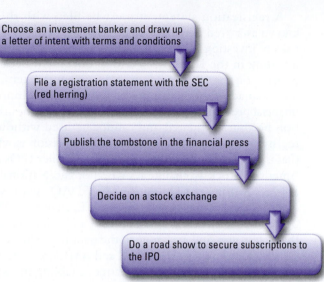

Choose an investment banker and draw up a letter of intent with terms and conditions

File a registration statement with the SEC (red herring)

Publish the tombstone in the financial press

Decide on a stock exchange

Do a road show to secure subscriptions to the IPO

on either a firm commitment or a best efforts basis. Best effort suggests that this will not be a strong IPO and should serve as a warning to investors. A commitment, by contrast, means that the investment bank will purchase shares at a discount and resell them at full price to institutional investors primarily, but also to individuals.

The importance of investigating the reputation and track record of any underwriter cannot be overemphasized. Investment banking has become a very competitive industry, and the lure of large fees from IPOs has attracted some firms of questionable character. You should also examine the investment mix of the bank. Some underwriters focus solely on institutional investors; others, on retail customers or private investors. It is often useful to have a mix of shareholders; private investors tend to be less fickle than institutional investors, so their presence contributes more stability to the stock price in the market. The investment bank should also be able to support the IPO after the offering by giving financial advice, aid in buying and selling stock, and assistance in creating and maintaining interest in the stock over the long term.

Once chosen, the underwriter draws up a letter of intent, which outlines the terms and conditions of the agreement between the underwriter and the entrepreneur/selling stockholder. It normally specifies a price range for the stock, which is a tricky issue at best. Typically, underwriters estimate the price at which the stock will be sold by using a price/earnings multiple that is common for companies within the same industry as the IPO. That multiple is then applied to the IPO's earnings per share. This is only a rough estimate; the actual going-out price will not be determined until the night before the offering. If the entrepreneur is unhappy with the final price, the only choice is to cancel the offering, an action that is highly unattractive after months of work and expense.

A registration statement must be filed with the SEC. This document is known as a "red herring," or prospectus, because it discusses all the potential risks of investing in the IPO. This prospectus is given to anyone interested in investing in the IPO. It is a critical document because the SEC will render a decision on the IPO based on this statement. After filing the registration statement, an advertisement called a "tombstone" announces the offering in the financial press. The prospectus is valid for nine months; after that, the information becomes outdated and cannot be used without officially amending the registration statement. Another major decision is where to list the offering— that is, on which exchange. In the past, smaller IPOs automatically listed on the American Stock Exchange (AMEX) or the National Association of Securities Dealers Automated Quotation (NASDAQ) because they couldn't meet the qualifications of the New York Stock Exchange (NYSE). Today, with technology companies such as Amazon.com and Qualcomm listed on NASDAQ, it is the fastest-growing exchange in the nation. NASDAQ operates differently from the other exchanges. The NYSE and AMEX are auction markets with securities traded on the floor of the exchange, enabling investors to trade directly with one another. NASDAQ, by contrast, is a floorless exchange that trades on the National Market System through a network of broker–dealers from respected securities firms that compete for orders. In addition to these three, there are regional exchanges (such as the Boston Stock Exchange) that are less costly alternatives for a small, growing company.

The high point of the IPO process is the road show, generally a two-week whirlwind tour of all the major institutional investors by the entrepreneur and the IPO team to market the offering. This is done so that once the registration statement has met all the SEC requirements and the stock has been priced, the offering can be sold virtually in a day, before its value has a chance to fluctuate in the market. The coming-out price determines the amount of proceeds to the IPO company, but those holding stock prior to the IPO often see the value of their stock increase substantially immediately after the IPO. The final price is typically agreed upon by the company and its underwriters the day before the offering. In some cases, IPOs reach the final stage only to be withdrawn at the last minute. For example, in August 2006, The GoDaddy Group Inc., a prominent Internet domain registrar, pulled its IPO filing after the SEC had declared it a go. CEO/founder Bob Parsons explained that there were three reasons for the decision: (1) IPO market conditions were not favorable due to volatile global conditions such as the Iraq War, rising oil prices, and poor performance by tech stocks in general; (2) the quiet period (required from the time a filing is made until one month after the stock is available in the market) posed a significant problem for the CEO, who had a regular radio show that would have to be discontinued; and (3) the company really didn't have to go public because the sole investor was Bob Parsons. At the start of the process, it looked like a good thing to do, but by the time the IPO was to occur, the environment had changed.[35] An entrepreneur who is considering doing an IPO should look at the condition of the market and very carefully weigh the pros and cons of becoming a public company at that time.

Every new venture needs to plan for resource gathering throughout its life. The kind of money you need to secure those resources and the timing for seeking it is a function of the type of business you have and how much revenue you can generate early on. The longer you can go without giving up equity, the more control you will have over the direction of your company. However, it is also the case that if you grow too slowly, you may leave the door open to competitors who are able to move more quickly. Growth is the subject of Chapter 17.

New Venture Action Plan

- Calculate how many personal resources you have to help fund a new venture.
- Determine ways to bootstrap the startup of your new venture.
- Network to come in contact with potential "angels."
- Identify an attorney who can help structure any legal documents.
- Investigate the sources of debt financing in the community.
- Determine if any of the non-dilutive sources of funding are appropriate for your business.

Questions on Key Issues

1. How does bootstrap financing fit into the strategic plan of a new venture?
2. What is the role of angels as a source of new venture funding?
3. Contrast funding with equity and funding with debt or non-dilutive sources.
4. Why are commercial banks not usually a reliable source of new venture financing?
5. What are the benefits of a private offering as compared to a public offering?

Experiencing Entrepreneurship

1. Make a list of all the sources of friendly money, including your personal resources, that you can tap to start a new business. How much startup money could you reasonably raise?
2. Interview an angel and a banker to learn what his or her expectations are when reviewing business plans for new ventures. In a two-page report, compare their criteria for choosing to fund or not fund the new business.

Relevant Case Studies

Case 1 AdRoll
Case 7 HomeRun

CHAPTER 17

Planning for Growth and Change

"The great thing in this world is not so much where we stand, as in what direction we are moving."

—OLIVER WENDELL HOLMES

CHAPTER OBJECTIVES

- Explain the stages of growth in a new venture.
- Discuss the differences between market exploitation and market exploration.
- List three ways to grow within your industry.
- Explore ways to go global.
- Identify the various risks facing a growing venture and how to mitigate them.
- Discuss how to plan for harvest and exit.

PROFILE

17.1

ANNIE'S HOMEGROWN: A STORY OF SUCCESSFUL, IF NOT BUMPY, GROWTH

It is a rare CEO who can take his or her entrepreneurial company through extraordinary growth and remain CEO as the company transitions to a public company. But CEO of Annie's Homegrown, John Foraker, takes nothing for granted. He may actually subscribe to the dictum of the great baseball player Satchel Paige who once said, "Don't look back. Something might be gaining on you." Foraker doesn't have to look back because he knows that he always has the big food companies like Kraft and the smaller consumer packaged goods (CPG) like Back to Nature Foods on his tail. In fact, the better the job he does growing the company, the more competitors he seems to gain.

Foraker is not the founder of Annie's. That honor goes to Annie Withey who in 1989 sold her company Smartfood to Frito-Lay for $15 million. She and her husband then started a new business, Annie's Homegrown, which in 1995 did a direct public offering that raised $1.3 million. By 1998, with the company approaching $6 million in sales, they met Foraker who had built a $10 million company around olive oils and mustard. Foraker wanted to expand and Annie's need to raise some growth capital, so in 1999, Foraker and his company invested $2 million on the agreement that he could buy out the couple over time. He then began distributing their products to Costco, Kroger, and Safeway. By the time 2002 rolled around Foraker decided that he needed expansion capital. Nothing eats up more money than growth. Out of the blue came Molly Ashby whose VC firm Solera Capital bought a majority share in the company for $23 million, taking it private, and promptly moved the headquarters from Boston to Berkeley, California, the home of the organic movement. Within three years Ashby and Foraker acquired Annie's Naturals, which produced organic salad dressings and condiments.

Annie's Inc.'s continuing strategy has been to stay ahead of trends. So, for example, in 2010 when the value of whole grains was getting a lot of attention, Annie's changed all of its cookie products to include at least 8 grams of whole grains. Annie's spends 1.6 percent of sales on R&D, a paltry amount compared to Kraft, but they also let their suppliers come up with new products that they test and often bring to market. In 2012, Annie's went public again, raising $109 million. The next frontier to tackle was mainline product placement, moving out of the natural foods section to also see placement in the mainline aisles. They tried their macaroni and cheese product first and for the 52 weeks that ended January 19, 2013, sales had increased 39 percent year over year. It is still a struggle to get conventional grocers to put natural and organic products among the mainstream products, but that challenge is slowing dissipating. For Annie's, growth has been a series of steps to create awareness and secure shelf space in mainline grocers. All of those steps required new financial resources, and fortunately for Annie's, their story was attractive to investors.

Sources: Casserly, M. (October 28, 2013). "The Homegrown Success (And Mild Indigestion) of Annie's Natural Foods, *Forbes*; Schroeder, E. (September 6, 2013). "Annie's Makes Move to Mainline," *Food Business News*. http://www.foodbusiness-news.net/articles/news_home/Business_News/2013/09/Annies_makes_move_to_mainline.aspx?ID=%7B24C97179-D3BD-403F-A61F-7E2CCFCA89D4%7D&cck=1

Expansion is a natural by-product of a successful startup. Growth helps a new business secure or maintain its competitive advantage and establish a firm foothold in the market. It is the result of a strong vision on the part of the entrepreneur and the founding team that guides decision making and ensures that the company stays on course and meets its goals. Some entrepreneurs shy away from growth because they're afraid of losing control. That fear is not unfounded; many businesses falter during rapid growth because of the enormous demands placed on the company's resources. In fact, The Startup Genome report, which looked at more than 650 Silicon Valley Web startups, found that premature scaling of the venture was the most common reason for failure.[1] In other words, if you grow quickly before your business is ready, it can be a disaster. Furthermore, it is unlikely that any business can consistently grow over its life without ever faltering.[2] Of the original *Forbes* 100 list of most powerful companies in 1917, only 18 companies remained in the top 100 by 1987, and 61 had ceased to exist. Of the remaining group, only General Electric Co. and Eastman Kodak Co. outperformed the S&P 500's 7.5 percent average return over the 70-year period, and they surpassed it by only 0.3 percent.[3] A pretty dismal record overall, but the truth is that all companies have periods in which they appear to stall—the larger a company gets the more its growth rate slows.[4] What this means to an entrepreneur is that sustaining double-digit growth over the long term is probably not possible. But with solid planning in place before growth occurs, many of the pitfalls of rapid growth can be avoided, and growth can continue for a longer time than otherwise would be possible.

The *Inc.* 500 companies are representative of rapidly growing private ventures, and the statistics about them reveal some interesting patterns. It is particularly relevant to view the 2013 crop of companies that have over the past decade seen multiple wars, the September 11, 2001, tragedy at the World Trade Center in New York, a financial disaster in 2008, and two recessions. According to *Inc.* magazine's annual survey for 2013, the average three-year growth rate from 2009–2012 for the top 500 entrepreneurial companies was 2,926 percent. The industries with the most companies in the high growth category were energy and consumer products and services; however, currently the health care sector is on the rise. The states with the most *Inc.* 500 companies were California, Texas, Florida, New York, and Illinois. Table 17.1 displays the top 10 companies by growth rate and it provides a sense of the diversity in types of businesses that grow rapidly. To meet the *Inc.* 500 criteria, a company had to be a U.S.-based, privately held, for-profit company founded and in revenue by March 31, 2009. The minimum revenue to qualify was $100,000 in 2009 and $2 million by 2012. *Inc.* measured the three-year growth rate from 2009 to 2012.[5]

Growth requires a successful strategy, but it's not the same type of strategy that businesses have followed in the past. Why? Because the business environment has changed so that what we used to see as sustainable competitive advantage—a unique product, a market niche, a brand, or relationships with customers—in many industries is becoming less possible. In their 2012 book, *Repeatability: Build Enduring Businesses for a World of Constant Change*, capturing 10 years of research on how companies grow, Zook and Allen point to three ways that strategies for growth are changing. First, just like we've seen

TABLE 17.1 Top 10 *Inc.* 500 Companies by Growth Rate

	Company	Location	3-Year Growth Rate	Revenue (in millions)	What the Company Does
1	Fuhu	El Segundo, CA	42,148%	$117.9	Creates Nabi Android tablet for kids
2	FederalConference.com	Dumfries, VA	24,831%	$49.6	Government event planning and execution
3	The HCI Group	Jacksonville, FL	24,545%	$25.5	Healthcare IT consultancy
4	Bridger	Addison, TX	23,308%	$1,900.0	Midstream oil and natural gas industry services.
5	DataXu	Boston, MA	21,337%	$87.0	Big data solutions for marketers
6	MileStone Community Builders	Austin, TX	17,938%	$45.7	Sells homes in planned communities
7	Value Payment Systems	Nashville, TN	17,404%	$25.5	Electronic payments with proprietary platform
8	Emerge Digital Group	San Francisco, CA	17,064%	$23.9	Digital marketing for Web and mobile publishers
9	Goal Zero	Bluffdale, UT	16, 981%	$33.1	Solar power recharging kits
10	Yagoozon	Warwick, RI	16,689%	$18.6	E-commerce retailer of discount costumes and part supplies.

© Cengage Learning®

with business plans, growth strategy is now more about the general direction in which you want to take your company based on its capabilities that you plan to consistently improve on. They call it a "strategy on a page," rather than the traditional three-inch thick binder holding a detailed plan. The reason that strategy is more fluid today is due to the speed at which the business world operates. Change is constant, so no well-honed plan will survive in the near term, let alone the long term. Second, because of increasing uncertainty, it is no longer possible to predict the future with any degree of confidence. That means your company has to be set up for change—fast product development, testing, learning, and adapting. Finally, it's now difficult to separate strategy from structure, that is, your company's organizational structure. Maintaining a flatter structure that puts you, your operational team, and the customer in close contact will help you respond quickly to change.

Before we consider specific categories of growth strategies, it's important to understand the stages of growth that your company might experience and where your company needs to be before you can focus on growth.

17.1 STAGES OF GROWTH IN A NEW VENTURE

Rates and stages of growth in a new venture vary by industry and business type; however, there appear to be some common issues that arise during growth that suggest areas of strategic, administrative, and managerial problems. The importance of knowing when these issues will surface cannot be overstated, for it should be part of your well-orchestrated plan to anticipate events and requirements before they occur. Research results suggest that organizations

FIGURE 17.1

Stages of Growth and
Company Focus

Startup	Early Growth	High Growth	Stable Growth
Capital Customers Distribution	Cash flow Marketing	Resources Growth Capital Management	Innovation Maintaining success

© Cengage Learning®

progress sequentially through major stages in their life and development.[6] Still other studies have noted that at each stage of development, the business faces a unique set of problems.[7] The stages of growth (see Figure 17.1) can be described as four phases through which the business must pass. (1) Startup is characterized by concerns about capital, customers, and distribution; (2) initial growth, by concerns about cash flow and marketing; (3) rapid growth, by concerns about resources, capital, and management capabilities; and (4) stable growth, by concerns about innovation and maintaining success. Let's explore these stages in more depth.

17.1a   Startup Success

During startup, your main concerns are to ensure sufficient capital, seek customers, and design a way to deliver your product or service. At this point, you really are a jack-of-all-trades, doing everything that needs to be done to get the business up and running. This includes securing suppliers, distributors, facilities, equipment, and labor. Your primary goal in the first year or so is survival. But you will also need to prepare for the moment when your business is ready to grow. Some of the signs that you're at the point where it's time to think about growth are the following:

- Customers are coming to you faster than you expected; you don't have to go out and get them like you did in the beginning.
- You're easily meeting your goals.
- Your sales have caught up to the capital invested and you have enough money to spend on growth. You have the right team on board with the skills you will need to expand.

17.1b   Initial Growth

If your new venture survives startup, you now have a business that is probably generating revenue and your focus shifts to the issue of cash flow. Can your business generate sufficient cash flow to pay all its expenses and at the same time support the growth of the company? At this point, your venture is usually relatively small, there are few employees, and you are still playing an integral role in all facets of the business, but particularly in securing the resources for growth. This is a crucial stage, for the decisions made here will determine whether your business will remain small or move into a period of rapid growth, which calls for some significant changes in organization and strategy. You and your team need to decide whether you are going to grow the business to a much larger revenue level or remain stable yet profitable.

17.1c   Rapid Growth

If the decision is to grow, sufficient resources must be gathered together to finance that growth. This is a very risky stage because growth is expensive, and there are no guarantees that you will be successful in the attempt to reach the next level. You need a plan for scaling production and distribution, and you need control systems in place to monitor quality. You also need the right talent in place because there will be no time to do effective hiring during a period of rapid growth. The problems during this stage center on maintaining control of rapid growth. They are usually solved by delegating control and accountability at various levels; failure is typically due to uncontrolled growth, lack of cash, and insufficient management expertise to deal with the situation. If growth is accomplished, it is at this stage that entrepreneurs often sell the company at a substantial profit. It is also at this stage that some entrepreneurs are displaced by their boards of directors, investors, or creditors because the skills that made them so important at startup are not the same skills the company needs to grow to the next level. As a result, many entrepreneurial ventures reach their pinnacle of growth with a management team entirely different from the one that founded the company. To the extent that you are a vital part of the vision of the company and can identify an appropriate new role in the now larger company, you can remain the primary driver of the business. Jeff Bezos, Amazon's founder, is one example of an entrepreneur who actually stayed at the helm and took his company from startup to global corporate giant. But that outcome is not as common as you might think.

17.1d   Stable Growth and Maintenance

Once your business has successfully passed through the phase of rapid growth and you are able to effectively manage the financial gains of growth, your business has reached Phase 4, stable growth and maintenance of market share. Here the company, which is usually large at this point, can remain in a fairly stable condition as long as it continues to be innovative, competitive, and flexible. If it does not, sooner or later it will begin to lose market share and could ultimately fail or become a much smaller business.

High-tech companies seem to be an exception to traditional growth patterns. Because they typically start with solid venture capital funding and a strong management team (dictated by the venture capitalists), they move out of Phases 1 and 2 very rapidly. During Phases 3 and 4, if the structure is effective and their technology is adopted in the mainstream market, they can become hugely successful. If, on the other hand, the structure is weak and the technology is not readily adopted, they can fail quickly.

17.1e Factors That Affect Growth

To comprehend the role of growth in a company's evolution, it is important to understand the factors that affect the success of your growth strategy. There are three major factors: market and industry factors; management factors; and scale factors.

Market and Industry Factors

The degree of growth and the rate at which a new venture grows are dependent on market strategy. If the niche market that a company is entering is by nature small and relatively stable in terms of growth without new avenues to expand, it will of course be more difficult to achieve the spectacular growth and size of the most rapidly growing companies. On the other hand, if a product or service you're offering can expand to a global market, growth and size are more likely to be attained.

Entering a market dominated by large companies is not in and of itself an automatic deterrent to growth. A small, well-organized company is often able to produce its product or service at a very competitive price while maintaining high quality standards, because it doesn't have the enormous overhead of the larger companies. Moreover, if the market is an old, established one, a firm entering with an innovative product in a niche can experience rapid rates of growth. In some industries, such as the wireless industry, innovation is a given, so merely offering an innovative product is not enough to be successful. In highly innovative industries such as this, the key to rapid growth is the ability to design and produce a product more quickly than competitors do. By contrast, in an industry that is stable and offers commodity products and services, entering with an innovative product or process will provide a significant competitive advantage.

At startup it was definitely important to position your company where the competitive forces were relatively weak. In general, finding an unserved niche accomplished that because by definition no one was currently competing in that space. However, as your company grows, that isn't always possible; so you will need to take the challenges you find and turn them into advantages. Michael Porter, famous for his Five Forces analysis of industry competitiveness, finds that there are a number of ways you can tackle forces that may work against you.[8]

- *Supplier power.* To avoid being controlled by a supplier that can negatively impact your cost structure, you can consider standardizing your parts so it's easier to switch to another vendor.

- *Customer power.* To lessen customer churn, expand your offerings in both products and services, so the customer has an incentive to avoid high switching costs by moving to a competitor.

- *Established competitors.* Look to innovation and new products that are significantly different from what your competitors are offering.

- *New entrants.* Increasing your R&D spending is one way to establish a barrier to new entrants.

- *Substitutes.* Consider offering more convenience or availability with valuable add-on products and services and counter the availability of substitutes.

Intellectual-property rights, like patents, copyrights, trademarks, and trade secrets, offer a competitive advantage to a new venture because they provide a grace period in which to introduce a product or service before anyone else can copy it. However, relying on proprietary rights alone is not wise. It is important to have a comprehensive marketing plan that enables your new business to secure a strong foothold in the market before someone attempts to reproduce your product and compete with it. True, an owner of intellectual property has the right to take someone who infringes on those proprietary rights to court, but the typical small company can ill afford this time-consuming and costly process when it needs all its excess capital for growth. See Chapter 7 for a more in-depth discussion of intellectual property.

Some industries, simply by virtue of their size and maturity, are difficult for a new venture to enter and penetrate enough to make a profit. Other industries prohibit new entries because the cost of participating (plant and equipment, fees, and/or compliance with regulations) is so high. Yet in the right industry, a new venture can erect barriers of its own to slow down the entry of competing companies. Patent rights on products, designs, or processes, for example, can effectively erect a temporary barrier to permit a window of opportunity to grow.

Management Factors

Along with market and industry factors, management factors influence a company's growth. When a new company has survived and is successful, even as a small business, there is a tendency to believe that it must be doing everything right and should continue in the same manner. That is a fatal error on the part of many entrepreneurs who don't recognize that change is a by-product of success. Many times it isn't until the venture is in crisis that entrepreneurs realize that the time has come to make a transition to professional management, a step that requires a fundamental change in attitudes and behaviors. Rapid growth requires skills that are very different from startup skills.

It is an unfortunate fact that with very few exceptions, most entrepreneurs do not scale—meaning, they have a difficult time moving from the entrepreneur role to the executive role, which requires adapting their leadership capabilities to the needs of the growing company. Four leadership tendencies seem to be a problem for entrepreneurs attempting to manage growing organizations.[9]

1. *Loyalty to the original founding team.* While this trait may appear to be admirable and is necessary in the earliest stages of a new venture, it can become a problem in a larger organization where the original founders may need to step aside in favor of more professional management with large-company skills and experience.

2. *Task orientation—Focus.* In an entrepreneurial venture, driving forward with single-minded focus is an advantage, but in a growing company, excessive focus on details can result in losing the big picture. A good example is Dogswell, a dog treats company whose CEO focused so much on raising money to fund growth and the launch of a new product that he didn't see that the company's coupon campaign to get customers to try the

new product was eating up the profits in the core business. Fortunately, he caught the error in time and the company has gone on to do well.

3. *Single-mindedness of vision—Discipline.* A new venture needs the strong vision of its founder to enable it to survive all the challenges of startup; however, you need to make sure that at the same time you are not plagued by tunnel vision and unable to clearly see what's coming. An effective CEO must listen to and communicate with employees in all areas of the company to insure their loyalty and productivity.

4. *Working in isolation.* Entrepreneurs have to be careful not to isolate themselves and their business from all the stakeholders in the business. Cutting themselves off from the external stakeholders is often a way to stay in the more comfortable planning mode. It takes courage to face analysts, media people, and most importantly customers. You must learn to communicate and work with a diverse group of interests beyond those with which you're most comfortable.

Entrepreneurs who grow into leaders do so because they're open to the feedback of board members, mentors, investors, employees, and customers; and they're eager to address their weaknesses, leave behind the skills that are no longer needed, and develop new skills that will facilitate the growth of the company.

Scaling Factors

It is a sad fact that many entrepreneurial ventures that start with great concepts and experience early success eventually hit a wall. Growth stalls and the firm flounders. Studies have found that among all the factors affecting growth, the most critical appears to be the inability to understand and respond to the business's environment.[10] That is, the entrepreneur did not recognize the opportunities and challenges developing outside the company and their potential to harm it. For example, in its first eight years, one manufacturer's representative firm with 30 highly trained salespeople grew to $20 million in sales and came to dominate its Midwestern market. But at the eight-year point, the firm stopped growing and sales hit a plateau. Its founder thought the problem was an internal one, sales effectiveness. What really happened, however, was that the firm's competitors had changed their marketing and distribution strategies. One competitor had moved into direct sales; another had developed a strong social media capability. The effect of these changes was to depress the sales of the entrepreneur's company in a matter of just months. This entrepreneur had failed to recognize the changes in the environment and respond rapidly to them. What this suggests is that you must continually scan your environment and assess it for changes and emerging competitors.

Sustaining growth is important but finding ways to scale the business is arguably more important. Growing requires adding resources to generate equivalent revenue--growing is expensive. By contrast, scaling adds revenue at an exponential rate relative to the resources used and serves to increase your margins, which results is more profit. Google is an excellent example of a company that adds customers (revenue) at a rapid rate while employing minimal resources to service those customers. To effectively scale your business, you need to find areas of your business model that can be replicated and applied in new ways quickly and at relatively low cost. The notion of selling more to the same customers is one way to do that. Incorporating software-based products is another because once the initial development costs are paid for, replication costs go to virtually zero.

Table 17.2 provides a simple framework for planning the growth of your business. Think of it as a checklist of things to consider as you think about growth. Today we can identify three major categories of growth strategies: (1) growing within the current market through exploitation or exploration strategies; (2) growing within the industry through vertical integration, horizontal integration, and strategic alliances; and (3) going global with support from alliances, agents, and intermediaries. See Figure 17.2 for an overview of these strategies.

TABLE 17.2
A Framework for Growth

Strategies	Tactics
Scan and assess the environment.	1. Analyze the environment.
	a. Is the customer base growing or shrinking? Why?
	b. How are competitors doing?
	c. Is the market growing?
	d. How does your company compare technologically with others in the industry?
	2. Do a SWOT analysis (strengths, weaknesses, opportunities, threats).
Plan the growth strategy.	3. Determine the problem to be solved. Where is the pain?
	4. Brainstorm solutions.
	a. Don't limit yourself to what you know and have done in the past.
	b. Think about how you can innovate strategically.
	c. Choose two or three solutions to test.
	5. Set a major goal for significant change in the organization.
	6. Set smaller, achievable goals that will put you on the path to achieve the major goal.
	7. Dedicate resources (funding and staff) toward the achievement of these goals.
	8. Examine your business model for scalable aspects that will allow your company to grow rapidly at lower cost.
Hire for growth.	8. Put someone in charge of the growth plan.
	9. Bring in key professional management with experience in growing companies.
	10. Provide education and training for employees to prepare them for growth and change.
Create a growth culture.	11. Involve everyone in the organization in the growth plan.
	12. Reward achievement of interim goals.
Build a strategy advisory board.	13. Invite key people from the industry who can keep you apprised of changes.
	14. Make industry partners and customers part of the planning process.
	15. Invite more outsiders than insiders onto the advisory board.

© Cengage Learning®

FIGURE 17.2   Categories of Growth Strategies for Entrepreneurs

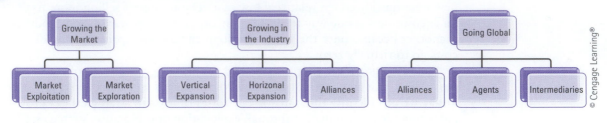

© Cengage Learning®

17.2   GROWING THE MARKET

Entrepreneurs are often faced with the choice of maximizing the value from the current market versus seeking new value from new markets. In the earliest stages of a new venture, the choice is certainly clearer: find the first customer and own that market. However, as the company grows, we have learned that "enduring success is not about the choice of market, but about the essential design of a company."[11] It's about continuous improvement and innovation in products, markets, business models, and the company itself. It needs to capture markets beyond the first target market and begin to look at adjacent markets. If a growing company spends too long in its target market, ignoring exploration beyond what it knows, it could end up in an inertial situation that will ultimately destroy its business model and its competitive advantage. One of the critical tasks of growth is to constantly monitor and refine your business model and the marketing strategy that helps you execute that model.[12]

There are generally two broad methods for implementing growth in the market: market exploitation and market exploration.

17.2a   Market Exploitation

With market exploitation, you attempt to increase sales by using more effective marketing strategies within the current target market. This is a common growth strategy for new ventures because it enables entrepreneurs to work in familiar territory and grow their businesses while they're getting their systems and controls firmly in place. Under this strategy, the company would expand gradually from the initial target market, whether it is a geographic area or a customer base. For example, the initial target market for a portable electronic travel guide might be travel agencies. Efforts and resources would be focused on getting those customers solidified and then gradually moving on to other target customers, such as hotels and convention bureaus. Another way to employ market exploitation is to attract customers from competitors by offering a value proposition that better meets their needs. Yet another approach is to go after noncustomers who typically have not purchased because the product or service is too costly, has too steep a learning curve, or has high switching costs. Once your first product is firmly established in its market, you can think about how to now meet the needs of noncustomers with a less costly version that might be simpler and easier to adopt.

17.2b Market Exploration

Market exploration strategies involve "challenging prior approaches to interfacing with the market."[13] What this means is that you will seek out new markets, use new approaches, or launch new products or channels of distribution.

Market exploration consists of taking a product or service to a broader geographic area or innovating new products even in areas where the company has not played previously. For example, a company that has been marketing on the East Coast may decide to expand across the rest of the United States. In the case of a company like Google, moving into the tablet and cell phone market was a form of market exploration as were Google Glass and the driverless car. Recognizing that revenue from AdWords was not sustainable in the long term, Google moved out of its dominant market to attack new products and markets to counter the common problem of sticking to a core value driver too long so that customers do not accept the inconsistency when you do something different.[14]

One of the most popular ways to expand a market geographically is to franchise, because this approach is generally less costly than setting up a national distribution system. The next section explores franchising in more detail and the succeeding section deals with licensing—another effective way to grow.

Franchising

Franchising enables a business to grow quickly into several geographic markets at once. The franchiser sells to the franchisee the right to do business under a particular name; the right to a product, process, or service; training and assistance in setting up the business; and ongoing marketing and quality control support once the business is established. The franchisee pays a fee and a royalty on sales, typically 3–8 percent. For this fee, the franchisee may get:

- A product or service that has a proven market
- Trade names and/or trademarks
- A patented design, process, or formula
- An accounting and financial control system
- A marketing plan
- The benefit of volume purchasing and advertising

Franchises generally come in three types: dealerships, service franchises, and product franchises. Dealerships enable manufacturers to distribute products without having to do the day-to-day work of retailing. Dealers benefit from combined marketing strength but are often required to meet quotas. Service franchises provide customers with services such as tax preparation, temporary employees, payroll preparation, and real estate services. Often the business is already in operation independently before it applies to become a franchise member. The most popular type of franchise is one that offers a product, a brand name, and an operating model. Examples include LA Boxing, Supercuts, and Servpro. Although it is a popular vehicle for growth, franchising a business is not without its risks. It is much like creating a whole new business, because the entrepreneur (franchiser) must carefully document all processes and procedures in a manual that will be used to train the franchisees. Potential franchisees need to be scrutinized to ensure that they are qualified to assume the responsibilities of operating a franchise. Moreover, the cost of preparing a business to franchise is considerable and includes legal, accounting, consulting, and training expenses. Then, too, it may take as long as three to five years to show a profit.

Not all businesses should use franchising as a means for growth. A successful franchise system will need to have the following characteristics:

- A successful prototype store (or preferably stores) with proven profitability and a good reputation so that the potential franchisee will begin with instant recognition
- A registered trademark and a consistent image and appearance for all outlets
- A business that can be systematized and easily replicated many times
- A product that can be sold in a variety of geographic regions
- Adequate funding, because establishing a successful franchise program can cost upwards of $150,000
- A well-documented prospectus that spells out the franchisee's rights, responsibilities, and risks
- An operations manual that details every aspect of running the business
- A training and support system for franchisees, both before they start the business and that continues after startup
- Site selection criteria and architectural standards

Some examples of successful franchises that can be studied as models include Curves for Women (fitness), Supercuts (salon), and Jackson Hewitt Tax Service. All have been around long enough to demonstrate their effectiveness as franchises.

Developing a franchise program requires the assistance of an attorney and an accountant, both of whose advice should be carefully considered before undertaking the effort. One of the things that will be developed with the aid of an attorney is a franchise agreement. This document is often 40–60 pages in length and deals with a variety of legal issues, which you need to understand before you go down the path of selling franchises of your business.

Licensing

Like franchising, licensing is a way to grow a company without investing large amounts of capital in plant, equipment, and employees. A license agreement is a grant to someone else to use your company's intellectual property and exploit it in the marketplace by manufacturing, distributing, or using it to create a new product. For example, your company may have developed a new patented process for taking rust off machinery. That process could be licensed to other companies to use on their equipment in return for paying a royalty back to your company. Conversely, you may have an idea for a new line of promotional products and want to acquire a license for a famous name and likeness to use on them to make them more attractive to consumers. This would entail seeking a license agreement from the owner of the trademarked name and likeness to use it commercially. An example is seeking a license from the Walt Disney Company to use Mickey Mouse on a line of products.

But licensing is much more than this, and you need to understand fully the value of intellectual property and how it can provide income in a variety of different ways. For the purposes of this discussion, anything that can be patented, copyrighted, or trademarked, and anything that is a trade secret, has the potential to be licensed. Many entrepreneurs don't realize that frequently in the conduct of their business, they gather valuable data on customers, markets, methods, and processes, but rarely do they package that data as intellectual property for sale. Restaurant Technologies, based in Eagan, Minnesota, is a supplier of cooking oil to restaurant and fast-food chains and grocery stores. To better understand when a customer needed to be restocked, the company installed sensors that tracked oil usage at the customer's site. Over time, the company realized that it had amassed very valuable data—intellectual property—that its customers might appreciate benefitting from. Using password-protected websites for each customer, it began posting the information. Then the company sold solutions to the customer to fix problems their telemetry had detected; in this way, the company was helping its customers become more efficient.[15] If your company has intellectual property that someone else might pay to use or commercialize in some way, certain steps should be taken to ensure that both parties to the transaction win. Licensor and licensee depend very much on each other for the success of the agreement, so the outcomes must be worthwhile at both ends of the deal.

The following are steps that potential licensors should take to ensure a successful transaction:

Step 1: Decide exactly what will be licensed. The license agreement can be for a product, the design for a product, a process, the right to market and distribute, the right to manufacture, or the right to use the licensed product in the production of yet another product. It will also be important to decide whether the licensee may only license the product as is or may modify it.

Step 2: Understand and define the benefits the buyer (licensee) will receive from the transaction. Why should the licensee license from your company? What makes the product, process, or right covered by the license unique and valuable? The licensee should be convinced that dealing with you offers many advantages and will be much more profitable than dealing with someone else.

Step 3: Conduct thorough market research to make certain that the potential customer base is sufficient to ensure a good profit from the effort. Of course, the licensee will also have done market research, particularly if he or she approaches your company with a proposal for a licensing agreement. But the latter situation is typical only with intellectual property that is well recognized in the marketplace—characters, for instance (Batman, Harry Potter). If you hold new intellectual property that is unproven in the marketplace you may need to seek out licensing agreements to get your product commercialized.

Step 4: Conduct due diligence on potential licensees. It's important to make certain that any potential licensee has the resources to fulfill the terms and conditions of the license agreement, can properly commercialize the intellectual property, and has a sound reputation in the market. A license agreement is essentially a partnership, and choosing partners carefully is vital.

Step 5: Determine the value of the license agreement. The value of a license agreement is determined by several factors: (1) the economic life of the intellectual property—that is, how long it will remain viable as a marketable product, process, or right; (2) the potential that someone could design around the intellectual property and compete directly; (3) the potential for government legislation or regulation that could damage the marketability of the IP; (4) any changes in market conditions that could render the IP valueless. Once the monetary value of the license has been calculated on the basis of these four factors, the license becomes negotiable. Generally, you will want some money up front, as a sign of good faith, and then a running royalty for the life of the license agreement. The amount of this royalty will vary by industry and by how much the licensee must invest in terms of plant, equipment, and marketing to commercialize your license.

Step 6: Create a license agreement. With the help of an attorney who specializes in licenses, draw up a license agreement or contract that defines the terms and conditions of the agreement between licensor and licensee.

17.3   GROWING WITHIN THE INDUSTRY

There are many opportunities for entrepreneurs to pursue integrative growth strategies—to grow their ventures through acquisition. Acquisition is in many respects less about your financial ability to purchase another company and more about the ability to negotiate a good deal. With several research studies reporting that upwards of 75 percent of all acquisitions damage shareholder value, it is clear that this approach to growth must be taken very carefully.[16] In general, you want to target opportunities that integrate well with your core business, that can be implemented quickly, and that ensure the continuation of smooth operating processes. Traditionally, when entrepreneurs have wanted to grow their businesses within their industries, they have looked to vertical and horizontal integration strategies, but now that it is important to run leaner operations, they have been looking, more often than not, to alliances. This section examines all three strategies—vertical, horizontal, and alliances.

17.3a   Vertical Integration Strategies

An entrepreneurial venture can grow by moving backward or forward within the distribution channel. This is called *vertical integration*. With a backward strategy, either the company gains control of some or all of its suppliers or it becomes its own supplier by starting another business from scratch or acquiring an existing supplier that has a successful operation. This is a common strategy for businesses that have instituted a just-in-time inventory control system.

By acquiring the core supplier(s), you can streamline the production process and cut costs. With a forward strategy, your company attempts to control the distribution of its products by either selling directly to the customer (that is, acquiring a retail outlet) or acquiring the distributors of its products. This strategy gives your business more control over how its products are marketed. Surface Technology, Inc. (STI) is a Trenton, New Jersey–based nickel-plating shop working in a very competitive business. To continue to grow, STI had to find broader uses for its customers' parts, so it talked to customers to find out exactly what the various processes are that their parts go through before coming to STI for coating, and then where they go after leaving the STI plant. For example, STI found that before certain steel parts came to its shop, they were hardened in a process conducted by another vendor. STI saw a value in developing its own trademarked process and eliminating one vendor from the

GLOBAL INSIGHTS

Africa Focuses on Startups

It might surprise most people to learn that between 2001 and 2008, Africa was one of the fastest growing regions in the world at about 5.6 percent per year. This growth is attributed in large part to the wealth of commodities in the country, but also to the privatization of state-owned enterprises and the lowering of barriers to competition. The African Development Bank, as well as other multinational financial institutions, has worked to improve the business climate by financing private businesses and public–private partnerships. The strongest economies in Africa are found in Botswana, Mauritius, Morocco, South Africa, and Tunisia where the average per capita GDP of $10,000 exceeds the combined per capita GDP of Brazil, Russia, India, and China. In these areas, entrepreneurs are creating wealth and jobs that are lifting these economies out of poverty. Christian Ngan, a Cameroonian, returned to his home country after working in Europe to start an African hand-made bio cosmetic company called Madlyn Cazalis, producing body oils, natural lotions, and soaps. Sangu Delle, a Ghanaian, founded Golden Palm Investments, which invests in early-stage companies across Africa.

However, not all of Africa is well suited to startups. Of the "Ten Worst Countries for Startups" list compiled by the World Bank, most are located on the African continent. The main problems in places such as the Republic of Congo and Chad are extremely high costs, lack of access to financing, and lack of protections for investors and lenders, in addition to the daunting political and economic challenges.

Sources: Mfonobong, N. (February 4, 2014). "30 Most Promising Young Entrepreneurs in Africa 2014," *Forbes*, http://www.forbes.com/sites/mfonobongnsehe/2014/02/04/30-most-promising-young-entrepreneurs-in-africa-2014/; Kaberuka, D. (2010). "Capturing Africa's Business Opportunity," *McKinsey Quarterly*, June, 2010, 1–4; and *Doing Business: Measuring Business Regulations*, 2010, www.doingbusiness.org/Rankings.

customer's process. A side benefit was that quality for the customer went up because STI now controlled how the two processes worked together. Similarly, STI developed downstream processes so that eventually it became more of a one-stop shop for the customer.[17]

17.3b   Horizontal Integration Strategies

Another way to grow your business within the current industry is to buy up competitors or start a competing business (sell the same product under another label). This is *horizontal integration*. For example, suppose you own a chain of sporting goods outlets; you could purchase a business that has complementary products, such as a batting cage business, so that customers can buy their bats, balls, helmets, and the like from your retail store and use them at your batting cage. Another example of growing horizontally is agreeing to manufacture a product under a different label. This strategy has been used frequently in the major-appliance and grocery industries. Likewise, many major food producers put their brand name food items into packaging labeled with the name of a major grocery store.

17.3c   Alliance Strategies

Another way for your company to grow within its industry is for you as an entrepreneur to focus on what you do best and let others do the rest. You do this by forming alliances or partnerships with entities that offer some capability or product that they need. An alliance is then formed for the mutual benefit of both parties. Typically, an alliance involves less interaction and coordination than a merger but more than a license agreement. They are usually formed as joint ventures to develop new technology, conduct research, produce products, or co-market products, to name a few. If, for example, the core activities of your business include designing and developing new products for the consumer market, other companies can make the parts, assemble the products, and market and deliver them. In essence, your company and its core activities become the hub of the wheel, with the best suppliers and distributors as the spokes. This alliance strategy helps both businesses grow more rapidly, keep unit costs down, and turn out new products more quickly. In addition, for the entrepreneur, the capital saved by not having to invest in fixed assets can be directed to those activities that provide a competitive advantage. The electronics and apparel industries used this growth strategy long before it became trendy. Today many other industries are beginning to see the advantages of an alliance approach.

   Much like a merger, it is important that the two or more companies seeking an alliance have cultures, values, and ways of doing things that are not in conflict with each other because to the marketplace, the companies must appear as one. Moreover the alliance has to start at the top of the companies. Without buy-in from the CEO and his or her counterpart in the other company, the chances of the alliance succeeding are threatened.

17.4   GROWING BY GOING GLOBAL

Today the question for a growth-oriented company is not "Should we go global?" but "When should we go global?" There are many reasons why you must consider the global market even as early as the development of your original business plan. Some entrepreneurs will launch companies that are born global. The term *born global* usually denotes a company that generates at least 25 percent of its sales in the first three years from the international marketplace and that derives a competitive advantage from outsourcing and selling in several countries.[18] Entrepreneurs who attend world trade shows know that their strongest competition may as easily come from a country in the Pacific Rim as from the company next door. They also know they may have to rely on other countries for supplies, parts, and even fabrication to keep costs down and remain competitive.

A number of years ago in a seminal research project, Oviatt and McDougall studied a dozen global startups and followed them over time. Four failed, for a variety of reasons, but those that failed tended to exhibit fewer of the "success characteristics" that the researchers found in those that survived. Those success characteristics included:[19]

1. A global vision from the start
2. Internationally experienced managers
3. Strong international business networks
4. Preemptive technology
5. A unique intangible asset, such as know-how
6. Closely linked product or service extensions (i.e. the company derives new and innovative products and services from its core technology)
7. A closely coordinated organization on a worldwide basis

However, going global is also a risky proposition. Building a customer base and a distribution network is difficult in the domestic market; it is a colossal challenge in foreign markets. Moreover, financing is more difficult in global markets because of currency fluctuations, communication problems, and regulations that vary from country to country, to name just a few of the challenges.

Savvy entrepreneurs understand that they can't simply land in a country and immediately do business. It takes time to establish relationships and build trust before a sale can be made. Developing a network of resources that include the following will help you get to the right people who can make things happen.[20]

- The U.S. Commerce Department Commercial Service
- U.S. Chambers of Commerce
- International law firm
- One of the Big Four accounting firms
- Large institutional investment bank
- International trade representative

17.4a   Finding the Best Global Market

Finding the best market for a product or service can be a daunting task, but consulting certain sources of information can make the job easier. A good place to start is the *International Trade Statistics Yearbook of the United States*, which is available in any major library or online at http://unstats.un.org/unsd /trade/default.htm. With the United Nations Standard Industrial Trade Classification (SITC) codes found in this reference book, it is possible to locate information about international demand for a product or service in specific countries. The SITC system is a way of classifying commodities used in international trade. Entrepreneurs should also be familiar with the Harmonized System (HS) of classification, which is a 10-digit system that puts the United States "in harmony" with most of the world in terms of commodity-tracking systems. If an international shipment exceeds $2,500, it must have an HS number for documentation. The district office and the Washington, DC office of the International Trade Administration are also excellent sources, as is the Department of Commerce (DOC). The commerce department's online database links all the DOC International Trade Administration offices and provides a wealth of valuable research information.

17.4b   Export Financing

To make a sale in the global market, your company needs funds to purchase the raw materials or inventory to fill the order. Unfortunately, many entrepreneurs assume that if they have a large enough order, getting financing to fill the order will be no problem. Nothing could be further from the truth. Export lenders, like traditional lending sources, want to know that you have a sound business plan and the resources to fill the orders. Entrepreneurs who want to export can look for capital from several sources, including bank financing, internal cash flow from the business, venture capital or private investor capital, and prepayment, down payment, or progress payments from the foreign company placing the order. A commercial bank is more interested in lending money to small exporters if they have secured a guarantee of payment from a governmental agency such as the Export-Import Bank of the United States, because such a guarantee limits the risk undertaken by the commercial bank. It is very similar to an SBA loan guarantee. Asking buyers to pay a deposit up front, enough to cover the purchase of raw materials, can also be a real asset to a young company with limited cash flow.

Another financial issue that plagues companies doing business overseas is currency fluctuation. In a very short time frame, as little as a couple months, currency in a country can move up or down 5 to 10 percent, which is challenging for entrepreneurs who don't have margins that can withstand that kind of volatility. An international bank can help you find ways to mitigate the risk of currency fluctuation. For example, you may be able to take advantage of a forward contract that will lock in the price at which the foreign currency will be converted to U.S. dollars. Some entrepreneurs choose to use local banks and collect and spend the money they earn in the country in which they earn it to avoid having to convert it.

17.4c   Foreign Agents, Distributors, and Trading Companies

Every country has a number of sales representatives, agents, and distributors who specialize in importing U.S. goods. It is possible to find one agent who can handle an entire country or region, but if a country has several economic centers, it may be more effective to have a different agent for each center. Sales representatives work on commission; they do not buy and hold products. Consequently, you are still responsible for collecting receivables, which, particularly when one is dealing with a foreign country, can be costly and time-consuming.

Using agents is a way to circumvent this problem. Agents purchase a product at a discount (generally very large) off list and then sell it and handle collections themselves. They solve the problem of cultural differences and the related difficulties inherent in these transactions. Of course, using an agent means losing control over what happens to the product once it leaves your hands. You have no say over what the agent actually charges customers in his or her own country. If the agent charges too much in an effort to make more money for himself or herself, the entrepreneur may lose a customer.

Entrepreneurs who are just starting to export or are exporting to areas not large enough to warrant an agent should consider putting an ad in U.S. trade journals that showcase U.S. products internationally. For manufactured products, it may be possible to find a manufacturer in the international region being targeted that will let you sell your products through its company, thus providing instant recognition in the foreign country. Ultimately, that manufacturer could also become a source of financing for your company. Another option is to use an export trading company (ETC) that specializes in certain countries or regions where it has established a network of sales representatives. ETCs often specialize in certain types of products. What typically happens is that a sales representative may report to the ETC that a particular country is interested in a certain product. The ETC then locates a manufacturer, buys the product, and sells it in the foreign country. Trading companies are a particularly popular vehicle when a company is dealing with Japan.

17.4d   Choosing an Intermediary

Before deciding on an intermediary to handle the exporting of products, you should undertake some due diligence. Specifically, you should check the intermediary's current listing of products to see whether there is a good match, understand the competition and question whether the intermediary also handles these competitors, and find out whether the intermediary has enough representatives in the foreign country to handle the market. You should also look at the sales volume of the intermediary, which should show a rather consistent level of growth. And you should make sure the intermediary has sufficient warehouse space and up-to-date communication systems, examine the intermediary's marketing plan, and make sure the intermediary can handle the servicing of your product.

Once a decision has been made, an agreement detailing the terms and conditions of the relationship should be drafted. This is very much like a partnership agreement, so it is important to consult an attorney who specializes in overseas contracts. The most important thing to remember about the contract is that it must be based on performance, so that if the intermediary is not moving enough product, the contract can be terminated.

17.5   PREPARING FOR CHANGE

Change is a certainty that every entrepreneur can count on. There is no way to avoid it in today's global environment; therefore, you must be ready and willing to adapt to new conditions, new threats, and new opportunities. Many entrepreneurs have started a business with a vision and a plan for where that business would go but quickly have found that things change along the way. Forces beyond their control push their ventures in new directions, and a new set of plans has to be constructed. Consider the highly volatile technology market during the first two years of the new millennium. How many entrepreneurs who had developed business plans for new e-commerce ventures and were seeking capital in early 2000 knew that their window of opportunity to secure those investments was about to close? In April of that year, the stock market plummeted, foreshadowing an enormous shakeout in the dot-com world and the end of "money for nothing." In a matter of months, hundreds of potential new e-commerce ventures failed to make it to the marketplace because they had no backup plan in place. Some would argue that the signs were there all along, but the easy availability of venture capital inspired the notion that all an entrepreneur needed was a great idea that could scale out to a huge market. In any case, most entrepreneurs were not prepared for the change and had no contingency plans in place.

One of the events for which entrepreneurs often fail to plan is the harvest or exit from the business. Knowing in what manner you want to realize the benefits of having created a successful business guides decision making throughout the life of the business. Moreover, if you have taken investment capital during the growth of your business, the investors will be looking for an exit strategy that involves some type of liquidity event. This section looks at contingency planning, alternatives for harvesting the wealth of the venture, and alternatives to consider if the venture should fail.

An effective contingency plan will answer several important questions:

1. In the event of a problem, which suppliers will be willing to extend the entrepreneur's repayment time and for how much?
2. What nonessential assets does the business have that can be turned into cash quickly?
3. Is there additional investment capital that can be tapped?
4. Does the business have customers who might be willing to prepay or purchase earlier than planned?
5. Has a good relationship with a banker and accountant been established? How can they help the business get through the crunch?

After answering these questions, you can (1) identify the potential risks associated with your venture; (2) calculate the probability that those identified risks will in fact occur; (3) assign a level of importance to the losses; and (4) calculate the overall loss risk. In the next section we consider some of the major categories of risk that entrepreneurs face. Figure 17.3 summarizes the process for addressing risk.

17.5a   Identifying Potential Risks

Risk is a fact of business life, and your company's exposure to risk increases as it grows. Understanding where the risk lies enables you to respond effectively through process improvement strategies and buffer strategies. *Process improvement strategies* involve reducing the probability that the risk will occur by forming strategic alliances with strong partners[21] or by developing backup suppliers and better communication with suppliers.[22] However, even with process

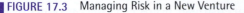

FIGURE 17.3   Managing Risk in a New Venture

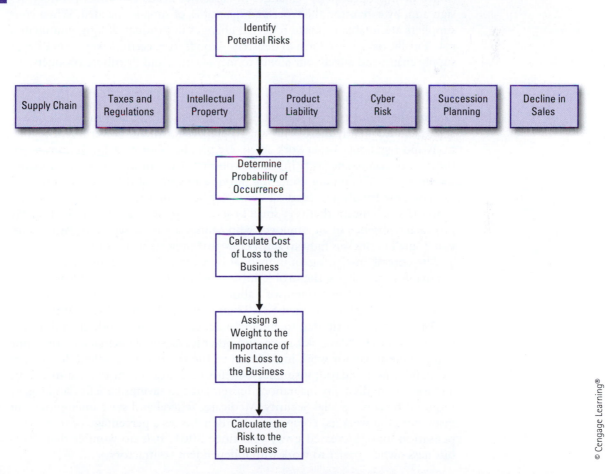

improvement strategies in place, it is impossible to eliminate risk completely. *Buffer strategies* are used to protect a company against potential risk that can't be prevented. Maintaining sufficient inventory and alternative sources of supply are two examples of buffer strategies.

Supply Chain Risks

The common practice of outsourcing the upstream activities of the business—raw materials, manufacturing, assembly, inventory—presents advantages and risks to entrepreneurs. The financial health of a supplier is critical to the stability of the business. When a supplier faces financial hardships and cannot provide supplies, raw materials, and so forth in a timely manner and you have no backup, the results can be loss of customers and, in some cases, the failure of the your business. Supplier capacity constraints are another source of risk for entrepreneurs. When demand fluctuates or increases precipitously, suppliers may not be able to ramp up quickly enough to meet the demand.[23] Quality-related risks and the inability of suppliers to keep up with technological change can have ramifications throughout the entire value chain, including raising the cost of producing a product.[24] Changes in customer needs can affect product design and, by extension, the types and quantities of supplies needed. When your suppliers are unable to make required changes in product design, you incur a risk. Finally, risks in the form of disasters—floods, fire, earthquakes—can disrupt supply chains and affect your ability to manufacture and distribute products.

Taxes and Regulations

During the life of every business, new laws, regulations, and rules will be enacted, and frequently there is no way to prepare for them. Government regulations and regulatory paperwork are severe problems for growing ventures, and the cost of compliance is rising to the point where entrepreneurs are looking for ways to avoid coming under the purview of some of these regulations. For example, the Family and Medical Leave Act has a threshold firm size of 50 employees, which means that very small businesses are now faced with the possible protracted absence of an employee who cannot easily be replaced. As a result, many small businesses fight to stay below that important number.

The cost of employing an individual is becoming so prohibitive that many companies are solving the problem by subcontracting work and leasing employees. The U.S Department of Labor reports that employers' costs for employee compensation averaged $31.93 an hour in March 2014.[25] Of this cost, 31.2 percent was attributed to employee benefits, which include such things as paid vacations, holidays, sick leave, and other leave; supplemental pay (overtime and premium pay for work in addition to the regular work schedule, such as weekends and holidays); insurance benefits (life, health, short-term disability, and long-term disability insurance); retirement and savings benefits; and legally required benefits (Social Security, Medicare, federal and state unemployment insurance, and workers' compensation). Benefits, as a percentage of total compensation, have increased every year since 2001. It is no wonder that many business owners prefer to work with independent contractors.

Intellectual Piracy

For all the benefits of globalization, one of the biggest negatives has been intellectual piracy. The U.S. Chamber of Commerce reports that piracy costs the United States alone more than $250 billion annually and 750,000 lost jobs every year.[26] The industries that suffer the most seem to be the software, film, and pharmaceutical industries. Although piracy cannot be completely stopped, small companies can fight back by investigating suppliers and manufacturers before doing business with them, contractually requiring their foreign partners to submit to international binding arbitration so you won't have to navigate the local courts of a country, and registering all trademarks in whatever country your company is doing business in.

Product Liability

The chances are fairly good that any company that manufactures products will face a product liability suit at some point. More and more of the risk of product-related injuries has been shifted to manufacturers, creating a legal minefield that could prove disastrous to a growing company. Even if your company carefully designs and manufactures a product and covers it with warnings and detailed instructions, your company may still be vulnerable if misuse of the product results in injury. For a company to be legally liable, the product must be defective and an injury must have occurred. But in a litigious society, those requirements don't stop people from initiating lawsuits even when there are no grounds. Most product liability insurance covers the costs of defense, personal injury, or property damage, but not lost sales and the cost of product redesign. Moreover, if the insurance company must pay on a claim, the entrepreneur's premiums will no doubt increase.

A growing company must plan for potential litigation from the very inception of the business. One proven method is to establish a formal safety panel that includes people from all the major operational areas of your business. During the startup phase, that panel may consist of only you and one or two outside advisers with experience in the area. It is the job of the panel to review safety requirements on a regular basis, establish new ones when necessary, and document any injuries or claims made against the product. Prior to product introduction in the marketplace, the panel should see that careful records are maintained of all decisions regarding final product design, testing, and evaluation procedures. Advertising of the product should contain no exaggerated claims or implied promises that may give customers the impression that the company is claiming more safety features than the product actually possesses. Implied promises can be used against the entrepreneur in a court of law.

Cyber Risk

One of the more recent and insidious risks a company that is doing business online faces is cyber risk: hacker attacks that could bring the business network down, phishing attacks (acquiring sensitive information such as user names and passwords), spybots, and the ever-present viruses and worms. More recently, cyber militias have emerged—groups of hackers that act in the national interests of the country that sponsors them to provide nearly constant attacks on the national security infrastructure of countries like the United States. In 2012, Verizon did a Data Breach Investigations Study that found that of the 855 data breaches they studied, 71 percent happened in businesses with fewer than 100 employees. Furthermore, their 2013 report found that attacks on small businesses were rising.[27] With so many small businesses now relying on computers and online data, there are a few things you must do to protect your business.

- Back up all your data to a secure location whether to cloud storage or an offsite server.
- Work with your website developer to ensure that the platform you're using is secure.
- Be forewarned that if you publicize your big company client list, it may make your company vulnerable to attack as hackers may find you to be an easier target than your much larger client.
- Use different passwords for every account that you have.

Many businesses have secured cyber insurance policies to attempt to mitigate the risk. However, these policies are often difficult to understand and contain so many exclusions that one company figured that the insurance policy price was close to what it would cost them to do what they could to reduce their cyber risk on their own. However, entrepreneurs with companies that rely heavily on Internet-based systems will want to get advice about securing a policy that protects the company against liability for security breaches, crisis management (notifying customers about the theft of information), business interruption, and the cost associated with restoring information that has been corrupted.

Decline in Sales

When sales decline and positive cash flow starts looking like a memory, entrepreneurs often go into a period of denial. They start paying their suppliers more slowly to preserve cash, they lay people off, they stop answering the phone, and they insulate themselves against the demands of their creditors. Their panic frequently causes them to make poor decisions about how to spend the precious cash they do have. They figure that if they can just hold on long enough, things will turn around. Unfortunately, this attitude only makes the problem worse, effectively propelling the business toward its ultimate demise. How can an entrepreneur lose touch with the business and the market so much that he or she puts the business at risk? What often happens is that entrepreneurs get so wrapped up in the day-to-day operations of the business that they don't have time to contemplate the "big picture" or stay in tune with their customers. Consequently, all too often they don't see a potential crisis coming until it's too late.

When sales decline, lowering prices isn't necessarily the solution. If your company's customers understand the value of your product or service, any such sudden discounting will confuse them. When there is a decline in sales, it is especially important to look at all possible sources, not just the economy. You may have been lax about checking the credit status of customers and distributors, or the inventory turnover rate may have changed. You may have failed to notice an emerging competitor offering a product or service more in line with current tastes and preferences. When a growing business first notices a dip in sales, it is time to find the cause and make the necessary changes. This will be easier if the business has a contingency plan in place. To prepare the best defense against a cash flow crisis, you must remain committed to producing exceptional-quality products; controlling the cost of overhead, particularly where that overhead does not contribute directly to revenue generation (expensive cars, travel, excessive commissions); controlling production costs through subcontracting and being frugal about facilities; making liquidity and positive cash flow the prime directive, so that your company can ride out temporary periods of declining demand; and having a contingency plan in place.

17.5b Calculating Risk Probability and the Cost to the Business

It is extremely difficult to calculate the probability that a given risk will occur with any degree of accuracy. Consequently, any cost-benefit analysis conducted will probably contain flaws and may even cause you to decide that the cost of protecting the business is nearly equal to the cost of the loss.[28] Nonetheless, it is important to gauge, based on industry and customer knowledge, the chance that a particular risk will occur and what the impact of that occurrence will be on the company. For example, you might want to know how many widgets to order for the summer season. You know you can sell 50 in a day and that you make a profit of $10 each. The average number of days in the season is 95. Thus you multiply 4,750 widgets times $10 to get the average profit for the season. You have just committed a common error that has been called the "flaw of averages."[29] The problem with averages is that they mask risk. Average inputs don't always produce average outputs. For example, if a lower-than-average demand produces lower-than-average revenues, then a higher-than-average demand is not possible because the company would have made only enough product to satisfy an average demand. This kind of error is quickly exposed when doing probability modeling such as the Monte Carlo simulation, which models behaviors under multiple uncertainties within a specified period. It is often used in the insurance industry to model accident risk. Working with this type of modeling software is an effective way to get a feel for the risk inherent in any business. Understanding the magnitude of a potential loss is important in deciding where to devote limited resources to protecting against a particular loss. Assigning a level of significance is again an arbitrary exercise, because the weight given to any risk impact is based on the company's goals, core competencies, and focus.

The overall risk of loss is simply the product of the probability of occurrence times the cost of the impact to the business times the level of significance of that impact:

$$\text{Risk of Loss} = (P \times C \times S)$$

For example, suppose you determine that there is a 40 percent chance that you will lose a key person to a competitor. The financial cost of that loss is the cost of doing a search for a new hire, which you estimate at $10,000 (this does not include the nonfinancial costs, such as loss of tacit knowledge). You assign a weight of 80 percent, on a scale of 1 percent to 100 percent, to reflect the importance of this risk to the company. Thus, the overall risk of loss is approximately

$$\text{Risk of Loss} = (\$10{,}000 \times 0.40 \times 0.80) = \$3{,}200$$

If this calculation is done for all the identified risks, it will be easier to decide on which risks to concentrate efforts and focus resources, remembering at all times that the risk-of-loss numbers are merely educated guesses. While it is true that these calculations don't insure against risk, they do help you make decisions about where to focus your risk mitigation efforts.

17.6   LEADERSHIP SUCCESSION

No company can count on keeping the same management team over the life of the business—or even after the startup phase. The demand for top-notch management personnel (particularly in some industries, such as those in the high-tech sector) means that other companies will constantly be trying to woo the best people away from the best firms. Losing a CEO in times of high turnover is not uncommon. In 2013, 14.4 percent of the largest 2,500 public companies lost their CEOs.[30] But key employees are often lost for other unpredictable reasons like death or illness. In fact, some estimates suggest that the chances of losing a key executive to death are significantly greater than losing a business to fire.

Succession planning—identifying people who can take over key company positions in an emergency or in a change of ownership—is an important part of planning for change. Ideally your replacement will come from within the company, but in the case of a growing entrepreneurial company that has been operating in a "lean and mean" mode, promoting from within may not always be possible, so outsiders must be found. Succession planning for small enterprises and for the unique issues of family businesses is the subject of the next two sections.

17.6a   Change of Ownership in Small Enterprises

The big question that existing small enterprises face is whether to promote from within or hire from the outside when replacing a CEO. Entrepreneurs who have adopted succession planning as one of their roles will have identified insiders with potential to lead at some point in the future and who also have spent sufficient time outside the company in the industry and market so that they also bring an outsider's view to the table.[31] Employing a simple process for succession planning will increase the likelihood that the process will actually result in an effective succession plan. One such simple process was advanced by the research of Pasmore and Torres.[32] It calls for a four-step plan:

1. *Situation assessment.* You need to determine the timing of succession, the criteria for selection, the likely internal candidates, a plan for identifying possible external candidates, and plans for engaging the appropriate stakeholders in the process.

2. *Announcement of the process.* Once the company's situation is assessed, you should announce the plans and process to relevant stakeholders such as board members, advisors, and employees. Making people aware of how the selection will be made will go a long way toward preventing unsubstantiated rumors and misunderstandings.

3. *Execution of the search.* At this stage, management moves forward to search and select either an internal or external candidate.

4. *Transition.* Once the selection has been made, you need to help the new leader during the transfer of power, smooth the transition with important stakeholders, and make a graceful exit at the appropriate time.

To prepare for the possible unexpected loss of a key employee, it is a good idea to purchase "key-person insurance," which will cover the costs associated with abruptly having to replace someone. Bringing in a consultant to guide your management team in succession planning is a valuable exercise for any growing venture. Often consultants are hired temporarily to take over a vacant position for a specified period, during which they train a permanent successor. Another solution is to cross-train people in key positions so that someone can step in, at least for the short term, in the event of an emergency. Cross-training is generally an integral and critical part of a team-based approach to organizational management.

17.6b Succession Planning in Family-Owned Businesses

Entrepreneurs who head family-owned companies face special problems because they tend to look to a son, daughter, or other family member to succeed them. Succession in a family-owned business will not happen unless it is planned for, however. In fact, the Family Firm Institute of Boston reports that less than a third of all family businesses survive the transition from first to second generation ownership.[33] This is partly because the owner must deal not only with business issues related to succession—ownership, management, strategic planning—but also with the unexpected, such as a death or relationship issues with family members, a much more difficult task. Succession planning tends to expose family issues that may have been kept in the background but have been building over time. For example, the daughter who the entrepreneur assumed would take over the business may have no interest in doing so but may never have told her entrepreneur father. Or, a child may believe himself or herself capable of simply stepping into a managerial role with no previous experience. If an entrepreneur has created a plan for succession, a problem like this may be solved by making it a requirement that a child or potential successor work for another company for several years to gain some business savvy and to decide whether he or she wants to take over the family business. Many sports enterprises are family businesses that face these same issues. When the iconic George Steinbrenner, owner of the New York Yankees baseball team died in July 2010, he left the ownership of the team to his two sons. He began planning for succession and preparing his sons starting in 1973.[34] Although the family business could look outside the family for their next leader, they are not likely to do that as research has found that most family businesses want to retain control within the family.[35]

Succession planning in family businesses takes a long time due to three key issues:

- Physiological and emotional issues that stem from the interrelations of family members
- The complexity of succession, particularly since the owner typically has no experience in this area
- Relevant laws and taxation that impact the financial status of the company

To start the process of succession planning, all the active family members should participate on a committee to explore the options. Some of the questions to examine are the following:

- Is the next generation being sufficiently prepared to take over the business when the time comes?
- What is the second generation's expectation for the future of the business, and is it congruent with the company's vision?
- What skills and experience does the second generation need to acquire?
- What would the ideal succession plan look like?

Then, with the help of an attorney, buy-sell agreements should be developed to ensure that heirs receive a fair price for their interest in the business upon an owner's death and to protect against irreparable damage in the event of a shareholder's permanent disability by outlining provisions for buying out the disabled shareholder's interest. An estate planning professional can help evaluate the impact of any changes in the business on the entrepreneur's personal assets. Given that most privately owned businesses in the United States are family-owned businesses, this succession planning strategy is useful for any business that wants to be prepared for the loss or retirement of its leader.

17.7   PLANNING FOR HARVEST AND EXIT

Many first-time entrepreneurs have questioned the need for an exit plan, or harvest plan, because they are more concerned with launching the business and making it a success than with thinking about how they're going to get out. But even though some entrepreneurs stay with their ventures for the long term, the majority enjoy the challenge of startup and the excitement of growth and abhor the custodial role of managing a stable, mature company. Consequently, exiting the business does not necessarily mean exiting the role of entrepreneur. It may in fact mean taking the financial rewards of having grown a successful business and investing them in a new venture. And there are serial entrepreneurs who do that very thing over and over again throughout their lives, starting businesses and then selling them or letting others run them. Whether or not you intend to exit your business at any point, you should have a plan for harvesting the rewards of having started the business in the first place. There is another important reason why a harvest plan is essential. Many entrepreneurs take investor capital at some point in the growth of their companies, and investors require a liquidity event so that they can exit the business with their principal and any return on investment they have accrued.

The following paragraphs examine several methods by which you can achieve a rewarding harvest.

17.7a Selling the Business

Selling the business outright to another company or to an individual may be the goal if you are ready to move on to something else and you want to be financially and mentally free to do so. Unfortunately, however, selling a business is a life-changing event because for several years, you have probably devoted the majority of your time and attention to growing the business, and it played an important role in structuring your life. After the business has been sold, you may experience a sense of loss, much like what accompanies the death of a loved one; without preparation, emotional stress could be the consequence. Therefore, planning for this enormous change will be vital.

The best way to sell a business is to know almost from the beginning that selling is what you eventually want to do, so that you will make decisions for the business that will place it in the best position for a sale several years later. For one thing, your business will need audited financial statements that lend the business forecasts more credibility. The tax strategy will not be to minimize taxes by showing low profits but, rather, to show actual profits and pay the taxes on them, because that will provide a higher valuation for the business. Throughout the time that you own the business, its expenses and activity should be kept totally separate from your personal expenses. It will also be important to plan for the amount of time it will take to sell the business and wait to sell until the right window of opportunity has opened.

Smaller businesses for sale often use the services of business brokers; however, a high-growth venture is more likely to employ the services of an investment banking firm that has experience with the industry. Investment banks normally want a retainer to ensure the seriousness of the commitment to sell, but that retainer will be applied against the final fee on the sale, which could average about 5 percent of the purchase price. When your business is sold, you do not have to sell all the assets. For example, the building could be held out of the sale and leased back to the business purchaser, with you staying on as landlord.

While the potential purchaser is conducting due diligence on you and the business, you need to do the same with the purchaser. The purchasing firm or individual should be thoroughly checked out against a list of criteria you have developed. The purchaser should have the resources necessary to continue the growth of the business, be familiar with the industry and with the type of business being purchased, have a good reputation in the industry, and offer skills and contacts that will ensure that the business continues in a positive direction. In order to compare one buyer with another fairly, it is often helpful to make a complete list of criteria and then weight them to reflect their relative importance.

17.7b   Cashing Out but Staying In

Sometimes entrepreneurs reach the point where they would like to take the bulk of their investment and gain out of the business but are not yet ready to cut the cord entirely. They may want to continue to run the business or at least retain a minority interest. There are several ways this can be accomplished. If your company is still privately owned, the remaining shareholders may want to purchase your stock at current market rates so that control doesn't end up in other hands. In fact, the shareholders' agreement that was drafted when you set up the corporation may have probably specified that shareholders must offer the stock to the company before offering it to anyone else.

If your company is publicly traded, the task of selling the stock is much simpler; however, if you own a substantial portion of the issued stock, strict guidelines set out by the SEC must be followed when liquidating a shareholders' interests. If your company had a successful IPO, founders' stock will have increased substantially in value, which presents a tax liability that should not be ignored. That is why many entrepreneurs in such situations cash out only what they need to support whatever goals they have. This strategy, of course, is based on the presumption that the company stock will continue its upward trend for the foreseeable future.

Entrepreneurs who want to cash out a significant portion of their investment and turn over the reins to a son, daughter, or other individual can do so by splitting the business into two firms, with the entrepreneur owning the firm that has all the assets (plant, equipment, vehicles) and the other individual owning the operating aspect of the business while leasing the assets from the entrepreneur's company. See Figure 17.4.

A Phased Sale

Some entrepreneurs want to soften the emotional blow of selling the business, not to mention softening the tax consequences, by agreeing with the buyer—an

FIGURE 17.4
Restructuring the Family Business

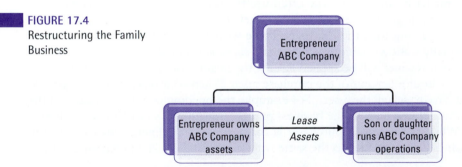

individual or another firm—to sell in two phases. During the first phase, you sell a percentage of the company but remain in control of operations and can continue to grow the company to the point at which the buyer has agreed to complete the purchase. This approach gives you the ability to cash out a portion of your investment and still manage the business for an agreed-upon time, during which the new owner will probably be learning the business and phasing in. In the second phase, the business is sold at a prearranged price, usually a multiple of earnings.

This approach is fairly complex and should always be guided by an attorney experienced in acquisitions and buy-sell agreements. The buy-sell agreement, which spells out the terms of the purchase, specifies the amount of control the new owner can exert over the business before the sale has been completed and the amount of proprietary information that will be shared with the buyer between Phases 1 and 2.

In recent times, the consolidation play has become a way for many small business owners to realize the wealth they have created in their businesses. This is how it works. A large, established company finds a fragmented industry with a lot of mom-and-pop–type businesses. The consolidator buys them up and puts them under one umbrella to create economies of scale in the industry. The local management team often stays in power, while the parent company begins to build a national brand presence. The payoff for you comes when the consolidator takes the company public and buys out all the independent owners. It is important to conduct due diligence on any potential consolidator, because one's ability to cash out will be a function of the consolidator's ability to grow the company and take it public.

17.7c   Being Acquired

For decades the end-of-the-rainbow scenario for entrepreneurs was to do an initial public offering (IPO) for all the benefits it provided: overnight wealth (if successful); clout in the market; access to larger amounts of capital; and more credibility with partners and the supply chain. However, today, the IPO is no longer the Holy Grail; in fact, a report by Ernst & Young found that the number of IPOs by startups is down about 75 percent this decade over the previous decade.[36] In any case, you should probably not suggest that you're planning for an IPO when you go for your first seed round. The IPO is discussed more fully in Chapter 16.

In the past decade, the number of mergers and acquisitions has increased significantly. The first three quarters of 2013 saw $865.1 billion in acquisitions and mergers, a 39 percent increase over the same period in 2012.[37] Compare that to an annual volume of $41.27 billion for IPOs in 2013.[38]What is driving this change? Some of it can be explained by the fact that a private company that goes public is essentially on its own whereas if it is acquired, it now can access the resources and support of the acquiring company, which may be a large public company. This becomes increasingly important in a highly competitive landscape where joining forces with another company makes the entrepreneurial venture more competitive. Another reason is that many ventures today do not offer complete solutions to problems; they offer a part of a solution that needs to be combined with a technology or product held by another company. In that scenario, an acquisition may be the best strategy. In general, if your company is capital intensive and you will derive more benefit from managing it, the IPO may be the better way to go. It is a fact that the valuations of companies that go public are generally larger than the valuations of those that are acquired, principally because the acquirer is in a better bargaining position. Nevertheless, many entrepreneurs choose the lower valuation of an acquisition because they are not confident that their high IPO valuation will be sustainable long enough for them to liquidate any shares due to the standard lock-up provisions that prevent insiders from selling their shares after an IPO for a period of time.

Acquirers can be categorized in two ways: financial acquirers such as private equity or buyout firms that provide growth capital with the intention of selling for a profit, and strategic acquirers, which are large, often public, firms that are established in the market. In general, if your business is doing well but needs substantial resources to grow to the next level, a strategic acquirer will likely be your choice.

Acquisition is not without its challenges; after all, you are integrating two companies that may have different cultures and processes and may be located in different parts of the country or world. It is the job of the acquirer to complete the integration of the entrepreneurial venture as quickly and seamlessly as possible. At the same time, it is the responsibility of the entrepreneur to make the integration as easy as possible for the acquirer. Some of the reasons why acquisitions do not go well are the following:

- The products of the two companies are not complementary
- Getting the salesforce up to speed on the new products being acquired
- R&D approaches and expertise are very different
- The cultures of the two companies don't mesh

By all accounts, being acquired will continue to be the most common way that entrepreneurs and investors harvest the wealth they have created.

17.7d   Dealing with Failure: Bankruptcy

Death is certainly part of any business life cycle, and, therefore, some entrepreneurs must exit their businesses through liquidation. For whatever reasons, the business could not manage a down sales cycle, find new sources of revenue, pay its obligations, or secure capital to float the business until conditions improved. Certainly no entrepreneur starts a business with liquidation in mind as the exit strategy, but sometimes the forces working against the business are so great that you must have an exit vehicle so you can move on to do something else. What forces a company into bankruptcy is difficult to pinpoint. The immediately precipitating cause is the failure to pay debt; however, myriad other events contributed to that cause. They include a lack of understanding of economic and business cycles, carrying excessive debt and surplus overhead, shifts in demand, excessive expenses, poor dividend policies, union problems, supplier problems, and poor financial management. Of course, the common denominator for all these factors is poor management.

The Bankruptcy Reform Act of 1978 and Public Law 95–958 provide for more than just liquidation of the business in the event of failure, so that businesses owners might have the opportunity to save their businesses through a process of restructuring. Therefore, it is important to have a clear understanding of the bankruptcy mechanisms available if you are faced with financial adversity. The bankruptcy code consists of several chapters, but two chapters are relevant to entrepreneurs: Chapter 7 and Chapter 11. A Chapter 7 bankruptcy is essentially the liquidation of the assets of the business and the discharge of most types of debt. The debtor files a petition and several required schedules of assets and liabilities with the bankruptcy court serving the area in which he or she lives. A trustee is appointed to manage the disposition of the business, and a meeting of the creditors is held after the petition is filed. The goal of the bankruptcy is to reduce the business to cash and distribute the cash to the creditors where authorized. After exemptions, the monies derived from liquidation go first to secured creditors and then to priority claimants, such as those owed wages, salaries, and contributions to employee benefit plans. Any surplus funds remaining after this distribution go to the entrepreneur.

By contrast, a Chapter 11 reorganization under the bankruptcy code is really not a bankruptcy in the commonly used sense of the word. It is simply a reorganization of the finances of the business so that it can continue to operate and begin to pay its debts. Only in the case where the creditors believe that management is unable to carry out the terms of the reorganization plan is a trustee appointed to run the company until the debt has been repaid. Otherwise, the entrepreneur remains in control of the business while in a Chapter 11 position.

Before considering bankruptcy as an option to either exit a troubled business or restructure the business in an effort to survive, entrepreneurs should seek advice from an attorney and/or a specialist in turnarounds in the industry. Turnaround consultants are good at putting an unhealthy business on a diet; setting small, achievable goals; and making sure the business stays on track until its finances are in the black. Private equity firms often operate in this capacity.

In the end, knowing how to harvest the wealth the business has created can help in structuring a growth plan that will get you where you want to go. Preparing for the unexpected—contingency planning—will go a long way toward ensuring that the business stays on the path to achieving its goals.

17.8 SOME FINAL THOUGHTS

Entrepreneurship as a field of study has been in vogue for more than 40 years. There is hardly a media source today that does not talk about entrepreneurs. In fact, the term is in real danger of becoming a cliché and losing its value because it is used to describe all kinds of ventures, from the small "mom-and-pop" to the Fortune 500 conglomerate. It has been used to define successful artists, scientists, and journalists whether or not they start a business. This book has focused on the birth and early growth of innovative, growth-oriented new ventures and has used a classic definition of the term *entrepreneurship*: the creation, evaluation, and exploitation of opportunities that are innovative, growth oriented, and that create new value for customers. These ventures face unique opportunities and challenges, but their relatively small size and lean structure also make them particularly adaptable to an uncertain and rapidly changing environment. Entrepreneurs are the source of breakthrough innovation, economic growth, and job creation. Startups and the entrepreneurs who create them stand out from the crowd. However, entrepreneurship is more than just new venture creation; it is a way of viewing the world and a skill set that can be learned. Adopting an entrepreneurial perspective is valuable for corporate entrepreneurs, small business owners, and those who want to take charge of their lives, their careers, and their businesses and differentiate themselves in a way that enables them to realize their dreams. In that sense, entrepreneurship is for everyone who wants to experience the freedom and independence that come from knowing that opportunities and the resources to make those opportunities a reality are within their grasp.

New Venture Action Plan

- Identify market, management, and scale factors that may affect the growth of your business.
- Determine which growth strategy is most appropriate for your business.
- Identify potential international markets for the product or service.
- Develop a plan for globalization of the company at some point in the future.
- Think about an exit or harvest strategy and what impact your choice might have on your business decisions.

Questions on Key Issues

1. What are four characteristics of high-growth companies?
2. How can both market and management factors affect the growth of a new venture?
3. What questions should you ask at each level of the new venture's growth?
4. What advantages does growing within the current market have over integrative and diversification strategies?
5. Why is it important to start a growth-oriented business with a plan for globalization from the beginning?
6. What are the possible exit strategies that entrepreneurs can employ?

Experiencing Entrepreneurship

1. Visit an export center in your area and talk to a Department of Commerce trade specialist who can advise you on how to become prepared to export. What did you learn that you hadn't learned from reading this text?
2. Interview an entrepreneur whose new venture is in its early stages, and question him or her about the growth strategy and exit plan for the business. Can you identify the type of strategy being used?

Relevant Case Studies

Case 3 Raising a CleanBee Baby
Case 5 The Case of Google, Inc.

CASE STUDIES

ADROLL: A CASE STUDY OF ENTREPRENEURIAL GROWTH*

Introduction

In 2013, AdRoll was the fastest growing online advertising company in the United States. The founding team consisted of CEO, Aaron Bell, President, Adam Berke, COO, Peter Krivkovich and Chief Architect, Valentino Volonghi. The innovative company provided customers with critical information that could benefit their bottom line through advertisement retargeting. AdRoll had the capabilities to track each person's online shopping behavior on certain websites. For example, if a consumer looked at a pair of Nike running shoes online and then went back to that same site to look at colors, AdRoll would recognize this information. This information would then be sold and that consumer would experience Nike advertisements specifically targeted at them as they navigated through other websites. The potential market for services such as this was enormous. As a result, AdRoll was ranked the seventh fastest growing private company in the United States by *Inc. Magazine* in 2013. *Forbes Magazine* ranked the AdRoll as the #1 fastest growing company in San Francisco.

*This case was written by Todd A. Finkle, Pigott Professor of Entrepreneurship, Gonzaga University, as a basis for class discussion. Reprinted by permission.

Source: Copyright © 2014 Todd A. Finkle, Pigott Professor of Entrepreneurship, Gonzaga University. All Rights Reserved.

Despite the unbelievable success of the company, the company faced challenges related to growth. The founders knew that uncontrollable growth could lead to disaster. They had to figure out a plan for how to grow their company.

Background of Adroll

AdRoll was founded in 2007 as a means to make advanced display advertising techniques available for brands of all sizes. In 2013, the original founders were still at the company along with two additions that included: Suresh Khanna, Vice President of Sales, and Greg Fulton, Senior Product Director and 150 employees. It was projected that the company would have 450 employees by January 2014.

The company's focus was on retargeting, which kept track of consumer's online browsing behavior. Once this information was collected, AdRoll would then display ads of interest to customers as they traveled around the web. Without retargeting, only 2% of potential customers return to a site. Using retargeting, AdRoll had the potential to bring back the other 98 percent of those customers who otherwise would have never returned. AdRoll also displayed ads for products the consumer had never seen but could potentially be interested in. For example, if a customer looked at ads for basketball shoes, ads by that same site would follow that potential customer around the web.

At the beginning of 2013, AdRoll was in the growth stage of the industry life cycle. The company infiltrated the online marketing industry before the Great Recession of 2008. AdRoll chose to enhance the quality and performance of its products versus focusing on sales. AdRoll's exponential growth started in 2009 when it went into advertisement retargeting. In 2008, AdRoll's revenue was $111,000 and by 2012 it had sales of $50 million for a 45,000 percent increase over four years.

AdRoll captured 500 new customers a month with a 97 percent customer retention rate. The company began a partnership with Facebook that allowed most of AdRoll's clientele to advertise on the largest social networking site in the world. With the ability to advertise on Facebook, customers received a 1,600% return on their investment.

AdRoll received $15 million dollars in funding in July, 2012. With this injection, the company had plans to hire additional employees and expand its office space. The company was also in the process of creating high performance products in the mobile, video and social markets.

AdRoll was a subsidiary of Semantic Sugar Inc., a technology company. Semantic Sugar, Inc. provided online advertising services. The company was incorporated in 2006 and was based in San Francisco, California. Semantic Sugar Inc. owned more than 50 percent of AdRoll.

SWOT Analysis

Strengths

AdRoll's strengths included a 97 percent customer retention rate along with cutting edge display products. The company also had products for all sizes of businesses. AdRoll was one of eight companies to advertise through the Facebook platform. The company had a high return on investment for customers and a skilled and experienced management team. Finally, the firm had a simple navigation platform.

Weaknesses

The weaknesses that confronted AdRoll included seven other competing companies that were also a part of the Facebook platform. Some feedback from consumers had been negative. The company would have a hard time sustaining its growth rate of 11,082 percent like it had in the past 3 years. AdRoll was a young company that did not have extensive experience in the growth process. The company also had a lack of presence in the competitive mobile market.

Opportunities

Opportunities for AdRoll included possible expansion from retargeting retail into retargeting for movies, gaming, sporting events, business-to-business marketing, and other social media sites (Twitter, Pinterest, etc.). In addition, the company could (1) partner with other search engines to track consumers' searches and get a more specific idea of the ads that would be effective; (2) provide search retargeting, a product that is sold by most of AdRoll's competitors; (3) continue the development of RollFace in connection with Google Glass; and (4) further expand into international markets.

Threats

Threats to AdRoll included the possibility of lawsuits if consumers felt that their privacy had been infringed upon, competitors entering the market and replicating its products and services, the possibility of Facebook's presence in the social media world diminishing, and the potential for an economic turndown.

Strategies & Competitive Advantage

AdRoll's business level strategy was overall low cost leadership. Before AdRoll was founded, retargeting advertisements were primarily used by wealthy customers. AdRoll expanded their target market to include small businesses, retailers, and *Fortune* 500 companies. Furthermore, AdRoll had a heavy emphasis on customer service. The company always made itself available to its customers to gain a competitive advantage through ease of use.

AdRoll had a "hands on" management team. They were not afraid of getting their hands dirty to make things work. Due to the smallness of the company there was a lot of transparency and they had a very creative and innovative culture.

AdRoll's primary competitive advantage was the quality of its products. The company claimed that the ads it placed on Facebook were two to three times as effective as the ads of the other seven competitors involved in the Facebook exchange. Additionally, AdRoll showed an extremely high return on investment, which made existing customers unwilling to switch away from AdRoll.

Management Team

AdRoll needed to continue building and attracting a quality management team as they grew. AdRoll's management team was all young men who came from both Stanford and Harvard and who had worked on start-ups in one way or another in the past. They created a culture that could be described as "forward thinking, fun, and hardworking."

AdRoll did not have a hard time finding employees; however, to keep up with the fast growth, they needed to select the right future team members. If AdRoll chose the wrong people, it could be detrimental to their company. Because AdRoll already had smart, young, fun, and risky managers, it may have been beneficial for AdRoll to hire older and more conservative members for their management team. However, more conservative managers might not have worked well with the fast growing and innovative starting team. Therefore, AdRoll put forth the effort to find adaptable managers with open minds and a willingness to take risk, but also not afraid to ask the starting management team to give an idea or decision another consideration.

According to Erin Lockhart, AdRoll's PR Manager, its mission was "to make powerful performance advertising techniques simple for businesses of all sizes." Therefore, AdRoll needed to select managers that knew how to interact with small businesses and meet their needs while also knowing how to meet the needs of large *Fortune* 500 companies. AdRoll also needed managers that were technical experts who had the ability to simplify their technology so any business or individual could use AdRoll's services.

Future of Adroll

Due to its success, AdRoll had a lot of room for growth. While the potential for increasing its customer base was exciting, it posed many challenges for the firm. Thus, AdRoll needed to manage the expansion of the company in a controlled way.

During the expansion stage, AdRoll opened a new office in New York and projected that by January 2014, it would have more than 450 employees. AdRoll was faced with the challenge of growing at a controlled rate without losing customers. Not only that, it faced competition against larger more experienced companies that had already been through the kind of growth that AdRoll was experiencing.

AdRoll began to be recognized as a serious competitor. More established companies had the opportunity to steal much of AdRoll's potential customers before AdRoll had the time to reach them because they could not keep up with their growing customer base. To survive in this market, AdRoll needed to continue to retain customers by providing excellent customer service and selecting a growth team to manage its expansion so that the rest of the company could focus on the customer base and creativity.

AdRoll's expansion meant a lot for the company in terms of changes to its organizational structure and culture. AdRoll's office was set up in a large room with lots of young people and dogs all working in a fast-paced environment, which also facilitated creativity. The question for AdRoll was would it be able to maintain this structure and culture as the company expanded and grew?

As AdRoll expanded and grew, it was either going to have to work hard to maintain this open room structure or change it to a more functional specialization structure. The problem with this was that the more functional structure might result in less creativity. This was dangerous for AdRoll given that much of the company and its ideas thrived on AdRoll's allowance for creativity and innovation.

Since big companies were starting to recognize AdRoll, the company needed to focus on its product to keep customers. AdRoll needed to select a small team to focus on growth and the maintenance of its culture so it could simultaneously be successful at both things.

With this continued growth, AdRoll faced several risks. One of these risks was that many of AdRoll's competitors, such as Chango, offered search retargeting. AdRoll focused mainly on site retargeting and contextual retargeting, which was also done by many of AdRoll's competitors. Therefore, potential customers could choose elsewhere if AdRoll did not have what they were looking for. This risk could have been managed by expanding and innovating AdRoll's product line. The company needed to continue hiring qualified advertising experts that had experience in the social media industry. This would allow for AdRoll to stay competitive by introducing new and innovative approaches to retargeting.

Another risk facing AdRoll was the fickle nature of social media. Much of AdRoll's success could be attributed to being a part of the Facebook exchange. During this time, Facebook was the most popular and widely used social media platform. But that could change in the future.

Additionally, AdRoll was the exclusive retargeting partner on Google Glass, an unreleased glasses product that customers wear and use their personal vision as the screen. AdRoll was working with the company to develop EyeRoll and Roll-Face, which would retarget advertisements based on items consumers looked at and their interest level. For example, if a consumer's friend was wearing a NorthFace jacket, EyeRoll would detect this item. Then, RollFace would identify the consumer's interest in this product by their facial expression and advertise this product right in the view of their personal vision.

The list of competitors for AdRoll would only grow as others saw the potential in the industry. New competitors would imitate the retargeting techniques AdRoll had developed, and would attempt to narrow the gap between their products and others. If competitors figured out how to provide the same service for a cheaper option, it could have really hurt AdRoll's high retention rate of customers. This was especially troubling for AdRoll since much of its focus was on small to medium sized businesses. If new competitors focused solely on small business, and provided a better product with better services, AdRoll was in trouble. However, AdRoll could combat that risk by staying up to date with its innovations in retargeting, and by ensuring that its existing customers were pleased with the products and services they were receiving.

Regardless of competitors, AdRoll still needed to finance the growth of its company. Fortunately, AdRoll had a couple of key advantages in addition to its amazing growth. It had a highly regarded team and had already made crucial relationships with venture capital firms and the "movers" in the Silicon Valley and greater San Francisco area. The growth of the company relied less on the money they were able to generate than on funds from venture capital investments.

AdRoll sought any necessary financing through relationships with venture capital firms including: Foundation Capital, Merus Capital and Accel Partners. AdRoll's early attraction of these venture capital firms and the amazing return on initial capital put them in a great position to acquire additional capital requirements. Yet, it was not financing that was AdRoll's main obstacle to significant growth but rather being able to get the required talent on board.

This was a similar problem that confronted other high technology companies like Google and Facebook. Google became famous for its hiring processes and its amazing employee benefits.

Facebook earned very high remarks including the "Best Place to Work" by GlassDoor.com. It was crucial that AdRoll focus its attention on moving its services forward and focusing on emerging technologies including the mobile spectrum.

Lastly it was important that AdRoll's founders be proactive in the potential harvest of their organization. Although it was typical for companies that have seen this amount of growth to eventually seek an IPO, this strategy did not turn out to be very valuable for some technology companies. In order to ensure their growth, AdRoll could incorporate an employee stock ownership plan (ESOP). This strategy might allow AdRoll to offer key talent and a clear incentive for working for such a fast growing company. Employees could be offered stock, which would give them ownership of the company and a vested interest in its success. This allowed AdRoll to stay away from the risks of an IPO and the regulation that comes from it.

Final Decision

AdRoll's founding management team met for dinner to discuss the issues related to growing pains in the company. Despite being the most successful and fastest growing small companies in the U.S. in 2013, they felt the stress that goes with growth. They talked well into the night on how to proceed.

Discussion Questions

1. Describe the background of AdRoll.
2. Perform a SWOT Analysis of AdRoll.
3. What is the current business level strategy that AdRoll uses? Is this the appropriate strategy? If not, what would you recommend? What other strategies are they using? For example, what types of functional (finance, marketing, management/HR, etc.) strategies are they using? Can you recommend any changes to help the organization?
4. Does AdRoll have a competitive advantage? If so what is the competitive advantage? Is the competitive advantage a sustainable competitive advantage? Why? If not, why?
5. What areas do you see as opportunities for growth, and what strategies do you recommend to AdRoll? Why?
6. As AdRoll grows, how will the structure of its organization change? What affect will that have on AdRoll? What affect will that have on the culture of AdRoll?
7. What recommendations would you make to the founder(s) of AdRoll in regards to harvesting its organization (sell, merge, selling to employees, IPO, etc.)?

References

AdRoll. "AdRoll Launches Retargeting on Google Glass." *AdRoll Blog*. p., 1 Apr. 2013. Web. 30 Apr. 2013.

"AdRoll." *Retargeting and Display Advertising*. Web. 10 May 2013. http://www.adroll.com.

"AdRoll Triples Revenue, Surpasses $50M Run Rate in 2012." *Prnewswire*. 24 Jan. 2013. Web. http://www.prnewswire.com/news-releases/adroll-triples-revenue-surpasses-50m-run-rate-in-2012-188186831.html.

"Chango." *Â·Real-time Marketing Solutions*. Web. 10 May 2013. http://www.chango.com.

"Comparing the Top 4 Retargeting Companies." *SEOmoz*. Web. 24 Jan. 2012. http://www.seomoz.org/blog/comparing-the-top-4-retargeting-companies.

"FetchBack - The Targeted Display Company." *FetchBack*. Web. 10 May 2013. http://fetchback.com.

"Retargeting and Audience Targeting Solutions." Web. 10 May 2013. http://retargeter.com.

B2P: MICRO-BIOINFORMATICS TECHNOLOGY AND GLOBAL EXPANSION[*]

"That's fantastic," Dr. Rosemary Sharpin said as she hung up the phone. Dr. Sharpin was ecstatic and could not wait to share the news with the researchers. She had just found out that her company, B2P, which makes bacteria testing systems for water and food, had been selected as one of the finalists in the New Zealand Focus on Health Challenge, a contest for companies specializing in innovative health technology. Because the challenge focused on helping New Zealand based companies commercialize their products in the United States, Dr. Sharpin knew that expanding outside of New Zealand—something that she has always wanted B2P to do—was eminent.

The international opportunities for B2P had grown in recent years as stories of contaminated food and drinking water had become more and more common. Outbreaks of disease traced to tainted supply chains and careless agricultural practices had caused panics among consumers and led the government to crack down on the industries that controlled the nation's food supply. With thousands of illnesses or deaths and millions of dollars in losses associated with food recalls, insurance claims, and lawsuits every year, the problem had reached critical mass.

A potential solution for the problem lay in the process used to test food and water for contaminants. Current methods of testing for *E. coli* and related bacteria required a professional laboratory,

skilled staff, and up to three days for results to be received. These limitations slowed down the testing process and could contribute to outbreaks. However, B2P Micro-Bioinformatics Technology (B2P), Dr. Sharpin's company, had developed a portable, one-time use, self-contained testing device that enabled almost immediate detection of bacteria present in or on anything.

Before taking advantage of the opportunity, Dr. Sharpin had to answer a number of questions. Although the publicity from the New Zealand Health Challenge might help her gain a foothold in the international market, she had to decide whether to expand her efforts in Australasia, where she had already made some progress, concentrate on the more lucrative European and North American markets, or look for opportunities in the third world market. Dr. Sharpin had to identify which industries had the greatest need for B2P's products and where the barriers to entry might cause problems. And most importantly, Dr. Sharpin had to develop a strategy for entry to these new markets that maximized her chances for success while minimizing the risk to her young company.

Company Background

In 1983, Dr. Rosemary Sharpin formed ICPbio International Ltd., New Zealand's first biotech company. ICP developed and marketed products related to embryo transfer in animals, bio-chemical extraction from animal blood, and quality assurance

[*] This case was written by Melissa Wu, a graduate of the Marshall MBA program at the University of Southern California, as a basis for class discussion. Reprinted by permission.

testing for the dairy industry. It was at ICP that Dr. Sharpin learned of the need for better *E. coli* and coliform testing. As a result, in conjunction with NZDRI (the New Zealand Dairy Research Institute), ICP began to research and develop the innovative biotechnology that would become the foundation for B2P's testing products.

After 20 years with the company as the Joint Managing Director responsible for product development, international sales, and marketing, Dr. Sharpin was ready to begin another startup. In 2002, she bought the intellectual property that was the basis of the B2P product suite from ICP, and she and business partner Maxine Simmonds "spun off" B2P Ltd. from the successful biotech manufacturing company. Wanting to focus fulltime on B2P, Dr. Sharpin also sold her shares in ICP.

As the sole owner of B2P technology and products, Dr. Sharpin had several different options for setting up the company. One of her goals in organizing was to not over extend the company too much in the initial stages. As a result, B2P's structure was straightforward and leveraged outsourced resources including contract manufacturing, marketing, and non-essential design and development. While the company had initially been headquartered in Auckland, New Zealand, B2P expected to eventually move its corporate headquarters to Europe to be closer to larger markets.

Due to her experience at ICP, Dr. Sharpin knew what the market needed: a fast, simple, portable bacteria testing system. B2P's solution—essentially a large bottle in which the contents turn either pink or white, depending on the bacteria present—effectively filled that need and quickly became popular in the New Zealand dairy and shellfish industries. As a result of this success, B2P developed multiple products varieties and complementary products, all with the same testing concept. The products included:

- B2P WaterCheck™: Tests for *E. coli* and coliforms in water. Requires 100 ml of water sample for testing in a self-contained unit.

- B2P FoodCheck™: Tests for *E. coli* and coliforms in solids, including whole shellfish, meat, chicken, yogurt, and leafy greens. Similar to WaterCheck but features wide neck opening to easily add 10 g of sample food.

- B2P DairyCheck™: Tests for *E. coli* and coliforms in dairy liquids.

- B2P COLIQUIK™: Tests for *E. coli* and coliforms in salt water, chemically-treated water, wash from food products, and any other sample with a matrix which may interfere with growth of bacteria or which could spontaneously cause oxidation or reduction in the system (e.g. lemon juice, vitamin C, etc.).

- B2P Swab-It™: Tests for *E. coli* and coliforms on surfaces. Features a moist swab to wipe sample and test for bacteria.

- B2P MicroMagic (rental-financed): Test reader and analyzer. Incubates up to four COLIQUIK samples and illuminates the sample every minute, measures the light responses, plots the readings, and calculates all changes. The system features optional GPS and GPRS technology and battery unit for remote messaging to a central location. Can transmit compressed, encrypted data to nominated personnel (via SMS text message) and/or to a data management system (the MicroWizard™).

- B2P MicroWizard: An on-line interface used to track and verify results.

The Food and Water Testing Industry

Consumer concern and government involvement have caused an increased opportunity within the testing industry as demand for safer products grows.[1] Two ongoing developments that affect *E. coli* and coliform testing are the growth

---

[1] The testing may occur in a laboratory or on-site. Research and testing can be carried out within the laboratory environment or it may involve field studies. Much of the testing in this sector involves the maintenance of utility, agricultural, food, and industry/product standards. The research is carried out and used by industry, government, universities, colleges, individuals, and non-profit organizations.

EXHIBIT 1
U.S. Laboratory Testing
Services by Product/Service

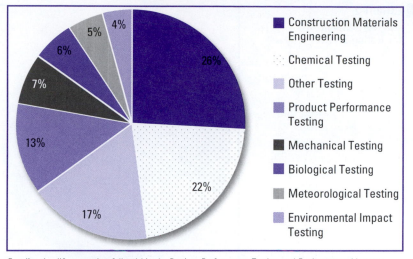

E. coli and coliform testing falls within the Product Performance Testing and Environmental Impact Testing categories (depending on the product on which the tests are being conducted).

Source: Adapted from data found in Laboratory Testing Services in the U.S., IBISWorld Industry Report, August 19, 2009.

in the environmental testing activities industry (Exhibit 1) and an increase in agricultural testing, with both areas benefiting from additional government funding and increased competition. Overall, it is estimated that the general testing industry grew 2.6 percent from 2004 to 2009, despite the recession.[2]

The U.S. *E. coli* and coliform testing space is segmented, with laboratory services divided by size and industry focus (Exhibit 2). There are no large companies that dominate the industry; instead, the industry is comprised of many small players (nearly 70 percent of laboratories have fewer than 10 people).[3] Much of the industry is comprised of regional and national companies that require samples from around the country to be shipped to central laboratories. Many of the smaller labs will employ a few staff members who perform industry-specific tests of water, beef, leafy greens, or dairy products. The larger labs also tend to be industry focused but many have multiple products capable of testing additional contaminants besides *E. coli* and coliform. It is

worth noting that several of the larger labs will outsource specific tests to smaller facilities. IBIS World predicts that existing companies will expand their operations, either by the acquisition of a complementary or rival business or by entering into joint ventures.[4] As such, industry concentration is likely to increase in the future.

Within the *E. coli* and coliform testing industry there are several "areas of pain." Overcoming them can place an organization ahead of the other testing outlets. They include:

Breadth of services: A testing laboratory that can provide a broad array of services often has a competitive advantage over smaller labs. This flexibility enables customers that require a range of different tests to get them all performed at one laboratory.

Reliability: Reputation and reliability are extremely important within the testing world.[5] According to Eric Gorman, a Senior Geologist with GSI/water, laboratory reputation is so important that he will frequently

---

[2] Laboratory Testing Services in the U.S., IBISWorld Industry Report, August 19, 2009.

[3] Laboratory Testing Services in the U.S., IBISWorld Industry Report, August 19, 2009.

[4] Laboratory Testing Services in the U.S., IBISWorld Industry Report, August 19, 2009.

[5] Laboratory Testing Services in the U.S., IBISWorld Industry Report, August 19, 2009.

EXHIBIT 2
U.S. Market Segments
for Testing Services

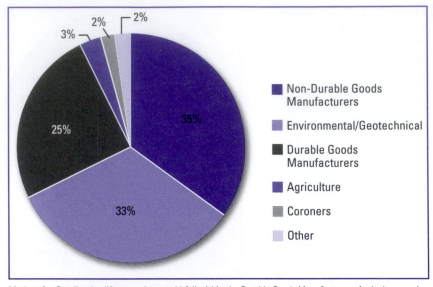

- ■ Non-Durable Goods Manufacturers
- ■ Environmental/Geotechnical
- ■ Durable Goods Manufacturers
- ■ Agriculture
- ■ Coroners
- ■ Other

Markets for *E. coli* and coliform testing would fall within the Durable Goods Manufacturers, Agriculture, and other categories (depending on the product on which the tests are being conducted).

Source: Adapted from data found in Laboratory Testing Services in the U.S., IBISWorld Industry Report, August 19, 2009.

test labs with "blanks" of a known contaminant in order to cross reference the final lab results for validity.[6] Because many tests require skilled, knowledgeable technicians, labs that have more highly skilled technical teams may have the advantage.

Technology: Not surprisingly, proprietary technology can also be an advantage in the testing world. New discoveries and testing methodologies can help save time and money, and improve the accuracy of results. Patents can protect the intellectual property and provide an added competitive advantage to the testing organization.

Time: Slow turnaround time has plagued laboratories for years. While many labs can complete tests within 24 hours, transportation time and/or backlog can result in delays of more than 72 hours. In 2007 it was estimated that only 8 percent of the entire testing industry's tests were performed onsite.[7]

Price: While the price charged for services can be a critical point of competition, many clients are more concerned with accuracy and timeliness. They are often inclined to pay a premium to feel certain that their testing will be reliable and prompt.

The Opportunity

As a result of continuing outbreaks and extensive media coverage, *E. coli* in food and water remained at the top of mind for many Americans. In a 2007 survey funded by *The Beef Check-Off* and managed by the National Cattlemen's Beef Association, *E. coli* was the food borne pathogen with the highest consumer recognition and the highest consumer concern.[8] Every new incident and media report raised consumer fears, which in turn resulted in consumer demand that the government and food industry ensure the safety and quality of their

[6] Gorman, Eric. "Follow up questions. Re: question about water." Email to Melissa Wu, 13 January 2010.
[7] Laboratory Testing Services in the U.S., IBISWorld Industry Report, August 19, 2009.

[8] Food poisoning from *E. coli* and vegetables most concerning, by Rick McCarty, Executive Director, Issues Management—NCBA, accessed via web www.beef.org/uDocs/foodpoisoningfromecoliandvegetablesmostconcerning631.pdf.

products. In fact, government entities such as the CDC, EPA, and FDA had all indicated that clean drinking water and safe recreational water were ongoing priorities.

Current methods of testing for *E. coli* and related bacteria required a well-equipped laboratory, skilled staff, and 22 to 72 hours for results to be received. Sending samples to the lab meant that production managers lost control of the testing process, and the ability to make rapid responses to problems that invariably arose might compromise the product and cause health issues. Sample integrity was also frequently compromised. These obstacles could force companies such as fresh food suppliers, who must ship their products out immediately, to bypass key steps in the testing process or even to move on without waiting for results. There was an opportunity in the marketplace, therefore, for a company and product that could avoid these pitfalls entirely by producing results quickly, on site, and without a trained staff.

Dr. Sharpin believed that B2P's simple, electronic, and field-ready automated bacterial testing systems were perfectly suited to solve the current global crisis. The self-contained units could be used in any environment to detect, count, and report *E. coli* and related bacteria. The products did not require the presence of a skilled technician and reduced the results delivery time to fewer than 2 hours for highly contaminated material and 12 to 14 hours for a confirmed negative test. According to Dr. Sharpin, "There is no user-friendly product on the global market that operates with this speed, specificity, sensitivity and reporting immediacy. This has a huge impact on marketability into existing and new markets in the hospitality and pre-prepared/fast food markets, as well as Third World and 'aid' markets and emergency management."

Any area that could be affected by *E. coli* could be considered a potential market. Based on consumer demand and government intervention, the two markets with significant opportunities were within the water and food industries' supply chains. These included:

- Water testing for:
  - Drinking/ground water
  - Private wells
  - Oceans, lakes, rivers, etc.
  - Amusement parks
  - Hotels, cruise ships
  - Post-disaster

- Food testing:
  - Suppliers of products related to:
    - Beef
    - Dairy
    - Leafy greens
    - Chicken, other meats
  - Restaurants
  - Hotels, convention centers, etc.

Within the larger markets were a number of different opportunities, each with a different business model based on audience type. On a high level, they included:

Suppliers: For suppliers, time is money. Waiting for test results means holding back inventory and adding delays to their operations. The USDA did not require certain tests to be conducted and as a result, much of the industry was self-regulated.[9] Many suppliers were hesitant to perform non-required tests due to fear of being "found out" and losing potential revenue. Additionally, because tracking *E. coli* contamination could be time consuming and difficult, it was easier for suppliers to "play the blame game" when outbreaks occurred. While most did not want to self-test, more and more companies, such as Tyson Chicken, were taking the initiative. Making it easier for suppliers to test their products and reducing the test result time could only help this audience.

Commercial Retail Outlets: If contaminated food makes its way through the supply chain to retail outlets (hotels, stores, fast food restaurants) or commercial recreational water becomes contaminated, companies' reputations can be seriously damaged. While many outlets preferred to rely on heath inspectors to regulate their facilities, a growing number were taking control of the situation. Companies such as Costco, Nestle, and Trader Joe's had taken an active and public

---

[9] Moss, M. (2009, November 12). E. coli Outbreak Traced to Company That Halted Testing of Ground Beef Trimmings. *The New York Times*. Retrieved from www.nytimes.com/2009/11/13/us/13ecoli.html?_r=0.

stance regarding self-testing and/or only working with suppliers who tested their products. For these outlets, the B2P web connected RFID/bar code product tracking tags found in the Micro-Magic device would help reassure the outlet and the consumer that the product had sufficiently passed *E. coli* tests.

Cities, Towns, Utilities: In general, the testing of drinking water was heavily regulated and a number of tests had to be passed before the water was considered potable. Because of these requirements, using B2P's products alone would not be sufficient. However, B2P's kits could still act as a vital step in the testing process. For example, Mr. Gorman was required to send water samples to a specialized lab for final testing. However, he also wanted the convenience of being able to test the water for contamination and treat it accordingly before sending in the sample. In essence, he could use the kit to determine whether or not to disinfect a well before taking the final sample, possibly saving additional money and time. B2P products, such as the MicroMagic and testing containers, could be used to regularly monitor city water supplies and conduct "pre-tests" before sending the water to a lab for a final report. Additional revenue could be generated by charging for data management and the sale of additional containers.

Beaches, Lakes, Rivers: Testing for *E. coli* in beaches, lakes, and rivers can be challenging due to their distance from water testing facilities. This causes delays in results and increases the possibility of contamination. The B2P product was ideal for this situation as local organizations could easily test the water and obtain the necessary results quickly. Dr. Sharpin, keen to enter the recreational water market, noted that "If every lifeguard did a test at night, then in the morning they would know whether the water was safe for swimming, right then and there." As with testing for drinking water sources, revenue could be generated by charging for data management and the sale of additional containers.

Testing Laboratories: With the consolidation of labs within the industry, partnerships with local and regional laboratories will create an advantage to those labs that want to expand their product line. While there may be some issue with IP, a joint venture or license agreement may be a good short-term advantage to introducing the product to the U.S. market.

Consumers: Americans are increasingly concerned about food and water safety and there is a growing market within the U.S. for do-it-yourself water and food testing kits. Consumers are familiar with the Brita model of purchasing a primary water filtration unit and additional filters. This model could work well for B2P with the sale of kits that include an incubator and testing containers and subsequent sales in containers. Because B2P did not have established operation and distribution systems within the U.S., a practical option would be for the company to establish a joint venture with a consumer water filtration company. These agreements could be entered exclusively or openly. Some water options included: Culligan International Co; RainSoft Water Conditioning Co; EcoWater Systems, LLC; Kinetico, INC; Brita; Everpure; William R. Hague, INC; Atlantic Ultraviolet Corp; CUNO; and GE Water and Process Technologies. Food partnerships could also be explored.

Competition and Challenges: The *E. coli* testing market had a mixture of company types, from large laboratories to consumer-oriented products, and no single company dominated the industry.[10] The majority of these organizations had aligned themselves with one industry or another. Competitive product in the existing market was in the form of test kits which had to be used in some form of laboratory with significant additional equipment and skilled personnel. While there was no direct competitor that offered B2P's combination of self-contained, reliable, do-it-yourself, fast result tests, there

[10] Laboratory Testing Services in the U.S., IBISWorld Industry Report, August 19, 2009.

were organizations that did offer similar products. Bluewater Biosciences in Canada offered a do-it-yourself kit that did not require incubation. It differed from the B2P product because it took 2–3 days to obtain results and could be hazardous due to the lack of protection against breakage and spillage. Colitag, a product from CPI International, was another similar product. It had been on the market for several years and featured a do-it-yourself test with results in 2–24 hours. This product required an incubator and did not offer a solution to dispose of the billions of dangerous bacteria that could be found in the test solution.

When considering the testing market, and specifically the U.S. testing market, there were several key challenges that had to be considered. They included:

- **Breadth of Services.** Many labs offered multiple types of testing. By sending samples to a lab of this kind, a company could obtain lab results for more than one contaminant.
- **Reputation.** Without a proven American track record, entering the testing market could be a challenge.
- **Regulation.** The U.S. was a highly regulated market and obtaining government approvals was expensive.[11]
- **Requirement.**[12] When possible, companies sometimes chose not to test their products at all. If testing was not required and its cost exceeded the cost of a product recall, many—especially in the meat industry—chose not to test their products.

The Future of B2P

The frightening threat of *E. coli* contamination in food and water will always be a problem. Fortunately, serious outbreaks can easily be prevented if the contamination is caught quickly and dealt with immediately. Thus, the need for a reliable, convenient, quick method of testing food and water provides an ample opportunity for B2P to expand its business. Their *E. coli* and coliform testing kits are more reliable, more efficient, and more convenient than any other product on the market, and the company has made successful inroads in Australasia. However, breaking into the lucrative European and American markets will likely take a serious commitment of both time and resources.

To maximize its chances for success, Dr. Sharpin knows B2P must answer a number of questions before moving forward. Specifically, what industries should they focus on and is the U.S. the best place to start? What kinds of challenges will the company face and how are they best overcome? And which of the many opportunities the company has available should it pursue first?

Discussion Questions

1. What are some of the challenges the company faces when entering the U.S. testing market and how can B2P overcome them?
2. Is the B2P product an industry game changer? Is the product better than the other testing devices on the market? Why? Why not?
3. What are some of the opportunities for B2P?

[11] Generally speaking, the Testing Services industry is subject to regulation by numerous government agencies and international groups. The major regulating bodies affecting the industry include: American National Standards Institute (ANSI); National Institute of Standards and Technology (NIST); U.S. Food and Drug Administration (FDA); Occupational Safety and Health Administration (OSHA); Environmental Protection Agency (EPA); and the U.S. Department of Agriculture (USDA).

[12] *Source:* Laboratory Testing Services in the U.S., IBISWorld Industry Report, August 19, 2009.

RAISING A CLEANBEEBABY*

Sitting in CleanBeeBaby's brand new loft space in Venice, California, Jennifer Beall took a few minutes to pause and reflect on her company's first few years of life. In 2010, her idea for a mobile stroller and car seat cleaning service had taken the winning prize in her school's MBA business plan competition—surprising a lot of people. She also was surprised—very surprised—to have won. "I was concerned," she said, "that investors wouldn't be excited about it, because most investors are not my customer." More generally, the idea was one whose growth potential many had questioned. Drive a van fully stocked with cleaning supplies and equipment to places where moms can drop off dirty seats and strollers for one- or two-hour eco-friendly cleaning? Make it a different place each day? It was the sort of concept that many deemed too simple and too small to merit attention. When people talked about entrepreneurship, they wanted growth and scalability! CleanBeeBaby seemed more mom-and-pop (or mom-and-poop) than gazelle.

Now, more than three years after the company's official launch and more than five years after she had begun work on the idea, Beall was looking at a company whose potential seemed huge. She had a van operating all day, every day, in Los Angeles—plus additional vans operating in Orange County and San Diego, California; she also had a courier service (pick up, clean, and deliver back) operating in New York City. She was overseeing a staff of 22 individuals, including five full-time employees. Stores like Nordstrom's and Babies "R"

Us had asked if she might work with them to provide in-store cleaning services for their customers. Hundreds of inquiries, both domestic and international, had come in from individuals seeking to franchise the operation. She couldn't even keep pace with local demand—as the owners of boutiques in her existing cities wanted more van visits than a regular schedule could accommodate. And that was just the beginning. Beall was also getting more and more questions from retailers and parents seeking advice about safe cleaning supplies and related products.

With so many questions coming at Beall from so many different directions, she was left to ponder an age-old parental question: How might she help her baby—CleanBeeBaby—grow up?

An Idea is Born

When Jennifer Beall steps in front of a group and shares the CleanBeeBaby story, she almost immediately explains that she does not yet have children of her own. She says it unapologetically and with a grin—knowing that her audience often presumes parenthood for those helming baby businesses. In fact, it is the first indication that Beall has never been all that interested in building a small company.

Raised in Austin, Texas, Beall attended Duke University and then the Kellogg School of Management at Northwestern University. Though she began college thinking she would become an engineer, she chose instead to pursue a degree in mathematics. Thereafter, she accepted a position in management consulting. Eventually, she started working at Roll International—a

*This case was written by Elissa Grossman, Associate Professor of Clinical Entrepreneurship at the University of Southern California, as a basis for class discussion. Reprinted by permission.

privately held company whose global holdings include Fiji Water and the in-house consulting group in which she worked. It was Roll that partially bankrolled her MBA degree and, thus, Roll to which she had to return upon graduating. Nonetheless, her graduate school focus involved entrepreneurship.

> I spent my whole first year of business school looking for a business idea, and I decided my thesis was about helping improve work-life balance for busy moms. I put together 50 ideas on a spreadsheet. One idea was a clip that would hook a portable DVD player onto your stroller or onto a restaurant table. (Of course, this was pre-iPad.) Another was a co-working space for new moms, with daycare down the hall. That way, you could work, but still have access to breastfeed every few hours. I spent my second year narrowing down the list. This idea about cleaning car seats quickly floated to the top because every mom who we talked to wanted it—and we couldn't find anyone else out there who was doing it.

That Beall was not a mom was, in her view, irrelevant to the underlying inspiration or the business itself. What mattered was that she might someday want the sort of work-life balance that she did not see those around her finding. At her first management consulting job, for example, Beall noticed that her female colleagues often tried to start a family and make partner at the same time; she also noticed that, ultimately, none had chosen to stay on the partner track.

> I thought to myself, 'I want to have a career and a family. Maybe this isn't the right career for me.' I started paying attention to the blogs and magazines. I decided I needed to figure out the macro trend. Millennials care about work-life balance in their 20s. They want to work at Google so they can play ping pong. I decided, 'I think this issue is going to balloon for them.'

Beall's belief in this insight guided her MBA choices. She recruited more than 40 classmates across five or six different classes, such that their project work could explore different aspects of her idea—either directly or indirectly.

> I took a market research class where we did a survey of over 1,500 parents nationwide. I took entrepreneurial finance, a business law class, a service operations class. I took service as marketing. And I took a class called "New Venture Formation." All of the classes were useful—even when they didn't allow us to work on our own business ideas. In my service operations class, for example, I got my team to do Stanley Steemer. We visited their vans and trucks—learning how a mobile business is run, how they work as a part of a franchise system. Everything built on itself. As a student, I could get anyone's time. A buyer at Target might give me a half hour interview when I was in school; out of school, I'd have trouble reaching that same person.

Concerns about potential competitors ran a distant second to fact-finding for Beall, who shared her concept with anyone she hoped might offer insight. She observed, with a laugh, "I've never been worried about people copying my idea because, as they tell us in business school, ideas are worth nothing. Also, there was no serious business person attacking this as a big opportunity. Nobody else was passionate about cleaning baby poop the way I was!"

Beall believed that her business plan competition victory was driven less by the idea itself than by the depth and breadth of the research she had completed. The win secured her sufficient credibility to raise, in 2010, a first round of funding—a friends and family round that provided $80,000 in convertible debt. Despite those funds, she was committed to return to the employer who had supported her degree.

Cleaning Up by Getting One's Hands Dirty

Upon receiving her MBA, Beall went back to Roll—continuing her full-time job as a consultant for 18 months. At the same time, "flying under the radar," she began to proactively pursue launch of her own company. Many work days ended at 3 AM, a schedule that took a toll on her energy and her relationships ("my boyfriend dumped me"). Those costs aside, her entrepreneurial efforts began paying off quickly and quite literally. She used the seed funds to purchase a van, first supplies, and the equipment needed to start a Los Angeles operation. Within four months of hitting the road, her business was cash flow positive.

> In school, we tried to figure out where moms would want to use this service—at the park, at the grocery store, at the baby stores, at the car wash. Where? It turned out that not all of these places were good. We tried parks, for example, and kept getting kicked out—no permits, no generators for, say, a vacuum. So I got in my car and drove to ten baby stores and said, 'can I do free cleanings here'? Every one said yes. That's how we got started. It cost me the cost of providing the cleaners, but nothing else. And they promoted the heck out of it—social media, whatever. The goal was to go viral, where people were forwarding it to their friends. We had big wait lists from those events. Over time, retailers started telling us that their daily revenues would increase on days when we were there.

Beall started realizing that the value of her service was so great to retailers, who told her their sales tripled or quadrupled on days when she visited, that she had no need to pay them for "placement." With this insight in hand, she began to barter for free space at baby expos and trade shows. The event organizer would get more sales, while CleanBeeBaby would get free marketing to a large group of prospective and targeted customers. She would also trade free cleaning services for mommy blogger attention. She observed, "The few times I've spent money on marketing, I've felt that I've not gotten my money's worth." In addition to bartering for space, she eradicated what would otherwise be the second largest cost for her company (after labor)—convincing cleaning product manufacturers to sponsor CleanBeeBaby. At different points in time, both BabyGanics and The Honest Company provided free cleaning supplies to Beall; doing so helped them market their own wares.

By July 2012, when Beall felt ready to leave the safety net of her "regular" day job, she also began noticing some of the challenges of growth. Among her discoveries: in the same way that her classmates had little passion for baby poop, those cleaning it (and other baby-related "stuff") weren't all that passionate either. They also didn't love having to drive to a different location every day. Good and committed cleaning technicians were challenging to find—and, in the early days, almost impossible to keep on board. Beall spent four months driving her own van, cleaning a seemingly endless supply of seats and strollers, and meeting her customers. At the same time, she tried to build the business beyond its launch location. When Beall started the New York branch, she initially did it without local staff—instead moving there for a summer to build the business herself.

> To launch in New York was a twofold challenge in that, on top of just expanding, I had to figure it out operationally. How does it work in bad weather? When there's no space in retail stores? When there are no parking lots in which to put a van? It is the second biggest market, but you need your own space in Midtown. We now have a courier who does pickups from retailers between 10 and 11 each morning—dropping off for customer pick-up by 6 PM.

In the fall of 2013, after returning to LA from New York, Beall turned her attention to the development of systems for more effective hiring and retention. She brought on a Senior Director of Operations, a Regional Manager for Southern California, and two full-time field supervisors.

She brought in part-time consultants to serve as CFO and to provide marketing support. She also began to be more proactive about hiring for fit—working with her senior managers to identify and carefully train a large team of technicians likely to remain with the company.

Freed by her senior staff to turn away from the minutiae and focus on higher level strategy, she began exploring her options. As a first step, she started conducting extensive research about if and how CleanBeeBaby might be turned into a franchise operation. Beall had long believed that there might be huge upside in franchising; residential cleaning franchisor Merry Maids had 1,432 operating units globally (2014 data), for example, while Molly Maids had 632 (2010 data). When she further factored in the many unsolicited inquiries that she received from prospective franchisees worldwide, her confidence increased. She initiated the legal paperwork and process to become a franchisor. On the heels of taking this step, she closed an angel funding round for $500,000 (with an expressed investor interest in a subsequent investment for the same amount).

She also began to pursue work with Nordstrom, after a buyer contacted her to see if CleanBeeBaby might partner with them on an in-store promotion. They proposed, specifically, a test in which they would pay for a fixed number of cleanings to be offered as free gifts with purchased strollers. In October, the pilot program ran, with great success, in three Southern California branches. Four more events followed in May 2014. On the heels of this second success, Nordstrom asked Beall to scale her efforts to encompass 17 stores in Southern California. They also expressed a desire, over the longer term, to expand the program nationally. In parallel with this, Beall began communicating with Babies "R" Us about other in-store concepts.

Decisions, Decisions

As the summer of 2014 drew to a close, Beall found herself confronted with a number of significant growth options. Which to choose and how to prioritize those options were foremost in her mind, always with an eye to retaining her own work-life balance. Her vision clearly included the formal establishment of a franchise offering. But creating that offering came with many executional decisions. How much should they charge? What sort of person constituted a high potential franchisee? Should she start by pursuing the hundreds of unsolicited franchisee inquiries already received—or by targeted marketing to candidates? Which geographic regions, if any, should she choose to assign to franchisees? Which might she keep corporate-owned? How should those locations be chosen? She hoped to sell two or three franchises by the end of 2014—and to have between 10 and 15 by the end of 2015.

Not content to stop there, she wondered how she might build out other revenue streams to make the business more robust and long-lived. She had begun, in Los Angeles, to experiment with stroller repair as well as cleaning; she had begun to clean other items too. Maybe it was time to launch her own cleaning product line—one that was eco-friendly and organic like the others, but whose profits would fuel her own business. If not that, or maybe at the same time, her growing profile as a baby expert (she had received significant press coverage in outlets such as *Entrepreneur* magazine and MSNBC) suggested that she might be able to start charging for items previously secured through barter—including long-term product sponsorships and retail relationships. She began to wonder, for example, if she could stop providing her services to boutiques for free and instead request a commission on sales achieved on CleanBeeBaby days. For retailers like Nordstrom and Babies "R" Us, she wondered if she should start exploring the possibility of dedicated in-store service centers. She also wondered if her email list, now many thousands strong, could be used to advertise others' products. Beall commented,

> What I'd really like, at some point, is to be the Geek Squad of the baby industry. In the same way that the Geek Squad spends time solving all sorts of technology problems, and includes both mobile and in-store components, we could be the go-to source for parents—car seats, strollers, cleaning products, and other things as well. That's where I'd like to head.

Tending to a Growing (CleanBee)Baby

As much as Beall could envision a promising CleanBeeBaby future, and felt ready to get there immediately, she also recognized that a misstep in the present could derail her plans. And Clean-BeeBaby's present—as a very active, very young company—required a great deal of founder attention. Requests for appointments and cleaning advice, plus reports from the field, seemed to hit her cell phone every few minutes. She also was kept occupied by her legal team—hard at work on the franchising opportunity—and the challenges of managing her team and ongoing business operations. A few minutes of pause and reflection were all, thus, that Beall would allow herself in the midst of yet another crowded day. Her phone buzzed and brought her back to reality. It was a cleaning technician in New York texting her that a vacuum had broken. As she reached to text back, a mom walked in the door to drop off a baby seat. That week, Beall had started offering drop-off cleanings at the new Los Angeles headquarters. Through the door of her office, Beall waved to the customer, shouting, "Just leave your seat on the table. We'll get to it right away!"

EXHIBIT 1   CleanBeeBaby Cleanings*

Location	Year	Strollers	Car Seats
Los Angeles	2011	400	600
	2012	1000	1500
	2013	1800	2800
New York	2013	800	400
Additional	~ 800–1000 bottles of stain remover per year (across all markets), plus multi-surface cleaner, dish soap (for stroller tires), laundry detergent, etc.		

*Estimates only, to provide a sense of initial market size and growth rate.

EXHIBIT 2   Sample Monthly Schedule (LA)

CLEANBEEBABY LOS ANGELES EVENTS						
Sunday	Monday	Tuesday	Wednesday	Thursday	Friday	Saturday
SUN	MON	TUE	WED	THU	FRI	SAT
Aug 31	Sep 1	Sep 2	Sep 3	Sep 4	Sep 5	Sep 6
Rosie Pope Santa Monica 11 to 4	Babies RUs Porter Ranch 10 to 3	Gelson's Valley Village 10 to 4	Romp Hollywood 10 to 4	Pampered Tot Hermosa Beach 10 to 3.	Pump Station Santa Monica 10 to 4	Granola Babies OCCosta Mesa 11 to 4
	LABOR DAY					
Sep 7	Sep 8	Sep 9	Sep 10	Sep 11	Sep 12	Sep 13
Pumpkinheads Brentwood 11-4 Kidsland – Ktown 11-3 Car Seat Safety Only	Gelson's Hollywood 10 to 4	Pamper 6 Play Westwood 10 to 4	Whole Foods Woodland Hills 10 to 4	Whole Foods El Segundo 10 to 4	Amy's Playground South Pasadena 10 to 3	Rosie Pope Santa Monica 10 to 3

(Continued)

Sunday	Monday	Tuesday	Wednesday	Thursday	Friday	Saturday
SUN	**MON**	**TUE**	**WED**	**THU**	**FRI**	**SAT**
Sep 14	**Sep 15**	**Sep 16**	**Sep 17**	**Sep 18**	**Sep 19**	**Sep 20**
Babies R Us Calabasas 11 to 4	**Gelson's** Valley Village 10 to 4	**My Little Sunshine** Culver City 11 to 3	**Xpecting Maternity** OCJCosta Mesa 10 to 4	**Juvenile Shop** Sherman Daks 10 to 4	**Buttercup** Pasadena 10 to 4	**Natural and Holistic Baby Expo** Long Beach *(no appointments can be made online)*
Sep 21	**Sep 22**	**Sep 23**	**Sep 24**	**Sep 25**	**Sep 26**	**Sep 27**
Pump Station Santa Monica 11 to 4	**Children's Orchard** Manhattan Beach 10 to 3	**Babies R Us** Porter Ranch 10 to 3	**Open for House Calls**	**Pump Station** Hollywood 10 to 4	**Mia a Dragonfly** Burbank 11 to 4	**Bellies** Glendale/ Montrose 11:30 to 4
Sep 28	**Sep 29**	**Sep 30**	**Oct 1**	**Oct 2**	**Oct 3**	**Oct 4**
Red CARpet Even! Skirball Center *(no appointments can be made online)*	**Gelson's** Long Beach 10 to 4	**Pumpkin heads** Brentwood 10 to 4	**Romp** Hollywood 10 to 4	**Babies R Us** Glendale/Atwater 10 to 3	**Pump Station** Santa Monica 10 to 4	**Granola Babies** OCJCosta Mesa 11 to 4

EXHIBIT 3 The CleanBeeBaby Mobile Service

Discussion Questions

1. Who are CleanBeeBaby's target customers, and what is the value proposition that Clean-BeeBaby offers? What problem is Beall solving?

2. Why does it matter that smaller retailers are experiencing much higher sales on days when Beall visits?

3. Why, if CleanBeeBaby's service is so great, aren't others doing it?

4. If CleanBeeBaby can't be replicated easily, then is it a good idea for Beall to pursue a franchise model?

5. Of the many options available to Beall at the end of the case, which should she pursue in the short-term? Why? How?

6. Is CleanBeeBaby the right name for the business?

COMMAND AUDIO: THREE STARTUPS FOR THE PRICE OF ONE

Introduction

As Don Bogue, CEO of Command Audio, stood before the imposing assemblage of intellectual-property attorneys at the Marcus Evans November 2006 Conference in Washington, DC, he knew he was about to bring them a perspective of their field that only he, as an entrepreneur whose company developed and now licenses patents, could bring. He had facetiously titled his speech "Do Not Try This at Home: A Scarred Entrepreneur's View of Patent Licensing, Litigation, and Law." It was to be his version of how his company successfully developed a sustainable business model based on its intellectual-property assets.

> I am an entrepreneur, not a lawyer. Consequently, I see the world of patent law and litigation through a soda straw. My view of what is important out of the vast body of patent law is very narrowly focused: One company (mine), one technology, one portfolio of patents, and, at any given time, one lawsuit, one opponent, one set of facts, legal maneuvers, relevant law, prior art, etc., etc. While I may say things with which you disagree, just understand that they come from this tightly bounded perspective.

The attorneys listening to Bogue were about to hear an interesting and very unique case study of Bogue's company, Command Audio, which had been granted more than 60 U.S. and foreign patents and which had succeeded in leveraging its patent portfolio in each of the three principal ways that such a portfolio can be monetized: (1) attracting investment capital and protecting the technology position, (2) acquiring customers and strategic partners, and (3) licensing patent rights.

> We are unique (or nearly so) not only because we have had these three very intense, very high-risk business experiences, but also because we have lived to tell the story.

The Founding of a Company

Don Bogue grew up in a middle-class family with a father who worked in law enforcement; as a consequence, the family moved a lot. Nevertheless, Bogue, who was his high school's student body president, followed a reasonably straight path that took him to Harvard University, where he graduated *magna cum laude* with a bachelor's degree in economics. He then spent a decade at Ampex Corp, where he held a number of senior management positions.

In the early 1980s, while Bogue was at Ampex running its audio–video systems business, he met John Ryan, who was chief engineer for the camera group. John, it seems, was about to leave the company to start his own company, called Macrovision, which invented and patented anti-copying technology for VHS tapes, the popular mode of video storage at the time. While at Ampex, Ryan had learned the value of patents; so after filing his initial applications, he proceeded to file for patent protection on all the various ways that someone could defeat his original invention. Meanwhile,

Bogue had moved on to join a small publicly held microwave test instrument company, Gigatronics, as CEO. One day in June 1995, Ryan called Bogue to tell him about a new technology he had developed that didn't fit with the Macrovision portfolio. Bogue liked the technology and thought that he might have a good business model for commercializing it. The thought of leaving the relative security of a job in corporate America was a risk, but Bogue believed that as a founder and CEO of a start-up company, "If you're not scared, you're not paying attention. It's thrilling, which is the state between exciting and terrifying." Bogue had no personal start-up experience to follow: he had to learn it as he moved forward. "If you have any self-awareness at all, you realize you have been given a gift: great accountability, but you're in charge of building the entire company from the ground up. It's even more fun than just being CEO." Together Don and John decided in late 1995 to launch Command Audio.

> John Ryan invented the basic functionality of what has come to be known as the personal video recorder, or PVR; you may be more familiar with its best known branded version TiVo. John's inventions, expressed in a series of patent applications he began filing in early 1993, cover the audio elements of devices that receive broadcast multimedia content, then store it as a database in some sort of random access memory for later replay at the convenience of the user. What you want, when you want it. (Don Bogue)

The technology that Ryan had invented would receive a broadcast signal and store all of it or only those parts that were of interest to the particular user. In other words, Command Audio would broadcast a variety of audio programming and the users could choose what they wanted to store and listen to. The receiver provided the users with an electronic program guide that let them select from the broadcast stream what they wanted to hear. A small hand-held device that was always on automatically captured the latest editions of the users' preferred programs for instantaneous access every time they got into their cars.

> I, for instance, had my receiver set up to give me, whenever I got in my car, instantaneously at a single press of a single button, the latest traffic report for my commute route, NPR's most recent top-of-the-hour newscast, a roundup of NFL action, today's "What's News Business and Finance Column" from the *Wall Street Journal* (in audio, of course), last night's Jay Leno monologue, and *News Hour with Jim Lehrer*. In short, with an RCA Audio-on-Demand receiver and a subscription to the Command Audio service, car commuters could listen to what they wanted whenever and wherever they were. (Don Bogue, Marcus Evans Conference, November 2006)

The receiver's interface was designed for "someone who is essentially blind and paralyzed, which, when you think about it, is a good analog for a person whose primary activity is driving a car at speed and only secondarily wants to access and listen to entertaining content: eyes on the road, not on a complex LCD display; hands on the wheel, not engaged in locating and pushing a dozen or more buttons." CA's research with consumers using driving simulators found, for example, that when people attempted to access content by navigating a three-level information hierarchy they invariably crashed. Two-level hierarchies in conjunction with distinctively shaped, tactile buttons and audio feedback were simple to use, at least as easy while driving as a conventional car radio. Who was the customer CA was trying to reach with its initial product and service? It wasn't the music listener, but rather car commuters who were looking for news and information in choices and amounts that fit their unique listening preferences during their morning and afternoon commute times. They already satisfied their on-demand music needs through conventional methods like tapes and CDs. The CA system would essentially do the same for non-music categories, and the content would be both local and national, although traffic, sports, and weather would have more detailed reports at a local level. The service would carry advertising, but the user would be able to opt out of listening to it. Bogue's market research determined that users actually wanted advertising if it was relevant to their interests and occurred at convenient times. CA placed advertising links at the end of program segments where they might logically occur according to the content presented. Users could also access advertising through a separate product information content menu. To provide such a service, CA had to acquire the content from broadcasters, acquire the rights to broadcast, and actually broadcast an interactive version. CA would receive an automated feed of broadcast material, for example, an NPR show. Then a technician would go through the broadcast and provide segment markers so the listener could choose the parts they wanted to listen to. This could actually be accomplished in a matter of seconds. CA broadcast 80 hours of content every day and, to this day, it believes it is the only company to which NPR has licensed broadcast rights to its "crown jewel" programs: *Morning Edition, Talk of the Nation,* and *All Things Considered.*

Audio content was ubiquitous, inexpensive, and provided by many companies. Moreover, in popular content areas like traffic, weather, news, sports, and business, users were indifferent to brand name, which further contributed to the low cost of the service. The CA system was most threatening to the AM band, which was the primary carrier of news, sports, and talk shows. And, to broadcast the signal, CA could use small pieces of idle spectrum in the FM band. In 1996, there were more than 7,000 licensed FM transmitters.[1]

About 16 percent of those were in the top 100 metro areas that CA was targeting. Bogue figured that leasing the idle spectrum would provide the stations with incremental income at no cost. The amount of money involved might not be significant to leading stations, but to stations in smaller markets and to public radio, it would be enormously attractive.

The Command Audio system consisted of three main components:[2]

- A database of news and non-music entertainment material in audio form, which was then compressed, encrypted, and broadcast to hand-held receivers
- Receivers that sifted the incoming material and stored in memory those portions that were of interest to the user
- Specific items that, at the user's convenience, he or she could recall from memory for listening

Implementing the system required a program center where content was gathered, edited, formatted, and distributed by satellite link to local markets for transmission. CA then leased idle frequency spectrum from a network of local FM radio stations and pushed it to users' receivers.

The Industry

Just 30 years ago, most of what we rely on today for entertainment, networking, collaboration, and communication did not exist. With the advent of digital technology in the mid-1990s, the surge in new consumer electronics has been unprecedented. Digital TV (DTV) products emerged in 1998 after being adopted as the industry standard in 1996. As of 1998, one in four U.S. households had the basic equipment to put together a home theater system; VCRs were a commodity item, as were personal computers. In 1996, digital cellular communications became available in the United States, and in June 1998, the first Internet-enabled phones appeared.

The consumer electronics industry actually began with radio, which was commercialized by Radio Corporation of America (RCA), a joint venture of General Electric, Westinghouse, and AT&T; and Telefunken, a joint venture of European companies

---

[1]"By the Numbers." *Broadcasting & Cable* (March 4, 1996), p. 76.

[2]Command Audio Business Plan, 1996.

Siemens and AEG.[3] RCA later led the commercialization of television worldwide, but failed in the 1970s from an ineffective effort to become a conglomerate. Meanwhile, by the late 1980s, Japanese companies Sony and Matsushita became the most important commercializers of electronics, in particular, the Walkman, Triton Color TV, the VCR, the CD, and the DVD, and succeeded in driving American companies out of their own domestic markets.

The personal video recorder industry grew rapidly when in 2001 the satellite and cable television companies began integrating the PVR function into their marketing packages in competition with existing PVR companies. In 1999, TiVo Inc. and ReplayTV Network Inc. were the industry leaders and the first to mass-market to consumers. Their technologies enabled consumers to pause and record live TV as well as enjoy instant replay. Because TiVo developed many strategic alliances with huge consumer product companies like Sony, Toshiba, GE, DirecTV, and Philips, it gained market share over ReplayTV, which struggled after being acquired by SONICblue. Unit sales of digital video recorders are depicted in Figure 1.

The Market and the Competition

In 1996, Bogue determined that approximately 120 million people in the United States commuted to work each day by car, and of those, 18 million spent 60 minutes or more commuting in their cars. His market research also indicated that more than 90 percent of those commuters were interested in CA's on-demand service. Bogue knew that a new consumer product might take years to be adopted by the mass market. Figure 2 depicts the comparative projected U.S. household penetration of radio-on-demand (ROD) against VCR and CD adoption patterns.

The "early adopters" of CA's service were defined as people who

- Resided in the 100 largest metropolitan areas[4]
- Spoke English as their primary language
- Commuted to work by car
- Spent an aggregate of 60 minutes per day commuting

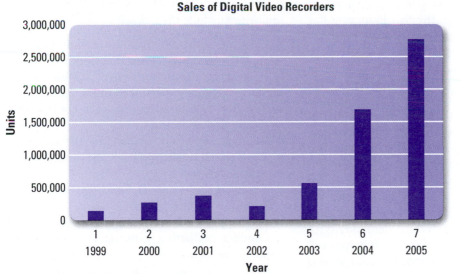

FIGURE 1 Sales of Digital Video Recorders

Source: Media Trends Track, Television Bureau of Advertising, Inc., www.tvb.org.

---

[3]A. D. Chandler. "Gaps in the Historical Record: Development of the Electronics Industry." *Working Knowledge* (October 20, 2003), http://hbswk.hbs.edu/item/3738.html.

[4]Top 100 Metropolitan Areas per "Metro Market Ranks." *Radio Advertising Source* (December 1995).

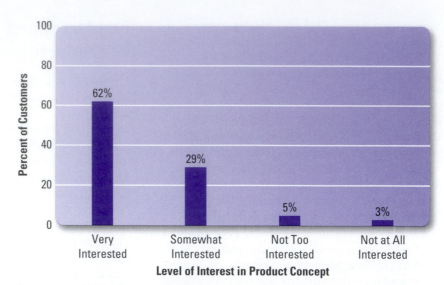

FIGURE 2 Overall Interest in Command Audio Concept

Source: Command Audio Business Plan, 2005, p. 33.

Bogue believed that this target group represented the best chance for entering the market, and it consisted of 18 million people. Customers were disproportionately male, more inclined to purchase electronic devices, and had higher incomes. To validate his estimates and gauge demand, Bogue commissioned an independent market study. In a test in the San Francisco Bay area of 625 residents, respondents were favorably accepting of the concept. Figure 3 depicts the response pattern for this group.

As part of the follow-up to the telephone survey, the participants took part in focus groups where they were able to understand the CA concept more in-depth. Their response was similarly positive, with their evaluation rising after they had viewed a demonstration of the system. Conjoint analysis, which asked participants to make explicit trade-offs between various product or service functions, features, and prices, further substantiated the conclusion relative to demand. With premium content, a free receiver, $30 per month subscription, and a Sony brand, the analysis was able to achieve gross penetration rates as high as 75 percent. Even with these positive results, however, Bogue knew that the actual penetration rate of the CA service would depend on the marketing campaign, the scope of the distribution

channel, the quality of the programming, and the quality of the individual experience in accessing the programming.

His model for the adoption of the CA system was Hughes Electronics Corporation's DIRECTV®, which has been called the most successful product launch in the history of consumer electronics. The similarities include the following:[5]

- CA is an advanced version of a universally accepted consumer service that does not require the mastery of a complex new technology.
- There appears to be a need in the market.
- The CA system gives the user control over timing and content.
- There appears to be demand for the system.
- Users purchase the receivers and then subscribe to the service.
- Receivers are manufactured by well-known consumer electronics firms.
- Service providers and hardware manufacturers conduct marketing campaigns to build consumer awareness.

Bogue understood the need to license to other radio-on-demand service providers and media and entertainment companies seeking

[5]Command Audio Business Plan, 1996, p. 38.

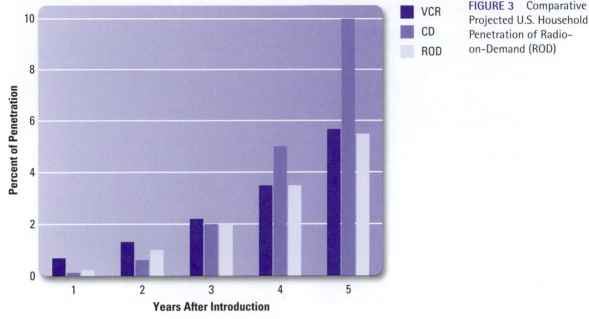

FIGURE 3   Comparative Projected U.S. Household Penetration of Radio-on-Demand (ROD)

Source: Command Audio Business Plan, 1996.

new channels for content distribution if he was ever going to reach mass adoption. He figured that these additional service providers could capture about 40 percent of the market by 2002. Figure 4 displays total system demand and Command Audio's revenue projections.

The Competition

Bogue saw his primary competition as conventional radio, which was free to users because of its advertising business model and because it no longer had a learning curve. Nevertheless, he believed that users wanted more control over what they listened to and they wanted to avoid a clutter of advertising that was not relevant to their interests. For a low price and through a simple method, users could gain that control. Because CA's system could determine audience demographics, it would be easier for CA to convince prospective advertisers to use its medium over conventional radio in order to closely target ads to the interests of specific demographic groups.

One competitor was RBDS (Radio Broadcast Data System), a low data rate data broadcasting service that, in 1996, was being adopted by some FM stations. The service enabled "listeners with specially equipped car radios to receive supplementary program data and text messages that [could] be displayed on the receiver to show station call letters, programming format . . . title and artist of a current piece as well as playlists of the next several selections. In addition the radios could receive and display pager messages and low data rate information such as sports scores."[6] In 1995, approximately 5 percent of licensed stations were broadcasting some RBDS data, and fewer than 800,000 car radios were RBDS compatible.

In 1996, when Bogue wrote the Command Audio business plan, a few companies had announced intentions to bring satellite broadcast radio to market through point-to-multipoint systems that would transmit music and non-music programming to cars equipped with special receivers. These services promised better quality sound, the ability to select a station by format, a broader range of programming, and freedom from

[6]Command Audio Business Plan, 1995, p. 48.

FIGURE 4   Command Audio (CA) Plan Revenue Summary

	1998	1999	2000	2001	2002
Radio-on-demand subs, avg (000)	98	596	1,501	2,778	4,589
U.S. household penetration, end (%)	0.2	1.0	2.0	3.5	5.5
CA market share (%)	100.0	90.0	88.0	70.0	60.0
CA subs, avg (000)	98	556	1,320	2,264	3,428
Activation fee ($)	10.00	10.00	10.00	10.00	10.00
Basic sub fee ($/month)	19.95	19.95	19.95	19.95	19.95
Premium sub fee ($/month)	9.95	9.95	9.95	9.95	9.95
Premium buy rate (%)	80.0	80.0	80.0	80.0	80.0
CA sub revenue ($ million)	38	209	487	835	1,265
Avg revenue per sub ($/mo)	29.28	28.71	28.28	28.17	28.12

© Cengage Learning®

terrestrial-induced signal interference. However, satellite radio would not give the user control of what they listen to, how much, and when.

In 1996, wireless communication (cellular or PCS) was facing the same barriers to adoption, and their high cost to install or expand made them an unlikely delivery mechanism for on-demand radio because they could not match CA's pricing. Moreover, wireless did not have the bandwidth to deliver a program at a sufficient level of quality. The other potential competitor was Internet search engines and browsers, but they were not yet capable of providing simple and safe access to program material while driving. With this approach, users could not gain immediate access to current information and breaking events, and downloading would necessarily occur at a particular time when the user was connected to the Internet. So users would have to carry their receivers from the car to their computers and back. In addition, users would have to pay based on how much content they downloaded or they would be required to listen to advertisements. The biggest threat might come with the convergence of the Internet and wireless capability, which in 1996 was still several years away.

A significant advantage that Bogue saw for CA was its low infrastructure costs, which reduced its capital requirements significantly when compared to other information and entertainment service providers. "For example, in 1996 major direct-to-home satellite TV programmers spent between $0.5 billion and $1.5 billion each to purchase transmission licenses and launch satellites. Command Audio, by comparison, [spent] in total just $10 million on facilities and equipment in order to commence service . . . and only $23 million annually to lease the necessary FM subcarriers."[7]

Business Model #1: Raising Investment Capital and Protecting the Technology Position

In December 1999, just before CA launched its service, Audio on Demand, it raised $56 million in venture capital. Although this was a time of intense investment by the venture capital community, CA's funding was successful by any measure. It was designed to provide launch financing into four lead markets and to begin the exploration of another six markets.

The service was officially launched in January 2000, running 24 hours a day, 7 days a week. In March, CA began its media campaign to a lukewarm response; the customer acquisition rate was not nearly as fast as projected. To make matters worse, the service suffered a 25 percent

[7]Command Audio Business Plan, 1996, p.14.

churn because of the battery, which was too large and didn't have a long enough life span. Initially, CA charged $200 for the receiver and $9.99 per month for the service, but within three weeks they were forced to lower the price of the receiver to $99 and make adjustments to the service pricing and programming.

As the company also optimistically prepared for a potential initial public offering (IPO) of $150 million to roll out to the top 50 markets, April 2000 brought the crash of the public equity markets, especially for pre-profitability technology companies, and the investment banks CA had chosen to lead the IPO advised the company that the window of opportunity for companies like CA had closed but would likely open again in spring 2001. Although that was only a year away, if their predictions were correct, Bogue couldn't figure out how things would change fast enough to keep the company alive. They would be out of money by September 2000.

> Our senior management team realized very quickly that a seismic and very negative shift in our prospects had occurred. Though crushingly disappointed, we decided almost immediately to shut down our service and downsize the company to conserve capital for a strategic redirection towards software development and licensing. In this new model, we generalized the tools and technologies we already had developed and licensed them to others who wanted to offer similar on-demand media services.

Business Model #2: Licensing Their Tools and Technologies

With a portfolio of valuable technologies and a determination not to give up, Bogue repositioned the company as a software development and licensing company that would license the systems and tools it had developed to companies that wanted to offer on-demand media services. Initial success with digital radio pioneers XM Satellite Radio and iBiquity encouraged Bogue that he had made the right decision. CA's growing patent portfolio was demonstrating to licensees, strategic investors, and partners that CA was the technology leader in broadcast on-demand media.

However, as optimistic as Bogue was, he soon discovered that his software licensees' plans had also been rather optimistic. Development delays resulted in these industry leaders deciding not to deploy CA's technology for three more years, which meant that CA would not be receiving any royalties for three years. Once again the company was faced with the possibility of a cash shortfall and once again Bogue downsized the company with a plan to reorganize yet again. In August 2002, Bogue sold CA's software development business to iBiquity Digital and licensed to that company all of CA's patents and software. iBiquity had the right to sublicense CA's patents in the terrestrial digital radio field, but CA retained the exclusive rights to license its intellectual property in every other field of use.

Business Model #3: Enforcing Existing Patents and Licensing Agreements

Still searching for a strategy that would enable CA to return its shareholders' capital, Bogue was about to undertake the most unconventional and risky business model of all: licensing and, where necessary, enforcing CA's patents. With digital and satellite radio already under license, Bogue turned his attention to personal video recorders, the sort of device pioneered by TiVo and ReplayTV. This market was potentially very large, but it would prove extremely difficult to penetrate. For the next 15 months, Bogue and his team, now a very small company, worked hard to conserve CA's remaining cash and began to approach the major consumer electronics companies as well as manufacturers of cable and satellite television set-top boxes. Although these companies had an interest in personal video recorders and saw them as the next big thing, they were reluctant to accept the fundamental nature of CA's intellectual property and the need to acquire a license to use it. They figured that if they ignored CA, the company would eventually disappear.

Bogue had not gone into this effort without preparation. The response of the big consumer electronics companies was expected, and it was time to draw a line in the sand. It was clear that TiVo and Replay were using the audio time-shifting functionality embodied in John Ryan's inventions, even though they were focused on television. Their use of the technology could well have been inadvertent; they may simply have been unaware at the time they began developing their products that the same idea had occurred to Ryan a few years earlier. TiVo's founders came out of Silicon graphics and apparently, in their own way, had reached the same solution as John Ryan had. Bogue also foresaw that, down the road when video was delivered to cell phones, it would be delivered through broadcast rather than point-to-point technology and would be cached on the handset by users. That, too, would require manufacturers and service providers to obtain licenses to CA's patents. So now he had two choices: He could either shut down the company or he could fight the big boys. He chose the latter.

Bogue quickly realized that the key to his company's success was in having the money to go after the companies that were infringing his patents, and he had to have enough funding to outlast them. His current investors, as committed as they were, would not be supplying any more capital for this latest business model; in any case, the amount that Bogue needed was significantly higher than they might provide. An exhaustive search produced the answer: an insurance policy that covered the cost of offensive patent litigation and provided several million dollars of financing at a price the company could afford. CA would pay an up-front premium and, upon settlement of the lawsuit, would repay what had been put out plus a premium. This policy was the turning point because the company was now competing on a level playing field with the major electronics manufacturers.

With financing in place, Bogue began to study companies coming into the PVR market and selected a target to focus on for litigation: Sony Corporation. Bogue figured that if he could win this suit, the other companies infringing his patents would be more likely to fall in line and pay royalties rather than risk infringement litigation. On February 1, 2002, CA filed a patent infringement action against Sony Corporation. The litigation took four years, during which CA prevailed in multiple Markman rulings, summary judgment motions, and a bench trial on inequitable conduct. After the two companies had spent over $15 million, Sony decided to settle the lawsuit. It paid an up-front financial settlement and signed a royalty-bearing license for the use of CA's patents around the world.

This was a monumental win for Command Audio. The personal video recorder market, which consists of cable and satellite TV set-top boxes, DVD recorders, game consoles, and PCs, is perhaps twenty times as large as the digital and satellite radio market. And right behind that is television delivery to cell phones that incorporate broadcast tuners and PVR functionality, which is an order of magnitude larger than personal video recorders. Analysts estimate that in 2006 alone, more than 25 million PVRs were sold, and that number would grow by 30 percent in 2007.[8] In April 2007, CA signed a license agreement with Scientific Atlanta, a leader in cable television set-top boxes and a Cisco company. They intend to use CA's technology in all of their PVR set-top box products. Bogue knows that even with this pivotal win, the game is not over. Although he has aligned his patent and business strategies and prepared his company's financing, will every company infringing his patents agree to pay royalties? Is this a sustainable strategy?

Discussion Questions

1. What was the source of the opportunity for Command Audio?
2. What were the problems with the first business model: building and selling the CA box and service to consumers?
3. Why did the second business model fail? Could that failure have been avoided?
4. Was it necessary for the company to go through three business models before it found the right one to build a sustainable company?

[8]"Scientific Atlanta Purchases License to Use Command Audio's PVR Technology." Press release (April 24, 2007).

CORPORATE ENTREPRENEURSHIP AND INNOVATION IN SILICON VALLEY: THE CASE OF GOOGLE, INC.*

Introduction

In May 2009, Sergey Brin and Larry Page, co-founders of Google, Inc., watched Green Day in concert at the famous Shoreline Amphitheatre in Mountain View, California. The brilliant young entrepreneurs had many things on their minds. They tried to determine how they were going to navigate Google during the worst recession the United States had seen since the Great Depression (Willis, 2009). The Standard and Poor's 500 (S&P 500), one of the most popular indicators of the U.S. economy, had dropped to an intra-day low of 666.79 on March 6, 2009, from an intra-day high of 1576.09 on October 11, 2007, for a collapse of 57.7 percent (S&P 500 Index, 2009). World-wide stocks had decreased on average by approximately 60 percent.

Warren Buffett, Chairman of Berkshire Hathaway and one of the most prolific investors of all time, foresaw the current economic turmoil in early 2008. Buffett stated, "Even though the numbers do not state it, the United States was in for a deep long-lasting recession" (*USA Today*, 2008).

By early 2009, U.S. retirement accounts also dropped by an average of 40 percent or $3.4 trillion (Brandon, 2009). Many U.S. retirees saw their pensions cut in half and many were forced to go back to work or rely on their families to support them.

Brin and Page had never witnessed anything like this in their young lives. Even the ever successful company they created in 1998, Google, Inc., was feeling the effects of the crisis. At its low point, Google's stock price dropped 51.35 percent from an intra-day high of $713.58 on November 2, 2007, to an intra-day low of $259.56 on November 20, 2008. The stock price picked up momentum recently and traded at $410 as of May 28, 2009.

As the young entrepreneurs listened to the Bay Area band Green Day, they pondered their next moves. Google had problems. The company's primary problem was how to maintain the culture of corporate entrepreneurship and innovation in the face of flat net profits from 2007 to 2008. As a result of this, the firm had to fire several employees for the first time in the company's history and eliminate products that made no money (Blodget, 2009). Furthermore, employees left for a variety of reasons (e.g., lack of mentoring and formal career planning, too much bureaucracy, low pay and benefits, high cost of living in the area, desire to start their own business, etc.).

EXHIBIT 1   Google Income Statements 2004–2008 (in Millions)

	2008	2007	2006	2005	2004
Period End Date	12/31/2008	12/31/2007	12/31/2006	12/31/2005	12/31/2004
Period Length	12 Months	12 Months	12 Months	12 Months	12 Months
Revenue	21,795.55	16,593.99	10,604.92	6,138.56	3,189.22
Total Revenue	**21,795.55**	**16,593.99**	**10,604.92**	**6,138.56**	**3,189.22**
Cost of Revenue, Total	8,621.51	6,649.09	4,225.03	2,577.09	1,468.97
Gross Profit	**13,174.04**	**9,944.9**	**6,379.89**	**3,561.47**	**1,720.26**
Selling/General/Administrative Expenses, Total	3,748.88	2,740.52	1,601.31	854.68	483.9
Research & Development	2,793.19	2,119.99	1,228.59	599.51	395.16
Depreciation/Amortization	0.0	0.0	0.0	0.0	0.0
Interest Expense (Income), Net Operating	0.0	0.0	0.0	0.0	0.0
Unusual Expense (Income)	1,094.76	0.0	0.0	90.0	201.0
Other Operating Expenses, Total	0.0	0.0	0.0	0.0	0.0
Operating Income	**5,537.21**	**5,084.4**	**3,550.0**	**2,017.28**	**640.19**
Interest Income (Expense), Net Non-Operating	0.0	0.0	0.0	0.0	0.0
Gain (Loss) on Sale of Assets	0.0	0.0	0.0	0.0	0.0
Other, Net	4.52	−4.65	3.46	4.14	25.09
Income Before Tax	**5,853.6**	**5,673.98**	**4,011.04**	**2,141.68**	**650.23**
Income Tax—Total	1,626.74	1,470.26	933.59	676.28	251.12
Income After Tax	**4,226.86**	**4,203.72**	**3,077.45**	**1,465.4**	**399.12**
Minority Interest	0.0	0.0	0.0	0.0	0.0
Equity in Affiliates	0.0	0.0	0.0	0.0	0.0
U.S. GAAP Adjustment	0.0	0.0	0.0	0.0	0.0
Net Income Before Extra. Items	**4,226.86**	**4,203.72**	**3,077.45**	**1,465.4**	**399.12**
Total Extraordinary Items	0.0	0.0	0.0	0.0	0.0
Net Income	**4,226.86**	**4,203.72**	**3,077.45**	**1,465.4**	**399.12**

Source: www.google.com/finance?fstype=bi&cid=694653.

EXHIBIT 2   Google Cash Flow 2004–2008 (in Millions)

	2008	2007	2006	2005	2004
Period End Date	12/31/2008	12/31/2007	12/31/2006	12/31/2005	12/31/2004
Net Income/Starting Line	4,226.86	4,203.72	3,077.45	1,465.4	399.12
Depreciation/Depletion	1,212.24	807.74	494.43	256.81	128.52
Amortization	287.65	159.92	77.51	37.0	19.95
Deferred Taxes	−224.65	−164.21	0.0	0.0	0.0
Non-Cash Items	2,055.44	489.44	−112.83	656.47	682.66
Changes in Working Capital	295.32	278.8	43.96	43.74	−253.21
Cash from Operating Activities	**7,852.86**	**5,775.41**	**3,580.51**	**2,459.42**	**977.04**
Capital Expenditures	−2,358.46	−2,402.84	−1,902.8	−853.04	−355.9
Other Investing Cash Flow Items, Total	−2,960.96	−1,278.75	−4,996.35	−2,505.16	−1,545.46
Cash from Investing Activities	**−5,319.42**	**−3,681.59**	**−6,899.15**	**−3,358.19**	**−1,901.36**
Financing Cash Flow Items	159.09	379.21	581.73	0.0	4.3
Total Cash Dividends Paid	0.0	0.0	0.0	0.0	0.0
Issuance (Retirement) of Stock, Net	−71.52	23.86	2,384.67	4,372.26	1,195.03
Issuance (Retirement) of Debt, Net	0.0	0.0	0.0	−1.43	−4.71
Cash from Financing Activities	**87.57**	**403.07**	**2,966.4**	**4,370.83**	**1,194.62**
Foreign Exchange Effects	−45.92	40.03	19.74	−21.76	7.57
Net Change in Cash	**2,575.08**	**2,536.92**	**−332.5**	**3,450.3**	**277.88**
Net Cash—Beginning Balance	6,081.59	3,544.67	3,877.17	426.87	149.0
Net Cash—Ending Balance	8,656.67	6,081.59	3,544.67	3,877.17	426.87

Source: www.google.com/finance?fstype=bi&tcid=694653.

In a little over 10 years, Google had grown to a company with over 20,000 employees. If Google wanted to continue its main strategy of growth through innovation, it would have to find a way to recruit the best employees and retain them.

Background of Founders

Google was founded by Larry Page and Sergey Brin who met in 1995 while they were Ph.D. students in computer engineering at Stanford University. Page was born in Lansing, Michigan, on March 26, 1973, and was the son of a computer science professor at Michigan State University who specialized in artificial intelligence. Page's mother also taught computer programming at the Michigan State University (Thompson, 2001, page 50).

Page spent his youth learning about computers and immersed himself into multiple technology journals that his parents read. Page had a very impressive educational background. He attended a Montessori school initially, and then went to a public high school. He later went on to earn a Bachelor of Science Degree (with honors) in computer engineering from the University of Michigan. Page was then accepted to graduate school at Stanford where he met Brin and began his study of website linkages. Nicola Tesla, a Serbian inventor who was a contemporary of Thomas Edison, was Page's inspiration. Tesla was superior to Edison in some respects; however, he failed at commercializing his inventions. Page wanted to do both.

EXHIBIT 3   Google Balance Sheet 2004–2008 (in Millions)

	2008	2007	2006	2005	2004
Period End Date	12/31/2008	12/31/2007	12/31/2006	12/31/2005	12/31/2004
Assets					
Cash & Short Term Investments	15,845.77	14,218.61	11,243.91	8,034.25	2,132.3
Total Receivables, Net	2,642.19	2,307.77	1,322.34	687.98	382.35
Total Inventory	0.0	0.0	0.0	0.0	0.0
Prepaid Expenses	1,404.11	694.21	443.88	229.51	159.36
Other Current Assets, Total	286.11	68.54	29.71	49.34	19.46
Total Current Assets	**20,178.18**	**17,289.14**	**13,039.85**	**9,001.07**	**2,693.47**
Property/Plant/Equipment, Total—Net	5,233.84	4,039.26	2,395.24	961.75	378.92
Goodwill, Net	4,839.85	2,299.37	1,545.12	194.9	122.82
Intangibles, Net	996.69	446.6	346.84	82.78	71.07
Long Term Investments	85.16	1,059.69	1,031.85	0.0	0.0
Note Receivable—Long Term	0.0	0.0	0.0	0.0	0.0
Other Long Term Assets, Total	433.85	201.75	114.46	31.31	47.08
Total Assets	**31,767.58**	**25,335.81**	**18,473.35**	**10,271.81**	**3,313.35**
Liabilities and Shareholders' Equity					
Accounts Payable	178.0	282.11	211.17	115.58	32.67
Payable/Accrued	0.0	0.0	0.0	0.0	0.0
Accrued Expenses	1,824.45	1,575.42	987.91	528.94	269.29
Notes Payable/Short Term Debt	0.0	0.0	0.0	0.0	0.0
Current Port. of LT Debt/Capital Leases	0.0	0.0	0.0	0.0	1.9
Other Current Liabilities, Total	299.63	178.07	105.51	100.87	36.51
Total Current Liabilities	**2,302.09**	**2,035.6**	**1,304.59**	**745.38**	**340.37**
Total Long Term Debt	0.0	0.0	0.0	0.0	0.0
Deferred Income Tax	12.52	0.0	40.42	35.42	0.0
Other Liabilities, Total	1,214.11	610.53	88.5	72.05	43.93
Total Liabilities	**3,528.71**	**2,646.13**	**1,433.51**	**852.86**	**384.3**
Common Stock	0.32	0.31	0.31	0.29	0.27
Additional Paid-In Capital	14,450.34	13,241.22	11,882.91	7,477.79	2,582.35
Retained Earnings (Accumulated Deficit)	13,561.63	9,334.77	5,133.31	2,055.87	590.47
Other Equity, Total	226.58	113.37	23.31	2115.0	2244.03
Total Equity	**28,238.86**	**22,689.68**	**17,039.84**	**9,418.96**	**2,929.06**
Total Liabilities & Shareholders' Equity	**31,767.58**	**25,335.81**	**18,473.35**	**10,271.81**	**3,313.35**
Total Common Shares Outstanding	315.11	313.28	309.0	293.03	266.92

Source: www.google.com/finance?fstype=bi&cid=694653.

EXHIBIT 4   Google's Stock Price From IPO Through May 28, 2009

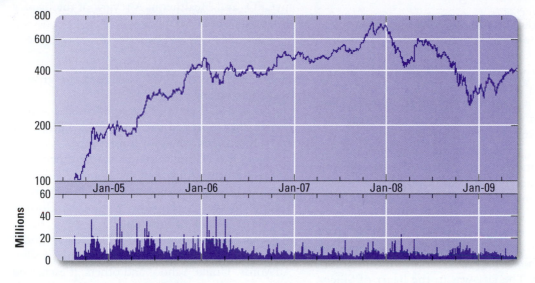

In 1973, Sergey Brin was born in Moscow Russia. At age six, Brin and his family who were Jewish, fled Russia to the United States to escape anti-Semitism. Brin's father was a mathematics professor at the University of Maryland and his mother was a research scientist at NASA's Goddard Space Flight Center. Brin attended a Montessori high school and graduated with a degree in computer science and mathematics with honors from the University of Maryland. He then began to study computer science at Stanford University until he dropped out to form Google with Page. Brin was the more gregarious; however, both were strong willed and opinionated.

At Stanford they began their quest to "organize the world's information and make it universally accessible" (Miller, 2006, page 10). Google began as a research project at Stanford University in January, 1995.

Page started his research under the tutelage of Dr. Terry Winograd, a computer science professor at Stanford. His research focused on which web pages linked to a given page. His initial problem was trying to determine the number of citations in academic publishing. He called his research project "BackRub." Brin soon joined Page

on the project. Page began exploring the web in March 1996 by using Page's Stanford home page. It was at this point that Page and Brin developed PageRank, an algorithm that ranked the importance of the sites that were relevant to the entry.

Page and Brin did not create the algorithm with the intention of making money, but they wanted to have a significant impact on the world. As time went on they decided that they did not want to create their own company, but they wanted to sell their invention to one of the existing search companies (e.g., WebCrawler, AltaVista, Yahoo!, etc.). However, all of these companies stated that there was no money in search and rejected them.

By 1996, Brin and Page had servers and computers stacked in their dorm room. Initially targeted at Stanford students, the two consulted with two former Stanford students that started Yahoo!, Jerry Yang and David Filo. They encouraged Brin and Page to create their own company. So the two decided to drop out of school and start their own business. In 1998, Sun Microsystems co-founder Andy Bechtolsheim, who also dropped out of Stanford to become a successful entrepreneur, wrote a check for $100,000 to Brin and Page and they formed a new company called Google, Inc.

Growth of Google

Since its founding in 1998, Google was one of the most innovative companies in the world. The company ranked at the top with other leading companies like Apple in the development of innovative products and technologies. Corporate entrepreneurship and innovation was the heart and soul of the company's success.

Google initially set up its business in a garage at 232 Santa Margarita, Menlo Park, California in 1998. Later that year, Google was named Search Engine of Choice by *PC Magazine* in the Top 100 Sites of 1998 (Lowe, 2009, page 282). In 1999, Google moved to a new office space in Palo Alto to make room for several new employees. Palo Alto was the location of Stanford University. The city was in the heart of Silicon Valley and was the location where the first semiconductor chip was created in 1956 by Fairchild Semiconductor.

In 1999, Google received its first significant influx of capital, $25 million in venture capital financing from Sequoia Capital and Kleiner, Perkins, Caufield, and Byers, both located in Silicon Valley. Members of both firms sat on the board of directors of Google.

In 1999, the term "googler" was termed for "people who used Google." In August 1999 Google moved to Mountain View, just south of Palo Alto. Google moved into an empty building next door to Silicon Graphics, a firm that was founded by a former Stanford electrical engineering professor, Dr. James Clark, and seven graduate students and staff from Stanford. Clark would go on to found Netscape Communications, myCFO, and Healtheon. A review of the history of Google can be seen below.

Stages of Growth

Hamel and Breen (2007) described the growth of Google into five stages:

Google 1.0: Brin and Page invented a search engine that searched the Web, won millions of eyeballs, but generated no real revenue.

Google 2.0: Google sold its search capacity to AOL, Yahoo!, and other major portals. These partnerships generated revenue and sparked a surge in search requests. Suddenly, Google started to look like a business.

Google 3.0: Google crafted a clever model for selling ads alongside search results called AdWords. Unlike Yahoo! and others, it eschewed banner ads, and took a newspaper's "church-and-state" view of advertising and content by clearly differentiating between ads and search results. Moreover, advertisers paid only when users actually clicked on a link. Google was well on its way to becoming the Internet's leading retailer of ad space.

Google 4.0: Google's initially controversial Gmail service, which served up ads based on a computer analysis of each incoming message, provoked a serendipitous bit of learning that led to the creation of AdSense. This breakthrough gave Google the ability to link its ads to virtually any sort of Web content, not just its own search results. AdSense gave webmasters a new way of monetizing content and vastly expand the scope of Google's business model.

EXHIBIT 5   Google's Corporate History

Aug-98	Sun co-founder Andy Bechtolsheim writes a check for $100,000 to an entity that doesn't exist yet: a company called Google, Inc.
Sep-98	Google files for incorporation in California on September 4. Larry and Sergey open a bank account in Google's name and deposit check.
Dec-98	"PC Magazine" reports that Google "has an uncanny knack for returning extremely relevant results" and names it the search engine of choice.
Jun-99	Google's first press release announces a $25 million round from Sequoia Capital and Kleiner Perkins.

(continued)

EXHIBIT 5   Google's Corporate History *(continued)*

May-00	The first 10 language versions of Google.com are released targeting the Western European market from Spain up to Denmark. (New Market)
Jun-00	We forge a partnership with Yahoo! to become their default search provider. (Partnership)
Sep-00	We start offering search in Chinese, Japanese and Korean, bringing our total number of supported languages to 15. (New Market)
Oct-00	Google AdWords, the self-service ad program with keyword targeting, launches with 350 customers—revenue stream. (New Product)
Dec-00	Google Toolbar is released. It's a browser plug-in that makes it possible to search without visiting the Google homepage. (Innovation)
Feb-01	Acquires Deja.com's Usenet Discussion Service, adds search and browse features, and launches it as Google Groups. (Acquisition)
Mar-01	Google.com is available in 26 languages. (Foreign)
Jul-01	Image Search launches, offering access to 250 million images. (New Product)
Aug-01	Google opens its first international office, in Tokyo. (International)
Aug-01	Eric Schmidt becomes CEO, and Larry and Sergey are named presidents of products and technology, respectively.
Oct-01	A new partnership with Universo Online (UOL) makes Google the major search service for millions of Latin Americans. (Partnership)
Feb-02	The first Google hardware is released, the Google Search Appliance. (Related Diversification—Hardware)
Feb-02	Google releases a major overhaul for AdWords, including new cost-per-click pricing. (Innovation)
May-02	Partnership with AOL to offer Google search and sponsored links to customers using CompuServe, Netscape, and AOL.com. (Partnership)
Sep-02	Google News launches with 4000 news sources. (New Product)
Oct-02	Google opens its first Australian office in Sydney. (International)
Dec-02	Google launches Froogle to buy stuff (later called Google Product Search). (New Product)
Feb-03	Acquires Pyra Labs, the creators of Blogger. (Acquisition)
Mar-03	We announce a new content-targeted advertising service called AdSense. (New Product)
Apr-03	Acquires Applied Semantics, whose technology bolsters AdSense. (Acquisition)
Apr-03	Google launches Google Grants, an advertising program for nonprofit organizations to run ad campaigns for their cause. (New Product)
Dec-03	Google launches Google Print (later renamed Google Book Search), indexing small excerpts from searched for books. (New Product)
Jan-04	Google launches Orkut as a way to tap into the sphere of social networking. (New Product)
Mar-04	Google formalizes its enterprise unit with the hire of Dave Girouard to run the enterprise search business. (Related Diversification)
Mar-04	Google introduces Google Local (later part of Google Maps), offering business listings, maps, and directions. (New Product—Maps)
Jul-04	Acquires Picasa, a digital photography company. (Acquisition)
Aug-04	Google's Initial Public Offering of 19,605,052 shares of Class A common stock with opening price of $85 per share. (IPO)
Oct-04	Google opens an office in Dublin, Ireland. (International)
Oct-04	Google launches SMS (short message service) to send search queries to GOOGL or on a mobile device. (Related Diversification—Phone)

(continued)

EXHIBIT 5   Google's Corporate History *(continued)*

Oct-04	Google opens new engineering offices in Bangalore and Hyderabad, India. (International—Outsourcing)
Oct-04	Google Desktop Search is introduced so users can search for files and documents stored on their own hard drive. (New Product)
Oct-04	Acquires Keyhole, a digital mapping company whose technology will later become Google Earth. (Acquisition—Maps)
Dec-04	Google opens an R&D center in Tokyo, Japan, to attract bright Asian engineers. (International—Outsourcing)
Feb-05	Google Maps goes live. (New Product—Innovation—Maps)
Mar-05	Google launches code.google.com, a new place for developer-oriented resources, including all of our APIs. (New Product)
Mar-05	Acquires Urchin, a web analytics company whose technology is used to create Google Analytics. (Acquisition)
Apr-05	Google Maps features satellite views and directions. (Innovation—Maps)
Apr-05	Google Local goes mobile, and includes SMS driving directions. (Related Diversification—Phone)
May-05	Google releases Blogger Mobile, enabling mobile phone users to post and send photos to their blogs. (Related Diversification—Phone)
May-05	Google launches Personalized Homepage (now iGoogle) enabling users to customize their own Google homepage. (New Product)
Jun-05	Google Mobile Web Search is released, specially formulated for viewing search results on mobile phones. (Related Diversification—Phone)
Jun-05	Google launches Google Earth: a satellite imagery-based mapping service. (New Product—Innovation—Maps)
Aug-05	Google launches Google Talk, which enables Gmail users to talk or IM over the Internet for free. (New Product)
Sep-05	Google opens new R&D center in China. (International—Outsourcing)
Sep-05	Google Blog Search goes live to facilitate finding current and relevant blog postings. (New Product)
Oct-05	Google launches Google.org, a philanthropic arm of the firm, to address energy and environmental issues. (Diversification—Charity)
Oct-05	Google introduces Google Reader, a feed reader. (New Product)
Nov-05	Google releases Google Analytics, formerly Urchin, for measuring the impact of websites and marketing campaigns. (Innovation)
Nov-05	Google opens our first offices in São Paulo, Brazil, and Mexico City, Mexico. (International)
Dec-05	Gmail for mobile launches in the United States. (Innovation—Phone)
Jan-06	Acquires dMarc, a digital radio advertising company. (Acquisition—Unrelated Diversification)
Jan-06	Google launches Google.cn, a local domain version of Google in China. (International—Multi-domestic Competition)
Jan-06	Google introduces Picasa in 25 more languages. (New Market)
Feb-06	Google releases Chat in Gmail, using the instant messaging tools from Google Talk. (New Product)
Feb-06	Google launches Google News for mobile launchers. (New Product—Phone)
Mar-06	Acquires Writely, a web-based word processing application that subsequently becomes the basis for Google Docs. (Acquisition)
Mar-06	Google launches Google Finance, our approach to an improved search experience for financial information. (New Product)
Apr-06	Google launches Google Calendar, complete with sharing and group features. (New Product)
Apr-06	Google releases Maps for France, Germany, Italy and Spain. (New Market)
May-06	Google releases Google Trends, a way to visualize the popularity of searches over time. (New Product)

(continued)

EXHIBIT 5 Google's Corporate History *(continued)*

Jun-06	Google announces Picasa Web Albums, allowing Picasa users to upload and share their photos online. (Innovation)
Jun-06	Google announces Google Checkout, a fast and easy way to pay for online purchases. (New Product)
Jun-06	Gmail, Google News and iGoogle become available on mobile phones in eight more languages. (New Markets—Phone)
Aug-06	Google releases Apps for Your Domain, a suite of applications including Gmail and Calendar for any size organization. (New Product)
Aug-06	Google Book Search begins offering free PDF downloads of books in the public domain. (Innovation)
Oct-06	Acquires YouTube. (Acquisition)
Oct-06	Acquires JotSpot, a collaborative wiki platform, which later becomes Google Sites. (Acquisition)
Dec-06	Google releases Patent Search in the U.S., indexing more than 7 million patents dating back to 1790. (New Product)
Jan-07	Google partners with China Mobile, world's largest mobile telecom carrier, to provide mobile searches in China. (International—Partnership)
Feb-07	Gmail is opened up to everyone, no longer by invitation only. (New Market)
Feb-07	Google launches Google Apps Premier Edition, bringing cloud computing to businesses. (Innovation)
Feb-07	We introduce traffic information to Google Maps for more than 30 cities around the U.S. (Innovation—Maps)
Jun-07	Google partners with Salesforce.com, combining that company's on-demand CRM applications with AdWords. (Partnership)
Jul-07	Acquires Postini. (Acquisition)
Aug-07	Google launches Sky inside Google Earth, including layers for constellation information and virtual tours of galaxies. (New Product—Maps)
Sep-07	Google introduces AdSense for Mobile, giving sites for mobile browsers the ability to host same ads as on computers. (Innovation—Phone)
Sep-07	Google adds Presently, a new application for making slide presentations, to Google Docs. (New Product)
Nov-07	Google (with Open Handset Alliance) announces Android, first open platform for mobile devices. (Related Diversification—Phone)
Nov-07	Google.org announces RE<C, an initiative designed to create electricity from renewable sources. (Unrelated Diversification—Energy)
Mar-08	Acquires DoubleClick, which provides internet ad services. (Acquisition)
May-08	Google releases Google Health to the public, allowing people to manage their medical records and health information online. (New Product)
Jul-08	Google releases first downloadable iPhone app. (Related Diversification—Phone)
Sep-08	Unveils G1, the Google Phone on the Android operating system, available through T-Mobile. (Forward Vertical Integration—Hardware)
Oct-08	Google introduces Google Earth for the iPhone and iPod touch. (New Market)
Jan-09	Google launches Picasa for Mac. (New Market)
Feb-09	Google introduces Google Latitude, that lets users share their location with friends. (New Product—Maps)
Feb-09	Adding new languages enables Google Translate to accommodate 41 languages, covering 98% of Internet users. (Innovation—New Markets)

Source: Google Milestones (2009). Retrieved on March 31, 2009, www.google.com/corporate/history.html.

Google 5.0: Google used its windfall from advertising to fund a flock of new services, including Google Desktop (a cluster of information utilities accessible directly from a user's PC screen), Google Book Search (an ambitious plan to digitize the books from the world's greatest libraries), Google Scholar (a tool for searching academic papers), and Google Chrome, a new Internet search browser.

The company also purchased a number of other firms over the years including Keyhole (which became Google Earth), Writely (which became Google Docs), YouTube, and Android (which went on to become the Android Operating System for Google's new phone launch called the Android in 2008).

In 2008, Google had more than $4 billion in revenues with the majority of it coming from the company's AdWords business model or click through advertising. AdWords was one of the most revolutionary developments in the media world since television itself, said author John Battelle (2009): "AdWords was what made Google ... Google." AdWords was what generated the ads—or "Sponsored Links," you see on a Google results page. You only have to pay for the link when someone actually clicks on the link and goes to the advertiser's website. It was called "pay-per-click."

Strategies at Google

Google's primary corporate strategy was related diversification. Google achieved its diversification strategy through corporate entrepreneurship and innovation and acquisitions. This enabled Google to increase its offerings and decrease its competition. As the industry leader, Google used offensive strategies by constant innovation of its product lines and expansion into other industries like mobile phones, maps, blogging, news, health, etc.

Google provided internet users with the most relevant search results on as many topics as possible. This included going international to outsource and expand markets by providing its products in foreign languages. Google's business level strategy was a broad differentiation strategy, because it offered features that other search engines did not, such as translating from one language into another, while still providing the most relevant search results.

Philanthropy at Google

Philanthropy was widespread at Google. The company gave 1 percent of its equity and yearly profits to philanthropy. Google's five primary areas that it focused on were: (1) Google.org which used Google's information and technology to build products and advocate for policies that address global challenges; (2) Engineering Awards and Programs that supported the next generation of engineers and maintained strong ties with academic institutions worldwide pursuing innovative research in core areas relevant to its mission; (3) Information and Tools to Help You Change the World that were used to promote causes, raise money, and operate more efficiently; (4) Charitable Giving that supported efforts in the local communities and around the globe; and (5) Google Green Initiatives where Google gave back to the community through financing humanitarian efforts in Africa and research on alternative fuels and global warming (Google.org, 2010).

Competition

Google operated in markets that changed rapidly. Google faced the possibility of new and disruptive technologies and faced formidable competition in every aspect of their business, particularly from companies that sought to connect people with information on the web. The company considered Microsoft Corporation and Yahoo! Inc. to be their primary competitors.

Google faced competition from other web search providers, including start-ups as well as developed companies that were enhancing or developing search technologies. Google competed with internet advertising companies, particularly in the areas of pay-for-performance and keyword-targeted internet advertising. The company also competed with companies that sold products and services online because these companies were trying to attract users to their websites to search for information about products and services. Google also provided a number of online products and services, including Gmail, YouTube, and Google Docs, which competed directly with new and established companies offering communication, information, and entertainment services integrated into products or media properties.

EXHIBIT 6   Google Philanthropic Initiatives

Google.org

Google.org *used Google's strengths in information and technology to build products and advocate for policies that address global challenges.*

Google Flu Trends—A tool that uses aggregated Google search data to estimate flu activity in near real-time for 20 countries.

Google PowerMeter—A home energy monitoring tool that gives you the information you need to use less electricity and save money.

Earth Engine—A computational platform for global-scale analysis of satellite imagery to monitor changes in key environmental indicators like forest coverage.

RE<C—An effort to develop utility-scale renewable energy at a price cheaper than that of coal.

Google Crisis Response—A team that provides updated imagery, outreach through our web properties, and engineering tools such as the Person Finder application, in the wake of natural and humanitarian crises.

All for Good—A service, developed by Google and other technology companies, that helps people find volunteer opportunities in their community and share them with their friends. All for Good provides a single search interface for volunteer activities across many major volunteering sites and organizations.

Engineering Awards and Programs

Google supported the next generation of engineers and maintained strong ties with academic institutions worldwide pursuing innovative research in core areas relevant to its mission.

Google Research—Awards for world-class, full-time faculty pursuing research in areas of mutual interest.

BOLD Scholarships—Diversity internships to encourage those who are historically under-represented in the technology industry to explore a new career opportunity.

Google Code University—Tutorials and sample course content so computer science students and educators can learn more about current computing technologies and paradigms.

Google PhD Fellowship Program—Recognition for outstanding graduate students doing exceptional work in computer science, related disciplines, or promising research areas.

Google RISE Awards (Roots in Science and Engineering)—Awards to promote and support science, technology, engineering, mathematics (STEM) and computer science (CS) education initiatives.

Google Scholarships—Scholarships to encourage students to excel in their studies and become active role models and leaders.

Summer of Code—Stipends to student developers to write code for various open source software projects.

Information and Tools to Help You Change the World

Google tools were used to promote causes, raise money, and operate more efficiently.

Google for Non-Profits—Information on free Google tools for creating awareness, fundraising, and operating more efficiently.

Google Grants—In-kind online advertising for non-profit organizations.

Apps for EDU/Non-Profits—Free communication, collaboration and publishing tools, including email accounts, for qualifying non-profits.

Checkout for Non-Profits—A tool to increase online donations for non-profit organizations.

Custom Search for Non-Profits—A customized search experience for non-profit organizations.

(continued)

EXHIBIT 6   Google Philanthropic Initiatives *(continued)*

Sketchup for EDU—A product allowing educators to create, modify, and share 3D models.

YouTube for EDU—An educational channel for two- and four-year degree granting public and private colleges and universities.

YouTube for Non-Profits—A designated channel, premium branding, and additional free features to drive non-profit fundraising and awareness.

YouTube Video Volunteers—A platform to connect non-profit organizations with volunteers who can help them to create videos.

Google Earth Outreach—Resources to help non-profits visualize their cause and tell their story in Google Earth and Maps.

Google MapMaker—A tool that allows users to contribute, share and edit map information for 174 countries and territories around the world.

Charitable Giving

Googler-led giving to support efforts in our local communities and around the globe.

Corporate Giving Council—A cross-Google team that coordinates support for Googler-led partnerships on causes such as K-12 science/math/technology education and expanding access to information.

Holiday gift—A $22 million donation in 2009 to a couple dozen deserving charities from around the globe in order to help organizations who have been stretched thin by increasing requests for help at a time of lower donations. Gift was in lieu of giving holiday gifts to clients and partners.

Community Affairs—Investments in local communities where Google has a presence, creating opportunities for Googlers to invest their time and expertise in their communities, engage in community grant making, and build partnerships with stakeholders in the community.

Google employee matching—Up to $6,000 company match for each employee's annual charitable contributions and $50 donation for every 5 hours an employee volunteers through the "Dollars for Doers" program.

Google Green Initiatives

Google implemented innovative and responsible environmental practices across the company to reduce its carbon footprint, to ensure efficient computing, and to help its employees be green.

Source: Philanthropy at Google. Accessed May 18, 2010, www.google.org/googlers.html.

Google competed to attract and retain relationships with users, advertisers and Google Network members and other content providers in different ways (see below, Google's 2008 Annual Report):

- *Users.* Competed to attract and retain users of their search and communication products and services. Most of the products and services Google offered to users were free, so the company did not compete on price. Instead, the company competed in this area on the basis of the relevance and usefulness of search results, features, availability, and ease of use of products and services.

- *Advertisers.* Google competed to attract and retain advertisers. Google competed in this area principally on the basis of the return on investment realized by advertisers using the company's AdWords and AdSense programs. Google also competed based on the quality of customer service, features and ease of use of its products and services.

- *Google Network members and other content providers.* Google competed to attract and retain content providers (Google Network members, as well as other content providers for whom the company distributed or licensed content) primarily based on the size and quality of its advertiser base, and its ability to help these partners generate revenues from advertising and the terms of the agreements.

EXHIBIT 7   Yahoo! Financial Ratios 2004–2008

Liquidity Ratios

Liquidity Indicators	2008	2007	2006	2005	2004
Quick Ratio	1.97	1.12	1.7	1.79	1.1
Current Ratio	2.78	1.41	2.54	2.86	3.46
Operating Cash Flow Ratio	.007	.302	.638	.919	.583
Debt to Equity	.217	283	.257	.265	.295

Profitability Ratios

Profitability Indicators	2008	2007	2006	2005	2004
ROA	3.27	5.56	6.73	18.95	11.08
ROE	4.07	7.06	8.48	24.21	14.61
ROI	0.12	7.15	9.79	12.9	10.59
EBITDA Margin	12.29	21.64	25.49	50.46	37.24
Revenue per Employee	528,589	487,362	563,656	536,497	469,046
Net Profit Margin After Tax	(2.31)	7.35	9.96	36.1	20.9

Asset Management Ratios

Asset Management	2008	2007	2006	2005	2004
Total Asset Turnover	0.55	0.59	0.58	0.53	0.47
Receivables Turnover	6.79	7.02	7.78	8.75	9.35
Accounts Payable Turnover	43.83	48.86	71.63	88.74	89.01

Silicon Valley

Culture and Location

Google was located in the heart of Silicon Valley, Mountain View, California. According to Randy Komisar, an entrepreneur-turned-venture capitalist at Kleiner, Perkins, Caufield, and Byers, "In Silicon Valley we have created a culture that attracts the sort of people who prosper in ambiguity, innovation, and risk taking" (Harris, 2009). Other parts of the U.S. have also been successful at building innovative technology corridors like Boston, Massachusetts, and Austin, Texas.

Silicon Valley was often called South San Francisco, but was really comprised of about 60 miles of suburbs immediately to the south of the city of San Francisco. Some of the more prominent cities and companies included (North to South) South San Francisco (Amgen and Genentech), San Mateo (YouTube), Redwood Shores (Oracle Corporation, Electronic Arts, and Sun Microsystems), Menlo Park (most venture capital firms), Palo Alto (Hewlett-Packard and Facebook), Mountain View (AOL, Intuit, RedHat, Symantec, and VeriSign), Sunnyvale (Yahoo!, Ariba, NetApp, and Advanced Micro Devices), Santa Clara (Applied Materials and Nvidia Corporation), Cupertino (Apple, Inc.), San Jose (McAfee, eBay, Adobe Systems, and Cisco Systems), and Los Gatos. Hundreds of prestigious high technology companies were located here.

Cost of Living

Silicon Valley was one of the most expensive places to live in the U.S. During the recent housing boom, the average house in the region sold for $800,000. Prices differed depending on the city. For example, during the height of the housing boom an average house in San Jose sold for $710,000. However, by 2009, the price had fallen to $475,000 or a 33 percent plunge. Real estate in Palo Alto held up better than other parts of Silicon Valley. The average price of a home at the housing peak was $1.2 million versus $1.1 million in early 2009. Several factors contributed to Palo Alto's resilience: (1) The city was sunny and beautiful; (2) its proximity to Stanford; (3) the limited amount of housing available (no space for new homes); (4) its proximity to all of the top high-tech companies in the region (Google and Apple were 15 minutes away), and (5) the prestigious K-12 school system. Steve Jobs, CEO of Apple Inc., Steve Young, former star quarterback of the San Francisco 49ers, and Page all lived in Palo Alto.

The average per capita personal income in the U.S. was $39,751; however, in Silicon Valley salaries were 30 percent above the average. While this may sound encouraging, the cost of living in Silicon Valley was significantly higher than most places in the U.S. For example, if you made $100,000 a year in Dallas, Texas, and took a job at Google and moved to Palo Alto you would have to make a salary of $252,226 to afford the same lifestyle. The high cost of living was a barrier that the company had to overcome when recruiting employees.

Education and Employees

There were a number of universities and colleges in the San Francisco area; however, there were only two world class research universities; Stanford University and the University of California at Berkeley. Some of the brightest minds from all over the world came to Silicon Valley to work and/or attend these schools. San Jose State University, which was also located in Silicon Valley, was also a major feeder of engineers to high tech companies in the region. Furthermore, several of these engineers went on to become leaders in their respective companies (e.g., Gordon Moore, founder of Intel Corporation in 1968).

The region was a breeding ground for some of the brightest minds in the world. The area had a forward looking energy. People were more entrepreneurial because they had witnessed great wealth creation. According to Bill Powar, one of the founders of VeriSign, "I worked at Visa for 30 years, but when the internet was created we saw an opportunity to create the first internet security system that is still used today." Powar made millions on the initial public offering and retired.

Access to Capital and Legal Infrastructure

Money was another key variable for the success of Silicon Valley. Sand Hill Road in Menlo Park was famous for the large number of venture capital firms in a very small area. During the dot.com boom, real estate there was the most expensive in the world. A small number of employees worked in very small office buildings that were often hidden by trees and brushes. At Kleiner, Perkins, Caufield, and Byers, one of the premier venture capital firms in the world, bottlebrush trees hid the name of the firm. Other prestigious venture capital firms there were Sequoia Capital, InterWest Partners, Kohlberg Kravis Roberts, Draper Fisher Jurvetson, etc. This proximity to venture capital gave Google a competitive advantage since venture capital firms liked to be close to their investments and sit on their boards.

As Silicon Valley grew, the number of law firms specializing in funding, litigation, resolving disputes, high tech companies, and intellectual property grew enormously. Many of these firms were located in San Francisco and Palo Alto.

EXHIBIT 8 Map of Silicon Valley

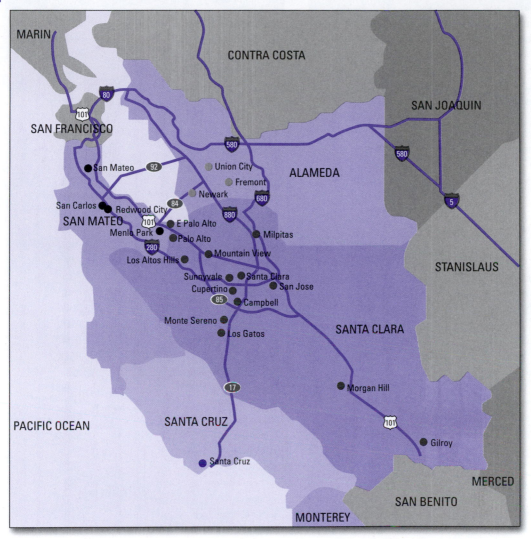

Source: Silicon Valley Cities and Counties. Retrieved May 19, 2009, www.siliconvalleyonline.org/cities.

EXHIBIT 9 Leading Public Companies in Silicon Valley

Company	Symbol	Company	Symbol
Agilent Technologies, Inc.	A	Altera Corp	ALTR
Apple	AAPL	Applied Materials	AMAT
Actel	ACTL	Applied Micro	AMCC
Adobe Systems	ADBE	Advanced Micro Devices	AMD
Adaptec	ADPT	Applied Signal Tech	APSG
Affymetrix	AFFX	Ariba	ARBA
Align Technology	ALGN	Aruba Networks	ARUN

(continued)

Company	Symbol	Company	Symbol
Atheros Comms	ATHR	Macrovision Solns	MVSN
Bigband Networks	BBND	Nanometrics Inc	NANO
Brocade Comm	BRCD	Netflix	NFLX
Cadence Design	CDNS	Nektar Therapeutics	NKTR
Chordiant Software	CHRD	National Semiconductor	NSM
Credence Systems Corp	CMOS	Netapp	NTAP
Coherent	COHR	Netgear	NTGR
Cisco Systems	CSCO	Nvidia	NVDA
Cypress Semiconductor	CY	Novellus Systems	NVLS
Cybersource	CYBS	Omnicell	OMCL
Data Domain	DDUP	Oplink Comms	OPLK
DSP Group	DSPG	Openwave Systems	OPWV
Ebay	EBAY	Oracle	ORCL
Electrs for Imaging	EFII	Omnivision Tech	OVTI
Echelon	ELON	Palm	PALM
Equinix	EQIX	Verifone Holdings, Inc.	PAY
Electronic Arts	ERTS	PDL Biopharma	PDLI
Extreme Networks	EXTR	PMC-Sierra	PMCS
Foundry Networks, Inc.	FDRY	Power Integrations	POWI
Finisar	FNSR	Pericom Semicondctr	PSEM
Gilead Sciences	GILD	Quantum Corporation	QTM
Google-A	GOOG	Rackable Systems	RACK
Granite Construction, Inc.	GVA	Robert Half International, Inc.	RHI
Harmonic	HLIT	Rambus	RMBS
Hewlett-Packard Company	HPQ	Silicon Graphics, Inc.	SGIC
Integr Device Tech	IDTI	Silicon Image	SIMG
Informatica	INFA	Symyx Technologies	SMMX
Intel	INTC	Sandisk	SNDK
Intuit	INTU	Synopsys	SNPS
Ipass	IPAS	Synnex Corporation	SNX
Intersil-A	ISIL	Sunpower-A	SPWR
Intuitive Surgical	ISRG	Silicon Storage Tech	SSTI
Integr Silicon Sol	ISSI	Symantec	SYMC
Intevac	IVAC	Symmetricom	SYMM
Interwoven, Inc.	IWOV	Synaptics	SYNA
Sun Microsystems	JAVA	TiVo	TIVO
JDS Uniphase	JDSU	Trident Microsystem	TRID
Juniper Networks	JNPR	Trimble Navigation	TRMB
KLA-Tencor	KLAC	Tessera Tech	TSRA
Linear Technology	LLTC	Varian Medical Systems, Inc.	VAR
Lam Research Corp	LRCX	Varian	VARI
LSI Corporation	LSI	VMware, Inc.	VMW
Micrel	MCRL	VeriSign	VRSN
McAfee, Inc.	MFE	Xilinx	XLNX
Monolithic Power	MPWR	Yahoo	YHOO

Corporate Entrepreneurship and Innovation

Corporate entrepreneurship (Guth & Ginsberg, 1990) is a term used to describe entrepreneurial behavior inside established mid-sized and large organizations. Corporate entrepreneurship can be formal or informal activities aimed at creating new businesses in established companies through product and process innovations and market developments (Zahra, 1991). Innovation is a key ingredient of corporate entrepreneurship where one can take an idea or invention and create something new of value. For example, an innovation of the toothbrush is the electric toothbrush.

Rule and Irwin (1988) stated that companies established a culture of innovation through: the formation of teams and task forces; recruitment of new staff with new ideas; application of strategic plans that focused on achieving innovation; and the establishment of internal research and development programs that were likely to see tangible results.

The roots of corporate entrepreneurship proliferated at 3M Corporation. 3M was the first company that introduced "organizational slack" as a key factor enabling their engineers and scientists to spend 15 percent of their time on projects of their own design. As a result of this many inventions came out of 3M (e.g., Post-it Notes and Scotch Tape).

Corporate Entrepreneurship and Innovation at Google

Google's mission was not based on money alone; rather it was to improve the world. The heart and soul of Google was based on entrepreneurship and innovation. The philosophy of the company started at Stanford University. Stanford had a program dedicated to the formation of technology oriented ventures called the STVP or the Stanford Technology Ventures Program in the School of Engineering. The school had a rich 100 year history of students and faculty that created fledging organizations like Federal Telegraph and

Telephone, Hewlett-Packard, Varian Associates, SRI International, Yahoo!, Cisco, Sun Microsystems, Silicon Graphics, Varian Medical Systems, and VMware.

Stanford encouraged their professors to create companies based on their research. According to Dr. Thomas Lee, the founder of Stanford's Integrated Circuits Laboratory, "Entrepreneurship is built into the DNA of Stanford." When Lee arrived, he said that colleagues told him that he would have to do a startup. He said there was a kind of peer pressure on campus to start a business. The President, John L. Hennessey, had prospered as an entrepreneur in MIPS Computer Systems (now MIPS Technologies) and Silicon Graphics (Harris, 2009). Stanford also encouraged their professors to take equity stakes in companies. This culture fostered entrepreneurial ventures throughout the region. In the 2009 student business plan competition there were 235 entries, double the amount during the dot.com boom.

Google's management model was similar to other high-tech companies like Microsoft, Apple, and Cisco. Google bought many of the buildings around its original office. The make-up, location, and culture of the company were similar to that of a college or university. It was not uncommon to see many bicycles around the campus traveling from building to building along with people playing volleyball outdoors.

According to current CEO Eric Schmidt (2009), "I looked at Google as an extension of graduate school; similar kinds of people, similar kinds of crazy behavior, but people who were incredibly smart and who were highly motivated and had a sense of change, a sense of optimism. It was a culture of people who felt that they could build things; they could actually accomplish what they wanted and ultimately people stay in companies because they can achieve something."

Brin and Page created a company that had some of the brightest minds in the world. Similar to a top flight university, they hired the brightest minds, worked in small teams, received feedback, and their mission was to improve the world. The culture of Google had similar values as academia in the sense that everything was questioned. Ideas were critiqued by your peers not just your managers. At Google, position and hierarchy seldom won an argument, and the founders wanted to keep it that way (Hamel and Breen, 2007).

Another factor that contributed to the success of Google was their flat, open organizational structure. Typical corporate models had many layers of management and strategy was driven top down. However at Google, the company was highly democratic and employees were encouraged to question anyone. Strategy tended to come from bottom up. Company President, Eric Schmidt, stated that he talked with many employees every day about their various projects. The culture and structure of Google initiated from Brin and Page's attitude, "We do not like authority and we do not like being told what to do." Brin and Page understood that breakthroughs come from questioning assumptions and smashing paradigms (Hamel and Breen, 2007).

In order to increase the effectiveness of communication, the company developed an intranet, called "MOMA," or "Message Oriented Middleware Application." MOMA was a Web page and threaded conversation for each of the company's several hundred internal projects, making it easy for teams to communicate their progress, garner feedback, and solicit help. The company also created a program called Snippets; a site where all Google engineers could post a summary of their activities. Any Googler could search the Snippets list to locate individuals working on similar projects, or to simply stay abreast of what was happening (Hamel and Breen, 2007).

Google also had a policy of giving outsized rewards to people who came up with outsized ideas, a team-focused approach to product development, and a corporate credo that challenged every employee to put the user first (Hamel and Breen, 2007).

Support from Top Management

Google sought out the best and brightest from all over the world. Google was committed to having one of the most open and entrepreneurial environments in the world. Evidence of this could be seen in a recent study of MBA graduates who were interviewed about which company they wanted to work for and Google was number one, where 20 percent of all MBA graduates said they wanted to work for Google after graduation (CNNMoney.com, 2009).

Corporate Culture and Employees

The most critical factor in stimulating entrepreneurship within Google was the culture. Keys to success included forming an innovative and loose structure with quality employees. It was also essential to reward entrepreneurship and innovation.

Google's hiring process was based upon the belief of Brin and Page that A-level talent wanted to work with A-level talent and B-level talent tended to hire B-level talent or lower. This can ruin an organization. As a result, Google's hiring process could be painful to applicants. Interviews often extended several weeks and potential employees were often given scientists, Mensa-level problems to solve on the spot. Decisions on candidates were made by veteran associates and executives. It was an admittedly brutal process, but it weeded out anyone who was merely average (Hamel and Breen, 2007).

Brin and Page tried to keep the layers of management to a minimum. They also tried to keep the communication channels narrow so people could act quickly. They disliked taking orders from people and hated being managed. According to Brin and Page, "Our management philosophy amplified that quality employees who are motivated do not need to be managed." Similar to academia, Google gave their employees a lot of freedom.

Google's website stated that its philosophy was, "Never Settle for the Best." Google's persistence, along with enormous amounts of energy and ambition, brought about its success. The company's website listed "Ten Things Google Has Found to Be True":

1. Focus on the user and all else will follow.
2. It is best to do one thing really, really well.

3. Fast is better than slow.
4. Democracy on the web works.
5. You do not need to be at your desk to need an answer.
6. You can make money without doing evil.
7. There is always more information out there.
8. The need for information crosses all borders.
9. You can be serious without a suit.
10. Great is not good enough.

(*Source*: www.google.com/corporate/tenthings .html, accessed May 17, 2009.)

Page and Brin placed heavy emphasis on providing a relaxed and fun work environment. They believed that employees should create their own hours and work them as they felt they were most productive. Google's staff worked 80 percent of their hours on regular work and the other 20 percent on noncore projects (organizational slack). The company estimated that it developed 10–12 new service offerings every quarter. According to Marisa Mayer (2009), Vice President of Search Product and User Experience and the first female engineer hired at Google, "The 20% was one of the keys to our success. It gave the engineers the ability to work on whatever they were passionate about. You never know when you are going to create great products. That was why we gave them the opportunity to be creative. That was how Google News and Gmail were born. You have to try a number of different things. Certainly we are in the business of searching and advertising, but basically we are in the business of innovation. Our innovation strategy has been three fold: (1) allow small teams to work together, (2) allow ideas to come from everywhere, and (3) give employees 20% free time to work on any projects they have a passion for. These have all contributed to our success."

Google prided itself on its open, social environment but many people felt that Google had turned increasingly "corporate." The environment in which engineers were able to create their own products and services was decreasing since it had to go through a full review process that could take months before the product was released to market. Although engineers enjoyed being creative, they might as well create a product/service that they can monetize on their own.

Despite these factors, Google had problems related to the rapid growth of the company. As of May 2009 Google had over 20,000 employees. This had a negative effect on the company's ability to maintain an entrepreneurial culture. The most often heard complaint was that the employees' skills were not being utilized. As one Ivy League graduate stated, "I have an Ivy League education and I was hired to shuffle papers in Human Resources. I quit after six months."

Small, Self-Managed Teams

The majority of Google's employees worked in teams of three engineers when working on product development. Big products like Gmail could have 30 or more teams with three to four people on a team. Each team had a specific assignment (e.g., building spam filters or improving the forwarding feature). Each team had a leader; however, leaders rotated on teams. Engineers often worked on more than one project and were free to switch teams. According to Shona Brown, Google's VP for operations, "If at all possible, we want people to commit to things, rather than be assigned to things" (Hamel and Breen, 2007).

Reward Structure

Google was called a playground on steroids where there were 18 cafes staffed with 7 executive chefs. Google was known for offering its staff incredible free perks: volleyball court, gyms, gourmet lunches and dinners (although leaving after eating dinner was frowned upon), Ben & Jerry's Ice Cream, yoga classes, employees could bring their dogs to work, onsite masseuse, office physician, laundry service, travel back and forth to work, etc. This made Google one of the most sought after companies to work for. Google offered great perks to their employees because they wanted the brightest and most qualified employees focusing their attention on their jobs all of the time.

Google employees earned a base salary that was on par with, or slightly lower than the industry average; however the standard deviation around that average was higher at Google than it was at most other companies. At Google, annual bonuses amounted to 30 to 60 percent of base salary, but the financial upside could be much, much bigger for those that came up with a profit-pumping idea (Hamel and Breen, 2007).

Google understood that entrepreneurs were motivated by money. Therefore in 2004, they created the "Founders Awards." These were restricted stock options (sometimes worth millions) that were given quarterly to teams that came up with the best ideas to increase the profitability of the company. The largest such award to date went to a team led by Eric Veach. His team created a new advertising algorithm, dubbed "SmartAds" and won $10 million (Hamel and Breen, 2007).

Decision Point

As Brin and Page sat through the concert they thought, "Look at Green Day. These guys have been successful for years and they still ROCK!! If Green Day can do it, so can Google." But Brin and Page realized that in order to accomplish their goals they would need to figure out how to solve their corporate problems. Their primary problem was how to maintain their culture of corporate entrepreneurship and innovation in the face of flat net profits from 2007 to 2008. Additionally, a multitude of other issues faced the company: (1) a decrease in advertising revenue, (2) the firing of several employees for the first time in the company's history and the elimination of products that made no money, and (3) the loss of employees for a variety of reasons (e.g., lack of mentoring and formal career planning, too much bureaucracy, low pay and benefits, high cost of living in the area, desire to start their own business, etc.). If Google wanted to continue its main strategy of growth through innovation, it would have to find a way to recruit and retain the best employees.

Google had to figure out how to maintain its culture of corporate entrepreneurship and innovation in an era of stagnant profitability. Furthermore, the company had grown to over 20,000 employees. How could it maintain its culture with so large an organization?

Discussion Questions

1. What are the major problems facing Google in 2009?
2. Given the economic environment in 2009 as described in the case, what implications, opportunities, and threats does this context pose for Google currently? What about in 2012?
3. Based on the content of the case, what was the primary Strategic Inflection Point for Google? Why did you select this point?
4. A. Calculate the key profitability, liquidity, and asset management ratios for Google over the past five year period and compare them with Yahoo! Based on the financial ratios, what advantages does Google have over Yahoo!? What vulnerabilities does Google have versus Yahoo!?
   B. Is Google financially healthy? Why or why not?
5. What were Google's keys to success?
6. What recommendations would you make to Google? Why?

References

100 Top MBA Employers. CNNMoney.com. Accessed May 28, 2009, http://money.cnn.com/magazines/fortune/mba100/2009/full_list.

Battelle, J. (2009). Inside the Mind of Google. CNBC Interview. December 3, 2009.

Blodget, H. (2009). Google Announces Layoffs (GOOG). *Silicon Valley Insider.* Accessed May 15, 2009, www.businessinsider.com/2009/1/google-announces-layoffs-goog.

Blodget, H. (2009). Google Announces Layoffs (GOOG). *Silicon Valley Insider.* Accessed May 15, 2009, www.businessinsider.com/2009/1/google-announces-layoffs-goog.

Brandon, E. (2009). Retirement Accounts Have Lost $3.4 Trillion. USNews.com. Accessed May 28, 2009, www.usnews.com/blogs/planning-to-retire/2009/03/13/retirement-accounts-have-now-lost-34-trillion.html.

Buffett: Economy in a Recession Will Be Worse Than Feared. USAToday.com, April 4, 2008. Accessed May 15, www.usatoday.com/money/economy/2008-04-28-buffett-recession_N.htm.

Christie, L. (2009). Homes Almost 20% Cheaper. CNNMoney.com. Accessed May 24, 2009, http://money.cnn.com/2009/05/26/real_estate/CaseShiller_home_prices_Q1/index.htm?cnn=yes.

Google Milestones (2009). Accessed on March 31, 2009, www.google.com/corporate/history.html.

Google.org (2010). Philanthropy at Google. Accessed May 18, 2010, www.google.org/googlers.html.

Guth, W., and Ginsberg, A. (1990). "Guest Editors' Introduction: Corporate Entrepreneurship." *Strategic Management Journal*, 11, 297-308.

Hamel, G., and Breen, B. (2007). Aiming for an Evolutionary Advantage. *Harvard Business Review*. Harvard Business School Press, Boston, MA.

Harris, S. (2009). Stanford's Rich Entrepreneurial Culture Still Bursting with Ideas, Nurturing Minds. *San Jose Mercury News*, May 10, pages 1, 19.

Lowe, (2009). *Google Speaks: Secrets of the World's Greatest Billionaire Entrepreneurs*. John Wiley & Sons. Page 282.

Miller, M. (2006). *Googlepedia: The Ultimate Google Resource*. Que. Page 10.

Pinchot, G., and Pellman, R. (1999) *Intrapreneuring in Action: A Handbook for Business Innovation*. Berrett-Koehler.

Pohle, G., and Chapman, M. (2006). IBM Global CEO Study 2006: Business Model Innovation Matters. *Strategy and Leadership*, 34, 5, 34-40.

Rule, E., and Irwin, D. (1988). Fostering Intrapreneurship: The New Competitive Edge. *Journal of Business Strategy*, 9, 3, 44-47.

S&P 500 Index (2009). Accessed October 24, 2009, http://finance.yahoo.com/q/hp?s=^GSPC&a=0&b=3&c=1950&d=9&e=25&f=2009&g=d&z=66&y=132.

Schmidt, E. (2009). Inside the Mind of Google. CNBC Interview. December 3, 2009.

Thompson, C. (2001). *Current Biography Yearbook*. H.W. Wilson Co. Page 50.

Willis, B. (2009). U.S. Recession Worst Since Great Depression, Revised Data Show. Accessed November 27, 2009, www.bloomberg.com/apps/news?pid=20601087&sid=aNivTjr852TI.

Wolcott, R., and Lippitz, M. (2007). The Four Models of Corporate Entrepreneurship. *MIT Sloan Management Review*, Fall, 49, 1, 74–82.

Zahra, S. (1991). Predictors and Financial Outcomes of Corporate Entrepreneurship: An Exploratory Study. *Journal of Business Venturing*, 6, 4, 259-285.1

ANDREW MASON & GROUPON, INC.*

Introduction

On November 29, 2012, Andrew Mason just got approved by the board of directors of Groupon, Inc., to remain the CEO of the company despite its poor performance. Since Groupon went public in November, 2011, at $20 a share, its shares were down nearly 80%.

Investors lost faith in the five-year-old Internet company once touted for transforming local business advertising by marketing Internet discounts on everything from spa treatments to dining. Analysts questioned whether Mason had enough business experience to run a fast-growth company with thousands of employees across the globe. Europe had been a particular problem as its debt crisis sapped demand for higher-priced deals and merchants balked at the steep discounts Groupon offered there. Groupon and rivals in the daily deals business, like Amazon.com-backed LivingSocial, have been forced to revamp their business models as daily deal fever waned. Groupon had lost money in the third quarter of 2012. LivingSocial, Groupon's biggest competitor, cut almost 10 percent of its staff during that period (Barr, 2012).

As Mason walked along the waterfront in Chicago, he pondered what direction the company should take. At one time, Groupon had an offer from Google to be purchased for $6 billion;

*This case was written by Todd A. Finkle, Pigott Professor of Entrepreneurship, Gonzaga University, as a basis for class discussion. Reprinted by permission.

however, the company passed on the deal. Now the company was struggling to survive. Mason had to figure out what strategic direction the company should take in order to survive and grow in the future.

Andrew Mason & Groupon, Inc.

Andrew Mason, who recently turned 31 years old, was the co-founder of the Internet company Groupon. Mason had a casual style and was a very humble person. He had a great deal of creative energy, was stubborn, and looked at problems in different ways. Mason started showing signs of being an entrepreneur at a young age. Born in Pittsburgh, as a kid he painted house numbers on curbs and bought candy at retail stores to resell to classmates in the lunchroom (Briggs, 2010). Mason started a Saturday morning bagel delivery service when he was 15 years old (Coburn, 2010). He coined his small business with the name Bagel Express and served many local houses and businesses in his childhood town of Mount Lebanon, a suburb of Pittsburgh, Pennsylvania. Mason later made money in high school repairing computers. After high school Mason moved to Illinois to attend Northwestern University where he graduated with a degree in music in 2003 (Coburn, 2010). Mason claimed that not only did being a music graduate from Northwestern benefit him but also being in a rock band undoubtedly helped him to achieve success. According to Mason, "Being in a band makes you learn how to disagree with people and hold onto a kind of uncompromising belief. You have to stick to doing what you believe is right. I think that is probably core to the culture of this company" (Cutler, 2010).

Prior to Groupon, Mason worked in Web design at several Chicago-based startups. He assisted in the startup and promotion of a number of online businesses in the late 90s and early 2000s. He worked for venture capitalist and serial entrepreneur Eric Lefkofsky, who co-founded the startup, Starbelly.com, which was sold to a company for $240 million right before the dot-com bust of January 2000.

Mason returned to school in 2006 to work on a degree from the University of Chicago's Harris School of Public Policy. While on scholarship there, he began to experience problems with his cell phone provider. He started to brainstorm for an idea for a website devoted to promoting change based on a large number of participants desiring the same thing. Mason was offered $1 million to fund the implementation of his idea by Lefkofsky (Coburn, 2010). He immediately dropped out of school to pursue this idea and started developing what would become ThePoint. ThePoint was a Web platform that allowed anyone to write a campaign exhorting others either to do something (stage a demonstration) or to give money to a cause (make Election Day a national holiday) (Coburn, 2010).

Due to a lack of profitability, Mason ended up innovating ThePoint. Mason noticed that the site's most popular campaigns involved group buying so he decided to create a sub-business on the site dedicated to this concept. This was the beginning of Groupon, which launched its first offer—a two-for-one pizza deal—on October 22, 2008. Twenty-four Chicago residents bought the deal, and Groupon was off and running. After six months of operating solely in Chicago, it expanded to Boston, New York, Toronto, and Washington, D.C. (Etter, 2011).

Groupon's foremost objective was to provide its members a website that allowed them collective buying power or "power in numbers." Groupon was a service that offered consumers select discounts to local businesses, categorized by city. According to Mason's 2010 interview with Charlie Rose, each discount, presented in the form of a coupon purchased from Groupon, "offered a big discount of 50% or more" for items from these local businesses (Mason, 2010). Participating businesses can be anything from spas to movie theaters, restaurants to art studios, and virtually anything in between. However, in order for consumers to obtain coupons for these businesses, Groupon required a minimum number of people to purchase the coupons, hence the term *collective buying power*. Collective buying power also benefited these local businesses. By establishing a minimum performance level, these businesses could guarantee that enough customers would purchase their coupons in order for their side of the deal to be worth their time, money, and effort. In doing this, Mason was able to make the claim that through Groupon, "for the first time, local businesses got performance based marketing. They only paid when these customers walked in the door. We got them in the door then it was up to them to give them an amazing experience" (Mason, 2010).

By the end of 2009, after only 14 months, Groupon had 1.8 million subscribers (Groupon, 2011). In 2010, the company expanded into several new cities each month in addition to international expansion. It received and rejected multibillion dollar offers from both Yahoo! and Google in the late 2010 (Harris, 2010) and closed the year with 50.5 million subscribers (Groupon, 2011).

Groupon's growth continued at a torrid pace into 2011; the company had more than doubled its subscriber count in the first half of 2011, reporting 115.7 million subscribers as of June 30, 2011. In the two and a half years from January 1, 2009, to June 30, 2011, over 23 million different customers purchased a Groupon and over half have purchased more than one. In 2011, the company went public at $20/share, making the company worth $30 billion. By 2012, the company reported that it had 11,471 employees with sales of $1.6 billion.

Industry

Groupon competed in the discount group-buying service industry, or the "social group-buying" industry that was characterized by "daily deals." This was an emerging industry that Groupon single-handedly brought back into the limelight after it had all but died online by early 2001. Groupon had some group-buying coupon competitors or Groupon clones that generated excellent traffic at times but not necessarily revenue or profit like Groupon did. Their biggest competitor was LivingSocial of which Amazon. com was an investor. LivingSocial had a market value of $3 billion as of 2011. Other competitors included YouSwoop, Scoop St., BuyWithMe, Tippr, Gilt Groupe, and DailyCandy, all of which offered daily local deals. Google had been building and beta-testing a Groupon clone called Google Offers, something it began after Groupon rejected its offer to purchase the company.

Groupon's Strategies

Groupon employed a multicountry, multiregional strategy that tended to focus on getting people to buy into currently popular or potentially popular products or services from vendors in their urban area and from online merchants. Groupon formed many temporary alliances with businesses in order to gain access to offerings for its own members and thus bring in revenue worth up to 50% of the deal purchase price. These businesses could be thought of collectively as Groupon partners that were vital for the continuation and success of Groupon's business. Groupon also had its vendors or partners sign a year-long contract that locked them into getting placement with Groupon and no one else during that time. Groupon also had a highly efficient and very active sales team that tended to stay ahead of its competitors and worked hard to get quality deals for Groupon members.

Groupon employed largely the same strategies throughout its very short life, which included: broad market penetration; clever, interesting e-mails that promoted each Groupon; simple core technology that focused on delivering e-mails containing Groupon pitches and processing transactions quickly for deals that reached the tipping point; word-of-mouth and paid referrals (in Groupon dollars) as well as mass marketing/advertising to bring in new members (especially for newer markets overseas); affordability of all deals offered by Groupon (price sensitivity); and a large, growing group of talented staff who acted as salespeople, writers, and brokers for Groupon.

To diversify its product base, Groupon launched Groupon Goods in 2011 as a forum to sell discounted products. Groupon Goods had a diverse product mix. The offering was a quick success as Groupon sold $2 million worth of goods in its first week. Goods surpassed $200 million in revenue during the second quarter of 2012, and the marketplace was expected to sell between $600 million and $800 million worth of goods in 2012 (Stambor, 2012). That placed Groupon among the largest North American online retailers. For the sake of comparison, Saks Direct was No. 38 in the *Internet Retailer Top 500 Guide*, with Internet Retailer–estimated 2011 online sales of $748.6 million while Abercrombie & Fitch was No. 45 with online sales of $552.6 million (Stambor, 2012).

Groupon in 2012

The average Groupon user was a single female between the ages of 18 and 34. More than half of them held college degrees, and two-thirds of them made between $50,000 and $100,000 (Coburn, 2011). Although there were many critics of Groupon, there were also an abundance of success stories. Wendella Boats, located on the Chicago River, was one of those success stories. It sold 19,850 coupons for its Chicago River architectural boat tour for $12 a ticket when the tour was normally $25. The director of operations for the company mentioned that the deal with Groupon significantly helped the company's cash flow due to receiving its cut of the deal up front. Other success stories included 9,258 Groupons sold for $5 in pizza that was worth $10,719; Groupons sold for $185 in teeth-whitening services that was worth $600; and 1,269 Groupons sold for $50 at a denim boutique that was worth $125.

The managing editor of the website Bundle provided a critical look at Groupon based on her website's findings. The website dealt with tracking consumers and their relationship with money. She called it the *cult of Groupon*, because those who subscribed to Groupon's daily deals were addicted to the daily hit and sometimes people wound up buying coupons that seemed attractive due to the savings but were not really needed. A similar issue dealt with customer loyalty. Businesses used Groupon in an attempt to expand their customer base. For example, restaurants wanted users of Groupons to turn into regular diners. However, Groupon's customer base oftentimes was merely seeking the best deal, only to move on to the next best deal. Also, due to the nature of Groupon, some restaurants became overwhelmed by the coupon diners, which led to an overall loss on the deal. This was especially problematic for restaurants when coupon users were basing their tips for meals on the discounted price of the meal. Groupon has since addressed this issue and reminded its customers to tip the restaurants based on the menu price.

One other major concern with Groupon was its lack of profitability. It had been caught using questionable accounting methods, which made the corporation look better off than it actually was. Another concern for investors stemmed from when Groupon initially filed papers. Founders and early employees sold a huge amount of stock instead of holding on to it. This was potentially a bad indication that the company has already reached its peak.

The average Groupon subscriber spent $18 in the first half of 2011 compared with $21 in the first half of 2010 (McNaughton, 2011). There was also a possibility that the competition was affecting margins as a number of companies were trying to compete in the same market, such as DealSwarm, DealOn, DealFind, GoDailyDeals, and YourBestDeals.

It was well documented that Groupon required strategic partners to offer a minimum 50 percent off the deal they came to terms with. In addition, Groupon's take (the amount of revenue it kept on each Groupon it sold) was at 41 percent as of the first 9 months of 2011, which was down slightly from 43 percent in 2009. That margin was being squeezed further in 2012. Essentially what this meant for the merchants that were dealing with Groupon was that they had to be willing to sell their product or service at a price that was 25 percent of the listed price (*Forbes*, 2012). This posed a threat for Groupon because there was a chance that other companies could find ways to take a percentage that was less than Groupon's, which would be more attractive in the eyes of merchants because they would be able to keep more money in their own pockets.

An additional threat was that merchants got fed up with sites like Groupon and refused to use them. In one instance, Ms. Bengel of Wellpath said, "Every day, we get an e-mail or phone call saying, Can we match someone else's price? We're not Wal-Mart" (Streitfeld, 2011). A study by researchers at Harvard and Boston University also discovered that the long-term reputation of the merchant was at risk; fans of daily deals were on average hard to please. What did that mean exactly? Well, "after they ate at the restaurant or visited the spa, they went on Yelp and grumbled about it. This pulled down the average Yelp rating by as much as half a point" (Streitfeld, 2011). Since this audience was so critical of the merchant, offering a Groupon put the merchant's reputation at risk.

Despite these issues in 2012, Groupon maintained 50 to 55 percent of the industry's market share, followed by LivingSocial with 20 to 25 percent (Pepitone, 2012).

Groupon's Problems in 2012

One critical problem Groupon faced was the ease of replication of its business model. Groupon had to ensure that it remained attractive and profitable for all of the partner businesses that it worked with to bring deals to the consumer. Groupon faced many threats from foreign markets where it had limited or no experience (e.g., Australia, India, and Japan). As result, Groupon was often pressured into either expending more resources to gain a foothold in those markets or perhaps paying top dollar to acquire a first-mover advantage.

Groupon's biggest future competitor would be Google Offers. However, Google had yet to establish itself in any meaningful markets the way both Groupon and LivingSocial had done.

Another problem with Groupon was that the merchants that it was doing business with were failing to get any brand loyalty, which was what many of them were hoping to accomplish with the Internet coupon site. Instead, coupon users were drawn to the company for one-time use and once they had used their coupon, say for a day at the spa, they just looked for a deal at a spa somewhere else (Streitfeld, 2011). The reason behind this inevitable disappointment with retailers was that customers on the site realized that they would never have to pay full price again. On the other hand, merchants were told that these coupon deals would lead to new customers who would stick around and pay full price (Streitfeld, 2011).

The co-founder of Bloomspot, Jasper Malcolmson, compared the deal offers with merchants to that of marketing subprime loans during the housing boom that led to the economic recession. According to Malcolmson, "They were giving these mortgages to every consumer regardless of whether he could handle it. But sooner or later you find that you can't make great offers to people if they're not making you money" (Streitfeld, 2011). This led Malcolmson to change Bloomspot's focus to merchant profitability.

In addition to the problem of brand loyalty, coupon fatigue seemed to be setting in. With the revenue-generating model that Groupon had created, countless other companies entered the market in hopes of creating some of their own revenue. Copycat sites such as DoubleTakeDeals, YourBestDeals, DealFind, DoodleDeals, DealOn, DealSwarm, and GoDailyDeals emerged among hundreds of others. In fact, according to Local DealSites.com, there were 40 active coupon sites solely in New York City (Streitfeld, 2011). The strange thing was that 80 percent of subscribers to the website's daily e-mails had never actually bought a deal. Recognizing this as a huge problem, Groupon made attempts to increase purchases by offering $10 off the first coupon bought. This number has since increased to $15.

As mentioned earlier, another problem for Groupon was that although it had been growing in terms of the number of subscribers, the actual percentage of those subscribers who were making a purchase was low. In many ways it meant that the huge sums of money that were spent on marketing Groupon paid off, but the company was failing when it came to getting the customer active with its service. The amount of spending by subscribers was also low, which presented an opportunity for Groupon. The dollars spent by customers needed to increase if Groupon expected to make a profit.

Groupon also had financial problems. The company lost about $3 million in the third quarter of 2012. In the beginning of 2011, Groupon's gross billings of $668 million were growing by over *1,400* percent year over year; but by the third quarter of 2012, the $1.2 billion in billings represented a mere 5 percent annual increase. In the same time period, the number of customers who had purchased a Groupon in the previous year rose from 15.4 million to just under 40 million. But the gross billing per customer had fallen by just under 12 percent, from $169 to $149. The year-on-year growth rate of the company's quarterly revenues slumped from 1,358 percent in early 2011 to 33 percent in the third quarter (Zeitlin, 2012).

Furthermore, Groupon's marketing expenses were going up. As a result, the company laid off 954 workers in the third quarter.

David Reibstein, a marketing professor at the Wharton School at University of Pennsylvania, argued that the business would eventually suffer because merchants would realize that the coupons were not a great deal. Reibstein argued that Groupon's customers were likely "price-sensitive," meaning they searched for the best deal they could find. This meant that they were not likely to turn into repeat customers. So the merchants offered a deal, sometimes at a loss, but then got little future business (Zeitlin, 2012). Moreover, companies could alienate current customers by offering coupons. For example, a woman had paid full price for a spa treatment and

EXHIBIT 1
Groupon Revenue and Gross
Billings Growth

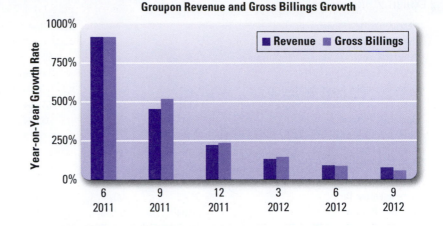

Groupon Revenue and Gross Billings Growth

then she saw someone come in at half price off. She would feel insulted or ripped off. Reibstein stated, "Nothing irritated people more than finding that they were paying a premium over what other people were paying. Even those customers who were perfectly willing to pay the full price for a spa treatment could get a Groupon instead, making the spa take a loss on a customer who was willing to pay full freight. The last group you want to offer coupons to are your existing customers" (Zeitlin, 2012).

The Future of Groupon & Mason

Since Groupon was founded, the company had grown into a major company with about 11,471 employees, millions of subscribers, and over a billion dollars in revenue in the 2012 alone. The reason for the success of Groupon was that the CEO and co-founder, Mason, recognized that there was an opportunity for the creation of collective buying power in order for customers to receive discounts on products and services. This simple idea would have customers interested because of the great deals they would be receiving and businesses intrigued because of the opportunity to reach a wide audience and acquire repeat customers. Unfortunately for Groupon, its model of receiving half of the sales dollars from the company offering the Groupon has yet to provide a profit. The company has continued to make necessary strides to correct this huge problem and seem to be inching closer to "righting the ship." Mason has to determine what his next moves will be to increase the profitability of the company.

EXHIBIT 2 Groupon Inc. Income Statement

In Millions of USD (except for per share items)	3 Months Ending 2012-09-30	3 Months Ending 2012-06-30	3 Months Ending 2012-03-31	3 Months Ending 2011-12-31	3 Months Ending 2011-09-30
Revenue	568.55	568.34	559.28	492.16	430.16
Other Revenue, Total	-	-	-	-	-
Total Revenue	568.55	568.34	559.28	492.16	430.16
Cost of Revenue, Total	181.79	135.18	119.50	96.27	68.05
Gross Profit	386.77	433.15	439.79	395.90	362.12
Selling/General/Admin. Expenses, Total	358.90	388.30	400.20	410.62	367.15

EXHIBIT 2   *(Continued)*

Research & Development	-	-	-	-	-
Depreciation/Amortization	-	-	-	-	-
Interest Expense (Income)—Net Operating	-	-	-	-	-
Unusual Expense (Income)	2.43	−1.64	−0.05	0.26	−4.79
Other Operating Expenses, Total	-	-	-	-	-
Total Operating Expense	543.11	521.85	519.64	507.14	430.40
Operating Income	25.44	46.48	39.64	−14.97	−0.24
Interest Income(Expense), Net Nonoperating	-	-	-	-	-
Gain (Loss) on Sale of Assets	-	-	-	-	-
Other, Net	-	-	-	-	-
Income Before Tax	25.92	100.42	30.97	−25.48	−3.18
Income After Tax	−0.94	33.55	−3.59	−59.68	−14.42

Source: Google Finance—Groupon Inc. Financials. Retrieved December 3, 2012, from http://www.google.com/finance?q=NASDAQ:GRPN&fstype=ii#

EXHIBIT 3   Groupon Inc. Balance Sheet

In Millions of USD (except for per share items)	As of 2012-09-30	As of 2012-06-30	As of 2012-03-31	As of 2011-12-31	As of 2011-09-30
Cash & Equivalents	1,201.01	1,185.80	1,160.99	1,122.93	243.94
Short-Term Investments	-	-	-	-	-
Cash and Short-Term Investments	1,201.01	1,185.80	1,160.99	1,122.93	243.94
Accounts Receivable—Trade, Net	110.06	98.67	122.64	108.75	109.85
Receivables—Other	-	-	-	-	-
Total Receivables, Net	110.06	98.67	122.64	108.75	109.85
Total Inventory	-	-	-	-	-
Prepaid Expenses	121.34	116.14	101.28	91.64	103.86
Other Current Assets, Total	-	-	-	-	8.00
Total Current Assets	1,432.41	1,400.61	1,384.91	1,323.33	465.64
Property/Plant/Equipment, Total—Gross	141.44	111.44	80.88	66.43	51.78
Accumulated Depreciation, Total	−37.56	−28.15	−21.17	−14.63	−10.41
Goodwill, Net	196.98	192.02	185.34	166.90	169.15
Intangibles, Net	51.45	54.30	56.84	45.67	50.14
Long-Term Investments	131.04	131.18	48.48	50.60	45.19
Other Long-Term Assets, Total	117.07	121.69	135.59	136.18	24.06
Total Assets	2,032.81	1,983.10	1,870.86	1,774.48	795.57
Accounts Payable	60.02	60.36	40.62	40.92	40.60
Accrued Expenses	818.56	802.18	810.26	732.73	622.14
Notes Payable/Short-Term Debt	0.00	0.00	0.00	0.00	0.00
Current Port. of LT Debt/Capital Leases	-	-	-	-	-
Other Current liabilities, Total	246.62	237.63	215.50	221.51	103.95
Total Current Liabilities	1,125.20	1,100.18	1,066.38	995.16	766.69
Long-Term Debt	-	-	-	-	-
Capital Lease Obligations	-	-	-	-	-
Total Long-Term Debt	0.00	0.00	0.00	0.00	0.00
Total Debt	0.00	0.00	0.00	0.00	0.00

EXHIBIT 3   *(Continued)*

Deferred Income Tax	28.59	25.84	12.47	7.43	4.79
Minority Interest	5.37	2.99	4.17	−1.42	−0.94
Other Liabilities, Total	74.64	74.77	75.19	70.77	39.72
Total Liabilities	1,233.80	1,203.78	1,158.20	1,071.93	810.26
Redeemable Preferred Stock, Total	-	-	-	-	-
Preferred Stock—Non Redeemable, Net	-	-	-	-	0.01
Common Stock, Total	0.07	0.07	0.07	0.06	0.00
Additional Paid-In Capital	1,459.48	1,437.16	1,401.58	1,388.25	1,414.39
Retained Earnings (Accumulated Deficit)	−672.49	−670.85	−703.18	−698.70	−633.95
Treasury Stock—Common	-	-	-	-	−808.67
Other Equity, Total	11.96	12.94	14.19	12.93	13.52
Total Equity	799.01	779.32	712.66	702.54	−14.70
Total Liabilities & Shareholders' Equity	2,032.81	1,983.10	1,870.86	1,774.48	795.57
Shares Outs—Common Stock Primary Issue	-	-	-	-	-
Total Common Shares Outstanding	654.90	651.57	645.25	644.15	637.80

Source: Google Finance—Groupon Inc. Financials. Retrieved December 5, 2012, from http://www.google.com/finance?q=NASDAQ:GRPN&fstype=ii#

EXHIBIT 4   Groupon Inc. Cash Flow

In Millions of USD (except for per share items)	9 Months Ending 2012−09−30	6 Months Ending 2012−06−30	3 Months Ending 2012−03−31	12 Months Ending 2011−12−31
Net Income/Starting Line	29.02	29.96	−3.59	−297.76
Depreciation/Depletion	39.84	24.53	11.72	32.05
Amortization	-	-	-	-
Deferred Taxes	9.61	13.00	−0.88	32.20
Noncash Items	6.49	−15.83	30.30	100.61
Changes in Working Capital	116.17	107.38	46.16	423.34
Cash from Operating Activities	201.12	159.03	83.71	290.45
Capital Expenditures	−55.81	−39.80	−13.09	−58.33
Other Investing Cash Flow Items, Total	−86.41	−66.80	−33.35	−89.11
Cash from Investing Activities	−142.23	−106.60	−46.44	−147.43
Financing Cash Flow Items	12.78	11.83	−8.00	−7.90
Total Cash Dividends Paid	−3.06	−1.61	−0.65	−5.53
Issuance (Retirement) of Stock, Net	8.87	5.66	0.38	880.63
Issuance (Retirement) of Debt, Net	-	-	-	0.00
Cash from Financing Activities	18.59	15.88	−8.28	867.21
Foreign Exchange Effects	0.59	−5.45	9.06	−6.12
Net Change in Cash	78.08	62.86	38.05	1,004.10
Cash Interest Paid, Supplemental	-	-	-	0.00
Cash Taxes Paid, Supplemental	-	-	-	1.64

Source: Google Finance—Groupon Inc. Financials. Retrieved December 5, 2012, from http://www.google.com/finance?q=NASDAQ:GRPN&fstype=ii#

Discussion Questions

1. Discuss the childhood, background, education, and personality of Andrew Mason.
2. Discuss the history of Groupon from startup until today. What strategies did Mason and Groupon employ to grow their business?
3. In what industry(ies) does Groupon compete? What companies does Groupon compete against? Perform a SWOT analysis of Groupon. What is Groupon's competitive advantage?
4. What were the major problems Groupon, Inc. faced in 2012?
5. What recommendations would you make to Andrew Mason? Why?

References

Barr, A. (2012). Groupon Says Mason Remains Ceo, Shares Slide. Retrieved November 29, 2012, From http://www.chicagotribune.com/business/sns-rt-us-groupon-ceobre8a-s1eq-20121129,0,4417430.story

Briggs, B. (2010, December 10). Quirky CEO 'genius' behind Groupon's success. Retrieved January 20, 2012, from http://www.msnbc.msn.com/id/40494597/ns/business-us_business/t/ quirky-ceo-genius-behind-groupons-success/

Coburn, L. (2010, March 24). Groupon CEO Andrew Mason talks growth, clones, and why Groupon isn't a coupon site [Web log message]. Retrieved September 6, 2011, from http://thenextweb.com/location/2010/03/24/groupon-ceo-andrew-mason-talks-growth-clones-groupon-coupon-site/

Cutler, K.–M. (2010, May 7). *Groupon CEO: Being in a band made my business rock*. Retrieved September 6, 2011 from SocialBeat: http://venturebeat.com/2010/05/07/groupon-andrew-mason/

Etter, L. (2011, August). Groupon Therapy. *Vanity Fair*. Retrieved November 29, 2012, from http://www.vanityfair.com/business/features/2011/08/groupon-201108

Forbes. (2012, January 5). Groupon Still Chasing $25 Billion Mirage. *Forbes.com*. Retrieved February 29, 2012, from http://www.forbes.com/sites/greatspeculations/2012/01/05/groupon-still-chasing-25-billion-mirage/

Groupon's S-1 Filing with the SEC. Retrieved August 8, 2011, from http://www.sec.gov/Archives/edgar/data/1490281/000104746911005613/a2203913zs-1.htm

Harris, M. (2010, November 21). Groupon Shopping Itself? Buzz Is that the Chicago-Based Deal Site Is in Talks with Google. *Chicago Tribune*. Retrieved December 5, 2012, from http://articles.chicagotribune.com/2010-11-21/business/ct-biz-1121-confidential-groupon-20101121_1_yahoojapan-google-news-yahoo-finance

Mason, A. (2010, December 10). The Rise to Wealth (C. Rose, Interviewer).

McNaughton, M. (2011, August 12). Groupon Doubles Subscribers in 2011, But Only 20% Have Made Purchases. *The Realtime Report*. Retrieved February 25, 2012, from http://therealtimereport.com/2011/08/12/groupon-doubles-subcribers-in-2011-but-only-20-have-made-purchases/

Pepitone, J. (2012, November 30). Problems at Groupon, LivingSocial Make Daily Deals Market Look Bleak. *CNNMoney.com*. Retrieved December 5, 2012, from http://money.cnn.com/2012/11/30/technology/groupon-livingsocial-daily-deals/index.html

Stambor, Z. (2012). Groupon Turns Its Business Model on End. *Internet Retailer*. Retrieved November 29, 2012, from http://www.internetretailer.com/2012/09/04/groupon-turns-its-business-model-end

Streitfeld, D. (2011, October 1). Coupon Sites Are a Great Deal, but Not Always to Merchants. *The New York Times*. Retrieved February 12, 2012, from http://www.nytimes.com/2011/10/02/business/deal-sites-have-fading-allure-for-merchants.html?_r=3ref=business

Zeitlin, M. (2012, November 12). Why Groupon and Living Social Are Doomed. *The Daily Beast*. Retrieved December 1, 2012, from http://www.thedailybeast.com/articles/2012/11/30/why-groupon-and-living-social-are-doomed.html

HOMERUN.COM: BREAKING INTO A SATURATED MARKET*

"Business is terrific," reflected HomeRun.com CEO Jared Kopf, as he reviewed his first quarter profits. Kopf had just celebrated the opening of a satellite office in Phoenix, managed by former Go Daddy Vice-President of Business Operations Bob Olson. Hiring Olson was a coup for Kopf, who had spent several months hunting for the right executive to lead his sales organization.

The past several months had been a crucial time for HomeRun, an Internet business that had opened its doors in Fall 2009. The group buying market, which remained largely untapped in early 2009, was now erupting, with more than 200 copycat businesses offering daily deal emails and local discounts.[1] All of the companies were built around a similar model: a daily email to users with an offer that featured a deep discount on anything from a restaurant dinner to a series of yoga classes. As long as a certain number of people decided to opt in to buy the discounted item, the deal would "tip." This group dynamic ensured the product would go viral, as friends and family shared in the deal. "I think that the web today is very much about delivering personalized and relevant offers to people and helping people find the things that are actually meaningful to them," said Kopf, who believed that his business had huge potential to grow in a down market.

Company Background

HomeRun was the brainchild of Jared Kopf and Matt Humphrey, two entrepreneurs who met in San Francisco in October 2008. Kopf was the former co-founder of digital content publisher Slide, and chairman of the self-service advertising platform, AdRoll. Humphrey was a Carnegie Mellon prodigy (starting at the university at the age of 13) and founder of the social gaming company, Kickball Labs. Kopf and Humphrey became friends while working for Internet companies that shared office space in early 2008. The two met up again in November 2009, when both were looking for new ventures to launch. Over lunch, Kopf and Humphrey discovered their mutual interest in group buying. The net result? HomeRun.com.

Naming the company was no easy task, but in the end Kopf and Humphrey chose to go with HomeRun and acquired the domain name for $131,000. The team believed that the name immediately differentiated their venture from other group buying startups (or local e-commerce startups as they were also known) that were opting for more complicated monikers like Group-Swoop and Deals2Buy. HomeRun was "simple,

*This case was written by J.C. Ford as a basis for class discussion. Reprinted by permission.
[1]"Meet the Fastest Growing Company Ever." Forbes.com. August 17, 2010, www.forbes.com/forbes/2010/0830/entrepreneurs-groupon-facebook-twitter-next-web-phenom.html.

memorable, and transmittable," noted Kopf. He also liked that the name didn't carry any money-saving connotations such as "deal" or "coupon" and promoted the ideals of teamwork and winning. Kopf wanted to "appeal to deeper emotions as a way to differentiate."

Initially, the company moved forward with Kopf, Humphrey, and two talented engineers who had previously worked with Humphrey. In December 2009, it became apparent that more help would be needed to hire and train a competent sales staff, so Kopf brought on Noah Lichtenstein, a business development executive from WeatherBill. With heavy personnel costs, Kopf needed to conserve capital, and he chose to farm out the initial content and graphic needs, keeping the full-time team as lean as possible.

HomeRun.com went live in late January 2010 in the local market of San Francisco and offered the following products:

Daily Steal: One amazing thing to do in the city every day.

Beginner's Luck: Great offers for members within their first thirty days of membership.

Private Reserve: Unique experiences reserved for top point-earning members.

Most of the deals were given "avalanche pricing," which meant that the more inventory the customer bought, the lower the price fell. To keep other group buying sites from using "avalanche pricing," they had plans to trademark the name.

On the engineering side, Humphrey's team developed a versatile platform that worked not only for the HomeRun site, but also as a deal engine for other businesses. The team also worked diligently to make the daily offers available for redemption via mobile phones.

In June 2010, the team expanded to include account managers, sales representatives, content writers, and developers. Soon the demand for sales and customer service staff outweighed the existing manpower, so Kopf began searching for a customer service professional who could handle the rapidly expanding sales staff and customer base. His search brought him to Bob Olson, the

legendary sales guru of GoDaddy.com. The problem? Olson was firmly rooted in Phoenix, Arizona, where he lived with his wife and children. Dedicated to making the situation work, Kopf met with his executive team and they decided that sales and customer service teams would relocate to Arizona where Olson would run the office and where the costs of doing business were considerably lower.

The Local E-Commerce Industry

The local e-commerce or group buying industry is based on a simple premise: businesses are always seeking new ways to connect with local consumers. At the same time, consumers are always searching for ways to save money. Companies involved in the local e-commerce space find local restaurants, spas, or other businesses that are willing to offer substantial discounts, as long as their brand is shared with a large number of new customers. The company offers the discount online to their user base and then takes a cut of the profits (often as much as 50 percent). As the company grows, it continually expands to new markets, offering duplicate services in major cities around the country and eventually the world.

The local e-commerce industry works particularly well in a down market. In late 2010, the recession was still going strong, with a 9.6 percent unemployment rate.[2] Consumers were opting to keep their cash in the bank, preferring to eat at home rather than eating out. The climate was ripe for the local e-commerce model, because people still wanted to enjoy their pre-recession lifestyles, as long as it was affordable.

Several key components of the local e-commerce industry set the successful companies apart from their competitors: socialization, technology, service, inventory, and pricing.

Socialization

Local e-commerce success relies on the power of group buying, which springs from the premise

---

[2]"United States Unemployment Rate." TradingEconomics .com. October 2010, www.tradingeconomics.com/Economics/ Unemployment-Rate.aspx?Symbol=USD.

that people typically trust products recommended by friends and family. Coming together as a community means that consumer purchases garner more significance than items acquired by individuals. Successful group buying companies encourage social interaction on multiple platforms, including Twitter, Facebook, and mobile phone applications. They also incorporate social feeds on their websites that display what friends are buying and when. "It's addictive," claims Jay Gleason, a writer from San Francisco, who has spent more than $1,000 on dozens of daily deals in the past year.

Simply offering a daily deal isn't enough to capture the market at this level of market saturation, however. Companies need to add elements of serendipity to acquire a larger user base while also making the product more social. Free offers, VIP memberships, and website games are just some of the ways that group buying companies are staying competitive in the market.

Technology

Many local e-commerce sites offer real-time redemption through iPhone and Android applications. Most are integrated with Facebook and all employ a simple, deal-a-day email as their primary method of outreach. To stand out, a company must create proprietary technology that differs from the daily email standard that has become a norm in the industry. Local e-commerce company Tippr has gone so far as to secure ten patents for the technology its Seattle-based team has created to drive their site.

Successful local e-commerce companies must also develop and employ technologies that enable them to personalize their products. Generic deals geared for the masses result in a decline in memberships. By contrast, companies that engineer personalized alerts stay a step ahead of their competitors, cutting through the noise to deliver the offers that fit individual user needs.

Service

Anybody can start a local e-commerce company by sourcing merchant inventory and creating a simple redemption process. Success, however, lies in developing an effective customer service organization. At a minimum, companies must have one customer service person for every market, which creates an expansion problem for startups that want to compete against larger group buying companies, such as Groupon and Living Social. In 2010, Groupon employed more than 300 customer service representatives and sales associates.

Focusing on service also helps to improve the company's customer retention. According to *The Wall Street Journal*, Groupon's research found that only 22 percent of Groupon buyers make a return visit to businesses that don't offer a second discount.[3] A business that can surpass that percentage stands to gain interest from merchants, who are losing faith in the ROI of the group buying model.

Inventory and Pricing

As the market becomes more saturated, diversity of inventory becomes increasingly important. For example, when a merchant is found on multiple deal sites, the deal site's brand becomes secondary to the discount offered. Some companies have overcome this challenge by creating exclusivity agreements with merchants. However, the merchants, seeing multiple deal platform opportunities available, rarely acquiesce to these agreements. Companies that choose to hire a telemarketing expert have the upper hand on companies that opt to learn the art of consumer telemarketing on the job. The pricing of the company's inventory is also a key differentiator. Most deal buying companies offer prices that are discounted by fifty percent or greater. This creates price sensitivity among consumers, who may use a new discounter once, but will not return until another similar discount is offered. This behavior may be due to the consumer's inability to afford full price merchandise or to a lack of desire to pay full price for anything.

---

[3]"Online Coupons Get Smarter." WallStreetJournal.com. August 25, 2010, http://online.wsj.com/article/SB100014 24052748703447004575449453225928136.html.

The Opportunity

Although the market is over-saturated, there is still an opportunity for a strong group buying platform like HomeRun to earn substantial revenues if they closely examine their core markets: business owners and consumers. Struggling business owners are the bread and butter of the group buying industry because they are generally looking to unload excess inventory, and the opportunity to show that inventory to a large number of potential customers is very attractive. At the same time, the commission structure of the deal works in favor of the group buying company, which typically earns fifty percent of the proceeds from the inventory sold within a 24-hour period.

Struggling businesses are not the only beneficiaries of the group buying process. Given the high unemployment rate, it's no surprise that consumers are continually on the lookout for great deals and offers. In a saturated market, however, consumers trade brand loyalty for the largest discount they can find. If the group buying company can personalize the deal, it gains a chance to increase its customer retention rate.

If a company creates proprietary technology, potential B2B opportunities emerge. HomeRun's deal platform offered an opportunity for other companies to run offers to their customers under their proprietary branding without having to build their own e-commerce platform.

Successful companies create incentives for all their customers to share their offers. For example, Groupon encourages its customers to share news about deals through email, Facebook, and Twitter; it also promises that if one of its users sends a Groupon link to a friend, and the friend buys a Groupon item within 72 hours, the one who sent the link receives $10 worth of Groupon credits in their account.

Competition and Challenges

The biggest challenge in the group buying space is the ease with which these types of companies start up. There are no clear barriers to entry, and success lies in the ability to source deals and acquire consumer email addresses. For many deal companies, branding, coupled with massive email lists, is the only differentiator between success and failure.

In 2010, the most formidable competitor in the deal buying space was Groupon, with a valuation of more than $1 billion.[4] Besides offering a deal of the day email for more than 150 cities, Groupon sourced national deals accessible to all Groupon members. For example, a nationwide deal with Gap, Inc., offering $50 worth of clothing for $25 nabbed Groupon $11 million in revenue.[5] According to a report by Morgan Stanley, Groupon cleared more than $500 million in 2010. Following Groupon was Living Social, a company that in 2010 closed a $40 million round of funding to begin their international expansion.[6]

Although discounts for nationwide brands may work for all parties involved, they are not as ideal for local businesses. Platforms such as Facebook and Twitter provide a broader context for consumer engagement, branding, product introduction, and customer service. With group buying companies, it's not as clear what a local business would do to encourage deal-buyers to revisit their location.

As companies grow in popularity, they deal with an inevitable backlog of merchants who want to be featured but can't. In 2010, Groupon was struggling with a six-month backlog of eager merchants. HomeRun's opportunity to fill that void was clear, but the path to doing so was less obvious. The backlogged merchants at Groupon often sought refuge at smaller group buying companies that offered more advantageous margins and faster placement.

---

[4]"It's Official: Groupon Announces That $1.35 Billion Valuation Round." TechCrunch. April 18, 2010, http://techcrunch.com/2010/04/18/its-official-groupon-announces-that-1-35-billion-valuation-round.

[5]"Walmart Takes Page From from Groupon." *Chicago Business*. October 27, 2010, www.chicagobusiness.com/article/20101027/NEWS07/101029899/walmart-takes-page-from-groupon.

[6]"Meet the Fastest Growing Company Ever." Forbes.com. August 17, 2010, www.forbes.com/forbes/2010/0830/entrepreneurs-groupon-facebook-twitter-next-web-phenom.html.

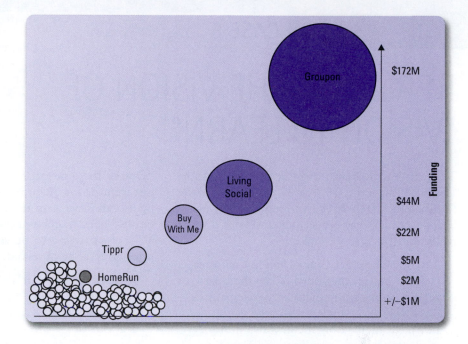

The Future of HomeRun

People will always buy things and there will always be interest in discounts. However, in a saturated market, consumers are less likely to be loyal to a deal company and more likely to use an aggregator service to find the best deals.

To combat this, HomeRun competitor Groupon created a self-service platform known as Groupon Stores. The service enabled local businesses to create Facebook-like pages where fans could follow the company and access deals. The business customers were allowed to create their own deals, bypassing Groupon's average six-month waiting period. The catch? They were still required to pay Groupon's standard commission rate.

Similarly, HomeRun offered the HomeRun Merchant Scoreboard, which ranked local businesses in a city by how many potential "customers" they were able to reach through HomeRun. The customers counted as a composite score of followers and purchasers of that merchant's deals. The score produced the total number of new customers that the merchant could now access. Each merchant had a HomeRun page where fans could follow the brand and tap into new, special discounts.

To ensure a successful future for HomeRun, Kopf must examine several possibilities before executing a strategy. He wonders if he has considered all the possibilities and debates with his team about the criteria they should use in making the decision.

Discussion Questions

1. What criteria should the HomeRun team use in selecting among the many strategic possibilities for the company?
2. Should HomeRun expand its merchant pages to allow merchants to run their own deals, similar to the Groupon Stores idea, or should the company differentiate itself by diving deeper into social gaming and membership rewards?
3. Should HomeRun continue to diversify by entering the global market or concentrate on national partnerships with large corporations?
4. Given the saturation in the market and difficulty maintaining brand equity, does it make sense to create a self-service platform that other companies can use to run their own proprietary deals?

REALIZING THE VISION OF "VISION TO LEARN"*

To hear Austin Beutner speak about Vision to Learn (VTL), the 501(c)(3) organization he founded in March 2012, is to hear a social problem described very powerfully and with a great many statistics. For example,

> 250,000 elementary school kids in California lack the glasses they need to see the board, read a book, study math or participate in class. 95% of 1st graders who need glasses do not have them. Low income and minority students are disproportionately affected. . . . 80% of learning during a child's first 12 years is obtained by vision.[1]

Beutner is quick to follow any statement of the problem with an impassioned explanation of his solution: a non-profit venture that provides underserved children with free eye examinations and free prescription glasses that they need. A successful businessman and public servant long before he began to develop the vision for VTL, Beutner helped fund the start of VTL using a grant from his family foundation. Thereafter, he quickly hired another person—Gaye Williams, former chief of staff to Los Angeles Mayor Antonio Villaraigosa—to take on the role of executive director.

It was thus on a very hot afternoon in August, with temperatures in excess of 90 degrees, that Williams hung up the phone, sighed, and said,

"One of the generators in our mobile eye clinic just went down. At some point soon, we need to figure out if we want to keep repairing that clinic or if we need to get a new one instead." Running VTL was proving to be very different from her prior career. She observed,

> In a lot of ways, it's simpler. In a lot of ways, it's harder. At City Hall, money comes in whether or not people are doing a good job. We try to do a good job, of course, but, at some level, revenue continues to come in; decisions have to be made on how best to spend it. Here, every grant application we file, every funding request we make, we have to prove—to ourselves and somebody else—that we are providing a very critical service that is meeting an unmet need. It's a different kind of bottom line, and it requires a lot of attention.

At the micro level, Williams was referring to the day-to-day details that required decisions, some of which could deplete funds that were challenging to find. The generator in question, for example, powered the oldest mobile eye clinic owned by VTL—a specially outfitted bus that had been driven thousands of miles over several years to bring optometrists and opticians to kids throughout the Los Angeles Unified School District (LAUSD). It was essential for operations, but at a time when VTL was looking to grow, it wasn't clear that vehicle replacement should be prioritized over other initiatives.

At the macro level, Williams was referring to the challenges of organizational growth. In just

---

* This case was written by Elissa Grossman, Associate Professor of Clinical Entrepreneurship at the University of Southern California. Reprinted by permission.

[1] http://www.visiontolearn.org/images/docs/howwework.pdf

over two years since VTL's launch, the organization had provided more than 22,000 exams and distributed more than 18,000 pairs of glasses to kids in need. As big as these numbers might seem, they addressed a tiny fraction of a larger problem, and solving that larger problem was Williams and Beutner's real goal.

From City Hall to Study Hall: Making a Different Kind of Difference

For Williams, taking on the leadership of VTL was a non-obvious step after working for the Los Angeles mayor. When invited to VTL's initial launch by Beutner, she was still busy in politics—too busy to attend the event. Thereafter, when invited to lead the organization, her response was non-committal—"I said I'd consider it only after the administration ended." Williams at last agreed to get involved after a third invitation—when she attended a press conference staged in partnership with the LA Dodgers. She got involved not solely or even primarily because she had a personal connection to the problem (she did not need glasses as a child or have a child who needed glasses), but because she realized that it aligned with her long-term interest in serving the public good. Too, she believed in and admired Beutner—whose many career successes and extensive Los Angeles political and community involvement she found inspiring.[2]

Even after accepting the job offer, however, her initial commitment remained more professional than personal. It took time—and an opportunity to see others get the opportunity to see—to become more emotionally involved.

> When I was first asked to come over here, I thought, "Glasses on kids? Really? It doesn't pull my heartstrings. I don't know.

It sounds alright." I thought it was so matter of fact. Part of being a nonprofit, however, is pulling heartstrings. I kept thinking, "Who's going to care about that? Do I even care about it?" And, then, I went to a school and saw the kids putting their glasses on for the first time. And I started tearing up. You could tell they were seeing things—really *seeing things*—for the very first time. Even thinking about it now, I'm tearing up. Just seeing it. It changed my perspective entirely.

It became clear too that, in delivering glasses to children in need, VTL was providing benefits well beyond "just" happiness and improved eyesight. In a study run by UCLA, VTL kids showed improved confidence, increased classroom participation, improved focus, greater ease with homework, and improved academic performance overall. Teacher testimonials echoed these findings, suggesting that other behavioral improvements were also seen, resulting in easier classroom management.[3]

As Williams reflected on the future, she also reflected on the problem: An estimated 20 percent of all children have correctable vision and hundreds of thousands of whom go without glasses for logistical or practical reasons associated with accessing expert medical care. Initial success in Los Angeles and in a few other parts of California implied great potential elsewhere. But not all school districts looked like LAUSD, and not all of VTL's efforts had gone smoothly, as great as its early aggregate numbers were. It was clear that VTL was much like any other new organization in that its growth involved both challenges and successes and required careful operational management and an additional influx of capital.

A View of the Details

VTL recognized not solely that some children lacked independent access to qualified eye care but also that these children might be disinclined—for reasons of self-consciousness or

---

[2] Beutner, a former investment banker, has served as the chairman of several organizations, including CalArts and the Broad Stage (and has sat on a variety of other LA, California, and U.S. boards). In addition, he has held various political roles (e.g., an appointment as LA's deputy mayor for economic development). In 2014, Beutner became owner, CEO, and publisher of *The Los Angeles Times*.

[3] http://visiontolearn.org/index.php/our-impact/vtl-at-school

embarrassment—to wear corrective lenses. To address these issues, Beutner created a model that involved (1) bringing free medical expertise, via a mobile eye clinic (a specially outfitted bus), directly to the schools (a reverse of the traditional approach, in which the patients went to the doctors) and (2) providing the children a social way to experience eye exams and celebrate their sight together.

The system was straightforward but involved a great many details. On an almost daily basis, each of VTL's three mobile eye clinics was sent to a partner school—having scheduled and announced the visit date well in advance. Prior to VTL's arrival, school staff (typically, the school nurse) would conduct preliminary screenings to identify children with potential problems, distribute parental consent forms, and collect the signed forms. On the day of the visit, each child would see a qualified optometrist to be examined and fitted (if necessary) for glasses. The child would then work with VTL staff to select his or her own frames from a large set of cool, fashionable, and age-appropriate choices. Two weeks later, VTL would return to the school—delivering all ordered eyeglasses and ensuring that they fit correctly.

Staffing

When Williams began working at VTL, she was the only paid person on the full-time staff. Operations were supported with contractors (i.e., drivers, optometrists, opticians, and accounting and finance support) as well as two volunteers. The full-time staff subsequently grew from one to three, including a financial analyst who could provide the organization with undivided attention and real-time number crunching. In 2014, VTL continued to staff its clinics with part-time drivers and medical staff, each of whom was provided benefits in addition to an hourly wage. Administrative oversight and paperwork was handled through a personnel service.

VTL recruited many of its part-time optometrists straight out of graduate programs at schools such as the University of California at Irvine and the University of California at Davis. In hiring, VTL paid particular attention to the candidate's alignment with the organization's mission and took great care to provide a realistic job preview to those with an interest. As Williams observed,

> What we're doing is great, but the conditions aren't always that great. You're on a playground with lots of kids. It's hot. And when something happens—like a generator breaking down—it gets really, really hot. The kids can be a handful. The administrators of some of these schools sometimes forget we're supposed to be there that day, which can mean they're not organized when we show up. Lots of moving pieces. It's also very different than in an office. One patient after the next. People have to be committed to it, or they won't last very long.

Funding

VTL initially launched used philanthropic dollars. Considerable press attention and school adoption followed thereafter, leading to VTL's receiving, in March 2013, a $1.2 million First 5 LA grant. (First 5 LA administers a fund, derived from state tobacco taxes, to support initiatives that help children thrive and learn in their first five years of life.) Donations supplemented this grant, bringing VTL's annual 2013 operating budget to $1.6 million—13 percent of which was spent on overhead. The efficiency of VTL's cost structure was, and remains, closely tied to patient volume (i.e., how many children can get through the process in a given day).

Locations

In the first year of its operations, VTL focused all of its efforts on those in the LAUSD. In March 2013, the mayor of Sacramento announced, in his State of the City address, a plan to launch VTL programming there. VTL subsequently visited several schools in Oakland and San Jose. The official Sacramento launch of VTL followed a few months later, in November 2013, with a high-profile press event at Jefferson Elementary School, attended by governor of California Jerry

Brown and former U.S. secretary of commerce (and VTL board member) Mickey Kantor.

In September 2014, VTL began to expand more broadly, moving beyond LAUSD to Southern California schools in Compton, Inglewood, and Long Beach, plus Northern California Schools in San Jose, Oakland, the San Francisco Unified School District, Fremont, and other smaller school districts with high Title I populations. (Title I schools are identified by the federal government as meriting additional funding support to help close the gap between disadvantaged students and students elsewhere.)

Growing Pains: Seeing the Forest, Not the Trees

Shortly after the Sacramento announcement was made, Williams came on board in her full-time role. Immediately, she learned that the announcement had pre-dated completion of a formal agreement with the Sacramento City Unified School District (which had the largest school-aged population in the city). Though this timing did not appear to be problematic on paper, it was problematic in reality when it became clear that the school district was going to opt out of the program.

For Williams, the district's decision not to partner with VTL was instructive. Though she managed to identify and close deals with multiple area schools—and, ultimately, to oversee an examination program for more than 8,000 Sacramento children—she also realized that growth might be more difficult and slower than she had initially anticipated.

> You might think that every school district would open its doors to us. That's what I thought. But it turned out that wasn't the case. Not every school sees the value of what we offer and not every school nurse wants to support the extra work involved in bringing us on site. School nurses already have too much on their plates. And while we do hire people part-time, we also hire them with a long time horizon. You can't

hire staff for three months. They come on board with the idea that there's work and so you feel a responsibility to the employees to keep things going.

Sandra Waite, Healthy Start Coordinator in Sacramento's Elk Grove Unified School District, characterized the nurses' perspective succinctly, "It's a great program, but it is very tough to just get enough staff—particularly after there have been budget cuts—to get the kids screened and ready for when the van comes. Everyone wants it, but making it happen can be tough." Waite, a huge proponent of VTL, was one who had made it work. As she explained,

> So many of us have to jump through hoops to help the kids. Kids sometimes have to, for example, wait for months to get the care they need. It's frustrating for us as nurses. But, here, it's immediate and for everyone. It doesn't matter if they're documented, undocumented, insured, or uninsured. As long as they're at our school, they will be seen. If they fail the test, they will be provided glasses. And they're nice glasses. It is a lot of work for the staff, but the rewards are great. I think it's a fantastic program.

Despite the support of Waite and numerous others, VTL was unable to find a sufficiently large student population to make the costs work. Williams thus temporarily shut down the Sacramento VTL clinic and brought it back to LA. She acknowledged, in the process, that VTL's existing cost structure was such that more kids meant greater efficiency; there were structural limitations that implied a need for very careful forethought in selecting new locations.

> We learned a lot including the importance of being able to access a bigger pool of kids and a bigger pool of funders. Our decision to target the Bay Area this year came out of the Sacramento experience. Agreements signed up front. Memorandums of understanding signed with eight school districts. Signed, ready to go, nurses ready to do screenings.

There was a significant downside to the Sacramento closure: VTL had to let go of the staff retained to implement its Sacramento plans. There was an unanticipated upside as well: It allowed one mobile eye clinic to be taken offline and brought in for a long overdue refurbishment.

Building a Sustainable Non-profit

As Williams pondered the growth path and potential of VTL, she observed that there were several different challenges to address. She noted,

> We want to keep our mobile clinics running year round, but schools are closed in the summer. Also, different regions have different educational systems; you need a lot of kids to keep us busy. There are also issues of how to provide the funding essential for long-term growth. To date, we've relied quite substantially on philanthropic contributions. But that isn't sufficient—and isn't a strong basis for growth. We know what the issues are, but we need to figure out how to manage them.

Williams and her staff had begun to discuss what constituted the fundamental characteristics of regions most conducive to supporting VTL. They also had begun to identify what sorts of organizations they might help when the school year ended, with the hope that they could identify a strategy that wouldn't leave them scrambling every summer. Williams emphasized,

> Finding the right location and the right partners can be difficult. Consider a fair, for example. Maybe there are 1,000 people who could benefit from our service, but only 50 can be examined in a day. We have to be careful about putting ourselves out there and not being able to provide the service. We want to make a promise to a group of children and be true to that promise. We want to reach 100% of those to whom we offer help.

In addition to these practical operational challenges, there was always the funding question. Philanthropic dollars would be insufficient to support the desired growth. Grants would also be insufficient (in part because grantors preferred to support ventures with the ability to find an independently sustainable path over the long term).

For Williams (and Beutner), denizens of the political world, the best solution lay in enacting and passing new legislation. Williams said,

> Having our clinic in Sacramento, which allowed the Governor to come out and see it, piqued his interest in helping to solve the problem. They put in legislation that was passed, that will allow for a pilot project allowing for [Medicaid] reimbursement of mobile vision clinics. That got us to start working with managed care providers and to answer key questions—for example, what would that look like, how would it work. It also got us to start talking to people in other states.

What Next?

In mid-2014, the decision was made to expand to Delaware—in large part because the state's governor and one of its senators bought in to the notion that Medicaid reimbursement could be directed toward vision programs like the one offered by VTL. "They want us to come," said Williams. "They also can make the Medicaid piece work. That can fund 75% of our business, with the remaining 25% offered through philanthropy and foundations. That can assure us long-range sustainability." Even with Delaware's support, however, Williams acknowledged that a laundry list of questions remained unanswered. What was the likelihood that other states would follow? How should so distant a launch be staffed? What would be involved in securing similar legislative support in different states? The vision remained inspiring, but bringing clarity to that vision, particularly given so many questions, was going to require a closer look.

Williams stared at the wall of VTL's conference room as she reflected on the challenges ahead. Behind her was a spectacular view of the

Pacific Ocean that she paid no heed. The wall—festooned with hundreds of colorful thank-you notes from children now able to see—offered a more inspirational view. "This is fun," Williams said. "At City Hall, you're trying do things for people. At the end of the day, you're not sure you accomplished those things. Vision to Learn is something to go home and feel good about."

Discussion Questions

1. What problem is VTL trying to solve? How does VTL solve this problem?
2. What accounts for VTL's early and quite substantial success?
3. Identify the central lessons of the Sacramento experience, and clarify how those lessons should inform VTL's next moves.
4. How does VTL's status as a non-profit hinder or help its growth prospects?
5. What business problems is VTL facing at the end of the case? In what priority should those be resolved moving forward?

¢URRENCY13*

Enabling Bank Trusted
Peer-to-Peer Payments

Whitney Kalscheur

Bryan T. Walley

*The Currency13 feasibility study was completed to meet, in part, the requirements for a graduate level course. It is intended for discussion purposes only and should not be considered a "model" for how to do feasibility analysis. Rather, it offers the opportunity to discuss various elements of a new venture prior to launch.

Source: Reprinted by permission of the authors.

By the year 2016, peer-to-peer payments are expected to reach $1.6 trillion, and global mobile payments are expected to reach $600 billion by 2011. However, with this growth comes an increase in fraud.[1] The solution is Currency13, a proprietary payments platform that issues unique, onetime use codes through its closed system to enable safe and easy payments. This patent-pending technology can be white-labeled by small- and medium-sized financial institutions to offer peer-to-peer payments to end users while continuing to enjoy use of funds. It's a winning scenario for banks, bank customers, and consumers.

Market Pain and Currency13 Opportunity

Peer-to-peer payments are a burgeoning industry; however, it is imperfect and poses problems for both consumers and banks. Rapid expansion has shown that current service providers have focused on convenience as the key benefit for the consumer while other very real concerns still persist.[2] When making online payments, consumers still have the very real threat of identity theft. The Federal Trade Commission has stated that identity theft is the fastest growing crime, with 10 million people becoming victims each year. That equates to approximately 19 people per minute.[3] Additionally, consumers are charged almost 3 percent per transaction for exchanges under $3,000 by the most dominant players such as PayPal. This decreases the appeal of online shopping and electronic payments.[4]

Not only are peer-to-peer payments problematic for consumers, they are also cumbersome for financial institutions. Currently, when a transaction is in progress using some of the current popular systems, banks lose the opportunity to use member funds for lending and investment. The challenge is that many banks do not have a method for creating a network that allows consumers to make funds transfers with people who are not members of the consumer's institution.

Currency13 Solution

While these very real concerns may seem insurmountable, there is a solution: Currency13. Currency13 is a proprietary online software that issues unique onetime use codes per transaction. The process is simple. Consumers authenticate a bank account through their online banking interface. If a consumer's bank does not currently use Currency13, an account can be set up directly through the system's website. Once authenticated, a consumer can begin issuing codes to other consumers within the Currency13 system. The payee enters the amount of the transaction and is issued a code. The receiver of funds inserts the code received from the payee into their Currency13 account and enters the amount of the transaction. The money is then transferred.

Currency13 completely eliminates the security threat to consumers. By having to enter both a code and the dollar amount, the system guarantees the authenticity of the receiver. Additionally, in order to receive payment, one must be a member of the Currency13 system. Therefore, the company is able to track where money is sent. Lastly, should a consumer lose the unique code, the threat is mitigated because the code has an expiration date. Once a code expires and cannot be used, a new code can be issued for payment.

---

[1] "Alternative Payment Schemes: Leveraging ACH." The Santa Fe Group. April 7, 2009.

[2] Agrawal, Mohit. "Mobile Payments: Will the Consumers Adopt?" Telecom World. Accessed 18 November 2009, www .mohitagrawal .com/2009/04/mobile-payments-will-consumers-adopt.html.

[3] "Chilling Facts about Identity Threats." Identity Theft Information Center. Accessed 03 October 2009, www.scambusters .org/identitytheft.html.

[4] "Transaction Fees for Domestic Payments." PayPal.com. Accessed 3 November 2009, www.paypal.com/cgi-bin /webscr?cmd=_display-receiving-fees-outside.

Consumers also have the benefit of making payments without charge. This is because banks will pay one dollar per member using Currency13 through their online banking interface. In return, financial institutions will be provided access to their members' Currency13 account funds and also have a large network of banks that have been interconnected due to Currency13.

Once Currency13 is adopted for online banking transfers, the company will begin to market the product as a way to make payments to small businesses both online and through a consumer's cell phone. Additionally, because of the unique nature of Currency13, the product can be used for gift certificates, international payments, loan transfers, and payroll as the most secure form of currency.

Target Market and Currency13 Approach

In-depth research has shown that Currency13 is a desirable product for both consumers and financial institutions. The primary online consumers are middle- to upper-class women, but the industry is fragmented. Therefore, Currency13 interviewed 9 women with household incomes of $62,000 or greater and 6 men with the same household income. The age of all consumers interviewed ranged between 25 and 60.

Through these 15 one-hour interviews, Currency13 ascertained that consumers are interested in a reliable way to make payments and transfers to their peers while also being provided a sense of security and no transaction fees. On average, consumers are making purchases online at least one time per month, with the purchase amount being $200 or less. Typically, consumers pay using PayPal or a credit card.

Through these discussions, the company learned that consumers remain apprehensive about inputting personal information online, especially through websites that are not well known and established. This sentiment is also consistent with consumers who use ebay.com as they are not familiar with the consumer on the receiving end. PayPal does assist in alleviating the security concern; however, 3 consumers interviewed had their PayPal accounts breached and now are reluctant to use it. When asked if they would ever return to PayPal upon increased security, they were hesitant saying they were very nervous about dealing with the breach of security again.

Although security is a concern, it is not so prevalent that consumers are avoiding online shopping. Therefore, in order for Currency13 to be a reasonable alternative, adoption of the software must be streamlined and easy. Currency13 has solved that issue by looking at partnering with financial institutions and implementing the software on online banking interfaces. This entry strategy will allow banks to feel secure in that they will be rewarded their use of funds and members can easily "click" to opt into the system. Because consumers had concerns using unknown websites and entering personal information, the company is also looking at online banking interfaces as a way to get around the hurdle of building trust with Currency13. Consumers mentioned that they typically trust their online banking platforms as there are several security passwords that need to be utilized in order to reach their accounts. Therefore, the online platform is the perfect place to begin implementing Currency13.

There are more than 8,000 financial institutions in the United States, and while the largest banks are well known, the vast majority of these would be considered small- to medium-sized, community, or local banks and credit unions. These institutions do not have the resources or time to develop their technology in-house and, therefore, leverage third party systems to provide core accounting, online banking, and other critical technical services to their customers. Within this context, Currency13 has spoken with multiple sources, including Online Banking and Bill Pay Product Managers at City National Bank, Metavante (now part of FIS), Corillian (now part of Fiserv), and Digital Insight (an Intuit company). All of this primary research has indicated that financial institutions are actively looking to offer peer-to-peer, mobile payments that integrate with their online banking platform, and the service providers listed are all in the process of rolling out a flavor of this service. What is clear is the demand, but what is not is the model that will enable the financial institutions and the service providers to offer a compelling and easy to use service to the end customer.

Competition and Currency13 Advantages

In the financial institution industry, peer-to-peer and mobile payments are "hot" spaces right now. There are many competitors for the Currency13 technology. These competitors range from established players, such as Visa, MasterCard, PayPal, and Google Checkout, to more recent entrants, such as Obopay, CashEdge, and WebMoney, to new startups that are coming online almost daily, such as PayQuicker. The competitive landscape is fierce, but none of these companies is focused on serving the small- and medium-sized financial institutions, which is where Currency13 will play. Visa, MasterCard, Obopay, and CashEdge are currently targeting the largest financial institutions and/or mass consumers directly. Google Checkout and WebMoney are focused on online ecommerce sites. And PayQuicker, still in a beta phase, has yet to make its strategy known. So, although there are similar technologies, these companies are not positioned to serve the small- and medium-sized bank at this time.

Currency13's unfair advantage is twofold: (1) The payment system is patent pending and (2) The model is bank friendly. In terms of the technology, one of the differentiators is that Currency13 leverages the concept of coupon payments, which decouples the sensitive information, such as name and sender's account number, from the transactional information, such as the dollar amount and reason for payment. Another Currency13 technology advantage is that the sender can place an expiration date on the payment, so there is a risk mitigation element to the system that other platforms do not offer.

The Currency13 business model is also unique in the market, in that the company does not rely on Use of Funds to remain profitable nor does it charge a per-transaction fee for financial institution users. To date, the primary reason that banks have not partnered with PayPal to offer peer-to-peer payments, an obvious choice in this arena, is that PayPal and the bank would fight for which account holds the funds. PayPal, in essence, is a competing bank and uses the excess funds to earn float revenue. To incentivize small- and medium-sized financial institutions to adopt the Currency13 technology, there is no per transaction fee for FI users, which is not common across the industry. The strategy with this model is to drive user volume and allow the banks to determine the per-transaction pricing structure for the end customer.

Currency13 Business Model

Currency13 has a unique and simple monetization model. Unlike current peer-to-peer payment systems, consumers who utilize Currency13 will not be charged per transaction. Currency13 consumers will be able to utilize the benefits of the system for free if they are members of financial institutions that opt into the software. The banks will be charged one dollar per user per month. Upon installation of the system onto a bank's interface, consumers will be able to select Currency13 for transfers when they log into their banking account. The consumer information will be sent to Currency13 so that the company can accurately monitor consumer use. When a consumer is inactive for more than six months, Currency13 will no longer charge the bank for that particular member. Consumers who are not members of Currency13 banks will still be able to utilize the software directly through the company website. Those consumers will be charged a 1.0 percent transaction fee when receiving funds.

Product Development Plan

Currency13 has an aggressive development plan. The online software has already been developed and can be utilized directly by consumers via the Internet. Because consumer findings derived from in-depth interviews showed concern about entering personal information onto unknown websites, Currency13 has decided to move forward on the white-labeled version of the product for banks. At the same time, the company will work diligently to contract with financial institutions interested in the software. At that juncture, Currency13's white-labeled product will be uploaded onto each bank's online interface. The company believes that installation can occur as soon as six months. After working with the first few institutions, Currency13 will hire an additional marketing employee in month ten to procure more accounts. From month twelve on, the company will continue to acquire skilled sales and customer representatives to assist with the rapid movement of the product. Currency13's unique closed system of onetime use codes is patent pending both nationally and internationally, and the success of the company is predicated upon building relationships with well known financial institutions. These relationships will help create consumer awareness and security in the brand. Additionally, those relationships are also key for the product's rapid adoption.

Management Team

Ian James currently serves as Currency13's CEO and software programmer after co-founding the company in late 2007. He has over seven years of software and web programming experience in addition to a strong research capabilities. Christy Matson serves as the company's Chief Financial Officer and co-founder. She has over seven years of business experience, including serving as the accounting and financial expert during the startup phase of iOffer.com. Christy Matson and Ian James will be responsible for developing the company's white label software and managing the day to day operations of Currency13, including customer service. Whitney Kalscheur has over seven years of marketing, brand management, and entrepreneurial experience that will help to propel Currency13 forward. In addition to beginning her own sunglasses company, her expertise will enable the company to develop the essence of the company's brand image and strategically determine how to best approach potential partners. Bryan Walley has 10 years of technology and banking experience, with a track record of delivering technical and process improvement results for both external clients and internal stakeholders. The company has one foreseen gap within its management team that can be easily overcome: a valuable sales manager. This person will assist in developing a team of qualified sales representatives responsible for building relationships with local banks in order to build the Currency13 network.

Financial Projections and Forecast

The financial projections rely on the following assumptions:

Financial Institution Assumptions	
Monthly Fee/FI User	$ 1
Average Number of Users/FI	7,500
Integration Fees/FI	$40,000

The $1.00 per FI User is at or below the expected cost per user for an online banking or online bill pay user that many of the competitors listed above charge financial institutions. The 7,500 users per financial institution is an industry average number for online banking and bill pay usage for a bank with more than 12,000 total customers.

Consumer Transactions Assumptions	
Average Payment Amount	$20.00
Fee per Consumer Transaction	0
Net Consumer Transaction Growth Rate	14.0% (includes 1.0% churn)

And as a result, the following metrics are a result:

Cash Flow Positive	Month 15
Breakeven	Month 34
Total FI's on Month 36	46
Total FI Users on Month 36	$322,500

In order to achieve the forecasts above, Currency13 estimates the following capital raise will be required:

Startup Capital Needs (SUCN)	$ 532,172
Safety Factor (SF)	$ 120,000
Total Startup Capital (SU)	**$ 652,172**

Timeline and Major Milestones

In conjunction with the financial projections above, Currency13 has laid out the capital, human, and physical resources plan against the major milestones below.

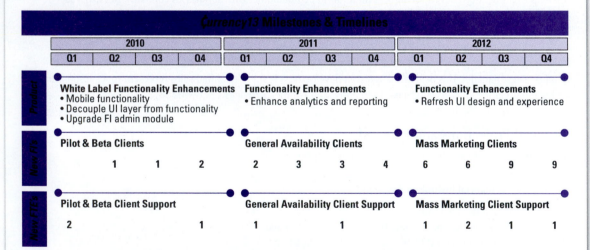

Harvest Strategy

To exit the peer-to-peer payment industry, acquisition would be the most viable option. This option becomes even more important once the company acquires consumers and financial institutions because they will rely on the product for transfers. This will enable the company's management team to maintain their reputations for future entrepreneurial business opportunities and allow the financial institution to continue to use the product for its peer-to-peer payments. An IPO is also possible; however, because Currency13 will rely heavily upon relationships with financial institutions, it would be challenging to receive approval from each institution within the network. If acquisition were not possible, the steps to shutting down the business would be to shift the funds from consumer's Currency13 accounts into their checking accounts prior to shutting down the system. For consumers who are not part of member banks, Currency13 would take measures to notify consumers in order to enable them time to empty their Currency13 accounts. The company would reduce its staff to the original two founders so that they could monitor consumer account elimination.

Exhibit 1 Key Management Team Bios

The Key Management for Currency13 includes:

- Ian James – Ian has 7 years of software and programming experience in addition to strong research capabilities. This experience includes working as a network consultant at Mark Chow Insurance and Investment planning and as a programmer at GizmoLabs. In addition, he has experience in directing and managing a software development team. He holds a B.S. in Physics from the University of California at Berkeley and is the co-founder and CEO of Currency13.

- Christy Matson – Christy has 7 years of management and financial experience, including several years as the lead accountant and financial expert at the startup iOffer.com. She has worked as an auditor at State Street Corporation in Boston, MA, holds a B.A. in Legal Studies from the University of California at Berkeley, and is the co-founder and CFO of Currency13.

- Bryan T. Walley – Bryan has 10 years of technology and banking experience with a track record of delivering technical and process improvement results for both external clients and internal stakeholders. He is currently enrolled in the USC Marshall MBA.PM program and has an undergraduate degree from the USC Marshall School of Business with an emphasis in Entrepreneurship and Information Systems.

- Whitney Kalscheur – Whitney has over 7 years experience within marketing and brand management. In addition, she began and was the co-owner of Oculus Eyewear until July 2008, upon which time the business was sold. She is currently enrolled full time at the USC Marshall School of Business with an emphasis in entrepreneurship and marketing and holds a B.A. from the University of California at Berkeley.

Exhibit 2 Advisory Board

The Advisory Board for Currency13 includes:

- Keith Matson – Keith has over 30 years of business experience. In addition to being a retired naval aviator, Keith has begun and sold several businesses within the realm of real estate and is an owner of the Padres. He received his bachelor's from the University of California at Berkeley in 1976. He became an angel investor in iOffer.com in 2001 and in OpenCuro.com in 2007. He also serves at the company's lead advisor.

Exhibit 3 Industry Analysis, Value Chain, and Business Process

Life cycle and industry demographics

NAICS 52232: Industry is established but growing as consumers become increasingly more reliant on ecommerce to meet their shopping needs. Ecommerce and online auctions are the means by which online payment software is typically utilized, and the industry is highly fragmented. The most well recognized payment system is PayPal. The focus within payment systems are convenience and safety. Consumer disposable income and changes in technology are the biggest areas of volatility. Household consumers and individuals make up 80 percent of the market and tend to be affluent, followed by online small businesses making up the second largest group at 8.9 percent. The online consumer is typically middle- to upper class educated women. Market estimates that alternative payments could reach $1.6 trillion by 2016, with global mobile payments volume could reach $600 billion by 2011.

Source: IBIS World.

Trends, gaps, and disruption possibilities

Banks/Financial institutions need to capture low-cost deposits and most competitor systems do now allow use of funds. Financial institutions are still dealing with the aftermath of credit crunch and recognize technology as a means to reduce costs and/or increase revenue. They are grappling with how to serve younger demographics and are looking at mobile technology as a means to do so via the nearly 3 billion mobile phones worldwide. More robust mobile content and increasing functionality of phones will help drive mobile payments adoption. There is also a gap within Internet banking that also has strong youth adoption as they are comfortable with ecommerce. There is an overall shift to electronic payments but also a merchant pricing revolt which will allow Currency13 to being adopted due to the company's reasonable pricing model. Prior to the 2008 recession, the money transferring industry grew by an average annual rate of 6.2 percent due to an increase in consumer spending and improvements in technology.

Barriers to entry

They are low but include:

- R&D costs – minimal
- Security concerns
- SAS 70 II audit
- Banks can be very slow to adopt
- Regulations
- Integration to online banking platforms
- Insurance
- Liability for consumer information
- Driving traffic to site
- Consulting fees
- No reputation in established industry

3 Industries and at least 6 customers where solution can be deployed

Industries:

- Banking/consumer-oriented financial institutions
- Telecommunications (mobile payments)
- Ecommerce

Customers:

- Online marketplaces (eBay/iOffer)
- Online gaming
- Blogs
- Credit unions
- Small online businesses
- Peer-to-peer payments/bank transfers

Five forces

Rivals: PayPal, Obopay, WebEx, WebMoney, Electronic Payment Systems, eBillme, Moneta, Secure Vault Payments, Noca, Mazooma, Revolution Money, Bill Me Later, Acculynk, Google Checkout, Amazon Payments, Decoupled Payments

Suppliers: Developers, hardware, infrastructure

Buyers: Financial institutions via established partnerships, financial institutions, new ecommerce sites, new small businesses, blogs, online gaming systems, consumers

Subs: Cash, credit cards, ACH, bill pay, debit

Comps: Online banking and mobile apps, ecommerce

Lead informants

- Alex Falk and Steven Wildemuth, City National Bank Product Managers
- Eric Jamison, FIS P2P Initiative Leader
- Rob Killoran, Fiserv Sales Manager
- Janice Cheung, Intuit Senior Product Manager
- Bank Technology News
- FierceFinanceIT and FierceMobile
- CNET
- Gartner, Tower, Javelin, etc.
- NACHA
- OpenCuro Founders – Christy and Ian
- Hoover's
- IBISWorld
- GonzoBanker

Primary and Secondary Research Summary

The Financial Institution Industry Research conducted included speaking with Alex F. and Steven W., the Online Banking and Bill Pay Product Managers at City National Bank, Eric J., the P2P Initiative Leader at Metavante (now part of FIS), Rob K., Sales Manager at Corillian (now part of Fiserv), and Janice C., Senior Product Manager at Digital Insight (an Intuit company). Some of the highlights from these conversations include:

- Alex F. noted repeatedly that he is already looking for a solution of this type, that there is strong demand for this type of product in the market, and that City National Bank would be a candidate for the Currency13 offering. Further, he helped with ensuring that the business model is bank friendly.

- Steven W. brought a commercial, not consumer, perspective to the interview. And from that vantage, he felt that there is a convergence of commercial functionality, like being able to pay anyone from anywhere, that is heading down market toward the consumer.

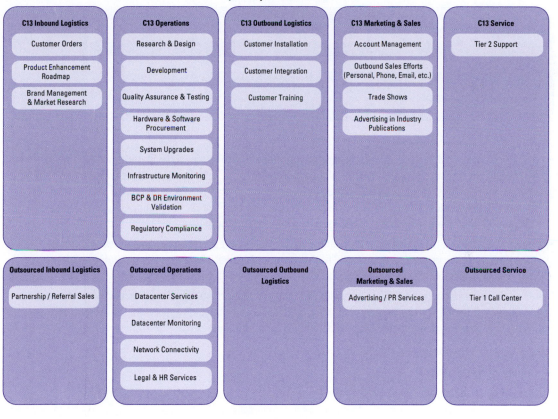

Currency13 Value Chain

C13 Inbound Logistics	C13 Operations	C13 Outbound Logistics	C13 Marketing & Sales	C13 Service
Customer Orders	Research & Design	Customer Installation	Account Management	Tier 2 Support
Product Enhancement Roadmap	Development	Customer Integration	Outbound Sales Efforts (Personal, Phone, Email, etc.)	
Brand Management & Market Research	Quality Assurance & Testing	Customer Training	Trade Shows	
	Hardware & Software Procurement		Advertising in Industry Publications	
	System Upgrades			
	Infrastructure Monitoring			
	BCP & DR Environment Validation			
	Regulatory Compliance			

Outsourced Inbound Logistics	Outsourced Operations	Outsourced Outbound Logistics	Outsourced Marketing & Sales	Outsourced Service
Partnership / Referral Sales	Datacenter Services		Advertising / PR Services	Tier 1 Call Center
	Datacenter Monitoring			
	Network Connectivity			
	Legal & HR Services			

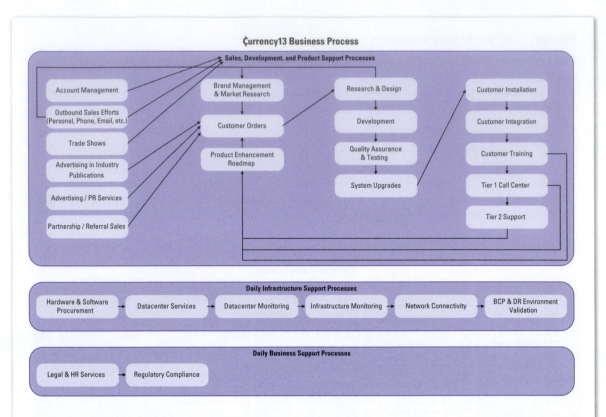

- Eric J. was interested in the coupon aspect of the Currency13 technology, as he stated that it is a unique offering in the market. He noted that the biggest hurdles this type of technology faces is brand recognition and number of users on the system (i.e., the positive network effect). He also commented that the typical rollout strategy for Metavante/FIS on this type of technology involved 3X the number of clients that Currency13 was forecasting, so that was a safe and sound projection.

- Janice C. offered many industry resources and reports, noting that peer-to-peer payments, both for the consumer and the commercial space, was "hot" these days. She was also extremely helpful in validating the cost and support structure in our financial model.

Based on the information gathered in the company's industry analysis posted above, Currency13 performed 15 one-hour interviews with consumers who make electronic payments and/or electronic banking. The information represents an aggregate of the most important information derived from these findings.

Demographics of Interviews

- *Gender*: 9 Female, 6 Male
- *Age*: 25 to 60 for Female, 33 to 58 for Male
- *HH Income*: $62,000+

The results of these interviews include:

- *Online Shopping Habits*: Shop online at least 1 time every two months, spending on average $50 but typically no more than $200. They pay using PayPal or credit card.

- *Mobile Highlights*: None had made peer-to-peer payments through their mobile phone but were interested. Seems cumbersome to log into current peer-to-peer payment accounts. 11 interviewees had phones that could be classified as smartphones.

- *Banking Habits*: 8 out of 15 consumers consistently banked online. They had mentioned that they could transfer money within their own accounts. None had made transfers to other consumers using their online banking platform. They were intrigued by the concept of a way to transfer money between bank accounts but were skeptical of the security of the operations. Consumers felt comfortable logging into the bank's platform because there were typically several security measures a consumer had to go through prior to reaching his personal account information.

- *Fraud*: 3 consumers had their PayPal accounts breached. Only one had lost money because of the breach. The other two were able to update their profiles after being notified by PayPal of the breach. They are all reluctant to use it and prefer to use credit cards. When asked why they felt comfortable using credit cards, they mentioned they did not have many other options and felt comfortable that the credit card company would rectify any wrongdoing. One consumer had her car broken into and her credit cards were stolen. They were charged several thousand dollars. She was able to get the funds returned; however, the process was a hassle.

- *Overall Sentiments about Pricing*: Consumers would prefer to not be charged a fee to make peer-to-peer payments and felt that 3 percent was exorbitant. Several were not aware that PayPal charged a Purchase Payment upon receiving money in a transaction. "PayPal is becoming a credit card company."

- *Overall Sentiments about Shopping on Unfamiliar Websites*: Consumers will not shop on unfamiliar websites that require personal information. They would especially be hard pressed to enter banking information onto an unfamiliar site.

- *Overall Sentiments about Shopping Online*: Consumers love it. It is convenient and a big time savings. While they are concerned about security, it is not a large enough deterrent to stop consumers from entering personal information/credit card information to make purchases. They mentioned that they would definitely be willing try a new more secure product as long as using the product was seamless and streamlined.

Exhibit 4 Pro Forma Financial Statements

Below are the summary section and the assumptions section for the Currency13 financial model.

Total Startup Capital	**652,172**
Capital Expenditures (CE)	**450,000**
R&D Expenses	450,000
Soft Costs (SC)	**465,495**
Net 30 AR Balance	465,495
Startup Costs (SU)	**3,925,410**
Salaries	880,000
Commissions	522,460
FTE Workstations	25,000
Office Space w/Utilities	186,250
Office Equipment	27,000
Advertising	40,500
Travel & Entertainment	81,000
Accounting	36,000
Legal	54,000
Insurance	36,000
FTE Load	308,000
Server Lease	794,700
Transportation	805,500
Installation Costs	41,000
Cell Phones	44,000
Internet	44,000
Working Capital (WC)	**4,308,733**
Working Capital Needs	4,308,733
Startup Capital Needs (SUCN)	**532,172**
Startup Capital Needs	532,172
Safety Factor (SF)	**120,000**
Safety Factor	120,000

Note: SC is Month 36 A/R, SF is 3 x Installation Fees.

Assumptions

Monthly Fee/FI/User	$1.00
Average OLB & BP Users/FI	7,500
Server Lease/FI	$1,500.00
FI Integration Fee	$40,000.00
Salary/Month/FTE	$5,000.00
FTE Load	35.0%
Sales Commission	10.0%
Office sq. ft./FTE	500
Office Cost/sq. ft.	$2.50
Income Tax Rate	45.0%
Average Payment Amount	$20.00
Fee per Consumer Transaction	1.0%
Consumer Transaction Growth	15.0%
User Churn Rate	1.0%

Model Results

Cash Flow Positive Month	15
Breakeven Month	34
FI's Month 12	4
FI's Month 24	16
FI's Month 36	46
FI Users Month 12	22,500
FI Users Month 24	105,000
FI Users Month 36	322,500
Consumer Transactions Month 12	2,132
Consumer Transactions Month 24	10,270
Consumer Transactions Month 36	49,480

Assumptions

Monthly Fee per FI User	$1.00		Average Payment Amount		$20.00
OLB & BP Users per FI	7,500		Fee per Consumer Transaction		1.00%
Server Lease / FI	$1,500		Consumer Transaction Growth		15.00%
FI Integration Fee	$40,000		User Churn Rate		1.00%

Milestones	Mo.1	2	3	4	5	6	7	8
New FI's on System	0	0	0	0	0	1	0	1
Cumulative FI's	0	0	0	0	0	1	1	2
Consumer Transactions	500	575	656	747	852	971	1,107	1,262
Salaried FTE	2	2	2	2	2	2	2	2
Lease Office Space	0	0	0	0	0	0	0	0

Cash Inflows	Mo.1	2	3	4	5	6	7	8
FI Revenue								
FI Users (Net 30)	0	0	0	0	0	0	7,500	7,500
FI User Churn	0	0	0	0	0	0	0	0
Total FI Users (Net 30)	0	0	0	0	0	0	7,500	7,500
Integration Fees (Net 30)	0	0	0	0	0	40,000	0	40,000
Total FI Revenue	0	0	0	0	0	40,000	7,500	47,500
Consumer Revenue								
Transactions (Net 30)	0	100	115	131	149	170	194	221
Total Consumer Revenue	0	100	115	131	149	170	194	221
Total Cash Inflows	0	100	115	131	149	40,170	7,694	47,721

Cash Outflows	Mo.1	2	3	4	5	6	7	8
Fixed Costs								
Salaries	10,000	10,000	10,000	10,000	10,000	10,000	10,000	10,000
Commissions	0	0	0	0	0	4,000	750	4,750
FTE Workstations	5,000	0	0	0	0	0	0	0
R&D Costs	250,000	0	0	0	0	0	0	0
Office Space w/ Utilities	0	0	0	0	0	0	0	0
Office Equipment	500	500	500	500	500	500	500	500
Advertising	750	750	750	750	750	750	750	750
Travel & Entertainment	1,000	1,000	1,000	1,000	1,000	1,000	2,000	2,000
Accounting	1,000	1,000	1,000	1,000	1,000	1,000	1,000	1,000
Legal	1,500	1,500	1,500	1,500	1,500	1,500	1,500	1,500
Insurance	1,000	1,000	1,000	1,000	1,000	1,000	1,000	1,000
FTE Load	3,500	3,500	3,500	3,500	3,500	3,500	3,500	3,500
Total Fixed Costs	274,250	19,250	19,250	19,250	19,250	23,250	21,000	25,000
Variable Costs								
Server Lease	1,200	1,200	1,200	1,200	1,200	2,700	2,700	4,200
Transportation	1,500	1,500	1,500	1,500	1,500	3,000	3,000	4,500
Installation Costs	500	500	500	500	500	1,000	500	1,000
Cell Phones	500	500	500	500	500	500	500	500
Internet	500	500	500	500	500	500	500	500
Total Variable Costs	4,200	4,200	4,200	4,200	4,200	7,700	7,200	10,700
Total Cash Outflows	278,450	23,450	23,450	23,450	23,450	30,950	28,200	35,700

Total Cash In/Outflows	Mo.1	2	3	4	5	6	7	8
Net Cash In/Outflow	−278,450	−23,350	−23,335	−23,319	−23,301	−220	−20,506	12,021
Tax Liability	0	0	0	0	0	4,149	0	5,410
Cumulative Cash Flow	−278,450	−301,800	−325,135	−348,454	−371,754	−366,683	−387,189	−380,577

Metrics	Mo.1	2	3	4	5	6	7	8
Revenue / User	0	0	0	0	0	0	6.3	12.7
Cost / User	0	0	0	0	0	0	57.5	62.3
Margin / User	0.0%	0.0%	0.0%	0.0%	0.0%	0.0%	289.0%	−79.7%

Assumptions

Salary / FTE	$5,000	Office sq.ft. / FTE	500
FTE Load	35.00%	Office Cost / sq.ft.	$2.50
Sales Commission	10.00%	Income Tax Rate	45.00%

9	10	11	12	13	14	15	16	17	18	19
0	1	0	1	1	0	1	1	1	1	1
2	3	3	4	5	5	6	7	8	9	10
1,439	1,640	1,870	2,132	2,430	2,770	3,158	3,600	4,104	4,679	5,334
2	3	3	3	4	4	4	4	4	4	5
0	0	0	0	1	1	1	1	1	1	1

9	10	11	12	13	14	15	16	17	18	19
15,000	15,000	22,500	22,500	30,000	37,500	37,500	45,000	52,500	60,000	67,500
−75	−75	−150	−150	−225	−225	−300	−375	−375	−450	−525
14,925	14,925	22,350	22,350	29,775	37,275	37,200	44,625	52,125	59,550	66,975
0	40,000	0	40,000	40,000	0	40,000	40,000	40,000	40,000	40,000
14,925	54,925	22,350	62,350	69,775	37,275	77,200	84,625	92,125	99,550	106,975
252	288	328	374	426	486	554	632	720	821	936
252	288	328	374	426	486	554	632	720	821	936
15,177	55,213	22,678	62,724	70,201	37,761	77,754	85,257	92,845	100,371	107,911

9	10	11	12	13	14	15	16	17	18	19
10,000	15,000	15,000	15,000	20,000	20,000	20,000	20,000	20,000	20,000	25,000
1,493	5,493	2,235	6,235	6,978	3,728	7,720	8,463	9,213	9,955	10,698
0	2,500	0	0	2,500	0	0	0	0	0	2,500
0	0	0	0	100,000	0	0	0	0	0	0
0	0	0	0	5,000	5,000	5,000	5,000	5,000	5,000	6,250
500	500	500	500	750	750	750	750	750	750	750
750	750	750	750	1,000	1,000	1,000	1,000	1,000	1,000	1,250
2,000	2,000	2,000	2,000	2,000	2,000	2,000	2,000	2,000	2,000	2,500
1,000	1,000	1,000	1,000	1,000	1,000	1,000	1,000	1,000	1,000	1,000
1,500	1,500	1,500	1,500	1,500	1,500	1,500	1,500	1,500	1,500	1,500
1,000	1,000	1,000	1,000	1,000	1,000	1,000	1,000	1,000	1,000	1,000
3,500	5,250	5,250	5,250	7,000	7,000	7,000	7,000	7,000	7,000	8,750
21,743	34,993	29,235	33,235	148,728	42,978	46,970	47,713	48,463	49,205	61,198
4,200	5,700	5,700	7,200	8,700	8,700	10,200	11,700	13,200	14,700	16,200
4,500	6,000	6,000	7,500	9,000	9,000	10,500	12,000	13,500	15,000	16,500
500	1,000	500	1,000	1,000	500	1,000	1,000	1,000	1,000	1,000
500	750	750	750	1,000	1,000	1,000	1,000	1,000	1,000	1,250
500	750	750	750	1,000	1,000	1,000	1,000	1,000	1,000	1,250
10,200	14,200	13,700	17,200	20,700	20,200	23,700	26,700	29,700	32,700	36,200
31,943	49,193	42,935	50,435	169,428	63,178	70,670	74,413	78,163	81,905	97,398

9	10	11	12	13	14	15	16	17	18	19
−16,765	6,020	−20,257	12,289	−99,226	−25,416	7,084	10,844	14,683	18,466	10,513
0	2,709	0	5,530	0	0	3,188	4,880	6,607	8,310	4,731
−397,342	−394,031	−414,288	−407,529	−506,755	−532,172	−528,276	−522,311	−514,236	−504,080	−498,297

9	10	11	12	13	14	15	16	17	18	19
7.3	11	8.3	11.1	10.6	9.5	11.6	11.5	11.6	11.8	12.1
33.3	36.5	26.3	28.5	27	23.3	25.2	22.7	20.9	19.7	18.9
−78.0%	−69.9%	−68.3%	−61.1%	−60.6%	−59.2%	−54.1%	−49.1%	−44.4%	−39.8%	−36.0%

Milestones	20	21	22	23	24	25	26	27
New FI's on System	1	1	1	1	2	2	2	2
Cumulative FI's	11	12	13	14	16	18	20	22
Consumer Transactions	6,081	6,932	7,903	9,009	10,270	11,708	13,347	15,216
Salaried FTE	5	5	5	5	5	5	6	6
Lease Office Space	1	1	1	1	1	1	1	1
Cash Inflows	**20**	**21**	**22**	**23**	**24**	**25**	**26**	**27**
FI Revenue								
FI Users (Net 30)	75,000	82,500	90,000	97,500	105,000	120,000	135,000	150,000
FI User Churn	2600	2675	2750	2825	2900	2975	21,050	21,200
Total FI Users (Net 30)	74,400	81,825	89,250	96,675	104,100	119,025	133,950	148,800
Integration Fees (Net 30)	40,000	40,000	40,000	40,000	80,000	80,000	80,000	80,000
Total FI Revenue	114,400	121,825	129,250	136,675	184,100	199,025	213,950	228,800
Consumer Revenue								
Transactions (Net 30)	1,067	1,216	1,386	1,581	1,802	2,054	2,342	2,669
Total Consumer Revenue	1,067	1,216	1,386	1,581	1,802	2,054	2,342	2,669
Total Cash Inflows	115,467	123,041	130,636	138,256	185,902	201,079	216,292	231,469
Cash Outflows	**20**	**21**	**22**	**23**	**24**	**25**	**26**	**27**
Fixed Costs								
Salaries	25,000	25,000	25,000	25,000	25,000	25,000	30,000	30,000
Commissions	11,440	12,183	12,925	13,668	18,410	19,903	21,395	22,880
FTE Workstations	0	0	0	0	0	0	2,500	0
R&D Costs	0	0	0	0	0	100,000	0	0
Office Space w/ Utilities	6,250	6,250	6,250	6,250	6,250	6,250	7,500	7,500
Office Equipment	750	750	750	750	750	1,000	1,000	1,000
Advertising	1,250	1,250	1,250	1,250	1,250	1,500	1,500	1,500
Travel & Entertainment	2,500	2,500	2,500	2,500	2,500	3,000	3,000	3,000
Accounting	1,000	1,000	1,000	1,000	1,000	1,000	1,000	1,000
Legal	1,500	1,500	1,500	1,500	1,500	1,500	1,500	1,500
Insurance	1,000	1,000	1,000	1,000	1,000	1,000	1,000	1,000
FTE Load	8,750	8,750	8,750	8,750	8,750	8,750	10,500	10,500
Total Fixed Costs	59,440	60,183	60,925	61,668	66,410	168,903	80,895	79,880
Variable Costs								
Server Lease	17,700	19,200	20,700	22,200	25,200	28,200	31,200	34,200
Transportation	18,000	19,500	21,000	22,500	25,500	28,500	31,500	34,500
Installation Costs	1,000	1,000	1,000	1,000	1,500	1,500	1,500	1,500
Cell Phones	1,250	1,250	1,250	1,250	1,250	1,250	1,500	1,500
Internet	1,250	1,250	1,250	1,250	1,250	1,250	1,500	1,500
Total Variable Costs	39,200	42,200	45,200	48,200	54,700	60,700	67,200	73,200
Total Cash Outflows	98,640	102,383	106,125	109,868	121,110	229,603	148,095	153,080
Total Cash In/Outflows	**20**	**21**	**22**	**23**	**24**	**25**	**26**	**27**
Net Cash In/Outflow	16,827	20,659	24,511	28,388	64,792	−28,523	68,197	78,389
Tax Liability	7,572	9,296	11,030	12,775	29,156	0	30,688	35,275
Cumulative Cash Flow	−489,043	−477,680	−464,199	−448,586	−412,950	−441,474	−403,966	−360,851
Metrics	**20**	**21**	**22**	**23**	**24**	**25**	**26**	**27**
Revenue/User	12.4	12.8	13.1	13.5	14.3	14.2	14.2	14.3
Cost/User	18.3	17.9	17.6	17.4	17.3	17	16.2	15.6
Margin/User	−32.3%	−28.7%	−25.3%	−22.1%	−17.2%	−16.7%	−12.6%	−8.6%

28	29	30	31	32	33	34	35	36	TTD
2	2	2	3	3	3	3	3	3	
24	26	28	31	34	37	40	43	46	
17,346	19,774	22,543	25,699	29,296	33,398	38,074	43,404	49,480	
7	7	8	8	9	9	10	10	10	
1	1	1	1	1	1	1	1	1	

28	29	30	31	32	33	34	35	36	TTD
165,000	180,000	195,000	210,000	232,500	255,000	277,500	300,000	322,500	
−1,350	−1,500	−1,650	−1,800	−1,950	−2,100	−2,325	−2,550	−2,775	
163,650	178,500	193,350	208,200	230,550	252,900	275,175	297,450	319,725	
80,000	80,000	80,000	120,000	120,000	120,000	120,000	120,000	120,000	
243,650	258,500	273,350	328,200	350,550	372,900	395,175	417,450	439,725	5,224,600
3,043	3,469	3,955	4,509	5,140	5,859	6,680	7,615	8,681	
3,043	3,469	3,955	4,509	5,140	5,859	6,680	7,615	8,681	69,965
246,693	261,969	277,305	332,709	355,690	378,759	401,855	425,065	448,406	5,294,565

28	29	30	31	32	33	34	35	36	TTD
35,000	35,000	40,000	40,000	45,000	45,000	50,000	50,000	50,000	880,000
24,365	25,850	27,335	32,820	35,055	37,290	39,518	41,745	43,973	522,460
2,500	0	2,500	0	2,500	0	2,500	0	0	25,000
0	0	0	0	0	0	0	0	0	450,000
8,750	8,750	10,000	10,000	11,250	11,250	12,500	12,500	12,500	186,250
1,000	1,000	1,000	1,000	1,000	1,000	1,000	1,000	1,000	27,000
1,500	1,500	1,500	1,500	1,500	1,500	1,500	1,500	1,500	40,500
3,000	3,000	3,000	3,000	3,000	3,000	3,000	3,000	3,000	81,000
1,000	1,000	1,000	1,000	1,000	1,000	1,000	1,000	1,000	36,000
1,500	1,500	1,500	1,500	1,500	1,500	1,500	1,500	1,500	54,000
1,000	1,000	1,000	1,000	1,000	1,000	1,000	1,000	1,000	36,000
12,250	12,250	14,000	14,000	15,750	15,750	17,500	17,500	17,500	308,000
91,865	90,850	102,835	105,820	118,555	118,290	131,018	130,745	132,973	2,646,210
37,200	40,200	43,200	47,700	52,200	56,700	61,200	65,700	70,200	794,700
37,500	40,500	43,500	48,000	52,500	57,000	61,500	66,000	70,500	805,500
1,500	1,500	1,500	2,000	2,000	2,000	2,000	2,000	2,000	41,000
1,750	1,750	2,000	2,000	2,250	2,250	2,500	2,500	2,500	44,000
1,750	1,750	2,000	2,000	2,250	2,250	2,500	2,500	2,500	44,000
79,700	85,700	92,200	101,700	111,200	120,200	129,700	138,700	147,700	1,729,200
171,565	176,550	195,035	207,520	229,755	238,490	260,718	269,445	280,673	4,375,410

28	29	30	31	32	33	34	35	36	TTD
75,128	85,419	82,270	125,189	125,935	140,269	141,137	155,620	167,733	919,155
33,808	38,439	37,021	56,335	56,671	63,121	63,512	70,029	75,480	675,721
−319,531	−272,550	−227,302	−158,448	−89,184	−12,036	65,589	151,180	243,433	243,433

28	29	30	31	32	33	34	35	36	TTD
14.5	14.7	15	15.5	15.5	15.6	15.7	15.9	16.2	
15.3	15	14.8	14.7	14.3	14	13.8	13.6	13.6	
−5.10%	−1.70%	1.10%	4.90%	8.20%	11.40%	14.20%	16.90%	19.40%	

Exhibit 5 Narrative Assumptions for Financial Statements

The table below lists the line item, value, and reasoning behind the assumptions contained within the financial statements rendered above.

Revenue Figures

FI Adoption Rate	See Model	The forecast for the FI Adoption Rate is based on conversations with Eric J. as well as experiences of multiple product rollouts at City National Bank.
Monthly Fee/FI User	$1.00	Market rates for online banking and bill pay users in a similar model are above or near this value.
Average OLB & Bill Pay Users	$7,500.00	OLB and BP penetration rates across in the industry averages 60+%. Target FI's have more than 12,000 customers, which lead to an average user base of 7,500.
FI Integration Fee	$40,000	This is a professional services arrangement for 320 hours at $125 / hour. This time would be allocated across 2–3 individuals.
Server Lease/FI	$1,500	This is a dedicated hardware fee per financial institution.
Monthly Salary/FTE	$5,000	This rate yields a $60,000 salary to allow employees to live but also keep them very motivated.
FTE Load	35%	This is to account for taxes and other costs associated with full time employees.
Sales Commission	10%	This is to incent the sales representatives.
Office sq. ft./ FTE	$500	Nate C., a Commercial Real Estate professional, stated that this would be a conservative estimate.
Office Cost/sq. ft.	$2.50	Nate C., a Commercial Real Estate professional, stated that this would be a conservative estimate and include utilities.
Income Tax Rate	45%	This includes both CA State (9%) and Federal (35%) corporate tax rates.
Average Payment Amount	$20.00	This average payment amount was based on several different factors: Current usage patterns in the OpenCuro.com platform, a sampling of check payments from City National Bank, and the assumption that if users did not have cash on hand, this would be the smallest amount owed to a peer where the peer would demand payment.
Fee per Customer Transaction	1.00%	This is below or near industry average, as credit cards and online payment systems can charge up to 2.5% of the transaction amount in fees.
Consumer Transaction Growth	15%	This figure is taken from the trends being shown in the OpenCuro.com system to date.
User Churn Rate	1.00%	This is to allow a percentage of users to opt out of the system after a 90 day period.

Cost Figures Not Already Discussed Above

FTE Workstations	$ 2,500	This is a new computer expense during the month of hire.
R&D Costs	$450,000	This is a development fee to enhance the product. In Month 1, there is a $250,000 spend. And there are $100,000 spends in Year 2 and Year 3.
Office Equipment	$ 500	This is an allocation for paper, supplies, and miscellaneous work equipment.
Advertising	$ 750	This is a monthly allocation to build brand awareness, which increases in Year 2 and Year 3.
Travel & Entertainment	$ 1,000	This is a monthly allocation to allow Currency13 employees to travel and meet with prospects and customers. It increases in Year 2 and Year 3.
Accounting	$ 1,000	This is a monthly allocation based upon a price quote from Schubert & Company.
Legal	$ 1,500	This is a monthly allocation based upon a price quote from Good, Wildman, Hegness & Walley.
Insurance	$ 1,000	This is a monthly allocation based upon a price quote from Aon Insurance.
Transportation	$ 1,500	This a monthly allocation that increases in line with the total number of financial institutions on the system.
Installation Costs	$ 500	This is the expense that would be incurred to procure a new domain name and other technical requirements when a new financial institution comes onto the system.
Cell Phones	$ 500	This is an allocation of $250 per FTE for their work related mobile phone.
Internet	$ 500	This is an allocation of $250 per FTE for internet access at home.

Exhibit 6 Success and Risk Factors

Success Factors:

- Reputation – It is important to build a reputation within the banking community and with consumers. Currency13 is a company that consumers can trust and that values identity protection. In addition, the company stands behind all agreements.

- Marketing/Sales – Because Currency13 is a closed system and is monetized per consumer, rapid adoption is key. Therefore, having the right marketing and sales team is imperative to drive sales.

- Bank Partnerships – Without these relationships, the software will not get over the hurdle of consumer trust with the product. Additionally, it is imperative for adoption.

- Pricing – Consumers dislike current pricing models for peer-to-peer payment transactions. Currency13 has the simple model of charging banks one dollar per user. This pricing model will be a success factor in increasing adoption of the product.

Risk Factors:

- Security Breaches – While the company is currently confident in the Currency13 business model, security breaches are an area of concern. The company has consumer information stored offsite at a high security location and takes many steps to monitor information, therefore this risk factor is low.

- Competition – Currency13's niche is within the online banking realm; however, key competitors have the resources to build relationships quickly and may attack that niche fast. Because the product is superior to competitor products, competition may slow down adoption but not stop it completely.

- Technology – Changes in technology may be the largest threat to Currency13. In order to mitigate this risk, the company has patented its system. Once a network of banks is developed, the likelihood that a new technology will take over is low as the company plans to contract with institutions for an extended period of time.

- Cyclicality in Consumer Disposable Income – Currency13 has mitigated this risk because the banks will pay the company per consumer per month. The consumer lapses after six months and by that time, new consumers will likely utilize the product.

NOTES

Chapter 1

1. Schumpeter, J.A. (1934). *The Theory of Economic Development*. Cambridge: Harvard University Press.
2. Schendel, D. (1990). "Introduction to the Special Issue on Corporate Entrepreneurship." *Strategic Management Journal*, Summer Special Issue 11: 1–3.
3. Gartner, W.B. (1985). "A Conceptual Framework for Describing the Phenomenon of New Venture Creation." *Academy of Management Review, 10(4)*: 702.
4. Churchill, N.C., and D.F. Muzyka. (1994). "Defining and Conceptualizing Entrepreneurship: A Process Approach." In Hills G.E. (ed.), *Marketing and Entrepreneurship*. Westport, CT: Quorum Books, 11–23; Shane, S.A., and S. Venkataraman. (2000). "The Promise of Entrepreneurship as a Field of Research." *Academy of Management Review*, 25: 217–226; and S. Venkataraman. (1997). "The Distinctive Domain of Entrepreneurship Research." In Katz J., and J. Brockhaus (eds.), *Advances in Entrepreneurship, Firm Emergence and Growth*. Greenwich, CT: JAI Press, 119–138.
5. Stevenson, H.H., and J.C. Jarillo. (1990). "A Paradigm of Entrepreneurship: Entrepreneurial Management." *Strategic Management Journal*, Summer Special Issue 11: 17–27.
6. Lumpkin, G.T., and G.G. Dess (January 1996). "Clarifying the Entrepreneurial Orientation Construct and Linking It to Performance." *Academy of Management Review*, 21(1): 135.
7. Schumpeter, J. (1934). *The Theory of Economic Development*. Cambridge: Harvard University Press; Solow, R.M. (1970). *Growth Theory: An Exposition*. Oxford: Oxford University Press; and Grossman, G.M., and E. Helpman. (Winter 1994). "Endogenous Innovation in the Theory of Growth." *Journal of Economic Perspectives*, 8(1): 23–44.
8. Romer, P. (1986). "Increasing Returns and Long-Run Growth." *Journal of Political Economy*, 94: 1002–1037.
9. Flurry Analytics. (January, 2014). PricewaterhouseCoopers. http://www.pwc.com/gx/en/technology/mobile-innovation/download-customised-report.jhtml
10. Jovanovic, B., and G. MacDonald. (1994). "The Life-Cycle of a Competitive Industry." *Journal of Political Economy*, 102(2): 322–347.
11. U.S. Department of Commerce, Bureau of the Census and International Trade Admin., Advocacy-funded research by Kathryn Kobe. (2007). www.sba.gov/advo/research/rs299tot.pdf; and Advocacy Small Business Statistics and Research. http://web.sba.gov/faqs/faqIndexAll.cfm?areaid=24, accessed September 26, 2010.
12. Acs, Z., William Parsons, and Spencer Tracy. (June 2008). "High-Impact Firms: Gazelles Revisited," U.S. Small Business Administration, Office of Advocacy, http://archive.sba.gov/advo/research/rs328tot.pdf. The term gazelles was used to describe rapidly growing firms in Birch,D.L., and James Medoff. (1994). "Gazelles." In Solmon, L.C., and Alec R. Levenson(eds.), *Labor Markets, Employment Policy and Job Creation*. Boulder, CO: Westview Press, 159–168.
13. Acs, Z., William Parsons, and Spencer Tracy.(June 2008). "High-Impact Firms: Gazelles Revisited," U.S. Small Business Administration, Office of Advocacy, pp. 1, 16, 17, http://archive.sba.gov/advo/research/rs328tot.pdf
14. Source: U.S. Small Business Administration. "Statistics of U.S. Businesses, U.S. Dynamic Data, U.S. Data: Employer Firm Births and Deaths by Employment Size of Firm, 1989-2010," http://www.sba.gov/advocacy/849/12162; U.S. Bureau of the Census.(November 2011). "Statistics of U.S. Businesses: Latest SUSB Annual Data, 2009,

U.S. & States Totals," http://www.census.gov /econ/susb/historical_data.html; and U.S. Bureau of the Census.(October 2012). "Statistics of U.S. Businesses: Latest SUSB Annual Data, 2010, U.S. & States Totals," http://www.census.gov/econ/susb/

15.   U.S. Small Business Administration. "Statistics of U.S. Businesses, U.S. Dynamic Data, U.S. Data: Employer Firm Births and Deaths by Employment Size of Firm, 1989-2010," http://www.sba.gov /advocacy/849/12162

16.   Acs, Z., William Parsons, and Spencer Tracy.(June 2008). "High-Impact Firms: Gazelles Revisited," U.S. Small Business Administration, Office of Advocacy, p. 14, http://archive.sba.gov/advo /research/rs328tot.pdf

17.   Dilger, R. J. (January 30, 2013). "Small Business Administration and Job Creation," Congressional Research Service. http://www.fas.org/sgp/crs /misc/R41523.pdf

18.   Amoros, J.E., and N. Bosma. "Global Entrepreneurship Monitor 2013," http://www.gemconsortium.org/docs/3106/gem-2013-global-report

19.   Schumpeter, J. (1934). *The Theory of Economic Development.* Cambridge: Harvard University Press.

20.   Kirchhoff, B. (1994). *Entrepreneurship and Dynamic Capitalism.* Westport, CT: Praeger.

21.   Reinertsen, D.G. (1999). "Taking the Fuzziness Out of the Fuzzy Front End." *Industrial Research Institute, Inc.* (November/December): 25–31.

22.   Townsend, D.M., L.W. Busenitz, and J.D. Arthurs (in press). "To Start or Not to Start: Outcome and Ability Expectations in the Decision to Start a New Venture." *Journal of Business Venturing*, JBV-05466

23.   "Frequently Asked Questions," (September 2012). SBA Office of Advocacy. http://www.sba.gov /sites/default/files/FAQ_Sept_2012.pdf

24.   Shane, S. (December 17, 2012). "Startup Failure Rates: The Definite Numbers," *Small Business Trends*, http://smallbiztrends.com/2012/12 /start-up-failure-rates-the-definitive-numbers.html

25.   Wagner, E.T. (September 12, 2013). "Five Reasons 8 Out of 10 Businesses Fail," *Forbes*, http://www .forbes.com/sites/ericwagner/2013/09/12 /five-reasons-8-out-of-10-businesses-fail/

26.   Headd, B. (January 2001). *Factors Leading to Surviving and Closing Successfully.* Center for Economic Studies, U.S. Bureau of the Census, Working Paper #CES-WP-01-01; and Advocacy-funded research by Richard J. Boden (Research Summary #204).

27.   Cohen, W., and R. Levin (1989). "Empirical Studies of Innovation and Market Structure." In Schmalensee, R., and R. Willig (eds.), *Handbook of Industrial Organization*, 2nd ed. New York: Elsevier, 1059–1107.

28.   Case, J. (1992). *From the Ground Up.* New York: Belknap Press, p. 44.

29.   Ibid., 46.

30.   Ibid., 64.

31.   Gupta, U. (1989). "Small Firms Aren't Waiting to Grow Up to Go Global." *The Wall Street Journal* (December 5): B2.

32.   McDougall, P.O., S. Shane, and B.M. Oviatt (1994). "Explaining the Formation of International New Ventures: The Limits of Theories from International Business Research." *Journal of Business Venturing*, 9: 469–487.

33.   Reuber, A.R., and E. Fischer (1997). "The Influence of the Management Team's International Experience on the Internationalization Behaviors of SMEs." *Journal of International Business Studies*, 28: 807–825.

34.   Ibid.

35.   Meeker, M. "Internet Trends 2013," Keiner Perkins Caufield & Byers

36.   Manufacturing Barometer. (January 2014), PricewaterhouseCoopers, http://www.pwc.com /us/en/industrial-manufacturing/barometer-manufacturing/index.jhtml

37.   Schwartz, N.D. (September 23, 2013). "More Manufacturing Coming Back to the U.S." *Economix, New York Times*, http://economix.blogs .nytimes.com/2013/09/23/more-manufacturing-coming-back-to-the-u-s/?_php=true& _type=blogs&_r=0

38.   Jopson, B. (June 9, 2013). "New Stamping Ground for Nike and Adidas as 3D shoes kick off," *Retail*, http://www.ft.com/intl/cms /s/0/1d09a66e-d097-11e2-a050-00144feab7de .html#axzz2wLlCaKVI

39.   Spindell, A. (June 18, 2013). "Conditions are Ripe for Manufacturing Entrepreneurs," *Thomasnet News*, http://news.thomasnet.com /IMT/2013/06/18/conditions-are-ripe-for-manufacturing-entrepreneurs/

40.   Staff. (December 3, 2012). "The Rise of Big Data," *Entrepreneur*, http://www.entrepreneur. com/article/224977-2

41.   The Lean Startup, http://theleanstartup.com /principles, accessed March 19, 2014.

42. Blank, S. (May 2013). "Why the Lean Start-up Changes Everything." *Harvard Business Review*, http://hbr.org/2013/05/why-the-lean-start-up-changes-everything/ar/1

43. Egusa, C. (December 17, 2013). "Beyond Lean Startups: Eric Ries' Movement Heads to Fortune 500, Government, and Beyond," *Venture Beat*, http://venturebeat.com/2013/12/17/beyond-lean-startups-eric-ries-movement-heads-to-fortune-500-government-and-beyond/

Chapter 2

1. Vogelstein, F. (2004). "14 Innovators," *Fortune* (November 15).
2. Goodman, M. (October 15, 2013). "Real World Work-Life Balance: How to Find Your Entrepreneurial Zen," *Entrepreneur*, http://www.entrepreneur.com/article/227963
3. Eng, S. (July 10, 2001). "Impress Investors with Your Firm's Endgame," *The Wall Street Journal Startup Journal*, www.startupjournal.com
4. Davidsson, P. (2005). "The Types and Contextual Fit of Entrepreneurial Processes," *International Journal of Entrepreneurship Education*, 2(4): 407–430.
5. Aspelund, A., T. Berg-Utby, and R. Skejevdal. (2005). "Initial Resources' Influence on New Venture Survival: A Longitudinal Study of New Technology-Based Firms," *Technovation*, 25(11): 1337.
6. Roberts, M.T., and L. Barley (December 2004). "How Venture Capitalists Evaluate Potential Venture Opportunities," *Harvard Business School Press*.
7. Lessin, J.E. (April 3, 2013). "Age Rises for Some Tech Founders," *The Wall Street Journal*, http://online.wsj.com/news/articles/SB10001424127887324000704578389103697378458
8. "All in the Mind," (March 14, 2009). *Special Report on Entrepreneurship. The Economist*, p. 5.
9. Farrell, C. (April 30, 2012). "Older Entrepreneurs Start companies Too," *Bloomberg Businessweek*, http://www.businessweek.com/articles/2012-04-30/older-entrepreneurs-start-companies-too
10. Drucker, P.E. (1985). *Innovation and Entrepreneurship*. New York: Harper & Row.
11. Nicolaou, N., S. Shane, L. Cherkas, J. Hunkin, and T.D. Spector (2008). "Is the Tendency to Engage in Entrepreneurship Genetic?" *Management Science*, 54(1): 167–179.
12. Abdul, A., I.E. Allen, C. Brush, W.D. Bygrave, J. DeCastro, J. Lange, H. Neck, J. Onochie, O. Phinisee, E. Rogoff, A. Suhu, and Global Entrepreneurship Monitor. (2008). *2008 National Entrepreneurial Assessment for the United States of America, Executive Report*.
13. Shane, S., and S. Venkataraman (2000). "The Promise of Entrepreneurship as a Field of Research." *Academy of Management Review*, 25(1): 217–226; and Begley, T., and D. Boyd (1987). "Psychological Characteristics Associated with Performance in Entrepreneurial Firms and Smaller Businesses." *Journal of Business Venturing*, 2: 79–93.
14. "Home-Based Businesses," The U.S. Small Business Administration, http://www.sba.gov/content/home-based-businesses, accessed April 14, 2014.
15. Colao, J.J. (October 28, 2012). "The Ten Best Serial Entrepreneurs You've Never heard Of," *Forbes*, http://www.forbes.com/sites/jjcolao/2012/10/29/the-ten-best-serial-entrepreneurs-youve-never-heard-of/
16. Westhead, P., D. UcBasaran, and M. Wright (2005). "Decisions, Actions, and Performance: Do Novice, Serial, and Portfolio Entrepreneurs Differ?" *Journal of Small Business Management*, 43(4): 393.
17. Rosa, P. (1998). "Entrepreneurial Processes of Business Cluster Formation and Growth by 'Habitual' Entrepreneurs," *Entrepreneurship Theory and Practice*, 22: 43–61.
18. Unite for Sight, http://www.uniteforsight.org/about-us/board, accessed March 20, 2014.
19. Zahra S.A., D.F. Karutko, and D.F. Jennings. (1999). "Guest Editorial: Entrepreneurship and the Acquisition of Dynamic Organizational Capabilities," *Entrepreneurship Theory and Practice*, 23(3): 5–10.
20. Wolcott, R.C., and Lippitz, M.J. (Fall 2007). "The Four Models of Corporate Entrepreneurship," *MIT Sloan Management Review*, 49(1): 75–82.
21. Barnett, William P., H.R. Greve, and D.Y. Park (1994). "An Evolutionary Model of Organizational Performance," *Strategic Management Journal*, 15 (Winter Special Issue): 11–28; and Baum, Joel A.C., and O. Christine. (1991). "Institutional Linkages and Organizational Mortality," *Administrative Science Quarterly*, 36: 187–218.
22. Ramesh, G. (July–September 2005). "Entrepreneurial Traps: Autobiography of an Unknown Entrepreneur," *South Asian Journal of Management*, 12(3): 79.
23. Aldrich, H., and C. Zimmer (1986). "Entrepreneurship through Social Networks." In D.L.

Sexton and R.W. Smilor (eds.), *The Art and Science of Entrepreneurship*. Cambridge, MA: Ballinger, 2–23.

24. Granovetter, M. (1982). "The Strength of Weak Ties: A Network Theory Revisited." In P.V. Marsden and N. Lin (eds.), *Social Structure and Network Analysis*. Beverly Hills, CA: Sage, 105–130.

25. Burt, R.S. (2004). "Structural Holes and Good Ideas," *The American Journal of Sociology*, 110(2): 349.

26. Fisher, D., and S. Vilas (2000). *Power Networking: 59 Secrets for Personal and Professional Success*. Marietta, GA: Bard Press.

27. Hatala, J.P. (2005). "Identifying Barriers to Self-Employment: The Development and Validation of the Barriers to Entrepreneurship Success Tool," *Performance Improvement Quarterly*, 18(4): 50.

28. Lounsbury, M., and M. Glynn (2001). "Cultural Entrepreneurship: Stories, Legitimacy, and the Acquisition of Resources," *Strategic Management Journal*, 22: 545–564.

Chapter 3

1. Brown, T. (June, 2008). "Design Thinking," *Harvard Business Review*, http://hbr.org/2008/06/design-thinking/

2. Gryskiewicz, S.S. (1987). "Predictable Creativity." In S.G. Isaksen (ed.), *Frontiers of Creativity Research: Beyond the Basics*. Buffalo, NY: Bearly, 305–313.

3. Noller, R.B. (1979). *Scratching the Surface of Creative Problem Solving*. Buffalo, NY: DOK.

4. Isaksen, S.G., M.I. Stein, D.A. Hills and S.S. Grayskiewicz. (1984). "A Proposed Model for the Formulation of Creativity Research," *Journal of Creative Behavior*, 18: 67–75.

5. Singh, B. (1986). "Role of Personality versus Biographical Factors in Creativity," *Psychological Studies*, 31: 90–92; Barron, F., and D.M. Harrington. (1981). "Creativity, Intelligence, and Personality," *Annual Review of Psychology*, 32: 439–476; and Gardner, H. (1993). *Frames of Mind*. New York: Basic Books.

6. Amabile, T.M. (1988). "A Model of Creativity and Innovation in Organizations." In B.M. Staw and L.L. Cummings (eds.), *Research in Organizational Behavior*, Vol. 10. Greenwich, CT: JAI Press, pp. 123–167; Oldham, G.R., and A. Cummings. (1996). "Employee Creativity: Personal and Contextual Factors at Work," *Academy of Management Journal*, 39: 607–634; Mumford, M.D., and S.B. Gustafson. (1988). "Creativity Syndrome: Inte-

gration, Application, and Innovation," *Psychological Bulletin*, 103: 27–43; and Payne, R. (1990). "The Effectiveness of Research Teams: A Review." In M.A. West and J.L. Farr (eds.), *Innovation and Creativity at Work*. Chichester, England: Wiley, pp. 101–122.

7. Wallas, G. (1926). *The Art of Thought*. New York: Franklin Watts.

8. Seeff, N. (2010). *The Triumph of the Dream*. Norman eeff Productions.

9. Reuters. (February 23, 2006). "Work More, Do Less with Tech," *Wired News*, www.wired.com/techbiz/media/news/2006/02/70274.

10. Ophira, E., C. Nass, and A.D. Wagner. (August 25, 2009). "Cognitive Control in Media Multitaskers," *Proceedings of the National Academy of Sciences*, 106(34), 14181–14182.

11. Kanter, R.M. (Winter 2005). "How Leaders Gain (and Lose) Confidence," *Leader to Leader*, 35: 21.

12. Ibid.

13. Girotra, K., C. Terwiesch, and K.T. Ultrich. (April 2010). "Idea Generation and the Quality of the Best Idea," *Management Science*, 56(4): 2.

14. Stroebe, W., and M. Diehl. (1994). "Why Are Groups Less Effective Than Their Members: On Productivity Losses in Idea Generation Groups," *European Review Of Social Psychology*, 5: 271–303.

15. Op. cit. Girotra et al. (April 2010), p. 23.

16. Liedtke, J., and Obilvie, T. (2011). *Designing for Growth*. New York: Columbia Business School Publishing, p. 53.

17. Shane, S. (2003). *A General Theory of Entrepreneurship: The Individual-opportunity Nexus*. Northampton, MA: Edward Elgar.

18. Kirzner, I. (1973). *Competition and Entrepreneurship*. Chicago, IL: University of Chicago Press, p. 17; and Shane, S. (2003). *A General Theory of Entrepreneurship: The Individual-opportunity Nexus*. Northampton, MA: Edward Elgar.

19. Alvarez, S.A., and J.B. Barney. (2007). "Discovery and Creation: Alternative Theories of Entrepreneurial Action," *Strategic Entrepreneurship Journal*, 1: 11–26.

20. Baker, T., and R. Nelson. (2005). "Creating Something from Nothing: Resource Construction through Entrepreneurial Bricolage," *Administrative Science Quarterly*, 50:329–366; and Sarasvathy, S.D. (2001). "Causation and Effectuation: Toward a Theoretical Shift from Economic Inevitability to Entrepreneurial Contingency," *Academy of Management Review*, 26(2): 243–263.

21. Op. cit. Alvarez and Barney (2007), p. 15

22. Isaksen, S.G., K.B. Dorval, and D.J. Treffinger. (2011). *Creative Approaches to Problem Solving*, 3rd ed. Thousand Oaks, CA: Sage Publications, p. 31.

23. Isaksen et al. (2011), p. 44.

24. Jones, M.D. (1998). *The Thinker's Toolkit*. New York: Three Rivers Press.

25. Rogers, M. (May 1998). "The Definition and Measurement of Innovation," *Melbourne Institute of Applied Economic and Social Research, The University Melbourne*, Working Paper No. 10/98.

26. OECD. (1997). *The Oslo Manual: Proposed Guidelines for Collecting and Interpreting Technological Innovation Data*. Paris: OECD, p. 28.

Chapter 4

1. Kirsner, S. (July 6, 2008). "Incubator Polishes Gem of an Idea," *Boston.com*, www.boston.com/business/articles/2008/07/06/incubator_polishes_gem_of_an_idea

2. Porter, M.E. (2008). "Total Strategy: From Planning to Execution," *Presentation Given to HSM Expomanagement, Buenos Aires*, http://docs.google.com/viewer?a=v&q=cache:rTAJVFXNu9MJ:ar.hsmglobal.com/adjuntos/15/documentos/000/052/0000052960.pdf+Profitability+of+Selected+US+Industries+1992-2006&hl=en&gl=us&pid=bl&srcid=ADGEESge0regu2t0ZOqlYgYQbO1RRMnXwIhixf7dZiKFKuU_u1-smm_BH-3MTYPajDi2BIacWZWn0Ghg2_T1Bea8NbjvdFcO_8-_RS32ivprL99SdOXeL0LRGBEGz3z-ufOy7cQxpTm&sig=AHIEtbSUFdnE0K6H0MTKWcR_7JC7kmDcvA

3. Bisson, P., E. Stephenson, and S.P. Viguerie. (June 2010). "Global Forces: An Introduction," *McKinsey Quarterly*, www.mckinseyquarterly.com/Strategy/Globalization/Global_forces_An_introduction_2625

4. Downes, L., and P.F. Nunes. (March 2013). "Big-Bang Disruption," *Harvard Business Review*, HBR.org, Reprint R1303B.

5. Afeyan, N. (February 26, 2014). "Top 10 Emerging Technologies for 2014," *World Economic Forum*, http://forumblog.org/2014/02/top-ten-emerging-technologies-2014/

6. Schrage, M. (2006). "The Myth of Commoditization," *MIT Sloan Management Review*, 48(2): 12.

7. Jin, J.Y., J. Perote-Pena, and M. Troege. (2004). "Learning by Doing, Spillovers and Shakeouts," *Journal of Evolutionary Economics*, 14: 85–98.

8. McGahan, A.N. (2004). *How Industries Evolve*. Boston, MA: Harvard Business School Press.

9. Ibid., 10.

10. Porter, M.E. (1980). *Competitive Strategy: Techniques for Analyzing Industries and Competitors*. New York: The Free Press, p. 3.

11. Rivkin, J.W., and A. Cullen. (January 7, 2009). "Finding Information for Industry Analysis." HBS 9-708-481, p. 19.

12. Slater, S.F., and E.M. Olson. (January–February, 2002). "A Fresh Look at Industry and Market Analysis," *Business Horizons*, p. 20.

13. Hammersley, M. (1990). *Reading Ethnographic Research: A Critical Guide*. London: Longman.

14. Gray, R. (May 18, 2000). "The Relentless Rise of Online Research," *Marketing*, ProQuest.

15. "Survey Response Rates," (January 28, 2010). *Survey Gizmo*, http://www.surveygizmo.com/survey-blog/survey-response-rates/

16. Kennedy, B. (December 23, 2013). "The Worst Product Flops of 2013," *24/7 Wall Street*, http://247wallst.com/special-report/2013/12/23/the-worst-product-flops-of-2013/3/

17. Ulwick, A.W. (2002). "Turn Customer Input into Innovation," *Harvard Business Review*, product number 858X

18. Chen, M.I. (1996). "Competitor Analysis and Intercompany Rivalry: Toward a Theoretical Integration," *Academy of Management Review*, 21(1): 100–134.

19. Bergen, M., and M.A. Peteraf. (June–August 2002). "Competitor Identification and Competitor Analysis: A Broad-Based Managerial Approach." *Managerial Decision Economics*, 23(4/5): 157–169.

20. Op. cit. Slater, S.F., and Olson, E.M. (2002), p. 18.

Chapter 5

1. Drucker, P.F. (2008). *The Five Most Important Questions You Will Ever Ask about Your Organization*. San Francisco: Jossey-Bass.

2. Chesbrough, H.W. (2010). "Business Model Innovation: Opportunities and Barriers," *Long Range Planning*, 43(2–3): 354–363.

3. Shafer, S.M., H.J. Smith, and J.C. Linder. (2005). "The Power of Business Models," *Business Horizons*, 48: 199–207.

4. Zott, C., and Amit, R. (2010). "Business Model Design: An Activity System Perspective," *Long Range Planning*, 43(2–3): 216–226.

5. Cavalcante, S., Kesting, P., and Ulhoi, J. (2011). "Business Model Dynamics and Innovation: Re Establishing the Missing Linkages," *Management Decision*, 48(8):1327–1342.

6. Osterwalder, A., Pigneur, Y., and Tucci, C.L. (2005). "Clarifying Business Models: Origins, Present,and Future of the Concept," *Communications of AIS*, 2005 (16): 1–25.

7. Hamermesh, R.G., Marshall, P.W., and Pirmohamed, T. (January 22, 2002). "Note on Business Model Analysis for the Entrepreneur," *Harvard Business School*, 9-802-048.

8. Hamel, G. (2000). *Leading the Revolution*. New York: Plume.

9. Linder, J., and S. Cantrell. (2001). "What Makes a Good Business Model, Anyway?" *Accenture Institute for Strategic Change*, www.accenture.com/SiteCollectionDocuments/PDF/business_model_pov.pdf

10. Kaplan, R.S., and Norton, D.P. (1996). *Balanced Scorecard: Translating Strategy into Action*. Boston, MA: Harvard Business School Press.

11. Stuart, A. (December 2002). "This Year's Model," *Inc. Magazine*, www.inc.com

12. Niraj, R., M. Gupta, and C. Narasimhan. (July 2001). "Customer Profitability in a Supply Chain." *Journal of Marketing*, 65(3): 1–16.

13. Shafer, S.M., H.J. Smith, and J.C. Linder. (2005). "The Power of Business Models," *Business Horizons*, 48: 199–207.

14. Chanal, V. (Ed.) (April 6, 2011). "Rethinking Business Models for Innovation," http://www.rethinkingbusinessmodel.net

15. Friedman, T.L. (2005). *The World Is Flat*. New York: Farrar, Straus & Giroux.

16. Linder, J., and S. Cantrell. (2001). "What Makes a Good Business Model Anyway? Can Yours Stand the Test of Change?" *Outlook: Point of View*, www.accenture.com/SiteCollectionDocuments/PDF/business_model_pov.pdf

17. Helmer, H.W. (2005). "A Lecture on Integrating the Treatment of Uncertainty in Strategy," *Journal of Strategic Management Education*, 1(1): 94.

18. French, N., and L. Gabrielli. (2005). "Uncertainty and Feasibility Studies: An Italian Case Study," *Journal of Property Investment & Finance*, 24(1): 49.

19. Simon, M., and S.M. Houghton. (2003). "The Relationship between Overconfidence and the Introduction of Risky Products: Evidence from a Field Study," *Academy of Management Journal*, 46(2): 139–149.

20. Op. cit., Helmer, 2005, 193–114.

21. Taleb, N.N. (2012). *Antifragile: Things That Gain from Disorder*. New York: Random House, p. 161.

22. Kim, W.C., and Mauborgne, R. (2004). *Blue Ocean Strategy*. Boston, MA: Harvard Business Review Press.

23. Wauthy, X. (2008). No Free Lunch sur le Web 2.0 ! Ce que cache la gratuité apparent des réseaux sociaux numériques. Regards Économiques

24. Allen, L.H., and C.K. Prahalad. (May–June 2004). "Selling to the Poor," Foreign Policy, 142: 30–37.

25. Merkle, R.C. (April 2001). "That's Impossible." Foresight Nanotech Institute, www.foresight.org/impact/impossible.html

Chapter 6

1. Nauyalis, C.T., and M. Carlson. (March 2010). "Portfolio Pain Points," *PDMA Visions Magazine*, p. 13.

2. Zassenhaus, M. (May 1, 2013). "What 'Lean UX' Looks Like–A Story of Product Development," *The Ladders*, http://info.theladders.com/our-team/what-lean-ux-looks-like-a-story-of-product-development-part-i

3. Ulrich, K.T., and S. Pearson. (1998). "Assessing the Importance of Design through Product Archaeology," *Management Science*, 44(3): 352–369.

4. Nauyalis, C.T., and M. Carlson. (March 2010). "Portfolio Pain Points," *PDMA Visions Magazine*, p. 13.

5. "Industry Trends 2014," Vector Consulting Services, http://www.vector.com/portal/medien/vector_consulting/publications/Industry-Trends_VectorConsultingServices_2014.pdf

6. Ries, E. (2011). "The Lean Startup Methodology," http://theleanstartup.com/principles, accessed April 26, 2014.

7. Stevens, G.A., and J. Burley. (2003). "Piloting the Rocket of Radical Innovation," *Research Technology Management*, 46(2): 16–26.

8. Teece, D.J. (1986). "Profiting from Technological Innovation," *Research Policy*, 15(6):285–305.

9. Pisano, G.P., and D.J. Teece. (Fall 2007). "How to Capture Value from Innovation: Shaping Intellectual Property and Industry Architecture," *California Management Review*, 50(1): 277–296.

10. Ibid, p. 281

11. Cooper, R.G., and S.J. Edgett. (2003). "Overcoming the Crunch in Resources for New Product

Development," *Research Technology Management*, 46(3): 48.

12. Cooper, R.G. (2001). *Winning at New Products: Accelerating the Process from Idea to Launch*, 3rd ed. Boston: Perseus Publishing.

13. Crawford, C.M. (1992). "The Hidden Costs of Accelerated Product Development," *Journal of Product Innovation Management*, 9(3): 188–199.

14. Mankin, E. (2004). "Is Your Product-Development Process Helping—or Hindering—Innovation?" *Strategy & Innovation. Harvard Business School Press*, 4.

15. G. Bacon, S. Beckman, D. Mowery, E. Wilson. (Spring 1994). "Managing Product Definition in High-Technology Industries: A Pilot Study," *California Review*, 36(3): 32–56.

16. Rose, E.P. (2013). "Managing NPD Project Tradeoffs," *Visions*. 35(4), 4.

17. Ibid.

18. Earle, M., and Earle, R. (2008). *Case Studies in Food Product Development*. Cambridge, England: Woodhead.

19. Thompson, N.T. (September 11, 2013). "Building a Minimum Viable Product? You're Probably Doing It Wrong," *Harvard Business Review*, http://blogs.hbr.org/2013/09 /building-a-minimum-viable-prod/2/2

20. Cooper, B., and Vlaskovits, P. (February 4, 2013). "Three Reasons Not to Build a Minimum Viable Product," *Pandodaily*, http://pando .com/2013/02/04/three-reasons-not-to-build-a-minimum-viable-product/

21. Quinn, J.B. (2000). "Outsourcing Innovation: The New Engine of Growth." *Sloan Management Review*, 41(4): 13–29.

22. Lieberman, J. (November 22, 2013). "Thinking Beyond Cost-Cutting: 5 Trends Driving Adoption of Offshore Product Development," *Wired: Innovation Insights*, http://insights.wired.com /profiles/blogs/5-trends-driving-adoption-of-off -shore-product-development-1#axzz301iHBReV

23. Mitra, S. (March 6, 2014). "Outsourced Product Development Gaining Popularity among Small Businesses," *Small Business Trends*, http://small -biztrends.com/2014/03/outsourced-product -development-small-business.html

24. Portnoy, E. (December 31, 2013). "How to Outsource Product Development and Build Great Products," *Forbes*, http://www.forbes.com/sites/ eliportnoy/2013/12/31/how-to-outsource- product-development-and-build-great-products/

25. Reynolds, E.B., and Hiram, S. (November 2013). "Invented in America Scaled Up Overseas: Manufacturing Startups," *Mechanical Engineering*, 135(11): 36.

Chapter 7

1. Chaplinsky S. (2002). "Methods of Intellectual Property Valuation," *Darden, University of Virginia*, UVA-F-1401, http://faculty.darden. virginia.edu/chaplinskys/PEPortal/Documents /IP%20Valuation%20F-1401%20_watermark_pdf

2. Malackowski, J.E., Cardoza, K., Gray, C., and Conroy, R. (February 2007). "The Intellectual Property Marketplace: Emerging Transaction and Investment Vehicles," *The Licensing Journal*, 27(2):1.

3. "Trade Secrets Law in California," *Digital Media Law Project*, May 12, 2014, www.dmip .org/legal-guide/trade-secrets-law-california

4. Trademark Act of 1946, 15 U.S.C. § 1127.

5. AMBRIT, INC., v. KRAFT, INC., United States Court of Appeals, Eleventh Circuit, 812 F.2d 1531 (1986).

6. "Trademark Appeal Board Says 'Pretzel Crisps' Is Generic," *Eye on IP*, March 21, 2014, http://www.usip.com/Publications/EyeonIP /140321.html

7. Brown, J.D., and J.E. Prescott. (2000). "Product of the Mind: Assessment and Protection of Intellectual Property," *Competitive Intelligence Review*, 11(3): 60.

8. "Trademark Registration in China Brings Challenges and Rewards," *Eye on IP: Sheldon Mak & Anderson PC*, November 14, 2013, www.usip .com/Publications/EyonIP/131114.html

9. "Amazon Found to Infringe Trademark in UK Based on 'Lush' Searches," *Eye on IP*, February 28, 2014.

10. 2001 Duke L. & Tech. Rev. 0018, May 31, 2001.

11. "Some Online Retailers May Not Qualify for DMCA Safe Haven in Copyright Cases," *Eye on IP*, May 7, 2014, http://www.usip.com/Publications EyeonIP/140507.html

12. General Information Concerning Patents, United States Patent and Trademark Office, November 2011.

13. *Diamond v. Chakrabarty*, 447 U.S. 303 (1980).

14. Whitford, D. (2006). "Vision Quest," *Fortune Small Business* (April): 46.

15. "Qualifying for a Patent," *NOLO Law for All*, www.nolo.com/legal-encyclopedia/faqEditorial-29120.html

16. Reitzig, M. (Spring 2004). "Strategic Management of Intellectual Property," *Sloan Management Review*, 45(3): 35.

17. Love, J.J., and W.W. Coggins. (2001). "Successfully Preparing and Prosecuting a Business Method Patent," www.immagic.com/eLibrary/ARCHIVES/GENERAL/AIPLA_US/A010510L.pdf

18. Sheldon, J.G. (2013). *The Manager's Guide to Intellectual Property*. Amherst MA: HRD Press.

19. Oddi, A.S. (1996). "Un-Unified Economic Theories of Patents: The Not-Quite-Holy Grail," *Notre Dame Law Review*, 71: 267–327.

20. Mullin, J. (May 14, 2014). "The Year in Patent Litigation: More Trolling, More Texas," *Ars Technica*, http://arstechnica.com/tech-policy/2014/05/the-year-in-patent-litigation-more-trolling-more-texas/

21. Jones, A. (July 8, 2012). "Patent Troll Tactics Spread," *The Wall Street Journal*, http://online.wsj.com/news/articles/SB10001424052702303292204577514782932390996

22. Lemper, T. (2012). "The Critical Role of Timing in Managing Intellectual Property," *Business Horizons*, 55:339–347.

23. Somaya, D., Teece, D.J.U., and Wakeman, S. (September/October 2012). "Business Models and Patent Strategies in Multi-Invention Contexts," *Ivey Business Journal*, http://iveybusinessjournal.com/topics/innovation/business-models-and-patent-strategies-in-multi-invention-contexts#.U3QayvldV8E

Chapter 8

1. Davidsson, P., and B. Honig. (2003). "The Role of Social and Human Capital among Nascent Entrepreneurs," *Journal of Business Venturing*, 18: 201–331.

2. Ruef, M. (2002). "Strong Ties, Weak Ties, and Islands: Structural and Cultural Predictors of Organizational Innovation," *Industrial and Corporate Change*, 11: 427–429.

3. Bird, B.J. (1989). *Entrepreneurial Behavior*. Glenview, IL: Scott Foresman; and Kamm, J.B., J.C. Shuman, J.A. Seeger, and A.J. Nurick. (1990). "Entrepreneurial Teams in New Venture Creation: A Research Agenda," *Entrepreneurship Theory and Practice*, 14(4): 7–17.

4. Ensley, M.D., J.W. Carland, and J.C. Carland. (2000). "Investigating the Existence of the Lead Entrepreneur," *Journal of Small Business Management*, 38(4): 59–88.

5. Venture Atlanta. (May 23, 2013). "Oracle to Buy Vitrue for $300 Million," http://ventureatlanta.org/2012/05/oracle-to-buy-vitrue-for-300-million/

6. Aldrich, H., and C. Zimmer. (1986). "Entrepreneurship through Social Networks." In D.L. Sexton and R. W. Smilor (eds), *The Art and Science of Entrepreneurship*. Cambridge, MA: Ballinger, 3–23.

7. Dubini, P., and H. Aldrich. (1991). "Personal and Extended Networks Are Central to the Entrepreneurial Process," *Journal of Business Venturing*, 6(5): 305–313.

8. Pentland, A. (April 2012). "The New Science of Building Great Teams," *HBR's 10 Must Reads on Teams by Harvard Business Review*, p. 3.

9. Ibid. Pentland, 2012.

10. Ibid. Pentland, 2012, p. 8

11. Hackman, R. (May, 2009). "Why Teams Don't Work," *Harvard Business Review*.

12. Wasserman, N. (2013). *The Founder's Dilemmas*. Princeton, NJ: Princeton University Press.

13. Gorman, M., and Sahlman, W.A. (1989). "What Do Venture Capitalists Do?" *Journal of Business Venturing*, 4(4): 231–248.

14. Kaplan, S.N., and Stromberg, P. (2004). "Characteristics, Contracts, and Actions: Evidence from Venture Capitalist Analyses," *Journal of Finance*, 59: 2173–2206.

15. Seifert, R., and B. Leleux. (December 2007). "Shape Up Your Technology Start-ups." *Perspectives for Managers*, 153:1.

16. Anonymous. (2002). "Making Virtual Collaborations Work," *Research Technology Management*, 45(2): 6–7.

17. Gersick, C.J.G., and J.R. Hackman. (1990). "Habitual Routines in Task-Performing Groups," *Organizational Behavior and Human Decision Processes*, 47: 65–97.

18. Kozlowski, S.W.J., S.M. Gully, P.P. McHugh, E. Salas, and J.A. Cannon-Bowers (1996). "A Dynamic Theory of Leadership and Team Effectiveness: Developmental and Task Contingent Leader Roles." In G.R. Ferris (ed.), *Research in Personnel and Human Resource Management*. Greenwich, CT: JAI Press, pp. 253–305.

19. Ibid. Wasserman (2013).

20. Ibid Wasserman (2013).

21. Roure, J.B., and M.A. Madique. (1986). "Linking Prefunding Factors and High-Technology Venture Success: An Exploratory Study," *Journal of Business Venturing*, 1(3): 295–306.

22. Murray, A.I. (1989). "Top Management Group Heterogeneity and Firm Performance," *Strategic Management Journal*, 10: 125–141.

23. Kamm, J.B., J.C. Shuman, J.A. Seeger, and A.J. Nurick. (1990). "Entrepreneurial Teams in New Venture Creation: A Research Agenda," *Entrepreneurship Theory and Practice*, 14(4), 7–17.

24. Venture Source. (n.d.). *The Next Big Thing 2012*. Retrieved from the *Wall Street Journal*: http://online.wsj.com/news/interactive/NBT092012?ref=SB100008723963904448131045780189 40187057924

25. Op.cit. Wasserman (2013).

26. Wasserman, N. (February, 2008). "The Founder's Dilemma," *Harvard Business Review*. http://hbr.org/2008/02/the-founders-dilemma/ar/1

27. Hamm, J. (2002). "Why Entrepreneurs Don't Scale," *Harvard Business Review*, R0212J

28. Fiegner, M., B. Brown, D. Dreux, and W. Dennis. (2000). "CEO Stakes and Board Composition in Small Private Firms." *Entrepreneurship Theory and Practice*, 24: 5.

29. Kidwell, R.E., and N. Bennett. (1993). "Employee Propensity to Withhold Effort: A Conceptual Model to Intersect Three Avenues of Research." *Academy of Management Review*, 18(3): 429–456.

30. Goodstein, J., K. Gautam, and W. Boeker. (1994). "The Effects of Board Size and Diversity on Strategic Change," *Strategic Management Journal*, 15(3): 241–250.

31. Barthelemy, J. (Spring 2001). "The Hidden Costs of Outsourcing," *Sloan Management Review*, 42(3): 60–69.

32. Sovereign, K.L. (1999). *Personnel Law*, 4th ed. Upper Saddle River, NJ: Prentice-Hall.

33. Butcher, D.R. (June 22, 2010). "Cooperative Purchasing: Buy More for Less?" *Industry Market Trends*, http://news.thomasnet.com/IMT/archives/2010/06/cooperative-purchasing-procurement-more-for-less.html

Chapter 9

1. Blank, S. (July 22, 2010). "The Phantom Sales Forecast—Failing at Customer Validation," http://steveblank.com/2010/07/22/what-if-the-price-were-zero-failing-at-customer-validation.

2. Gilbert, C.G. and M.J. Eyring. (May 2010). "Beating the Odds When You Launch a New Venture," *Harvard Business Review*, http://hbr.org/2010/05/beating-the-odds-when-you-launch-a-new-venture/ar/1.

3. Ibid.

4. "After the Techcrunch Bump." *Redeye VC*, http://redeye.firstround.com/2008/01/after-the-techc.html, accessed July 22, 2010.

5. Faris, R. and R. Heacock. (November 2013). "Measuring Internet Activity: A Selective Review of Methods and Metrics," *Internet Monitor Special Report Series No. 2*, http://cyber.law.harvard.edu/publications/2013/measuring_internet_activity.

6. Christensen, C. (2012). "Jobs to Be Done," Clayton Christensen Institute, http://www.christenseninstitute.org/key-concepts/jobs-to-be-done/, accessed June 10, 2014.

7. Walters, D. (2002). *Operations Strategy*. Houndmills, Hampshire: Palgrave Macmillan.

8. Hogan, J.E. and J. Zale. (February 15, 2005). "The Top 5 Myths of Strategic Pricing," MarketingProfs.com, www.marketingprofs.com/5/hoganzale1.asp.

9. Docters, R.G. (September/October 1997). "Price Strategy: Time to Choose Your Weapons." *The Journal of Business Strategy*, 18(5): 11–15.

10. Fishman, C. (February 2003). "Which Price Is Right?" *Fast Company* 68: 92.

11. Johnson, W.K. and B.T. Walley. (Fall 2009). *Currency13, Enabling Bank Trusted Peer-to-Peer Payments*, a feasibility studying conducted at the University of Southern California as part of the requirements for a course in technology feasibility.

Chapter 10

1. "Startup Business Failure Rate By Industry," (January 1, 2014), *Statistic Brain*, http://www.statisticbrain.com/startup-failure-by-industry/.

2. Gage, D. (September 20, 2012). "The Venture Capital Secret: 3 Out of 4 Startups Fail," *The Wall Street Journal*, http://online.wsj.com/news/articles/SB1000087239639044372020457800498 0476429190.

3. Gumpert, D.E. (2002). *Burn Your Business Plan! What Investors Really Want from Entrepreneurs*. Needham, MA: Lauson Publishing.

4. Kelly, P. and M. Hay. (2000). "The Private Investor—Entrepreneur Contractual Relationship: Understanding the Influence of Context." In E. Autio et al. (eds), *Frontiers of Entrepreneurship Research*. Wellesley, MA: Babson College.

5. Ibid., 65.

6. Logan, D. and H. Fischer-Wright. (Fall 2009). "Micro Strategies: The Key to Successful Planning in Uncertain Times," *Leader to Leader*, 43–52.

7. Ibid, p. 46.

8. Kahneman, D. and G. Klein. (March 2010). "Strategic Decision: When Can You Trust Your Gut?" *McKinsey Quarterly*, 2: 58–67.

9. Ibid

10. Hankin, R.N. (July 17, 2000). "Creating and Realizing the Value of a Business," *Entrepreneur's Byline*, www.entrepreneurship.org/en/resource-center/creating-and-realizing-the-value-of-a-business.aspx.

11. Mason, C.M. and R.T. Harrison. (2000). "Investing in Technology Ventures: What Do Business Angels Look for at the Initial Screening Stage?" In E. Autio et al. (eds), *Frontiers of Entrepreneurship Research*. Wellesley, MA: Babson College, p. 293.

Chapter 11

1. Ward, A., E. Runcie, and L. Morris. (2009). "Embedding Innovation: Design Thinking for Small Enterprises," *Journal of Business Strategy*, 30(2/3): 78–84.

2. Liedtka, J. and T. Ogilvie. (2011). *Designing for Growth: A Design Thinking Tool Kit for Managers*, New York: Columbia University Press.

3. Kaplan, R.S. and D.P. Norton. (2002). *The Strategy-Focused Organization: How Balanced Scorecard Companies Thrive in the New Business Environment*, Boston: Harvard Business School Press; and Mankins, M.C. and Steele, R. (July–August 2005). "Turning Great Strategy into Great Performance," *Harvard Business Review*, 83(7): 64–71, 191.

4. Martin, R. (Winter 2004). "The Design of Business," *Rotman Management*, Rotman School of Design, Toronto, Canada.

5. Hanks, S.H. and G.N. Chandler. (1994). "Patterns of Functional Specialization in Emerging High Tech Firms," *Journal of Small Business Management*, 32(2): 22–37; and Jennings, P. and G. Beaver. (1997). "The Performance and Competitive Advantage of Small Firms: A Management Perspective," *International Small Business Journal*, 15(2): 63–75.

6. Lorsch, J.W. (1999). "Note on Organization Design," *Harvard Business School*, Case No, 476-094.

7. Reed, M.I. and M. Hughes, eds. (1996). *Rethinking Organizations: New Directions in Organization Theory and Analysis*. London: Sage; Hassard, J. and M. Parker. (1993). *Postmodernism and Organizations*. London: Sage; and Boje, D.M. (1996). *Postmodern Management and Organization Theory*. Thousand Oaks, CA: Sage.

8. Gumm, D.C. (September–October 2006). "Distribution Dimensions in Software Development Projects: A Taxonomy," *IEEE Software*: 45.

9. Martin, R. (Fall 2005). "Embedding Design into Business," *Rotman Magazine*, Rotman School of Design, Toronto, Canada.

10. Bryne, J.A. (February 8, 1993). "The Virtual Corporation," *Business Week*: 98–102.

11. Fitzpatrick, W.M. and D.R. Burke. (2000). "Form, Functions, and Financial Performance Realities for the Virtual Organization," *S.A.M. Advanced Management Journal*, 65(3): 13–25.

12. Garaventa, E. and T. Tellefsen. (2001). "Outsourcing: The Hidden Costs," *Review of Business*, 22(1/2): 28–32.

13. Watkins, M. (2004). "The First 90 Days," *Association Management*, 56(8): 44–54.

14. Smircich, L. (1983). "Concepts of Culture and Organizational Analysis," *Administrative Science Quarterly*, 28: 339–358.

15. Davis, S. (1984). *Managing Corporate Culture*. Cambridge, MA: Ballinger.

16. Deal, T. and A. Kennedy. (1982). *Corporate Cultures: The Rites and Rituals of Corporate Life*. Reading, MA: Addison-Wesley.

17. Ulrich, D. and D. Kale. (1990). *Organizational Capability: Competing from the Inside/Out*. New York: John Wiley & Sons.

18. Frei, F. and A. Morriss. (2012). *Uncommon Service: How to Win by Putting Customers at the Core of Your Business*. Boston: Harvard Business School Publishing Corporation, Chapter 5.

19. Tosti, D.T. (2007). "Aligning the Culture and Strategy for Success," *Performance Improvement*, 46(1): 21.

20. Wortmann, C. (2008). "Can Stories Change a Culture?" *Industrial and Commercial Training*, 40(3): 134–141.

21. Zappos Family. (2014). "Zappos Family Core Values," accessed June 24, 2014, http://about.zappos.com/our-unique-culture/zappos-core-values.

22. Osborne, R.L. (1992). "Minority Ownership for Key Employees: Dividend or Disaster?" *Business Horizons*, 35(1): 76.

Chapter 12

1. Murray, A. (August 21 2010). "The End of Management," *The Wall Street Journal*, www.wsj.com.

2. Hammer, M. (April 2004). "Deep Change," *Harvard Business Review*: 1.

3. Knowledge@Wharton. (September 6, 2006). "You Can't Manage What You Can't Measure: Maximizing Supply Chain Value," http://knowledge.wharton.upenn.edu/article.cfm?articleid=1546.

4. Abrams, R. (May 26, 2011). "Entrepreneurs, Don't Let Stuff Control Your Business," *USA Today.com*.

5. Magretta, J. (1998). "Supply Chain Management, Hong Kong Style," *Harvard Business Review*, Reprint 98507.

6. Ferdows, K., M.A. Lewis, and J.A.D. Machuca. (November 2004). "Rapid-Fire Fulfillment," *Harvard Business Review*, Reprint R0411G.

7. Anderson, E. and B. Weitz. (February 1992). "The Use of Pledges to Build and Sustain Commitment in Distribution Channels," *Journal of Marketing Research*, 29: 18–34; and Doney, P.M. and J.P. Cannon. (April 1997). "An Examination of the Nature of Trust in Buyer–Seller Relationships," *Journal of Marketing*, 61: 35–51.

8. Lusch, R.F. and J.R. Brown. (October 1996). "Interdependency, Contracting, and Relational Behavior in Marketing Channels," *Journal of Marketing*, 60: 19–38; and Noordewier, T.G., G. John, and J.R. Nevin. (October 1990). "Performance Outcomes of Purchasing Arrangements in Industrial Buyer–Vendor Relationships," *Journal of Marketing*, 54: 80–93.

9. "Feigenbaum's 40 Steps to Quality Improvement," www.scribd.com/doc/23251743/Armand-V-Feigenbaumrename-1.

10. Ibid.

11. American Society for Quality. (2004). "Basic Concepts: Process View of Work," accessed April 22, 2007, http://asq.org/learn-about-quality/process-view-of-work/overview/overview.html

12. Challener, C. (July 16, 2001). "Six Sigma: Can the GE Model Work in the Chemical Industry?" *Chemical Market Reporter*, www.findarticles.com.

13. Bartholomew, D. (September 2001). "Cost v. Quality," *Industry Week*, www.industryweek.com.

14. "Play Big." (November 2006). *Fortune Small Business*: 30.

Chapter 13

1. Cole, R.A. (April 2011). "How Do Firms Choose Legal Form of Organization?" *SBA Office of Advocacy*, under contract number SBAHQ-09-M-0254.

2. "The 2012 Statistical Abstract," U.S. Census Bureau, http://www.census.gov/compendia/statab/cats/business_enterprise/sole_proprietor-ships_partnerships_corporations.html.

3. Davidoff, H. (April 2006). "Understanding Buy-Sell Agreements," *The CPA Journal*, www.nysscpa.org/cpajournal/2006/406/essentials/p58.htm.

4. Toder, E. and J. Koch. (August 6, 2007). "Fewer Businesses Are Organized as Taxable Corporations," *Tax Policy Center, Urban Institute and Brookings Institution*, p. 491.

5. Bort, J. (May 12, 2014). "Why Startup Founders Happily Give Up 90 Percent of Their Companies," Inc.com, http://www.inc.com/julie-bort/why-startup-founders-give-up-90-percent-of-their-companies.html.

6. Forms of Organization Overview. (June 2013). *Law for Change*. Washington, DC: Steptoe & Johnson LLP.

7. "How to Start a Nonprofit, Step 2: Key Questions to Ask before Getting Started," National Council of Nonprofits, accessed June 27, 2014, http://www.councilofnonprofits.org/knowledge-center/how-start-nonprofit/step-2-key-questions-ask-getting-started.

Chapter 14

1. Cecere, L. (December 11, 2013). "New Products: More Costly and More Important," *Forbes*, http://www.forbes.com/sites/loracecere/2013/12/11/new-products-more-costly-and-more-important/.

2. Dahlstrom, P. and D. Edelman. (April 2013). "The Coming Era of On-Demand Marketing," *McKinsey Quarterly*.

3. Court, D., D. Elzinga, S. Mulder, and O.J. Vetvik. (June 2009). "The Consumer Decision Journey," http://www.mckinsey.com/insights/marketing_sales/the_consumer_decision_journey.

4. Golder, P.H. and G.J. Tellis. (Spring 2004). "Growing, Growing, Gone: Cascades, Diffusion, and Turning Points in the Product Life Cycle," *Marketing Science*, 23(2): 207–218.

5. "The Diffusion Process," Ames: Agriculture Extension Service, Iowa State College, Special Report No. 18, 1957; and Rogers, E. (1962). *Diffusion of Innovations*. New York: The Free Press.

6. Moore, G. (1999). *Crossing the Chasm: Marketing and Selling High-Tech Products to Mainstream Customers*. New York: Harper Business.

7. Temkin, B.D. (February 5, 2010). "Mapping the Customer Journey," *Forrester Research*, p. 6.

8. Woodruff, R. (1997). "Customer Value: The Next Source for Competitive Advantage," *Journal of the Academy of Marketing Science*, 25(2): 139–153.

9. Cooper, R.G. (2001). *Winning at New Products*, 3rd ed. New York: Perseus.

10. Woodall, T. (2003). "Conceptualization 'Value for the Customer': An Attribution, Structural and

Dispositional Analysis," *Academy of Marketing Science Review*, 12.

11. Op. cit., Woodruff, 1997, 141.

12. Smith, J.B. and M. Colgate. (2007). "Customer Value Creation: A Practical Framework," *Journal of Marketing Theory and Practice*, 15(1): 7.

13. Frey, D. (February 19, 2002). "Your Seven-Step, One-Day Marketing Plan," accessed April 27, 2007, www.marketingprofs.com.

14. MacInnis, D. (2006). "Just What Is a Brand, Anyway?" *Marketing Guides*, accessed April 29, 2007, www.marketingprofs.com.

15. MacInnis, D. and C.W. Park. (2006). "Branding and Brand Equity: Clarifications on a Confusing Topic," *Marketing Guides*, accessed April 29, 2007, www.marketingprofs.com.

16. Shipley, M. (March 13, 2007). "Keeping the Brand Health: The Annual Brand Checkup,", accessed April 29, 2007, www.marketingprofs.com.

17. Zeisser, M. (June 2010). "Unlocking the Elusive Potential of Social Networks," *McKinsey Quarterly*, www.mckinseyquarterly.com/Unlocking _the_elusive_potential_of_social_networks_2623.

18. Ellis, D. (October 13, 2009). "Are Your Marketing Dollars buying Customers—or Just Renting Them?" *MarketingProfs.com*, www.marketingprofs .com/articles/2009/3083/are-your-marketing -dollars-buying-customersor-just-renting-them.

19. YouTube press statistics. http://www.youtube .com/yt/press/statistics.html.

20. Berger, J. (2013). *Contagious: Why Things Catch On*. New York: Simon & Schuster.

21. Naziri, J. (August 16, 2013) "Dollar Shave Club Co-founder Michael Dubin Had a Smooth Transition," *Los Angeles Times*, http:// articles.latimes.com/2013/aug/16/business /la-fi-himi-dubin-20130818.

22. "Surviving Silly Bandz: Prolonging the Shelf Life of Fads," *Knowledge @ Wharton*, July 21, 2010, http://knowledge.wharton.upenn.edu/article .cfm?articleid=2551.

23. "Turning Social Capital into Economic Capital: Straight Talk about Word-of-Mouth Marketing," *Knowledge @ Wharton*, July 21, 2010, http://knowledge.wharton.upenn.edu/article .cfm?articleid=2554.

24. MarketShare and the Keller Fay Group. (October 25, 2012). "Quantifying the Role of Social Voice in Marketing Effectiveness," http://pages .marketshare.com/rs/marketshare/images/Mar ketShare-KellerFay_SocialVoice_Executive- Summary.pdf?mkt_tok=3RkMMJWWfF9wsRonua

%2FJZKXonjHpfsX56usvWqW%2BlMI%2F0ER3f OvrPUfGjI4AScZ0aPyQAgobGp5I5FEPQrbYTK Nht6wIXg%3D%3D

25. McConell, B. and J. Huba. (November 26, 2002). "Top 6 Tips to Understanding Customer Evangelism," www.marketingprofs.com.

26. *IAB Internet Advertising Revenue Report Conducted by PricewaterhouseCoopers (PWC)*. (2013). http://www.iab.net/research/industry _data_and_landscape/adrevenuereport.

27. Chui, M. et al. (July 2012). "The Social Economy: Unlocking Value and Productivity through Social Technologies," *McKinsey Global Institute*.

28. Ibid, p. 11.

29. Smith, K. (August 16, 2012). "Look at How Many Fake Followers the Most Popular People on Twitter Have," *Business Insider*, http://www .businessinsider.com/see-how-many-fakers-are -following-your-favorite-celebrity-on-twitter -2012-8?op=1.

30. Kaushik, A. "Best Social Media Metrics: Conversation, Amplification, Applause, Economic Value," *Occam's Razor*, accessed July 9, 2014.

31. Sciortino, J. (October 2006). "Sharing a Lobster." *Fortune Small Business*, 45.

32. Corey, C.W. (August 10, 2010). "Africa: Agoa Ministers Learn Importance of Adding Value to Commodities," allAfrica.com, http://allafrica .com/stories/201008110794.html.

33. Kuman, R., J.A. Petersen, and R.P. Leone. (October 2007). "How Valuable Is Word of Mouth?" *Harvard Business Review*, Reprint R0710J.

34. Clark, C. (June 2013). "The Start Experiment," CorieClark.com, http://corieclark .com/2013/07/10/the-start-experiment/.

Chapter 15

1. Bazerman, M.H., and A.E. Tenbrunsel. (April 2011). "Ethical Breakdowns," *Harvard Business Review*, http://hbr.org/2011/04/ethical-breakdowns /ar/1

2. Raghavan, A. (January 11, 2014). "In Scandal's Wake, McKinsey Seeks Culture Shift," *The New York Times*, http://www.nytimes.com/2014/01/12/ business/self-help-at-mckinsey.html?_r=0

3. United States Sentencing Commission. "Guidelines Manual," http://www.ussc.gov/guidelines-manual /guidelines-manual, accessed July 28, 2014.

4. Adler, P. (2010, June 7). "Ethical Action: The ABCs of IOUs," Workshop presented at the University of Southern California.

5. Ibid.

6. Klitzman, R. (July 7, 2014). "Why Facebook Should Follow Ethical Standards—Like Everybody Else," *The Huffington Post*, http://www.huffingtonpost.com/robert-klitzman-md/why-facebook-needs-to-fol_b_5557862.html

7. Baker, S.L. (May 22, 2009). "Cancer Studies Published in Respected Journals Biased by Medical Industry Money," *Natural News*, www.naturalnews.com/026314_cancer_research_studies.html

8. Brodsky, N. (October 2002). "Street Smarts: The Unkindest Cut of All," *Inc.*

9. Brown, M. E., and T.R. Mitchell. (2010). "Ethical and Unethical Leadership: Exploring New Avenues for Future Research," *Business Ethics Quarterly*, 20(4): 583–616.

10. Eisenbeib, S.A., and F. Brodbeck. (2014). "Ethical and Unethical Leadership: A Cross-Cultural and Cross-Sectoral Analysis," *Journal of Business Ethics*, 122: 343–359.

11. Evan, W., and R.E. Freeman. (1996). "A Stakeholder Theory of the Modern Corporation: Kantian Capitalism." In T. Beauchamp and N. Bowie (eds.), *Ethical Theory and Business*. Englewood Cliffs, NJ: Prentice Hall, 97–106.

12. McDonald, G.M., and R.A. Zepp. (1989). "Business Ethics: Practical Proposals," *Journal of Business Ethics*, 81: 55–56.

13. Josephson Institute for Ethics, http://character-counts.org

14. Kant, I. (1964). *Groundwork of the Metaphysics of Morals*. New York: Harper & Row.

15. Cavanaugh, G.F., D.J. Moberg, and M. Valasquez. (1981). "The Ethics of Organizational Politics," *Academy of Management Review*, 6(3): 363–374.

16. Sharma, R., and M. Sharma. (June 2014). "Some Reflections on Business Ethics and Corporate Social Responsibility," *Asia Pacific Journal of Management and Entrepreneurship Research*, 3(2): 89–96.

17. Dees, J.G., H.J. Emerson, and P. Economy. (2001). *Enterprising Nonprofits: A Toolkit for Social Entrepreneurs*. New York: Wiley.

18. Fenugreen, www.fenugreen.com, accessed July 15, 2014.

19. Lane, R. (December 17, 2012). "30 Under 30: Social Entrepreneurs," *Forbes*, http://www.forbes.com/pictures/ekeg45kfk/maggie-doyne-26/

20. Ransom, D. (September 12, 2008). "Starting Up: Funding Your Social Venture," *The Wall Street Journal*, http://online.wsj.com/article/NA_WSJ_PUB:SB122124827514029295.html

21. Roper, J., and G. Cheney. (2005). "Leadership, Learning, and Human Resource Management: The Meanings of Social Entrepreneurship Today," *Corporate Governance*, 5(3): 95.

22. Thompson, J.L. (2002). "The World of the Social Entrepreneur," *International Journal of Public Sector Management*, 15(4/5): 412–431.

23. Working Assets, www.workingassets.com/About.aspx, accessed July 28, 2014.

24. Collins, J., and J. Porras. (1997). *Built to Last: Successful Habits of Visionary Companies*. New York: Harper Business; Collins, Jim. (October 15, 2001). *Good to Great*. New York: HarperBusiness.

25. Reingold, J., and Underwood, R. (2004). "Was 'Built to Last' Built to Last?" *Fast Company*, http://www.fastcompany.com/50992/was-built-last-built-last

26. Whole Foods Market, www.wholefoodsmarket.com/mission-values/core-values, accessed July 15, 2014.

27. Nash, L. (March–April 1988). "Mission Statements—Mirrors and Windows," *Harvard Business Review*: 155–156; and Schermerhorn Jr., J.R., and D.S. Chappell. (2000). *Introducing Management*. New York: John Wiley.

28. "Drucker Foundation Self-Assessment Tool: Content—How to Develop a Mission Statement," *Leader to Leader Institute*, www.leadertoleader.org

29. Boyd, D.P., and D.E. Gumpert. (March–April 1983). "Coping with Entrepreneurial Stress," *Harvard Business Review*: 44–64.

Chapter 16

1. Lussier, R.N., and C.E.Halabi. (2010). "A Three-Country Comparison of the Business Success Versus Failure Prediction Model," *Journal of Small Business Management*, 48(3): 360–377.

2. Akin, M. (2011). "Does Venture Capital Spur Patenting? Evidence from State-Level Cross-Sectional Data for the United States," *Technology and Investment*, 2(4): 295–300.

3. Venkataraman, S. (1997). "The Distinctive Domain of Entrepreneurship Research," *Advances in Entrepreneurship Research: Firm Emergence and Growth*, 3: 119–138, JAI Press.

4. Moore, G. (2002). *Crossing the Chasm*. New York: HarperBusiness.

5. "Business in a Bag," *VisionSpring*, www.visionspring.org/blog, accessed February 10, 2011.

6. "Impact Investing: Harnessing Capital Markets to Drive Development at Scale," *Beyond Profit*

Magazine, http://beyondprofit.com/impact
-investing-harnessing-capital-markets-to-drive
-development-at-scale, accessed March 5, 2010.

7. GrayGhost Ventures, www.grayghostventures.com,
accessed July 18, 2014.

8. Ransom, D. (September 12, 2008). "Starting Up:
Funding Your Social Venture," *The Wall Street
Journal*, http://online.wsj.com.

9. Bhide, A. (1992). "Bootstrapping Finance: The
Art of Startups," *Harvard Business Review*, 70(6):
109–117.

10. Siriwardane, V. (September 20, 2010). "How to
Build a Bootstrapping Culture," *Inc.*, www.inc
.com/guides/2010/09/how-to-build-a-boot-
strapping-culture.html

11. Wellner, A.S. (December 2003). "Blood Money,"
Inc., www.inc.com

12. Suster, M. (July 22, 2014). "The Changing Structure
of the VC Industry," *Both Sides of the Table*, http://
www.bothsidesofthetable.com/2014/07/22
/the-changing-structure-of-the-vc-industry/

13. *MoneyTree™ Report*, (Q4 2013/Full-year 2013).
Pricewaterhouse Coopers/National Venture Capital Association, http://www.pwc.com/en_US
/us/technology/assets/pwc-moneytree-q4-and
-full-year-2013-summary-report.pdf

14. Ibid. p 5.

15. Franke, N., M. Gruber, D. Harhoff, and J. Henkel.
(September 2006). "Venture Capitalists' Evalu-
ations of Start-up Teams: Trade-offs, Knock-out
Criteria, and the Impact of VC Experience." *Entrepreneurship Theory and Practice*, 12: 8–20.

16. Shepherd, D. (1999). "Venture Capitalists' Intro-
spection: A Comparison of 'In Use' and 'Espoused'
Decision Policies," *Journal of Small Business Management*, 27: 76–87.

17. Mayer, M. (December 2003). "Taking the Fear
Out of Factoring," *Inc.*: 90–97.

18. Ordanini, A., L. Miceli, M. Pizzetti, and A.
Parasuraman. (2011). Crowd-Funding: Transforming Customers into Investors Through Innovative Service Platforms," *Journal of Service
Management*, 22(4): 443.

19. Steinberg, S., and R. deMaria. (May 2012) "The
Crowd Funding Bible," *Read.me:* 1–90.

20. Kickstarter Stats, https://www.kickstarter.com
/help/stats, accessed July 21, 2014.

21. Voelker, T.A. and R. McGlashan. (2013). "What Is
Crowdfunding? Bringing the Power of Kickstarter
to Your Entrepreneurship Research and Teaching

Activities," *Small Business Institute Journal*, 9(2):
11–22.

22. Mollick, E.R. (January 2014). "The Dynamics of
Crowdfunding: An Exploratory Study, *Journal of
Business Venturing*, 29:1, pp.1–16.

23. Lipper, G. (2007). "Is Valuation a Key Issue in
Funding Startups?" *In Valuing Pre-revenue Companies*, Kauffman Foundation, www.eVenturing.
org, p. 11.

24. Villalobos, L., and W.H. Payne. (2007). "Startup
Pre-money Valuation: The Keystone to Return on
Investment," *In Valuing Pre-revenue Companies*,
Kauffman Foundation, www.eVenturing.org, p. 9.

25. Villalobos, L. (2007). "Valuation Divergence," *In
Valuing Pre-revenue Companies*, Kauffman Foundation, www.eVenturing.org, p. 21.

26. Baker, M., and J. Wurgler. (February 2002). "Market Timing and Capital Structure," *Journal of Finance*, 57(1): 1–32.

27. Reardon, M. (June 4, 2006). "Investors Sue Vonage over IPO," www.zdnet.com/news/investors
-sue-vonage-over-ipo/148306?tag=content;
search-results-rivers

28. Renaissance Capital, www.renaissancecapital.com,
accessed February 10, 2011.

29. Hamm, A.F. (February 11, 2005). "Small Startups Look to Foreign IPO Markets," *Silicon Valley
/San Jose Business Journal*, www.bizjournals.com
/sanjose/stories/2005/02/14/story3.html

30. Ritter, J.R. (July 9, 2014). "Initial Public Offerings: Updated Statistics," http://bear.warrington
.ufl.edu/ritter/IPOs2013Statistics.pdf

31. Welbourne, T.M. (2010). "Want to Make Money
on the New Initial Public Offerings?" *Center for
Effective Organizations, Marshall School of Business,
University of Southern California, HRM, the Journal*, http//ceo.usc.edu/pdf/IPOs_HRM.pdf

32. PricewaterhouseCoopers, (September 2012). *Considering an IPO?* http://www.pwc.com/en_us
/us/transaction-services/publications/assets/pwc
-cost-of-ipo.pdf

33. Feldman, A. (September 2005). "Five Ways That
Smart Companies Comply," *Inc.*, www.inc.com

34. "2014 Sarbanes-Oxley Compliance Survey,"
http://www.protiviti.com/en-US/Documents
/Surveys/Infographic-2014-SOX-Compliance-
Survey-Protiviti.pdf

35. Parsons, B. (August 8, 2006). "GoDaddy Pulls
Its IPO Filing! Why I Decided to Pull It," www
.bobparsons.com/WhyIPOPulled.html

Chapter 17

1. Empson, R. (May 28, 2011). "What Makes a Startup Successful? Blackbox Report Aims to Map the Startup Genome," *TechCrunch*, http://techcrunch.com/2011/05/28/what-makes-a-startup-successful-blackbox-report-aims-to-map-the-startup-genome/

2. Kaplan, S., and R. Foster. (2001). *Creative Destruction: Why Companies That Are Built to Last Underperform the Market—and How to Successfully Transform Them*. New York: Doubleday/Currency.

3. Mackey, J., and L. Valinkangas. (2004). "The Myth of Unbounded Growth," *Sloan Management Review* (Winter): 89–92.

4. Stanley, M.H.R., L.A.N. Amaral, S.V. Buldyrev, S. Havlin, H. Leschhorn, P. Maass, M.A. Slainger, and H.E. Stanley. (1996). "Scaling Behaviour in the Growth of Companies," *Nature*, 379: 804–806.

5. "How the 2013 Inc. 5000 Companies Were Selected," Inc.com, http://www.inc.com/magazine/201309/leigh-buchanan/how-the-inc.500-companies-were-selected-2013.html, accessed July 22, 2014.

6. Roberts, M.J. (1999). "Managing Growth." In *New Business Venture and the Entrepreneurs*. New York: Irwin/McGraw-Hill.

7. Hannan, M., and J. Freeman. (1984). "Structural Inertia and Organizational Change," *American Sociological Review*, 49: 149–164; and McKelvey, B., and H. Aldrich (1983). "Populations, Natural Selection, and Applied Organizational Science." *Administrative Science Quarterly*, 28(1): 101–128.

8. Porter, M.E. (January 2008). "The Five Competitive Forces That Shape Strategy," *Harvard Business Review*, R0801E.

9. Hamm, J. (December 2002). "Why Entrepreneurs Don't Scale," *Harvard Business Review*, 2–7.

10. Terpstra, D.E., and P.D. Olson. (1993). "Entrepreneurial Startup and Growth: A Classification of Problems," *Entrepreneurship Theory & Practice* (Spring): 5–20.

11. Ibid.

12. Kapferer, J. N. (2012). "Abundant Rarity: The Key to Luxury Growth, "*Business Horizons*, 55(5), 453–462.

13. Logman, M. (2013). "Limits to Growing Customer Value: Being Squeezed between the Past and the Future," *Business Horizons*, 56: 655–664.

14. Op. cit. Zook, C. (2012).

15. "2014 Minnesota Business Ethics Award Honors Restaurant Technologies, Inc. (June 3, 2014). "MarketWatch," *The Wall Street Journal*, http://www.marketwatch.com/story/2014-minnesota-business-ethics-award-honors-restaurant-technologies-inc-2014-06-03

16. Mannion, M.J. (July 2003). "Advice on Acquisition Advisors," *Inc.*, www.inc.com

17. Kline, S.R. "Growth and Diversification Through Vertical Integration," *PF Online*, www.pfonline.com/articles/growth-and-diversification-through-vertical-integration, accessed February 10, 2011.

18. Karra, N., and N. Phillips. (2004). "Entrepreneurship Goes Global." *Ivey Business Journal* (November/December): 1.

19. Oviatt, B.M., and P. McDougall. (1995). "Global Start-ups: Entrepreneurs on a Worldwide Stage." *The Academy of Management Executive*, 9(2): 30–44.

20. Owens, J.B. (2007). "Who You Need to Know and How to Find Them: Building a Global Network," *Inc.* (April): 116.

21. Smeltzer, L.R., and S.P. Siferd. (1998). "Proactive Supply Management: The Management of Risk." *International Journal of Purchasing and Materials Management*, 34(1): 38–45.

22. Krause, D.R. (1999). "The Antecedents of Buying Firms' Efforts to Improve Suppliers." *Journal of Operations Management*, 17(2): 205–224.

23. Lee, H.L., V. Padmanabhan, and S. Whang. (1997). "The Bullwhip Effect in Supply Chains." *Sloan Management Review*, 43(4): 93–102.

24. Robertson, T.S., and H. Gatignon. (1998). "Technology Development Mode: A Transaction Cost Conceptualization." *Strategic Management Journal*, 19(1): 515–531.

25. "Employer Costs for Employment Compensation, March 2014," Bureau of Labor Statistics, U.S. Department of Labor, June 11, 2014.

26. "Navigating Legal Challenges," Fortune.com (January 2007): S3.

27. Conner, C. (September 14, 2013). "Are You Prepared? Record Number of Cyber Attacks Target Small Business," *Forbes*, http://www.forbes.com/sites/cherylsnappconner/2013/09/14/are-you-prepared-71-of-cyber-attacks-hit-small-business/

28. Zsidisn, G.A., and A. Panelli (2000). "Purchasing Organization Involvement in Risk Assessments, Contingency Plans, and Risk Management: An Exploratory Study," *Supply Chain Management*, 5(4): 187.

29. Buchanan, L. (May 2003). "How to Take Risks in a Time of Anxiety," *Inc.*, www.inc.com

30. Favaro, K., P. Karlsson, and G.L. Neilson. (May 30, 2014). "The Lives and Times of the CEO," *Strategy + Business*, Columbia Business School, http://www.strategy-business.com/article/00254?pg=all#ceo_turnover

31. Bower, J.L. (November 2007). "Solve the Succession Crisis by Growing Inside-Outside Leaders," *Harvard Business Review*, R0711E.

32. Pasmore, W., and R. Torres. (2007). "The Best Next CEO," *Leadership Excellence, 24* (8), 16–17.

33. The Family Firm Institute of Boston, www.ffi.org, accessed October 21, 2010.

34. Needleman, S. (July 16, 2010). "In Sports, Managing the Team Is Often a Family Affair." *The Wall Street Journal*.

35. Astrachan, J.H., S.B. Klein, and K.X. Smyrnios. (2002). "The FPEC Scale of Family Influence: A Proposal for Solving the Family Business Definition Problem," *Family Business Review*, 15(1): 45–58.

36. Ernst & Young, "Turning the Corner: Global Venture Capital Insights and Trends 2013," http://www.ey.com/Publication/vwLUAssets/Global_VC_insights_and_trends_report_2012/$FILE/Turning_the_corner_VC_insights_2013_LoRes.pdf

37. Burrows, D. (December 11, 2013). "Mergers and Acquisitions—The 10 Biggest Deals of 2013," *Investor Place*, http://investorplace.com/2013/12/mergers-and-acquisitions-biggest-deals-2013/#.U9kkzvldV8F

38. "2014 IPO Report, Wilmer Cutler Pickering Hale and Dorr LLP," http://www.wilmerhale.com/uploadedFiles/Shared_Content/Editorial/Publications/Documents/2014-WilmerHale-IPO-Report.pdf

INDEX

Note: *f* indicates *figure*, *p* indicates *profile*, and *t* indicates *table*.